PRAISE FOR
RICH MARAZZI and LEN FIORITO'S
AARON to ZUVERINK

"YOU HAVE GOT TO READ THIS BOOK."
New York Daily News

"One of the most unique baseball books ever written"

Baseball Bulletin

"Entertaining and informative"
Chicago Tribune

"Not only great for quick reference on the players of the era—but also plain enjoyable reading."

—Frank Messer,
Yankee announcer

"A valuable book"

—Mel Allen, Yankee announcer

"Do yourself a favor—
read AARON TO ZUVERINK."
New York Post

Other Avon Books by
Rich Marazzi and Len Fiorito

AARON TO ZUVERINK: *Baseball Players of the Fifties*

AARON TO ZIPFEL

RICH MARAZZI
AND
LEN FIORITO

 AVON
PUBLISHERS OF BARD, CAMELOT, DISCUS AND FLARE BOOKS

AARON TO ZIPFEL is an original publication of Avon
Books. This work has never before appeared in book form.

AVON BOOKS
A division of
The Hearst Corporation
1790 Broadway
New York, New York 10019

First Avon Printing, May 1985

AVON TRADEMARK REG. U. S. PAT. OFF. AND IN
OTHER COUNTRIES, MARCA REGISTRADA, HECHO EN
U. S. A.

Printed in the U. S. A.

WHF 10 9 8 7 6 5 4 3 2 1

Acknowledgments

We would like to express our thanks and appreciation to the following who have made an important contribution to this book:

Ron Liebman: one of the most respected baseball statisticians in the Society For American Baseball Research and its most renowned trivia expert, for his valuable contribution in the areas of historical accuracy plus statistical and anecdotal information. Ron has been a contributor and assistant editor of *The Sporting News Baseball Record Book* since 1968 and has also worked as a baseball statistician in the New York offices of the Associated Press. Mr. Liebman who is currently employed as a senior statistician for the New York City Housing Authority has written the most comprehensive articles ever published on "Consecutive Game Hitting Streaks" and "Winning Streaks by Pitchers."

Russ Dille: for use of several *Sporting News* editions and help in providing information regarding players' occupations.

Tom Zocco: a fellow SABR member who supplied interesting anecdotal information and assisted with the accuracy of the content of the book. Thanks to Tom also for providing several team press guides from the 1960s that aided our research.

Howard Giacomazzi: for the use of several *Sporting News* editions and for providing anecdotal information.

Stan Farber: for help in acquiring occupations.

Frank Messer: N.Y. Yankee announcer who provided much anecdotal information.

John Gordon: N.Y. Yankee announcer for providing anecdotal information.

Ron Siegel: for providing information taken from several college press guides.

Ted DiTullio: a SABR member who aided in statistical research.

Foxy Gagnon, Ralph Winney and Louis Rodriguez Mayoral: for help in acquiring occupations.

Bob Rosen: statistician at the Elias Sports Bureau for updating the lifetime batting averages and pitching records of active players in this book.

Loisann Kelly Marazzi: for typing a part of the manuscript and aiding in the sociological research of the 1960s.

Joanne Wilson: for typing a major part of the manuscript.

To the following players who consented to interviews and supplied additional information about the current status of several players profiled in the book: Jim Campbell, Tim Cullen, Tom Haller, Bob D. Johnson, Jeoff Long, Marcelino Lopez, Roger Repoz, Don O'Riley, Jerry Stephenson, Bob Saverine, Nick Willhite and Bud Zipfel.

A great deal of information that appears in this book is the direct result of interviews with the following players: Fritz Ackley, Gene Alley, Dave Bakenhaster, Jack Baldschun, Dave Baldwin, Norm Bass, Rich Beck, Rick Bladt, Ray Blemker, "Hoss" Bowlin, Gary Boyd, Ron Brand, John Braun, Ed Brinkman, Tom Brown, Cal Browning, Fred Burdette, Don Buschorn, Bill Butler, Bert Campaneris, Clay Carroll, Ted Davidson, Dick Dietz, John Donaldson, Paul Doyle, Bill Edgerton, John Ellis, Sammy Ellis, Mike Fiore, Larry Foster, Ralph Garr, Joe Grzenda, Jack Hamilton, Wynn Hawkins, Mike Hegan, Bob Hendley, Steve Hertz, Jim Hibbs,

Jess Hickman, Pat House, Ken Hunt, Charlie James, Ray Jarvis, Larry Jaster, Rex Johnston, Mack Jones, Steve Jones, Duane Josephson, Dick Joyce, Mike Jurewicz, Steve Kealy, Van Kelly, Bill Kern, Bill Kirk, Bobby Knoop, Bill Kunkel, Em Lindbeck, Frank Linzy, Jim Lonborg, Al Luplow, Bill MacLeod, Jerry May, Dick McAuliffe, Joe McCabe, Brian McCall, Sam McDowell, Bob Meyer, Gene Michael, Joe Moock, Cotton Nash, Dave Nelson, Syd O'Brien, Dennis O'Toole, John Papa, Fritz Peterson, Wayne Redmond, Jack Reed, Ron Reed, Jay Ritchie, Daryl Robertson, "Cookie" Rojas, Bob Sadowski, Chuck Schilling, Johnnie Seale, Charlie Shoemaker, Morrie Steevens, Dick Stigman, Ron Stone, Gary Timberlake, Jeff Torborg, Dick Tracewski, Tom Tresh, Bill Wakefield, and Roy White.

To the following public relations representatives of the various major league teams for supplying information regarding the current job status of several former players: Dennis D'Agostino (Mets), Larry Shenk (Phillies), Joe Safety (Yankees), Tom Mee (Twins), Gerry Clarke (Cubs), Rich Bresciani (Red Sox), Jim Toomey (Cardinals), Richard Griffin (Expos), Charles Shriver (White Sox), Mickey Morabito (A's), Dean Vogelaar (Royals), Wayne Minshew (Braves), Steve Brener (Dodgers), Tom Skibosh (Brewers), Mary Memmo (Pirates), Duffy Jennings (Giants), Dan Ewald (Tigers), Mike Ryan (Astros) and Bob Chandler (Padres).

To the following for help and support: Nick Fiorito, Jeanne Kelly, Bill Haber, Rose Vandemore, Don Kosakowski, Kevin Grace, Anthony Papalas, Raul Galvin, Irwin Cohen, and the staff at the University of Washington Library.

To Larry Donald (editor/publisher) and Mike Sheridan (managing editor) of the *Baseball Bulletin* for use of pictures.

Also, *Dave Weiner:* a friend whose inspiration and respect for this type of material helped *Aaron to Zipfel* become a reality.

and

John Douglas: our editor at Avon Publishers who spent countless hours refining the contents of this book.

TO THE READER

The authors are frequently asked how they located and acquired the occupations of over one thousand players profiled in this book and a similar number in *Aaron to Zuverink*. A variety of methods were used.

Their primary reference was *The Sport Americana Baseball Address List* by Jack Smalling and Denny Eckes. From this text they were able to obtain the addresses of most of the players profiled herein. In some cases the name listed in the book was that of the player's parent which proved to be equally valuable.

The authors wrote letters and made a multitude of phone calls throughout the country. Frequently, players gave leads as to the whereabouts of several individuals.

For players that could not be located in this manner, a list was drawn up and sent to the public relations directors of the various major league teams. Their assistance proved quite helpful.

Other methods included an attempt to locate relatives in the birthplace city of the player in question or contacting the individual's high school or college.

As mentioned in the acknowledgment section, the authors were also aided by certain individuals who provided information. A weekly check of organization updates provided by *The Sporting News* was also a meaningful source.

Although the authors have attempted to report the current job status and area residence for each player, it's inevitable that some changes will have occurred since they collected the information for the manuscript. Also, a player's residence is listed only when his job location isn't mentioned or his place of employment is other than his residence.

There are approximately 30 active players profiled in this book. Their lifetime statistics are computed through the 1984 season.

To qualify for inclusion in *Aaron to Zipfel*, a player had to debut in the major leagues between 1960–1969.

If you can enlarge or refine any of the facts cited in this publication, we will be happy to hear from you. You may drop a letter to either Rich Marazzi or Len Fiorito in care of the publisher.

INTRODUCTION

Baseball to me is still one of the toughest sports there is. I believe that anyone who reaches the "big leagues" knows this to be true. There are many obstacles and hurdles to overcome in order to be successful in the game. Having met the challenge has enabled me to go on in my career, after baseball, with the same determination, hustle, desire and will to win as I had while playing the game. I have many a scout, coach, manager, fellow teammate and fan to thank for their time and care in teaching me these lessons of life.

Baseball has always had a positive and rewarding place in my life. The game has taught me a great deal. I thank the game of baseball for giving me the opportunity to shine in its light and in the light of the fans, as well.

To all the fans, coaches, and players I say it has been great having had the opportunity to play eleven seasons in professional baseball. To all the young people coming up in organized baseball I say give it 100 percent and you'll have no regrets.

To Rick and Len, thank you for giving me this opportunity to read and hear about many of my old teammates. I was delighted to find that most of the players have turned out well since their baseball days.

I want to give personal and special thanks to John Schulte. A gentleman and the person who scouted me early in high school—he is a great man. Thank you John Schulte.

Bud Zipfel

A

AARON, Tommie
Died Aug. 16, 1984, at age 45 in Atlanta, GA

It's been said that "the worst misfortune that can happen to an ordinary man is to have an extraordinary father." Ditto for all the ordinary men in the world who have a famous brother, especially when that brother is Hank Aaron.

Hank was already an established star in 1962 when Tommie joined him as a first baseman-outfielder with the Milwaukee Braves. To compare the two is grossly unfair to both, but in a sport that feeds on statistics and comparisons it was only natural that Tommie would always be Hank's little brother.

From 1962–1971, Tommie was in and out of the majors with the Milwaukee and Atlanta Braves. When Hank, who carried a lifetime .305 mark, made his exit in 1976 with a .229 avg., it matched Tommie's overall log. Unfortunately, Tommie felt that a personality conflict with manager Bobby Bragan (1963–66) hindered his career.

But Tommie did have moments when it didn't matter who his brother was. On April 26, 1962, he hit a single, triple and homer as the Braves demolished the Phils, 10-4. A month later he tied a record by starting three double plays as a first baseman.

Tommie's highlight season in organized baseball came in 1967 when he led the Braves' Richmond team to the International League pennant and was named the league's MVP. The ex-Braves' coach could also boast that he hit the first homer ever in Atlanta-Fulton County Stadium in a exhibition game against Detroit prior to the '65 season.

Hank and Tommie combined for 768 home runs, the most of any brother combo in big league history. Henry carried the load with 755. The Aarons connected in the same game three different times, all during the '62 campaign. On Sept. 24, 1968, they pulled off a rare brother double steal against the Mets.

Tommie's career in the majors was at best mediocre. But then again, how do you follow such an extraordinary brother?

Prior to his death, Tommie was an Atlanta Braves' coach. He began receiving treatments for leukemia in 1982.

ACKLEY, Fritz
Liquor salesman for Saratoga Liquor
Haywood, WI

Florian "Fritz" Ackley surfaced with the White Sox in parts of '63 and '64, winning his only big league decision. His finest hour came in '63 when he led the International League in wins, going 18-5 with Indianapolis. Fritz, who used to own a hunting and fishing resort, said, "When I started to play ball, I wanted to throw one pitch in the big leagues." His goal was accomplished.

ADAMS, Doug
Maintenance employee with Certified Parts
Janesville, WI

In 1968, "Adam 12" began an eight-year run on NBC. A year later Doug Adams had an eight-game run in which he hit .214 as a catcher with the White Sox.

ADAMSON, Mike
Budget Director for Systems Development Corp.
Santa Monica, CA

Mike doesn't speak well for first-round draft choices. A right-handed pitcher, he was the Phillies' first-ever No. 1 draft choice in the first free agent draft in 1965. But he elected to remain at USC where he was a second-team All-American.

Following graduation, Mike was the Orioles' No. 1 selection in the special phase of the 1967 free agent draft. Without any minor league experience, he found himself in a

Baltimore uniform. Mike's euphoria was short-lived as he found himself in Rochester by the end of the season.

From 1967–1969 he was in 11 games for the Orioles and lost all four of his decisions.

ADLESH, Dave
Race track press steward
Long Beach, CA

A catcher who signed a reported $95,000 bonus with Houston, Dave spent parts of six seasons (1963–1968) with the Astros, hitting .168 in 106 games. His moment of glory came in '67 when he was behind the plate for Don Wilson's no-hitter over the Braves.

AGEE, Tommie
Owns the "Outfielder's Lounge" located near Shea Stadium in New York

In 1969, "Tommy" was a popular rock opera produced by The Who. It was also a year that Tommie Agee and the Mets rocked the baseball world. In Game Three of the World Series against the Orioles, Agee homered and made two circus catches in leading the Mets past Baltimore, 5-0. His fingertip grab of Ellie Hendricks' drive in the fourth inning was classic. Orioles' manager Earl Weaver said, "I've seen outfielders make great catches in World Series play before, but I've never seen two such great catches by the same player in the same game."

The Grambling University product started his 12-year sprint with Cleveland in 1962. His first full big league season came in 1966 as a member of the White Sox. Following a 22-home run, 86-RBI season, he was named the A.L. Rookie of the Year.

At one point in his career he went on what has been called one of the "worst hitting streaks of all times," a 22-game streak in which he picked up 23 hits and was actually in somewhat of a slump. During the stretch he reportedly used 22 different bats.

He went on a home run tear in June of 1970, banging out 11 roundtrippers. But his career-high .286 avg. that year

helped New York to only a third-place finish in the N.L.
East Division race.

After stops with the Astros and Cardinals in '73, he departed with a .255 average and memories of a '69 season
that allowed the Mets, a team of destiny, to go from ninth
place in '68 to the world championship a year later, the
biggest leap in big league history.

AKER, Jack
Manager at Buffalo in the Eastern League in 1984

Known as the "Chief," Jack does have a slight trace of Indian blood. But the nickname came more for his effective-
ness as a late-inning relief pitcher in a well-traveled
11-year (1964–74) trip. His finest season was in '66 with
the K.C. Athletics as he was 8-4 with a 1.99 ERA and a
league-leading 32 saves. For his efforts, he was named the
A.L. Fireman of the Year.

The following season, as the Kansas City player representative, Aker was caught in the middle of the turmoil between owner Charlie Finley and his teammates over an
airplane flight drinking incident which resulted in the firing of manager Alvin Dark and the release of slugger Ken
Harrelson.

Jack was transferred to the Seattle Pilots in '69 and after a stop with the Yankees, he finished his career in the
N.L. with the Cubs, Braves, and Mets. Overall, the "Chief"
went 47-45 with 123 saves in 495 games, all from the
bullpen.

ALCARAZ, Luis
Player-manager at Poza Rica in the Mexican League

A cousin of Orlando Cepeda, Luis was around big league
ballyards long enough (1967–70) to see action in 115
games with the Dodgers and Royals. The Puerto Rican-
born infielder led the Texas League in batting with Albuquerque in 1967. His mark of .328 was well above his
lifetime .192 in the biggies.

The federal prison at Alcatraz closed in 1963. An embarrassed public address announcer once apologized to Luis

for announcing him as Luis Alcatraz, adding, "I should have known that no man is an island."

ALLEN, Bernie
Vice-president and sales manager of Olympia Sport Shop
Lake Worth, FL

In 1960 Bernie Allen was completing touchdown passes for the Purdue Boilermakers. An outstanding quarterback, Bernie led Purdue to an upset victory over Minnesota that year, the Gophers' only defeat.

Two years later, Minnesota fans were cheering for Bernie as the Twins' regular second baseman. The exuberant rookie enjoyed his finest season of a 12-year jaunt with career highs in home runs (12) and batting average (.269). Defensively he combined with Zoilo Versalles for an amazing 236 double plays.

Before he made his exit in 1973 with a .239 lifetime mark, he wore the uniforms of the Senators, Yankees and Expos.

ALLEN, Bob
Construction worker in Tatum, TX

This left-hander pitched in 204 games with the Indians from 1961–63 and again in 1966 and 1967. He finished 7-12 with 19 saves.

ALLEN, Dick
Owns racehorses; stablehand at Santa Anita race track

"If horses can't eat it, I don't want to play on it." (Dick Allen's response to artificial turf.)

Dick (don't call me Richie) Allen's penchant for horses was always quite evident throughout a 15-year gallop (1963–77) frequently harnessed by turmoil. Allen signed with the Phillies for $70,000 out of Wampum High School in Pennsylvania.

Richie (as he was called then) didn't disappoint the Philadelphia brass. The thoroughbred copped N.L. Rookie of the Year honors in 1964 playing at third base, a position he never played in the minors. He swung his lethal bat to the tune of a .318 average, 201 hits, 29 homers and 91 RBIs.

In '65, Allen hit the first official N.L. home run in the Astrodome off Bob Bruce. The following year Dick hit a career high 40 roundtrippers. Cooperstown appeared a sure bet for the guy who played defense wearing a batting helmet.

But baseball's rising young star had another side. Apparantly plagued with inner racial tensions, Allen's behavior became unpredictable. His battles with teammates and management distracted from his abilities as a player. During the '65 season he squared off with teammate Frank Thomas around the batting cage before a game over an alleged racial remark. Later that evening Thomas was placed on waivers even though he pinch-hit a game-tying homer against the Reds.

If Richie had a major weakness as a hitter it was his high strikeout rate. He also had a high frequency rate of missing team planes, showing up late for games, or in some instances not at all. In 1969 he was fined $2,500 by Phillies' skipper Bob Skinner for missing an exhibition game near the end of the season. When Philly owner Bob Carpenter dismissed the fine, Skinner resigned. This further agitated the fans who made Allen a target of their wrath.

Late in the '67 season he suffered serious cuts on his right hand when the headlight of an old automobile he was pushing broke. The injury sidelined him for the remainder of the season.

Dick Allen's frustrations over baseball's reserve clause, white managers, and authority in general, were often made public. He once said, "Baseball is a form of slavery. Once you step out of bounds, that's it, they'll do everything possible to destroy your soul."

The stormy marriage between Allen and the Phils dissolved after the '69 season. His next stops were with the Cardinals ('70) and Dodgers ('71). Once again the unhappy superstar could not find harmony. In '72 he switched over to the White Sox and joined manager Chuck Tanner, a long-time friend. On the surface it appeared that Allen had discovered inner peace when he established a Chisox club record of 37 home runs in '72. He became the first White Sox player to homer into the centerfield bleachers at Comiskey Park when he teed off against Lindy McDaniel and the Yankees. That year he was voted the A.L. MVP with 37 home runs, 113 RBIs, and a .308 average, marking the first time a Chicago White Sox player ever led the A.L. in homers and RBIs.

His stay in Chicago lasted until '74 when he led the A.L. in four-baggers with 32. Allen's abuse of a relaxed discipline system was too much for Tanner and his bosses to handle. Back to Philadelphia (1975–76) for another futile try, Dick rode into the sunset with the Oakland A's in 1977. A career saddled by controversy had ended. In his satchel he carried a lifetime .292 average and 351 home runs.

Former Phils' manager Gene Mauch once said, "Richie Allen walks to the beat of a different drummer."

At Santa Anita racetrack, Dick Allen creates his own beat.

ALLEN, Hank
     Trains horses
     Upper Marlboro, MD

Hank was more of a long shot than his brother Richie. His career with the Senators, Brewers and White Sox (1966–73) was much more serene than his restless younger sibling, and so were his overall statistics—.241 average and 6 home runs in 389 games. Hank was a teammate of Richie's with the White Sox in '72 and '73.

A scholastic All-American in basketball, Hank did his hooping for Baldwin-Wallace University. He broke in with Richie at Elmira in the N.Y.-Penn League in 1960. During his major league stay he played all positions with the exception of pitcher and shortstop.

A third brother, Ron, completed the Allen trifecta in '72 with the Cardinals. He was around for just seven games as a first baseman and had just one hit, but that was a home run.

ALLEN, Lloyd
Bakery business in Chicago, IL

In 1969, Commander Lloyd Bucher and the Pueblo were captured off the coast of North Korea. That same year Lloyd Allen escaped from the minors and hung around for seven seasons (1969–75) with the Angels, Rangers and White Sox.

The right-handed reliever struggled to an 8-25 record, but did some effective work out of the Angels' bullpen in 1971 when he picked up 15 saves in 54 appearances.

ALLEY, Gene
Sales representative for Nagels, a firm supplying printing plates for corrugated industries
Rockville, VA

Hall of Famer Pie Traynor called the Gene Alley-Bill Mazeroski double play combo of the Pirates in the mid-1960s, "the best of all time." In 1966 the two combined for 215 twin killings, an N.L. record. That year Gene hit .299 and was a Gold Glove winner for his dazzling play at shortstop.

A good hit-and-run man and an accomplished bunter, Gene was the comsummate all-round player. Although plagued by various injuries in his 11-year trek (1963–73), he managed 999 basehits to go along with his .254 avg. When asked about his falling one hit shy of a thousand he replied, "It would have been nice to get a thousand hits. But missing the .300 mark by one point in '66 was probably more important to me."

ALOMAR, Sandy
Owns a Mobil gas station
Salinas, PR

This durable little second baseman was with the Braves, Mets, White Sox, Angels, Yankees, and Rangers from

1964–74. It was with the Angels that Sandy found his mark. He once played in 648 consecutive games in the A.L.

The versatile infielder ranks as one of the toughest players in the history of the game to double up. Sandy grounded into just 58 double plays in 4,780 at-bats while batting .245.

ALOU, Jesus
Montreal Expos Scout in the Dominican Republic

The youngest of the three Alou brothers, "Jay" signed with the Giants as a 16-year-old. The native of the Dominican Republic spent his first season in pro ball as a pitcher, but soon converted to the outfield.

He came up with San Francisco in 1963. On Sept. 10 that year he was part of a rare brother triple-team in a game against the Mets when Carlton Willey retired all three Alou brothers in order. Five days later Jesus joined Matty and Felipe at the same time in the Giants' outfield, another baseball first.

Although his 14-year career does not quite match those of his older brothers, he finished with a .280 mark and the reputation of a fine pinch-hitter with 82 pinch-hits. On July 10, 1964, he enjoyed a 6-for-6 day vs. the Cubs with each of his hits coming off a different pitcher. When Jesus collected his 1,000th hit, it made the Alous the only brother trio to each attain 1,000 or more hits.

When it all ended he had played with the Giants, Astros, A's, Mets, and one last time with Houston in '78.

ALOU, Matty
Manager at Cuidad Trujillo in the Dominican Republic winter league

If Bobby Thomson's dramatic home run in the 1951 N.L. playoffs could be labeled "the shot heard 'round the world," Matty's pinch-hit lead-off single in the ninth inning of the final game of the '62 playoffs might be termed "the shot heard 'round California." Alou's single ignited a four-run rally that carried the Giants to the N.L. pennant over the Dodgers once again.

But the achievements of Mateo Rojas Alou go much farther than the '62 playoffs. A lifetime .307 hitter in 15 seasons (1960–74) spent mostly with the Giants and Pirates, he captured the N.L. batting title in 1966 with a .342 average, an improvement of 111 points over his final season in San Francisco. Pirates' skipper Harry Walker got Matty to choke up on the bat and the rest was history. During that '66 campaign, Felipe (.327) finished second in the batting race, marking the first time that brothers ever finished 1-2 in a major league batting race. He was the second Latin (Roberto Clemente was the first) in the N.L. to win a batting title, and the first Dominican.

Matty never won another batting title, but he did hit for such averages as .338, .332, and .331 the next three seasons. He became one of five players in N.L. history to collect 200 or more hits in one year and not reach the .300 level when he went 201-for-677 (.297) with the '70 Pirates.

Joining the A's down the stretch in 1972, he had several timely hits in their race for the A.L. pennant. Matty then hit .381 in the playoffs before slumping (1-for-24) in the World Series despite the fact that the A's beat the Reds. In the '62 WS with the Giants he hit a beefy .333.

ALVARADO, Luis
Playing in Mexican League

The book on Luis was that he had the knack of getting his throws away quicker than any shortstop in the A.L. since Phil Rizzuto.

Alvarado joined the Red Sox in 1968 as an ambitious-looking shortstop. The following season he was the Player of the Year in the International League for Louisville. But his career in the big top (1968–76) lurched and stumbled its unpredictable way (.214) in 462 games mainly with the Red Sox and White Sox.

ALVAREZ, Rogelio
Cement truck driver in Miami, FL

Famous columnist Red Smith once wrote, "Dying is no big deal. The least of us will manage that. Living is the trick."

That could be true about staying alive in the majors.

Just ask Rogelio Alvarez, who hit .189 in 17 games for the Reds in brief stays in 1960 and 1962. The Cuban first baseman did some heavy hitting for the PCL pennant-winning San Diego team in the early '60s, but life in the big time was a bit different.

ALVIS, Max
Executive Vice President of First National Bank
Jasper, TX

Max was the Cleveland Indians third baseman for most of the sixties (1962–69). His best season was his first full year with the Tribe in '63 when he had career highs of 22 home runs and a .274 average. Max also led the A.L. in being hit by pitches that year, getting plunked 10 times.

The tough Texan overcame a case of spinal meningitis which sidelined him for much of the '64 season.

Teammates have belted pinch-hit home runs in the same inning 28 times in baseball history. Max joined Leon Wagner during the '65 season as both hit pinch-roundtrippers in a game against the Twins. In 1967 he was elected by the Cleveland writers as the Indians "Man of the Year." His last shot was with the Brewers in 1970 before he drifted away with a lifetime .247 avg.

ALYEA, Brant
Box person for craps table at the Tropicana Hotel and
Casino in Atlantic City, NJ

Garrabrant Ryerson (Brant) Alyea, who also has a floor person license for blackjack, had the hot hand on several occasions in his relatively short—but at times explosive—big league career.

A basketball star at Hofstra University in the early Sixties, Brant signed with the Reds, but emerged with the Senators in '65. On Sept. 12, "Lady Luck" was with him as he became the first player in A.L. history to hit a pinch-hit home run on the first pitch he ever saw in the majors, a three-run blast off the Angels' Rudy May. His homer came on a rainy day in the nation's capital and was witnessed by a total of 840 fans.

On Opening Day of the 1970 season he came out of the gate like a raging bull with two homers and two singles (7 RBIs) to pace the Twins to a 12-0 win over the White Sox. His hot early-season hitting put him on the cover of *The Sporting News* in early May.

Brant's luck ran out with the A's and Cards in '72. Career-wise he rolled a mediocre .247 avg. with 38 home runs, but he'll never forget that first one.

ANDERSON, Craig
>   Athletic Director at Lehigh Univ.
>   Bethlehem, PA

Craig's career (1961–64) is loaded with trivia. A right-hander who spent his 4-3 rookie year with the Cardinals, Anderson went to the Mets in the 1962 expansion draft.

As a spot starter and reliever in '62, he suffered through a 3-17 season. Interestingly enough two of his wins came on the same day (May 12) in the Mets' first-ever sweep of a doubleheader. Craig was credited with both victories in relief as the Mets swept the Milwaukee Braves, 3-2 and 8-7. The Lehigh graduate, who received a master's degree from Southern Illinois University, proceeded to lose his next 16 games that season. He went 0-2 in '63 and 0-1 in '64 which meant he lost his last 19 decisions in a row.

One of his losses came in the final game ever played at the Polo Grounds when Chris Short and the Phillies dumped the Mets, 5-1, on Sept. 18, 1963 before 1,752 fans.

ANDREWS, Mike
>   Vice-president of The Jimmy Fund; operates a baseball camp
>   Peabody, MA

Mike's opening performances came as a Red Sox second baseman in 1966. The regular second baseman for the "Impossible Dream" team of 1967, Mike hit .263 for the A.L. champs. Probably the best Bosox second sacker since Bobby Doerr, Mike's top season with the stick was in 1969, when he hit .293.

After the '70 season he was traded to the White Sox for

Luis Aparicio. Mike joined the Oakland A's down the stretch in '73 and became the center of controversy during the Fall Classic that year when the A's matched up with the Mets.

In Game Two of the Series he committed two errors which prompted A's owner Charlie Finley to force Andrews into signing a medical report that would place him on the disabled list.

Oakland players and the media came to Mike's defense as did Commissioner Bowie Kuhn, who restored him to the A's active roster. Andrews' triumph came when he received a standing ovation when he stepped out of the dugout to pinch-hit in Game Four.

The A's eventually won the Series, but manager Dick Williams publicly aired his feelings about Finley's interference and resigned. For Mike it was his grand finale. His younger brother, Rob, was a second baseman with the Astros and Giants in the late 1970s.   .258

ARCHER, Jim
    General sales manager for a Chevrolet-Oldsmobile
    dealership
    Tarpon Springs, FL

A southpaw, Jim Archer was mired in the minors for a decade before getting his chance with the Kansas City A's in 1961. In his debut he beat the Angels, 3-2, but ended the year at 9-15.

On Aug. 11 of his maiden season, Jim hooked up in a classic pitching duel with Billy Pierce, the crafty White Sox southpaw. Neither pitcher issued a single walk or allowed a count to reach 3-and-2. But all went for nought as far as Archer was concerned since Chicago won, 1-0, on Luis Aparicio's home run. The time of the well-pitched contest was just one-hour and thirty-two minutes.

The luckless hurler tried again the following year and lost his only decision in 18 games to finish at 9-16.

ARCIA, Jose
   Kansas City Royals scout
   Miami, FL

The city of Chicago was the site of the Democratic National
Convention in 1968 when 685 wild protestors were arrested in what has been referred to as the "Battle of Chicago." The Windy City was also the site that year of Jose's first
big league job when he joined the Cubs as an infielder.
   A native of Havana, Cuba, Jose began his pro career as a
pitcher with Modesto in 1962. Three years later he was
converted into an infielder. Selected by the Padres in the
N.L. expansion draft, Arcia hit .215 while with San Diego
in '69 and '70.

ARDELL, Dan
   President of D.A. Management Consultants, a firm
   involved in real estate planning and pension fund
   raising
   Huntington Beach, CA

Dan starred for the NCAA champion USC Trojans in 1961
as an outfielder. Later that same summer he appeared in 7
games with the expansion Angels, picking up one hit in
four at bats (.250).
   At a time when "Teen Angel" and "Devil or Angel"
were hit songs, Dan was suddenly an ex-Angel.

ARLICH, Don
   Math teacher and baseball coach at Park High School
   in Cottage Grove, MN
   St. Paul, MN

Computing this math teacher's big league stats is quite
simple since he lost his one decision in eight games with
the Astros in 1965–66.
   Actually, Don arrived with a damaged left wing which
he hurt at Jacksonville in '61. He says, "My fastball was
better in high school." Called up to Houston at the end of
the '65 season, he started his first game ever against the
Cards. When he left the contest after six innings he was

ahead, 3-2, but to Don's dismay, the Astros blew the lead
and his only chance to record a win in the big time.

ARLIN, Steve
    Dentist
    San Diego, CA

Steve won All-American honors at Ohio State in 1965 and
1966. He was voted the MVP of the College World Series in
'66 as he led the Buckeyes to the NCAA championship.
Steve then signed with the Phillies and worked his way
through their minor league system before he was taken by
the expansion Padres in 1969.

In '71 and '72 he led the league in defeats with 19 and 21
respectively, frequently the victim of weak hitting. The
Ohio State Dental School grad was drilled for 10 consecutive losses in '72. He closed with Cleveland in 1974.

Steve's grandfather, Harold Arlin, is credited with being the first announcer to broadcast a major league baseball game when he did the play-by-play on KDKA in
Pittsburgh as the Pirates hosted the Phillies on Aug. 5,
1921, at Forbes Field. Over 50 years later on Aug. 30,
1972, he returned to the broadcast booth at the invitation
of Pirates' announcer Bob Prince to broadcast a few innings during a game in which the Pirates were playing
San Diego with his grandson Steve on the mound.   34-67

ARRIGO, Jerry
    Bartender
    Amelia, OH

Early in his career with the Twins (1961-64), Jerry twice
just missed hurling a no-hitter. On June 26, 1964, he beat the
White Sox, 2-0, on a one-hitter, a ninth-inning single by Mike
Hershberger. Pitching for the Reds, he one-hit the Mets with
Jerry Grote's infield single the only hit he allowed.

Arrigo, who also saw action with the Mets and White
Sox with a return trip to Cincinnati in between, was
blessed with outstanding ability. According to Sammy
Ellis who pitched with Jerry at Cincy, "He had as good a
stuff as anybody in the N.L."   35-40

AUST, Dennis
   New York Yankee scout
   Tampa, FL

"Mission Impossible" began a long run on TV at the time Dennis was facing his own impossible mission of cracking the Cardinals' pitching staff. The right-hander from the University of Florida lost his only decision in 15 games with St. Louis in 1965–66.

AZCUE, Joe
   Salesman for Sears; owns a bar in Kansas City, Mo. called "The Catcher's Mitt"

"The immortal Cuban" began his 11-year odyssey with the Reds in 1960. He then made a stop at Kansas City before joining the Indians from 1963–69. The hard-nosed catcher also served behind the dish with the Red Sox, Angels, and Brewers, with his best season in '68 when he hit .280 for the third-place Indians.
   On July 30, 1968, Joe had the misfortune of hitting into an unassisted triple play, the last major leaguer to do so.
   The Cuban backstop is one of a handful of players who followed up a threat of holding out for an entire season over a salary dispute with the Angels in 1971. Instead he took a job pouring concrete.   .252

B

BAHNSEN, Stan
   Head of U.S. Operations for Caribbean Components, an electronics firm
   Pompano Beach, FL

This hard-throwing right-hander out of the University of Nebraska was first up with the Yankees in 1966, then was named the A.L. Rookie of the Year in '68 in his first full season, when he posted a 17–12 record with an excellent 2.06 ERA.

The Yankees' No. 1 selection in the first free agent draft in 1965, Stan pitched in front of his parents for the first time in pro ball in a 1966 game for Toledo. He didn't disappoint them as he hurled a no-hitter, but it wasn't until after the game that he knew he had pitched the masterpiece. In the sixth inning a slow-hit ground ball to third baseman Mike Ferraro bounced off his glove into the hands of shortstop Bobby Murcer, who threw wildly to first base. Originally scored a hit and an error, it was later changed to an error on Ferraro.

Traded to the White Sox after the '71 campaign, Stan went 21-16 in '72, but almost did a reversal a year later going 18-21. Pitching for Chicago on June 21, 1973, he shut out the Indians, 2-0, allowing 12 hits, 2 hits shy of the record for hits allowed while pitching a shutout. In August he pitched 8 2/3 innings of no-hit ball until Walt "No Neck" Williams hit safely.

Bahnsen also spent time with Oakland, Montreal, and California before winding up his long journey (146-149) in 1982.

BAILEY, Bob
    Manager at Columbus (Southern League)

Bob was signed off the Long Beach, Calif., sandlots by the Pirates for an estimated $175,000, which is reputed to be one of the biggest bonuses ever paid to a young prospect. After winning the International League Player of the Year and Sporting News Minor League Player of the Year honors for Columbus in 1962, Bob went aboard ship with the Pirates on a cruise that also included time with the Dodgers, Expos, Reds, and Red Sox into the late 1970s.

The most publicized deal of the 1966–67 trading season saw the Dodgers send Maury Wills to the Pirates for Bailey and Gene Michael. He was remarkably consistent, if not proficient, in L.A. as he was 73-for-322 for a .227 avg. in both 1966 and '67.

After two years in the California sun he became an original member of the expansion Expos and had his finest season in 1970 with 28 home runs and a .287 average.

Not the most fleet-footed guy around, he grounded into 216 career double plays en route to a .257 lifetime mark.

BAILEY, Steve
Director of Parks and Recreation
Lorain, OH

Steve Bailey, who earned a master's degree from Kent State, had a brief (1967–68) stay with the Indians, for whom he compiled a 2-6 record.

BAIRD, Bob
Died April 11, 1974, at age 32 from gunshot wounds suffered in an altercation in Chattanooga, TN

Bob's story is an amalgam of sweetness, bitterness, and tragedy. The left-hander once fanned a league record 20 batters pitching for Pensacola in a class D Alabama-Florida League game in 1962. At the end of the season he was elevated all the way to the big leagues. In 8 games with the Senators in parts of the '62 and '63 season, he was 0-4.

He died tragically when shot to death in 1974.

BAKER, "Dusty"
Active player with San Francisco Giants

Johnnie B. Baker, Jr., better known as "Dusty," was the Atlanta Braves' 25th-round choice of the 1967 Free Agent Draft. He came on the big league scene in 1968 as a teenager and made brief appearances with Atlanta the next three seasons.

The former Marine came up to stay in '72 when he hit a surprising .321 to finish third in the N.L. batting race. On Sept. 20 he tied a major league record for most times facing a pitcher in one inning (three) and most at bats in one inning (three) as the Braves scored a baker's dozen 13 runs in the second inning of the nightcap of a twinbill against

the Astros. Oddly enough, those were all the runs Atlanta
scored in its 13-6 victory. Dusty doubled to lead off the inning, hit a 3-run homer, and grounded out to end the inning with the bases loaded.

Traded to the Dodgers the following season, the southern California native chose to wear No. 12 after his idol,
Tommy Davis. In 1977 the Dodgers became the only club
in history to have four players with 30 or more home runs.
They were Steve Garvey (33), Reggie Smith (32), Ron Cey
(30) and Baker (30).

A *Sporting News* All-Star outfielder in 1981, Dusty wore
Dodger blue from 1976–83 and hit 144 homers before
going to San Francisco.   .280

BAKER, Frank
Somerset, NJ

In 1969 this Vietnam veteran prepared to do battle against
A.L. pitchers as a member of the Indians. In his first game
ever the outfielder collected four hits and was on cloud
nine. Following another brief try with Cleveland in '71, he
came down to earth with a lifetime .232 avg.

This Frank Baker is not to be confused with the Yankee
and Oriole shortstop of the early 1970s.

BAKER, Tom
Died March 9, 1980, in Port Townsend, WA at age 45

Pitching for Hawaii in the PCL in 1961, Tom met with
misfortune in his home state when he was injured in an
automobile accident in Seattle. Later that summer he suffered a broken arm in Spokane.

Finally, in '63 he made it with the Cubs where he
pitched 10 games, but all he got for his forbearance was a
tough 2-1 defeat to the Reds, the result of two unearned
runs. It was his only decision.

BAKENHASTER, Dave
Warehouseman for Nabisco Brands Food Co.
Columbus, OH

The Rolling Stones had their first big hit, "It's All Over Now," in '64. Dave was singing that tune after pitching in just two games with no decisions for the Cardinals that summer.

In retrospect, he says, "I never achieved what I really set out to do. My abilities were not as good as I thought they were." He admits, "I felt sorry for myself when I first got out. But when I got my head screwed on right, I was okay."

BALDSCHUN, Jack
Salesman for Lumber Dealer Supply
Green Bay, WI

As a rookie with the Phillies in '61, this right-handed relief specialist led the N.L. with 65 appearances and was the only Phils' flipper to post a winning record (5-3) that season. At one point he came out of the bullpen eight straight games, one short of the then major league record. From '61 to '65 he led the Phils in appearances.

His 12 victories in '62 made him the winningest reliever in the N.L. On April 14, 1963, Jack was credited with both wins in a doubleheader sweep over the Cardinals. But he's quick to remember that, "I once lost two games in one day to the Mets at the Polo Grounds."

Perhaps the most bitter year in Phillies' history was 1964. Baldschun spoke candidly about the Phillies' collapse, pointing the finger at manager Gene Mauch. "He (Mauch) used two men (Jim Bunning and Chris Short) too many times the last two weeks of the season. They pitched about every other day. Gene was trying to win it early. He would come to see me every day and told me to be ready. But I wasn't used." With a career-high 71 appearances and 21 saves in '64, that was a tough pill for Jack to swallow.

The fireman deluxe spent time in Cincinnati and San Diego before calling it quits in 1970. Overall he was 48-41, plus 60 saves in 457 games, all as a reliever.

BALDWIN, Dave
   Systems engineer for Phelps Dodge Corp. in Phoenix.
   Also writes humor, children's stories, and scientific
   articles.
   Tucson, AZ

Former basketball coach Al McGuire says, "Superintelli-
gent people can't be superb athletes. They're too aware."
   This intellectual sidearming right-hander had an articulate plan to make it big, but when it all ended he showed a
6-11 mark and a fine 3.09 ERA in 176 games from 1966–73.
   The University of Arizona graduate, who worked as an
anthropologist during the off-season, led the Senators'
bullpen in '67 with a dozen saves and a 1.70 ERA. Baldwin, who probably had as many college degrees as he had
pitches, earned a Ph.D in genetics at Arizona in 1979, and
received an M.S. in systems engineering in 1983.
   Looking back, he says, "Mine was certainly an up-and-
down career. This was due in large part to being a sidearm
relief pitcher in a day when both sidearmers and relievers
were highly suspect according to many managers."
   Dave carried his books with him to such cities as Washington (Senators), Milwaukee (Brewers) and Chicago
(White Sox).

BALES, Lee
   General Manager for Rauscher-Pierce, a stock brokerage firm, in Houston, TX

On Aug. 7, 1966, this switch-hitting Braves' infielder
made an ignoble debut as he became the fourth man in
major league history to strike out four times in his first big
league contest. Apparently haunted by the number 4, he
picked up just 4 singles in 43 at bats with the Braves and
Astros ('67).
   Lee's bat and glove were in harmony on July 25, 1965, in
a game for Austin in the Texas League as he went 6-for-6.

BALSAMO, Tony
      Co-ownor of Lenny's Clam Bar and Restaurant in
      Rockville Centre, NY

"Whatever Happened to Baby Jane?" starring Joan Crawford and Bette Davis was one of the big flicks in 1962, the
year this Brooklyn-born right-hander out of Fordham University lost his only decision in 18 relief appearances for
the Cubs. Fans were soon asking, "Whatever happened to
Tony Balsamo?"

BANDO, Sal
      Milwaukee Brewers' special assistant to the general
      manager

It's been said that statistics are like a girl's bikini. They
show a lot, but they don't reveal anything. Sal's stats do
not adequately recall the story of "Mr. Clutch."
      The third baseman and captain of the Oakland A's dy-
nasty years in the early 1970s, Sal set the standard for the
team's success. Voted the MVP in the 1965 College World
Series while playing for Arizona State, Bando found himself with the Kansas City A's the following year although
his first full season came in '68. Statistically his best year
was in '69 when he ripped 31 home runs and 113 RBIs, his
career high in both categories. That year he played every
inning at third base, a feat not repeated until Cal Ripken
played every inning at shortstop in 1983.
      Sal contributed many clutch hits for the A's, but none
probably bigger than the home run he hit in Game Three
of the 1974 A.L. Playoffs vs. the Orioles. With the series
tied, 1-1, after the first two games in Oakland, his fourth-
inning homer proved to be the only run of the contest as
Vida Blue outdueled Jim Palmer to give the A's a 2-1 edge
in the series.
      Following the '76 season he left Charlie Finley's trou-
bled franchise. When asked if it was difficult leaving, he
replied, "Was it difficult leaving the Titanic?"
      After spending the next five years with the Brewers, he
retired with 242 four-baggers and a .254 average.

BANEY, Dick
    Employed with Wickes Furniture Store
    Anaheim, CA

Dick was one of 25 pitchers who took the mound for the
Seattle Pilots in 1969. He will forever more remain the
only pitcher in Pilots' history to go undefeated, winning
his only decision in nine games.

Sent back to the minors for more seasoning, he returned
to win three more games with the Reds in 1973–74 and
wound up 4-1.

Described as "a real work of art" by Jim Bouton in *Ball
Four,* Dick was in an artistic mood when he posed in
Playgirl Magazine a few years back.

BANKS, George
    Currently disabled with amyotrophic lateral sclerosis
    (Lou Gehrig's Disease); formerly employed with the
    Kohler Co.
    Pacolet, SC

George was around from 1962–66 with the Twins and Indians. However, the highlights of this third baseman's career came in the minors. In 1961 he led the Eastern
League with 30 home runs and was the PCL All-Star third
sacker in '65 with 35 home runs for Portland.

George struggled against big league pitching for a .219
average, but his biggest battle has been his nine-year fight
with A.L.S.

BARBER, Steve
    Owns a car care center
    Las Vegas, NV

This hard-throwing left-hander struggled in the minors,
but found life in Baltimore more to his liking. In 1960 he
vaulted directly from Class D to become a member of the
Orioles' "Kiddie Korp."

There was no doubt that Steve could "hum that seed"
(he was clocked at 95.5 mph), but the only problem was
where it would land. However, the big time appeared to

have a somewhat settling affect on the 21-year-old lefty as
he went 10-7, but still had control problems leading the
league in walks with 113. In 1963 Steve became the first
20-game winner in Orioles' history, going 20-13.

Plagued by tendonitis in his left elbow in '66, the
flamethrower was never the same. Frustration accompanied Steve along the remainder of his travels, which took
him to the Yankees, Pilots, Cubs, Braves, Angels, and
Giants with some time spent in the minors.

On April 30, 1967, he was on the losing end of a game
against the Tigers despite combining with Stu Miller to
hurl a no-hitter. Steve pitched the first 8 2/3 innings, but
lost the game, 2-1, on a wild pitch and an error. He proved
to be his own worst enemy that day, surrendering 10
walks. That same season he had a no-hitter going against
California with one out in the ninth when Jim Fregosi doubled. Barber got the next two batters and the win.

A different pitcher with the same name was on the
Twins' roster in 1970-71.

Unaffected by superstition, Steve wore No. 13 on his uniform jersey. Ironically as a reliever, he had 13 saves in his
career.   121-105

BARBIERI, Jim
      Sporting goods salesman
      Spokane, WA

Many former stars have been honored to throw out the
first ball at World Series games. Jim was given the honor a
dozen years before he ever played in the majors.

Jim's life was brought up to date in Martin Ralbovsky's
1974 book, *Destiny's Darlings,* about the 1954 Schenectady, NY, world champion Little League team. Captain of
the team which captured the title at Williamsport, PA, by
defeating a California team of which future Cubs' rookie
star Ken Hubbs was a member, Barbieri made it to the
Dodgers in '66. His .280 average in 39 games helped the
club to the N.L. pennant. It was his only season in the
biggies.

In the '66 Series, the Orioles swept the Dodgers. For
Baltimore's Boog Powell it was sweet revenge since Boog

was a member of a Florida team that was defeated by
Jim's "Destiny's Darlings" in '54.

BARKER, Ray
Security officer for General Motors
Martinsburg, WV

"Buddy" had his first taste of honey with the Orioles in
1960. He wasn't seen again until '65, when he performed
his services with the Indians and Yankees.

A first baseman, Barker was used mostly in a pinch-
hitting role, which he played well for the Pinstripers in
'65, connecting for three pinch-hit home runs, including
two in succession. .214

BARNOWSKI, Ed
Director of sales and promotions for the Rochester I.L.
team

Ed had a rather benign six-game experience with the Orioles in 1965–66, failing to gain a decision. But his minor
league portfolio resembles that of Walter Johnson.

The Syracuse University product once struck out 20 batters in a game in 1963 at Stockton in the California
League. The following year he fired two no-hitters for the
same team.

BARONE, Dick
Route salesman for American Bakeries
San Jose, CA

The 1960 Pirates had their share of heroes. Dick Groat hit
.325 to win the N.L. batting title while Bill Mazeroski's
dramatic home run in the bottom of the ninth in Game
Seven of the World Series gave the Bucs the championship
over the Yankees.

As the heroes went by, Dick Barone sat on the curb of
the dugout and clapped. The shortstop was hitless in 3
games and 6 at-bats that year during his brief stay in

Pittsburgh. It was ironic that he celebrated his 28th birthday on October 13th, the day of Mazeroski's homer.

BARRAGAN, Cuno
        Insurance salesman for Cal Western Life Insurance
        Co.
        Sacramento, CA

"Cuno" was nearly 30 years old when he had his first shot
in the majors with the '61 Cubs. Unfortunately he suffered
a fractured ankle while sliding into third base in spring
training and wasn't activated until September.
    Barragan then connected for a home run in his first big
league at-bat. It turned out to be his only homer in his
three-year jog.   .202.

BARRY, Rich
        Automobile salesman
        Kaneohe, HI

Do you remember Rich Barry, the Phillies' outfielder in
1969 who self-destructed after 20 games with a .188 average?

BARTON, Bob
        Insurance broker specializing in commercial property
        casualty insurance
        San Diego, CA

An outstanding high school basketball player in Kentucky, Bob was all set to accept a scholarship from Adolph
Rupp at the University of Kentucky when he decided to
sign a pro baseball contract with the Giants. Rupp was so
upset he barred all future Giant scouts from the Kentucky
campus.
    Bob's baseball jaunt as a catcher (.226) spanned the
years 1965–74 with the Giants, Padres and Reds.

BASS, Norm
    Computer Operations for McAuto Company
    Inglewood, CA

The year 1961 was a memorable one for Norm and his brother Dick, who became the first Los Angeles Rams running back to ever rush for over 1,000 yards in a season. In his first big league start, Norm picked up his first win in a 20-2 rout of the Twins as the A's established a record for most runs in a game while the team was lodged in Kansas City.
    After going 11-11 his rookie year, he was just 2-6 in '62 and was out of the majors the following year after only three appearances, finishing 13-17.

BATEMAN, John
    Houston, TX

Batman became a national craze as a TV show in 1966 when John Bateman had the finest season of an otherwise mediocre career, batting .279 while catching for the Astros.
    Throughout his career he battled excess pounds along with curve balls and sliders. It is estimated that he paid over $2,000 in fines for being overweight during much of his 10-year stay which began in Houston in '63.
    The chunky backstop went to Montreal in the 1969 expansion draft, then signed out with the Phils in '72.
    On Sept. 29, 1970, John hit the final home run ever at Connie Mack Stadium in Philadelphia.
    During the late '70s he traveled with Eddie Feigner's King and His Court 4-man softball team. John batted a bit more than his listed weight as he tipped the scales with a .230 lifetime avg.

BATES, Dick
    Scottsdale, AZ

Playing for Mobile in a minor league contest in 1917, a player named Johnny Bates hit a fly ball about 200 feet in the air over second base. To the amazement of everyone in the park, the ball got stuck in the fuselage of a passing plane. The umpire, who obviously had a good sense of humor, ruled the stowaway clout a home run, using the following logic. "When last seen, the ball was traveling out of the park in fair territory."

Dick Bates never lost a batted ball to a passing plane, but when Peter, Paul, and Mary were singing "Leaving On A Jet Plane," they might have been singing about Dick. The southpaw jetted out after appearing in one game for the Seattle Pilots in which he accumulated a sky-high ERA of 27.00!

BAUTA, Ed
Location unknown

The Cuban right-handed reliever was the losing pitcher in the first game ever played at Shea Stadium as the Mets lost to Bob Friend and the Pirates, 4-3, before 48,736 fans. By the way, Friend was also the winning pitcher when the Giants played their last game in the Polo Grounds before their move west. Bauta was 6-6 with the Cardinals and Mets (1960–64).

BEARNARTH, Larry
Montreal Expos pitching coach

Larry was 32-2 at St. John's University before the New York City native pitched for the Mets from 1963–1966.

While playing in the Venezuela Winter League following the '65 season, he answered heckling fans by throwing the ball into the stands. The incident so angered the crowd that four policemen had to escort Larry back to his hotel. His ball-tossing caper prompted Larry to leave the country.

Five years after toiling with the Mets, he returned to the bigs for a couple of appearances out of the Brewers' bullpen in '71.   13-21

BEAUCHAMP, Jim
Manager at Durham (Carolina League)

Nat King Cole sang "Ramblin' Rose" in '63, the year this ramblin' journeyman first baseman-outfielder arrived with

the Cardinals. For the next 11 years he was in and out
with the Cards, Astros, Braves, Reds and Mets. He earned
his ticket to the majors by hitting .337 with 31 homers for
Tulsa, good enough for MVP honors in the Texas League
in '63.

An Oklahoma cattle rancher during his playing days,
Jim Beauchamp (pronounced Beach-um) was used primarily as a pinch-hitter in the majors. He celebrated his 33rd
birthday on Aug. 21, 1972, by hitting two home runs as the
Mets beat the Astros, 4-2. The following night he homered
again and drove in all four of the Mets' runs in another 4-2
victory over Houston.   .231

BECK, Rich
     Manager of the Seattle First National Bank (Odessa,
     WA branch)

Frank Sinatra sang *It Was a Very Good Year* in 1965 and
for Rich Beck it was. The right-hander hurled a no-hitter
for Columbus in the Southern League that summer. In the
final game of the season he pitched a two-hit shutout to
give his team the pennant.

Rich joined the Yankees in September and won two of
three decisions, including a shutout while posting an excellent 2.14 ERA. But '65 proved to be his swan song. After
a two-year stint in the army, he never returned.

Beck has the distinction of tossing a 7-inning no-hitter
in his first professional game with Idaho Falls in 1962.

He says, "Baseball continues to be my first love. How
can you ask for a better job than to play a kid's game and
get paid for it."

BECKERT, Glenn
     Trades commodities as a member of the Chicago
     Board of Trade
     Palatine, IL

Glenn could probably be considered the Joe Sewell of his
day. One of the toughest ever to strike out, Beckert led the
N.L. from 1966–69 with the least strikeouts for players
with 400 at-bats or more. During that period the nifty

Cubs' second baseman with the fine bat control fanned a slim total of 105 times.

In '68 he led the N.L. in runs scored with 98, the first player to lead the league in that department with less than 100 since George Burns of the 1919 Giants led with 86. Glenn, who almost always got a piece of the rock, enjoyed a 27-game hitting streak in '68, when he was named "Chicago Player of the Year" by the Chicago baseball writers.

Beckert's 11-year story (1965–75) was spent mostly with the Cubs. He checked out with the Padres with a .283 career average, his finest year coming in 1971 when he hit .342. He was voted to the N.L. All-Star team four consecutive years.

BEDELL, Howie
Kansas City Royals Coordinator of Player Development

During the 1968 season, Don Drysdale held N.L. opponents scoreless for 58 ⅔ consecutive innings from May 14th to June 8th. Playing for the Phils on June 8th, Howie pinch-hit for pitcher Larry Jackson in the fifth inning and hit a sacrifice fly to put an end to "Big D's" streak. It was his only RBI of the season.

In 1963 Bedell had a streak of his own as he tied the American Association record by hitting in 43 consecutive games while at Louisville. Three years later he took Eastern League batting honors and was voted the circuit's MVP.

Overall Howie hit .193 in 67 games with the Milwaukee Braves (1962) and Philadelphia Phillies (1968).

BEENE, Fred
Milwaukee Brewers' scout in the Southwest
Oakhurst, TX

"Do what you can, with what you have, where you are," said Theodore Roosevelt.

Little Freddie Beene did what he could with what he had wherever he went. The 5'9", 150-lb. right-hander pitched

Sam Houston State to the 1963 NAIA championship before entering pro ball.

He used all of his tools on May 8, 1965, in a memorable Eastern League game when he pitched four-hit shutout ball in relief over the last 12 innings as Elmira beat Springfield, 2-1, in a 27-inning marathon.

Fred was up with the Orioles for brief stays (1968–70), but spent most of those years at Rochester. On Opening Night in 1969 he had a shutout going until the ninth inning when he suffered a fractured leg when hit by a line drive.

Beene wore Yankee threads from 1972–74 before closing with the Indians in '75. Owner of a lifetime 12-7 mark, he was particularly effective in '73, going 6-0 with a 1.68 ERA in 19 games.

BELANGER, Mark
> Represents pro athletes with Professional Management Associates
> Timonium, MD

Mark had the assignment of replacing the legendary Luis Aparicio at shortstop for the Orioles. One of the slickest fielding shortstops ever, he won eight Gold Gloves tying Aparicio for the most ever won by a shortstop.

Belanger was labeled the next Marty Marion because of his tall and lithe (6'2"–170-lb.) appearance and his grace on the field.

Mark had brief trials in Baltimore from '65–'67, but was around for keeps from 1968–81. Granted free agency after the '81 season, he signed with the Dodgers, then was released after the '82 campaign with a .228 lifetime mark.

The 1976 A.L. All-Star shortstop appeared in four World Series and six ALCS all with the Orioles. His 21 ALCS games for the Orioles is a club record for most games played with one team.

BELINSKY, Bo
   Drug and alcohol abuse counselor in Hawaii

"Going to bed with a woman never hurt a ballplayer. It's staying up all night looking for them that does you in."
                                        —Casey Stengel.

   The screwball with the screwball, Bo Belinsky was the subject of Maury Allen's marvelous book in 1973, *Bo: Pitching and Wooing*.
   Signed originally by the Orioles, Belinsky was acquired in the 1961 expansion draft by the California Angels. The Trenton, NJ, native arrived with the Angels in 1962. The self-styled King of the Twist carried with him his colorful and controversial reputation as a pool shark and womanizer. Irv Kaze, the publicity director for the Angels at the time, commented, "He's a handsome son of a bitch. He's got that lean and hungry look they all like to mother. You can almost feel the animal sex in him."
   The Angels soon realized that Robert "Bo" Belinsky had a business side to him when he proceeded to become a holdout before he had ever pitched in a major league game. But he eventually signed for the $6,000 minimum after a bit of acrimony.
   Bo won his first start on April 19, 1962, with relief help from Art Fowler, a free spirit in his own right. Undefeated after three starts, the unpredictable southpaw no-hit the Orioles, 2-0, on May 5, 1962, before a crowd of just over 15,000 at Chavez Ravine. Following his no-hitter, he fired a verbal blast at Paul Richards, the Baltimore manager. He said, "I wonder how Paul Richards liked that. The only thing that man ever said to me the year I was in spring training with the Orioles was, 'Maybe I'll see you again sometime.' Well, he did."
   The fame generated from his no-hitter and flamboyant lifestyle gained him entry into some of Hollywood's swankiest parties, several of which were arranged by columnist Walter Winchell. Belinsky's dates ranged from unknown local beauties to starlets like Ann-Margaret, Connie Stevens, Tina Louise, Mamie Van Doren, and even Queen Soraya of Iran. His romance with Mamie Van Doren was a lengthy one. In the late '60s he married Jo

Collins, *Playboy's* Playmate of the Year in 1965. Bo's second marriage (and divorce) was to a member of the Weyerhaeuser family after he reportedly saved her from drowning.

Belinsky finished 10-11 in '62. The next year he was 2-9, spending a portion of the season in Hawaii (P.C.L.). In 1964 he actually pitched well with a 9-8 record and 2.86 ERA, but spent part of the year suspended for breaking club rules.

In the late '60s Bo made stops with the Phillies, Astros, Pirates and Reds in between trips to Hawaii, where he pitched another no-hitter on Aug. 18, 1968, defeating Tacoma, 1-0. Belinsky believes he was blackballed out of the A.L. by his Angels' manager, Bill Rigney, because he once hit a reporter in his hotel room. His last attempt was with the Cardinals, but he never made it north with St. Louis.

Belinsky's acting career deserves mention. He appeared in "Damn Yankees" at Melodyland in Anaheim with his Angels' roommate, Dean Chance. Bo did several episodes of *77 Sunset Strip, Dakota,* and *Surfside Six* as well as some cowboy flicks.

He finished 28-51 lifetime, but baseball statistics do not come close in telling the story of one of the most colorful personalities in sports' history.

BENCH, Johnny
> Has a Coors Beer distributorship for three Ohio counties with a group of associates; does promotional work for the Cincinnati Reds.

In the first major league free agent draft in '65, there were seven catchers drafted before Bench. Most of the seven never set foot on a big league diamond.

Johnny first came up as a 19-year-old late in the '67 season with the Reds. Wearing uniform No. 53 he hit an anemic .163 in 26 games. The next season he switched to No. 5 and hit 15 homers to go along with his .275 average to cop N.L. Rookie of the Year honors. He also won the first of what would be 10 consecutive Gold Gloves behind the dish.

During his rookie year he established a major league record for most games caught by a rookie (154).

The catcher supreme enjoyed exalted status in 1970,
winning MVP honors with league-leading career highs of
45 home runs and 148 RBIs. He won MVP honors again in
'72 after leading the senior circuit in homers (40) and RBIs
(125). In the NLCS that fall his dramatic ninth-inning
roundtripper tied the fifth and final game against the Pirates which eventually was won by the Reds.

That winter Johnny's fans and friends were shocked to
learn he needed surgery for a lesion on his lung. Fortunately, there was no malignancy.

Three times in his career he hit three home runs in a
game. The first two times (July 26, 1970, and May 9, 1973)
all three of his roundtrippers came off future Hall of
Famer Steve Carlton.

Bench appeared in four World Series with the Reds. In
1976 he destroyed the Yankees with a .533 mark. He
batted .370 in 11 All-Star Games. Johnny is the only
player in major league history with at least three career
home runs in the All-Star Game (3), League Championship
Series (5) and World Series (5).

On June 10, 1983, the 35-year-old Cincinnati legend announced his retirement. He took with him 325 lifetime
home runs as a catcher, the most of any backstop in big
league history. Overall he hit 389 four-baggers.

Johnny Bench won't be elected to the Hall of Fame at as
young an age as Sandy Koufax, but he will still be only 41
years old during the induction ceremonies at Cooperstown
in the summer of '89.

Sparky Anderson, his former manager, says, "No man
should be compared to Johnny Bench."

BENNETT, Dave
      Carpenter for Truttman Construction Company
      Yreka, CA

The Lovin' Spoonful were singing, *Do You Believe in
Magic* in 1964. The Bennett brothers may have been singing it also that summer when they were both members of
the Phillies' pitching staff. But for Dave the magic was

brief since he disappeared after just one inning of one
game out of the bullpen.

BENNETT, Dennis
Employed in a lumber mill
Klamath Falls, OR

When Dennis came up with the Phils in '62, the hard-
throwing southpaw had already been a participant on the
rodeo circuit, competing in bareback bronco events. He
also had been a forest fire fighter in California. But then it
came time to burn opposing batters and compete in pitching duels.

His first major league victory on June 2, 1962, was a
memorable one as he hurled a 4-hit shutout and struck out
11 to crush the Dodgers, 7-0, and snap their 13-game winning streak. Following his 9-9 rookie season, he pitched
winter ball in Puerto Rico and severely damaged an ankle
in an auto accident in which the driver of the car was
killed.

Traded to the Red Sox in '65, Dennis finished in '68 after
pitching briefly with the Mets and Angels.   43-47

BERRY, Ken
Kansas City Royals minor league hitting instructor

This outstanding defensive centerfielder was with the
White Sox (1962–70) and Angels (1971–73) during his long
journey. He departed in '75 at .255 after stops with the
Brewers and Indians.

Ken is well-remembered for his numerous leaping
catches at Comiskey Park at the centerfield wall, robbing
opposing hitters of home runs. Twice a Gold Glove winner
('69 and '72), he played errorless ball both seasons. His
best years at the plate came in '72 and '73 when he hit .289
and .284 respectively with the Angels. In '67 he had a
20-game hitting streak with Chicago.

BERTAINA, Frank
> Operates a travel bureau leading hunting trips to
> Africa
> Santa Rosa, CA

Frank qualifies as your typical flaky lefty chucker. Former pitcher Moe Drabowsky nicknamed Frank "Toys In
The Attic" after the 1963 movie for his daffy behavior.

The eccentric southpaw was on target when he won his
first big league game for the Orioles on Sept. 12, 1964, as
he matched one-hitters with K.C.A.'s hurler Bob Meyer.
After winning just three more in Baltimore over the next
three seasons, he was traded to Washington in '67.

Frank stayed in the nation's capital until '69, then returned to Baltimore before engaging in his last shootout
with the Cardinals in '70 to finish at 19-29.

BERTELL, Dick
> Salesman for Willamette Industries
> Mission Viejo, CA

Television personality Jack Paar walked off the "Tonight
Show" in 1960 when Dick walked on a big league diamond
for the first time as a catcher with the Cubs where he made
his living until 1965. His best season in the Windy City
came in '62 as he batted .302. Dick spent the first half of
that season commuting on weekends between Army service at Fort Knox, Ky., and various N.L. parks. He was discharged on July 13, 1962, and celebrated his return to
civilian life with a pinch-hit home run the following day.

Bertell also spent time with the Giants before walking
off with the Cubs in '67.

An All-American selection in his college days, Dick
paced Iowa State to the "Big Seven" championship in
1957. .250

BETHEA, Bill
> Assistant baseball coach at the University of Texas

In 1964 Billy Mills dramatically won the 10,000-meter run
in the summer Olympics in Tokyo. For Bill Bethea, 1964

was the year the former Texas Longhorn reached the majors as an infielder for an undramatic 10-game run with the Twins, hitting .167.

BETHKE, Jim
> Engineer for Missouri Pacific Railroad
> Kansas City, MO

In 1965 the Byrds sang *Turn, Turn, Turn* when Jim was an 18-year-old right-handed reliever with the Mets. Strangely, after winning his only two decisions in 25 appearances, there were no more turns for Jim.

BILLINGHAM, Jack
> Sporting goods business
> Winter Park, FL

A distant cousin of Christy Mathewson, Jack broke in with the Dodgers in '68. The Expos selected the tall right-hander in the expansion draft, but he was traded to the Astros before ever throwing a pitch in Montreal.

Billingham spent most of the '69 season working out of the Astros' bullpen. He was converted to a starter the following year before traded to the Reds at the end of the '71 campaign. It was in Cincinnati that he made his mark as the most durable and dependable member of the rotation for the "Big Red Machine" the next several years, winning 19 games in '73 and '74. On Opening Day of the '74 season Jack served up Hank Aaron's 714th home run which tied Aaron with Babe Ruth's career mark.

In World Series competition Billingham shows a microscopic ERA of 0.36 in 7 games pitched, winning both of his decisions.

Jack joined the Tigers and his former Cincy manager Sparky Anderson at Detroit for a couple of years before bowing out with the Red Sox in 1980 after a 145-113 record.

Visiting the Tigers' spring training camp in 1981, he told Sparky, "I wish you'd let me talk to the players about what's in store for them when they hit the outside world. On second thought, forget it. I wouldn't have believed it last spring if someone told me."

BILLINGS, Dick
      Real estate business in Dallas, Texas area

Dick was the regular catcher with the last Washington
Senators team and the first edition of the Texas Rangers.
      A graduate of Michigan State with a degree in educa-
tion, he had brief trials with the Senators as an outfielder
in 1968–69, then volunteered to go to Denver the following
year to study catching skills. He learned his lessons well
and returned to Washington, then moved with the team to
Texas until 1974. He closed the book on his career in '75
with the Cards.   .227

BLACKABY, Ethan
      General Manager at Phoenix in the Pacific Coast
      League

Over the years baseball has had such zany characters as
Rabbit Maranville, Casey Stengel and Jimmy Piersall.
Add Ethan Blackaby. Once while playing in a Texas
League game, he took a sign in the batter's box standing
on his head. Ethan was simply trying to get the sign from
manager Rocky Bridges who was standing on his head in
the third base coaching box!
      A running back at Illinois, Ethan once ran 80 yards for a
touchdown against Wisconsin. But Blackaby decided to
shed his thigh pads for sliding pads.
      As a member of the Braves in '62, the mod dresser hit
the first pitch he ever saw in the biggies for a double. But
the speedy flychaser managed just two more hits in his
15-game scamper with Milwaukee in 1962 and 1964.   .120

BLADT, Rick
      Construction worker
      Silverton, OR

Rick constructs large farm elevators today. He says, "A lot
of high rope and scaffold work is involved."
      After a look into his baseball past, one would think that
Mr. Bladt would be doing private detective work because
of his history of searching for missing baseballs.

Playing for Syracuse in a game against Memphis on July 30, 1976, Art Gardner of Memphis hit a shot off the centerfield wall in the bottom of the third inning and circled the bases for an apparent inside-the-park home run. While Gardner was racing around the bases, Bladt searched frantically for the ball. The umpires had Gardner return to second and called the case of the missing baseball a ground-rule double.

Life wasn't always so bizarre for Rick. He first saw action with the Cubs in '69 after hitting .312 for Tacoma in the P.C.L. Six years later he returned with the Yankees. After 62 games and a missing baseball, this elevator builder got the shaft with a .215 avg.

BLAIR, Paul
Minor league instructor in the Houston Astros' organization; named Commissioner of the North American Baseball League (1986)

Known as "Motormouth," Paul actually let his skills do the talking during his impressive 17-year (1964–80) trek. Originally Mets' property, Paul was drafted by Baltimore, where he eventually earned the reputation as the premier centerfielder in the A.L.

A lifetime .250 swatter, Paul's career high came in 1967 when he hit .293 and led the A.L. in triples with 12. Two years later he banged out 26 homers, his high in that department.

Blair usually made his presence felt during post-season play. In the 1966 Series against the Dodgers he collected only one hit, a titanic 430-foot moon shot which gave the O's a 1-0 victory in Game Three en route to a four-game sweep. He then made a dramatic leaping catch in the eighth inning of the fourth game to rob Jim Lefebvre of a homer, preserving another 1-0 Birds' victory.

In the 1969 ALCS against the Twins, his suicide squeeze bunt brought home the game-winning run in the 12th inning of the first game, scoring Mark Belanger to beat Minnesota, 4-3. The event was historic as it marked the first game ever of an American League Championship Series. In the third contest he paced the Orioles to an 11-2

pasting with a big 5-for-6 day on a pair of singles, two doubles and a home run.

Blair's post-season assault continued in 1970 as he tied a
record for most base hits in a five-game Series when he
went 9-for-19.

It was during the '70 season that Paul's career dangled
by a thread after he was hit by a pitch from California's
Ken Tatum that caused serious eye and facial injuries. The
beaning left Paul a bit gun-shy in the batter's box. He appeared tentative, standing a good distance from the plate
and even tried switch-hitting for a brief period.

The classy outfielder added one more Series distinction
in '71 when, as the leadoff hitter in Game Four, he became
the first man to bat in a night World Series contest and
proceeded to single against Luke Walker.

Paul carried his October tradition with him as a member
of the Yankees in '77 and '78 when he batted .333 against
the Dodgers.

BLANCO, Gil
        Owns kennels and trains hunting dogs
        Phoenix, AZ

Happiness Is A Warm Puppy became a best seller with
over half a million copies sold at the time 19-year-old
southpaw Gil Blanco was barking modestly in the Bronx
with the Yankees in '65. The next year he scooted to
Kansas City. After a 2-4 showing in 11 appearances, he
was apparently sent to Charlie Finley's doghouse, from
where he never returned.   3-5

BLASINGAME, Wade
        Foreman for the Houston Construction Company
        Fairbanks, AK

Wade's profile is a bit uncanny. One of the few New
Mexico–born major leaguers, "Blazer" grew up in Fresno,
Calif., and attended the same high school as big league
hurlers Jim Maloney and Dick Ellsworth. Each would
have an important chapter in Blasingame's book.

Wade signed for a reported $100,000 bonus with the

Milwaukee Braves in 1961. Two years later he came up as a wide-eyed 19-year-old rookie. In his first full season in '64 he was 9-5 and ironically defeated Ellsworth and the Chicago Cubs for his first victory in the big show. On April 30, 1969, he was the starting and losing pitcher for the Astros when Jim Maloney of the Reds no-hit Houston, 10-0, at Crosley Field.

Blasingame wore Yankee pinstripes in '72 and he finished up at 46-51.

BLASS, Steve
Sells high school class rings for a jewelry company in Pittsburgh; Pirates' cable television announcer

From 1968–1972, Steve was one of the most effective hurlers in the N.L. His trademark of leaping and jumping on either his catcher or nearest teammate after the final out of a win became classic.

In '68, the right-hander was 18-6 (2.12 ERA) to lead the league in winning percentage. He also led the pack that year with 7 shutouts. Had it not been for a gimmick on Aug. 31st, he would have had 8 whitewashes. Here are the details.

The Pirates had arranged the sale of veteran relief pitcher Roy Face to the Tigers. Face was brought into the game early to pitch to one batter in order to tie the all-time record of 802 appearances for one team before being sold. To make room, Blass was sent to left field. Steve returned to the mound and proceeded to blank the Braves 8-0. But because he had not pitched the entire game, he was not credited with a shutout.

The following season he was involved in another unusual game (Sept. 5, 1969) in which he beat the Cubs, 9-2, on a 4-hitter with all 4 hits coming off the bat of Billy Williams. Steve also whacked his first homer in the big leagues that day.

Blass was the darling of Pittsburgh in '71. After going 15-8 during the regular season, he won Game Three of the Fall Classic against Baltimore after the O's took the first two games. Steve then pitched a clutch 4-hitter to win the seventh and deciding game for the Bucs.

It was in '73 that his woes began. Unable to throw strikes or get anybody out, he sought help through hypnosis and psychiatrists. A return trip to the minors was of no help. At age 31, Steve was all done, his engine destroyed by some unexplainable malfunction after a 103-76 record.

Blass, who is married to the sister of John Lamb, a pitcher with the Pirates in the early '70s, also conducts summer baseball camps. He commented, "When I was a kid I used to fantasize about pitching in the seventh game of a World Series." That he did—and did well.   103-76

BLEFARY, Curt
Nightclub owner of "Curt's Coo Coo Lounge"
Dania, FL

Someone once said, "The game is not about becoming somebody, it's about becoming nobody." That basically sums up the baseball life of Brooklyn-born Curt Blefary who went from a somebody to relative obscurity over the course of his 8-year slide.

Named *The Sporting News* and Baseball Writers Association Rookie of the Year in 1965 on the basis of his 22 home runs and 70 RBIs for the Orioles, Curt received praise from Baltimore fans and members of the media. The 6'2", 200-lb. strongboy was used primarily in the outfield and at first base in his first four years in Baltimore. In 1968 he caught 40 games, including a no-hitter thrown by Tom Phoebus.

On June 6, 1967 in the first game of a doubleheader against California he belted 3 homers, one a grand slam, in leading the Orioles to a 16-4 win.

His trade to Houston for Mike Cuellar at the end of the '68 season proved to be a one-sided deal in favor of Baltimore as Cuellar went on to become one of the leading pitchers in the A.L. while Curt stumbled with a .212 average. After visits with the Yankees, A's, and Padres, Curt split with a .237 mark.

BLEMKER, Ray
Compliance specialist with the U.S. Dept. of Labor
Henderson, KY

Jim Reeves topped the charts in 1960 with *He'll Have To Go,* which is what the K.C.A.'s must have said about "Buddy" Blemker after the left-handed hurler out of Georgia Tech made one appearance in relief at Boston in which he allowed three hits and three runs in one inning.

He lamented, "I don't think I was given enough of a chance."

BLOMBERG, Ron
Insurance business
Chicago, IL

Ron should be an expert in health insurance since he spent about as much time in the training room with an assortment of pulled muscles as he did on the playing field.

The Yankees' No. 1 selection in the 1967 major league free agent draft, this herculean-looking first baseman-outfielder never quite reached the superhuman heights expected of him.

His first taste was a sweet one in 1969 when he collected 3 hits in 6 at-bats. Ron's early success had Yankee fans salivating. As time went on he had Yankee fans yawning.

On Opening Day of the 1973 season, Ron became the first designated hitter in big league history. With the bases loaded in the first inning, he was walked by Red Sox pitcher Luis Tiant, but the Bosox went on to win, 15-5. Blomberg went 1-for-3 that day. He played in exactly 100 games in '73 and batted .329. His next few years in New York produced high averages, but limited action because of injuries.

In 1978 Ron became a free agent. Signed to a multiyear contract by the White Sox, he packed his tube of Ben-Gay and headed for his next whirlpool in Chicago. After hitting just .231 in 61 games, he was given his release in spring training the following year. His 107 games played in 1972 for the Yankees represented his season high.

Ron limped away with a lifetime .293 average.

BLOOMFIELD, Clyde
Restaurant owner
Rogers, AR

"Bud's" restaurant specializes in rainbow trout which he raises himself on his own trout farm. As an infielder in one game for the Cardinals in '63 and seven with the Twins in '64, this graduate of the University of Arkansas never specialized in hitting as he went 1-for-7.   .143

BLUE, Vida
Owns a 3,500-acre cattle ranch in the Shasta County community of Whitmore
Oakland, CA

Nick "The Greek" once said, "Remember this: The house doesn't beat a player. It merely gives him the opportunity to beat himself."

Vida Blue beat himself.

In 1983 four members of the Kansas City Royals pleaded guilty in a cocaine scandal that surrounded the team. They were Willie Wilson, Willie Aikens, Jerry Martin, and Vida Blue. Vida pleaded guilty of possession of cocaine (three grams, street value $450). His plea indicated that an undisclosed arrest had been made. Released by the Royals on Aug. 5, 1983, he was sentenced to a three-month prison term. It was also revealed that the former pitching ace underwent treatment for a drug dependency problem.

In his second start after returning to the Oakland A's from the minors in 1970, he beat the Royals, 3-0, on a one-hitter, losing the no-hit bid on a two-out, eighth-inning single by Pat Kelley. Two weeks later (Sept. 21, 1970), Vida became the youngest pitcher in modern major league history to pitch a full nine-inning no-hitter when he blanked the Twins, 6-0.

Blue's path to baseball eminence reached its zenith in '71 when he went 24-8 with a league-leading 8 shutouts and a glittering 1.83 ERA. Vida joined Don Newcombe, Sandy Koufax, Bob Gibson and Denny McLain as the fifth pitcher ever to win the Cy Young and MVP Award in the same year.

Then came the spring training holdout, temporary retirement, and contract dispute with Charlie Finley. After finally signing, he sputtered in '72, going 6-10. The A's went on to the World Championship, with Blue being used primarily in relief. In the fifth and deciding ALCS game against the Tigers, the hard-throwing southpaw saved the game from out of the bullpen.

He rebounded with successive seasons of 20, 17 and 22 wins. After two more years in Oakland, Blue went across the Bay to the Giants the next four years. His last job was with the Royals, where he was merely a shadow of his former self.

Vida appeared in four All-Star Games. He was the only A.L. pitcher to win the mid-summer classic during the period 1963–1982 when he was credited with the 6-4 A.L. victory at Tiger Stadium in 1971. He was also the winner in the '81 All-Star Game representing the Giants for the N.L., giving him the distinction as the only pitcher in major league history to start and win games for both leagues.

An extremely superstitious person, Vida changed his uniform number with the Giants from 35 to 14, the number he wore as a high school quarterback. When the change did not improve his pitching performance, he switched back to his old number.　　　　191-143

BOAK, Chet
Died Nov. 28, 1983, at age 48 in Emporium, PA

Route 66 starring George Maharis and Martin Milner had high TV ratings in 1960 when Chet drove in for five games with the Kansas City A's. The second baseman refueled and headed for Washington the following year and again played in five games.

Playing at Shreveport in the Southern Association on May 15–16, 1960, he connected for grand-slams in consecutive games, the summit of Chet's relatively short journey.　　　　.100

BOBB, Randy
> Died in Carnelian Bay, CA on June 13, 1982 at age 34
> in an auto accident

A member of the NCAA champion Arizona State team, Randy was called up to the Cubs late in '68 with just a little over one year of professional experience as a catcher.

His big chance came during the halfway point of a game between the Cubs and Reds on Aug. 18th. With Pete Rose on first base, Randy erased "Charlie Hustle" when he attempted to steal second base on the first pitch handled by the rookie receiver in the majors.

After another quick peek at Wrigley Field in '69, Randy left as a 10-game major leaguer.   .100

BOCCABELLA, John
> Appliance dealer representative for the Pacific Gas
> and Electric Co.
> San Rafael, CA

This is the tale of a man who left his heart in San Francisco and his bat in Pocatello.

John Dominic Boccabella was a 10-week sensation with Pocatello in the Pioneer League in 1963. The 6'3", 200-lb. Santa Clara College graduate tore the league apart, batting .365 to go with his 30 homers and 92 RBIs. His reward was a promotion to the Cubs where he stayed until 1968.

Big John joined the expansion Montreal Expos in '69. On July 6, 1973, he accomplished the rare feat of hitting two home runs in one inning.

A versatile player who was used as a catcher, first baseman, third baseman, and outfielder, he returned to his native San Francisco with the Giants in '74 where he finished up at .219.

BOEHMER, Len
> Boehmer Bros. Plumbing and Electrical Supply
> Flint Hill, MO

An infielder out of St. Louis University, Len hit .327 at Macon in 1964 to win the Southern League batting title.

He joined the Reds briefly three years later, then won a spot as a utility infielder for the Yankees in 1969. He was used as a utility player at every infield position that needed patching.

A typical good glove–no hit type of player, Boehmer went hitless in his first 26 major league plate appearances. His first big league hit helped to beat the Red Sox on June 22, 1969. Len had one more try with the Yanks in '71. Unfortunately, he couldn't repair the hole in his .164 lifetime bat.

BOGLE, Warren
    Junior H.S. physical education teacher
    Miami, FL

This 6'4", 200-pounder left-hander from the U. of Miami threw hard and averaged over a strikeout per inning (26 K's in 23 innings) with the Oakland A's in 1968. However, Warren never returned.

BOLES, Carl
    Insurance salesman
    Oakland, CA

A Willie Mays lookalike, a picture of Carl once went across the country through several newspapers mistakingly identifying him as Mays. In his brief stay with the '62 Giants, his 9-for-24 (.375) performance resembled the real Willie Mays.

The ex-sailor, who began in the Giants' organization in 1954, later played in Japan.

BOLIN, Bobby
    Owns a farm
    Six Mile, SC

Before Bobby arrived with the San Francisco Giants in 1961, he already had a pair of no-hitters to his credit in the minors. He almost threw a no-hitter in '66 against the Pirates, but Bill Mazeroski crushed his dreams with a bloop single.

The hard-throwing right-hander tied a major league record on Aug. 26, 1966, when he fanned the first five Dodgers to start a game. Although he had a strong year in '68 (10-5; 1.99 ERA), he ran into his share of hard luck. In one game he pitched 11 innings of shutout ball for the Giants, but was a victim of non-support as S.F. won the 17-inning marathon 1-0. Late in the season the sidearmer lost, 2-0, when Ray Washburn hurled his no-hitter at Candlestick.

Traded to the Brewers prior to the 1970 season, Bob was the winning pitcher in the team's first victory in Milwaukee following the franchise shift of the Seattle Pilots. He was traded to the Red Sox late that year and wound up his 13-year career in Beantown in '73. His final numbers read: 88-75 with 50 saves.

BOLLO, Greg
Owns heating and air conditioning business
Grosse Ile, MI

Lee Marvin won the Academy Award for best actor in *Cat Ballou* in 1965. Greg Bollo didn't win any awards, but did make it into 18 games with the White Sox in 1965–66, losing his only decision.

BOND, Walter
Died on Sept. 14, 1967, at age 29 in Detroit, MI

In life, a man has to play the cards he's dealt. Walt was dealt a bummer. Afflicted with leukemia in 1963, the disease finally conquered the 6'7", 230-lb. tower of strength. But his determination was like steel; it never rusted or crumbled.

Originally signed by the Cardinals in the mid-'50s, "The Bomber" was eventually released. He then played with the Kansas City Monarchs in the Negro American League before signing with Cleveland.

His heavy hitting in the Indians' 1960 spring training camp in Arizona prompted the controversial trade of popular Cleveland home run champion Rocky Colavito to the

Tigers for defending A.L. batting champ, Harvey Kuenn. General Manager Frank (Trader) Lane of the Indians said, "Rocky's expendable; the long ball will be supplied by Bond."

But big Walter hit just 5 roundtrippers and spent much of the season back in the bush leagues. Walt returned for parts of the '61 and '62 seasons. He went to Houston (1964–65) where he racked up 20 homers in '64, still a record for most homers in one season for Houston by a lefty batter. He had 8 in Colt Stadium and 12 on the road.

Bond was released by the Twins in '67 and was with Jacksonville in the International League when he had to go on the inactive list due to the illness which resulted in his death in September that year.

Better hands have been dealt.   .256

BONDS, Bobby
Cleveland Indians' hitting instructor

For most players, a .268 lifetime average and 332 home runs would be considered an enormous success. But for Bobby Bonds, a man targeted for superstardom, those career totals fall short for a player many considered Cooperstown material.

After hitting .370 at Phoenix (P.C.L.) in 1968, Bobby was brought up to San Francisco in mid-season. He made his debut on June 25, 1968, in a smashing way by belting a grand-slam off the Dodgers' John Purdin. The big blast was Bobby's first major league hit, coming in his third at-bat. He became only the second player in history, and the first since 1898, to hit a grand-slam in his first major league game.

The following year he hit 32 home runs and stole 45 bases. The talented outfielder looked like the second coming of Willie Mays. He would go on to become the only player in baseball history to hit 30 homers and steal 30 bases in the same season more than twice, accomplishing the feat in five different years.

In '71 he had a career-high 102 RBIs as the Giants won the N.L. West title. Bobby peaked in '73 when he hit .283 with 39 home runs, 43 stolen bases, and a league-leading

131 runs. Bonds was named by *The Sporting News* as the N.L. Player of the Year for his heroics.

Following the '74 season he was traded to the Yankees for Bobby Murcer. He later played for the Angels, White Sox, Rangers, Indians, and Cubs before closing in '81.

Like many big swingers, Bonds was a frequent strikeout victim, establishing a record-breaking 189 in 1970. Bobby joins Frank Robinson, Lee May, Frank Howard, Reggie Smith and Dave Winfield as the only players to collect 100 or more home runs in each league. He also shares the record with Ted Williams of hitting five 1-0 game-winning four-baggers.

Bonds comes from a strong athletic family. His brother, Robert, was a linebacker with the N.F.L. Kansas City Chiefs. His sister, Rosie, was a sprinter on the 1964 U.S. Olympic Team and established the U.S. Women's record in the hurdles.

BONIKOWSKI, Joe
Employed with the advertising dept. of a newspaper
Charlotte, NC

In 1964, Cassius Clay became Muhammad Ali when Joe Bonikowski became a major league pitcher with the Minnesota Twins. The 6-foot right-hander went 5-7 in 30 games, the extent of his big league life.

"Bongo" made his debut early that year, on April 12th, and was the winner in relief, going six innings in which he allowed just one run and three hits.

Two years earlier his father made the long journey from Philadelphia to see Joe pitch in a game for Wilson in the Carolina League and wasn't disappointed as Joe threw a no-hitter.

BOOKER, Rich
Furniture store owner
Brookneal, VA

Remember Booker T. and the M.G.'s with their big instrumental hit *Green Onions?* How about "Buddy" Booker, a catcher with the Indians (1966) and White Sox (1968), who hit .182 in 23 games?

BOOZER, John
Director of Lexington County Recreation Commission
Lexington, SC

A graduate of the University of South Carolina with a B.S. degree in business administration, John was the kind of guy who left behind a myriad of stories, such as eating bugs for kicks.

The right-hander pitched creditably in the minors, winning 19 games for Chattanooga in the Southern League. The 6'3", 205-pounder went 14-16 with the Phillies during the 1962–64 and 1966–69 seasons.

BORBON, Pedro
Active in the Mexican League

Pedro's world today as a Mexican League player consists of never-ending bus rides, shabby motels and greasy spoon restaurants. But it wasn't so long ago that the ace reliever of the "Big Red Machine" teams of the 1970s was flying in jumbo jets, lodging in the best hotels and dining in elegance.

Borbon broke in with the Angels in 1969. Traded to Cincinnati, he spent most of his time the next couple of years in the minors. But from '72 on he was the fireman deluxe of the Reds.

In the '72 Series against Oakland, Pedro appeared in six of the seven games and for the most part was very effective. Unfortunately, he was charged with the defeat in the seventh and final game.

The following year he had 11 wins, 14 saves, and a skimpy 2.15 E.R.A. in 80 appearances.

A native of the Dominican Republic, Pedro was known as "Dracula" around the league following an incident during the 1974 season when he bit an opposing player during a brawl.

Pedro also pitched with the Giants and Cardinals before creeping away at 69-39 with 80 saves.

BORK, Frank
  Manufacturer's rep for domestic items and home fur-
  nishings
  Columbus, OH

All three major television networks televised in color for
the first time in 1964 when this lefthander had a not-too-
colorful 2-2 record in 33 games with the Pirates. Frank did
beat the Phils in his first major league start, ending a
Pittsburgh six-game losing streak.

BORLAND, Tom
  Owns a tire business, "Pioneer Tire Center"
  Stillwater, OK

An All-American pitcher at Oklahoma State with a 11-0
record, Tom was the MVP of the College World Series in
1955. Three years later he was the winning chucker for
Minneapolis of the American Association in the deciding
game of the Junior World Series.
  But the Red Sox couldn't get too much mileage out of
Tom in 1960–61. As a matter of fact, this tire business
owner looked more like a blowout, losing all four of his decisions.
  However, he was with the A.L. All-Star team in 1960
—but as the batting practice pitcher.

BOSCH, Don
  Land developer
  Napa, CA

A much-heralded minor league fielding whiz described by
veteran writer Maury Allen as an "ulcer-ridden, gray-
haired, twenty-five-year-old," this switch-hitting flychaser
hit just .164 in 146 games with the Pirates (1966), Mets
(1967–68) and Expos (1969).
  Don had just four home runs in his career, but when he
connected off Mike McCormick and Juan Marichal in a
series against the Giants in '68, he became the first Mets'
player to hit home runs from both sides of the plate.

BOSMAN, Dick
    Employed with J K J Chevrolet in Vienna, VA; assistant baseball coach at Georgetown University

"If you don't hustle when I'm pitching, I'll kick your ass."

—Dick Bosman

Those words were once spoken to a Washington teammate who Bosman was critical of because of a lack of hustle. They describe this hard-nosed right-hander out of the University of Wisconsin.

In 1966 he became the resident ace of the Senators' mound staff. In 1969 his 2.19 ERA led the A.L. while he compiled a 14-5 record for the fourth-place team managed by Ted Williams. The following year he won a career-high 16 games.

Bosman was the starting pitcher for the Senators on the last Opening Day in Washington (April 5, 1971) as Washington defeated Oakland, 8-0, before 45,000 at RFK Stadium. He moved with the franchise to Texas in '72, then wound up with the Indians and Oakland.

On July 19, 1974 he no-hit the world champion A's, winning 4-0, with his own throwing error costing him a perfect game.

When Dick was released by the A's in '77 he was quite bitter. He said, "Charlie Finley just cut my throat and left me to bleed. He didn't can me till the end of spring training when it was too late to catch on anywhere else."

Before his baseball career, Dick built and drove drag racers, reaching a speed of over 180 mph. He finished as high as second place in the National Drag Racing Championships.

BOSWELL, Dave
    Employed with the National Brewing Co.
    Baltimore, MD

Dave walked in with the Twins in 1964 as an eager 19-year-old fireballer. For the next few years he enjoyed steady winning seasons. Pitching with the Twins in 1967,

Dave joined Jim Kaat and Dean Chance to form the first
200-strikeout trio on the same major league team during a
season.

In 1969 he went 20-12 without recording a shutout,
but his big year was clouded by controversy. Midway
through the season he was involved in an off-the-field
scuffle with teammate Bob Allison which resulted in his
joining a long list of players to get punched out by Billy
Martin, his manager at the time at Minnesota. He later
commented in classic Yogi Berra style, "It's now just a
forgotten memory."

On Oct. 5, 1969, he was a tough-luck loser to the Orioles,
1-0, in 10 innings in the ALCS.

From then on it was all downhill. Released by the Twins
in 1971, Boswell hooked on with the Tigers where he was
briefly united with Martin, who was now the Bengals'
skipper. After refusing assignment to the minors, the slender right-hander signed with the Orioles where he did add
one more win (ironically over the Twins) before being released again. When Dave received his walking papers at
age 26, he was 68-56.

BOSWELL, Ken
        Automobile salesman
        Austin, TX

The Mets, born and nurtured in futility since their incep-
tion in 1962, had never finished above ninth place entering the '69 season. But then success came like an
avalanche. One of the reasons was Kenny Boswell, who
split the second base job with Wayne Garrett and Al
Weiss. His 101 hits that year (.279) all seemed to come at
the right time.

Boswell almost matched his season total of three home
runs when he homered twice in the '69 NLCS sweep over
the Atlanta Braves.

Ken also put his name in the record books for his
fielding exploits at the keystone position. In 1970 he established a major league mark for highest fielding average
(.996) for a second baseman. Boswell also set a N.L. record

for most consecutive errorless games in a season (85), from
April 30th to Sept 26th.

At the other extreme he established a N.L. record on
Aug. 7, 1972, for the longest game (13 innings) with no
chances by a second baseman.

When the Mets lost the '73 Series to the A's, Ken tied a
Series record with three pinch-hits. His 11-year career
with the Mets (1967–74) and Astros (1975–77) saw the
clutch second sacker hit .246.

BOTZ, Bob

> Owns a carpet cleaning business, Botz's Rug Doctors
> of Metro Milwaukee
> Milwaukee, WI

Steppenwolf took us on a *Magic Carpet Ride* in the late
Sixties. Bob "Butterball" Botz was on his magic carpet
ride in 1962 as a reliever with the Los Angeles Angels,
going 2-1 in 35 appearances.

BOULDIN, CARL

> Stockbroker for Paine, Webber in Cincinnati; also
> coaches Little League baseball
> Fort Thomas, KY

In March of 1961, Carl was the captain of the University of
Cincinnati Bearcats team which defeated the Jerry Lucas–
John Havlicek defending champion Ohio State for the
NCAA basketball championship. Carl scored 16 points in
the 70-65 victory.

Later that summer he pitched in a couple of games for
the Washington Senators. The right-hander saw part-time
duty with the Senators for the next three seasons.

Carl says, "I don't feel like I really made it since I was
Washington's yo-yo for three years. But my kids think that
it was great that I was on a bubble gum card. Actually they
thought it was great until they discovered the backside of
the card." It read 3-8 in 27 appearances!

BOUTON, Jim
Tapes conventions for business groups
Teaneck, NJ

Bouton pitched a 7-hit shutout in his first major league start, beating the Senators, 8-0, on May 6, 1962. In 1963, Jim (21-7) combined with Whitey Ford (24-7) to give the Yankees two 20-game winners in one year for the first time since 1951, when Ed Lopat and Vic Raschi turned the trick. The year before he was the winning pitcher of the longest game in the A.L. (7 hours) at Detroit on June 24, 1962.

After going 18-13 in '64, it was all downhill. Known for his clubhouse mimic act of Frank Fontaine's "Crazy Guggenheim" and his flying hat while on the mound, Jim plummeted to 4-15 in 1965 and was in the minors shortly after.

In 1968 he was with Seattle in the P.C.L. and his 4-1 win over Spokane on Sept. 2nd came in the last P.C.L. game ever played in Seattle. The next year Bouton was with the expansion Pilots before being sold to the Astros. That was the season he kept his infamous diary that led to *Ball Four*.

Jim went 4-6 with the Astros in 1970. It appeared that he hung up his gray sweaty flannels for the last time as he became a sportscaster in New York and *Ball Four* was made into a short-lived TV series.

But the controversial pitcher-turned-author had an itch to make a comeback. Atlanta Braves' owner Ted Turner signed him in '78 and he went to the low minors in hopes of perfecting a knuckleball that would carry him back to the majors. After five starts and a 1-3 log, Jim had scratched his itch—it was time to leave a game he dearly loved.

In recent years he has developed a product called "Big League Chew," a shredded bubble gum sold in a pouch, designed to look like chewing tobacco. Jim has also been involved with selling baseball card–style cards in which individuals can have their own photographs on a card.

Bouton continues to be viewed by several former players as somewhat of a villain who broke the unwritten law of the clubhouse confidence. The controversy generated by his book was heavy enough to warrant a follow up publication titled, *I'm Glad You Didn't Take It Personally.*

To Jim's chagrin, too many did! 62-63

BOWENS, Sam
Insurance agent
Baltimore, MD

Sam was in the habit of taking things nice and easy. Because of his slow, deliberate lifestyle, Pete Ward used to say, "He ought to wake up before coming into the locker room."

An outfielder with the Orioles (1963–67) and Senators (1968–69), Sam was wide awake in his first full season ('64) when he hit 22 of his career total 45 home runs. In the Orioles' four-game sweep over the Dodgers in the '66 Series, Bowens was one of a dozen eligible players who never made it off the bench. But all twelve did accept their full winner's share of over $11,000.

Over the years baseball players being called from the minor league club to the majors have been known to arrive from a long distance in a very brief amount of time. On the other hand, those being sent down are often "delayed." During the '69 season it took Sam 13 days to get from Washington to Buffalo.

Then again, Sam always enjoyed taking his time. .223

BOWLIN, "Hoss"
Baseball coach at Livingston University in Alabama

In 1969 Johnny Cash sang about *A Boy Named Sue.* Two years earlier a boy named Lois Bowlin picked up one hit in five at-bats in the two games he played as a third baseman for the K.C.A.'s.

How does a guy get a name like "Lois?" "After six children, my mother wanted a girl. When I was born she named me Lois," related Bowlin. Obviously, the name was an embarrassment to him. He said, "When I was in school I went by the name Louis. Since I used to run real fast as a kid, they called me 'Little Hoss.' "

Playing for Birmingham in the Southern League in 1967, "Hoss" was in the process of playing all nine positions in a game. However, after pitching in the eighth inning for his eighth position, that night he was forced to leave the contest when he suffered an eye injury. He recalled, "I went to catch for the last inning. As I was putting on the mask, a piece of wire from the mask cut me."

BOWMAN, Ernie
  Park and Recreation Department employee
  Johnson City, TN

Famed American novelist Ernest Hemingway died in 1961, the same year Ernie Bowman, a smooth-fielding but light-hitting utility infielder began a 3-year stay with the Giants in which he hit .190 in 165 games. His only home run came off Al Jackson to beat the Mets at the Polo Grounds, 2-1.

BOYD, Gary
  Broker for Investors Diversified Services, an investment insurance firm
  Gardena, CA

As the joke goes, "First prize: One Week in Cleveland. Second prize: Two Weeks in Cleveland."
  Gary would have been delighted to have a few more weeks in Cleveland. After going 0-2 in 8 games in '69, Gary's vacation in Municipal Stadium was over.
  He writes, "I wish my baseball career would have been longer and more successful. It was a good life—like being a kid forever."

BRABENDER, Gene
  Construction business
  Kewaskum, WI

Don't let the name fool you. This big strong macho relief pitcher used to playfully take the spikes that were used to fasten the tarpaulin and bend them.
  A trapper in the off-season during his playing days, Gene once caught a poacher robbing his traps. In a rage, he picked the guy up and tossed him into a pond.

But Gene was not so violent on the mound. Drafted by
the Orioles off the Dodgers' Spokane roster in the fall of
'65, Gene went 4-3 his rookie year in '66 for the World
Champion Birds.

The 6'5", 225-pound right-hander found himself with
the Pilots in '69, when he went 13-14, establishing a record
for most victories by a pitcher on a first-year club. With the
Brewers in '70 he got a chance to pitch in his home state,
but fell to 6-15 in his final year in the majors.

In 1983 an unfortunate story made the national wire
services that he had been forced to put his 1966 World
Series ring up for collateral in exchange for a business
loan for his construction business. For a period of time he
was unable to recover the ring from the bank. But the
story had a happy ending as Gene and his ring were re-
united.   35-43

BRADEY, Don
    Employed with the Ford Motor Co. as a parts coordina-
    tor
    West Bloomfield, MI

In 1964 Pepsi-Cola adapted the slogan, "Come Alive.
You're in the Pepsi Generation," when Don Bradey briefly
came alive as a major league pitcher with the Houston
Astros. To Don's dismay his big league career quickly died
after he went 0-2 in three games with a bruised ERA of
19.29.

BRADFORD, "Buddy"
    Ladera Heights, CA

The Vietnam military buildup reached 400,000 men in
1966 when Charles "Buddy" Bradford, a player whose career was frequently interrupted by military commitments,
broke in with the White Sox. Between injuries, military
trips, and shuttling back and forth from the minors,
"Buddy" had a very unsettling experience.

When the well-traveled outfielder walked his last mile
in 1976, he had seen action with the White Sox three different times, with stopovers in between with the Reds, In-

dians, and Cardinals. "Buddy" played in Japan after his
busy experience in the States.   .226

BRADLEY, Tom
Baseball coach at Jacksonville University (FL)

Tom experienced culture shock in 1969, playing with the
Angels. After spending most of the 1970 season in the trop-
ical breezes of Hawaii, he was traded to the White Sox, for
whom he had back-to-back 15-win seasons in '71 and '72.
Then it was off to San Francisco, where he fizzled after the
'75 season.
  The Maryland graduate departed at 55-61. In 1983 his
Jacksonville team defeated Akron, 35-24, and established
an NCAA record when they scored 20 runs in one inning.

BRANCH, Harvey
Part owner of a Firestone dealership
Memphis, TN

In the early 1960s Branch Rickey gave up his plans of
starting a third major league, the Continental League, after both the American and National Leagues expanded.
  Left-hander Harvey Branch may not have given up on
his plans of pitching in the majors, but after one game in
which he was charged with the defeat after giving up five
runs in five innings for the Cardinals, St. Louis gave up on
him.

BRAND, Ron
Owns a construction business
Roseville, CA

Ron Brand, who today has eight children ranging from
ages 2 to 22, had an 8-year swing with the Pirates (1963),
Astros (1964–68) and Expos (1969–71). Ron was primarily
a catcher, although he did play other positions in the infield and the outfield.
  The stocky 5'8", 175-pound member of the Mormon
Church participated in the first game ever played in the

Astrodome and picked up Houston's first hit there, a triple off Mel Stottlemyre of the Yankees in an exhibition game. He also saw action in the first game ever played in Philadelphia's Veterans Stadium and the first big league contest in Montreal.

Following his playing career, Brand managed in the minors for three years. He says, "I am grateful to God for having achieved the major leagues, and to have known and played with such great athletes."   .239

BRANDON, Darrell
Business estate planning manager for the Aetna Insurance Co.
Hanover, MA

"Bucky's" career represents a kind of schism. He began as an infielder-outfielder, but after hitting just .210 in the Alabama-Florida League in 1960 he switched to pitching. Six years later he found himself in the Hub as an 8-8 rookie Red Sox chucker. After a 5-11 season with the Bosox in '67 it was back to the minors.

The righthander wore the uniforms of the Pilots and Twins before sliding out with the Phillies (1971–73).   28-37

BRAUN, John
Salesman for the Frank Liquor Co.
Madison, WI

Among the beer slogans used in 1964 you might remember "Schlitz—real gusto in a great light beer." John was full of gusto in '64 when the Milwaukee Braves brought the hopeful right-hander up with the big club. He pitched two scoreless innings that year. But tragedy struck in spring training the following season when he ran into an outfield wall while chasing a fly ball, resulting in a dislodged nerve in his elbow.

From that point on things were shaky for John. He knew the next time he threw a fastball that his arm and life support system could come unplugged. Eventually it did and it was all over.

But John took with him a six-pack of memories. "Pitch-

ing for Quad Cities I once had a no-hitter for 8 2/3 innings
against Kokomo. Also, I'll never forget Bob Uecker leading calisthenics in spring training. He was an absolute,
positive clown. When he led 'cals' there was always some
sexual content," laughed John.

BRAVO, Angel
    Coach in the Venezuelan Winter Baseball League
    Maracaibo, Venezuela

Angel joined the White Sox in 1969 after hitting .342 at
Tucson to win the P.C.L. batting title.
    His 13 pinch-hits with Cincy in 1970 helped the Reds to
the N.L. pennant. Angel cooled off completely after his employment with the Padres in '71.   .248

BREAZEALE, Jim
    Juvenile probation officer; operates a group home for
    the mentally retarded
    Houston, TX

By definition, "xenophobia" is a fear of strangers. Actually,
nobody was too worried about this 64-game stranger who
showed up with the Atlanta Braves in parts of the '69, '71
and '72 seasons. Primarily a first baseman, Jim batted .234.

BREEDEN, Danny
    Employed with United Parcel Service
    Robertsdale, AL

This 28-game performer with the Reds ('69) and Cubs ('71)
most likely holds the record of having caught the least
amount of big league games while catching a no-hitter. He
was the catcher for the Cubs on June 3, 1971, when Ken
Holtzman no-hit the Reds.
    Danny's brother, Hal, was a first baseman with the
Cubs in '71, then spent time with the Expos.   .151

BREEDING, Marv
Manufacturer's representative
Decatur, AL

Marv seemed levitated after a good rookie season when he batted .267 with the Orioles and was their everyday second baseman. The next year he was struck by the sophomore jinx, hitting an ignoble .209. Following another year in Baltimore, he wound up his four-year glide with Washington and the Dodgers. .250

BRENNEMAN, Jim
Owns Saddleback Valley Insurance
Norco, CA

In the summer of 1965 the Beach Boys were singing *California Girls* when this California boy made three appearances on the mound for the Yankees. Jim escaped with no decisions while running up an 18.00 ERA.

BRETT, Ken
Miller Beer television commercials
Hermosa Beach, CA

Ken signed a bonus contract with the Red Sox out of high school. The following year (1967) he made it to Fenway late in the season when the Bosox were chasing their "impossible dream." As a raw 19-year-old, he appeared in just one game on the mound, but was named to the World Series roster to replace the injured Sparky Lyle. By the end of the '67 Series, he had pitched in more World Series games than he had regular season contests as he came in from the bullpen in two games. At this time, George Brett was just entering high school and was known as Ken Brett's younger brother. Eventually it would be changed to "Ken Brett is George Brett's older brother."

The well-traveled left-hander also pitched with the Brewers, Phillies, Pirates, Yankees, White Sox, Angels, Twins, Dodgers, and Royals.

Obviously good hitting runs in the family. Ken established himself as one of the premier hitting pitchers early in his career. Pitching for the Red Sox in a '69 game against the Yankees he had a single, double, and home run in a 4-3 win.

As a member of the Phils in 1973, he set a major league record for most consecutive games hitting a home run by a pitcher when he connected on June 9, 14, 18, and 23.

Ken last played with brother George and the Royals in 1981. He closed at 83-85 plus a .262 batting avg. The pitcher-slugger hit 10 career homers. He remains the last A. L. pitcher to get a hit when he delivered a pinch-hit single for the White Sox in 1976.

BREWER, Jim
    Pitching coach at Oral Roberts University
    Tulsa, OK

Shortly after arriving with the Cubs in 1960, to replace an injured Moe Drabowsky, Jim was placed on the disabled list himself when he suffered a broken jaw at the hands of Billy Martin. Billy, who was with the Reds at the time, charged the mound like a ferocious lion thinking the rookie pitcher was throwing at him.

The attack led to a two-week stay in the hospital for Brewer plus several painful facial operations. In court Brewer's own teammate, Don Zimmer, testified that Brewer was throwing at Martin. Jim, who sued for $1 million, eventually settled for $35,000 in damages.

Brewer struggled the next couple of years, but he then developed into one of the top relievers in the N.L. for several years. His finest season came in '72 with the Dodgers when he won 8 and saved 17 with a 1.26 ERA. He finished with the Angels in '76 at 69-65 and 132 saves. Possessor of an excellent screwball, he later was a coach with the Montreal Expos.

BRICE, Alan
    Chief Investigator with the Public Defender's Office;
    operates his own detective agency
    Bradenton, FL

Alan Shepard made the first U.S. space flight in 1961. After three trips to the mound and one loss for the Chicago

White Sox in '61, 6'5" Alan Brice found himself in ever-lasting orbit.

BRIGGS, John
  Employed with the Recreation Dept.
  Paterson, NJ

An All-State athlete in football, basketball, and baseball in New Jersey, Johnny came up with the stormy Phillies in 1964 after just one season at Bakersfield in the California League. But like so many fancy labeled rookies, Johnny never quite lived up to expectations.

The first baseman-outfielder endured a dozen years of big league life with the Phillies (1964–71), Brewers (1971–75) and Twins ('75). He took opposing pitchers deep 21 times in both 1971 and '72. His big day came on July 4, 1973, when he scalped the Indians with six hits.   .253

BRILES, Nelson
  Seattle Mariners' color commentator

Nellie, who was on hand as a member of the Cardinals for Jose Feliciano's controversial rendition of the national anthem before the start of a 1968 World Series contest, did some guitar playing and singing of his own. At times Nellie was found performing in nightclubs with his twin brothers Ray and Bob, who were known as—what else—the "Ray Bobs."

Briles was music to Cardinals fans in 1967–68. When Bob Gibson suffered a broken leg after being struck by a Roberto Clemente line drive in '67, Nelson picked up the slack, replacing Gibson in the starting rotation. Briles had his pitches in harmony, finishing the season with nine straight victories. In '68 he won a career-high 19 games, as the Cards repeated the N.L. title.

After two more years with St. Louis, he took his guitar to Pittsburgh. As a member of the World Champion Pirates in 1971, he shut out the Orioles on two hits in Game Five to put the Pirates up, 3-2, in a Series they won in seven games.

Nellie's 14-year career also included stops with the Royals, Rangers, and Orioles.   129-112

BRINKMAN, Chuck
    Executive with a toy company
    Chicago

Little boys and girls began watching *Sesame Street* in 1969 when this toy executive played with the idea of being a successful big league catcher with the White Sox. After parts of six seasons spent mostly in Chicago, Chuck decided that the toy business was more profitable than negotiating a contract with a .172 average.

BRINKMAN, Ed
    Chicago White Sox coach

Western Hills High School in Cincinnati has sent eleven players to the majors, the most celebrated ones being Pete Rose and Don Zimmer. Add Eddie Brinkman to the list.
    The older brother of Chuck Brinkman, Eddie was the brilliant-fielding Senators' shortstop from 1963–1970. The Brinkmans were never a threat to the DiMaggios as Eddie batted a career .224.
    In 1971 he went to Detroit with Aurelio Rodriguez and Joe Coleman. The following year Ed helped the Tigers to the A.L. East crown. Although he hit a typical .203, he established the one-season mark for defensive excellence at shortstop by going 72 straight games without a muff and handling 331 consecutive chances without an error. His .990 fielding average was the best ever for one year.
    After two more years with Detroit, he was with the Cardinals, Rangers, and Yankees before he left in 1975.

BRITTON, Jim
    FBI agent
    Atlanta

A big, strong Don Drysdale type, Jim turned down a football scholarship from Penn State to sign with the Orioles.

Britton pitched an opening night no-hitter for Austin in the Texas League to start the '67 season, fanning 15 and retiring the last 25 in a row after giving up a first inning walk. Promoted to Richmond in the International League that year, he blanked Rochester, 2-0, in a one-game playoff after both teams finished in a first place tie. Sadly for Jim, his father, who was present at the game, suffered a heart attack and died during the contest.

Jim made his living with the Braves (1967–69) and Expos (1971). His 7-5 mark in '69 contributed to Atlanta's West Division title.   13-16

BROCK, Lou
    Owns Brocworld Enterprises Inc.
    St. Louis

The Chicago Cubs didn't seem to be making that much of a mistake at the trading deadline on June 15, 1964, when they swapped this 25-year-old .251 hitter to the Cardinals, even though he helped the Cards to the World Championship. But 15 years later, when Lou collected his 3,000th hit against his original team, it simply reinforced the Cubs' miscalculation as Brock finished at .315.

"Larcenous Lou" began his assault on the stolen base record when he pilfered 74 bases in '66 to lead the N.L. for the first of eight times.

In 1967 Brock became the first player ever to hit at least 20 home runs and swipe 50 bases in the same season. The base stealing czar was spectacular in the '67 Fall Classic win over the Red Sox, batting a sultry .414 and swiping a record 7 bases. The following October the Cards lost to the Tigers, but Lou was awesome once again, batting .464 to go along with his 7 steals. No player has ever hit for the cycle in a Series contest, but Brock probably came the closest in Game Four when he had a double, triple and a home run in the Cards' 10-1 victory. His 14 stolen bases in Series competition ties him with Eddie Collins. Ironically, Collins and Brock are also the only members of the exclusive 3,000 hit club never to win a batting title. Lou is one of only three players to collect 3,000 or more hits and not at-

tain a lifetime batting average of .300. The others are Al
Kaline and Carl Yastrzemski.

The all-time base stealing champ with 938, Lou was not
your prototype slugger with a modest total of 149 home
runs between 1961–79. But on June 17, 1962, playing for
the Cubs against the Mets in the Polo Grounds, he hit a
480-foot shot off Al Jackson into the center field bleachers
to become the first left-handed hitter ever to hit a ball into
the right section of the centerfield bleachers in the Polo
Grounds. Brock joined Joe Adcock and Hank Aaron as the
only players to homer in the center field bleachers at that
park.

Among the products manufactured by Brocworld Enterprises Inc. is something called a capabrella—an umbrella
modeled after a baseball cap. Another is a key chain contain-
ing tiny leather products in the form of a baseball glove. Lou
was elected to the Hall of Fame in 1985.   .293

BROOKS, Bobby
    Confined to a wheelchair with a muscular disorder.
    Harbor City, CA

Bobby only had a 55-game shot with the A's and Angels, but
for a brief moment in 1969 he was perched on top of the world.

Playing at Birmingham in the Southern League, Bobby
got the word to report to the A's on Sept. 1st. On the last
day of August (at Birmingham) he singled in his first at-
bat to drive home his 100th run of the season. The young
outfielder anxiously left the game for the airport to board
his plane to Boston where he would join the Oakland club.

In his first at-bat in the majors he doubled off the
Green Monster. Four years later he would play his last
game.   .231

BROSSEAU, Frank
    Vice-president of the First Minneapolis Bank
    St. Paul, MN

This banker really had simple numbers to compute. In a
3-game count, this 6'2", 200-lb. right-hander had no decisions with the Pirates in '69 and '71. Things were more in-

tricate at the University of Minnesota where he led the
Gophers to the 1964 NCAA championship.

*During the 1960s the all-time leading runner in National
Football League history, Jimmy Brown, retired to make
movies. We listened to Herman's Hermits' Mrs. Brown,
You've Got a Lovely Daughter; Charlie Brown's All-Stars
began their everlasting losing streak; James Brown was the
reigning King of Soul, and we heard, "You won't have
Nixon to kick around anymore," after he lost the election for
Governor of California to Edmund Brown.*
   *Baseball had its share of Browns during that decade.
Let's take a look at a few.*

BROWN, Gates
   Detroit Tigers' hitting coach in 1984

"In high school I took a little English, some science, some
hubcaps and some wheel covers."
                                            —Gates Brown

   One of the more popular figures in the Motor City
during the Sixties, William "Gates" Brown struggled
through the early years of his life, serving time at the
Mansfield (OH) Reformatory. Upon his release he signed
with the Tigers. With a new lease on life and a lethal bat,
he became one of the league's premier pinch-hitters from
1963–1975.
   On June 19, 1963, he strolled to the plate for the first
time ever in the big show and swatted a pinch-homer, the
first of a lifetime total of 15 pinch-homers.
   Brown was a part of one of baseball's legendary pinch-
hit stories. It was around the fifth inning or so when he decided that a pinch-hitter wouldn't be needed for a couple of
innings. The chunky Bengal decided to satisfy his hunger
pangs and order a couple of hot dogs. Suddenly, Tiger manager Mayo Smith ordered Gates to pinch-hit. Surprised,
the rotund Tiger stuffed the weiners into his jersey.
   At bat, Gates ripped a liner to right-center. He decided
to stretch it into a double and made a head-first slide,
forgetting about the hot dogs. When he arose, his Detroit

jersey was a splattering of colors. The two dogs cost him a
$100 fine.

Gates was at his best when Detroit took it all in '68,
going 18-for-49 (.462) in his pinch-hitting role. His value
was never more evident than in a doubleheader sweep over
the Red Sox that year when his 14th-inning pinch-homer
won the first game and his pinch-single in the 9th inning
of the second game capped a winning four-run rally.

Brown continued to terrorize opposing hurlers that summer. On Aug. 9th and 11th he hit pinch-homers in consecutive at-bats.

In 1974 he became the A.L. all-time leader with 15
pinch-homers and 101 hits off the bench.   .257

BROWN, Ike
> Umpires high school and college baseball in the
> Memphis, TN area.

Former President Dwight D. Eisenhower died in '69, the
same year Isaac "Ike" Brown came to the major leagues.
After hitting .356 in the first half of the '69 season at
Toledo, Ike was summoned to Detroit.

Brown played every infield and outfield position during
his six years with the Tigers. He was a member of the
Kansas City Monarchs in the Negro League before signing
with the Tigers' organization.   .256

BROWN, Jophery
> Actor and stuntman in Hollywood, CA

A right-handed pitcher out of Grambling University where
he had a 26-1 record and was named to the N.A.I.A. All-
American team in 1966, Jophery found the going a little
tougher in organized baseball. Pitching for Lodi in the California League in '67, he lost his last 13 decisions to finish
7-17 but turned it around in '68, going 11-1 for Lodi, which
earned him a promotion to the Cubs for a couple of harm-
less innings.

While in the minors, he pitched two no-hitters and,
would you believe, lost both games!

BROWN, Larry
    Club pro at a country club
    Lake Worth, FL

The younger brother of Dick Brown, an A.L. catcher from
1957–65 who died in 1970 of a brain tumor, Larry rolled in
with the Indians in '63. In a game on July 31, 1963, he hit
the final home run of a record four the Indians hit in one
inning.

A versatile infielder who made his living for 12 years at
shortstop, Larry also saw time with the A's, Orioles, and
Rangers.   .233

BROWN, Ollie
    New York Yankees scout
    Buena Park, CA

Petula Clark went *Downtown* in the mid-Sixties when
"Downtown" Ollie Brown acquired the moniker for all the
home runs he hit in the direction of downtown Fresno
when he led the California League with 40 homers and 133
RBIs in 1964 and was named MVP of the league.

In the late 1960s he bounced between San Francisco and
the P.C.L. The first choice of the San Diego Padres in the
N.L. 1968 expansion draft, Ollie had his best season in
1970 with 23 homers, 89 RBIs and a .292 average for the
sputtering Padres. His 13-year hike was also spent with
the A's, Brewers, Astros and Phillies.   .265

BROWN, Oscar
    Employed with the Texaco Oil Co.
    Carson, CA

Oscar completes the second set of Brown brothers who appeared in the Sixties. The younger brother of Ollie, Oscar
helped lead his Long Beach, CA, team to the 1963 American Legion national championship. He then attended USC
before signing with the Atlanta Braves.

In his first year in pro ball, he hit .346 at Yakima in the
Northwest League to capture the batting title. After hitting .326 in the Texas League, he joined the Braves in '69.

The Browns had another brother, Willie, who made his
mark as a star running back at USC and later played for
the Rams and Eagles in the N.F.L.   .244

BROWN, Paul
    Cattle rancher
    Holdenville, OK

Paul Brown is quite an illustrious name in the annals of
football, but not in baseball. The Oklahoma Sooner spent
portions of four seasons with the Phillies from 1961–63
and again in '68. After 36 games he came up empty at 0-8.
    But every cloud has a silver lining. In 1961, the right-
hander pitched a one-hit shutout for Buffalo over Louisville
to give his team the championship of the Junior World Series.
    Paul's younger brother, Jackie, who is currently the
pitching coach for the Texas Rangers, pitched in the
majors from 1970–77.

BROWN, Randy
    Insurance Business
    Orlando, FL

Volkswagen vans made their pilgrimage to Woodstock,
NY, in the summer of '69. Among love bugs and drugs, a
contingent of 400,000 paid homage to the under-30 generation entertained by Jimi Hendrix, Jefferson Airplane,
Santana, and Janis Joplin.
    That same summer Randy reached his mecca as a
catcher with the California Angels. But nobody paid homage to Randy who, in parts of two seasons (18 games), was
not very entertaining with a .138 avg.

BROWN, Tom
    Operates a direct mail order business, "Golden
    Ponds"
    Salisbury, MD

Oscar and Ollie Brown had a well-known football-playing
brother. Paul Brown had a famous football name. Tom

Brown was an outstanding football player. As a matter of fact, he is the only man to play major league baseball and also appear in the Super Bowl. The University of Maryland alumnus played in 61 games with the Washington Senators in 1963. He then played with the Green Bay Packers in Super Bowls I and II.

Following a star-studded collegiate career on the gridiron and baseball diamond at Maryland, the first baseman-outfielder elected to sign a baseball contract with the Senators. After his hot hitting during spring training in '63, Tommy found himself in the Opening Day lineup against the Orioles, whose starting pitcher was a former high school teammate, Steve Barber. President Kennedy was in attendance for the traditional season opener and expressed his pleasure at seeing the former football hero in the lineup.

Tom recalled, "About 1½ weeks before the season started, John F. Kennedy asked if that Brown boy was going to start on Opening Day. General Manager George Selkirk became a bit concerned about the President's wishes." According to manager Mickey Vernon, Kennedy's statement had nothing to do with Brown being in the lineup.

Most young players would be elated to find themselves in the big leagues. But Tom was not totally prepared for the big party. He said, "I think I was rushed a little." By July of the '63 season, he was sent to the minors and returned in September. But after 61 games and a .147 average, his confidence was like a rubber band on the verge of snapping. He was hitting under .200 in the Eastern League the following season when the Packers drafted him.

Tom discussed his love for Vince Lombardi, his coach with the Packers. "He was by far the greatest individual I was ever associated with in athletics."

BROWNE, Byron
     Employed with a trucking company in Houston, TX

Playing for the Cubs in his first major league game on Sept. 9, 1965, Byron had the shocking experience of facing

Sandy Koufax who pitched a perfect game to win, 1-0. In his first full season the following year he hit .243 with 16 home runs and was named along with Tommie Agee and Cleon Jones to the Topps Rookie All-Star Team in the outfield.

If Byron had one bad habit it was striking out. He whiffed a league-leading 143 times in '66. On July 19-20 he tied a dubious major league record by fanning eight times in two games. The Reds' hard-throwing Jim Maloney sat him down five times in the first game.

He was also with Houston, St. Louis, and Philadelphia. When it ended in '72 Browne had a .236 avg.

One of fifteen children, Byron's brother, Dennis, played pro basketball with Dallas in the American Basketball Association.

BROWNE, "Pidge"
    Public relations work for a brewery
    Houston TX

Prentice Almont "Pidge" Brown emerged for a total of 65 games as a 33-year-old rookie first baseman with the Houston Colt .45s in 1962.

"My 13 years in the minors are worth it for this one in the majors," said "Pidge." "Pidge" had previously played in Houston as a minor leaguer, hitting .328 in 1956 and .350 in 1961.   .210

BROWNING, Cal
    Owns the Elks Supply Co. (a group of lumber yards)
    Clinton, OK

In 1960 Johnny Horton went to the top of the charts with *Sink the Bismarck* when Cal sunk after just one appearance in a relief role for the Cardinals. He lasted less than an inning and probably remembers the first pitch he ever threw in vivid living color: Don Hoak hit it out of the park. "It was disappointing," says Cal. No kidding!

BRUBAKER, Bruce
> Sales Manager at Paul Miller Ford in Lexington, KY

Bruce's father became the world's champion fly caster in the competition at the Brussels World's Fair in 1958 while Bruce was hurling nothing but no-hitters and one-hitters with a perfect 0.00 ERA on the scholastic level. In '64 he led the International League in victories (15) and ERA (2.63) for Syracuse.

After two games in the big leagues with the Dodgers (1967) and Brewers (1970), Bruce's hopes were dashed as he never got another chance. But he could brag that he played in two decades.

BRUCKBAUER, Fred
> Executive with the John Deere Company
> Holmen, WI

Fred is a member of a rather dubious group of hurlers who pitched in the majors and never retired a batter.

A right-hander, he signed a bonus contract with the Senators after pitching the University of Minnesota to a pair of Big Ten titles. When he made it to the big time in '61, it was back home in his native state following the Senators' transfer to Minnesota. Unfortunately, he allowed three basehits and a walk without retiring a batter in his only outing for the Twins.

BRUMLEY, Mike
> Pastor of the Gracemont Baptist Church in Tulsa, OK; heads an organization called Sports Ministries International

After a heavenly minor league beginning, Mike could have used some divine intervention in the majors. The All-Star catcher for three consecutive years in the minors, Mike caught three years with the Senators (1964–66) and hit .229. His son, Mike Jr., a shortstop from the University of Texas, was selected in the second round of the free agent draft by the Red Sox in 1983.

Rev. Brumley was designated Chaplain for the 1984 Summer Olympic Games in Los Angeles.

BRUNSBERG, Arlo
High school Physical Education teacher and coach
Blaine, MN

Alice's Restaurant, where you could get anything you want, was a popular song by Arlo Guthrie in the late Sixties. All Arlo Brunsberg could get was a chance to catch in two games with the Tigers in 1966, picking up one hit, a double off "Catfish" Hunter in three at bats.   .333

BRYAN, Billy
Recruiter for the Alabama National Guard
Opelika, AL

Although only about 300 people lived in Morgan, GA, two of them were in the majors during the Sixties. One was Billy Bryan, who arrived with the K.C. A's in 1961 and the other was pitcher Tom Cheney. Bryan, a National Guard recruiter, fought his battles with the A's (1961–66), Yankees ('66–'67) and Senators ('68) before pulling out for good.

The tallest catcher (6'4") in the majors in '63, Bill hit only .216, but tied a record on April 27, 1963 when he was walked intentionally three times in one game.

"I tried several different jobs after leaving baseball. My job now gives me a chance to work in high schools and colleges and stay close to athletic programs and meet a lot of young people," says Bryan.

BRYANT, Don
Barber in Jacksonville, FL

This 6'6", 220-pound "Bear" had a 59-game hunt with the Cubs and Astros. Called up to the Cubs in the middle of the '66 season, he went 3-for-5 in his first game in the major leagues.

On May 1, 1969, he was behind the plate when Don

Wilson no-hit Cincinnati. The towering Floridian, who went on to coach with the Red Sox and Mariners, hit his weight (.220) during his interrupted safari.

BRYANT, Ron
Poker and blackjack dealer in Harrah's Casino
Lake Tahoe, NV

"I am the master of my fate; I am the captain of my soul."
—William E. Henly

In 1973, Ron Bryant was the talk of the baseball world when he went 24-12 with the San Francisco Giants. Strangely enough, he did it without posting a shutout. Two years later he was gone, disappearing faster than Jimmy Hoffa did.

Signed out of high school by scout Eddie Montague, Ron pitched briefly with the Giants in '67, then gained more meaningful employment in San Francisco between 1970–74 before one last try with the Cardinals in '75.

Fighting the perils of alcoholism for several years, Ron injured his shoulder in a swimming pool accident. In 1979 he joined Alcoholics Anonymous in Lake Tahoe where he had found a job at Harrah's Casino as a poker and blackjack dealer. The stocky left-hander is hoping to return to school and patch the missing pieces of his life, and hopefully become master of his fate and captain of his soul.   57-56

BUCHEK, Jerry
Meat cutter
St. Louis, MO

In the 1967 filming of the movie *The Odd Couple* with Jack Lemmon and Walter Matthau, Jerry can be seen as the pivot man in the "triple play" scene.

Buchek signed with his hometown Cardinals out of high school and had a brief look with them as a teenager in 1961. He then prepped for a couple of years in the minors and was named to the International League All-Star team in '63. Back up the following year, he played a utility role

for the '64 World Champs and singled in his only at-bat in
the win over the Yankees.

After a couple of seasons with the Mets, he made a complete reverse pivot and walked out with a .220 average.

BUCKNER, Bill
  Active player with the Red Sox

"There's a kid who has the swing to lead the league in
hitting."

—Ted Williams, 1970

Of all the players to debut in the 1960s, "Billy Buck"
probably is the best bet to make it into a fourth decade
since in 1990 he will be only 40 years old in a sport where
old age has become as common as an April shower.

Bill began in the Dodgers' organization in '68 as an
18-year-old and led the Pioneer League in hitting with a
.344 avg. He had a brief glimpse of big league life in '69
when he made one pinch-hitting appearance with the
Dodgers. After tearing the P.C.L. apart in '70 he returned
to stay.

Buckner was the leftfielder when Hank Aaron hit his
historic 715th home run in April, 1974. Overall Bill had
good success in Dodger threads, hitting over .300 three different years.

In 1977 Los Angeles sent Bill to the Cubs along with
shortstop Ivan DeJesus for outfielders Rick Monday and
Mike Garman. Buckner, who attended Arizona State and
USC, enjoyed his best season in 1982 when he established
personal highs in hits (201), runs scored (93), homers (15),
RBIs (105), walks (36), games (161) and at bats (657). He became the first Cub since Billy Williams (1970) to have
more than 200 hits in a season. In 1980 he won the N.L.
batting title at .324.

At this writing his lifetime average is .294. Look for Bill
Buckner to be a four-decade player.

BUFORD, Don
    San Francisco Giants' coach in 1984

A star running back at USC, Don was also a member of the Trojans' 1958 NCAA baseball champs. The compact 5'7" barrel of dynamite had two careers, one in the U.S., the other in Japan.

Named the Minor League Player of the Year by *The Sporting News* in 1963 when he batted .336 at Indianapolis and led the I.L. in hitting, runs, hits, doubles, stolen bases, and assists, Don received his ticket to the White Sox and eventually replaced Nellie Fox at second base. Later, he switched to the hot corner.

Following the 1967 season he was involved in a trade to Baltimore which saw shortstop Luis Aparicio return to Chicago. Buford moved to the outfield and was the leadoff man for the pennant-winning Orioles from 1969–1971. He swung a dangerous stick in '69 and '71, when he hit .291 and .290 respectively.

What are the chances of a player scoring 99 runs three consecutive years? Don did it from 1969–1971, leading the league in '71. In the three ALCS during that period, Buford batted .357.

On April 9, 1970, the little outfielder became the first Oriole to hit home runs from each side of the plate in one game.

In the '69 World Series against the Mets he homered in his first Series at-bat against Tom Seaver in the opening game, then followed up with a double as the Orioles won, 4-1. But the Mets then clipped the Birds, winning four straight as Don took the collar the remainder of the Series, going 0-for-18.

During the '72 season Buford was making $70,000 a year. After a poor season in '72, the Orioles front office was planning to cut his salary 20 per cent. Don said Sayonara and went to Japan for a contract in the neighborhood of $120,000 plus free housing and other fringe benefits. He played with the Taiheiyo Lions in Japan from 1973–75.   .264

BUNKER, Wally
   Real estate business
   Everett, WA

There was Wally Cleaver, Archie Bunker, and, yes—Wally
Bunker!

Wally signed with the Orioles out of high school and
made his major league debut at age 18 in 1963, losing one
late-season start. In '64 the right-hander was voted the
A.L. Rookie Pitcher of the Year after a brilliant 19-5 mark
with a 2.69 ERA. His .792 winning percentage was the
best in the American League. Wally tossed one-hitters
that season against Kansas City and Washington.

But the luckless pitcher would never realize the heights
predicted of him after his freshman showing. Plagued by
elbow trouble for nine years, Wally's career met with un-
mitigated frustration and terminated at just age 26 at
60-52. To his credit he was the winner of the third game of
the 1966 Series on a six-hitter, defeating the Dodgers, 1-0.

Selected by Kansas City in the expansion draft, he was a
respectable 12-11 for the Royals in 1969. A couple of years
later he was just a memory.

BURBACH, Bill
   Salesman for Lubrication Engineer
   Johnson City, TN

Drafted No. 1 by the Yankees in the first free agent draft
in 1965, Bill struggled through a 2-9 season in the Appalachian League. Pitching for Greensboro in the Carolina
League in '66, Bill had a no-hitter going for ten innings,
but left the game and was not involved in the decision. The
following year at Binghamton in the Eastern League he
won a 5-0 no-hitter after coming off the disabled list.

The 6'4" righthander was only 21 years old in '69 when
he made it to Yankee Stadium. His first win was a 2-0
shutout over Denny McLain. Burbach was gone two years
later.   6-11

BURCHART, Larry
    Savings & Loan manager
    Tulsa, OK

I Dream of Jeannie, starring Larry Hagman, was a TV run in 1965 when Larry Burchart dreamed of a spot in the biggies after pitching Oklahoma State University to the NCAA baseball title and to a third-place finish in '66. He signed with the Dodgers, then was drafted by Cleveland.

This Savings and Loan manager would have liked the Indians to have given him more interest on his baseball investment. After 29 games and an 0-2 record, Larry appeared a poor risk and was dropped from sight.

BURDA, Bob
    Estimator for City Wide Maintenance, a paint contract-
    ing business
    Los Angeles

After helping Tacoma to the P.C.L. pennant in 1961 with 20 homers and hitting .307, this first baseman-outfielder from Southern Illinios University got his first taste of the bigs with the Cardinals in 1962. For the next 10 years, Bob's career was interrupted between stops in the majors and minors. Although most of his time was spent with the Giants, he also saw action with the Brewers, Cards (for a second trip), and the Red Sox.

The lefty swinger led the N.L. in 1971 with 14 pinch-hits while playing for the Cardinals. Bob can boast that he was a teammate at different times of four players who garnered 3,000 hits in their careers—Stan Musial, Willie Mays, Lou Brock, and Carl Yastrzemski.

BURDETTE, Freddie
    Employed with United Parcel Service
    Albany, GA

A distant cousin to Lew Burdette, the 1957 World Series pitching hero, Fred won his only decision in his 30-game career (1962–64) with the Cubs. During the '64 season Fred and Lew were together on the Cubbies.

Looking back, Fred laments, "I never could get Lew to tell me how to throw the spitter. Bob Buhl had a pretty good one, too, and he wouldn't tell me either. I know now how to throw it. It's easy, but it's too late."

BURGMEIER, Tom
   Active player with the Oakland A's in 1984

One of baseball's longest running acts, Tom began his lengthy, winding journey in 1962 in the Houston farm system. Released two years later, he was signed by the Angels, the team that brought him up in '68.

Plucked by the Royals in the fourth round of the expansion draft in '69, "Bugs" went 9-7 with 17 saves and 1.74 ERA for the second place Royals (West Division) in 1971.

From 1974–77 he earned his living in Minnesota and enjoyed an 8-1 mark in 1976. "Burgy" became a free agent after the '77 campaign and signed with Boston. His top year came in 1980 when he went 5-4 with 24 saves. Named to the All-Star team that season, he held the lead or tie in 37 out of 43 games for the Bosox.

On August 3, 1980, Tom played left field for the last out in a game against Texas, becoming the first Sox pitcher to play another position since Mike Ryba caught in 1942.

The crafty reliever pitched eight scoreless innings in Fenway Park's longest game (20 innings) vs. Seattle on Sept. 3–4, 1981.

Burgy, who joined the Oakland A's in 1983, is the last active member of the original Kansas City Royals.   79-55

BURRIGHT, Larry
   Carpenter for a construction company
   Newport Beach, CA

As a rookie second baseman with the Dodgers in 1962, Larry played in a total 115 games (109 at the keystone sack), spelling Jim Gilliam from time to time. This carpenter hammered four home runs that year, one

being the first inside-the-park job ever hit at Dodger
Stadium.

He took his tools to Shea Stadium in '63 and '64 where
his scaffold unfolded with a .205 avg. Larry got the only
two hits in Ernie Broglio's 7-0 two-hitter for the Cards
against the Mets on Opening Day (April 9, 1963), the last
Polo Grounds opener.

BURWELL, Dick
 Brewery employee
 Mesa, AZ

In 1960 the American Heart Association announced that
smoking was dangerous to one's health. Unfortunately,
nobody informed Dick that walking opposing batters was
dangerous to job security.

A right-handed pitcher, Dick lasted a total of 13 innings
with the Cubs in 1960–61. He struck out one batter and issued eleven walks.

BUSCHHORN, Don
 Operating engineer with J.C. Nichols
 Kansas City, MO

Don lost his only decision in 12 games with the Kansas
City A's in 1965, but anybody who played with the A's during the rancorous Finley years, has a scrapbook of memories.

The former A's chucker recalled, "One spring training
one of my teammates and I met a couple of girls and invited them to our room. We were both single then. We
hadn't been in there for a minute when we heard a knock
at the door. My teammate opened the door. It was Finley.
He saw me, but not my buddy because he was standing behind the door. Finley told the girls to leave—that it wasn't
very nice being in our room."

Maybe Don played out of position. As a batter he was
2-for-4 in the majors.

BUTLER, Bill
Salesman for the Southland Co.
Stephens City, VA

Bill was picked by the Royals from the Tigers in the '69 expansion draft. The southpaw proved to be a pleasant surprise as he went 9-10, including four shutouts, and was named to the Topps Rookie All-Star Team. One of his victories was a one-hitter against the Indians.

Fighting arm problems, he never matched his rookie season. He said, "I injured my arm in 1970. I had an ulna nerve transplant in my elbow. After that it was never the same. I usually pitched in pain."

Butler divided the next three years between the Royals and Omaha before transferring to the Twins, where he hung up his damaged arm with a 23-35 record.

BUTLER, Cecil
Commercial wallpaper business, M.C.S. Painting and
Decorating
Dallas, GA

"Slewfoot" made his first start with the Milwaukee Braves on May 13, 1962, and beat the Mets, 3-2. He won one more game that year, but like so many other pitchers, arm trouble spiraled his career into depression.

Cecil had one last gasp with the Braves in '64 before closing undefeated (2-0) in 11 games.

BUTTERS, Tom
Director of Athletics at Duke University

A graduate of Ohio Wesleyan University, Tom was in 43 games with the Pirates between 1962–65. The right-hander, who went 2-3, had his career marred by a serious auto accident.

Butters has developed a keen reputation as a fund raiser since he was largely responsible for securing $5.1 million to renovate the Wallace Wade Stadium at Duke University.

C

CAIN, Les
> Owns three laundromat/dry cleaning establishments, in Oakland, CA

The 1950s saw Bob "Sugar" Cain pitch to a midget. The 1960s saw Les Cain arrive on the scene briefly with the 1968 Tigers. Although Les wasn't around too long, his rather brief career ('68; '70–72), might be termed a tasty but short confection of sweet success.

Pitching for Montgomery of the Southern League in 1967, he hurled a no-hitter over Birmingham, with the final out of the game coming in very dramatic fashion. Birmingham's Reggie Jackson lined a shot into left field on which the left fielder had the ball bounce off his glove into the air, then caught it in his bare hand while lying on the ground.

Les won a landmark court battle against the Detroit Tigers claiming Billy Martin forced him to pitch with a sore arm which ended his career. The Michigan Bureau of Workmen's Compensation ordered the Tigers to pay Cain $111 each week for life. A lump-sum settlement has since been made.   23-19

CALMUS, Dick
> High school teacher
> Tulsa, OK

Dick signed with his brother Myrle out of Webster High in Tulsa in 1963. Because of the bonus player rule which was in effect at the time, the young right-hander was kept on the Dodgers' roster for the full season.

The Dodgers got some mileage out of this bright-eyed rookie as he defeated the Giants twice in relief and also beat the Mets. His one defeat came in his first start, in a game that matched him with 40-year-old Warren Spahn, who was making career start No. 601, which broke the all-time N.L. record of 600 held by Grover Cleveland Alexander.

Dick went out quietly, pitching one game with the Cubs
in '67.   3-1

CAMILLI, Doug
Manager of Greensboro (South Atlantic League)

The son of former Brooklyn Dodgers' first baseman Dolph
Camilli, Doug was with us through most of the decade of
the Sixties with the Dodgers and Senators. Three of Doug's
brothers also played professional baseball, but none made
it to the majors.

A catcher, Doug hit an anemic .199 overall but had better
memories behind the dish especially on June 4, 1964, when
he caught Sandy Koufax's no-hitter over the Phillies.

The Camilli family has a chance of being the first in
major league history to have three direct generations play
in the majors. Doug's son, Kevin, was drafted by the Red
Sox in the 1983 free agent draft.

CAMILLI, Lou
Securities business
Albuquerque, NM

In the summer of '69, Senator Edward Kennedy drove his
car off a bridge on Chappaquiddick Island and plunged
into the deepest waters of his political career when Mary
Jo Kopechne, a passenger in Kennedy's car, drowned in
the accident.

That same summer Lou Camilli plunged into a career
that might have been a little over his head. A graduate of
Texas A&M, Lou was with the Indians from 1969-72. The
utility infielder batted .146 and submerged from sight forever.

CAMPANERIS, Bert
California Angels' bunting and baserunning instructor

The long and colorful career of shortstop Dagoberto Campaneris has been marked by many unique distinctions. A

cousin of former outfielder Jose Cardenal, Bert broke in at
Daytona Beach in the Florida State League in 1962. On
August 13th that summer he took the mound and pitched
a couple of innings against Fort Lauderdale, striking out
four and allowing one run. There is nothing unusual about
that except for the fact the ambidextrous "Campy" pitched
right-handed to right-handed hitters and switched to the
port side against lefty swingers.

Bob Nieman of the 1951 Browns is the only man to hit
home runs in his first two at-bats in the big leagues.
Campaneris almost duplicated the feat on July 23, 1964
when he poked two home runs in a rousing debut for the
K.C.A's, homering on the first pitch he ever saw in the
majors against Jim Kaat of the Twins and connecting
again off Kaat in the seventh inning.

However, the native of Cuba usually beat you in other
ways. Bert led the A.L. in stolen bases six different seasons, his high coming in '68 when he pilfered 62 bases. The
versatile little guy played all nine positions for the K.C.A's
on September 8, 1965, against the Angels. In the eighth inning he allowed one run in his one inning on the mound
before going behind the plate for his ninth position in the
game during the last inning. Unfortunately, he had to
leave the contest after injuring his shoulder in a collision
at the plate with Ed Kirkpatrick.

On August 29, 1967, Bert had three triples in a game,
the first time that was accomplished in the A.L. since Ben
Chapman of Cleveland did it in 1939.

One of the key figures during the Oakland A's dynasty
years in the early 1970s, "Campy" was involved in a bat-
throwing incident during the 1972 ALCS when he flung
his stick at Detroit pitcher Lerrin LaGrow. He was ruled
eligible to play in the World Series, but was suspended for
the first seven games of the 1973 season.

In the '73 Series his 11th-inning RBI single led the A's
past the Mets, 3-2, in the third game. "Campy" continued
his assault on the Mets when he homered in the seventh
game as the A's took all the marbles.

After playing out his option with Oakland in '76, he
signed with Texas, then joined the Angels in '79. During
the '82 season he found himself in the Mexican League,
but experienced a rebirth of sorts when the Yankees

brought him up from the Columbus team during the 1983 campaign. He wound up his career at .258.

CAMPANIS, Jim
    General Manager for "Ford of Upland" automobile
    dealership
    Yorba Linda, CA

There was another "Campy" behind the plate for the Dodgers from 1966–68; that is, until Jimmy Campanis had the distinction of being traded away by his father, Al, the Dodgers' general manager. Al traded his son to the K.C. Royals in 1968 because he thought the Royals would allow Jimmy to catch regularly.

Al, who had a short stay with the Dodgers in '43, commented after the trade, "If we ever make a bad deal, I hope this is the one".

Actually, the deal wasn't all that bad as Jim finished with a .147 average in 113 games split among the Dodgers, Royals, and Pirates.

Andy Warhol turned Campbell's soup cans into a form of pop art during the 1960s. The Campbell kids served as Campbell's form of advertising during the period. Four Campbell kids played in the majors.

CAMPBELL, Dave
    San Diego Padres' announcer

Primarily a second baseman, Dave played a utility role during his 8-year travels with the Tigers, Padres, Cardinals, and Astros from 1967–74.

As a regular second sacker for the Padres in 1970, Dave was the N.L. leader in both assists and putouts at the keystone position. The Michigan graduate batted .213 overall.

CAMPBELL, Jim

Owns a textile distributing company and two retail
textile discount stores
Sunnyvale, CA

Jim caught with Houston in 1962–63, hitting .221 in 82
games. "When my son was born on Aug. 29, 1962, my wife
asked me to hit one out to celebrate the occasion," related
the former backstop. He did just that and it came in the
ninth inning to beat the great Bob Gibson and the Cardinals, 3-2.

CAMPBELL, Joe

Owns a Chevrolet dealership
Bowling Green, KY

Joe arrived burning with desire, but was a flameout after
appearing in one game for the '67 Cubs. An exercise in futility, Joe struck out three times in his only three big
league at-bats.

CAMPBELL, Ron

Employed with the Country Skillet Catfish Company
Isola, MS

Bewitched came on TV in 1964 when Ron started a somewhat bewildering 52-game run with the Cubs that carried
over a three-year period. An infielder, Ron had a big night
at Amarillo in the Texas League when he collected 9 RBIs
to lead his team to a 17-10 victory.   .247

CAMPISI, Sal

Senior communications consultant for General Telephone Co. of Florida
New Port Richey, FL

At a time when pushbutton telephones came along, this
communications consultant was at Long Island University, where his ERA of 0.21 was the best in the nation in
1964. The Brooklyn-born right-hander, who grew up in the

shadows of Ebbets Field as a Dodgers' fan, dialed some impressive digits in the minors (11-3, 12-3, 13-2). His major league numbers weren't too bad either (3-2; 50 games; 2.71 ERA) with the Cards and Twins from 1969–71.

Although the name Sal was short for Salvatore, some opposing hitters suggested it should have been for "saliva," feeling that Sal wet the ball up on occasion.

CANNIZZARO, Chris
Manager at Redwood City in the California League

Chris is the only player to be a regular with two first-year expansion clubs—the '62 Mets and '69 Padres. His son, Chris, the first Met baby born, is currently a second baseman in the Red Sox organization.

A catcher, Mr. Cannizzaro had a 13-year excursion between the years 1960–1974. After breaking in with the Cardinals he was selected by the Mets in the N.L. expansion draft in 1961 and was the team's regular catcher during their daffy, embryonic maiden season of 1962. With the Mets he was called "Canzoneri" by manager Casey Stengel, who may have been alluding to the onetime lightweight boxing champ, Tony Canzoneri.

In '69 he was the first Padre named to the N.L. All Star team, but didn't get into the game. Chris also played with the Pirates, Cubs, and Dodgers.

CARBO, Bernie
Hair stylist; owns a beauty salon
Detroit

Many consider the 1975 World Series between the Red Sox and Reds as the most exciting Series ever played. Bernie Carbo's contribution to that pulsating Fall Classic added to the drama of it all as he hit two pinch-hit homers for the Bosox, tying the record set by Chuck Essegian of the L.A. Dodgers in 1959. Bernie's shots came in the third and the sixth games, the latter a 3-run homer off Rawley Eastwick in the eighth inning to tie the score at 6-6, which led to Carlton Fisk's midnight wallop that gave Boston the 7-6 victory.

Cincinnati's first-ever selection in the original free agent draft in 1965, Bernie got his first look at big league pitching late in '69 with the Reds after hitting a stylish .359 at Indianapolis to cop the American Association batting title and the league's MVP award. After striking out in his only three at bats in '69, he picked up his first big league base hit on Opening Day in 1970 with a home run against Montreal. In the '70 Series he was involved in a memorable and controversial play when he was called out at home plate by umpire Ken Burkhart while Burkhart was on the ground after becoming entangled with Baltimore catcher Elrod Hendricks and Carbo. It appeared that Hendricks tagged Carbo with his glove while the ball was in his throwing hand, but the out stood.

Bernie's rookie campaign turned out to be his finest, hitting .310 with 21 home runs. Named *The Sporting News* N.L. Rookie of the Year, he suffered the ugly sophomore jinx and plummeted to .219.

Following a contract dispute, the outspoken outfielder was dealt to the Cardinals in '72. He moved on to Boston and also spent time with the Indians, Brewers, and Pirates.   .264

CARDENAL, Jose
Chicago Cubs' announcer on Spanish-speaking network

The second cousin of Bert Campaneris, Jose was the first California Angels' player to bat against "Campy" when Bert played all nine positions on Sept. 8, 1965.

A lifetime .275 hitter, Jose enjoyed a lengthy 18-year stay during his U.S.A. tour that covered such cities as San Francisco (Giants), Anaheim (Angels), Cleveland (Indians), St. Louis (Cardinals), Milwaukee (Brewers), Chicago (Cubs), Philadelphia (Phillies), New York (Mets), and Kansas City (Royals). The speedy flychaser broke in with the Giants in '63, but enjoyed his longest tenure in the Windy City with the Cubs from 1972–77, where he twice batted over .300.

Jose helped the Royals down the stretch in 1980, hitting .340 in 25 games. His only World Series came that year as the Royals were defeated by the Phils.

CARDENAS, "Chico"
    Employed with the Sohio Car Care Center
    Cincinnati, OH

From 1960–1975, Leo "Chico" Cardenas spent most of his
time in Cincinnati, where he dazzled opponents with his
bat and his Gold Glove.

The slender Cuban had his engine tuned up in June of
'66 when he connected for a pair of homers off Juan
Marichal of the Giants. A couple of days later he hit a pair
in both ends of a doubleheader. Over a four-game stretch
he had a total of six homers, overall eight in eight games.

Chico's 20 roundtrippers in 1966 still stand as a Reds'
record for homers in a season by a shortstop. It was the last
time a N.L. shortstop hit 20 until the Astros' Dickie Thon
did in 1983.

Cardenas serviced the Twins at shortstop from 1969–71,
helping Minnesota to back-to-back A.L. West titles in '69
and '70. After traveling with the Angels, Indians, and
Rangers, "Chico" finally ran out of gas with a .257 avg.

His son, Leo Cardenas, Jr. was drafted by the Twins in
the 1983 free agent draft.

CARDINAL, Randy
    Location unknown

Randy Cardinal certainly deserves a spot somewhere on
our Ornithology team with the likes of "Hawk" Harrelson,
Robin Yount, "Goose" Goslin, Craig Swan, and Johnny
Peacock.

Randy arrived in 1963 with the Colt .45s when the
motion picture *The Cardinal* opened in theaters. A right-
hander, he was hoping to flap his wings, but actually laid
an egg, going 0-1 in six games.

It would be nice to report that Conrad "Randy" Cardinal
is head of the Ornithology department at Harvard, but the
truth is his trail has left us cold.

CAREW, Rod
    Active with the California Angels

"Trying to sneak a pitch past him is like trying to sneak the sunrise past a rooster."

                —Amos Otis on Rod Carew

A seven-time batting champion, only Ty Cobb (12), Honus Wagner (8), Rogers Hornsby (7), and Stan Musial (7) have equaled or surpassed that feat. Rookie of the Year with the Minnesota Twins in 1967, this Panamanian-born future Hall of Famer, who was raised in Harlem, finished over .300 for 15 consecutive seasons before his streak was broken in '84. However, during the '84 campaign he became the fourth player to play 1,000 or more games lifetime at two different fielding positions (second base and first base) joining Stan Musial (OF; 1B), Ernie Banks (SS; 1B), and Ron Fairly (1B; OF).

Despite four straight batting titles from 1972–75, Rod was generally an unrecognized "superstar" until his sensational year in 1977 when he flirted with a .400 season. He finished at .388, winning A.L. batting and MVP honors.

Not known for power, he became the first A.L. batting champ in 1972 to go through an entire season without a home run.

In 1969 Rod was a terror on the basepaths when he tied a major league record by stealing home seven times. In one game he stole second, third, and home in the same inning to pull off the hat trick. He made an attempt for an eighth steal of home in '69 in a game against the Seattle Pilots and upended umpire Jim Honochick at home with his slide. He was called out by the "Lite Beer" ump, but catcher Gerry McNertney later admitted he never tagged him.

Carew handles a camera with as much expertise as his bat. He is a skilled portrait lensman, particularly when it comes to capturing his teammates. The batting champ also excels in animal and scenic shots.   .330

CARLOS, Francisco
      Division manager for a company which designs and
      manufactures kitchen cabinets
      Scottsdale, AZ

Along with finding himself situated between future Hall
of Famers Rod Carew and Steve Carlton in this book,
"Cisco" Carlos joined another future Cooperstown in-
ductee, Johnny Bench, on the cover of *Sports Illustrated* as
one of the "New Stars of 1968."

Carlos came up with the White Sox late in 1967 and
fashioned a sparkling 0.86 ERA, going 2-0 including a
shutout in eight games. The following year he struggled
(4-14), then was traded to the Senators in '69, where he finished the next year 11-18 overall.

Johnny Bench will most likely enter the Hall of Fame in
1989. He will not have "Cisco" on his side as he did
twenty-one years earlier.

CARLTON, Steve
      Active with the Philadelphia Phillies

After "Lefty" won his fourth Cy Young award, Jim Palmer
commented, "He's setting the standards they'll be chasing
years from now."

Signed for a measly $5,000 bonus by the Cardinals in
1963, Carlton has emerged as the all-time strikeout king.
The southpaw was at Tulsa in '66 when he joined the Cardinals and went the distance to defeat the Twins in the annual
Hall of Fame game at Cooperstown. A few weeks later Steve
beat the Mets, 4-1, for his first big league win.

A wine connoisseur, Steve's first full season came in
1967 when he went 14-9 for the World Champion Cardinals. He lost his only start in the '67 Fall Classic against
the Red Sox despite allowing no earned runs in six innings.

The most poignant defeat of his career came on Sept. 15,
1969, when he fanned a then-record 19 Mets, but lost, 4-3,
when he gave up two homers to Ron Swoboda.

A contract dispute prior to the '72 season resulted in his
being traded to the Phillies for Rick Wise. There must
have been some red faces in St. Louis as "Lefty" had a

bionic year in '72, going 27-10 with an ERA of 1.97 and 310
strikeouts, becoming the first pitcher to win at least 20 for
a last-place team in the National League since Noodles
Hahn of Cincinnati in 1901. Mr. Invisible put together
eight shutouts that year, the most for a Phillies' pitcher
since Grover Alexander had eight in 1917.

The six-time 20-game winner led the league in K's five different times. His 275 whiffs in 1983 at age 38 tied a major
league record for the oldest pitcher to accomplish the feat.

One of the all-time pitching greats, "Lefty" has never
pitched a no-hitter, although he does hold the National
League record for six one-hitters. Twice he has gone 8⅔ innings, but no cigar. Carlton has a 2-2 mark in NLCS play
and is 2-1 in World Series competition.

On Sept. 23, 1982, he won career victory No. 300. It was
poetic justice that it would come against his original team,
the St. Louis Cardinals.   313-207

CARPIN, Frank
> Employed with Paine Webber
> Richmond, VA

In 1965 *Green Acres* opened on TV when this green kid out
of Notre Dame landed a job with the Pirates. He was then
shipped to Houston in '66, but was forced to retire after the
season with a bone spur in his pitching elbow.

Signed originally by the Yankees, Frank was the winning pitcher in a relief role for Columbus (I.L.) on May 24,
1965. The following day he jumped on board with the Pirates and made his major league debut in relief, a win over
the Cubs to complete his two day-two-team parlay.   4-1

CARROLL, Clay
> Supervisor with Cochran Concrete
> Sarasota, FL

As a highly effective reliever with Cincinnati's "Big Red
Machine," Clay's job was to tear down and destroy the confidence of opposing hitters. Now his job is to supervise
construction crews that build precast panels for large
buildings such as the Epcot Center in Orlando, Florida.

The right-hander with the excellent sinking fastball was always a heavy-duty performer. "Hawk," who came up with the Braves in '64, led the league in appearances two years later. Traded to the Reds in the middle of the '68 season, he showed off his tireless arm late that year in a twinight doubleheader at Pittsburgh. Reds' manager Dave Bristol used Clay for one inning in the opener to help preserve a Reds' victory. In the nightcap he started the game and pitched nine strong innings without allowing an earned run before bowing out for a pinch-hitter in the tenth frame. The following year he was 5-0 in relief in both May and June. His ten-game win streak tied Tom Seaver for the longest N.L. win streak of the season.

In the 1970 World Series, which the Reds lost to the Orioles in five, Clay appeared in four games and was the winner in relief in the Reds' only victory. His self-esteem was as tall as some of the buildings he now constructs when he was named Fireman of the Year by *The Sporting News* in '72 after leading the National League in games (65) and saves (37).

Carroll was also the winning pitcher in the seventh and deciding game of the 1975 World Series against the Red Sox. Overall in post-season play "Hawk" was as tough as steel, going 2-1 (1.50 ERA) in NLCS and 2-1 (1.33 ERA) in World Series competition. Before it was over in 1978, he also pitched with the White Sox, Cardinals, and Pirates.

Clay hit just one home run, but it was a memorable one—in the tenth inning of a game on May 30, 1969, to beat Bob Gibson and the Cardinals, 4-3. "The count was 3-and-2. It was a high pitch. As I ran around the bases Gibson stared me down," laughed Carroll.

Carroll denies any accusations of throwing a spitter. "I never had to throw a trick pitch. Like Dizzy Dean said, 'I just threw hard natural stuff,'" he said.   96-73

CARTY, Rico
        Associated with Dominican League baseball;
        Honorary General in Army of Dominican Republic
        San Pedro De Macoris

Rico's career was never dull. Playing with Toronto in the International League in 1963 he once homered twice in the same at-bat. The first homer was nullified because "time" had been called prior to the pitch. Undaunted, Rico whacked another one over the fence. That same season he made his debut by striking out twice in both at bats as a pinch-hitter with the Milwaukee Braves.

Carty's rookie year (1964) was outstanding by any standards. He hit 22 homers, had 88 RBIs, and batted .330, but Rookie of the Year honors went to Richie Allen.

The talented Dominican missed the 1968 season while battling tuberculosis as he was hospitalized for six months. Rico was flown to Atlanta on September 6th where he dressed for a day game with Houston and presented the lineup card at home plate before the game.

Always popular with the Braves' fans, he suffered a separated shoulder early in the '69 season, but returned to hit .342 in helping the Braves to the National League West title.

If Rico has a scrapbook, the 1970 season would fill half the pages. All he did was hit a league-leading .366 wrapped around a 31-game hitting streak. In August he was involved in an altercation with an off-duty policeman and suffered a serious eye injury.

Snakebitten again, Carty missed all of the 1971 Campaign because of a badly fractured ankle incurred during a winter league game.

From 1973–79 he went on tour with the Rangers, Cubs, A's, Indians, and Blue Jays. Used often as a designated hitter during his final years, he had three seasons with Cleveland where he hit over .300.

His meandering stream of frustration haunted him upon retirement with a .299 average, just missing the magic .300 club.

CASANOVA, Paul

Operates a disco in Caracas, Venezuela called "Baseball Disco"

Good Lovin', You've Lost That Lovin' Feeling, and *Stop in the Name of Love* were all giant hit records in the mid-Sixties. After the 1966 season the Washington Senators were lovin' their catcher appropriately named Casanova to the extent he was called the team's only untouchable by General Manager George Selkirk.

The 6'5" backstop arrived for a brief trial in 1965, then became the regular Washington receiver in '66, winning All-Star honors from *The Sporting News* following the season. He was rewarded with a $5,000 raise from $12,000 to $17,000 for his efforts.

A fine defensive catcher with a strong arm, Paul stayed in Washington through '71, then played his last three years in Atlanta where he kissed us goodbye at .225.

On June 12, 1967, the Senators outlasted the White Sox, 6-5, in 22 innings in a game which then established a record as the longest night game in major league history, 6 hours and 38 minutes. Paul caught the first pitch of the game from Joe Coleman and hit the final one for a game-winning single.

Colorful and fun-loving, Paul also had the reputation as a big spender and once filed for bankruptcy. A man who enjoyed the luxuries of life, Casanova had a fondness for water beds. He had one in his bedroom, dining room, and a mini water bed in his bathroom.

CASH, Dave
     Account Executive with Century Commodity Corporation
     El Cajon, CA

With a name like Cash, how could we keep him off our All-Currency team with the likes of Don Money, Wes Stock, Norm Cash and Bobby Bonds. Dave's bat was on the money in 1975 (Phils) when he collected 213 base hits and batted .305, a year he also set a major league record for at-bats (699).

The second baseman surfaced in '69, eventually replacing long-time second baseman Bill Mazeroski in the Pirates' lineup. He sparked the Bucs to the N.L. pennant in the '71 NLCS, hitting .421 (8-for-19) against the Giants.

A good leadoff hitter, Dave was traded to the Phillies following the 1973 season. His 3-year stay in Philly was an enjoyable one. In '76 Dave collected a league-leading 12 triples.

After the '76 campaign he became a free agent and signed with the Expos. On May 21, 1977, he tied a major league mark with 11 at-bats in a 21-inning game. His next stop was San Diego where he played one year (1980), closing his account at .283.

CATER, Danny
> Employed with the State of Texas as Comptroller of
> Public Accounts
> Austin, TX

If there are two administrative moves that Red Sox fans
will never forget they are Babe Ruth being sold to the Yankees and Sparky Lyle being traded to the Yankees for
Danny Cater.
  A line drive hitter, Danny zigged and zagged from
1964–1975 with the Phils, White Sox, A's, Yankees, Red
Sox, and Cardinals. In 1968 with Oakland he hit .290 and
was runnerup to Carl Yastrzemski's .301 for the American
League batting title.
  Cater showed good pop in his bat in New York, hitting
.301 as an everyday first baseman in 1970. Following the
'71 season he went to Boston for Lyle, who became a folk
hero in New York.   .276

CHACON, Elio
> Caracas, Venezuela

Elio's father is a member of Cuba's Baseball Hall of Fame.
Although Elio's .232 lifetime average doesn't qualify him
for America's Hall of Shame, he will never be enshrined in
Cooperstown.
  The second baseman-shortstop, who broke in with the
Reds in 1960, went 3-for-12 in the '61 Series against the
Yankees. An original member of the Mets in '62, Elio was
in 118 games at shortstop for the "Can't Anybody Here
Play This Game" Mets.

CHAMPION, Billy
> Chicago Cubs scout
> Shelby, NC

It isn't easy to win a minor league game and lose a major
league contest on the same day, but Billy did it. On Aug.
15, 1970, the right-hander was a winner for Eugene of the
P.C.L. when a suspended game was completed while Billy

was with the Phillies. That same day, Champion was defeated by the Reds in the big show.

Buford Billy Champion, Jr. was around from 1969–
1976, splitting time between the Phillies and Brewers.
Well-known for his excellent balk move, Billy did not
champion great statistics, going 34-50. In 1974 he went
11-4 (Brewers), the best winning percentage in the A.L.

CHANCE, Bob
    Employed with the State Liquor Commission in West
    Virginia
    Oak Ridge, WV

If we had to pick an All-Weight Watchers team in the
1960s, Bob would certainly be on the roster. Sometimes
called "Fat" Chance, Bob came up with the Indians late in
'63 after leading Charleston to the Eastern League pennant. The first baseman-outfielder batted .343 with 26
homers and 114 RBIs as he became the first player to win
the triple crown in the Eastern League since 1925.

From Cleveland he went to the Senators, where he spent
his summers from 1965–67. After a few games with the
Angels in '69, he finished at .261—that's his batting average not his weight.

Bob's son, Tony, is currently a center fielder with the Pirates' organization.

CHANCE, Dean
    Has concession rights in a large carnival circuit
    throughout the U.S.; owns farm
    Canton, OH

"In every real man a child is hidden that wants to play."
                                                —F. Nietzsche

Put Dean on a pitcher's mound and he would show his
he-man strength by whizzing baseballs by opposing batters. Give him a playmate like Bo Belinsky, or a good old-
fashioned country fair where he could knock down lead
milk bottles and win prizes for his teammates, and the
frivolous child would emerge in this Ohio farm boy.

Signed out of high school by the Orioles after compiling 18 no-hitters, Chance was eventually drafted by the Angels. He caught brief glimpses of sunny California in '61 and became a regular the following year when his buddy, Bo Belinsky, was grabbing headlines plus other things in Hollywood. In 1964 Chance copped the Cy Young Award, the youngest ever (23) to win the coveted trophy. The American League became one big carnival for Dean, who finished 20-9 with a 1.65 ERA. Like a roller coaster he roared through the junior circuit by racking up eleven shutouts, six by 1-0 scores, making him the only major league pitcher to win six games in a season by 1-0 scores. Five of his whitewashings were complete game victories.

The big right-hander disassembled the Yankees like a child picks apart cotton candy. In 50 innings against the Yanks that year, he gave up just one run, a homer to Mickey Mantle. Dean defeated the American League champs four times in five starts. The only game he failed to gain a decision was one in which he left with no score after 14 innings. To add insult to injury the Yankee killer went on stage with Belinsky that winter in the play *Damn Yankees.*

After mediocre success the next couple of years, Dean took his act to Minnesota. Although he was the loser on the last day of the '67 season to the Red Sox, he showed his old form, going 20-14. On August 6th he set down 15 consecutive Red Sox in tossing a rain-shortened no-hitter. Less than three weeks later he no-hit the Indians, 2-1, allowing a first-inning run on a pair of walks and an error.

In 1968 the fun-loving chucker leveled off to 16-16 and as a batter he struck out 63 times, a record total for a pitcher. Since 1900 Dean holds the ignoble record for the lowest career batting average (.066) for a pitcher with more than 400 at-bats (44-for-662).

Before calling it quits at age 30, Chance frolicked around with the Indians, Mets, and Tigers. His bag of prizes include a 128-115 log, 33 shutouts, and a 2.92 ERA.

Following his career he managed heavyweight boxer Ernie Shavers for a short time.

CHANEY, Darrell
     Former Atlanta Braves announcer; real estate busi-
     ness in Atlanta, GA

Darrell was named quarterback on the 1966 All-American
High School football team. The Oliver Morton High School
(Hammond, Indiana) star spurned 35 football offers, including a personal visit to his home by Notre Dame coach
Ara Parseghian to sign with the Reds.
     The switch-hitting shortstop hit 23 home runs at Ashe-
ville in the Southern League in 1968, then came up to
Cincinnati in '69 where he filled a utility role over the
next several seasons. He participated in three World Series (1970, '72, '75) then was traded to Atlanta where he
became the Braves' regular shortstop in 1976. Chaney's
last hurrah was in '79 when he took his bat, glove, and
spikes with him at .217.

CHARLES, Ed
     New York Mets' minor league coach at Kingsport (Ap-
     palachian League)

In 1962 Ray Charles was singing *Born to Lose* when Ed
Charles won his way to the majors after dragging his feet
through the bushes for ten years. The 27-year-old Kansas
City A's rookie showed his appreciation, hitting .288 with
17 home runs. Traded to the Mets during the '67 season, he
became the darling of Flushing in '69, coming off the
bench with some key hits and filling in at third base when
needed.
     The Mets used "The Glider" as their third baseman in
the 1969 World Series against the Orioles. After the
Series, Ed drifted away forever with a .263 average.
     Charles is one of 14 players in National League history
to pinch-hit home runs in consecutive at-bats when he did
the trick for the Mets on June 1-2 (1968).
     When Ed first began his pro career in the early 1950s, he
quickly was tagged with the nickname "Ez" after the
heavyweight boxing champion, Ezzard Charles.

CHARTON, Pete
    College professor at Roane State
    Harriman, TN

Frank (aka "Pete") Charton lost both decisions in 25 games with the Red Sox in 1964. Noting little Frank's prominent teeth, his grandmother dubbed him "Peter Rabbit" and the nickname "Pete" endured.

Charton, who received a degree in geology from Michigan State, was gone at age 24 due to a shoulder injury.

CHAVARRIA, Ossie
    Wine salesman; scouts for Toronto Blue Jays
    North Burnaby, BC, Canada

"Be home real soon, Mom, they're beginning to throw the curve."

—Ring Lardner, *Alibi Ike* (1915)

This versatile Panamanian was a master with his glove and a disaster with his bat. Ossie played every infield position with the Kansas City A's in 1966–67 and also saw some action in the outfield.

After 124 games Chavarria batted a paltry .208.

CHAVEZ, Nestor
    Died Mar. 16, 1969, at age 21 in an airplane crash in Maracaibo, Venezuela

Nestor was only 16 years old when he signed with the Giants in 1964. The Venezuelan right-hander possessed excellent control and was one of the most highly regarded prospects in the Giants' organization.

In 1967 he was 12-5 including seven shutouts and an ERA of 1.33 pitching for Waterbury in the Eastern League. Promoted to San Francisco that year, he earned his first and only decision for the Giants at Candlestick Park. It was a 4-inning relief stint in which the Giants beat the Phils, 1-0.

Chavez was en route to the spring training camp of the Giants Triple-A team at Phoenix when he was among 155 passengers who died in what, at that time, was the worst disaster in aviation history.

CHOATE, Don
Firefighter
East St. Louis, IL

Suddenly Last Summer was a box office attraction in 1960 when right-hander Don Choate's big league stay ended almost as suddenly as it began with no decisions in four outings for the Giants.

CHRISTIAN, Bob
Died on Feb. 20, 1974, at age 28 in San Diego, CA

Like Walt Bond, profiled earlier, Bob lost his battle with leukemia. An outfielder, he hit .319 to help lead Toledo to the International League pennant, then was in three games for the Tigers in '68. He closed his career in his native Chicago with the White Sox in '68 and '69.
.224

CHURCH, Len
Assistant golf pro at Canyon Creek Country Club
Richardson, TX

Would you say that Len belongs on our All-Holy team with Max Bishop, Johnny Temple, Dave Pope, Johnny Priest, and Howie Nunn?

A Chicago native, Church once hurled a no-hitter for the Cubs in the Windy City at the age of 11. However, this was for his Little League team. With the Cubs in the National League in 1966 he was 0-1 in four games. He says, "My greatest thrill was pitching against Hank Aaron and Roberto Clemente and getting both out." Amen.

CIMINO, Pete
    Beer distributor
    Bristol, PA

In 1962 Wilt Chamberlain had a record 100 points in an
NBA game. Two years earlier Pete set the Pennsylvania
high school record when he scored 114 points in a game for
Bristol High School.
    The fireballing chucker, who passed up several scholar-
ship offers in basketball to play baseball, once struck out
20 batters in a game for Wilson (Carolina League) on his
way up to the majors.
    Pete worked out of the bullpen for the Twins (1965–66)
and Angels (1967–68), with a 5-8 record to go along with a
3.07 ERA.

CIPRIANI, Frank
    Co-owner of two restaurants, "Garcia's Irish Pub" and
    the "Macaroni Co."
    Buffalo, NY

Frank was the hitting sensation of the Kansas City A's
spring training camp in 1961. An outfielder, this restaura-
teur yearned for a tasty smorgasbord of big league success,
but walked away starving for more time after playing in
13 games.   .250

CISCO, Galen
    San Diego Padres pitching coach

A fullback and linebacker at Ohio State, Galen captained
the Buckeyes' 1958 Rose Bowl team that defeated Oregon,
10-7, en route to the mythical NCAA championship. The
rugged right-hander then decided to play the summer game.
    Cisco saw time with the Red Sox and Mets between
1962–65 as a starter and reliever. After struggling it was
back to Triple-A, then one more shot with the Bosox and
expansion Royal in 1969.   25-56

*In the 1960s the Dave Clark Five was among the top groups
in the English invasion of pop music; Petula Clark took us*

Downtown *(along with Ollie Brown), and Jimmy Clark* won the Indianapolis 500.

CLARK, Glen
Building contractor
Dallas TX

After spending several years as a solid-hitting outfielder in the minors, Glen was hoping to cement himself in the big time but instead got buried after going hitless in four at-bats, all as a pinch-hitter with the Atlanta Braves in 1967.

CLARK, Rickey
Owns a business which creates and designs business forms for credit unions
La Mirada, CA

So you don't believe in the sophomore jinx? In 1967 Rickey seemed to be one of the brightest pitching prospects in the American League when he went 12-11 with an ERA of 2.59 to lead the Angels in both categories. The next year this industrial engineering graduate almost did a 360-degree turn when he lost his first eight decisions and finished 1-11. His bright spot that season was August 20th when he combined with Clyde Wright to pitch a one-hitter against Baltimore.

Following a swing back to the minors the Western Michigan University alumnus spent portions of the next few seasons with California before becoming a memory at 19-32.

CLARK, Ron
Manager at Peninsula in Carolina League in Toronto Blue Jays' organization in 1983

The winner of over 100 bouts as an amateur boxer, Ron was a two-time Golden Gloves champion before jumping from the ring to the diamond. A versatile infielder, Ron sparred around mainly from 1966–72 with the Twins, Pilots, A's, and Braves.

Voted by his Minnesota teammates as the outstanding rookie in 1968, the slim Texan had one last jab with the Phils in '75 before his final knockout came with a punchless .189 average.

CLARKE, Horace
>Baseball instructor with the Department of Recreation
>St. Croix, Virgin Islands

"A 100% player. He wanted to play every day." Those were the words spoken by former Yankee outfielder Roy White about Horace Clarke, the quiet, private gentleman who occupied the keystone position for the Yankees from 1965–74. Horace led the league's second baseman in assists for six consecutive seasons (1967–72). Only Hall of Famer Charley Gehringer, with seven years (but not consecutive), did more.

Sandwiched between two graceful players, Bobby Richardson and Willie Randolph, in a line of Yankee second basemen, Clarke's greatest assets were his consistency and durability. He led the league in at-bats in both '69 and '70.

The native of the Virgin Islands hit only 27 home runs in his ten-year odyssey (1965–1974), but the first two were grand slams. Horace gained the reputation as a spoiler when within a month's span in 1970 he ruined no-hit bids by Joe Niekro, Sonny Siebert, and Jim Rooker with ninth-inning base hits.

After a brief fling with the Padres in '74, Mr. Consistency departed with a .256 average.

CLEMENS, Doug
>Personnel and sales manager for General Machine Products Co., Inc., a manufacturer of tools and accessories for the communications industry
>Churchville, PA

Contrary to popular belief, Lou Brock was not traded straight up for Ernie Broglio. The Cubs sent Brock, Jack Spring, and Paul Toth to the Cardinals for Broglio, Bobby Shantz, and

Doug Clemens. A boyhood admirer of Ted Williams, who even named his son (Theodore Williams Clemens) after the "Splendid Splinter," Doug enrolled at Syracuse University on a football scholarship, but a knee injury cut short his gridiron days and baseball became numero uno.

The energetic outfielder was around for parts of nine years with the Cardinals (1960–64), Cubs (1964–65), and Phillies (1966–68), hitting .229, 115 points below his hero's average. But Teddy would have been proud of Doug when he hit three consecutive pinch-hit doubles on June 5, 6, 7 (1967) tieing a record held by Bert Haas of the Dodgers in 1937.

CLENDENON, Donn
    Attorney
    Dayton, OH

Donn Clendenon, Esq., was on trial from 1961–1971 with the Pirates, Expos, Mets, and Cardinals. The judgment passed on this angular first baseman was most impressive after compiling numbers like a .274 lifetime average with 159 home runs.

An outstanding athlete who won 12 letters at Morehouse College in Atlanta, "Clink" had basketball offers from the Harlem Globetrotters and New York Knicks. He was also offered a tryout with the Cleveland Browns of the N.F.L. To the dismay of several N.L. pitchers, Donn chose baseball.

From 1963–68 he was the Pirates' first baseman. In '68 he could have been charged with assault with a deadly bat when he hit 28 homers and collected 98 RBIs.

The 1969 season proved to be his big one. Picked up in the expansion draft by the Expos, he was soon traded to Houston where he refused to report. The barrister tossed a wrench in baseball's legal system by announcing his retirement.

Houston wanted the trade voided, and new Commissioner Bowie Kuhn found himself involved in a knotty controversy when he refused to void the trade. The Astros decided to ship Clendenon to the Mets where he became a New York folk hero that fall by walloping three homers (a record for a five-game series) and batting .351. His 1.071 slugging average was the best ever in a Series by a N.L. player with 10 or more at-bats. He was named the Series MVP for his exploits.

"Clink" continued his heroics on Opening Day in 1970 when he pinch-hit a bases-loaded single, giving the Mets a 5-3 win over the Pirates, the first-ever Opening Day victory for the Mets. He went on to have a solid season, collecting 22 homers, 97 ribbies, and a .288 average.

His case was closed after playing with the Cardinals in '72.

CLEVELAND, Reggie
    Partner in car dealership "Best Used Cars"
    Mansfield, TX

This native of Swift Current, some 100 miles from Moose Jaw, in the Canadian province of Saskatchewan, arrived in the world of skyscrapers and air pollution in '69 with one appearance for the Cards after a 15-6 mark in the Texas League. Reggie was up for good in '71, a year he was named the Rookie Pitcher of the Year after a 12-12 season with St. Louis.

The 6'1" right-hander brought a blast of freshness to Boston when he went 13-9 in 1975 with the American League pennant-winning Red Sox. Reggie concluded his career with the Rangers and Brewers.   105-106

CLINE, Ty
    Owns and operates two Baskin-Robbins ice cream shops
    Charleston, SC

The owner of two ice cream stores, Ty's career cannot be described as a strawberry sundae, but more of a long-lasting (1960–71) double scoop cone with some sprinkles here and there. An All-American baseball player at Clemson, life was scrumptious in 1960 for Ty when he hit .311 at Mobile, his first year in pro ball. After a short look with the Indians in '60 and '61 he was around the remainder of the decade, also seeing action with the Braves, Cubs, Giants, Expos, and Reds where he took his last bite in '71.

Ty hit .302 for the Braves in 1964 and was the National League leader in pinch-hits with 14. In the opening game of the 1970 NLCS, his key pinch-hit triple in the tenth inning of what had been a scoreless tie, led to a 3-0 Reds victory over Pittsburgh's Dock Ellis, with Ty scoring the winning run. In the final NLCS game, he drew a walk and came around to score the winning run as the Reds beat the Pirates to clinch the National League pennant. In the World Series against the Orioles he banged out a pinch-hit triple in a losing effort.

When his career finally melted into the twilight, Ty had a .238 average.

CLINTON, Lu
      Oil equipment business
      Wichita, KS

"Sweet Lou," who was also known as "Ponca City Lou" after his native home city in Oklahoma, was around from 1960–1967 with the Red Sox, Angels, A's, Indians, and Yankees before he ran out of fuel with a .247 average.

Luciean Louis Clinton spent most of his time in Boston where he became an attraction equal to the Old North Church in 1962. Struggling with an .096 average in late June, he suddenly went on a hitting spree. On June 29th he blasted a grand-slam homer. In a July 4th twinbill against the Twins he connected for seven straight hits. Nine days later in Kansas City his father and three brothers were watching him play in the majors for the first time when he hit for the cycle. In his last 85 games that season he hit .326 for the Bosox to finish the year with a .294 average.

Traded to California in '64, the Angels later sold Lu to the Kansas City A's on waivers (Sept. 8, 1965) but the deal was nullified after Clinton played in one game for Kansas City because of an error in the waiver process. After the mess was settled, he was awarded to the Indians. His last stop came with the Yankees. He was the club's leading pinch-hitter in '66, going 6-for-14 off the bench.

CLONINGER, Tony
> Has a horse breeding ranch
> Iron Station, NC

Only seven pitchers in big league history have hit two
grand slams during their careers: Schoolboy Rowe, Tommy Byrne, Dizzy Trout, Camilo Pascual, Bob Gibson, Rick
Wise, and Tony Cloninger. But Tony is the only one to collect his two slammers on the same day.

It was July 3, 1966, when the Braves met the Giants at
Candlestick Park. In the first inning he hit a grand-slam
blast off the Giants' Bob Priddy and followed up with a
fourth inning bell-ringer off Ray Sadecki. Cloninger's bat
continued to sizzle as he later singled home another run—
good for a 9-RBI day. It was a new record for pitchers,
smashing the old mark of 7 by Vic Raschi of the Yankees.

A couple of weeks earlier he smashed another pair of
home runs in a 17-1 rout of the Mets. Several wondered if
this man was Babe Ruth reincarnated!

The right-hander signed with the Milwaukee Braves out
of high school for a reported $100,000 bonus. After a slow
start in the minors (0-9 at Cedar Rapids) he got his act together and produced winning seasons with the Braves in
the early Sixties. In 1965 he was 24-11, replacing Warren
Spahn as the all-time single-season winner for a Braves'
pitcher in Milwaukee.

Tony was plagued by injuries and infirmities in '67,
missing most of the campaign. He then was traded to
Cincinnati in '68, and helped the Reds to the National
League pennant in 1970. His career ended with the Cardinals in 1972 at 113-97.

In the 1983 free agent draft, his two sons, Darin and
Mike, both pitchers, were selected by the Padres and
Twins respectively.

CLOSTER, Alan
> Employed in the stemory department at Philip Morris
> Richmond, VA

We first heard the provocative words "Take it off, take it
all off" on a Noxzema shaving cream commercial. Alan

must have heard the same words concerning his Washington Senators' uniform after he walked two batters and allowed a hit in just a third of an inning in '66.

The southpaw from Iowa State University was able to put it back on a few years later with the Yankees (1971–72) and Braves ('73). After going 2-2 in 21 games overall, he stripped for good.

COGGINS, Frank
    Employed with the FBI
    Griffin, GA

Frank's gaudy wardrobe was much more colorful than his 87-game party with the Senators and Cubs in parts of three seasons from 1967–72. The second baseman had a penchant for wearing pink suits, big straw hats, and knickers that he tucked into high boots. He also made daily visits to a florist to purchase a boutonniere to hang on his flashy threads. But Frank vanished with a drab .215 average. He is unrelated to Rich Coggins, the former Baltimore outfielder.

COLBERT, Nate
    Minister at the Union Baptist Church in Yuma, AZ; public relations work and minor league hitting instructor for the San Diego Padres

When pitcher Bob Shirley went from San Diego to the Cardinals in 1981 he commented, "Tradition here is Stan Musial coming in the clubhouse making the rounds. In San Diego it's Nate Colbert coming in the clubhouse trying to sell you a used car." The remark would not seem to be a complimentary one toward either Colbert or the Padres. However, Colbert's name is linked to Musial's regarding an on-the-field accomplishment that took place Aug. 1, 1972. In a doubleheader between the Padres and Braves he led the Padres to a twin victory, blasting five home runs for a total of 13 RBIs and 22 total bases. His 13 RBIs over two games established a new record while his 22 total bases for the day broke Musial's record of 21. Ironically Nate was in the stands as an 8-year-old in St. Louis the day Musial enjoyed his five-homer show.

In '72 Colbert set an RBI record that has gone virtually unnoticed. That year the anemic Padres scored a paltry total of 488 runs. Since the slugging first baseman collected 111 RBIs, it meant that he batted in 22.75 percent of his team's runs. Nate broke Wally Berger's record of knocking in 22.61 percent of his team's runs (Braves, 1935). Colbert banged out 38 home runs in both 1970 and 1972.

Traded to the Tigers after the '74 season, an ailing back cut short his career at the age of 30 after also playing with the Expos and Oakland A's. He closed with 173 home runs, a .243 average, and a night to remember!

COLBORN, Jim
Pitching coach at Iowa (American Association) in Chicago Cubs' organization

Richard Nixon, a graduate of Whittier College, took the office of President in 1969 when Jim Colborn, a Whittier alumnus, made his major league debut, winning his only decision in six games for the Cubs. After dividing time between the Cubs and Tacoma the next two years, Jim was traded to the Brewers in 1973 and went 20-12 for his finest season.

During a time when Mr. Nixon was suffering his Watergate woes, Colborn also found life difficult, experiencing three successive losing campaigns. This prompted a trade to Kansas City where he posted an 18-14 record as the Royals repeated as American League West champs. On May 14, 1977 he no-hit the Texas Rangers. It all ended with the Mariners in '78.

The right-hander also studied at the University of Edinburgh in Scotland on a Rotary Foundation Fellowship and was a columnist for the *Baseball Bulletin*. 83-88

COLEMAN, "Choo Choo"
Rochester, NY

Clarence "Choo Choo" Coleman probably ranks second to Marv Throneberry as a symbol of the Mets' futility in their

early years. Although there is probably no truth to the
story that he once called for a pitchout with the bases
loaded and a full count on the batter, he does lay claim to
the fact that he hit the first home run ever by a Met. However, you won't find it in the record books because "Choo
Choo's" clout was hit in the Mets' second exhibition game
ever, a 4-3 victory over the Cardinals.

Coleman was first up with the Phillies in 1961 when
they lost 107 games and finished a distant last. Picked up
by the Mets in the expansion draft, he saw a lot of duty behind the plate for the team that lost 120 and 111 games
successively in '62 and '63. He returned for more punish-
ment in '66, then departed with a .197 average.

Conversationally, "Choo Choo's" reputation was about
as silent as his bat. During an interview, Mets' announcer
Ralph Kiner tried to get the conversation started by asking him how he got his nickname. "Choo Choo" responded,
"I don't know." Supposedly he was tagged with the name
because of his unusual speed.

COLEMAN, Joe
California Angels minor league pitching instructor

The son of former pitcher Joe Coleman, Sr., Joe and his
dad combined for 194 wins. Papa Joe went 52-76 and Junior improved the family picture going 142-135 making
the Colemans, the Bagbys (Jim, Sr. and Jim, Jr.), and the
Trouts (Dizzy and Steve), the only three father-son pitching combinations to win over 50 games each.

Joe, Jr. was the first round pick of the Washington Senators in the 1965 free agent draft. He was the youngest
player in the majors in '65 when he won two games for the
Senators at age 18.

Many players prove to be minor league heroes and major
league flops, but Joe's case is just the opposite as he struggled on the farm in his formative years and found early
success in the biggies. Washington dealt the right-hander
to the Tigers for Denny McLain after the '70 season. Twice
a 20-game winner with the Bengals, he peaked in 1973,
going 23-15. In the '72 ALCS he blanked the A's, 3-0, establishing a record 14 strikeouts.

Before calling it quits in '79, he was with the Cubs, A's, Blue Jays, Giants, and Pirates.

COLLINS, Kevin
Vice-president of Summa-Harrison Metal Products
Hazel Park, MI

An infielder with the Mets, Expos, and Tigers during the years 1965–71, Kevin's first of six major league home runs came in dramatic fashion on Aug. 6, 1968, when he hit a three-run poke with two out in the ninth inning to lead the Mets over the Astros, 4-1. The following night he paid for it when he was knocked unconscious by Doug Rader who came roaring into third base. The incident ignited a bench-clearing brawl.

Kevin's nine pinch-hits in '69 led the league in that department. He left with a .209 average and memories of a wild 24 hours against Houston.

COLTON, Larry
High school teacher/freelance writer
Portland, OR

Larry's book, *Idol Time,* describing the championship season of the NBA Portland Trailblazers was published in 1977. The son-in-law of glamorous movie star, Heddy Lamar, Colton had a great deal of "idle time" after pitching two innings of relief in one game for the '68 Phils.

COMER, Wayne
Owns a clothing store
Shenandoah, VA

Originally signed by the Senators, Wayne found himself in the black and orange hue of the Tigers in 1967–68. In the '68 World Series he went a neat 1-for-1, picking up a pinch-hit single in his only plate appearance.

With the expansion Pilots the next year, Wayne hit 15 home runs. Following stops with the Brewers and Sena-

tors, his career unraveled like a cheap sweater back in
Detroit after 316 games and a .229 average.

CONDE, Ramon
    Supervisor of Sports in Puerto Rico; managed in Mexi-
    can League
    Juana Diaz, PR

This Conde man found life sugar-coated at Indianapolis in
1962 when he led the American Association with a .348 average. The year before he was a Silver Glove winner as the
top fielding third baseman in the minors, making him the
first player to win the award three straight years.
    But bitter reality set in late in '62 when he was called up
to the White Sox and went hitless in 16 at-bats.

CONIGLIARO, Billy
    Manager of a camera store
    Nahant, MA

Billy signed with the Red Sox out of high school in June of
'65 when his 20-year-old brother Tony was hitting cannon
shots over the Green Monster with regularity. The Conig-
liaros were finally united in '69 and for a brief period they
resembled the DiMaggios.
    In Billy's first game he whiffed. Exhibiting all the signs
of the prototype slugger, the young outfielder then hit two
consecutive homers before striking out again. During the
1970 season Billy drove 18 over the wall, but was upset
with Red Sox management for trading away his brother
Tony to the Angels. It took away the glitter of being named
to the Topps Rookie All-Star Team.
    Upset over lack of playing time in '71, he was quoted,
"They're going to retire my uniform . . . with me in it."
Disgruntled, he quit the Brewers in the middle of the '72
season, but returned for one more season as a spare flychaser with the World Champion A's in '73. He appeared
as a pinch-hitter (0-for-4) in the Series, then disappeared at
age 26 with a .256 average.

CONIGLIARO, Tony
Recovering from near-fatal heart attack at the Shaughnessy Rehabilitation Center in Salem, MA

Tony's life is a mixture of dramatics and tragedy.

1963—Hit .363 and was named MVP of the New York-Penn League.

1964—Hit .290 with 24 home runs as a 19-year-old Red Sox rookie, the most homers by a teenager in baseball history.

1964—June 3rd: hit a bases-loaded homer off Dan Osinski of the Angels, giving Tony the distinction of being the youngest player to hit a grand-slam.

1964—Suffered broken arm when hit by a Pedro Ramos pitch.

1964—Late in season, a Wes Stock pitch cracked his wrist.

1965—Led American League in home runs with 32, the youngest (20) to ever lead the league in four-baggers.

1967—(Spring training)—Suffered a hairline arm fracture when teammate John Wyatt hit him in batting practice.

1967—Was enjoying a 20-homer season when a Jack Hamilton (Angels) pitch on August 18th broke his left cheekbone and so impaired his vision that he didn't return until 1969.

1969—Opening Day: Returned from Hamilton beaning and hit a tenth-inning homerun to beat the Orioles, 5-4.

1969—Voted Comeback Player of the Year, a season he hit 20 homers.

1970—Plunked on the elbow by a Fred Lasher pitch. Tony ran to the mound and delivered a karate kick to the Indian pitcher's left thigh.

1970—Had career-high 36 homers and 116 RBIs.

1971—As a member of the Angels, he called a middle-of-the-night press conference to announce his retirement because of eye problems and general dissatisfaction with the club's management.

1975—Attempted comeback with Bosox in '75. After 21

games and a .123 average it was over. He struck
out five times in his last game.

1982—On January 9th was riding in car with his brother
Billy when he suffered a massive heart attack. At
the time of his seizure Tony was en route to the
airport after being interviewed for a broadcasting
job with the Red Sox.

His numbers read: 166 homers; a .264 average.

CONNOLLY, Ed
Vice-president of Kidder, Peabody and Co.
Pittsfield, MA

Ed Connolly, Sr. was a Red Sox catcher from 1929–32. He
died in 1963, one year before his son, Ed Connolly, Jr., took
the mound for Boston. The southpaw was 4-11 that season,
then returned to go 2-1 for the Indians in '67.   6-12

CONNORS, Billy
Chicago Cubs pitching coach; co-partner in the Larry
Bowa Baseball School in St. Petersburg, FL

Billy was a teammate of Jim Barbieri's on the 1954
Schenectady, NY, world champion Little League team. He
pitched the semifinal games in the 1953 and 1954 Little
League World Series in Williamsport, PA, and won both
outings.

Prior to his pro career he was a standout at Syracuse
University, where he led the baseball squad to a third-
place finish in the College World Series.

The flashy dresser, who broke in as an infielder-pitcher
in the Cubs organization, made it to the big arena in 1966
and lost his only decision when he came into a game in relief and gave up a homer to Roberto Clemente. But the
chemistry between Connors and his manager Leo Durocher was not good. He said, "Durocher didn't like sharp
dressers. He wanted to be the sharpest dresser on the
team."

Billy was sold to the Mets, for whom he pitched briefly in
'67 and '68, finishing at 0-2 in 26 games.

COOMBS, Danny
    High school teacher/basketball coach
    Houston, TX

How The West Was Won was a popular movie title in 1963 when Danny won a job with Houston. The 6'4" southpaw reliever, who also played basketball at Seton Hall, never reached the apex of his dreams during a trek that ended with San Diego in 1970–71 at 19-27. With the Padres he won 10 games as a starter in '70 and led the club with a 3.30 E R A.

CORKINS, Mike
    Manager of a "Tool Shack" franchise
    Riverside, CA

Somewhere in the future there will be a book written about the history of the San Diego Padres. And you can bet that Mike Corkins will have a place in it.

In August 1969 he hurled a 16-strikeout no-hitter while at Elmira in the Eastern League, the first no-hitter ever pitched by a member of the Padres' organization. The right-hander brought his blazing fastball to the National League soon after, and on September 22, 1969 he served up career home run No. 600 to Willie Mays.

On April 22, 1970, Corkins pitched well for San Diego, but lost, 2-1 to the Mets on the day Tom Seaver had a record 19 strikeouts. That same season Mike uncorked a grand slammer off 20-game winner Jim Merritt.

Corkins' ride with San Diego ended in 1974 at 19-28.

CORRALES, Pat
    Cleveland Indians' manager

Pat was the skipper of the Philadelphia Phillies at the start of the '83 season, but was relieved of his duties on July 18th even though his Phillies were 43-42 and in first place at the time of his dismissal. It was the only time that a manager was fired while in first place. Picked up by the Indians in late '83, Pat became only the fourth manager since 1900 to manage in both the American League and

National League in the same season, joining John Mc-
Graw (Baltimore and New York, 1902); Rogers Hornsby
(St. Louis and Cincinnati, 1952); and Bill Virdon (Yanks
and Houston, 1975).

The scrappy catcher had a nine-year run in the National
League with the Phillies (1964–65), Cardinals ('66), Reds
(1968–72) and Padres (1972–73). A lifetime .216 hitter, he
caught for the same high school team in Fresno which produced future big leaguers Jim Maloney and Dick Ellsworth. In 1965 Pat set a major league mark when he was
awarded first base six times because of catcher's interference. The record was broken by Dale Berra in 1983.

Pat also managed the Texas Rangers for 2-plus seasons
(1978–80).

COSMAN, Jim
    Regional manager for Browning Ferris, Inc.
    Memphis, TN

"I used to throw garbage, now I pick it up," says Jim. As a
regional manager, Jim doesn't do too much buggy-lugging,
but he did carry his load in his big league debut with the
Cards in '66 when he hurled a 2-hit shutout over the Cubs.
The next year he won a game for the World Champion
Cards, beating Gaylord Perry and the Giants, 3-1, when he
knocked in the winning run with a base hit.

The 6'4½" right-hander, who studied business administration at Middle Tennessee State College, spent the next
couple of years in the minors. His last pickup was with the
Cubs in 1970. Overall, Jim was 2-0 in 12 games with a 3.05
ERA.

COUGHTRY, Marlan
    Manufactures and sells doll furniture
    Rogue River, OR

Marlan Coughtry will never be mistaken for Marlon Bran-
do, even though he was born in Hollywood, but he did take
part in his share of theatrics when he committed three errors in his major league debut with the Red Sox on Sept.
27, 1960. The following night he was in the starting lineup

for the Bosox when Ted Williams hit his last home run in his final career at-bat. Marlan contributed a couple of hits of his own that game to help Boston to victory.

In 1961 he became the Eddie Yost of the P.C.L. and was called the "Walking Man," establishing a P.C.L. season record for drawing bases on balls and also a record for walking five times in a game.

The following year he lived out of a suitcase, appearing in 20 games divided among the Angels, A's, and Indians.   .185

COULTER, Tom
> Employed with Ohio Edison Co.
> Toronto, OH

"Chip" was in just six games at second base for the Cardinals in '69, the extent of his major league stay. It appeared that his dreams of an extended career would be realized when he went 4-for-5 in his first start. Coulter shows a .316 average (6-for-19).

COWAN, Billy
> Real estate investment consultant; owns and operates
> apartments in California, Texas, and New Mexico
> Palos Verdes Estates, CA

Billy received the Minor League Player of the Year Award in 1963 and had a peek at the big time with the Cubs near the end of that season. It was during September '63 that memories were etched indelibly in Billy's mind. "My greatest thrills were getting a basehit on the first pitch I saw in the big leagues, and my first home run (Sept. 17, 1963), a ninth-inning shot to beat Pittsburgh, 2-1, after I was called up," says Cowan.

Primarily an outfielder, Cowan also danced around with the Mets, Braves, Phillies, Yankees, and Angels before it ended in 1972.   .236

COX, Bobby
    Toronto Blue Jays' manager

Bobby received a reported $40,000 bonus to sign with the
Dodgers in '59. His first job in the majors was with the
Yankees in 1968, a year he was chosen to the Topps Rookie
All-Star Team at third base. Bobby's last job came one
year later when he lost his position to his roommate,
Bobby Murcer.

The present Blue Jays' manager braved the maddening
bus rides of the minors for several years where he learned
his trade before landing a coaching job with the Yankees
prior to his first major league managing assignment with
the Braves (1978–81). He has been the Jays' skipper since
1982.   .229

COX, Casey
    Owns insurance agency
    Clearwater, FL

No, "Casey at the Bat" had nothing to do with pitcher
Casey Cox. If anything, his ineptness with a bat is a good
argument for the designated hitter rule. This insurance
man was a poor risk as a batter as he was in 130 games before he finally reached first base when he was walked by
Sam McDowell. The 6'5" basketball player out of Los Angeles State College collected the first five of his 15 career
hits during the '69 season, with four of the five coming off
Earl Wilson. Casey swung for a not-too-mighty .099.

But Casey was paid to retire batters, not swat four-baggers. From 1966–69 he was quite effective as a relief
pitcher with the Senators. He was 12-7 in '69 and the next
year was made a starter. Casey then shifted to Texas with
the franchise in 1972 and was the first player on the Rangers squad to set up residence in the Dallas area. Unfortunately there was nothing in his policy that protected him
from being traded. In '73 Cox found himself with the Yankees, where he struck out for the last time at 39-42.

CRAIG, Pete
> Manages the Raleigh operation of Southern Offices
> Furniture Distributors Corp.
> Raleigh, NC

Roger Craig (no relation to Pete) was liberated when he
joined the World Champion Cardinals in '64 after being in
bondage with the hapless Mets for two years where he lost
a league-high 24 and 22 games in succession. For Pete
Craig, a Canadian-born right hander out of the University
of Detroit, '64 was the first of three seasons that he made
brief appearances on the mound for the Washington Senators (0-3).

CRAM, Jerry
> Pitching coach for Omaha, a Triple-A affiliate of the
> Kansas City Royals

Webster describes "cram" as to fill beyond normal capacity by pressing or squeezing; to study for an examination
in a hurried way. Jerry did his cramming at Riverside College in California where he received the Man of Distinction Award in 1967.
> But in the majors his 23-game career (0-3) was muddled,
starting in Kansas City (1969) and ending there in '76
with an in-between stop with the Mets.   0-3

CRAWFORD, Willie
> Member of the Los Angeles Dodgers Speakers Bureau
> Los Angeles, CA

Willie received $100,000 out of high school in Los Angeles
to sign with the Dodgers.
> He was just 17 when he hit .326 in the California League
in 1964, a year the young flychaser was promoted to the
Dodgers and hit .313 in 10 games. His next two seasons
were divided between Chavez Ravine and the Texas
League. Willie became one of a few teenagers to play in a
World Series when he went 1-for-2 as a pinch-hitter in the
'65 Fall Classic.
> Haunted by a high frequency of strikeouts, Willie never

achieved royal status. Most of his .268 career was spent
with Los Angeles (1964–75) before going to the Cardinals
in '76, where he reached his stride batting .304. Willie
split the '77 campaign with the A's and Astros and played
also with the Giants. With Oakland he requested uniform
No. 99 saying, "I wanted one I knew wasn't already
taken."

CRIDER, Jerry
Owns a resort, "Jerry Crider's Hunting and Fishing"
Ciudad Obregon, Mexico

Easy Rider was a box office hit in '69 when Jerry Crider
reached his destination that summer as a member of the
Twins after spending a decade in the bush leagues. The
1968 P.C.L. co-leader in victories (18-10) with Denver,
Jerry also cruised around with the White Sox in '70 where
he came to a screeching halt.

The burly 6'2", 205-lb. right-hander went on an embarrassing ride once at Yankee Stadium. Minnesota manager
Billy Martin called for reliever Bob Miller from the bullpen, but Jerry was chauffered in by mistake. After consult-
ing with Yankee skipper Ralph Houk and the umpire,
Jerry was driven back to the pen.

CROWLEY, Terry
Baltimore Orioles' hitting coach

Nobody ever confused this first baseman-outfielder with
Stan Musial, but he quietly carved a niche for himself in
the majors from 1969–82.

Terry arrived with the Orioles in '69. With the exception
of brief stops with Cincinnati (1974–75), Atlanta ('76), and
Montreal ('83) the popular pinch-hitter spent his days with
Baltimore, giving American League hurlers fits.

In the '79 World Series against the Pirates, he appeared
in five of seven games off the bench. In Game Four at
Pittsburgh with the Orioles trailing, 6-3, he drove in the
tying and winning runs in Baltimore's six-run seventh inning.   .250

CUETO, Berto
  Havana, Cuba

Following the United States trade embargo imposed on
Cuba in 1961, a complete break in diplomatic relations between the two countries resulted. That summer Cuban-
born right-hander Dagoberto Cueto pitched in seven games
with Minnesota. After going 1-3, there was a complete
break in relations between Berto and the Twins.

CULLEN, Jack
  Supervisor for Pabst Brewing Co. in Newark, NJ

Jack's 19-game career in part of '62 and '65 came to a head
with a 4-4 mark and a fine 3.07 ERA. The Yankee right-
hander hurled a three-hit 1-0 shutout over the Orioles on
Aug. 20, 1965.
  Jack found '65 to be a year of real gusto when he logged
a 14-5 record at Toledo in the International League.

CULLEN, Tim
  Vice-president, Institutional Trading for Prudential-
  Bache Securities
  San Francisco, CA

Tim did his trading (or was traded) around the American
League between 1966–1972. As a second baseman he was
with the Senators two different trips, the White Sox and
Oakland A's.
  An All-American at Santa Clara University, Tim once
made three errors in a game playing for the Senators. He
said, "When I came to bat, the Washington crowd gave me
a standing boovation." Cullen went from the '72 World
Series with Oakland directly to retirement.
  A graduate in accounting, Tim's final totals were neat
and precise (.220 average in 700 games). He is also the California coordinator of the Major League Baseball Players
Alumni Association.

CULP, Ray
President of his own real estate management company in Austin, TX

Like fine wine, Ray seemed to get better with age. Signed by the Phillies out of high school for a $100,000 bonus, Ray struggled in the low minors. Following a 13-8 season at Williamsport in 1962, he was promoted to the Phillies for the '63 season and posted a 14-11 record including five shutouts. His achievements earned him National League Rookie of the Year honors from *The Sporting News*. The hot rookie, who pitched one inning in the All-Star Game in '63, followed up with three more winning seasons in the City of Brotherly Love.

The right-hander went to the Cubs and then to Boston, where he found Fenway to be quite friendly. He enjoyed his best years for the Red Sox, winning 16 and 17 back-to-back. In 1968 he went on a roll, pitching four consecutive shutouts for the Bosox and on May 11, 1970, he tied a record when he whiffed the first six batters he faced.   122-101

CULVER, George
Pitching coach for Portland in the P.C.L.

This soft-spoken chucker was a lavish spender when it came to the art of sartorial splendor. As the story goes, he once got dressed in a purple, two-button, double-breasted suit with matching accessories and stood in front of the Carlton Howe Hotel in Cincinnati where motorists stopped and gaped in disbelief. His 48-49 overall mark from 1966–74 was not so splendid, but then again not too shabby.

George took his wardrobe to Cleveland, Cincinnati, St. Louis, Houston, Los Angeles (Dodgers) and Philadelphia. The right-hander did have one glittering day in 1968 when he no-hit the Phils. For his efforts, he was honored by fans on "George Culver Night" at Crosley Field.

CUMBERLAND, John
    Auto paint and body shop business, also trains show
    horses; Mets' minor league pitching coach
    · Westbrook, ME

The Yankees scored a first in professional sports and entertainment in 1968 by selling reserved seats for their
games via use of a computer. That year southpaw hurler
John Cumberland joined the Yankees, where he spent
parts of the next two seasons. Unable to make a dent with
the Yankees, he was traded to the Giants where he did his
best repair work in 1971, going 9-6 and helping San
Francisco to the National League West title.
    John then pitched with the Cardinals and Angels before
hanging up his mallet in 1974 at 15-15.

CURRY, Tony
    Nassau, Bahamas

Tony never played baseball until age 16 when the sport
gained popularity in his native Bahamas.
    It is doubtful that any other player has the distinction of
playing under three different managers in his first three
major league games. The young outfielder made his debut
on Opening Day in 1960, going 1-for-2. Following the
Phillies' loss to the Reds, Manager Eddie Sawyer resigned.
Tony then played under interim manager Andy Cohen in
his second game and completed the hat trick in his third
contest when he was introduced to Gene Mauch, the new
Phillies' skipper.
    Curry finished his rookie year with a .261 average and
joined Dodger rookies Frank Howard and Tommy Davis as
the outfielders on the Topps Rookie All-Star team. He
played briefly with the Phils in '61, then was out of the
majors until 1966 when he appeared in 19 games as a
pinch-hitter for the Indians.   .246

CURTIS, Jack
      Supervisor for the Regal Manufacturing Co., a textile
      industry
      Granite Falls, NC

In 1963 this textile supervisor's 14-19 career folded, but it
did have its sleek moments. After posting 19 wins for San
Antonio and being named the Texas League Pitcher of the
Year in 1960, Jack found himself in Wrigley Field with the
Cubs in '61. His 10 victories earned him a spot on the
Topps Rookie All-Star team.
   The young southpaw was especially tough on the
Braves, beating them three times in '61. But the most pub-
licized decision vs. the Braves was the one he lost, since it
was Warren Spahn's 300th career victory. However, Jack
did pitch creditably, allowing seven hits in the 2-1 loss.
   Curtis was swapped to the Braves for Bob Buhl in '62
and drifted away with the Indians the following year.

D

DAHL, Jay
      Died on June 20, 1965, at age 19 in an automobile ac-
      cident in Salisbury, NC

On September 27, 1963, the then-Houston Colt .45s
started an all-rookie lineup in a game against the Mets. It
was the youngest lineup ever to start a major league game.
The infield consisted of Rusty Staub (19) first base, Joe
Morgan (20) second base, Sonny Jackson (19) shortstop,
and Glenn Vaughan (19) third base. Jerry Grote (20) was
behind the plate. The outfield had Jim Wynn (21), Aaron
Pointer (21) and Brock Davis (19), while Jay Dahl (17) was
on the mound.
   Houston's pink-cheeked, baby-faced lineup lost to the
Mets, 10-3. Jay's three-inning stint marked his lone ap-
pearance in the big leagues.
   Two years later tragedy struck a promising future.

Pitching for Salisbury in the Western Carolinas League, Jay upped his record to a spotless 5-0 with a victory on June 19, 1965. The following day he was killed in a car wreck. With his death at age 19, he is the youngest former major leaguer in history to die.

DAILEY, Bill
>   Hardware sales representative
>   Pulaski, VA

This right-handed relief specialist broke in with the Indians in 1961, then was jettisoned to Minnesota where he established himself as one of the premier firemen in the American League in 1963, going 6-3 with 21 saves and a 1.99 ERA. A year later it was all over at 10-7 plus 22 saves.

DAL CANTON, Bruce
>   Pitching coach in Atlanta Braves' organization

When Bruce received his master's degree in Biology from West Virginia he did his thesis on the subject of pitchers' arm ailments. Little did he know that such a malady would place his wing in the graveyard of chuckers.

The well-educated hurler did experience a longer survival than most (1967–1977). Bruce, who was a biology teacher during the off-season during his playing days, spread his theories with the Pirates, Royals, Braves, and White Sox. The California State (PA) grad finished 51-49.

DALRYMPLE, Clay
>   Regional sales manager for a plumbing company
>   Westminister, MD

A heavyweight boxer in college at Chico State, Clay caught with the Phillies throughout most of the Sixties. Maury Wills called the rifle-armed receiver the toughest catcher for him to steal against. From July 14, 1966, to June 6, 1967, Clay's mitt was sterling, handling a record 628 straight chances without an error.

Long before he started selling tools for a plumbing company, he threw a monkey wrench into the baseball rule book. The incident occurred on July 18, 1969, when Clay was a member of the Orioles in a game against the White Sox. In the first inning Dalrymple came out with his regular catcher's mitt on his left hand and a fielder's glove in his back pocket. The idea was to use the fielder's glove if there was a play at the plate since it would be easier to catch a thrown ball because of its added flexibility.

The umpires were perplexed over Dalrymple's tactics. Finally, the men in blue decided it was illegal to have any extra gloves on the field, according to rule 3.14.

Clay tied a National League record on July 4, 1967, when he walked six times in a doubleheader sweep over Houston. In the '69 World Series he was 2-for-2 as an Orioles' pinch-hitter.   .233

DAMASKA, Jack
       Foreman at Babcock and Wilcox Tubular Products Co.
       Beaver Falls, PA

Chances are you remember Damascus, the winner of the 1967 Preakness. Chances are you never heard of Damaska, a Cardinals' hopeful who went 1-for-5 for the Redbirds in 1963, the same year another Beaver Falls product named Joe Namath was grabbing headlines on the gridiron at Alabama.

DARWIN, Bobby
       Los Angeles Dodgers' scout
       Buena Park, CA

Dodger Vice-President Al Campanis, hurrying to the airport, became involved in a two-car collision shortly after the '68 season had ended. A member of the tow-truck crew which came to his aid was a 6'2", 190-pound, athletic-looking young man who had the kind of body you would order out of a catalogue. His name was Bobby Darwin. The Los Angeles native introduced himself to Campanis who remembered how the Dodgers had tried to sign him before the Angels did in 1962.

When the list of players subject to draft reached the

Dodger office prior to the '69 campaign, Bobby became No.
1 on the Dodgers "wanted" list.

Darwin's strange big league journey began as a 19-year-
old, when he hurled three innings for the Angels in '62. He
spent the next several seasons in the minors as an employee of the Orioles' organization before meeting Campanis in distress on the freeway. The flamethrower made
three appearances without a decision on the mound for the
Dodgers in '69, spending most of the summer in Spokane.

Tired of fighting arm miseries, he tried the outfield with
remarkable success in the minors. Traded to Minnesota after the '71 campaign, he became a regular in the Twins
lineup for the next three years. In his first seven games
with Minnesota he became the most popular citizen in the
Twin Cities after belting four home runs. The 29-year-old
reclamation project finished with 22 roundtrippers and 80
ribbies in '72, then followed up with 18 and 25 four-baggers the next two years, collecting 90 and 94 RBIs. He did,
however, lead the American League in striking out all
three years.

Before it was over he also played with the Brewers, Red
Sox, and Cubs. As a pitcher he was 0-1; his batting totals
read .251 with 83 home runs.

DAVALILLO, Vic
    Active in Mexican League

As did Bobby Darwin, Vic began as a pitcher, but his ability to use a bat like a marksman uses a rifle, prompted him
to alter his career and become an outfielder.

In 1962 the little 5'7" Venezuelan led the International
League in batting when he hit .346 for Jacksonville. The
next year he hit .292 as a Cleveland rookie and remained a
fixture in the Indians' outfield until he was shipped to the
Angels during the 1968 season. Vic reacted like a 10-year-
old in Disneyland, leading California in batting at .298.

Davalillo's next stop was with the Cardinals in '69
where he even pitched in two games without retiring a batter, giving up two hits and two walks. The following year
Vic led the National League in pinch-hitting (24-for-73)

with his 24-pinch-swats tying a single-season record held
then by Dave Philley and since broken by Jose Morales.

Vic then brought his odd step-in-the-bucket batting
stance to Pittsburgh, where he played a key role in the
Bucs' World Championship, hitting .333 as a pinch-hitter
and .285 overall. The following year he hit a career high
.318, then moved to Oakland where he played for his second World Champ in three years.

Following a two-year hiatus in Mexico, Vic returned to
the majors with the Dodgers (1977–80), where he teammed
with Manny Mota to give Los Angeles two valuable Span-
ish antiques off the bench.

Davalillo became one of a few players to participate with
three different teams in a World Series.   .279

DAVANON, Jerry
    Sales manager for a subsidiary of the Dover Co.; sells
    to oil industries
    Houston, TX

The Beatles' *Hello-Goodbye* could have been Jerry's theme
since he, a utility infielder, was on numerous rosters from
1969–1977. Originally in the Cardinals' organization, the
San Diego City College product was selected by the Padres
in the expansion draft, but before he completed his run,
Jerry played with the Cardinals on three different occasions. He also saw action with the Orioles, Angels, and
Astros.   .234

DAVIAULT, Ray
    Marketing Department of O'Keefe Brewery
    Montreal, Que.

Can you recall watching Ray Walston in TV's *My Favorite
Martian?* You have an excellent memory if you remember
Ray Daviault, a right-handed stranger from Canada who
was 1-5 in 36 games for the original Mets.

DAVIDSON, Ted
> Owner of the TNT silk screening business
> Santa Maria, CA

"After I was shot by my former wife, I was never the same," lamented Thomas Eugene (Ted) Davidson.

Prior to the 1967 season, Ted was sitting inside a bar when his estranged wife accosted him, pulled out a .25 caliber pistol, and shot him in the stomach and chest. Almost instantly his baseball career exploded like a powder keg of dynamite.

As a left-handed relief pitcher, the Las Vegas native was a shade luckier, rolling an 11-7 mark with the Reds and Braves from 1965-68. Especially tough on lefty swingers, Ted wasn't afraid to "load it up." The candid chucker said, "I picked up the spitball on my own. I threw it quite a bit the last year or so. I would like to see them legalize it."

Ted's life was again abruptly altered in 1983 when he suffered a massive heart attack that led to quadruple bypass surgery. But he emphasized, "Believe me, it was much tougher recovering from the shooting."

DAVIS, Bill
> Insurance business
> Minneapolis, MN

"The Jolly Green Giant" became a familiar figure in television commercials in the 1960s as well as a song when Bill Davis, standing 6'7" was given that designation by the fans at Portland. The behemoth first baseman terrorized P.C.L. pitchers in '65, pounding out 33 homers.

Davis joined the Indians briefly before roaming back to Portland in '66 where a "Jolly Green Giant" Night was held to celebrate his return. One last try with the Padres in '69 and this relatively unknown Goliath vanished from the face of the earth.

A graduate of the University of Minnesota, Bill led the Gophers to the Big Ten title and NCAA World Series championship in '64. Equally adept on the hardwood, Davis captained the Minnesota basketball team. Unfortunately his roundball playing led to his extinction when he

severed an Achilles tendon playing basketball in the
winter of '67.   .184

DAVIS, "Brock"
  Transit driver
  Los Angeles, CA

Nicknamed "Brock" by his Little League teammates who
couldn't pronounce his first name of Bryshear, the flychaser out of Los Angeles State College skyrocketed directly to the Astros in 1963, but he spent the next several
years shuttling between the majors and minors.

  A .260 hitter, Brock was in transit to the Cubs and
Brewers. Ironically, he closed in 1972, the year he hit his
career high, .318.

DAVIS, Jacke
  Baseball coach and athletic director at Panola Jr. Col-
  lege
  Carthage, TX

An All-American selection at Baylor, Jacke played in 48
games for the Phillies in '62. Jacke had two memorable
moments for his scrapbook. Number one was his first big
league hit, a triple against the Mets in the Polo Grounds.
The other was a three-run, pinch-hit homer in the ninth inning which deprived Sandy Koufax of a shutout.   .213

DAVIS, Ron
  Computer programmer and supervisor of operations
  with the Grant Geo-Physical Oil & Gas Co.
  Houston, TX

Ernie Davis won the Heisman Trophy as the nation's outstanding football player in 1961, a year in which Ron
Davis was a backup quarterback for the Duke team which
defeated Arkansas in the Cotton Bowl. It was a banner
year for Ron as he also led the Blue Devils' nine to the
ACC and NCAA District Three titles. Named as the cen-

terfielder on the All-American team, Davis signed with Houston and emerged for a few games in '62.

Ron was summoned to Houston again in 1966 to fill in for the injured Jim Wynn late in the season. In one game against the Giants he took Juan Marichal deep for his first home run.

Traded to the Cardinals in '68, Davis appeared in two games in the World Series and went hitless in seven at-bats subbing for Roger Maris. One last gasp with the Pirates ('69) and he was done at .233.

DAVIS, Willie
　　Night club business
　　Dallas, TX

It was once said of Willie, "He can run, hit, throw, and field. The only thing he's never been able to do is think."

Blessed with Olympian speed, superb defensive skills, and a lively bat, Willie remained an enigma to management, which felt he never lived up to his promise. Named the Minor League Player of the Year in 1960 after leading the P.C.L. with a .346 average at Spokane, "Will O' The Wisp" earned his promotion to Los Angeles, where he entertained the sun-kissed Dodger fans from 1960–1973 in unpredictable see-saw fashion. A daring baserunner, he tied a record with three stolen bases in a game during the '65 World Series. In the '66 Fall Classic, Davis suffered the ignominy of making three errors in the same inning of Game Two. Ugly memories of Willie's atrocity inning remain engraved in the minds of those who bleed Dodger blue.

During the '68 season Willie experimented with several batting styles. After a prolonged slump he viewed a motion picture on batting by Ted Williams. Call it coincidence or just plain good instruction, but Willie showed marked improvement during the next three years as he batted over .300 each campaign from 1969–71. Beset by personal problems in the early 1970s, he became a practicing Buddhist in search of happiness. Davis also had a role in a Jerry Lewis movie *Which Way to the Front*.

A member of the National League All-Star squad in '71

and '73, Willie's All-Star record is perfect, going 3-for-3 in midsummer competition.

Following the '73 season, Willie hopped around with the Expos, Rangers, Cardinals, and Padres. He then took his bat to Japan for two years. Upon his return he stated, "It's tough for an American to play there because they still remember the war."

Tired of Japanese baseball, he came back to the States where he suffered a personal tragedy. When vacationing in Hawaii, his wife fell to her death while sightseeing on a cliff.

His lengthy stay ended with the Angels in '79. By normal standards Willie's .279 average and 182 homers would constitute a successful career, but in the minds of many, not so for this talented guy from Mineral Springs, AR.

DAVISON, Mike
Insurance business
Hutchinson, MN

Portnoy's Complaint sold well in 1969, a year Mike had no complaints since he got his first taste of big league honey as a relief pitcher with the Giants. Signed originally with the Orioles, Davison was considered a top prospect in the Giants' organization in the mid-Sixties. In 1970 he went 3-5 with San Francisco, all in relief. If the southpaw had any complaints it would be that his career was interrupted three years (1966–68) due to military service.   3-5

DAY, "Boots"
Manager at Bristol in Appalachian League in Tigers' organization

Nancy Sinatra was singing *These Boots Are Made for Walking* in 1966 when Charles "Boots" Day started out in pro ball in the Cardinals' chain. The outfielder climbed up to St. Louis for 11 games in 1969.

"Boots" then kicked around with the Cubs and Expos. A .256 lifetime hitter, he enjoyed his finest year in '71 when he hit .283 in Montreal.

The native of Ilion, NY, later tried pitching at Evansville, but stumbled.

DEAN, Tommy
Superintendent of the National Geographic press room in charge of printing all ads and editorials
Iuka, MS

When Tommy was signed to a $60,000 bonus by the Dodgers, he insisted on splitting it with his brother Scotty, who was responsible for convincing local high school authorities in Iuka, Mississippi (pop. 1,527) to construct a baseball field and adding basketball to the school's athletic curriculum. Scotty's request was triggered by the overall abilities of his brother.

Tommy didn't let brother Scotty down, garnering a four-year average of .510.

Scholarship offers poured in from 19 major universities. There were so many baseball scouts on his trail the Dean family put numbers in a hat to set up a drawing by the scouts for their speaking "turn." The Dean sweepstakes was to have been held on a Saturday, but the Dodgers jumped the gun and arrived on Friday. They signed Tommy, leaving a dozen other bird dogs scratching their heads and doing a slow burn.

After watching Tommy perform in the Arizona Instruction al League, Buzzy Bavasi rated him the finest fielding youngster he had seen since Pee Wee Reese. Considered the best fielding shortstop in the P.C.L. in 1967, this minor league Cinderella turned into a big league pumpkin, hitting .180 in 215 games with the Dodgers ('67) and Padres ('69–'71).

DEBUSSCHERE, Dave
Executive vice-president and director of operations for the New York Knicks

"The pressure in baseball is much greater than basketball. You don't remember all the baskets scored against you, but one pitch can beat you in baseball,"—Dave DeBusschere.

By the age of 21 this University of Detroit gladiator had

been through big league wars as a basketball and baseball player. The 6'6" right-hander pitched in a dozen games, all in relief, with the White Sox in the summer of '62. The first batter he faced was Manny Jiminez of the A's. Dave recalled, "I threw the first pitch behind his head all the way to the screen." That winter he averaged 12 points per game for the Pistons in the NBA.

In 1963 he went 3-4 for the Chisox, including one shutout. Although this was his final season in the biggies, he continued to pitch in the minors for a couple of years, racking up 15 wins for Indianapolis in both the '64 and '65 seasons.

By 1966 he would concentrate exclusively on basketball. During the 1964–65 NBA season he was named player-coach for the Pistons, the youngest (24) to ever coach a major professional team in any sport. Traded to the Knicks, he was a key member of their 1969–70 championship team which included Walt Frazier, Willis Reed, and Bill Bradley.

Dave's book, *The Open Man,* a diary of the championship season, was published the following year. In 1983 he was elected to the Naismith Memorial Basketball Hall of Fame in Springfield, MA.

DECKER, Joe
    Pitching coach at Salt Lake City in the P.C.L.

Joe recorded his first triumph in the majors on the final day of the '69 season with four shutout innings of relief work for the Cubs against the Mets. For the next three years he was up and down between the Cubs and minors. After a 12-7 season at Wichita in '72 with the best ERA in the American Association, he was traded to Minnesota where he enjoyed moderate success for the Twins, winning 16 games in 1974.   36-43

DEES, Charlie
    Oil company supervisor
    Harbor City, CA

Remember Dick and Dee Dee, Joey Dee and the Starlighters, and Dee Dee Sharp with *Mashed Potato Time?* How about Charlie Dees, who performed with the Angels from 1963–65 to the tune of .265.

A first baseman, "Chuck" started out in the Giants' chain, but found the dance floor crowded, with both Orlando Cepeda and Willie McCovey blocking his way.

The jazz record collector and trumpet player was on key in 1962 for El Paso when he hit .348 to win the Texas League batting title. On August 20th that year he became the first player since 1903 to hit four home runs in a game in the Texas League.

DEGERICK, Mike
  Landscape design business
  East Hanover, NJ

As an 18-year-old, Mike hurled a no-hitter in the Appalachian League in 1961. It appeared that this landscaper's blueprint for success was on schedule. But after one game in '61 and another the next year for the White Sox, Mike's plans were scrapped without a decision.

DE LA HOZ, Mike
  Real estate business
  Miami, FL

It was show time for Mike on July 8, 1965, when he carried out one of the greatest pinch-hitting performances the game had ever seen as a member of the Milwaukee Braves. The quiet Cuban came off the bench in the eighth inning to collect a pinch-hit homer, then singled to tie the game in the ninth when the Braves scored three runs. In the 12th frame, he singled, advanced to second on a sacrifice, and scored on a single by Frank Bolling to give the Braves a 9-8 victory.

De La Hoz came up with the Indians in 1960. A handy utility infielder, Mike also played with the Braves and Reds in a career that spanned the entire decade.   .251

DEMPSEY, Rick
    Active player with the Baltimore Orioles

"Do not put your faith in what statistics say until you have
carefully considered what they do not say."
                                    —William W. Watt

   Rick will never gain entry to baseball's coveted Hall of
Fame on the basis of his offensive statistics, but if one were
to choose an "All-Clutch" team, there would be a spot reserved for Mr. Dempsey. Simply stated, the man is a winner. He may go 0-for-June, but come October the veteran
catcher becomes deadly. In two World Series he shows a
.324 average (11-for-34). Rick's crowning achievement was
his performance during the '83 Fall Classic (5-for-13, .385)
with a record five extra base hits for a five-game Series
and throwing out the Phils' Joe Morgan twice in three stolen base attempts. His heroics earned him the World
Series MVP Award, a Pontiac Trans Am from *Sport* magazine.
   Rick broke in with the Twins in '69. Following the '72
season he was traded to the Yankees and was assigned to
Syracuse before becoming the backup catcher to Thurman
Munson. Traded to the Orioles in the middle of the '76 season, he found a comfortable nest and has been there ever
since.
   Defensively, the clever backstop has led the majors in
fielding twice. His excellent eraser rate of throwing out enemy runners has made him one of the most respected receivers in the American League.
   Rick's parents, George T. Dempsey and the former June
Archer, performed on the vaudeville circuit. A bit of a thes-
pian himself, he has twice given his famous "Baseball So-
liloquy in Pantomine" during rain delays at Fenway Park.
His rendition of Carlton Fisk's home run trot in Game Six
of the 1975 World Series has become classic. Rick's brother, Pat, is also a catcher in the Orioles' organization and
his sister, Cherie, is a professional golfer.
   At this writing Dempsey has a .240 career average, but
if there is a lesson to be learned from Mr. Watt, don't put
too much faith in statistics.

DENEHY, Bill
> Baseball coach at the University of Hartford (Connecticut)

How many guys can boast that they struck out Willie Mays each time they faced him? How many can say they were traded for a manager? Bill Denehy can answer "yes" to both questions.

Following a 9-2 mark with a 1.97 ERA at Williamsport in '66, Bill leaped to the Mets in '67. He was just 1-7 in 15 games, but had the distinction of fanning Willie Mays the four times he faced him.

In one of baseball's more unusual trades, Bill was dealt to the Senators in exchange for manager Gil Hodges. Two years later Hodges became known as "The Miracle Worker" when he managed the Amazin' Mets to the World Championship. Bill needed a miracle as he struggled in Washington before being sent back to the farm for more seasoning. He returned in '71 with the Tigers, losing all three decisions for the Bengals.   1-10

DENNIS, Don
> Employed with the National Guard
> Uniontown, KS

When Don was brought up to the Cardinals in '65 from Jacksonville, he faced instant adversity. In his first appearance he was brought in to protect a lead in the ninth inning. He immediately surrendered a home run which tied the score. But when Bill White homered in the Cards' next at-bat it made a winner out of Dennis, despite an ERA of 18.00.

But this Guardsman did an about face, allowing no runs in his next nine straight appearances. The right-handed reliever finished the year at 2-3 with six saves. Don had 38 more relief stints the following season before clicking his boots and marching away forever at 6-5 over two seasons.

DICKEN, Paul
    Contractor
    Ridgeway, CO

Simon and Garfunkel sang *The Sounds of Silence* in 1966.
Could they have been singing about Paul Dicken's bat?
The outfielder went hitless in 13 plate appearances, all in
a pinch-hitting role.
    Paul, who designs the houses he builds, was formerly in
his own business in Lake Worth, FL.

DICKSON, Jim
    Driver's education teacher
    Astoria, OR

Petticoat Junction crossed the tube in '63 when this driver's ed teacher pulled in with the Astros. After a brief run
with the Reds the next year, Jim had his first full season in
'65 with the Kansas City A's. The hard-throwing right-
hander established an American League rookie record by
coming cut of the bullpen 68 times. After the '66 campaign, Jim drove away at 5-3.

DIDIER, Bob
    Oakland A's coach

Bob was a highly touted high school quarterback at a time
his father, Mel Didier, a former minor league pitcher, was
an assistant football coach at LSU. But the young Didier
chose to call signals from behind home plate rather than
on the line of scrimmage.
    In 1969 the 20-year-old backstop enjoyed a .256 rookie
season with the N.L. West champion Atlanta Braves and
was named to the Topps Rookie All-Star team. Unfortunately, Didier was an asset with his glove but a liability
with his bat as he struggled the next few years for the
Braves, Tigers, and Red Sox.   .229

DIERKER, Larry
 Houston Astros' announcer

Sept. 22, 1964, was a day of infamy for Larry Dierker. Not only did he celebrate his 18th birthday, it was a day in which he made his big league debut and struck out Willie Mays and Jim Hart in the first inning. After prepping only 39 innings in the minors, Larry was on his way to becoming the winningest pitcher (139-123) in Astros history.
 On Sept. 30, 1966, he had a perfect game through eight innings against the Mets, only to lose, 1-0, on a two-hitter. Pitching for the weak-hitting Astros in 1968, the luckless hurler was shut out six times and dropped three one-run decisions. The following year he became the first Houston chucker to win 20 games when he went 20-13. Larry finally hit the jackpot on July 9, 1976, when he no-hit the Expos, 6-0.
 However, an ailing 30-year-old right arm proved fatal to Dierker's career. After pitching in '77 with the Cardinals, it was lights out.   139-123

DIETZ, Dick
 President of Sports Clinics Unlimited; conducts sports clinics throughout Georgia

Dick was the central figure in a sizzling controversy involving Don Drysdale's record consecutive scoreless innings streak in 1968. The Giants' catcher was batting with the bases loaded in the ninth and none out with a 2-and-2 count. Drysdale's next offering hit Dietz, but umpire Harry Wendelstedt ruled that Dietz had made no effort to avoid being touched by the ball. Instead of permitting a run-scoring hit batsman, the ump ruled the pitch "Ball Three." Dick eventually flied out and Drysdale went to pitch a record 58⅔ scoreless innings, shattering Walter Johnson's 45-year record. When asked recently about the play, Dietz simply replied, "It was a bad call."
 Named the Texas League Player of the Year in 1963 at El Paso after a league-leading .354 average, Dick was called up to San Francisco from Phoenix in 1966. In 1970 he was on top of his game, batting .300 with 22 home runs

and 107 RBIs. As a late-inning replacement for Johnny Bench in the All-Star Game, he led off the ninth inning with a home run to spark the National League to a come-from-behind victory.

In '71 he contributed 19 roundtrippers and 72 RBIs as a member of the Giants' National League West championship team. He was quoted after the clinching victory, "I feel great and the Dodgers can go to hell." The day before the start of the '72 season he found himself sold to the Dodgers and arrived at Dodger Stadium with his foot in his mouth. Dick closed with the Braves in '73 at .261.

DILAURO, Jack
    Manager of Koening's sporting goods store
    Akron, OH

In 1969, Jack made a nebulous 1-4 contribution to the "Miracle Mets." But he did show an excellent 2.40 ERA and was awarded his full World Series winner's share of $18,338.18.

That winter he was assigned to Tidewater by the Mets and was drafted by Houston. Based on information fed into a computer, Jack graded out the highest of over 300 lefty pitchers available in the draft. In 42 games for Houston in 1970, Jack went 1-3 and never pitched in the majors again.

Could Mr. DiLauro have been a "computer error"?

DILLMAN, Bill
    Administrative assistant to the president in the investment division of a real estate company
    Richboro, PA

In 1964 running back Brian Piccolo of Wake Forest University led the nation in rushing. Three years later this colorblind pitcher was signed out of the same school by the Orioles. His debut was a sparkling one—five hitless innings of relief to gain a victory over the Kansas City A's. Dillman went on to win his first four decisions as a rookie. He was 5-9, then reappeared a few years later with the Expos. "Bill's Song" was 7-12.

DILLON, Steve
      Policeman
      New York, NY

"No—my name's not 'Marshal or Matt'!"
    Gunsmoke was about midway through its 20-year run as
one of television's most popular shows when this southpaw
pitched one game for the Mets in '63 and two more the next
year without a decision.

DISTASO, Alec
      Policeman
      Los Angeles, CA

When Alec was selected as the No. 1 pick in the January
1967 free agent draft by the Cubs out of high school in Los
Angeles, he was said to resemble Dodger ace Don Drysdale
both physically and in the way he could fire the pellet. But
this blazing darling of the media turned into a brush fire
after making two appearances out of the Cubs bullpen in
'69.

*Two pitchers named Dobson took the mound in the Sixties.
Although probably not as confusing as the three Bob Mill-
ers who all pitched a few years earlier, the Dobsons (Chuck
and Pat) both were right-handers of the same size who
worked as starters. They are unrelated.*

DOBSON, Chuck
      Pitching instructor in California Angels' organization

Chuck pitched in high school just a few blocks away from
where he would be employed as a member of the Kansas
City A's and enjoy a steady (74-69) career that began in
1966. Dobson moved with the team from his hometown to
Oakland and became a dependable starter for the A's in
their first four seasons in the Bay Area. In 1970 he led the
American League in games started (40) and shutouts (5).
    Following elbow surgery, the 6'4" right-hander re-
turned to the minors, then made one last attempt with the
Angels before he called it quits.

DOBSON, Pat
    Milwaukee Brewers' minor league pitching coach in
    1984

In the beer commercial they filmed together, Pat Dobson
doesn't let Sparky Lyle finish talking. He interrupts Lyle,
stating, "You never let me finish." The reference is made
to 1974 when Pat was a 19-game winner for the Yankees
with relief help in a few from Lyle.

Pat began his not too "Lite" 11-year (1967–77) trip with
Detroit. He appeared in three games in the '68 World
Series without a decision. He then traveled across the hin-
terlands to San Diego before returning east a year later
with Baltimore. In 1971 he joined Jim Palmer, Dave
McNally, and Mike Cuellar as 20-game winners. The only
other team in baseball history to produce four 20-game
winners was the 1920 White Sox.

Dobson started the fourth game of the '71 Series against
the Pirates, the first night game in World Series history.
He pitched 6⅔ innings, but was not involved in the decision. Pat also made relief appearances in Games Six and
Seven. At one point during the regular season he won 12
consecutive starts, finishing 20-8.

Before the right-hander ran out of gas, he made stops
with the Braves, Yankees, and Indians.   122-129

DONALDSON, John
    Painting and wallpaper business
    Charlotte, NC

"I led the American League in sunflower seed eating and
also led the league in 'hang in there, get 'em next time,' "
quipped John.

The year 1967 was a memorable one for John in more
ways than one. Not only did he become the regular second
sacker with the Kansas City A's, he married the Miss
Missouri representative in the Miss Universe contest. He
moved to Oakland with the A's, then was traded to Seattle
the following year. It was back to Oakland in '70 and one
last try four years later when John decided there would be
"no next time," leaving with a .238 average.

DONOHUE, Jim
> Manufacturer's representative with Hillerich and
> Bradsby, producer of The Louisville Slugger bat
> Louisville, KY

You might think that a pitcher with a lifetime 6-8 mark
and a .147 batting average would be selling insurance instead of bats.

A 6'4" right-hander, Jim chose pro baseball over college
basketball scholarship offers out of high school. He arrived
with Detroit in 1961 and picked up his first victory and
save on the same day in a doubleheader sweep over the expansion Angels. Traded to the Angels shortly after, his
last hurrah came in '62 with the Twins.

What's in a number? Jim had a .429 winning percentage
and a 4.29 ERA!

DOTTER, Gary
> Part-owner of BDS Associates, a data processing com-
> pany
> Wichita Falls, TX

Among the popular music groups who had songs ringing
the charts in the 1960s were Gary U.S. Bonds, Gary Lewis
and the Playboys, and Gary Puckett and the Union Gap.

Among the not-so-popular baseball players in this era
was Gary Dotter, a southpaw chucker who appeared in a
total of seven games in brief trials with Minnesota in '61,
'63, and '64.

DOWLING, Dave
> Dentist
> Longview, WA

David B. Dowling, D.D.S., P.S. pitched in two big league
games, one in relief for the Cards in '64, the other a complete game victory for the Cubs two years later.

The 6'2" southpaw was named the "Sandlotter of the
Year" by the National Baseball Congress after averaging
18 strikeouts per game in the National Tournament for
the Alaska Goldpanners.

DOWNING, Al

> Real estate business in Santa Monica, CA; cable TV
> commentator for the Los Angeles Dodgers

Al has the distinction of being the only player in uniform
when Hank Aaron belted his historic 715th home run on
Apr. 8, 1974, and when Roger Maris hit home run No. 61
on Oct. 1, 1961. He was also the first black pitcher in Yankee history.

Downing was brought up briefly by the Yankees in
1961, but was up to stay in '63 when he put together consecutive 13-game winning seasons at the tail end of the
Yankee dynasty years. His 217 strikeouts topped the
American League in 1964. Three years later Downing battled adversity when he snapped his elbow delivering a
pitch. In retrospect, all was stormy before the calm.

In 1970 Al divided the season between the Oakland A's
and Milwaukee Brewers and finished the year with a
career-threatening 5-13 mark. Owner of an excellent pick-
off move, he started out as a long reliever with the Dodgers
in '71 where he experienced a rebirth. After pitching effectively in that role, Al was moved into the starting rotation
and responded by finishing 20-9 with a 2.68 ERA and a
league-leading five shutouts. His turnaround made him
the recipient as *The Sporting News* Comeback Player of
the Year. He departed in 1977 at 123-107.

DOYLE, Paul

> Owns business that manufactures parts for heavy
> trucks
> Huntington Beach, CA

"Our sales are well over a million a year, and it all started
with playoff money," says Paul Doyle in reference to his
successful parts business.

Paul's great American success story began in the low
minors in 1959. In 1968 he was working out of the bullpen
for Dallas–Fort Worth in the Texas League when he was
given his first start in late June and responded by pitching
a no-hitter over El Paso.

After beating the bushes for ten years, the 30-year-old

rookie was brought up by the Atlanta Braves. His 2-0 log plus four saves helped the Braves capture the National League West title in '69. Paul then made two separate stops with the Angels plus a visit in between to San Diego. 5-3

DRAGO, Dick
> Active in Mexican League in 1983; resides in Boston, MA

Quick now—Who gave up Hank Aaron's 755th and last home run of his career? Answer: Dick Drago.

Dick signed with the Tigers after his first year at the University of Detroit. On May 15, 1966, he was part of a double no-hitter parlay while pitching for Rocky Mount in the Carolina League. His teammate, Darrell Clark, hurled a no-hitter in the other end of the twin bill.

Plucked by the Royals in the expansion draft, the right-hander was a regular member of the club's starting rotation their first five years (1969–1973). Traded to Boston, he worked out of the bullpen in '75, picking up 15 saves in helping the Red Sox to the American League pennant. In the '75 ALCS against Oakland, Dick worked five innings of scoreless relief to gain saves in Games Two and Three. He made two appearances in the classic '75 World Series against the Reds and was tagged with the loss in the second game.

Dick moved around with the Angels, Orioles, and back to Boston, before drifting out to sea with the Mariners in 1981. 133-142

DRAKE, Sammy
> Physical education teacher
> Los Angeles, CA

Let's play more trivia.
> Question: Can you name the first set of black brothers to reach the big leagues after 1900?
> Answer: Solly and Sammy Drake. (Before 1900 Moses and Welday Walker played in the American Association.)

Though neither Solly or Sammy had a very distinguished career, they did make it to the big show. During

the Fifties, Solly shagged flies with the Cubs, Dodgers, and
Phillies while Sammy spent his time scooping up ground-
ers with the Cubs and Mets between 1960–62. An alumnus
of Philander Smith College in Little Rock, AR, where he
lettered in baseball, football, and track and was named
All-Conference on the gridiron, Sammy hit .153 in 53
games.

DUCKWORTH, Jim
    Instructor at the California Highway Patrol Academy
    in Sacramento, CA

Jackie Jensen's fear of flying was well publicized. Jim
Duckworth's was not. His aversion to flying was such that
he once walked off a plane and never got back on. Re-
sponding to a story that he had not only conquered his
fear, but had become a licensed pilot, Jim said, "I continue
to enjoy being on the ground rather than in the air, and
will not fly." During one stage of his pitching career, he
even went on the disabled list to seek help to overcome his
fear.
    Born in National City, CA, Jim toured American League
airports from 1963–66 with the Senators and A's.   7-25

DUFFALO, Jim
    Real estate agent
    Lancaster, TX

Can you recall the Buffalo Springfield? How about Jim
Duffalo who did some of his best pitching at Springfield
when he went 16-5 in 1960.
    For what it's worth he earned his living with the Giants
and Reds (1961–65) and closed a nice 15-8.

DUFFIE, John
    Duffie and Company Remodelling
    Decatur, GA

During the course of the '67 season, this 6'7" right-hander
was "Big Bad John" to opposing hitters in the Texas

League, being named the league's "Pitcher of the Year" after going 16-9. But in the majors he was knocked down a peg or two, losing both starts as a member of the Dodgers at the end of the '67 campaign despite an impressive 2.79 ERA.

Battling a sore arm in '68, John came to Los Angeles for medical examination and ran into deeper problems. Attempting to start Alan Foster's car by pushing it, he somehow got himself run over and suffered a torn ligament in the right knee. Surgery was performed in August of that year, but "Big Bad John's" season was over.

Patty Duke played identical twin cousins in a TV series, and Gene Chandler had a hit song called The Duke of Earl *in the Sixties when a pair of unrelated pitchers named Dukes appeared in the majors.*

DUKES, Jan
    Subcontract Administrator—Lockhead Aero Missile
    and Space Company
    Sunnyvale, CA

"Hope is merely disappointment deferred."
    —W. Burton Baldry

After pitching the Boulder, CO, team to the National Baseball Congress championship in 1966, Jan was bubbling with hope. The southpaw was further encouraged when he gained All-American honors at Santa Clara University in 1967.

But life in the big time was a disappointment. In a 16-game span, Jan was 0-2 as a member of the Senators and Rangers between 1969–72.

DUKES, Tom
    Associate vice-president for the Dean Witter Investment Company
    Arcadia, CA

A marketing major at the University of Tennessee, Tom placed himself with the Astros, Padres, Orioles, and An-

gels between 1967–72. In 1968 he tied a National League
record when he appeared in nine straight games out of the
Houston bullpen from July 3–July 12. The western music
buff hurled four scoreless innings in relief covering two
games for the Orioles in the '71 World Series.   5-16

DUNCAN, Dave
   Chicago White Sox pitching coach

More trivia! Who was the last player to hit a home run for
the Kansas City A's?
   Of course, it was Dave Duncan on Oct. 1, 1967. Dave is
also the last player to hit four consecutive doubles (June
30, 1975).
   The lanky catcher signed with the Kansas City A's for a
reported $65,000 bonus out of high school. In 1966 he led
the California League in home runs (46) and was voted the
league's MVP.
   Duncan's first taste of the big top came in '64 with the
A's, but he returned to the farm for more cultivation. He
returned three years later and stayed with the A's for five
years. The good-glove, light-hitting (.214) backstop was
gone following the '76 season after stops in Cleveland and
Baltimore.

DUSTAL, Bob
   Owns irrigation and plumbing business
   Lakeland, FL

Bob continued to tingle for 15 years to the rituals of a game
that had lanced him with pain and frustration. With the
exception of seven games in 1963, all in relief for the Tigers, the persistent right-hander spent the remainder of
his career in the minors.
   But Bob's goodbye was memorable, the kind found in fic-
tion. On June 8, 1968, a night was held in his honor at
Montgomery in the Southern League. Elated, Dustal defeated Birmingham following the ceremonies, then retired
as a player to take over as manager for the Batavia Tigers
in the New York-Penn League.

DYER, Duffy
     Manager at Kenosha (WI), (Midwest League)

Duffy had a sobering experience when he hit his first home run in organized ball. In 1967 at Williamsport, he poked an apparent grand-slam, but he had to settle for a single when he passed the runner on first base.

Dyer, who came up with the Mets in 1968 and stuck around for seven years, brought his catcher's tools to Pittsburgh, Montreal, and Detroit before becoming an ex-big leaguer in 1981.

The scrappy receiver played on three division championship clubs, and earned one World Series ring as a member of the '69 Mets.   .221

E

EARLEY, Arnold
     Former sheriff in Flint, MI

What are the chances of a relief pitcher making 56 consecutive appearances without a decision? Arnold Earley did that in 1965 coming out of the Red Sox bullpen. On the final day of the season he made his 57th trip and was charged with the defeat.

Arnold made his Boston debut in 1960. The southpaw reliever spent most of his time at the Fens in the early Sixties. Before leaving in '67, he was also with the Cubs and Astros.

Currently disabled after suffering a massive heart attack, Arnold owns a 12-20 career mark.

EDGERTON, Bill
     Labor employee with LTV
     South Bend, IN

"He crushed me like a ladybug."
                    —Bill Edgerton talking about Charlie Finley

Bill appeared to be on the brink of a long-lasting career after going 17-4 at Mobile in 1966 and was part of a bank of warriors the A's were nurturing for their future dynasty years. But Edgerton wasn't one of the big money boys in the A's system. He says, "The guys they invested a lot of money in you knew would make it. I was a borderline case."

Bill made another mistake. He banged heads with "der Boss"—Charles Finley. Things were never the same. Looking back, Edgerton spoke about the boorish former A's owner. "There was so much dissension on the A's club in 1966-67. I think we could have won the league if there wasn't." Edgerton also admits that Finley did many good things for baseball.

The left-handed hurler pitched with the K.C. A's in '66-'67. He found himself in the P.C.L. the following year with Seattle, then made history when he became the first player to sign a contract with the Seattle Pilots.   1-2

EDMONDSON, Paul
Died Feb. 13, 1970, at age 27 in an auto accident in Santa Barbara, CA

When one reads about the Paul Edmonsons of this world, one has to ask, "Why?"

A bright pitching prospect in the White Sox organization, Paul no-hit Montgomery early in the '69 season while pitching for Columbus in the Southern League. Later that year he was 1-6 for the White Sox in 14 games. His debut was a good one, a two-hit, 9-1 victory over California.

A product of San Fernando College, a memorial fund was established in his name following his death.

EDWARDS, "Doc"
Manager at Maine in International League

Ben Casey, starring Vince Edwards, came on TV in the early 1960s at about the time Howard Edwards, better known as "Doc," began to operate with the Indians (1962-63). Edwards, who picked up his nickname after serving in the Medical Corps in the Marines, also made visitations with the K.C. A's and Yankees before a five-year hiatus that found him missing from the big league scene.

In 1970 "Doc" was summoned to the Phillies to help an ailing catching corps as Tim McCarver and Mike Ryan each suffered a broken hand in the same game on May 2nd. He immediately applied the proper antidote, delivering three game-winning hits.

"Doc" began his managerial career in 1973 and was named Manager of the Year. His Charleston team was on the losing end of the 33-inning marathon game against Pawtucket in 1981, the longest game in professional baseball history.   .238

EDWARDS, John
Assistant manager in charge of quality control for Cameron Iron
Houston, TX

John established a much longer residence (1961–74) than did "Doc," the other Edwards backstop in the Sixties. A graduate of Ohio State University, Johnny preceded Johnny Bench as the regular Reds' catcher from 1961–67.

During his freshman season in '61, he only batted .186 but in the World Series vs. the Yankees, he led all Cincinnati batters with a .364 average (4-for-11).

John also caught for the N.L. champion Cardinals in '68 before his final fling with the Astros from 1969–74.   .242

EGAN, Dick
With the Major League Scouting Bureau
Knoxville, TN

Dick lived his big league life quietly. After a noisy year in 1962 when he led the P.C.L. in wins (17) and strikeouts (201) pitching for Hawaii, this southpaw tiptoed in the majors in a total of 74 games from 1963–67 with the Tigers, Angels, and Dodgers. He virtually went unnoticed, going 1-2 overall.

EGAN, Tom
> Sales rep for a trucking company
> Hacienda Heights, CA

USC coach John McKay called Tom the best high school quarterback he had ever seen. He turned down numerous football scholarship offers to sign a reported $100,000 bonus with the Angels.

When Tom joined the Angels on August 23, 1968, the club wasted no time in testing Tom's mettle as he caught nine straight games including two doubleheaders during an eastern swing.

During the '69 season, Tom was hit by an Earl Wilson pitch in the left eye and was never able to regain full sight in the eye. On July 28, 1970, he established a dubious record of five passed balls in a game.

He spent the next two years with the White Sox before returning to the Angels for '74 and '75 after a year in the American Association.   .200

EILERS, Dave
> Transport driver for Bluefell Creameries
> Brenham, TX

By his minor league "stats" it appeared as if Dave was on the road to Cooperstown. The righty chucker was 15-3 in the Northwest League in 1963. In '64 he once made 18 straight relief appearances without allowing a run. From 1963–65 Dave's minor league record was 33-7—move over Cy Young.

But after four years in the big top with the Braves, Mets, and Astros he was a modest 8-6 in 81 games, all in relief.

ELIA, Lee
> Coach with Philadelphia Phillies

When Lee was fired as manager of the Cubs in 1983, he joined the Cubs' fans he had blasted earlier, declaring "They don't even work" of the team's followers who showed up at Wrigley Field for daytime baseball to boo the team. For that statement, Lee wins "the foot in the mouth award" for all the players profiled in this book.

A shortstop from the University of Delaware, Lee worked as a schoolteacher in the off-season while playing professional baseball. A football standout at Delaware, Lee's time in the majors was brief as he was primarily a reserve shortstop with the White Sox (1966) and Cubs (1968) playing for volatile managers, Eddie Stanky and Leo Durocher. .203

ELLIOT, Larry
    Schoolteacher
    Encinitas, CA

Del Shannon was singing *Hats off to Larry* in 1962 when Larry arrived with the Pirates. It was hats off to Larry Elliot from July 21–24 (1964) when the hustling outfielder connected for a home run in four consecutive games for the Mets.

Elliot tipped his cap for the last time in '66 with the Mets. .236

ELLIS, Dock
    Coordinator of The Substance Abuse Rehabilitation
    Program of the California Institute for Behavioral
    Medicine in Los Angeles

Flamboyant and controversial, Dock was referred to as the "Muhammad Ali of baseball." The outspoken right-hander made his first start with the Pirates on July 31, 1968, and was aided by a triple play as the Bucs went on to beat the Reds 10-1.

On June 12, 1970, Dock no-hit the Padres at San Diego when Bill Mazeroski's diving catch of Ramon Webster's liner in the seventh inning saved the day for Ellis—as did a little LSD. As reported in the *Pittsburgh Press,* Ellis said that he was so out of touch with reality that he did not know he was to pitch the game until six hours before it started.

Pirates' trainer Tony Bartirome disputed Ellis' story. He said, "I'd call him a liar to his face if I saw him."

Ellis also revealed that he was high on pep pills in May 1974 during a game in Pittsburgh when he hit three Cincinnati players and walked another before being removed from the game.

Dock enjoyed his finest year in 1971, going 19-9 and tying a Pirates' record of winning 13 straight games as a starter. It was during that banner year that his mouth got about as much attention as his arm. Ellis was 14-3 at the All-Star break. Vida Blue of the A's was named to start the All-Star Game for the A.L. and Ellis stated he wouldn't get a starting nod for the N.L. because "they" wouldn't start "two soul brothers." Not only was Ellis given the start, he was tagged with the defeat, the only N.L. chucker to lose an All-Star Game in the 20-year period from 1963–1982.

Dock redeemed himself by beating the Giants in the NLCS, 9-4, in the second game. In the Series he was defeated by the Orioles in the opening game and wasn't used again.

He was a steady winner the next few years, then fell to 8-9 in '75 and was traded to the Yankees where he won Comeback of the Year honors, going 17-8. Dock defeated the Royals in the third game of the ALCS, then lost to the Reds in Game Three of the '76 Series. Before closing in '79, he pitched with the A's, Rangers, Mets, and Pirates. Near the end of his career his life story was published in a book *In the Country of Baseball.*

Dock was hospitalized for chemical dependency in 1980.   138-119

ELLIS, Jim
    Row-crop farmer
    Tulare, CA

How's this for a big night? Pitching for Quincy in the Midwest League on May 9, 1965, Jim hurled a one-hitter while belting a single, double, and three home runs, one of which was a grand slam. His 11-RBI night led to a 25-0 win.

Brought up to the Cubs in '67, he never equaled his minor league heroics as his 10-game stay with the Cubs ('67) and Cardinals ('69) left him at 1-1.

ELLIS, John
    Owns real estate business, "John Ellis and Associates"
    New London, CT

A star fullback in high school, John turned down over 50
football scholarship offers to sign with the Yankees. He
was suddenly called up in 1969 while playing at Kinston
in the Carolina League because the Yankees were deci-
mated by injuries and military obligations.

Yankee Stadium became a fantasy island for John the
day he made his debut. All he did was leg out an inside-the-
park home run and catch a two-hit shutout by Stan
Bahnsen who worked on a perfect game into the seventh
inning.

The next couple of years big John was moved to first
base to make room for Thurman Munson. He recalled,
"Lee MacPhail (general manager) told me Munson was
going to catch and I was going to first base because
Munson was better than me. It was the first time anybody
in baseball was honest with me. I appreciated that."

Ellis was named to the Topps Rookie All-Star team in
1970 and Munson established himself as a Yankee hero.
But as time wore on John was not playing regularly and
wanted to get out of New York. His wish was granted. He
was traded to Cleveland. Three years hence, John went to
Texas where it ended in 1981.   .262

ELLIS, Sammy
    New York Yankees' minor league pitching coach

A flamethrower, Sammy came up with the Reds in 1962,
not long after he pitched a no-hitter over Tacoma while a
member of the San Diego club in the P.C.L.

In 1965 Sammy was the talk of the baseball world—and,
yes, of numerologists also! He won 22 games, had 2 shutouts, 2 saves, and allowed 222 base hits. On his 22-10 season he said, "The Reds scored a lot of runs for me. I thought
the year before (10-3) was a better year as far as being an
asset to the team."

Plagued by arm trouble in future years, his 28-year-old
wing was laid to rest in '69 after stays with the Angels and

White Sox. An excellent golfer who twice won the Baseball
Players Association Tournament, the Mississippi State
product was 63-58 overall.

EMERY, Cal
Chicago Cubs minor league hitting instructor

Not to be confused with Cal Ermer, the Twins' manager
(1967–68), Cal Emery was a left-handed hitting first baseman who showed up for 16 games in 1963 with the Phillies. Signed out of Penn State, Cal was 10-1 on the mound
for the Nittany Lions and was named MVP of the College
World Series in 1957.

Emery's express was in motion in 1960 when he hit .388
at Asheville. But he sputtered in the big time, batting a
slow .158.

EPSTEIN, Mike
Owns a business management and brokerage com-
pany
Bend, OR

When it comes to baseball, Jews have hardly been the
chosen people. Although Mike Epstein may not qualify as
the "Rabbi of Swat," he did manage to wallop 134 home
runs and bat .244 during his fairly lengthy career (1966–
74).

One of the Great Jewish Hopes in the 1960s, Mike was a
fullback for the University of California and played in the
same backfield with Craig Morton. He began his baseball
journey at Stockton in the California League in 1965 and
was tagged "Superjew" by San Jose manager Rocky Bridges after leading the league with 30 homers and a .338 average. Fans and media began comparing Epstein to
Mickey Mantle. But the 6'3", 230-lb. Bronx native snapped,
"People compared me to Mickey Mantle, and I knew I
couldn't carry his jock."

In 1966 Mike was named the International League MVP
and *The Sporting News* Minor League Player of the Year
after hitting .309 to go with his league-leading 29 homers
and 102 RBIs.

Baltimore brought him up in '66 for six games. The following year the Orioles wanted to send the independent-thinking slugger back to the minors, but he refused to report and proceeded to stage a 19-day sitdown strike. Finally Epstein and Frank Bertaina were traded to Washington for pitcher Pete Richert.

In 1969 it was "Hava Nagila" for Mike as he hit 30 roundtrippers and garnered 85 ribbies for the Senators. On May 16th he connected for three homers and drove in 8 runs.

Traded to Oakland early in '71, Mike helped the A's to the World Championship in '72 with 26 homers and 70 RBIs. On June 15–16 (1971) he flexed his muscles and went on a roll, hitting four consecutive roundtrippers. His last laps were with the Rangers and Angels.

ESTELLE, Dick
   Owns a carpet business
   Point Pleasant, NJ

Dick electrified minor league audiences, pitching three no-hitters. One was in the Northwest League and the other two were in the P.C.L. for Tacoma. But after going 1-2 in 12 games for the San Francisco Giants (1964–65), he had his cord unplugged.

Commenting on his playing days, he says, "The years I played were very rewarding as I met a lot of good people who still remain friends to this day."

To baseball card collectors, Dick is known as the other man on Masanori Murakami's popular SF Giants' rookie card in '65, the only gum card involving a Japanese player.

ESTRADA, Chuck
   Oakland A's minor league pitching coach at Tacoma
   (P.C.L.)

The Orioles have always cultivated a rich tradition of pitching talent. Chuck was part of the crop known as the "Kiddie Korp," a group of young hurlers on the Baltimore roster in the early Sixties.

As an Orioles' rookie in 1960, Chuck tied for the A.L.

lead in victories (18-11) and was named by *The Sporting News* as the A.L. Pitcher of the Year. He followed up his dazzling rookie campaign with a 15-9 mark and was part of some unusual baseball trivia. In '61 Jim Gentile hit an A.L. record five grand-slams for the O's. And would you believe that Chuck was the winning pitcher in each game that Gentile poked a bell ringer.

But storm clouds soon replaced the sunshine in Estrada's big league life. A victim of elbow and shoulder problems, he fell off to 9-17 and pitched sparingly the next couple of years. Following last-ditch efforts with the Cubs and Mets, his story ended sadly at age 29 in 1967.   50-44

ETCHEBARREN, Andy
Coach with the Milwaukee Brewers

Who can forget this hard-nosed catcher with the pronounced eyebrows? Hall of Famer Frank Robinson won't.

Andy had some big assists during his 15-year career, but the biggest came on Aug. 22, 1966, when the Baltimore Orioles were attending a private team swim party. Suddenly Andy jumped in the pool and saved Robinson from drowning.

After brief trials, Etchebarren became the Baltimore backstop in 1966. Andy later would platoon with Ellie Hendricks. The next year (June 4, 1967) he ended the longest game in Orioles' history with a 19th-inning homer to beat Bob Priddy and the Senators.

Not known for carrying a heavy stick to the plate (.235, 49 HRs lifetime), his lumber awoke from slumber during Game Four of the 1973 ALCS when he hit a 3-run homer late in the game off Vida Blue which tied the score, 4-4. The Orioles eventually won the contest, forcing a rubber match for the pennant.

After playing with the Angels and Brewers, the catcher of French-Basque descent closed his career.

ETHERIDGE, Bobby
    Recreation director
    Greenville, MI

Bobby made a passionate effort to make it with the S.F. Giants. But after 96 games and a .244 average, his career crashed like a paperback romance.

In '67 he was named as the third baseman on the Topps Rookie All-Star team despite the fact he played in just 40 games and hit only .226. Obviously, it wasn't a vintage year for rookie third sackers.

EVANS, Darrell
    Active player with the Detroit Tigers

Darrell came up with the Atlanta Braves in 1969. In 1973 he clubbed 41 homers, joining Hank Aaron and Davey Johnson as the only teammate trio in baseball history with 40 or more home runs in the same season.

He almost wore out his shoes walking in '76 when he drew free passes in 15 consecutive games. In '83 he cracked the 1,000-walk level.

Sent to the Giants in '76, he captured the hearts of San Francisco fans on the day of his debut by leading a double-header sweep of the Padres with two home runs, one a grand slam.

Darrell was on base when Aaron connected for No. 715 on Apr. 8, 1974. The steady third baseman set a N.L. record by taking part in 45 double plays in '74.

On Sept. 12, 1974, Evans (Braves) and Cesar Geronimo (Reds) hit grand slam homers in the second inning of the first game of a twi-night doubleheader. It was the last time that two grand slams were hit in one inning by members of different clubs.

EVERITT, Leon
    Taxi driver
    Dallas

Leon hacked around for five games with the expansion Padres in 1969. When he completed his call, his meter read: 0-1.

The hard-throwing right-hander began in the Dodgers' organization. In 1967, Leon was the strikeout king of the Texas League with 200 whiffs pitching for Albuquerque.

F

FAIREY, Jim
San Francisco Giants Scout in the Carolinas
Clemson, SC

This Erskine College All-American was involved in one of the most unusual interference calls in baseball history while playing for Spokane in a P.C.L. game against Hawaii in 1967.

After. stealing third base, the stocky outfielder was knocked unconscious by the throw from the Hawaii catcher. The ball rolled into left field after hitting Jim on the skull. Fairey then rolled past the bag in an unconscious state after being struck by the ball. Third base coach Gordy Coleman had compassion for the KO'd runner and lifted him back onto the base. At this point the umpire called "interference" on Coleman invoking rule 7.09(i) and Fairey was called "out" not realizing what had happened.

But the left-handed hitting larruper was awake long enough to spend six years in the big arena (1968–73). He hit his first major league home run on June 20, 1968, a pinch-hit blast off Pirates' relief ace Elroy Face to give the Dodgers a 3-2 win and snap a nine-game Pittsburgh winning streak.

Fairey was with the Expos their first four seasons before closing with the Dodgers in '73.   .235

FANOK, Harry
Tool and die worker
Chardon, OH

Harry's career was swift but devastating. Known as "The Flame Thrower," Harry was one of the hardest throwers in the game. In 1962 he led the I.L. in strikeouts with 191 in 184 innings and beat Louisville in the seventh game of the Junior World Series for Atlanta.

However, his major league stay with the Cards in '63 and '64 was terminated after only 16 games because of a torn rotator cuff. During his short stay he made his presence felt, racking up 35 K's in 33 innings.   2-1

FARLEY, Bob
   President of the Fayjan Co., an industrial distributor
   Montgomery, PA

Ricky Nelson had a big hit song with *Travelin' Man* in 1961 and Dion had another with *The Wanderer* in '62. It's likely that first baseman-outfielder Bob Farley could identify with both song titles since he wandered from the Giants to the White Sox to the Tigers during those two years. When his travels ended, he had hit .163 in 84 games.

FAST, Darcy
   Owns an employment agency, "Acme Personnel Service"
   Lacey, WA

What a great name for a pitcher! But the truth is the only thing fast about Darcy was his career (0-1 in 8 games) for the '68 Cubs.

FAUL, Bill
   Manages his daughter's rock band
   Pleasant Plain, OH

If you had to pick an All-Flake team in the 1960s, Bill would join names like Belinsky, Lee, Pepitone, and McLain. Among other things he professed to be a master of self-hypnosis, a Doctor of Divinity, and a karate instructor. Unimpressed with tradition, he wore uniform No. 13.

A right-hander with a blazing fastball, Bill arrived with the Reds in '62 after graduating from the University of Cincinnati where he was a sprinter in track and a chucker

on the baseball team. Pitching in his first game for the
Bearcats, he fanned 19 to top Sandy Koufax's school record
of 18. Later he set an NCAA mark with 24 K's against
Jacksonville.

In '65 Faul was 6-6 for the Cubs with three shutouts on
the days the hypnosis was evidently working. That season
he pitched in just 17 games for Chicago, but had no less
than three triple plays behind him while he was on the
mound. The only other pitcher in major league history to
be the recipient of three triple killings in one season was
Will White of Cincinnati's 1882 American Association
Club.

Bill was last seen with the Giants in 1970.   12-16

FAZIO, Ernie
      General Manager of S and R Pick Up, Inc.
      San Leandro, CA

"It's easier to carry back to the dugout after I strike out."
—Ernie Fazio after switching from a 33 to a 29-ounce bat

Little Ernie was signed off the Santa Clara University
campus in 1962 for $75,000 after helping lead the school to
a second-place finish in the College World Series. Among
his teammates were Bob Garibaldi and John Boccabella.

In 1965 he was the All-Star second baseman in the
P.C.L., hitting 23 home runs for Oklahoma City. The di-
minutive second baseman–shortstop participated with the
Astro's and A's, where it ended in 1966.   .182

FELSKE, John
      Philadelphia Phillies' manager

Big John's appearance was much more imposing than his
.135 average over 54 games with the Cubs and Brewers between 1968–1973, but he did produce some robust figures
at Portland (P.C.L.) in 1970 when he hit a cool .315 to go
with his 18 roundtrippers.

A native of Chicago, John attended the University of Illinois. Before being named as a Phillies coach (now Man-

ager), he managed Portland into the Junior World Series
in 1983.

FERNANDEZ, Frank
Longshoreman terminal manager
Staten Island, NY

Frank chiseled his name into the baseball encyclopedia as
a catcher with the Yankees, A's, Senators and Cubs from
1968–1972.

The Yanks thought they had a plum when Frank hit
safely in his first big league at-bat in '67. After going to
Oakland, he was the apple of Charlie Finley's eye in 1970
when he banged out 15 four-baggers. It wasn't the number
that tickled the A's owner, it was the timing as seven of
the home runs were game-winning blasts, one of which
was a three run pinch-hit swat with two out in the 9th inning which pleased Finley so much he gave Frank a $2,000
bonus.   .199

FERNANDEZ, Lorenzo "Chico"
Employed with the National Brewing Company
Miami

Midnight Cowboy was shown in cinemas in 1968, the year
this Cuban-born second baseman had a brief cup of coffee
with the Orioles at the eleventh hour of his career. In 1965
at Lynchburg in the Southern League, "Chico" went 99
consecutive games without committing an error at the
keystone sack. He also led the league with a .992 fielding
average and received The Rawlings Silver Glove Award.

After ten seasons of long bus rides and dining in greasy
spoons, "Chico" was given a chance with Baltimore at
shortstop where he hit .111 in 1968. The following year he
was a player-coach at Rochester (I.L.) when he suffered serious head injuries from a beaning that required a metal
plate to be inserted in his head.

FERRARA, Al
    Agent for Home Exteriors Textured Coating
    Los Angeles, CA

"He says he was a piano player, but more than likely he was a piano mover."
                                        —A former teammate

As a youngster Al appeared as a solo pianist at Carnegie Hall. But by age 16 he decided he liked the idea of pounding out base hits more than his keyboard.

Signed off the sandlots of Brooklyn, the Dodgers' old bailiwick, Al impressed with his desire and potential, despite hitting only .083 his senior year in high school.

During his career, the muscular flychaser was center stage on more than one occasion. In a 1965 game against Dick Ellsworth and the Cubs, he broke up a no-hitter in the eighth inning with a three-run, pinch-hit homer to give the Dodgers a 3-1 win. In 1967 he was named the Dodger of the Year, batting .277 with 16 homers. When Tom Seaver set a record for consecutive strikeouts (10) in one game against the Padres on April 22, 1970, Al became Seaver's tenth straight strikeout victim, ending the game. But Ferrara accounted for the only San Diego run that day with a second-inning homer in a 2-1 loss to the Mets.

Al's World Series record is perfect, going 1-for-1 as a pinch-hitter in the '66 Fall Classic. His on and off (Dodgers, Padres, Reds) career ended in 1971. The brawny pianist finished at .259.

"The Bull" was in close touch with the theater as a player. He had some acting roles including parts in the Batman series. Following the '66 season he launched his movie career. His one liner in a jungle picture was "Ugh." Al made it without even a rehearsal.

In reference to his piano background Al chuckles, "I was supposed to be a lousy fielder. I blame my mother. I was practicing the piano when I should have been catching fly balls."

FERRARO, Mike
    Kansas City Royals' coach

If any position needs a marriage of reflexes and confidence, it is third base. Mike had it all meshing on Sept. 18, 1968, at the hot corner for the Yankees when he picked up a record-breaking 11 assists against the Senators.

The MVP in the Florida State League in '64, "Pound-cake" spent four years in the majors with the Yankees, Pilots, and Brewers between the years 1966–1972.

A native of Kingston, NY, as is Geraldine Ferraro, Mike began a managing career with the Yankees organization in 1974. He guided Oneonta, West Haven, and Tacoma to league championships before joining the Yankees as a coach in 1979 under Dick Howser. In 1983 he piloted the Indians to a 41-60 mark before being relieved of his duties on July 31st.

Mike underwent a cancer operation before the '83 season for removal of a kidney.   .232

FINGERS, Rollie
    Active with Milwaukee Brewers

On Nov. 30, 1963, the instant replay camera was first used on TV during an Army-Navy football game after Army quarterback Rollie Stichweh rolled out and ran the ball in for a touchdown. Rollie Fingers never rolled into the end zone, but has rolled up a record 324 saves in his career. A quick look at the 6'4" reliever deluxe and his slick handle-bar mustache, one might think that Rollie was a reincarnated member of the 19th-century Cincinnati Red Stockings. But the truth is Rollie has been around since '68 with the A's, Padres, and Brewers.

In his first three seasons with Oakland, he made 35 starts before moving to the bullpen permanently in '72. During the 1970s the ace fireman appeared in 640 games, the most by any pitcher. His 209 saves for the decade were 19 more than his runner-up, Sparky Lyle.

Rollie's list of achievements are endless. A seven-time All-Star, he is a four-time winner of the Rolaids Relief Man of the Year Award. Also named *The Sporting News* Fireman of the Year four times, he was named Relief

Pitcher of the Decade by *Baseball Magazine*. He became the first relief chucker in major league history to win both the Cy Young and MVP award in the same season and joins Stu Miller as the only two relievers to capture the "Fireman of the Year" award in both leagues. In 1984 the bullpen ace had 23 saves when he was sidelined by a herniated disc on July 23rd.   113-112

FIORE, Mike
    Employed with the maintenance department in
    Malverne, NY

Mike hit the first home run in the history of the Kansas City Royals on Apr. 13, 1969. The lefty-swinging first baseman came to the Royals via the expansion draft from Baltimore where he played in six games in '68.

While at Rochester in '68 he overcame Dick "The Monster" Radatz when he hit three consecutive homers one night against the big right-hander. Mike recalled, "After I hit the first one I asked Steve Demeter if Radatz would throw at me. Demeter said, 'No.' But in my next at bat he threw the ball over my head." He continued, "After the game Radatz came into the clubhouse and said, 'What the hell are you doing in this league?'"

Mike closed in '72 at .226 after stints with the Red Sox, Cardinals, and Padres.

Fiore is a former Yankee batboy!

FISCHER, Hank
    Restaurant business
    West Palm Beach, FL

Known as "Bulldog", Hank was signed to a Braves' contract in 1959 by John "Honey" Russell, the cage coach at Seton Hall. Hank averaged 22 points per game for the frosh, but Russell, who doubled as a Braves' scout, recommended that the Braves sign him. Milwaukee's gain was Seton Hall's loss.

Overall, Hank was 30-39 from 1962–67 with the Braves, Reds, and Red Sox. His best season was in 1964 when he won 11 games, including all five of his career shutouts.

FISHER, Fred
  Banker
  Perrysburg, OH

Of the Fisher-men in the Sixties, Fred had the smallest catch. Fred "Fritz" Fisher pitched in just one game for the Tigers in 1964. After one-third of an inning this banker's big league interest diminished when his ERA escalated to an inflated 108.00.

  Things were a bit more stable for Fred in 1962 when he helped pitch the University of Michigan to the NCAA championship.

FISHER, Tom
  Indianapolis, IN

In 1967 Jackie Wilson sang *Your Love Is Lifting Me Higher And Higher* when Tom crashed after hurling 1⅓ scoreless innings against Washington for the Orioles in his only game. The year before he was the outstanding chucker at Elmira in the Eastern League as he led the league in five departments including an ERA of 1.88.

FISK, Carlton
  Active with Chicago White Sox

"Pudge" has always had a flare for the dramatic. His 12th-inning, game-winning home run off Pat Darcy in Game Six of the 1975 World Series has been voted one of the all-time great moments in baseball. With his fists raised high, he shuffled up the first base line and watched the ball sail over the Green Monster into the Boston night.

  Following a brief visit to Boston in 1969, he arrived to stay in 1972 and established himself as one of the top-flight catchers in the American League, winning a Gold Glove and Rookie of the Year honors. On Opening Day in '73 he hit two home runs to begin the season in dramatic fashion.

  But 1977 was his vintage year when he walloped 26 homers and had 102 ribbies to go along with his .315 average. That year he became one of only six catchers in baseball history to score 100 runs and drive in 100 in the same season.

Following the 1980 season, the New Hampshire resident was granted free agency by an arbiter's ruling after it was deemed the Red Sox had not sent him his contract soon enough.

The White Sox took advantage of the opportunity and plucked Carlton away from Fenway. On April 10, 1981, the Chisox opened the season at Fenway Park, Fisk's home for the previous 10 years. In storybook fashion, he hit a three-run homer in the eighth inning to lead Chicago over his old teammates, 5-3.

"Pudge" wore No. 27 during his time in Boston. When he changed his Sox from red to white he reversed his number to 72 stating, "That was the year my son Casey was born, was my rookie year in the majors, and represents a turnaround in my career."

During the 1984 season he caught all 25 innings in baseball history's longest game ever by time—8 hours and 6 minutes as Chicago beat Milwaukee 7-6. The game was spread over two consecutive nights.   .278

FITZMAURICE, Shaun
> Owner and Administrator of the Elwood Early Learning Center Inc., a day care center
> Richmond, VA

This bonus baby out of Notre Dame came up to the Mets in 1966 after hitting .316 at Williamsport in the Eastern League that season. With the Mets he found the test difficult, hitting only .159 in nine games.

FITZMORRIS, Al
> Employed with First National Bank
> Kansas City, MO

An accomplished guitar player, songwriter, and singer, Al has the distinction of joining Bobby Shantz as the only two-time selections in major league baseball's expansion drafts.

Al spent eight years with the Royals and was quite effective during the Seventies having just one losing record in eight seasons. Following the '76 season he was chosen by the Blue Jays, but was traded to Cleveland for catcher

Alan Ashby before the start of the '77 season. "Fitz" closed
with the Angels in '78.   77-59

FLAVIN, John
> Tax examiner for the Treasury Department
> Fresno, CA

Car 54, Where Are You was one of the most popular TV
comedies in the early Sixties when John Flavin (who wore
No. 54) was on the Reds' spring training roster in '61.

A close inspection of this tax examiner's career reveals
that John was 0-1 in five games with the '64 Cubs. After
that, it was "John Flavin, Where Are You?"

FLETCHER, Tom
> Finishing Supervisor for Teepack, Inc., an industry
> which makes the casing for meats
> Oakwood, IL

The year 1962 was notable for Maria Fletcher as she was
crowned Miss America. It was also a glamorous year for
Tom Fletcher, who hurled the University of Illinois to the
Big Ten Championship with an 8-0 record and a 0.37 ERA.

The southpaw signed a $60,000 bonus with the Tigers in
'62 and pitched a couple of scoreless innings for the Bengals that year before a blood clot in his arm sent his baseball career on a slide. Undaunted, Tom struggled for six
more years in the minors before calling it quits.

FLOYD, Bobby
> Manager at Calgary in the P.C.L.

Following a dismal .243 season at Rochester (I.L.) in 1967,
Bobby's emotional approach to the game hit rock-bottom.
But he returned refreshed in '68, hitting .287 after reading
Dr. Maxwell Maultz's bestselling book, *Psychocybernet-
ics—The Power of Positive Thinking.*

A utility infielder out of UCLA, Bobby was called up to
Baltimore in 1968. In 1970 he was sent to the Royals for
Moe Drabowsky, but spent most of the season with
Omaha, the American Association champions. The former

Bruin remained with the Royals for portions of four more
seasons.   .219

FOSNOW, Jerry
    Regional sales manager for Gulf Oil Company
    Orlando, FL

In 1964 the Supremes sang *Where Did Our Love Go?* when
this left-hander flirted with a 36-game career with the
Twins that went on the rocks the following year.   3-4

FOSS, Larry
    Insurance business
    Wichita, KS

The name Joe Foss was familiar as the Commissioner of
the American Football League throughout most of the
1960s until he relinquished his post to Pete Rozelle when
the league merged with the N.F.L. in '68.
    The name of pitcher Larry Foss was not so familiar,
going 1-2 in a total of eight games for the Pirates ('61) and
Mets ('62).

FOSSE, Ray
    Director of Speaker's Bureau for the Oakland A's; real
    estate business
    Tracy, CA

Ray could have starred in baseball's version of *General
Hospital.* After 11 years of mounting injuries, the ma-
ligned catcher became a walking medical journal and was
gone at age 30.
    The Indians' first-ever No. 1 selection in the 1965 free
agent draft, Ray is probably best remembered for his
major home plate collision in the 1970 All-Star Game
with Pete Rose. Rose commented on the play, "You
know, Ray Fosse is a friend of mine. On the evening before the game, Ray visited at our house in Cincinnati,
but when I saw that the play at home was going to be
close, with Ray trying to block the plate, I had no choice
except to knock him over."

A three-sport performer at Southern Illinois University, Ray was up with the Indians in '67 and '68 for a quick look. By '69 he was Cleveland's regular catcher, but was on the disabled list for over two months of the season.

In 1970 Fosse was hailed as one of the best young receivers in the game. However, a highly promising season was marred by his mid-summer accident with Rose. He had a 23-game hitting streak and batted .307 with 18 roundtrippers that year.

In the '74 World Series his homer in the fifth and final game helped Oakland to a 3-2 win over the Dodgers as the A's captured the Series.

Ray rolled out in '79 after another stay in Cleveland and brief shots in Seattle and Milwaukee.   .256

FOSTER, Alan
Owns The Face Factory—a store specializing in women's cosmetics
El Cajon, CA

In the mid-Sixties the Beach Boys sang about the *Little Old Lady From Pasadena* when this Pasadena native made it to Dodger Stadium. The son of a doctor, his dad wrote out a prescription for the Dodgers which brought Alan close to $100,000 in bonus money.

Walter O'Malley called him the "next Don Drysdale." Foster never lived up to that billing, but did manage to hang around from 1967–76 with the Dodgers, Indians, Angels, Cardinals, and Padres.

During the 1967 season he became the first pitcher in P.C.L. history to hurl two no-hitters in one season. Pitching for Spokane, he no-hit Seattle twice by 1-0 scores just two weeks apart. The Los Angeles Dodgers were so impressed, they offered to buy the mound at Sick's Stadium in Seattle for Foster.   48-63

FOSTER, George
Active player with New York Mets

It's not often that Little League teammates are united in the majors. But when George joined the Mets in 1982 he

rejoined Dave Kingman who had been a Little League
teammate in Hawthorne, CA.

George arrived for short stays with the Giants in the
late Sixties. When Willie Mays hit career home run No.
600 he did it as a pinch-hitter for Foster. In '71 the Giants
traded him to the Reds for shortstop Frank Duffy and
pitcher Vern Geishert. The Giants are not proud of that
deal, but had little reason to regret it for a few years as
George hit just 13 home runs in his first three seasons with
the Reds and even spent time back in the minors.

George became one of baseball's premier hitters in the
1970s. He led the National League in RBIs three consecutive seasons (1976–78). In '77 George established an unusual major league record for most home runs (31) by a
right-handed batter on the road. That season he reached
his pinnacle with 52 homers and 149 RBIs and was voted
the National League MVP.

George appeared in three World Series with the Reds
and owns a .326 Series average. His black bat has been
dubbed "black death" and he was quoted as saying, "I in-
tegrated the bat rack."   .277

FOSTER, Larry
    Pastor in the Lutheran Church in America, serving
    the Lebanon Lutheran Church
    Whitehall, MI

Rev. Larry Foster saw a message in the game of baseball.
He commented, "It sensitized me with the pressure to win
and to cope with losing. It has been useful and helpful in
relating to people."

Looking back on his one-game career in 1963 with the
Tigers, he said, "I played with most of those guys on the
champion '68 Detroit team in the minors. Once in spring
training three of us were seated behind a screen. Two of us
were tagged as 'can't miss': Doug Gallagher and myself.
The third was Mickey Lolich." The right hander eventually pulled a tendon in his shoulder which proved fatal to
his career.

FOX, Terry
Employed by Texaco Co.
New Iberia, LA

In 1960 the USS Triton surfaced after a 41,500 mile under-
water voyage. That same year Terry Fox emerged with the
Braves after struggling through the minors. He then went
to Detroit where he did some exceptional work as a short
reliever for five summers. In '61 and '62 Fox was a top-
notch relief specialist, saving a total of 28 games with an
ERA under 2.00.

Terry wound up with the Phils in '66. He submerged
with an overall mark of 29-19 plus 29 saves.

FOY, Joe
Counsels wayward children in the South Bronx; owns
a store
Bronx, NY

Joe survived a battle with alcohol and drugs. A loner who
reportedly traveled in the fast lane with a bad crowd, Joe's
life became a series of emotional cartwheels. But everything has apparently come together under one umbrella
for this former third baseman who was named *The Sporting News* Minor League Player of the Year in 1965 for
Toronto (I.L.) where he was the league's MVP and batting
champion.

From 1966–68, Foy was employed at Fenway Park,
where he manned the hot corner for the Bosox. After a
year with the expansion Royals in '69, it was back to his
native New York with the Mets before making his final
swing with Washington in '71.   .248

FRANCIS, Earl
Butcher
Pittsburgh, PA

Connie Francis continued with her string of hit songs in
1960 with *Everybody's Somebody's Fool.* The name Francis Gary Powers made headlines surrounding the U-2 incident in which his spy plane was shot down by the Russians.

Right-hander Earl Francis wasn't quite the same household name, but he did appear in 103 box scores with the Pirates (1960–64) and Cardinals ('65) in a career that stands at 16-23.

FREEHAN, Bill
Partner with Hank Aguirre in Mexican Industries; Tigers' cable TV announcer

Bill was signed by Detroit in 1961 for an estimated $100,000 after his sophomore year at Michigan, where he also performed on the gridiron. He spent his entire career (1961–1976) with his hometown Tigers.

The accomplishments of this former Wolverine are numerous. When Bill hit .300 in '64, he became the first Detroit catcher to hit that high since Mickey Cochrane. The winner of five Gold Gloves, Bill was also a four-time American League All-Star, catching the entire 15 innings in the 1967 July classic. A defensive dynamo, Bill finished with a .993 fielding average, the highest ever for a catcher. He also leads all backstops in putouts and chances accepted.

During the Tigers' big '68 campaign, Bill homered 25 times and collected 84 RBIs. That season he tied an American League record when he was hit by pitches 24 times. On August 24th he was plunked three times in the same game, tying an American League record.

Although his book *Behind The Mask* didn't cause as many shock waves in the baseball world as did Bouton's *Ball Four,* Freehan's diary of the same 1969 season did have impact on the Tigers. It's been speculated that Freehan's revelations of Denny McLain's not having to adhere to team rules as others did, led to McLain being traded and manager Mayo Smith being fired.

Bill departed with a .262 average and an even 200 home runs, including three in one game on August 9, 1971.

FREGOSI, Jim
Manager at Louisville in the American Association

Jim was the Angels' wunderkind from 1963-70. Voted the "Greatest Angel Ever," "Frego" was the team's shortstop throughout most of the Sixties. He became the first Angel in club history to hit for the cycle, which he did in '64 and '68.

In 1970 Jim had career highs of 22 homers and 82 RBIs. Two years earlier he led the junior circuit in triples with 13.

A symbol of consistency, Fregosi played in 145 or more games for eight consecutive years, leading American League shortstops in double plays (125) in 1966. Following an injury-ridden season in '71, he was traded to the Mets for Nolan Ryan. His next stay was in Texas (Rangers) where he stayed five years before finishing with the Pirates in '78. He was released by the Bucs that year in order to return to manage the Angels, a position he held until 1981. Jim led the Angels to their first division title in 1979.   .265

FRENCH, Jim
> Option trader on the Pacific Stock Exchange in San Francisco, California
> Penngrove, CA

1971 was a year the Academy Award-winning movie *The French Connection* played throughout the country. It was also a year that Jim French's big league connection (1965–1971) terminated as a Senators' catcher.

A graduate of Ohio University with a master's degree in Finance from the University of Indiana, Jim said about his career: "The highlight was playing under Ted Williams."   .196

FRISELLA, Danny
> Died Jan. 1, 1977, at the age of 30 as the result of injuries suffered in a dune buggy accident in Phoenix, AZ

Danny joins the small list of players in this book who have died tragically. Before his death he put together a 34-40 record plus 57 saves from 1967–76 with the Mets, Braves, Padres, Cardinals, and Brewers. Frisella's highlight year was '71 when he won 8 games with 12 saves and had an ERA of 1.98 for the Mets.

When Danny won his first big league game on August 11, 1967, for the Mets, he wasn't anywhere near the ballpark to enjoy it. After pitching 6⅔ innings against the Pirates at Shea Stadium, he left the park to catch a plane to California where he had an Air National Guard meeting the next day. Don Shaw saved the 3-2 win for Danny while he was en route to the airport.

Frisella, who attended Washington State University, led the Cougars to a third-place finish in the College World Series, going 10-0 before signing with the Mets.

FRYMAN, Woodie
   Tobacco and cattle farmer
   Ewing, KY

"When you win you're an old pro. When you lose you're an old man."

—Charlie Conerly

Woodie was 25 years old and pitching semipro baseball when the U.S. government reduced the subsidy on growing tobacco on his farm. He then decided that pitching baseballs would be more profitable than pitching hay. After just a dozen minor league games, the spirited southpaw joined the Pirates and went 12-9 in '66, a year Woodie hurled three straight shutouts, including a one-hit masterpiece in which the Mets' Ron Hunt led off the game with an infield single. Hunt was then thrown out attempting to steal. Fryman retired the next 26 hitters in a row.

After the '67 campaign Woodie was traded to the Phillies. In 1972 he was waived out of the National League. He joined the Tigers and went 10-3 helping them to the A.L. East title. Fryman then jumped around with the Expos, Reds, Cubs, and Expos again, where it ended in '83.   141-155

FUENTES, Miguel
> Died on Jan. 29, 1970, at age 20 in Loiza Aldea, PR, of
> gunshot wounds during a nightclub altercation

"Mickey" has the distinction of pitching the final inning
in the history of the Seattle Pilots, working the ninth inning against the Oakland A's on October 2, 1969.

When he was called up to Seattle, he was making headlines in the Midwest League at 8-2 and a 1.46 ERA. In his
debut with the Pilots he pitched a complete game, defeating the White Sox, 5-1. He finished 1-3 in eight games
before his untimely death.

FUENTES, Tito
> S.F. Giants' announcer on Spanish Network
> Foster City, CA

Tito was once quoted as saying, "They shouldn't throw at
me. I'm the father of five or six kids." They were throwing
at this Cuban-born infielder on Sept. 13, 1973, when he
tied a major league record of being hit by pitches three
times in one game.

The outgoing second baseman spent his career (1965–78)
with the Giants, Padres, Tigers, and A's. He was labeled a
"hot dog" for his showboating antics on the field.

Tito enjoyed a fine rookie season by the Golden Gate
with San Francisco in '66, but was sent to the minors after
the '67 campaign when he hit an anemic .209. At Phoenix
he became a switch-hitter and got off to a good start before
suffering a broken leg. The slick-fielding infielder returned to the Giants and played on a regular basis in the
early Seventies.

FULLER, Vern
> Manager of the Harley Hotels chain in Cleveland

In 1966 Bobby Fuller sang *I Fought the Law* while second
baseman Vern Fuller fought the long odds and made it to
the majors for good with Cleveland after a brief trial in '64.
His career ended in 1970.   .232

FUNK, Frank
> Kansas City Royals minor league operations manager; also manages Eugene (Northwest League)

Frank had a relatively short but effective stay (1960–63) as a relief pitcher with the Indians and Braves. Called up to Cleveland that year, he recorded victories in his first three appearances as he pitched 10 scoreless innings. In '61 he was 11-11 with 11 saves in 56 games.

Early in the '62 season he entered a game at Yankee Stadium with two out and two on in the ninth inning and the Tribe ahead, 7-5. The Indians had lost 19 straight games going back two seasons at the House That Ruth Built. Home run champ Roger Maris stepped to the plate and was well aware that Frank had recently been quoted as saying that "Maris was lucky to hit 61 homers in '61." Funk got Maris to look at a called third strike as the Indians ended their Bronx famine.   20-17

G

GABRIELSON, Len
> Vice President for Kidder-Peabody stock brokerage firm
> Los Altos Hills, CA

A member of the 1958 USC NCAA baseball champs, "Gabe" played throughout most of the '60s with the Braves, Cubs, Giants, Angels, and Dodgers. His first basehit in the majors came on April 13, 1963, a three-run homer which gave the Braves a 5-2 victory over the Mets. The husky (6'4", 205-lb.) outfielder demonstrated his power that year by becoming the first player in the history of County Stadium to hit the right field scoreboard. His best season came two years later when he divided his time between Chicago and San Francisco and hit .293.

Part of a baseball family, his father, Len Gabrielson,

was a hitting star in the P.C.L. who played briefly for the
Phillies in 1939. A younger brother, Doug, was in the
Giants' organization and his uncle, Bill Matheson, played
in the Yankees' farm system.   .253

GAGLIANO, Phil
    Executive with the Durbin Durco Tool and Die Co.
    St. Louis

A teammate of Tim McCarver at Christian Brothers' High
School in Memphis, Phil scooped 'em up as a utility infielder from 1963–74 with the Cards, Cubs, Red Sox, and
Reds. He made pinch-hitting appearances for St. Louis in
the '67 and '68 World Series. A solid, dependable-type
player, Phil took home a .238 average in 702 games.

GAGLIANO, Ralph
    Marketing director for Dicanale, a food distributor-
    ship
    Memphis, TN

Ralph's cup of coffee was instant. As an 18-year-old, his big
league stay was limited to one game as a pinch-runner
with the Indians in 1965. The younger brother of Phil,
Ralph never had another chance to show his stuff.
    Tony Gagliano (uncle of Ralph and Phil), a one-time
pitcher in the Giants' organization, was a legendary coach
in American Legion baseball in Memphis.

GAINES, Joe
    Clothing salesman
    Oakland, CA

This clothing salesman wore an assortment of colors in
parts of seven seasons (1960–66) with the Reds, Orioles,
and Astros. The speedy outfielder sported several fashionable .300-plus seasons in the minors, but when he hung his
threads on the rack for the last time, he showed a relatively plain .241 average.

GALLAGHER, Doug
    Salesman for B and P Manufacturing
    Fremont, OH

The term "generation gap" was coined in the '60s. With the exception of a nine-game gap, Doug spent his life in the minors.

Labeled a "can't miss" candidate, the southpaw chucker pitched a no-hitter in the Sally League playoffs for Knoxville in 1960. In '62 he crashed after going 0-4 with Detroit. Doug actually found more success at the plate, going 2-for-6.

GAMBLE, Oscar
    Active with Yankees in 1984
    Owns a discotheque called Oscar Gamble's Players
    Club in Montgomery, AL

In 1969 John Wayne won his first Oscar for his role in *True Grit*. That year teenager Oscar Gamble arrived with the Cubs when they went into a September swoon after trying to hold off the surging Mets. During the off-season he was traded with pitcher Dick Selma to the Phillies for outfielder Johnny Callison. On Oct. 1, 1970 "Big O" collected the last hit in old Connie Mack Stadium in Philadelphia.

During his career the lefty-swinging outfielder also played with the Indians, White Sox, Padres, and Rangers before making his second trip with the Yankees. Gamble's finest year came in 1977 with the White Sox when he batted .294 to go with his 31 homers and 83 RBIs.   .268

GARBER, Gene
    Active with Atlanta Braves

Baseball fans like to associate players with certain games or achievements. Gene Garber is known as the guy who stopped Pete Rose's 44-game hitting streak on Aug. 1, 1978 when he fanned Rose in his final at-bat that evening.

Gene found the going tough during his minor league days. He lived at home on his father's farm while pitching for York in '68. Gene would arise before dawn each morning to help with the chores on the farm. He would then leave for a full day of classes in college and then pitch at York when the team was at home. In a 1967 game at Raleigh (Carolina League), Garber hurled a four-hit shutout in a seven-inning game in which he had a double play executed by his defense in every inning.

The bearded right-hander, who came up with the Pirates briefly in '69, has also toed the rubber for the Royals and Phillies before going to the Braves in '78 for Dick Ruthven.

"Geno" is Atlanta's all-time leader in saves, holding the single-season mark (30), set in 1982. Characterized for his side-winding style he was quite effective in '76 and '77, helping to lead the Phils to National League East titles.

During the off-season Gene works on his farm in Lancaster County, PA.   77-88

GARDNER, Rob
       Schoolteacher
       Binghamton, NY

Richard Frank "Rob" Gardner had somewhat of a haphazard odyssey with six teams from 1965–73. He broke in with the Mets in '65 and became part of major league history on October 2nd when he started and went the first 15 innings against Chris Short of the Phils in the second game of a twi-night doubleheader at Shea Stadium. The game ended 0-0 and was stopped by a 12:50 A.M. curfew after the 18th frame. It was the longest scoreless night game in big league history.

Nothing came easy for Rob. He gained his first big league victory (2-1 over the Cubs) when he doubled home the game-winner with his first hit in the majors. The southpaw then sauntered around with the Cubs, Indians, Yankees (twice), Brewers, and a second time with the A's before departing at 14-18.

GARIBALDI, Bob
  Branch manager, Pepsi Cola; also PAC-10 basketball
  official
  Stockton, CA

The MVP of the 1962 College World Series from Santa
Clara University, Bob signed for an estimated $150,000
bonus with the San Francisco Giants. He spent the greater
part of the decade pitching for Phoenix and Tacoma in the
P.C.L., but found enough time to pitch in 15 games with
the Giants in parts of four seasons from 1962–69.
  Bob also played basketball at Santa Clara where his
brother, Dick, was the head coach.   0-2

GARMAN, Mike
  Fruit farmer
  Caldwell, ID

As a scholastic athlete, Mike was an All-State selection in
the three major sports. He was the Red Sox' first-round selection in the 1967 free agent draft. After brief stays in
Boston, Mike was sent to the Cards in '74 and found his
niche, going 7-2 with six saves out of the bullpen. Before it
was over in '78, he was also employed with the Cubs, Dodgers, and Expos. Mike won four games and chalked up 12
saves with the National League pennant-winning Dodgers
in '77 and was credited with a save in the third game of the
NLCS against the Phillies.   22-27

GARR, Ralph
  Co-owner of a Kaloche doughnut shop; Atlanta Braves
  base running coach
  Houston, TX

There was a time when Ralph Garr appeared to be destined for Cooperstown. Suddenly, he was mysteriously released at age 34 by the Angels with a glossy .306 average.
To this day the "Roadrunner" is bewildered and confused.
"I can't understand. I never complained. They weren't fair
with me. They're giving guys one million dollars a year to-

day that couldn't hold my jock." That's a tough pill for a guy whose top salary was $160,000.

A graduate of Grambling University, Ralph was the NAIA batting champion in 1967 with an astronomical .568 average. He won two I.L. batting titles with Richmond. His .386 mark in 1970 is a league record.

Garr's first full season with Atlanta was a success when he hit .343 in 1971, finishing second to Joe Torre's .363. Ralph was perched on top of the league in '74 when he copped the batting title (.353) and led the league in base hits with 214 and triples with 17. He became the first player since 1930 to reach 200 hits by the month of August, but injured his knee and missed about three weeks in September.

Traded to the White Sox after the '75 season, he became the first American League player to bat in Canada on April 7, 1977, when the Chisox met the Blue Jays. He showed a live stick in Chicago, batting .300 in two of his four years in the Windy City. He was sold to the Angels late in '79 and was released by California in June of 1980. The "Roadrunner" is still scratching his head.

Ralph never hit for power (75 homers), but he tied a major league record on May 17, 1971, when he belted two four-baggers in extra innings in the same game (in the 10th and 12th).

GARRETT, Adrian
Manager at Denver in the American Association

Adrian's strong-flowing minor league career, in which he won four different home run titles, meandered into a trickle (.185, 11 HRs) on the big league level. A catcher, first baseman, and outfielder, Henry Adrian Garrett led the Texas League in home runs twice, plus the P.C.L. and American Association in four-baggers.

Garrett, who swung from a rope between the minors and majors, traveled with the Braves, Cubs (twice), A's, and Angels from 1966–76. Adrian then played in Japan. His moment of glory occurred on Sept. 22, 1975, when he hit a 3-run homer in the 16th inning at Anaheim to beat Chicago's Rich Gossage by a score of 3-0.

GARRETT, Wayne
     Real estate salesman
     Sarasota, FL

As was his older brother, Ronald Wayne Garrett was known by his middle name. Wayne broke in with the Braves' organization, but was drafted by the Mets after the '68 season. He survived the Mets' revolving door third base situation long enough to put in 709 games at the hot corner from 1969–76. Of the dozens of third basemen who've attempted to play the hot corner at Shea, Wayne served the longest and the best.

His two-run homer in the third and final game of the 1969 NLCS against the Braves put the Mets ahead to stay. Wayne's best year was 1973 when he parked 16 and had 58 RBIs for the National League champs. In the World Series against Oakland he went 5-for-30, but two of his hits were homers.

In July of '76 the all-around infielder went to Montreal. He came back to hit a grand-slam off Tom Seaver on Sept. 29th, which cost Seaver his fourth ERA title. Garrett finished with the Cardinals in '78.   .239

GARRIDO, Gil
     Associated with the professional baseball program in
     Panama City, Panama

Fail Safe played in cinema theaters in 1964 when Gil had 14 games in a Giants' uniform. However, most of his playing time came with Atlanta (1968–72) to round out his .237, 334-game career.

He is best remembered for his sensational fielding. A three-time Silver Glove winner for his shortstop play in the P.C.L., Gil set a league record while with Tacoma in 1964 when he went 63 consecutive games without an error.

GARVEY, Steve
     Active with San Diego Padres

On Sept. 10, 1969, Steve picked up his first career hit via a pinch-hit single off Denny Lemaster at Houston. Ken

Boyer, who was nearing the end of his career with L.A., commented, "That's the first of 2,000." No. 2000 came on May 7, 1983.

An All-American baseball player and starting defensive back at Michigan State University, Steve was originally selected as a third-round choice by the Twins in '66, but went to college instead. He then signed with the Dodgers after being selected No. 1 in the secondary phase of the 1968 draft.

Garvey, who was originally a third baseman, tore up the minors with his bat, but did not come into his own in the majors until 1974 when he hit .312 and drove home 111 runs to capture the MVP award and lead the L.A. Dodgers to the National League pennant. The Tampa native was the write-in candidate at first base for the National League All-Star team that summer.

In 1983 Steve set a N.L. record of playing in 1207 consecutive games, breaking the mark of 1117 formerly held by Billy Williams.

Steve's six 200-hit seasons are surpassed by only seven other players in major league history. Garvey appeared in five NLCS and owns a .356 average with seven home runs. He has also appeared in five World Series and carries a .319 mark. During the '84 season he became the only first baseman to play an entire season without making an error. He also broke Mike Hegan's consecutive game mark (178) of not committing an error.

Steve has been around the game a long time, as his father drove the Dodger bus during spring training in the 1950s. In 1977 he had a junior high school named after him in Lindsay, CA.   .299

GASPAR, Rod
    Insurance salesman
    Mission Viejo, CA

Prior to the 1969 World Series, Orioles' star Frank Robinson commented "Rod who?", when he was told the Mets' switch-hitting rookie outfielder, who had hit .228 during the season, predicted New York would win in four straight. After the Series when the Mets won in four straight after dropping the opener, Rod asked "Frank Who?".

Buried in the Texas League in '68, Rod was left unprotected by the Mets for the 1969 expansion draft. But neither the Padres nor Expos were interested, and in spring training of '69 Rod surprisingly made the Mets on his hustle and determination. His 178-game jaunt took him to San Diego in '71 and '74 where it ended at .208.

GASTON, "Cito"
Toronto Blue Jays' hitting coach

The 30th and final pick of the 1969 expansion draft by San Diego, Clarence "Cito" Gaston turned out to be one of the better selections by the Padres. Originally signed by the Braves, "Cito" did his prepping with that organization before he had his first taste of the big time with Atlanta in 1967.

In 1970 the outfielder put together an all-star season, batting .318 with 29 home runs and 93 RBIs, all career highs for a single season. That summer he represented San Diego at the All-Star Game in Cincinnati.

Gaston was traded to the Atlanta Braves after the '74 season for pitcher Danny Frisella. He was used mostly as a utility outfielder and pinch-hitter in Atlanta.   .256

GATEWOOD, Aubrey
Insurance business
Little Rock, AR

Aubrey was selected by the Angels from Detroit in the December 1960 expansion draft. One year later he was drafted by the New York Mets from Dallas-Fort Worth, making him the only player involved in the player selection for the expansion of both Major Leagues. Aubrey returned to the American League where he made his debut on Sept. 11, 1963 and beat the Red Sox, 4-1, on a four-hitter.

Gatewood's last gasp came with the Braves in 1970 when he appeared in three games. The righthander finished 8-9 overall with an excellent 2.78 ERA.

GEISHERT, Vern
　　Stationary grinder for the Richland Center Foundry
　　Company
　　Richland Center, WI

In 1969 Three Dog Night's big hit was *One*. Vern was with
the Angels for 11 games that season and went 1-1. Traded
to the Reds' organization, the right-hander was involved
in a deal which brought his name to the surface during the
1970s when he was traded along with Frank Duffy to the
Giants for outfielder George Foster.

GELNAR, John
　　Oil leasing business
　　Frederick, OK

The World's Fair opened in New York in 1964 when John
opened a 111-game march with the Pirates, Pilots, and
Brewers. A good-fielding pitcher, John closed with a 7-14
mark after appearing sporadically between 1964–1971.

GENTRY, Gary
　　Real estate business
　　Phoenix, AZ

Bobby Gentry had quite a year in 1967 with her rendition
of *Ode to Billy Joe*. Gary Gentry also found success, being
named the NCAA baseball "Player of the Year" after
pitching Arizona State to the National Championship.

　　The right-hander, who signed with the Mets and joined
them in 1969, was 13-12 his rookie season, including a 6-0
victory over St. Louis on September 24th which clinched
the National League East title. In Game Three of the Fall
Classic he started and pitched shutout ball into the seventh inning and defeated the Orioles, 5-0, with relief help
from Nolan Ryan.

　　Gary hurled a two-hitter against the Giants on May 2,
1972. Oddly both base hits were triples by Bobby Bonds.

　　Gentry never really developed into the pitcher the Mets
hoped. Traded to Atlanta after the '72 campaign, he was

finished after the 1975 season at age 28 with arm problems.   46-49

GERARD, David
Salesman for Petroleum Products in Trenton, NJ

Remember Lt. Phillip Girard, the man who relentlessly
pursued Doctor Richard Kimball on the popular TV series,
The Fugitive, in the 1960s? David "Jug" Gerard pursued a
major league career which lasted one season. The right-
hander was 2-3 in 39 relief appearances with the Cubs in
1962.

GERBERMAN, George
Jeweler for Gerberman's Jewelers
El Campo, TX

Like "Jug" Gerard, George also pitched with the Cubs in
'62, the year that *Combat* began a five-year television run.
Unfortunately, George's stay was for a pale five innings,
all in one game. Although effective (allowing just one run),
George was never thrown back into combat again against
National League hitters.

GERONIMO, Cesar
Last active with Kansas City Royals in 1983
Santo Domingo, Dominican Republic

The odds of one player being the 3,000th strikeout victim
for two different pitchers are quite remote. However,
Cesar was the 3,000th strikeout for Bob Gibson (July 17,
1974) and Nolan Ryan (July 4, 1980). But there were many
bright moments for Cesar who was hidden among such lu-
minaries as Bench, Rose, Morgan, Foster, and Concepcion
on those "Big Red Machine" teams of the mid-Seventies.
  A native of the Dominican Republic, Geronimo broke in
with Houston in 1969, then was involved in a blockbuster
deal which also saw the Reds trade for Joe Morgan after
the '71 season. Cesar was in the Reds' lineup (1972–80) for
five championship series and three World Series. From

1974–77 he was named to *The Sporting News* All-Star
Fielding Team. The brilliant centerfielder also won four
Gold Gloves during this period.

Unfortunately, Cesar established several dubious records including striking out seven straight times during
the '75 NLCS, and going hitless in 30 consecutive plate appearances, but grades better in World Series play, hitting
.308 in '76 and .280 in '75.   .258

GIBBON, Joe
    Cattle rancher
    Newton, MS

When Joe was at "Ole Miss" he was a basketball star,
averaging 30 points per game in 1957 to finish second in
the nation in scoring, just ahead of Wilt Chamberlain and
Elgin Baylor. The 6'4", All-Southeastern Conference baseball and basketball performer signed with the Pirates and
in '59 won 16 games for Columbus while leading the I.L. in
strikeouts.

Joe, who arrived with the Bucs in 1960 and went 4-2 with
the World Champs, became the first of over 1,200 players
who debuted in the big leagues in the '60s to participate in
a World Series game when he relieved in the second game
of the 1960 autumnal classic. His M.L. debut was a dramatic one for the Pirates on April 17, 1960. In the second
game of a twinbill he pitched two scoreless innings, supposedly mopping up a 5-0 loss to Cincinnati. But the Pirates
scored six in the last of the ninth inning to give Gibbon a
6-5 win.

The big left-hander had the finest season of his 13-year
career when he won 13 games in '61.

Joe was traded to San Francisco after the '65 campaign,
then returned to Pittsburgh before closing with the Reds
and Astros in '72.   61-65

GIBBS, Jake
    Baseball coach at the University of Mississippi

While Joe Gibbon made his mark with the roundball,
Jerry Dean "Jake" Gibbs was a Saturday afternoon hero

on the gridiron, capturing All-American honors as the
"Ole Miss" quarterback in 1960. The MVP in the '61
Sugar Bowl, Jake scored both touchdowns in a 14-6 victory
over Rice. He finished third to Joe Bellino in the voting for
the Heisman Trophy in 1960.

An All-American third baseman, Gibbs passed up football
offers from the Cleveland Browns and Houston Oilers to sign
an estimated $100,000 bonus with the Yankees. He switched
to catching and shuttled between the I.L. and the Yankees
for a few years. Jake, who saw action with the Yanks from
1962–71 mainly as a backup receiver, was the regular
catcher for New York before the arrival of Thurman Munson.

During the off-season Gibbs would return to his alma
mater to help coach the quarterbacks, among them Archie
Manning.   .233

GIBSON, Russ
     Banker
     San Francisco

Few catchers in baseball history can relish the memories
that Russ had in his first starting assignment of a 264-
game career with the Red Sox and Giants from 1967–72. In
his debut he went 2-for-4 and was on the receiving end as
Billy Rohr worked on a no-hitter against the Yankees into
the ninth inning.   .228

GIGON, Norm
     Employed with a chemical company
     Oakland, CA

"A full mind is an empty bat."

                                          —Branch Rickey

  Norm, who earned his master's degree in history from
the University of Rhode Island, wrote his thesis on the role
of British Imperialism in East Africa, a subject not likely
to be discussed in baseball clubhouses. The infielder-
outfielder possibly should have researched the subject of
longevity in the big leagues since he was gone after hitting
.171 in 34 games with the '67 Cubs.

Gigon's first major league hit was his only big league home run, a three-run shot which beat Juan Pizarro and the Pirates.

GIL, Gus
On the staff of Yankee Baseball School, Inc. at Biscayne College, North Miami, FL

Tomas "Gus" Gil was a childhood friend to Cesar Tovar, who even named a son after "Gus." Both signed with the Reds in the late 1950s, but neither ever played in Cincinnati.

Gus began his adventure as a utility infielder with the Indians in 1967. The native Venezuelan was a member of the Pilots and Brewers also, hitting .186 in 221 games.

On Aug. 16, 1970, Gil gave the Brewers a 4-3 win with a pinch-hit single in the bottom of the ninth inning, sending a bat day crowd of over 44,000 fans home happy. Bernie Brewer finally came down from his perch atop the right field scoreboard where he had been for 40 days, vowing to stay there until the Brewers drew a crowd of at least 40,000.

GILLIFORD, Paul
Production control supervisor at Wood Plastics Co.
Malverne, PA

Gilligan's Island was on TV in the mid-Sixties when Paul "Gorilla" Gilliford found himself stranded after pitching in two games without a decision for the Orioles in '67.

GILSON, Hal
Location unknown

Remember "Hal," the computer, from the 1968 movie: *2001: A Space Odyssey?* Remember Hal Gilson, a southpaw with the Cards and Astros that same year? He was 0-2 in 15 games.

GIUSTI, Dave

> Sales representative for Millcraft Products, Inc., a machine and fabricating company
> Pittsburgh, PA

To reverse the phrase, all was stormy before the calm for Dave. The Seneca Falls, NY, native spent his first few seasons with the Astros, where he was 47-53 before being shuffled to the Cardinals. As a starter in Houston, he one-hit the Giants on Aug. 13, 1966, to post a 1-0 win. His perfect game was spoiled by a second-inning single by Cap Peterson. Eight days later he blanked the Reds, 11-0, and had a pair of bases-loaded doubles for six RBIs. The following year Dave tied a dubious record when he delivered three wild pitches in one inning.

The Cardinals placed the right-hander in the expansion draft before ever using him. He was then selected by San Diego, which traded him back to St. Louis, all before the start of the '69 season. After a dismal 3-7 year, he went to Pittsburgh where he was converted into a reliever. The move proved ingenious as Dave blossomed into one of the premier bullpen specialists in the 1970s.

In '71 Giusti had a league-leading 30 saves for the World Champion Bucs and was named by *The Sporting News* as the N.L. Fireman of the Year. In post-season play he was virtually untouchable, hurling five scoreless innings apiece in the NLCS and WS. On July 30th that year Dave yielded Dave Kingman's first big league homer, a grand slam in San Francisco, helping the Giants to a 15-11 victory.

After stints with the Cubs and Oakland he wound up his 15 years of service with a 100-93 mark and 145 saves.

Dave, who pitched Syracuse University to a third-place finish in the College World Series before signing with Houston, also lettered in basketball for the Orangemen. A substitute teacher in the off-season during his playing days, he received his master's degree in Education from Syracuse.

GLADDING, Fred
    Houston Astros minor league pitching instructor

"The Bear" began a slow climb in the minors to Detroit. Following brief trials in the early 1960s he went 24-10 for the Bengals from 1964–67 as a relief specialist before he was traded to Houston for Eddie Mathews. Unfortunately, he was unproductive his first year with the Astros due to an elbow injury.

In 1969 Fred benefitted from the new save rule which liberally stated that a relief pitcher who enters the game at any time with the margin of a lead and holds that lead for the rest of the game is credited with a save. That year Gladding recorded a league-leading 29 saves despite a 4-8 mark and an inflated 4.19 ERA.

One of baseball's all-time worst hitters, Fred appeared in 450 games from 1961–73 and collected only one hit. It came on July 30, 1969, as the Astros swept a doubleheader from the Mets, 16-3 and 11-5. His lone hit in 63 big league at-bats came in the opener, during an 11-run inning in which Houston's Denis Menke and Jim Wynn belted grand-slams. In the nightcap the Astros engineered a 10-run inning. Fred commented, "The word will get around that I have a hot bat."

He wound up at 48-34 with 109 saves and a .016 batting average.

GLEASON, Roy
    Automobile salesman
    Monterey Park, CA

We jump from Mr. Gladding's ignoble .016 to Roy Gleason's noble 1.000 lifetime average.

In 1963 Roy made it into eight games with the Los Angeles Dodgers. On seven occasions it was as a pinch-runner, and three times he crossed the plate. The 6'5", 220-pounder never played defensively, but did have one at-bat, a double in his lone plate appearance.

The handsome, switch-hitting outfielder, who signed a $60,000 bonus with the Dodgers in the early 1960s, also did some acting in the movies and on television. One role

he missed out on was that of a soldier in a war movie because he was considered to be too tall for the part. However, in the real world his baseball career was interrupted
by military service since he served in Vietnam where he
was wounded and oft-decorated. Roy returned with several
decorations, including the Purple Heart and Bronze Star.
He attempted a comeback after his tour of duty, but never
made it back to the majors.

GLENN, John
       Employed with a chemical company
       Beverly, NJ

John Glenn became a hero as the first American to orbit
the earth on Feb. 20, 1962. But there were no tickertape
parades for this John Glenn who orbited around the majors
in 32 games with the Cardinals in 1960. When he made his
landing, the flychaser showed a .258 average.

GOETZ, John
       Attorney
       Troy, MI

This lawyer was around the legal system for a long time.
As a 15-year-old he pitched against the Marquette prison
team inside the prison grounds and hit a batter in the ribs
with a fast ball. The irate inmate took about three steps
out toward the mound to attack John and collapsed. John
swallowed hard and continued.
   A native of Goetzville, MI, the right-hander appeared in
four games out of the Cubs' bullpen in 1968, but was not involved in any decisions, or any cases of assault and battery.

GOLDEN, Jim
       Works in quality control department at Goodyear
       Topeka, KS

In 1960 Jim Golden was a 20-game winner for St. Paul
(American Association) and won his first and only start
with the Dodgers.

Jim was in Los Angeles in '61, then with Houston the next couple of years, going 9-13 overall in 69 games. The right-hander looks back at June 22, 1962, as a golden day when he beat the Mets 16-3 and collected three basehits, including two triples. He scored three runs and drove in three at the Polo Grounds.

GOLDY, Purnal
Estimator in commercial building construction
Denver, CO

A graduate of Temple University, Purnal hit .342 at Knoxville to win the Sally League batting title in 1960. The next year he exploded with a .351 average at Birmingham. Goldy made it to Detroit in '62 after hitting over .300 at Denver.

On June 16th he replaced the injured Al Kaline in right field and responded with two home runs. One would estimate that at this pace Purnal would end up with a lifetime 500 home runs and a .325 mark. But the facts read: .231 in 29 games for Detroit in 1962-63.

GONDER, Jesse
Transit driver for Golden Gate Transit
Oakland, CA

Originally Yankee property, Jesse came up with New York in 1960 after hitting .327 at Richmond. After appearing briefly in '61 with the Yanks when he went 4-for-12 as a pinch-hitter, Jesse was traded to the Reds where he stayed for a short time. Most of the year was spent in San Diego, where he hit .342 to win the P.C.L. batting title. He also led the league in RBIs (116) and was named MVP.

Gonder began the '63 season in Cincinnati, then was traded to the Mets. That year he hit .304 split between Cincy and New York and was named the catcher on the Topps Rookie All-Star team.

Before closing at .251 in 1967 Jesse also made stops with the Braves and Pirates.

GONZALEZ, Pedro
     Manager at Bradenton in Gulf Coast Rookie League
in Atlanta Braves' organization

The Juan Marichal–John Roseboro incident in 1965, when
Marichal clubbed Roseboro over the head with a bat, received a tremendous amount of publicity. Shortly after,
but much less publicized, Pedro Gonzalez duplicated the
act on Larry Sherry after he was hit by a pitch.

     Primarily a second baseman, Pedro was around from
1963–67 with the Yankees and Indians. In '59 he hit .371
at Modesto and took the Eastern League batting title in
1960 at Binghamton when he hit .327.   .244

GONZALEZ, Tony
     Retired in Miami, FL. Ex Angels and Phils coach.

Unrelated to Pedro, Cuban-born Tony Gonzalez had a
much longer and more successful major league career.
Tony debuted with the Reds on Opening Day in 1960 and
went 2-for-4 against the Phils' Robin Roberts. In June he
was traded to the Phillies and became a fixture in the Philadelphia outfield through the 1968 season.

     Tony carried a lively stick, three times hitting over .300,
including a career-high .339 in 1967. His glove wasn't too
shabby either. From August 31, 1961, to June 27, 1963,
Gonzalez went 205 games, handling 421 chances without
an error.

     Gonzalez started '69 with the Padres, but was traded to
Atlanta during the season where he was a key factor in the
Braves' stretch run. He hit .489 in the team's 10-game
winning streak.

     Tony hit .357 in the NLCS against the Mets, going
5-for-14 including a home run, but unfortunately lost out
on a chance to play in the Series as the Mets swept the
Braves. He wound up his career with the Angels the next
two years with a lifetime .286 mark.

GOOSSEN, Greg
   Boxing trainer
   North Hollywood, CA

Okay number buffs, try this one on for size. During Greg's big league trek (1965–70) with the Mets, Pilots, Brewers, and Senators, he had 11 pinch-hits among his 111 base hits. He scored 33 runs and had 44 RBIs.

A catcher, first baseman, and outfielder, Greg turned down football scholarship offers from USC and other schools to sign with the Dodgers out of high school. After one season of minor league ball he was put on waivers by Los Angeles and was claimed by the Mets. Goosen was named the New York-Penn League's "Player of the Year" in '65. During the second half of the '69 season he was the Pilots' best hitter, finishing with 10 homers and a .309 average.

GOSGER, Jim
   Officiates high school baseball, football, and basketball; secretary of a local Sports Officials Association;
   president of the Babe Ruth League
   Port Huron, MI

Jim swung from a rope between the majors and minors from 1963–74 with the Red Sox, A's, Pilots, Mets and Expos.

On Sept. 27, 1967, the Athletics ended their stay in Kansas City with a doubleheader sweep over the White Sox as Jim went 5-for-8 to help shatter the Chicago pennant hopes. The flychaser visited Seattle in '69, but was swapped from the Pilots to the Mets that same season. He went north to Montreal, then back to the Mets where he closed his suitcase at .226. Jim played 10 games for the 1969 Mets and 38 games for the '73 Mets (his only other year was in '74), but was not on the post-season roster either year.

GOSS, Howie
    Automobile salesman for a Pontiac dealership
    Fort Myers, FL

Following Howie's baseball days, he has sold cars. However, during his stay in '62 and '63 with the Pirates and Houston Colt .45s, he had a difficult time selling his .216 avg.
    A long ball-hitting outfielder, he poked out 27 home runs and collected 142 ribbies at Vancouver (P.C.L.) in 1961.

GOTAY, Julio
    Physical Education teacher in Ponce, Puerto Rico; coaches Ponce in Puerto Rican Winter league

The word "taboo" comes from a Polynesian term meaning prohibition. Failure to observe a taboo or prohibition leads to undesirable consequences or bad luck. Julio's "taboo" was touching a cross.
    Julio was playing in the Puerto Rico Winter League. Willie Montanez and Felix Millan decided to have a little fun and try to spook the superstitious infielder by making a cross out of two tongue depressors and a shoelace. They left the cross exposed in the area of second base knowing Julio's fear of touching crosses. When Gotay spotted the cross, he wouldn't go near his second base position.
    Catcher Elrod Hendricks then picked up the cross and put it in his pocket. On the next pitch the hitter jerked the bat back on a checked swing, hit Hendricks in the head, and knocked him cold. While the players gathered around Hendricks, Gotay stood on second base shouting, "I told you. I told you. No touch. Evil."
    Fortunately, Julio wasn't so tentative as a player. His career spanned the decade of the Sixties with the Cardinals, Pirates, Angels, and Astros. In '67 he hit .282 in 77 games for Houston. From June 18–20, he collected eight consecutive hits.   .260

GRABARKEWITZ, Bill
   Insurance business
   San Diego, CA

"I was x-rayed so often, I glow in the dark." Those were Billy's words in '68 after he suffered a broken ankle and broken finger playing at Albuquerque. Basically, this was the picture of Billy's life in baseball.

After hitting .308 in the Texas League he suffered a broken ankle in August, the first in a series of injuries for the snake-bitten infielder.

The Dodgers brought up Billy in '69. In his first full season (1970) he responded by hitting .289 with 17 home runs. Grabarkewitz was a write-in candidate for the National League All-Star team with many fans just writing in "Billy G" instead of trying to spell his tongue-twisting last name.

But the next couple of years were filled with injuries. "Bulldog," as he was also known, was traded with Frank Robinson to the Angels for Andy Messersmith. His final stops were with the Phils, Cubs, and A's. In 1975 Billy placed his x-ray sheets in a bag and ambled away with a .236 average.

GRAHAM, Billy
   Cattle farmer
   Flemingsberg, KY

Billy Graham, the popular evangelist, has been known to deliver long sermons. This Billy Graham delivered baseballs instead—but not for too long.

The son of a country doctor, Billy left baseball briefly to study for a medical career, then returned and was with the Tigers in '66 and the Mets in '67. A product of the University of Florida, he went 1-2 in six games.

GRAHAM, Wayne
      Schoolteacher; baseball coach at San Jacinto Junior
      College
      Houston, TX

Consider the forces and time constraints operating against
the batter. A fast ball travels from the pitcher's mound to
the batter's box, 60 feet, 6 inches away, in three- to four-
tenths of a second. For only three feet of the journey, an ab-
surdly 2/100ths of a second, the ball is in a position where
it can be hit.
      The above facts might account for Wayne's .127 average
in 30 games as a member of the Phillies ('63) and Mets
('64). The third baseman-outfielder out of the University of
Texas had better luck in 1961 when he hit .331 at Chattanooga in the Southern League.

GRAMLY, Tommy
      Employed with Texas Instruments
      McKinney, TX

Tommy hails from a baseball family. His brother, Jerry,
was in the Phillies' farm system and his father pitched in
the minors several years ago. As for Tommy, his cup of coffee came in '68 with the Indians, losing his only decision in
three games.

GRANGER, Wayne
      President of a sporting goods company
      Orlando, FL

Wayne debuted with the Cardinals in 1968 in a rather auspicious way during a game against the Astros in Houston.
St. Louis held a 3-1 lead in the ninth inning when the 6'2"
right-hander was called upon to stifle a Houston rally. The
Astros had a runner on first base when Granger replaced
Larry Jaster. Granger struck out Bob Aspromonte, got Lee
Thomas to pop up and set Julio Gotay down on strikes,
ending the game and registering his first save.
      The Cards dealt the rangy chucker to Cincinnati along
with Bobby Tolan for outfielder Vada Pinson and for the

next three years, Wayne's name became synonymous with relief pitching. In '69, he led the National League in appearances with 90, going 9-6 plus 27 saves, then led the league in saves (35) the following year. Both seasons he was named "Fireman of the Year" by *The Sporting News*. On July 24, 1970, he was the winning pitcher as the Reds beat the Giants, 5-4, in the final game ever played at Crosley Field in Cincinnati.

After the '71 season he juggled around with the Twins, Cards, Yankees, White Sox, Astros, and Expos. The ace reliever was gone following the '76 campaign with an even 35-35 mark plus 108 saves. His 451-game trek was all out of the bullpen.

GRAY, Dave
    Industrial sales rep for Emerson Electric
    Sunnyvale, CA

We watched movies like *The Pink Panther* and *A Patch of Blue* in the Sixties. In 1964 Dave Gray wasn't able to add much color to the eighth-place Red Sox, appearing in nine games without a decision.

GREEN, Dallas
    Chicago Cubs' president

When Dallas managed the Phils to the World Championship in 1980, he became only the fourth rookie big league skipper to win a World Series, the others being Bucky Harris (1924 Senators), Eddie Dyer (1946 Cardinals), and Ralph Houk (1961 Yankees).

The 6'5" right-hander joined the Phils in 1960. His fast ball was compared to the hardest throwing pitchers of his era. Dallas gained his first major league win by blanking the Dodgers, 2-0, on a three-hitter. In 1963 he gave up Jimmy Piersall's 100th home run, the day the eccentric outfielder ran backward around the bases. Dallas also gave up Pete Rose's only grand-slam. He last pitched in '67 and compiled a 20-22 mark in 185 games for the Phils, Mets and Senators.

Dallas remained in the game as a minor league manager in 1968–69, then was an assistant farm director and minor league director with the Phillies before taking over as the Phils' manager late in '79 when Danny Ozark was fired.

GREEN, Dick
    Moving van business
    Rapid City, SD

This slick-fielding second baseman teamed with Bert Campaneris at shortstop for several years and was an integral part of the Oakland A's dynasty from 1972–74.

Although Dick came up in '63, he emerged on a full-time basis the following year with "Campy". He swung a cool stick (.275) in '69 and led American League second basemen in fielding.

After missing a good part of the '72 season following surgery for a herniated disc, Dick hit .333 in the World Series playing in all seven games as the A's beat the Reds.

His 12-year career ended in '74 with a .240 average.

GREGORY, Lee
    Schoolteacher
    Fresno, CA

What do you do with a guy who could hit and pitch? In some cases, nothing. Lee, who showed promise in both departments, arrived with the Cubs in 1964 and had no decisions in 11 relief appearances.

Gregory, who signed a $50,000 bonus out of Fresno State College, never made much noise with his arm or his bat.

GRIFFIN, Tom
    Investments business
    Los Angeles, CA

Tom was the 1969 National League Rookie Pitcher of the Year with an 11-10 record including three shutouts for the Astros. He recorded 200 strikeouts, joining Don Wilson

(235) and Larry Dierker (232) to form the second 200-strikeout trio (on the same team) in baseball history.

If anybody epitomized the sophomore jinx it was Tom. His numbers crashed as hard as the stock market did in '29 as he fell to 3-13.

After refueling in the minors, he returned to Houston and enjoyed his best season in '74, going 14-10. He pitched a one-hitter against the Pirates on May·7th, the only hit a Willie Stargell single in the second inning.

Sold to the Padres in '76, Tom skipped around with the Angels and Giants, where he closed in '81 at 76-91.

GRIFFITH, Derrell
    Owns a grocery store
    Anadarko, OK

The popular *Andy Griffith Show* was on the tube throughout the Sixties. Derrell Griffith wasn't around quite as long (1963–66) with the Dodgers.

A third baseman-outfielder, Griffith hit .260 in 124 games. Most of his playing time came in '64 after his recall from Spokane (P.C.L.), where he was hitting .318.

Derrell experienced one of baseball's most frustrating maladies in that there never seemed to be a position for him with the Dodgers.

GRILLI, Guido
    Employed in an administrative capacity with the Holiday Inn
    Memphis, TN

Johnny Rivers was singing about Memphis when this Memphis native came to the A.L. with the Red Sox and Kansas City A's in 1966. The southpaw chucker went 0-2 in 22 games.

GROTE, Jerry
    Owns a meat company
    Manager at Lakeland (Florida State League) Detroit
    Tigers affiliate
    New Braunfels, TX

When the Mets selected Hobie Landrith as their first pick
in the expansion draft, General Manager George Weiss
was quoted, "To build a ball club, you have to start with a
catcher." Jerry emerged as the catcher the Mets were looking for.

    Grote, who broke in with the Astros in '63, was the back-
bone of the Mets for a decade, enjoying his best years at the
plate in '68 (.282) and '75 (.295). Defensively he established
a major league record with 20 putouts in Tom Seaver's
19-strikeout game in 1970.

    In the '69 World Series he had two big hits. One was a
ninth-inning single in Game Two as the Mets won, 2-1, to
tie the Series. His tenth-inning double resulted in the winning run scoring in the fourth game.

    The San Antonio native went to the Dodgers in 1977 and
participated in two more Fall Classics. After retiring, he
returned after two years to play for the Royals and Dodgers in 1981.   .252

GRZENDA, Joe
    Maintenance employee for Gould Battery in Dun-
    more, PA; owns a clothing store
    Daleville, PA

For the purist who believes a game is never over until the
final out, major league baseball never really left Washington. In essence that was Merrell Whittlesey's brilliant
lead in the *Washington Star* following the Senators final
game on Sept. 30, 1971, before the transfer of the franchise
to Texas.

    Washington held a 7-5 lead over the Yankees when Joe
entered the game in the ninth inning. He recalled the historic night: "I was told to warm up. I was afraid to get into
the game realizing the fans would be coming on the field to

collect memorabilia. They told me after I got two out to hesitate and let the bullpen clear out.

"Bobby Murcer made the second out. I still have the ball. The fans poured on the field in all directions. Frank Howard had three guys on his back, but he knocked them off like little toys. There was a guard at home plate. Somebody picked him up like he was a pole and put him aside. Fans then dug out home plate with their bare hands." The Yanks were awarded a 9-0 forfeit win.

But life wasn't always so hectic for Joe Grzenda. The hard-throwing left-hander was in and out of the majors between 1961–1972 with the Tigers, A's, Mets, Twins, Senators, and Cardinals. The well-traveled pitcher went 14-13 in 219 games, all but three as a reliever.

Sometimes called "Shaky Joe" because of his nervousness, Grzenda was 4-1 for the A.L. West Champion Twins in 1969.

GUINDON, Bob
    Area director for Wang Laboratories, Inc.
    St. Louis, MO

Twelve O'clock High was a TV spot in 1964, a year when Bob had a quick high (1-for-8) for the Red Sox. Signed by Boston for an estimated $125,000, the lefty-swinging first baseman had consecutive three-run homer games on his way to a 36-homer, 134-RBI season and MVP honors in the New York-Penn League.

In 1967 he turned to pitching and had only a few innings of mound work behind him when he pitched a no-hitter for Pittsfield in the Eastern League. Bob had a memorable game for Tulsa in the American Association in 1970. When he entered the game in the seventh inning his team trailed, 11-1. Bob proceeded to pitch three scoreless innings and belted a bases-loaded double and a grand-slam. But Tulsa's rally fell short and they lost, 11-10.

GUINN, "Skip"
    Location Unknown

Drannon "Skip" Guinn had a much more interesting name than he did a baseball career. The southpaw went

1-2 in 35 games split between the Braves and Astros from
'68–'71.

GUTIERREZ, Cesar
   Texas Rangers scout in Mexico

On June 21, 1970, Cesar became a part of baseball history
when he collected seven hits as a member of the Tigers in a
9-8 victory over the Indians in 12 innings. The little infielder remembered, "After I got my sixth hit, Wally Moses (Detroit coach) told me I was close to a record. I didn't
know what he meant, but I knew I had six hits. So I said,
'Okay, I try for seven.' "
   He got the seventh by hitting a hard grounder off pitcher
Phil Hennigan's glove and beating it out for a hit. Cesar
had tied Wilbert Robinson's seven-hit performance in
1892. The following year Cesar had a total of 7 hits for the
season. Since 1900, Rennie Stennett is the only player to
get seven hits in a nine-inning game (Sept. 16, 1975).
   Gutierrez, who won the P.C.L. batting title in '67 when
he hit .322 for Phoenix, had trials with the Giants that
year and again in '69 before being traded to Detroit.
   Following Cesar's big game he won a regular job with
the Bengals the remainder of the season. After batting
.189 in 38 games the following year, Señor Gutierrez became a mere immortal in baseball trivia.   .235

GUZMAN, Santiago
   Auto mechanic
   San Pedro De Mar, PR

This hard-throwing right-hander was said to bear a striking resemblance to Cardinals' great Bob Gibson. He was
even hailed as "the next Bob Gibson." However, after four
big league campaigns from 1969–72, he remained just
plain old Santiago Guzman after going 1-2 in 12 games.

H

HAGUE, Joe
Building contractor
San Antonio, TX

Joe has the distinction of hitting a grand-slam in his first at-bat in organized baseball while playing for Cedar Rapids in the Midwest League. The first baseman-outfielder broke in with the Cardinals in '68 at the end of the season after helping Tulsa to the P.C.L. pennant with 23 homers and 99 RBIs.

Following a couple of years with the Cardinals, Joe was traded to the Reds for Bernie Carbo and contributed some timely pinch-hits in Cincy's drive to the National League pennant in 1972, but was gone after the '73 campaign hitting .239 in 430 games.

HAHN, Don
Real estate business
Campbell, CA

Don joined the Expos in 1969. At the end of the next season, he was traded to the Mets for outfielder Ron Swoboda.

Hahn see-sawed between the Mets and Tidewater for a couple of years, but became a regular in the Mets' lineup late in '73 as Willie Mays neared the end of his career. The scrambling outfielder appeared in all post-season games with the Mets and was a steady performer, batting .241 in the WS (7-for-29) against the A's.

"Hondo" spent one more season in Flushing by the Bay, then dashed out in '75 with the Phils, Cards, and Padres.   .236

HAIRSTON, John
Schoolteacher
Birmingham, AL

There have been several black "firsts" in baseball. John carved his niche as the first son of a former black major lea-

guer to make it to the majors when he appeared in three
games as a catcher and outfielder for the '69 Cubs, going
1-for-4. John's dad, Sam, was a catcher who was up with the
White Sox briefly in 1951. John's brother, Jerry, is still active at this writing as a member of the Chicago White Sox.

HALL, Jimmie
      Over-the-road trucker
      Denver, NC

Jimmie was among the home run brigade of the homer-hap-
py Twins of the mid-Sixties. After laboring in the obscurity of
the minors for several years, Hall was invited to Minnesota
in 1963 where he surprised everyone with 33 four-baggers.
Playing long ball was a popular Twins' pastime that summer
as Harmon Killebrew hit a league-leading 45 roundtrippers,
while Bob Allison and Earl Battey added 35 and 26 homers
respectively. The only other outfield trio to each collect 30
or more homers were Joe DiMaggio, Tommy Henrich, and
Charlie Keller of the '41 Yankees.
    The hustling outfielder hit 65 more homers over the
next three seasons before being shuffled to the Angels. In
'65 he stole 14 bases to go with his .285 average, 25 doubles, 20 home runs and 86 RBIs—not a bad year's work.
Before he checked out in 1970, Jimmie also wore the uniforms of the Indians, Yankees, Cubs, and Braves.   .254

HALL, Tom
      Post Office employee
      Riverside, CA

"The Blade" first came up with the Twins in 1968. The
6-foot, 158-pound southpaw, who looked more like a hunger strike victim than a strikeout artist, averaged nearly a
strikeout per inning during his 10-year career (1968–77).
In 1970 he was 11-6 with 184 K's in just 155 innings
pitched for the American League West champion Twins.
    Tom was traded to the Reds after the '71 season for
Wayne Granger. The thin man promptly went to work,
going 10-1 with eight saves for the N.L. champions. In the
NLCS against the Pirates he was the winner in Game Two

with four scoreless innings and went three more innings without allowing a run in the fifth game as Cincinnati came from behind for a 4-3 victory to clinch the pennant. Although the Reds lost to the A's in seven games in the '72 Series, "The Blade" was unscored on in four games and was credited with a save in the sixth contest.

Hall also pitched for the Mets and Royals before leaving with a 52-53 record plus 32 saves.

HALLER, Tom
Executive vice-president of baseball operations for San Francisco Giants

In a major league first (and maybe last), Tom was the catcher for the Tigers on July 14, 1972, while his brother Bill was umpiring behind the plate. When asked about that game Tom replied, "It was no problem. My brother was a great umpire."

A quarterback at the University of Illinois in the late 1950s, Tom signed a bonus contract with the Giants and first came up in '61. For the next six seasons, he was the Giants' regular backstop for the most part. In his first full season in '62, he shared the catching duties with Ed Bailey for the National League Champions and walloped 18 homers. In the World Series loss to the Yankees, Tom hit .286 with a homer in Game Four.

Prior to the '68 season he was traded to the Dodgers for infielders Ron Hunt and Nate Oliver. It was the first trade between the two clubs since 1956 when the then-Brooklyn Dodgers traded Jackie Robinson to the New York Giants for pitcher Dick Littlefield, a trade later cancelled when Robinson retired.

Tom found Dodger Stadium to his liking. During his four years in Los Angeles he hit for his highest averages of .286 and .285 before he was traded to Detroit where he finished in 1972.   .257

HAMILTON, Jack
    Owns nightclub-restaurant, "Jack Hamilton" Club-
    house
    Morning Sun, IA

Often it is the triumphs of one at-bat—or the tragedy of one
pitch—that determines how fans and the media remember
a player. Jack is probably best remembered for the pitch
that hit Tony Conigliaro in the eye. Jack spoke about the
ugly incident. "A lot of people don't realize the whole situation. There were two outs in the eighth inning. I didn't
want to put Tony on." But fans see what they want to see
and some cast Jack in the role of the villain who almost
rubbed out Tony C.
    The fact that Jack threw the spitter didn't get him any
votes as America's No. 1 citizen. "Sure, I threw it. I never
tried to hide it," said Hamilton.
    Jack was around from 1962–1969 with the Phillies, Ti-
gers, Mets, Angels, Indians, and White Sox. He hurled two
no-hitters in the minors and just missed pitching one for
the Mets on May 4, 1966, shutting out the Cards, 8-0. The
lone hit came on a Ray Sadecki bunt single. Hamilton recalled, "Ken Boyer was playing a deep third base. He
played with Sadecki at St. Louis and knew he would bunt
sometimes with two strikes. But Sadecki caught Ken
playing back. After the game, Ken apologized to me."
    Jack rates the grand slam he hit as a Met on May 20,
1967, against Larry Jackson and the Cardinals as one of
his highlights. But he adds, "I got knocked out of the game
the next inning."
    "Hairbreadth Harry," as he was sometimes called, com-
pleted his 218-game stay with a 32-40 record. For you esoteric buffs, he is the only pitcher to give up a big league home
run to Tommie Aaron, but not to Tommie's brother, Hank.

HAMILTON, Steve
    Baseball coach at Morehead State in Kentucky

Steve Hamilton had two fantasies as a kid. One was to
play in Yankee Stadium and the other was to play in the
old Madison Square Garden. Both fantasies were met. He

recalled, "The first time I played in Yankee Stadium I got goose bumps all over. But Madison Square Garden was a big disappointment. The dressing rooms were dirty and the court had dead spots. It was just an old creaky building that smelled bad."

Gene Conley is the only man to play on championship teams in two professional sports, as a member of the Milwaukee Braves and Boston Celtics. Steve came close. He played from 1958–60 with the Minneapolis Lakers (NBA). In 1959 the Lakers won the Western Division, but lost in the championship series to the Celtics. As a member of the Yankee pitching staff, he saw the pinstripers lose two World Series.

A graduate of Morehead State, Steve averaged over 23 points per game his senior year for the Eagles, leading them to a berth in the NCAA tournament. Nicknamed "Hambone" and "Professor," the lanky 6'7" tobacco-chewing southpaw broke in with the Indians, then was traded to Washington the next year. Steve's next stop was Yankee Stadium, his fantasy island, where he caught the tail end of the Yankee dynasty years before finishing with the White Sox, Giants and Cubs. His final year was '72.

The gangly lefty had two trademarks—his large chew of tobacco and his "folly floater."

Hamilton's overall mark was 40-31 plus 42 saves. During the 1960s he had the best record for lowest opponent's batting avg. vs. left-handed hitters of any relief pitcher.

HANDRAHAN, Vern
    Mailman
    Charlottetown, Prince Edward Island, Canada

On Sept. 15, 1966, A's Manager Alvin Dark set a record by using seven pitchers in a shutout as the A's beat Cleveland, 1-0, in 11 innings. Vern entered the game to retire the final batter in the 11th inning to gain the save.

That would have to be Vern's upbeat game. In 34 games with the A's in '64 and '66 he was 0-2.

HANDS, Bill

> Employed with an engineering and petroleum company
>
> Parsippany, NJ

If we could choose our all-currency and bird teams, why not an all-anatomy squad? Certainly Bill Hands would qualify along with names like Barry Foote (what a battery!), Rollie Fingers, Ed Head, and Elroy Face.

Bill strolled in with the Giants in 1965. At the end of the season, he and Randy Hundley were sent to the Cubs for Lindy McDaniel. By the late Sixties, Bill climbed to the top of his profession, going 20-14 with the '69 Cubs.

The right-hander wound up in 1975 after two seasons each with the Twins and Rangers. He was 111-110 during his 11-year career.

A weak hitter, Bill set a dubious record in 1968 when he struck out in 14 consecutive at-bats.

HANEY, Larry

> Milwaukee Brewers' coach

In the late Sixties Larry was considered the best defensive catcher in the Orioles' organization. An All-American high school quarterback in Virginia, Larry signed a $60,000 bonus out of high school. He spent a couple of years with Baltimore as a backup catcher.

Larry found himself in Sick's Stadium with the expansion Pilots after his Baltimore apprenticeship. Before it was over, he made a couple of stops with Oakland, with a visit to St. Louis in between. Haney finished as a player-coach with the Brewers in '78, compiling a .984 fielding average, committing only 29 errors in 1,836 chances.   .215

HANKINS, Jay

> Midwest supervisor for the Major League Scouting Bureau
>
> Raytown, MO

Jay has tasted baseball as an A's outfielder ('61 and '63), traveling secretary, and ticket department employee. He served as a Royals' scout and minor league manager before joining the Major League Scouting Bureau in 1975. He graduated from the University of Missouri where he also played football.   .184

HANNAN, Jim
  President of Major League Baseball Players Alumni Association; employed with the Dean Witter Reynolds stock exchange firm
  Annadale, VA

A graduate of Notre Dame with a master's degree in finance from New York University, "Harpo" wrote his thesis on the financial analysis of the major league's pension plan.

The intellectual right-hander broke in with Washington in 1962, and remained in Washington until 1970, giving him a club record of nine years with the expansion Senators. His final lap came with the Tigers and Brewers the following year. Jim established the A.L. record of whiffing in 13 consecutive at-bats in 1968, the same year Bill Hands struck out 14 straight times in the senior circuit.   41-48

HARDIN, Jim
  Employed with Xerox Corp.; operates a deep sea fishing charter boat
  Miami, FL

A catcher in high school in Memphis, Jim was a second team All-City pick behind Tim McCarver before switching to pitching and being signed by the Mets. Hardin was drafted by Baltimore and came up with the Birds in '67 to post an 8-3 record.

Following the season he played winter ball in Puerto Rico and visited a hypnotist. Jim learned self-hypnosis and went on to have his best year in the big top in '68 when he went 18-13 with the Orioles.

It was downhill after that for this right-hander, who finished at 43-32 after pitching with the Yankees and Braves in 1971–72.

HARGAN, Steve
    Owns Sanco Pumping Service
    Palm Springs, CA

One of the greatest fulfillments a pitcher can experience is
to pitch a shutout and win the game with his bat. On June
19, 1967, Steve (Indians) hooked up with Chuck Dobson of
the A's in a scoreless pitching duel. With two outs in the
ninth, Hargan hit the only home run of his career. It
couldn't have come at a better time.

Steve was around for a dozen seasons (1965–77) with the
Indians, Rangers, Blue Jays, and Braves. A nagging elbow
injury hampered his 87-107 career.

HARKNESS, Tim
    Operates a packaging and moving company
    Oshawa, Ontario

The first base hit in Mets' history was delivered by veteran
outfielder Gus Bell. But the first hit for the Mets at Shea
Stadium was stroked by Tim Harkness on April 17, 1964,
when the Mets were defeated by the Pirates!

That was a bright moment for Tim, but it was difficult to
top his 14th-inning grand-slam off Jim Brewer the year be-
fore, giving the Mets an 8-6 victory over the Cubs at the
Polo Grounds. The homer tied John Pramesa of the 1951
Reds for the latest extra-inning grand-slam in National
League history.

Overall, the Canadian-born first baseman hit .235 for
the Dodgers and Mets (1961–64).

HARMON, Terry
    Regional sales manager for the Prism Cable TV com-
    pany
    Medford, NJ

Terry was "Mr. Utility" for the Phillies from 1967–77.
Playing the keystone sack on June 12, 1971, he set a major
league record by handling 18 chances in a game. The Ohio
University graduate hit .233 in 547 games.

HARPER, Tommy
Assistant to the General Manager, Boston Red Sox

Tommy had a 15-year run with the Reds, Indians, Pilots, Brewers, Red Sox, Angels, A's, and Orioles from 1962–76, hitting .257 with 146 home runs and 408 stolen bases.

In 1965 Harper led the N.L. in runs scored with 126. Tommy was the Seattle Pilots' most valuable player, topping the American League with 73 stolen bases in 1969. That represented the highest total in the American League since Ty Cobb pilfered 96 in 1915.

The next year with the Brewers, Tommy walloped 31 home runs and stole 38 bases, joining the 30-30 club with Bobby Bonds, Wilie Mays, Hank Aaron, Ken Williams, and Dale Murphy. He hit six four-baggers that year as a leadoff batter, to tie the A.L. record.

In 1973 Harper swiped 54 bases for the Red Sox, breaking the 62-year-old club record held by Tris Speaker.

Tommy, who didn't have exceptional speed but had great instincts on the bases, studied pitchers religiously and was only caught stealing 116 times in his career.

HARRAH, Toby
Active with the New York Yankees

The name "Harrah" is a palindrome. That simply means his name is spelled the same forward and backward. Dick Nen, Eddie Kazak, "Truck" Hannah, and Johnny Reder are others.

Toby arrived with Washington in 1969 for eight games. After spending 1970 in the Eastern League, he played with the Senators in their last season in Washington, then with the Texas Rangers throughout most of the 1970s until his trade to Cleveland for Buddy Bell after the '78 season.

Harrah was named the top shortstop in the American League in 1974 by the UPI and *The Sporting News*. On Aug. 27, 1977, at New York he hit the first of successive-pitch inside-the-park homers off Ken Clay. Bump Wills followed Toby. In 1977 Harrah switched to third base on a full-time basis. On June 26, 1976 he played all 18 innings

at the hot corner in a doubleheader against the White Sox
without a chance in the field. Toby was traded to the Yankees in 1984.

HARRELL, John
Employed with United Parcel Service
Santa Clara, CA

In 1969 the Beatles were singing *Get Back*. Despite going
3-for-6 with a couple of RBIs in two games with the Giants,
John never did get back to the majors.

HARRELSON, Bud
Manager at Columbia in the South Atlantic League

Big league scouts showed little interest in this 5'7", 130-
pound shortstop from the Bay Area. But former catcher
Roy Partee, scouting for the Mets, recommended this spi-
dery little guy who became the glue of the Mets infield for
over a decade.

Derrel McKinley Harrelson took over at shortstop for
the Mets in '67 after short trials the previous two years.
His best overall season came in 1971 when he hit .252, was
named to *The Sporting News* N.L. All-Star team and won a
Gold Glove. In 1970 Bud played in 54 consecutive errorless
games, tying Don Kessinger's major league mark for
shortstops.

Harrelson was involved in one of the most dramatic episodes in Shea Stadium annals when he wrestled with Pete
Rose at second base in the third game of the '73 NLCS. The
incident so excited the crowd that the field was turned into
a sea of debris. Willie Mays and manager Yogi Berra had
to walk out to the left field area to calm the crowd. In the
'69 and '73 World Series, the diminutive shortstop played
errorless ball for the Mets.

Tom Seaver's roommate for many years, Bud literally
went from the diamond to the altar on Aug. 15, 1976. In
the afternoon he scored the only run in the Mets' 1-0 win
over the Reds and was married in the evening.

Bud wound up with the Rangers in 1980 after a stop
with the Phillies. He joins Jerry Grote and Cleon Jones as

the only three Mets to play in all 12 of the New York club's
World Series games.　　　　　　　　　　　　　　　.239

HARRELSON, Ken
　　Chicago White Sox announcer

"Hawk" would have to rate as one of the most colorful and
controversial players to cross our path in the Sixties. Stylish both on and off the field, baseball's flower child sported
long hair, love beads, and gaudy paisley shirts and pants.
In uniform he popularized the high cut stirrup stockings
and wrist bands.

From 1963–71, "Hawk" glided around with the A's
(twice), Senators, Red Sox, and Indians. It was during
his second tour with Kansas City that he banged heads
with Charlie Finley, the A's volatile owner when "Hawk"
reportedly described Finley as "a menace to baseball."
For his penance he was given his outright release. The
move proved to be a blessing as Harrelson reaped a financial windfall. Within a week he had offers from six
clubs, finally signing with the Red Sox for a reported
$75,000.

The Bosox were in the middle of the '67 pennant race
and had lost Tony Conigliaro to his beaning injury. Ken
hit only .200 down the stretch, but Boston did cop the A.L.
flag.

Harrelson's vintage year proved to be 1968 when he hit
35 homers and led the league in ribbies with 109. On June
14th "Hawk" hit three successive home runs in a game at
Cleveland, driving in all seven runs of the 7-2 Red Sox victory.

Early in '69 the flamboyant first baseman-outfielder
was traded to Cleveland. Shocked by the trade, Harrelson
announced his retirement, but a few days later decided to
join the Indians and finished the year with 30 homers and
92 RBIs.

Harrelson suffered a broken leg early in '70 and played
just 17 games the entire year. Midway through the '71
campaign he announced his retirement from baseball to
join the PGA Tour. He didn't last long as a pro golfer, but

never returned to baseball as a player, although he was just 29 years old.

The nickname "Hawk" was tagged on him by "Duke" Sims in the minors. Harrelson was a Red Sox announcer before switching to the White Sox broadcast booth.

HARRELSON, Bill
Owns "Fitness Gym of Bakersfield"; sales rep for an oil company
Bakersfield, CA

This part-Cherokee Indian won only one game in the biggies against six losses for the Angels in 1968, but his win was a memorable one. On August 27th he combined on a one-hitter with Andy Messersmith in New York against the Yankees.

HARRINGTON, Mike
Assistant baseball and basketball coach at Southern Mississippi University

In 1963 television viewers began following the trials and tribulations of the Harrington family on *Peyton Place*. However, there wasn't much gossip about Mike's career, as he made it into just one game with the Phillies as a pinch-runner that year.

HARRIS, Alonzo
Freight handler for Santa Fe Trails and Services
Los Angeles, CA

Fremont High School in Los Angeles has produced a lengthy list of major leaguers over the years including Bobby Doerr, Gene Mauch, Bob Watson, George Hendrick, Dan Ford, and Chet Lemon. Add Alonzo "Candy" Harris.

"Candy" reminded many of Willie Davis because of his slight build and quick reflexes, but the switch-hitter didn't get a chance to use his tools much as he struck out in his only at-bat with the Astros in 1967.

HARRIS, Billy
> Manages the New Hanover Cold Storage Co.; coaches
> American Legion baseball
> Wilmington, NC

Richard Harris had the hit song *MacArthur Park* at the
time Billy made a tour of the various American League
parks with the Indians ('68) and Royals ('69). The second
baseman, who overcame serious injuries in a family fire in
North Carolina, appeared in a total of 43 games and hit
.218.

HARRISON, Chuck
> Owns an oil company; operates a company which pro-
> vides lawn maintenance for apartment complexes
> Abilene, TX

Known as "Pound Cake" due to his stocky 5'10", 190-
pound build, Chuck was on a shuttle between the majors
and minors. The Texas Tech football star, who captained
the '62 squad, hit .238 in 328 big league games between
the years 1965–71 with the Astros and Royals.

It was the candlelights of the minors, not the bright
lights of the majors, where Chuck had his fondest moments. He says, "I am most proud of playing for five championship teams in the six years I spent in the minors."
Chuck contributed heavily to those teams, hitting 28
homers in '63 and 44 the next year for San Antonio's back-
to-back Texas League winners, 37 for Oklahoma City in
'65, and 50 roundtrippers in two years ('70–'71) in which
he helped Omaha to American Association pennants.

HARRISON, Tom
> Owns a trucking business
> Bell, CA

Rex Harrison was an Academy Award winner for his role
in *My Fair Lady*. Canadian-born Tom Harrison didn't win
any awards as he had a fairly quick stay, pitching in just
one inning of one game for the Kansas City A's in 1965.

HART, Jim Ray
> Automobile salesman
> San Francisco, CA

Jim went from the cotton fields of North Carolina to the battlegrounds of big league baseball in 1963. His debut on July 7th with the San Francisco Giants was an unforgettable one. In the first game of a doubleheader against St. Louis he was floating after connecting for a pair of hits. In the nightcap Bob Gibson officially welcomed Jim to the wars of the majors when he plunked the wide-eyed rookie with one of his sizzlers and broke his shoulder blade.

Back in action on August 12th, he was batting with an 0-2 count in the bottom of the ninth inning against Curt Simmons who held a 13-0 lead. On the next pitch the veteran southpaw hit Hart in the head, disabling him the rest of the season.

Fortunately, life wasn't always so violent for Jim. From 1964–68 he was at the hot corner for the Giants on a regular basis, averaging 28 home runs a season. In his first full year in '64, he stroked 31 homers and had a career-high 33 two years later. On July 8, 1970, Jim hit for the cycle tying a big league record with six RBIs in one inning.

By the late Sixties his batting skills began to rust. After several tutorial stops in the P.C.L. he was traded to the Yankees in 1973 and received his discharge papers a year later. His numbers read: .278 average and 170 homers.

HARTENSTEIN, Chuck
> Pittsburgh Pirates minor league pitching coach

This skinny right-hander from the University of Texas was known as "Twiggy" after the English model who created a sensation in the modeling business in the mid-Sixties. On June 18, 1965, in a game which lasted a Texas League record 25 innings, Chuck pitched the first 18 frames for Dallas–Fort Worth before leaving the game with a 1-1 score.

Hartenstein joined the Cubs that year. By '67 he was one of the top relief pitchers in the N.L., collecting nine victories and eight saves in 45 appearances as his amazing sinker ball made him a Wrigley Field delight. Two years later the lean chucker showed some beef when he had 10 saves in 56 appearances for the Pirates. In 1970 he brought his sinker to the Cards and Red Sox. It appeared that Chuck was a mere memory before he reappeared in '77 with the expansion Blue Jays, finishing 17-19 lifetime plus 23 saves, all as a reliever.

HARTMAN, JC
Sergeant in the Houston Police Department

In the 1960s O.J. Simpson came into prominence on the gridiron as did A.J. Foyt in auto racing. JC Hartman played shortstop in 90 games for the Houston Colt .45s in 1962–63, hitting an uncelebrated .185.

JC has no periods after his initials since the letters constitute his actual name.

HAWKINS, Wynn
Security officer with General Motors
Lordstown, OH

On June 17, 1960, Ted Williams hit home run No. 500. The pitcher he took deep was Wynn Hawkins. "I had a count of 'no balls' and 'two strikes' on him. I tried to waste an inside slider, but he hit it over the left-center field fence," recalled the victimized hurler.

Hawkins, the all-time leading basketball scorer at Baldwin-Wallace University, was 12-13 in 48 games as a member of the Indians from 1960–62. He later scouted for the Tribe and in the late '60s was the team's traveling secretary.

HAYWOOD, Bill
Seattle Mariners' Assistant Director of Player Development and Instruction

Spencer Haywood led the U.S. basketball team to an Olympic championship in 1968, a year Bill Haywood

joined the Senators at age 31. The graybeard right-hander
pitched in 14 games without a decision.

Haywood got a late start in pro ball after serving four
years in the Marines following graduation from the University of North Carolina.

HEALY, Fran
New York Mets' cable television announcer

Fran's career (1969–78) covered time with the Royals
(twice), Giants, and Yankees. With the Royals Fran was
behind the plate for both of Steve Busby's no-hitters.

A .250 lifetime hitter, the 6'5" backstop is a graduate of
American International College. Before announcing with
the Mets, he was a Yankee radio and cable television
broadcaster. His verbal exchanges with Phil Rizzuto frequently created some of the best entertainment in New
York.

"Heal" comes from a baseball family. His Uncle Frank
caught for John McGraw's Giants and the Cardinals,
while his father, Bernard, played in the St. Louis farm system.

HEATH, Bill
Owns his own insurance company, Heath and Associ-
ates
Houston, TX

When Ken Holtzman hurled a no-hitter for the Cubs on
Aug. 19, 1969, Bill was behind the dish. But he wasn't
around to enjoy the celebration on the field since he had to
leave the game in the eighth inning when he suffered a
broken finger on a foul tip.

Originally drafted by the Phillies out of USC, Bill
caught with the White Sox, Astros, Tigers, and Cubs from
1965–1969.   .236

HEBNER, Richie
     Active with Chicago Cubs

As a high school hockey player, Richie scored 80 goals and was selected to the High School All-America hockey team. He was offered a professional hockey contract by the Boston Bruins, but decided to slap base hits instead of hockey pucks.

Hebner had his first shot with the Pirates in '68 and for the next several seasons he anchored the Bucs' infield at third base, appearing on five National League East champion teams. He added two more Division winners with the Phillies in 1977–78, and another with the '84 Cubs, giving him a record eight years of appearing in the NLCS. However, many of these post-season parties bombed for Richie: He holds the record for participating for more losing teams in NLCS than any other player when he was on the losing end for the seventh time as a member of the '84 Cubs.

The off-season gravedigger put the Giants six feet under in the 1971 NLCS when he homered off Juan Marichal in Game Three to give the Pirates a 2-1 win. The following day his three-run blast buried the Giants for keeps.

The ex-Marine usually came out fighting on Opening Day with five home runs to his credit in curtain raisers. Richie also played with the Mets and Tigers before returning to the Steel City for a second time.   .277

HEDLUND, Mike
     Director of administrative services for the LTV Federal Credit Union in Grand Prairie, TX

Nicknamed "Booger Red" by former teammate Gary Bell, Mike was up briefly with the Indians in '65 and '69. From 1969–72 he did his pitching for the Royals, where he finished 25-24 lifetime, his best year coming in '71 at 15-8.

HEFFNER, Bob
  Branch manager for Stroh's beer
  Allentown, PA

During a period when Hugh Hefner was building his Playboy empire, "Butch" Heffner was piecing together a 114-game career split among the Red Sox, Indians, and Angels.

  One of the most difficult timing plays in baseball is when a ground ball must be fielded by the first baseman and tossed to his pitcher who is sprinting over to cover the bag. Would you believe that in the history of the game only three pitchers have made all three putouts in an inning in this manner! They are Jim Bagby, Jr. (1940), Rick Reuschel (1975), and Bob Heffner (1963). Like Bagby, Heffner did it with the Red Sox.   11-21

HEGAN, Mike
  Milwaukee Brewers' announcer

Mike and his dad (Jim) share the distinction as the only father-son combo to appear in two World Series. Although he was in just five games with the Yankees in '64, Mike was on the World Series roster and played in three games as a replacement for Tony Kubek. He also participated in the '72 Fall Classic with Oakland. Jim played in the '48 and '54 Series as a member of the Indians. Although no father-son team has ever played together in the majors at the same time, the Hegans came close, with Jim leaving in 1960 and Mike starting four years later.

  The current Brewers' announcer, who hit for the cycle on Sept. 3, 1976, was easily recognizable with the A's "mustache gang" as the one player without a mustache.

  Mike became the first player to homer for the Seattle Pilots. From Sept. 24, 1970, until May 20, 1973, the smooth-fielding first baseman established a major league record for most consecutive errorless games at first base (178).

  Mike made his exit in 1977 after playing with the Brewers for a second time.   .242

HEIDEMANN, Jack
> Real Estate salesman for Realty Executive Realtors
> Phoenix, AZ

Jack was heralded as the next Lou Boudreau when the Indians made him their No. 1 selection in the June 1967 draft out of high school in Brenham, TX. After jumping around with the Indians, Cardinals, Mets, and Brewers from 1969–77, he closed with a .211 average, certainly not Boudreau style.

Looking back at his first full season when he took over as the Cleveland shortstop in 1970, Jack says, "Being 19 and not mature enough, the season was a long one. But the benefits in baseball were many, including meeting a lot of people and seeing the country."

Heidemann retired from the game with a shoulder injury and was operated on for a torn rotator cuff.

HEISE, Bob
> State Corrections officer
> Sonoma, CA

Bob's 11-year voyage encompassed time with the Mets, Giants, Brewers, Angels, Cards, Red Sox, and Royals. He first came up with the Mets in '67 and was in hog heaven when he hit .323 in 16 games.

Heise epitomized the role player, appearing in over 100 games each at second, short, and third. The utility specialist hit .247 in 499 games. He had only one home run in over 1100 major league at-bats.

HEISER, Roy
> Employed with American Airlines
> Baltimore, MD

We heard a lot of Roy Orbison during the Sixties with his string of popular songs including *Pretty Woman* and *It's Over*. In 1961 Roy Heiser was crying "It's over" after pitching in three games without a decision for the Senators.

HEIST, Al
> San Francisco Giants scout
> Cookson, OK

Brooklyn-born Al Heist was a 32-year-old archaeological
ruin when he got the call to the majors. His three-year run
(1960–62) was split between the Cubs and Houston.

A superb defensive outfielder, Al's nirvana came in an
early season game in '61 when he hit a grand-slam with
two out in the ninth inning to give the Cubs a 9-5 win over
the Braves.

In 1958 Al set a P.C.L. record by playing 136 games
without an error.   .255

HELMS, Tommy
> Cincinnati Reds' coach

The National League "Rookie of the Year" in 1966, Tommy had the reputation of a good hit-and-run man who was
tough to strike out. He enjoyed a 14-year career spent
mostly with the Reds and Astros. His last flings came with
the Pirates and Red Sox.

Helms was named to *The Sporting News* All-Star fielding team three years (1968, '70 and '71).

On July 1, 1970, Tommy was the first Red to homer at
Riverfront Stadium when he hit his only four-bagger that
year.   .269

HEMAN, Russ
> Owner of Tri-City carpet service
> Santa Ana, CA

At the urging of the Kennedy administration, there was a
"Fallout Shelter" craze in the country in 1961. Russ could
have used a little protection that summer. After a dozen
games divided equally between the Indians and Angels,
without a decision, the right-hander fell out of the majors,
never to return.

HENDERSON, Ken
    Office furniture business
    Saratoga, CA

Ken signed a bonus contract with the Giants out of high
school. Before becoming a regular in the San Francisco
outfield in '69, the switch-hitter had a few peeks at the big
time. His finest season came in 1970 when he hit .294. In
1972 he tied a N.L. mark for most switch-homers in a
month.

Traded after '72, Ken missed a good part of the '73 campaign because of injuries. The following season he enjoyed
career highs in homers (20) and RBIs (95) with the White
Sox. Ken became only the fifth A.L. switch-hitter to have
20 or more home runs in a season, joining Mickey Mantle,
Tom Tresh, Reggie Smith, and Roy White.

Henderson's 14-year trek ended after time with the
Braves, Rangers, Mets, and Reds.   .258

HENDLEY, Bob
    Baseball coach and teacher at Stratford Academy
    Macon, GA

On Sept. 9, 1965, Bob one-hit the Dodgers while pitching
for the Cubs. Normally, that kind of performance would
ensure victory—unless your mound opponent was named
Sandy Koufax. That day dandy Sandy threw a perfect
game at the Cubs. Ironically, the game's only hit, a
seventh-inning Lou Johnson bloop double just out of the
reach of first baseman Ernie Banks, did not figure in the
game's only run. In the second inning Hendley walked
Johnson, who was sacrificed to second base, then scored
the game's only run when he stole third and came in as the
throw went awry into left field.

But Bob returned with a vengeance five days later and
beat Koufax, 2-1, on a four-hitter. Hendley spoke about
those games: "In the game Koufax pitched a no-hitter his
fastball was rising and his curveball was coming off a
tabletop. We knew he would be tough to hit that night.
That game certainly motivated me a little more when I
pitched against him a few days later."

Along with the memories of those two contests, the southpaw chucker, who went 48-52 lifetime (1961–67), will never forget Frank Howard. With the Braves in 1963 he gave up home runs to the big slugger the final four times he faced him. Early in '64 when Hendley pitched for the Giants, "Hondo" connected the first time he saw Bob, making it five homers in succession. After being retired two straight times, Howard took Bob deep again, making it six homers in eight at-bats off the shell-shocked hurler.

Today Bob is contented with imparting his knowledge to his high school players. He said, "I have considered coaching an extension of my baseball career and it has been a rewarding and satisfying experience." It sure has. Bob's teams have won seven regional championships and four state titles.

HENDRICKS, Elrod
     Baltimore Orioles' coach

One of the more jovial spirits of the Sixties and Seventies, always-smiling Ellie Hendricks was around from 1968–1978, including three different visits to Baltimore plus one each with the Cubs and Yankees. A lifetime .220 swatter, the Virgin Islands backstop came to life in October, batting .273 in 23 post-season games for the Orioles and Yankees. In the 1970 World Series he hit .364, including a key homer in the opener as the Orioles beat the Reds, 4-3.

Hendricks spent nine years toiling in the minors before getting his chance with the O's on the recommendation of Earl Weaver, who was a coach with the Birds at the time. In 1967 Ellie led the Mexican League with 41 home runs.

In 1967 the guy with the calypso tongue was traded to the Cubs. He played in just 17 N.L. games, but in one he tied a league record when he walked five times.

Ellie started the '78 campaign as an Orioles' coach, but was activated six weeks later. In one game that season he took to the mound and pitched 2⅓ scoreless innings for Baltimore, allowing only one hit and one walk.

HENNIGAN, Phil
  Bread truck driver
  Center, TX

After 12 months of discussion, a table was finally chosen
for the Vietnam peace talks in 1969, a year this former ar-
tilleryman in Vietnam was firing bullets in relief for the
Indians. The right-hander worked out of the Cleveland
bullpen for four years before finishing with the Mets in
1973.   17-14

HENRY, Bill
  Sales manager for ABC-TV in New York
  Darien, CT

Longevity in baseball belongs to an elite breed who can control their destiny. But for many like Bill Henry, a trip to the
majors is usually a one-time fling. The tall southpaw out of
Seton Hall made two relief appearances for the Yankees in
1966 and was not involved in a decision. He did leave un-
harmed, allowing no runs in the three innings he pitched.
  This Bill Henry is not to be confused with the one of the
same name who pitched for six clubs from 1952–69.

HENRY, Ron
  Singer
  Denver, CO

This entertainer, who also acts in plays, was on stage for a
total of 42 games with the Twins in 1961 and 1964 hitting
.130. Ron really hammed it up in '64 when he collected a
total of five hits, with four of them going for extra bases (a
double, triple, and two home runs).

HEPLER, Bill
  Construction superintendent for Batson-Cook
  Tampa, FL

When Bill arrived with the Mets in '66, he had more self-
assurance than a late-night TV evangelist. However, a

little luck would have helped the left-hander who went 3-3 with New York.

In his debut he pitched fairly well, but ran into Larry Jackson of the Phils and lost, 3-0. The win upped Jackson's career record to 15-0 against the Mets.

The following season Bill found himself pitching for Williamsport in the Eastern League and tossed a no-hitter against Elmira, but once again ran into tough luck as he lost, 1-0, because of a walk and an error.

HERBEL, Ron
Real estate business
Tacoma, WA

Any guy who pokes six hits in 206 at-bats for a .029 average better know how to pitch. Ron's skills as a pitcher (42-37) qualify him as a man who knew what he was doing on the mound.

Signed to a bonus contract with the Giants out of Colorado State in 1958 when he led his team to the NCAA World Series, Ron toured the National League from 1963–71 with the Giants, Padres, Mets, and Braves. Herbel, who spent most of his time in San Francisco, had a very unorthodox windup as he went into his motion with the ball in his glove instead of his pitching hand.

HERMOSO, Angel
Operates amateur baseball schools in Carabobo, Venezuela

When Angel joined the Braves in 1967 he looked like a perfect flash of marble, but the skills of this utility infielder were never sculptured. After hitting .211 in 91 games with the Braves, Expos, and Indians, Angel was among the missing.

HERNANDEZ, Jackie
    Truck driver for Boudini Company
    Miami, FL

Jacinto Zulueta Hernandez, better known as "Jackie," is
not to be confused with Enzo Hernandez, the former Padres' shortstop from Venezuela. Jackie made the rare
switch from catching to shortstop and scooped 'em up from
1965–73 with the Angels, Twins, Royals, and Pirates.
    In the '71 World Series he played in all seven games for
the Bucs, going 4-for-18 and fielding 1.000 as the Pirates
took it all.

HERNANDEZ, Ramon
    Operates a liquor store
    Carolina, PR

Ramon was around for nine seasons as a member of the
Braves, Cubs (twice), Pirates, and Red Sox between
1967–77. He picked up most of his checks with Pittsburgh,
helping the Buccos to the National League East title three
different years.
    Especially tough on left-handed batters, the southpaw
short relief artist was 23-15 overall. In '72 he enjoyed his
best season, going 5-0 with 14 saves and a 1.67 ERA.

HERNANDEZ, Rudy
    Owns a clothing store
    Rio Piedras, PR

In 1960 Clark Gable and Marilyn Monroe each made their
last film, *The Misfits*, when Rudy made his first appearance
with the Washington Senators. His 4-2 (28-game) career
ended a year later.

HERRERA, Jose
    Zulia, Venezuela

The Expos' first team ever in 1969 had names like Coco
Laboy, Mack Jones, Bill Stoneman, and Jose Herrera. A

native of Venezuela, Jose appeared in 47 games that year, mostly in the outfield and hit a respectable .286.

A second baseman-outfielder, Jose broke in with the Astros in 1967. His 80-game swing ended in 1970 in Montreal with a .264 mark. As a member of the Expos, he once walloped pinch-hit homers twice within three days to beat the Braves.

HERRMANN, Ed
Lawn sprinkler systems business
Poway, CA

1967 was a tumultuous year in American history. The United States had escalated its role in Vietnam; antiwar protestors marched on the nation's capital, and teachers' strikes kept 40 million kids out of school.

For Edward Martin Herrman it was the summer he fulfilled his dream of playing in the big leagues when the White Sox gave him a brief taste. When he returned in '69 the rugged 205-pound catcher stayed until 1978 with the Chisox, Yankees, Angels, Astros, and Expos. In '70 he hit .283 with 19 homers.   .240

HERRNSTEIN, John
Vice-president of a savings and loan company
Dayton, OH

John captained the University of Michigan football team in 1958, but because of a knee injury he opted to play baseball. A first baseman-outfielder, John spent most of his career (1962–66) with the Phillies and also made last-ditch stops with the Cubs and Braves.

Herrnstein, who hit .220 lifetime, spoke about today's player-management relations. "In the 1960s the Players Association was still formative. It's almost inconceivable to me how the pendulum swung from the absoluteness of ownership to today's state."

HERRSCHER, Rick
 Orthodontist
 Dallas, TX

When Mets' skipper Casey Stengel was asked by Rick whether he should go to dental school or play big league baseball, Stengel, a former dental student himself, advised, "Go to dental school."

 A basketball player at SMU, Rick appeared in 35 games with the Mets during their maiden season in 1962. On August 5th he collected his first major league hit, a three-run homer off Jim O'Toole which gave the Mets a 5-3 victory over the Reds. The infielder-outfielder batted .220, then took Casey's advice deciding that fitting people with braces might be easier than offering at curve balls.

HERSHBERGER, Mike
 Salesman for Ohio Art Company
 Canton, OH

A native of the football hotbed of Massillon, OH, Mike was a gridiron gladiator at the University of Cincinnati before turning to professional baseball. He then rolled his muscular frame through the minors. After hitting .310 for San Diego (P.C.L.) in '61, he was invited to join the White Sox.

 Hershberger's 11-year march ended after also playing for the A's and Brewers before his final return to Chicago. Possessed of a fine throwing arm, Mike led the American League in assists (17) in 1967.   .252

HERTZ, Steve
 Coaches baseball and teaches health and diversified
 cooperative education at Southridge High
 Miami, FL

It might be appropriate to say that this Hertz was in the driver's seat, but maybe he should have tried harder after a five-game drive with the Astros in 1964.

 During spring training that year, Steve looked so good at third base and at the plate that Houston General Manager Paul Richards was quoted, "He's too good to be true."

Unfortunately, Richards was right. The 19-year-old hopeful washed out after going 0-for-4. Steve recalled, "It was somewhat of an intimidating experience."

HIATT, Jack
    Houston Astros' minor league catching instructor

Jack carved his place in baseball history when he belted a pinch-hit grand-slam off Elroy Face on July 31, 1967, to give the Giants an 8-4 win over the Pirates. It marked the 100th pinch-hit grand-slammer in major league history.
    Another memorable clout for Jack came on April 30, 1965, when he hit his first big league roundtripper against a guy named Sandy Koufax.
    In '64 he entered the big arena with the Angels before being traded to San Francisco the next year. In the early '70s the handyman catcher also played with the Expos, Cubs, and Astros before terminating his nine-year career with the Angels.   .251

HIBBS, Jim
    Owner of a real estate company, Gold Key Realtors
    Ventura, CA

There is a fine line between obscurity and greatness. Jim never cracked that fine line after going 0-for-3 in three pinch-hitting appearances for the Angels in 1967. He says, "I found baseball the finest learning experience of my life, and also the hardest way to make a living." A past president of the Ventura Board of Realtors, Jim has over forty sales people working for him today.
    Hibbs was an All-American catcher at Stanford University in 1966 where he earned a B.A. degree in history.

HICKMAN, Jess
    Director of retail sales for Satellite Earth Station
    Mamou, LA

The miniskirt came into fashion in 1965 when right-hander Jess Hickman arrived for a mini career which totaled one loss in 13 games as a reliever with the Kansas City A's in '65 and '66.

His name, Jess Owens Hickman, was not taken after the former Olympic star. He says, "I was named after my doctor."

Reflecting on his short stay, which was interrupted by an arm injury, Jess smiled, "The first time I faced Harmon Killebrew he hit one about nine miles over the light tower in Kansas City."

Such memories make for a "mini" career.

HICKMAN, Jim
Farmer
Henning, TN

After laboring in the St. Louis organization for several years, Jim became a charter member of the Mets and was a regular in the team's outfield the first four years.

On Aug. 7, 1963, he became the first Met to hit for the cycle in a 7-3 victory over the Cardinals. Two days later he hit a two-out grand-slam in the ninth inning to beat the Cubs in the Polo Grounds, 7-3, which ended Roger Craig's 18-game losing streak.

Jim also has the distinction of being the last player ever to homer in the Polo Grounds (Sept. 18, 1963) as the Mets lost to the Phils, 5-1.

Hickman became the first Met to wallop three homers in a game as the Mets beat the Cards, 6-3, on Sept. 3, 1965, with all three coming off Ray Sadecki.

The lanky 6'3" flychaser was traded to the Dodgers after the '66 season. He appeared in one game as a pitcher for the Dodgers in '67 hurling 2 innings and surrendered 2 hits, for a 4.50 ERA. One of the hits was Willie Mays' 553rd homer.

After toning his skills in the minors, he returned in 1968 with the Cubs. In 1970 he was named the "Comeback Player of the Year" after hitting 32 home runs, with 115 RBIs and batting .315. Hickman played in the All-Star Game that summer and it was his 12th-inning single which gave the National League a 5-4 win when Pete Rose

came around to score after the collision at home plate with
catcher Ray Fosse.

   Hickman spent three more years in Chicago before making his exit with the Cardinals in 1974, the organization
he began with back in the mid-Fifties.   .252

HICKS, Jim
      Supervisor for Continental Airlines
      Houston, TX

Not to be confused with Joe Hicks, who played the outfield
with the White Sox, Senators, and Mets from 1959–63, Jim
(also an outfielder) roamed the garden with the White Sox,
Cards, and Angels (1964–70) with time between spent in
the minors.

   Signed out of the University of Illinois where he also
played basketball, Jim led Tulsa to the P.C.L. pennant in
1968 with a league-leading .366 average and was named
the league's MVP. He was the Silver Bat winner that season with the highest batting average in the minors.   .163

HIGGINS, Dennis
      Owns a sporting goods store, Central Missouri Ath-
      letic Goods
      Jefferson City, MO

Relief pitching attracts a rare breed of men. Only a handful can survive the pressures that rankle the nerves coming in from the bullpen into the pressure cooker.

   In 1969 Dennis was the ace of Ted Williams' relief corps
with a 10-9 record plus 16 saves in 55 games for the Senators.
His overall mark stands at 22-23 with 46 saves in 241 games,
all but two in relief roles from 1966–1972. Dennis also saw
action with the White Sox, Indians, and Cardinals.

HILGENDORF, Tom
      Manager of a truck stop facility
      Cottage Grove, OR

After spending virtually the whole decade of the Sixties in
the pickup truck life of the minors, Tom joined the Cardi-

nals in 1969. From that point until 1975, he enjoyed the Mercedes life of the majors for the most part.

The southpaw chucker did his tossing for the Indians (1972–74) before closing with the Phils in '75 in his most effective campaign, 7-3 in 53 relief appearances.   19-14

HILL, Garry
Salesman for Package Products
Charlotte, NC

During the 1960s *The Beverly Hillbillies* became one of the top television shows. Calvin Hill starred at Yale before transferring his skills to the N.F.L., and Englishman Graham Hill won the Indianapolis 500.

Right-hander Garry Hill is not as readily recalled since he appeared in only one big league game in 1969 for the Braves and was tagged with the loss after lasting two innings.

HILL, Herman
Died on December 14, 1970, at age 25 in
Magallanes, Venezuela

Herman, an aspiring outfielder, batted over .300 with Denver in 1969, and played in 43 games with the Twins in '69 and '70. He had been traded to the Cardinals following the 1970 season before he met his untimely death in a tragic drowning in the Caribbean Sea where he had been playing winter league baseball in Venezuela.   .083

HILLER, Chuck
San Francisco Giants coach

On Oct. 8, 1962, Don Larsen celebrated the sixth anniversary of his 1956 World Series perfect game by gaining a victory in relief in Game Four of the WS, beating his former team. The 7-3 win over the Yanks was settled by Chuck Hiller's grand-slam, the first grand-slam ever hit by a National Leaguer in World Series history. Chuck's big swat, which broke a 2-2 tie, came in the seventh inning off Yankee reliever Marshall Bridges.

"Iron Hands" worked his way up to the Giants in '61 after winning the Texas League batting title with Rio
Grande Valley the year before with a .334 average and
was also named the league's MVP.

Sold to the Mets during the '65 campaign, Hiller hit a
career-high .280 in '66 and led the National League in
pinch-hitting, going 15-for-45 (.333). On Sept. 28, 1966, the
swift-fielding second baseman was involved in the last
triple play ever executed by the Mets in a game against
the Cubs. The play went from Ed Bressoud to Hiller to Ed
Kranepool. He also played briefly with the Phillies and the
Pirates.　　　　　　　　　　　　　　　　　　　　　　.243

HILLER, John
　　　Insurance business
　　　Duluth, MN

John suffered a heart attack at the young age of 27 following the 1970 season. It appeared that his promising pitching career would be wiped out. Following his attack, John
had an operation that removed 7-feet of intestine to relieve
a cholesterol problem. Something helped. After missing
one full season he rebounded and in 1973 was eventually
named the Comeback Player of the Year and Fireman of
the Year with a 10-5 mark and a sparkling 1.44 ERA to go
along with his then major league record 38 saves for the
Tigers.

Discovered on the suburban sandlots of Toronto, John
signed with Detroit without a bonus. He made it up to
Motown for brief trials in '65 and '66, then helped the Bengals to the A.L. pennant in '68 going 9-6 as a spot starter
and reliever.

Following his heart attack, John was reactivated midway through the '72 season and compiled a fine 2.05 ERA
as the Tigers clawed their way to the A.L. East title. In the
championship series against Oakland he hurled three
scoreless innings and was credited with a victory.

After his banner year in '73 he set A.L. records by winning 17 games and losing 14 as a reliever. The left-hander
retired early in the '80 season with an 87-76 record and

125 saves. He is the all-time Detroit club leader in games pitched (545).

The courageous southpaw, who was known as a quick worker on the mound, tied a major league record on August 6, 1968 when he fanned the first six batters he faced in a game.

HINSLEY, Jerry
    Employed with a road construction company
    Las Cruces, NM

In spring training of 1964, Jerry wrote a daily series in the *New York Journal-American* titled "Diary of a Rookie." The right-hander didn't have too many pages in the diary as he was 0-2 in 11 games with the Mets in '64 and '67.

HINTON, Chuck
    Baseball coach at Howard University
    Washington, DC

Chuck was the central figure in a Baltimore ruse that was thwarted by a California newspaper. Here is what happened:

Hinton started out in the Orioles' organization and won batting titles in the Northern and California Leagues in '59 and '60 with sparkling averages of .358 and .369. Interestingly enough, both years he connected for exact totals of 22 doubles, 7 triples, and 20 homers.

The Orioles knew they would lose a player of Hinton's talents to the expansion draft. So Baltimore skipper Paul Richards instructed Earl Weaver who was managing in the minors to have Chuck fake an injury by running into a wall. The gimmick was to discourage the expansion teams from picking up Hinton, thinking he was damaged goods.

Weaver would not go along with the stunt so Richards approached Hinton personally. One day when Earl was hitting fungoes to the young blue-chipper, Hinton crashed into the wall in theatrical fashion, faking an injury that sent him home with his arm in a sling.

After a California newspaper reported that Hinton had not been injured, the Senators jumped in and drafted him.

In 1962 he batted .310 with 17 homers and lead the team
in most offensive categories. Chuck also played for the Indians (twice) and Angels during an 11-year (1961–71) run
which saw him hit .264. Primarily an outfielder, he also
saw action at every infield position and behind the plate.
Hinton came back to haunt the Senators in '67 when he
poked three grand-slams against his former club.

HIPPAUF, Herb
Atlanta Braves' minor league pitching instructor

Herb was 0-1 in three games with the Atlanta Braves in
1966 at a time the youth of America in the counterculture
element were referred to as Hippies.
    After his brief stay, the left-hander was "out of sight."

HISLE, Larry
Milwaukee Brewers' scout and minor league instructor

It would have been interesting to summarize the accomplishments of this extraordinary athlete who eventually
lost a four-year battle with a shoulder ailment.
    A teammate of Al Oliver on the same Portsmouth, OH,
baseball team, Larry was also a highly touted basketball
player whom Oscar Robertson personally tried to recruit
for the University of Cincinnati.
    Larry's initial glimpse of the big time came with the
Phillies in '68. The following year he spent his first full
season in the City of Brotherly Love and banged out 20
homers. After a couple of dismal seasons Hisle was shipped
to the Dodgers, but never made it to Chavez Ravine. After
he hit .325 in 1972 for Albuquerque (P.C.L.) he was sent to
the Cards, then to the Twins that winter.
    Minnesota proved to be his land of tranquility, a place
where Larry's talents developed into star-like status. In
'77 he hit 28 homers to go with his league-leading 119
RBIs. He then signed as a free agent with the Brewers and
smacked 34 home runs and 115 RBIs in '78 for the Brewmen. Both years Hisle was on the American League All-
Star squad and appeared to be on the brink of greatness

when he was plagued by a shoulder injury in 1979 that proved to be his doom.

Larry hung it up in 1982 at .273 with 166 homers. But we will always wonder!

HOBAUGH, Ed
> Health and physical education teacher; baseball and soccer coach at Dayton, H.S.
> Dayton, PA

Mr. Ed came to TV in 1961, the same year Mr. Ed Hobaugh joined the Senators for a three-year jog that saw him go 9-10 in 61 games.

The right-hander captained the 1954 Michigan State baseball team which won the Big Ten championship.

HOERNER, Joe
> Vice-president of the Cardinal Travel Agency
> St. Louis, MO

Ask Joe's former Cardinal teammates what they remember about him and they'll probably tell you about the night in Atlanta when he took control of the team bus for a wild ride which ended back at the team's hotel after smashing into a road sign.

Joe rated as high on the mound as he did a clubhouse prankster. From 1963-77 the lefty established himself as a first-class reliever, going 39-34 with 99 saves for the Astros, Cardinals, Phillies (twice), Braves, Royals, Rangers, and Reds.

The gagster was a key factor in the Cardinals' bullpen for the '68 N.L. champs when he went 8-2 and collected 17 saves to go with a sparkling 1.47 ERA. Remarkably he notched all 8 wins and one of his losses in extra innings. On June 1st that year he tied an N.L. record when he struck out the last six batters he faced in a 6-5 victory over the Mets. His consecutive whiffs equaled a N.L. mark for relief pitchers.

During his years with the Cardinals, Joe opened a travel agency with teammate Dal Maxvill. A cousin, Dick Hoerner, was a one-time member of the L.A. Rams while another cousin, Mike Reilly, is a linebacker with the Bears.

HOFFMAN, John
    Yard supervisor for Ashland Cement
    Seattle, WA

Yippie leader Abbie Hoffman, who received his share of
publicity in the tumultuous '60s, popularized the saying
"Never trust anyone over 30." He couldn't have been
talking about 20-year-old John Hoffman who hit .143 as an
eight-game catcher for the Astros in '64–'65.

HOLMAN, Gary
    Schoolteacher
    Brea, CA

After appearing in 75 games for the Senators in '68, Gary
looked to be on the verge of stardom when he hit .294, including 11-for-32 as a pinch-hitter. Those kinds of numbers
gained him a place on the Topps Rookie All-Star team.
    The next year he played in 41 games, then vanished
from sight with an overall .259 average. Gary helped lead
USC to the 1963 national championship.

HOLT, Jim
    Owns a business that manufactures firefighting equip-
    ment
    Graham, NC

Do you remember the 1974 World Series when the power-
laden A's destroyed the Dodgers in five games? In the
fourth game a relatively obscure player named Jim Holt
stroked a pinch-hit single off Andy Messersmith to provide
the winning runs as the A's took a 3-1 lead in the Fall Classic. Prior to Jim's timely hit he had been 0-for-26 after
coming to the A's from Minnesota that August.
    The first baseman-outfielder made his debut with the
Twins in '68. For the next few years he was on an elevator between the majors and minors. Jim concluded his
jaunt in 1976, hitting .265 lifetime. He led the A.L. in
1975 in both pinch-hits (10) and at-bats (43) as a pinch-
swinger.

HOLTGRAVE, Vern
> Salesman for Carlyle Distributors, a beer distributor
> Breese, IL

The game of baseball was once described as an exercise of survival. Vern made it to the bright lights in '65, but succumbed after his one and only mound appearance for the Tigers after he allowed two runs in three innings of work in relief.

The right-hander made the giant leap from Rocky Mount in the Class A Carolina League to Detroit.

HOLTZMAN, Ken
> Insurance business
> Lincolnshire, IL

Hailed as the "new Koufax" when he first arrived with the Cubs in '66, Ken never was quite another Koufax, but the Jewish left-hander did have his moments en route to a 174-150 mark that covered 14 years. Actually he won 9 more games than Sandy but also lost 63 more. He ranks second in victories among Jewish pitchers to Ed Reulbach who had 182.

The only man to play for three of the most colorful managers ever (Leo Durocher, Earl Weaver, and Billy Martin), Ken was an All-American at the University of Illinois where he signed a $65,000 bonus with the Cubs. His father was a friend of Cardinals' general manager Bing Devine, having played amateur basketball with him. Bing had the inside track at signing Ken for St. Louis, but feeling he wasn't a big league prospect, failed to do so. Devine later signed Ken's brother, also a pitcher, but did a belly flop since he never made it to the majors.

During the first month of the '67 campaign, Ken reeled off five straight wins before he was called to military service on May 20th. He then made scattered appearances on a week-end pass from his base at Ft. Sam Houston in Texas late in the season. On Sept. 25th Ken outdueled Sandy Koufax in a Hebrew classic by a score of 2-1 after holding the Dodgers hitless for the first eight innings. He finished the year 9-0, giving him the distinction as one of four pitchers in big league history to have had undefeated seasons with nine or more wins. The others are Joe Pate of the A's (9-0 in 1926), Tom Zachary of the Yankees (12-0 in 1929), and Howie Krist of the Cardinals (10-0 in 1941).

Holtzman's first of two no-hitters came on August 19, 1969, when he blanked the Braves, 3-0. His next was a 1-0 victory over the Reds on June 3, 1971. In his first no-hitter, Ken accomplished the feat despite recording no strikeouts in the game.

In 1971 Ken struggled (9-15) and publicly expressed his distaste for Wrigley Field, commenting: "I hate this ballpark, and never want to pitch here again." Durocher accommodated Holtzman by refusing to use him the rest of the season. He was then shipped to Oakland for Rick Monday. Ken joined Vida Blue and Catfish Hunter as key starters for Oakland's three-year run of world championships. From 1972–74 the crafty southpaw won 19, 21, and 19 games.

Despite a 2-3 record in ALCS competition from '72–'75, he had a 2.06 ERA. In World Series play he was 4-1. Ken was a 3-2 winner in the opener of the '72 Series against the Reds. The next year he beat the Mets, 5-2, in the seventh and deciding game.

He was traded to Baltimore in '76 along with Reggie Jackson. In mid-season he went to the Yankees. Although his wish was to never pitch in Wrigley Field again, Ken finished up his career with the Cubs in 1979.

HOPKINS, Gail
    Orthopedic surgeon
    Chicago, IL

One of the best educated players of his era, Gail combined his medical studies with a career in baseball. The first baseman was in the big arena for seven years (1968–74) with the White Sox, Royals, and Dodgers.

A .266 lifetime hitter, Gail had his best year in 1970 when he hit .286 for the Chisox. At the time, he also graduated from Rush Medical College and was a resident at the Loyola University Medical Center in Chicago. Hopkins, who won a batting title playing in Japan in the mid-1970s,

also attended UCLA, received a degree in biology from
Pepperdine, and a Ph.D in biochemistry from Illinois Tech.

HORLEN, Joel
Home construction business; golf coach at the University of Texas
San Antonio, TX

If you ever confused Joe Hoerner with Joel Horlen, join the
crowd. However, there were differences between the two.

Joel signed with the White Sox in 1959 after pitching
Oklahoma State to the NCAA championship. In his first
season in pro ball he struggled to a 1-9 mark in the low minors. Five years later he had the second-best ERA in the
American League in 1964 at 1.88.

Horlen was the talk of the Windy City in 1967 when he
logged a 19-7 record, leading the Junior Circuit in winning
percentage (.731) and ERA(2.06). He also led the league in
shutouts with six, including a no-hitter over the Tigers at
Comiskey Park on September 10th.

Released during the players' strike at the start of the '72
season, he signed with Oakland where he spent his final
year as a member of the World Champion A's.

His first attempt at a no-hitter came on July 29, 1963.
After holding the Senators hitless for 8⅓ innings, he gave
up a single. Then with two out Don Lock homered and
Horlen lost the game 2-1.

Joe claimed chewing gum bloated him and tobacco
made him sick, so he chewed tissue paper while on the
mound.   116-117

HORTON, Tony
Banker
Santa Monica, CA

Emotional problems brought to an end the promising career of this 25-year-old outfielder late in the 1970 season.
In recounting Tony's situation, his manager Alvin Dark in
his book *When in Doubt, Fire The Manager,* called it "the
most sorrowful incident I was ever involved in in my baseball career."

An outstanding scholastic athlete who was voted the Los Angeles High School Athlete of the Year in 1962, Tony signed with the Red Sox and surfaced in 1964. Traded to Cleveland during the '67 season, Tony had his finest year in '69 with 27 home runs and 93 RBIs. The following year he hit for the cycle in one game and on May 24th delivered three homers in a contest. When he departed he had a .268 avg.

Tony once demonstrated his embarrassment by crawling back to the dugout in Yankee Stadium after he hit a foul pop to Yankee catcher Thurman Munson on a Steve Hamilton "Folly Floater" pitch.

Tony was the only major league regular of the 1960s who did not consent to have his picture used on a Topps gum baseball picture card. He did allow his picture to be used on a 1971 Kellogg's Cereal card after illness ended his career.

HORTON, Willie
    Detroit Tigers minor league hitting instructor

If somebody ever picks an All-Superstitious team, Willie would certainly have a spot in the lineup along with Julio Gotay, who was profiled earlier. For some reason Willie would not part with his original batting helmet as a member of the Tigers. He carried it with him throughout his career which also included time with the Rangers, Indians, A's, Blue Jays, and Mariners from 1963–80. He simply applied a new coat of paint to his precious helmet wherever he went. Horton also kept the same shoes, carefully placing shoe trees in them after each game and making certain they suffered a minimum of wear.

But maybe Willie's eccentricities could be justified since he did have a good thing going with a lifetime .273 average and 325 home runs. In between he drove in 1,163 runs. Keep the helmet and shoes, Willie!

A native of Detroit, Willie was scouted carefully by the Tigers after a sensational high school and amateur career in Detroit. As a 16-year-old, he was labeled as a "must get" prospect after belting a homer into the Tiger Stadium right field pavilion.

Horton hit a pinch-hit single in his first big league at-bat, then hit a pinch-hit homer off Robin Roberts in his second major league at-bat. For the next several years he terrorized A.L. pitchers with his lethal stick. During Detroit's '68 championship season, Willie hit a career-high 36 four-baggers and in the World Series against the Cardinals he batted .304 with a home run.

Willie remained in the Bengals' outfield the next several years, but mounting injuries curtailed his playing time. He was the Tigers' designated hitter from 1975 until he was traded to Texas early in the '77 season. In '79 Horton was the Mariners' designated hitter in all of the team's 162 games. He managed to wallop 29 homers and hit .279 that year. In one game he was robbed of his 300th homer and had to settle for a single when he banged out a howitzer that struck a speaker in the Kingdome. His efforts, which included 106 RBIs, earned him the "Comeback Player of the Year Award."

Willie was accustomed to hitting foreign objects in the air. Long before Dave Winfield was picking off pigeons in Toronto, Willie mortally wounded a pigeon after hitting a towering fly ball near the area of home plate in a 1974 contest at Fenway Park. The pigeon crash landed and scared the Tiger out of Willie's tank.

After the Mariners traded him to the Rangers, he wound up hanging on in the P.C.L. and in Mexico before retiring.

HOUSE, Pat
  Owns an air conditioning company
  Boise, ID

At the time we listened to the Animals' hit *House of the Rising Sun,* left-hander Pat House was attempting to rise to the majors after signing with the Braves out of the University of Wyoming, where he graduated with a degree in mechanical engineering. He finally rose with the Astros in '67 and set the following year, going 2-1 in 24 games.

House commented, "I have been active in youth baseball programs as a director and coach. I have fond memories of my involvement in baseball. It was a large part of my life for many years and still is today."

HOVLEY, Steve
    Plumber
    Ojai, CA

In Jim Bouton's classic *Ball Four,* Steve came across as the long-haired intellectual with the Seattle Pilots in 1969 who went with the team to Milwaukee in 1970. In the return of major league baseball to the beer city, the Brewers were shut out, 12-0, by Andy Messersmith (Angels) on a 4-hitter with Steve managing three of the hits. In June he was fined by manager Dave Bristol for coming late to a practice, but refused to pay the fine and was traded to Oakland.

When it ended in 1973 with the Royals, the articulate outfielder posted a .258 average.

HOWARD, Bruce
    Owns the Bruce Howard Insurance Agency
    Sarasota, FL

The White Sox signed Bruce out of Villanova in 1962. They also inked Denny McLain at the time, and the two became friends while pitching for Clinton (Midwest League) that year. The rule then stated a team could keep just one designated first-year player on their minor league team and the White Sox elected to keep Bruce while McLain went to the Tigers on waivers.

Howard won nine games for the Chisox in both '65 and '66. Prior to the '68 season he made a friendly wager with McLain of $5 over who would win the most games. Bruce lost the bet, 31-1.

The right-hander closed with the Orioles and Senators in '68 for a lifetime mark of 26-31.

HOWSER, Dick
    Kansas City Royals' manager

Only four managers in the history of major league baseball have won 100 or more games as a first-year skipper— Ralph Houk (109 in '61), Sparky Anderson (102 in '70), Mickey Cochrane (101 in '34), and Dick Howser (103 in '80, when he led the Yankees to first place in the American League East). The skipper of the Royals since 1981, Dick broke into pro ball after graduating from Florida State University where he starred for the Seminoles from 1954–58, earning All-American honors as a shortstop in 1957–58. As a sophomore he set the school record with a .422 average.

Dick began his eight-year American League stay in 1961 with the Kansas City A's and was named the American League Rookie of the Year by *The Sporting News* after hitting .280 and pilfering 37 bases. He also played with the Indians and Yankees before hanging it up after the '68 season with a lifetime .248 mark.

At only 31 years old he was made the Yankees' third base coach, succeeding Frank Crosetti who had been associated with the Yankees as a player and coach for 37 years. Dick was the third base coach in the Bronx until 1978.

Howser took over as head baseball coach at his alma mater in 1979. The next year he was George Steinbrenner's skipper, but was caught up in the Yankees' swinging door of managers.

HRINIAK, Walt
Boston Red Sox hitting coach

When Carl Yastrzemski connected for career base hit No. 3,000, he presented Walt with a gold watch with the inscription, "I couldn't have done it without you."

Pronounced Rin-ee-ack, Walt has been in baseball since signing a reported $50,000 contract with the Braves in 1961. His 13-year pro playing career included two years with the Braves and Padres as a catcher in 1968–69, although he started in organized baseball as a shortstop.

Playing for Austin (Texas League) in 1964, he was injured in an auto accident which shelved him for most of the season. A teammate, Jerry Hummitzsch, was killed in the accident.

Today Walt is recognized as one of the best batting practice pitchers in the game and conducts a hitting school for several weeks in the off-season.   .253

HUBBS, Ken
> Died on Feb. 13, 1964, at age 22 in Utah Lake, Utah, where a private plane he was piloting crashed.

Ken first emerged with the Cubs for ten games in 1961 and in his first full season in '62 he was named the National League Rookie of the Year after hitting .260 in 160 games. His 661 at-bats was an N.L. record for a rookie. Hubbs also established N.L. records for fielding at second base, going 78 consecutive games and 418 straight chances without committing an error. His totals after the '63 season showed a .247 mark in 324 games.

Ken obtained his pilot's license just two weeks before his fatal crash. He was en route home to California from Chicago after signing his contract for the 1964 season.

His 1962 record of 418 consecutive errorless chances at second base held up until late in the 1978 season when it was broken by the Orioles' Rich Dauer. Ironically enough, Dauer is from the same small town of Colton, CA, as Ken. In 1962 when Hubbs set the record, Rich was playing Little League baseball in Colton, and his coach was Ken Hubbs' father.

HUDSON, Jesse
> Location unknown

Jesse James Hudson was somewhat of a bandit to Appalachian and Northern League batters in 1967 as the left-hander led the circuit in several categories, but was a quiet citizen in the majors, working just two innings of one game for the 1969 Mets.

HUGHES, Dick
> Cattle rancher
> Stephens, AR

The life expectancy of a 29-year-old rookie in the majors is normally not too long. Such was true with Dick, but the limited time he had was put to good use.

Signed out of the University of Arkansas in 1958, he toiled for nine years in the bushes before joining the Cardinals in 1966. The following year he was a key factor in the Cards' National League pennant with a 16-6 record, the best winning percentage in the National League. However, he didn't have much luck in the World Series against the Red Sox as he set a dubious WS mark by allowing three home runs in one inning.

An ailing shoulder cut short his late-blooming career after a 2-2 record in 1968. Dick's belated and relatively short stay shows a 20-9 mark with a 2.79 ERA.

HUMPHREYS, Bob
Milwaukee Brewers' Coordinator of Player Development

Hubert H. Humphrey was in Washington as Vice-President when Bob Humphreys arrived in the nation's capital as a relief specialist. The hard-throwing right-hander was around for nine years (1962–70) with the Tigers, Cardinals, Cubs, Senators, and Brewers. Most of his time was spent in Washington, where he went 21-15 from '66 to '70.

HUNDLEY, Randy
Operates adult fantasy baseball camps in Scottsdale, AZ; manager at Iowa (American Association)

Tall, wiry, and durable are words that appropriately describe Randy, who signed a bonus estimated at over $100,000 by the Giants out of high school in 1960. Following brief trials with the Giants in '64 and '65, he was traded to the Cubs, where his career blossomed. Randy broke into the Chicago lineup in '66 by establishing an N.L. record for games caught by a rookie (149). His 19 homers were the most by a Cubs' catcher since Gabby Hartnett hit 22 in 1934.

An outstanding defensive catcher and field leader, he set a major league record for catchers in 1967, appearing in 150 or more games and making only four errors, erasing a record held since 1949 by Cleveland's Jim Hegan.

He played in 160 of the Cubs' 163 games in '68, setting still another mark for most appearances by a catcher.

After four years of averaging over 150 games a season

he was set back by injuries with a chipped bone in his hand in 1970, then missed most of the '71 season following knee surgery. Following one season each with the Twins and Padres, he returned to Wrigley Field to close his career with the Cubs in 1976.

Randy's 14-year jaunt finished with a .990 fielding average, and a .236 batting average.

HUNT, Ken
    English teacher and basketball coach at Morgan High School
    Morgan, UT

In the 1961 World Series the Reds used a record eight pitchers in the fifth and final game against the Yankees. Pitcher number eight that day was Ken Hunt, who hurled a scoreless ninth inning of a game won by the Yankees, 13-5. The appearance proved to be his swan song as he subsequently developed a sore shoulder that put him out of baseball.

Ken was around for just that one year in '61 and made the most of it, chalking up nine wins halfway through the season. But after the All Star break he experienced arm miseries and finished the year 9-10. Hunt was named the N.L. Rookie Pitcher of the Year by *The Sporting News,* but never pitched again in the majors.

HUNT, Ron
    Cattle rancher
    Wentzville, MO

"Some people give their bodies to science; I gave mine to baseball," said Ron. The battle-scarred infielder mastered the art of getting hit by pitches and is the all-time leader with 243 nicks. Leo Durocher once said, "That Hunt is making a mockery of the rule. He's a Goddamn faker." In 1971 Ron was hit by pitches a record 50 times. From 1968–74 he led the majors in that department.

After hitting .272 as a Mets' rookie in 1963, Ron finished second to Pete Rose for the N.L. Rookie of the Year award. In '64 he became the first Met to ever represent the club as a starter for the National League in the All-Star Game, a season he hit .303.

Following the '66 campaign, the hard-nosed second baseman was traded to the Dodgers for Tommy Davis. It was a bit shocking to the Dodgers when Ron announced he was saddened by his trade from the Mets. After one year in L.A., Ron went to San Francisco with his black and blue marks.

From 1971–74 Hunt went north to Montreal before finishing his career in his native St. Louis. His 14-year battle saw him bat .273.

HUNTER, "Catfish"
    Farmer
    Hertford, NC

Eight All-Star games, seven championship series, and six World Series in 15 seasons briefly summarize this man's career in which he went 224-166 lifetime, all this without a day spent in the minors.

Signed by the Kansas City A's in 1964, Jim was on the Daytona Beach roster, but was sidelined after undergoing an appendicitis operation. "Catfish" pitched with the A's their last three years in Kansas City and never went over the .500 mark. On May 8, 1968, he was 13-13 when he pitched the 11th perfect game in major league history, defeating the Twins 4-0. The tobacco-chewing right-hander struck out 11, including Harmon Killebrew three times. Hunter also contributed two singles and a double to knock in three of the four runs that memorable day. Following the historic masterpiece, he faced the same Twins a few days later and was shelled for six runs, including three homers, without surviving the first inning.

Catfish peaked in the early Seventies when he had three consecutive 21-victory seasons, including a 21-5 mark in '73 which gave him a league-leading .808 winning percentage. From 1972–74 he was 4-0 in World Series competition. In '74 he copped the Cy Young Award, going 25-12.

It was at this point that Catfish took the A's to arbitration after a contract dispute with Charlie Finley. He was declared a free agent and signed with the Yankees. His total financial package came to about $3,750,000. Jim was with the Yanks until his retirement after the '79 season.

Hunter was the last pitcher of record for the K.C. A's when he lost to Mel Stottlemyre and the Yankees on Oct. 1, 1967, and is also the last K.C. A's player to appear in an All-Star Game when he pitched the final five innings of the 1967 15-inning marathon at Anaheim. Jim took the loss that night, 2-1.

As a kid Catfish greatly admired the pitching styles of Robin Roberts and Ed Lopat. Like Roberts he was known to serve up a fat one now and then. Because of his pinpoint control, batters dug in and nicked him for 374 home runs, an average of one every 9.22 innings.

Hunter was able to help himself as a batter. In 1971 he hit .350, making him the last A.L. pitcher to win at least 20 games and hit over .300 in a season.

Catfish is lucky to have stepped on a major league diamond. In November 1963 he was the victim of a hunting accident when his brother's gun accidentally misfired, wounding Hunter's right foot. Jim needed two operations to remove bullet fragments and his little toe had to be amputated.

HUNTER, Willard
>   Supervisor of computer operations at University Medical Hospital
>   Omaha, NE

Nobody ever confused Willard with "Catfish." The southpaw chucker showed his stuff with the Dodgers and Mets in 1962 and the Mets again in '64, compiling a 4-9 record in 69 games. On June 20, 1962, he pitched a two-hitter for the Mets against the Braves, but came up short when both of the hits he allowed were home runs by Hank Aaron.

Believe it or not, two of his four wins came on the same day when the Mets swept both ends of a doubleheader on Aug. 23, 1964, against the Cubs.

HUNTZ, Steve
    Office supplies salesman
    Cleveland, OH

The Cardinals had plans for Steve in 1965, but he broke his leg in a slide during spring training. He finally made it in '67 with the Redbirds en route to a 237-game career split among the Cards, Padres, and White Sox.

In 1969 with St. Louis, Steve was the only member of the two-time defending National League champions to hit two home runs in a game when he connected twice on September 26th.   .206

HUTTON, Tommy
    Montreal Expos' announcer

Tommy had a taste of just about everything as a professional baseball player. In 1966 he was voted the Texas League Player of the Year when he won the circuit's batting championship with a .340 average. After short stays with the Dodgers in '66 and '69, Tommy had a big year at Spokane, copping the P.C.L. batting title in '71 at .352. He was the consummate player that year, leading the league in hits, runs, doubles, and fielding with a .998 percentage. During the '69 season at Spokane, Hutton even played third base one game as a left-hander for manager Tom Lasorda.

Beginning in '72 Tommy was in the majors to stay as a member of the Phils, helping the club to the N.L. East title in '77 with a .309 average. After one year in the American League with Toronto he closed with the Expos in 1981 where he was used on the mound for one inning of relief work.

Tommy is the brother-in-law of pitcher Dick Ruthven as the two are married to twin sisters. Hutton appeared several times as a bachelor on the *Dating Game* television show but was never chosen.   .248

I

IZQUIERDO, "Hank"
Minnesota Twins' scout in Florida and Latin America
Miami, FL

Pronounced (iz-quar-dough), Enrique Roberto "Hank" Izquierdo was a Cuban refugee who spent several seasons as a bullpen catcher for the Cleveland Indians without actually being on the team's roster.

"Hank" eventually signed a playing contract with the Twins and made it into 16 games in 1967, hitting .269.

Five years before he ever played in a big league game, Izquierdo was thrown out of one. In 1962 umpire Ed Hurley asked "Hank" to retrieve a ball which had rolled onto the field from the Cleveland bullpen. "Hank" ignored Hurley who promptly threw him out of the game. The Indians argued it was a misunderstanding that he didn't understand English, but Hurley responded, "His English was excellent after I threw him out."

The Cuban backstop survived gunshot wounds from a robbery in the early 1970s when he was working as a cab driver in Miami.

J

JACKSON, Grant
Pittsburgh Pirates' pitching coach

Grant was around long enough (1965–82) to count among his teammates Tito Francona (Phils in '67) and Tito's son, Terry (Expos in '82). A veteran of over 18 seasons, Grant Dwight Jackson, known to his friends as "Buck," broke in with the Phils in '65. He moved to Baltimore in 1971 and stayed with the Birds until mid-1976. While with the Orioles he developed the reputation as a sound relief specialist.

Jackson appeared in the ALCS in '73 and '74 and in the 1971 World Series with the Orioles. In '73 he helped the O's to the A.L. East title going 8-0 with nine saves.

The left-hander had a knack of being in the right place at the right time. On June 15, 1976 he was traded to the Yankees as part of a 10-player deal, and went on to perform in the '76 ALCS and World Series with the Yanks after going 6-0 for them.

Although selected by the Mariners in the expansion draft, he never pitched for Seattle because he was acquired by the Pirates, where he was employed from 1977–1981. Grant teamed with Kent Tekulve and Enrique Romo to give the Pirates a formidable bullpen staff. In 1979 he racked up a win over the Reds in the NLCS and a World Series victory over the Orioles. Jackson shares the NLCS and World Series records by appearing in each with three different clubs. The only other players to appear in a World Series with three different teams are Andy Pafko, Eddie Stanky, and Vic Davalillo.

After finishing the '81 season with the Expos he made stops with the Royals and Pirates once again.   86-75

JACKSON, Reggie
      Active player with California Angels

"I don't want to be liked, I just want to be respected."
                                        —Reggie Jackson

Whether or not you like Reginald Martinez Jackson, you probably should respect him, at least between the foul lines. Labeled as Mr. October, the title appropriately fits the autumn achievements of this controversial superstar. From the time his career began in 1967 with the Kansas City A's, he has participated in 71 post-season games. While with the A's, Jackson-led teams appeared in five Championship and three World Series; with the Yankees four Championship and three WS, and one ALCS with the Angels. In five WS he owns a .357 average with 10 home runs and 24 RBIs. Overall he has 18 post-season home runs.

His three-homer show in Game Six of the 1977 Series against the Dodgers came on successive pitches off Burt Hooten, Elias Sosa, and Charlie Hough. The only other player to hit three homers in a World Series game was Babe Ruth in 1926.

He is one of a quartet of players to hit 400 or more home runs and steal 200 or more bases. The others are Hank Aaron, Willie Mays, and Frank Robinson. Of everything Jackson is remembered for, it is unlikely that he is recalled as the only player to ever steal home in a LCS when he pilfered the dish in the '72 LCS. On the play he suffered a pulled hamstring and was unable to take part in the Series.

Probably his most dynamic four-bagger was the moon shot he hit in the 1971 All-Star Game at Detroit which struck the transformer on top of the roof at Tiger Stadium.

Following one year in Baltimore (1976), George Steinbrenner brought Reggie to New York. For the next five years the Steinbrenner-Jackson-Martin skit developed into the longest running show on Broadway.

Jackson, who was signed out of Arizona State by the Kansas City A's for a bonus of $90,000, will be remembered in a variety of ways. It may be his top button opened on his shirt, his bent forward trot, the "Reggie Bar," or whatever.

At this writing Reggie has 503 homers and a lifetime .265 average.

JACKSON, "Sonny"
    Atlanta Braves' coach in 1983

Maury Wills wasn't the only Washington native breaking big league stolen base records during the mid-Sixties. In his first full season with the Astros in 1966, Roland "Sonny" Jackson hit .292 with a N.L. Rookie record 49 thefts. This also tied the M.L. mark of 49 set back in 1910 by Rollie Zeider of the White Sox. On the final day of the season he had a shot at breaking the record, but after drawing a base on balls in his final at-bat, Sonny was picked off first base.

Sonny was a highly recruited football star in high school. He turned down a scholarship offer to be the first black player at the University of Maryland to sign with Houston.

The speedy little shortstop hit just seven home runs in his 12-year career. Three of them came in his rookie season and all were first inning inside-the-park jobs in the spacious Astrodome.

After the '67 campaign he was dealt to Atlanta where it all ended in 1974 with a .251 average.

JACOBS, Lamar
    Financial planner with Corporate Benefit Planners Agency, Inc.
    Canfield, OH

"Jake" combined a career in professional baseball with work in the music business as a singer, composer, and recording artist. Among his recordings on the RCA label was a tune titled *Hey, Little Ducky*.

There wasn't much that was ducky about this flychaser's ten-game string in which he went 2-for-10 (.200) with the Senators and Twins in 1960–61.

JAECKEL, Paul
    Salesman for Rolled Steel Corporation
    Claremont, CA

Hey, Paula by Paul and Paula topped the music charts during the mid-Sixties, a time when Paul Jaeckel became a big league pitcher with the Cubs.

Paul started out as a shortstop in the Cubs' chain in 1960. After hitting an anemic .199 the Cubs' brass said, "Hey Paul—try pitching." He did and after compiling records of 5-12 and 10-18 "earned" a promotion to the National League.

Jaeckel won his only decision in four games and was credited with a save, his win coming on Sept. 24, 1964, against the Dodgers at Wrigley Field. During his mini

stay he allowed no runs in the eight innings he worked.
For some reason he was never used in the majors again.

JAMES, Charlie
President of Central Electric Co.
Fulton, MO

Charlie was often called "Stan Musial's caddy" when he
first came up with the Cardinals in 1960. "It didn't bother
me one way or another," responded Charlie when asked
about his "caddy" handle.

A native of St. Louis, James played in his hometown until 1964 before finishing with the Reds in '65. The outfielder swung at a .255 clip in 510 games.

Before entering pro baseball, Charlie dazzled pro football scouts as a running back at the University of Missouri
and was drafted by the New York Giants of the N.F.L. But
he chose baseball since the diamond sport was always his
first love.

Charlie received a B.S. and a master's degree in electrical engineering from Washington University in St. Louis,
where he later was an instructor.

JAMES, Cleo
Riverside, CA

Cleo made it into ten games with the Dodgers in 1968 after
spending several years scratching and clawing his way to
the big top. At Spokane in 1969 he was named "Player of
the Year" in the P.C.L.

Most of his time in the majors was spent with the Cubs.
On Sept. 3, 1970, he was in left field for the Cubbies and
had a 1-for-4 day at the plate in a 7-2 victory over the
Phillies. The significance in this is that he was replacing
Billy Williams in the Chicago lineup when Billy ended his
1,117 consecutive game playing streak, a record since
broken by Steve Garvey.   .228

JAMES, Jeff
　　Employed with a lumber company
　　Springfield, OR

Not as illustrious a product of Indiana State University as Larry Bird or Tommy John, Jeff signed with the Phillies and was up with them in 1968 and '69 to go 6-6 as a spot starter and reliever in 35 games.

JAMES, Rick
　　Home construction business
　　Panama City, FL

The Cubs selected Rick as their No. 1 draft choice in the first major league free agent draft in June of 1965. His selection was not a profitable one as the right-hander appeared in only three games for Chicago in 1967 and was a loser in his only decision.

JARVIS, Pat
　　Dekalb County Sheriff
　　Dunwood, GA

Prior to his baseball career, Pat had a background in rodeos as a bucking bronco rider. However, life in the biggies was rather smooth for this right-hander, who had an 85-73 record when his eight-year hitch ended.

Jarvis, who spent the first seven years of his career with the Atlanta Braves, came in kicking, winning his first five starts. For the next four years he was a steady member of the Atlanta starting rotation, twice winning 16 games. On June 30, 1970, Pat beat Cincinnati, 8-2, in the first game ever played in Riverfront Stadium.

During his playing days he began work in vocational rehabilitation centers in the Atlanta area. Jarvis spent his final season in Montreal where his ride ended in '73.

JARVIS, Ray
    Marketing manager for the U.S. and in charge of sales
    for Canada for U.D.N. America (United German Nick-
    el Works)
    North Providence, RI

The poster boom peaked in 1969 as an estimated $20 mil-
lion worth of posters were sold including the classic "Keep
On Truckin'."
    It was also a year Ray began a 44-game trek with the
Red Sox that ended at 5-7 the following year. The right-
hander hurt his arm in spring training and his wing never
came around. The Bosox apparently saw enough and Ray
was told to "keep on truckin."
    When asked about the highlight of his career, he says,
"The day I struck out five times in a nine-inning game
against Cleveland." That certainly is an unusual highlight for a pitcher!

JASTER, Larry
    Assistant baseball coach at the University of New
    Mexico

Larry's seven-year N.L. career is best remembered for
his mastery of the Los Angeles Dodgers in 1966. The
left-handed pitcher was a thorn to the Dodgers who
never did figure him out that summer. He faced the
World Champs five times and shut them out on all five
occasions, allowing 24 hits (all singles) for a cumulative
.157 batting average. Over the 45 innings he struck out
31 and walked just 8. Between his first and second shutouts Larry was optioned to Tulsa for six weeks. He finished the year at 11-5 with a 3.26 ERA. In 1905 Tom
Hughes of Washington blanked the Indians five times
and in 1916 Grover Cleveland Alexander shut out the
Reds five times but neither accomplished the feat in
succession. Larry was saluted on the *Ed Sullivan Show*
for his Dodger dominance.
    "There were several occasions when we turned the dou-
ble play. I also had success keeping Maury Wills and

Willie Davis off base. Plus the defense behind me was good."

Larry received a reported $60,000 to sign with St. Louis in 1962 out of high school, turning down a football scholarship offer to Michigan State. He arrived with the Cards in '65 and went to Montreal after the '68 season, disenchanted with his role as a relief pitcher with the Cardinals. Pitching for the Expos against his former team on April 14, 1969, he threw the first major league pitch in Canada.

Jaster's journey terminated with the Braves in '72. Larry's brother Danny was also a pitcher in the St. Louis chain, but never reached the majors.

JAVIER, Julian
    Retired
    Dominican Republic

"Hoolie" began in the Pirates organization, but found Bill Mazeroski blocking his way at second base in Pittsburgh.

On Aug. 9, 1961 Julian celebrated his 25th birthday with a grand-slam in a 4-0 Cardinal victory over the Pirates. Two years later he was part of an all-Cardinal infield to start the 1963 All-Star Game. Sept. 13, 1964, was the last time a major league team scored at least one run in all nine innings of a game when St. Louis did the trick against the Cubs in a 15-2 rout. Javier led the carnage with a home run and a pair of doubles.

During the Sixties the slick-fielding Dominican second baseman helped the Cardinals to three N.L. pennants and two World Championships. He suffered a late-season hip injury in 1964 and had to be replaced by Dal Maxvill in the World Series win over the Yankees.

Julian had a sparkling '67 season with the World Champion Cardinals. Javier drove in the winning run in the pennant clincher and the two games immediately preceding it. He hit .281 with a career-high 14 home runs. In the World Series against the Red Sox he hit .360 in the seven games. His two-out double in the eighth inning of Game Two was the only hit off Boston's Jim Lonborg as the

Bosox won, 5-0. In the '68 Fall Classic against Detroit
Javier hit .333 in a losing effort.

After a dozen seasons in St. Louis, Javier closed his impressive 13-year trip with the N.L. pennant-winning Reds
in 1972.   .257

JENKINS, Ferguson
     Owns farm and raises Limousin and Aberdeen Angus
     pedigree cattle for breeding stock bulls
     Blenheim, Ontario

Fergie's career (1965–83) was a prestigious one with a
never-ending list of milestones. After a brief time in Philadelphia he was traded to the Cubs for veteran pitchers
Larry Jackson and Bob Buhl early in '66. From 1967–72
Jenkins went on a six-year tear, winning 20 or more games
each season. In 1968, when he finished 20-15, he tied a
major league record for frustration by being on the losing
end of five 1-0 games. He is one of three right-handers with
at least seven 20-win years since 1920. The others are Bob
Lemon (7) and Jim Palmer (8).

In '71 he led the league in wins (24) and complete games
(30). The Cy Young Award winner that year, he also walloped six home runs.

Jenkins set a new Cubs' strikeout mark in '67 when he
fanned 236, breaking a 58-year-old club standard. In the
All-Star Game that summer Fergie tied a record with six
strikeouts in three innings of work. Ferguson's single-
season career high in strikeouts came in '69 when he
whiffed a league-leading 273 batters.

The 6'5" hurler always seemed to have a flare for the
dramatic in Chicago. When he made his debut with the
Cubs it was in a relief stint against the Dodgers in '66. He
shut them out for six innings, then hit a home run to win
the game, 2-0. He was the first Cub pitcher since Lon
Warneke (1934–35) to have back-to-back 20-win seasons
(1967–68).

In the late Sixties, Fergie gave up home runs on a
nightly basis during the off-season while on tour with the
famed Harlem Globetrotters. The batter each time was
Meadowlark Lemon, the renowned basketball clown. A

limited part-time player for the Trotters, he was a full-time advance publicity man for them.

Following a 14-16 year in '73 he was sent packing to the Rangers for Bill Madlock and responded with a 25-12 season in his first tour of the American League and was named "Comeback Player of the Year" for his accomplishments. He then shifted gears to Boston (1976–77), where pitching was a dirty word, then returned to Texas in '78. Pitching for the Rangers on May 15, 1981 Fergie recorded career win No. 261 with a 2-1 win over the White Sox, making him the winningest hurler in major league history to never participate on a pennant or division winner. The item was totally overshadowed when Len Barker of the Indians threw a perfect game the same night.

Released by the Cubs early in the '84 season, after spending the '82 and '83 seasons at Wrigley, Ferguson departed as the only pitcher to collect 3,000 strikeouts with less than 1,000 walks. He also owns the career record for most putouts (363) by a pitcher. Jenkins and Walter Johnson are the only two pitchers to have five consecutive seasons with both 20 wins and 200 strikeouts.

Fergie joins Gaylord Perry, Cy Young, and Jim Bunning as the only pitchers to win 100 games in both leagues. Lifetime he owns a 284-226 record to go with his 3,192 strikeouts and 3.34 ERA.

Jenkins' reputation was tarnished in 1980 after his bag, when inspected in a Canadian airport, revealed two ounces of marijuana, four grams of cocaine, and two grams of hashish. He was subsequently suspended by Baseball Commissioner Bowie Kuhn and found guilty in court. However, the Judge decided to erase the verdict due to Ferguson's clean record.

JENKINS, Jack
    Salesman for Spicola Hardware, a sporting goods dis-
    tributor
    Tampa, FL

Jack's real name is Warren Washington Jenkins. He was a
right-handed pitcher who appeared with the Washington
Senators in 1962 and 1963 and then made it back to the
majors with the Dodgers in 1969.   0-3

JESTADT, Garry
    Insurance business
    Sunnyvale, CA

Hurricane Camille caused quite a stir in 1969, the year
Garry blew in with the Expos. After stops with the Cubs
and Padres, Garry drifted out to sea in '72, having hit .260
in 176 contests. The infielder later played in Japan before
returning to Phoenix (he attended Arizona State), where
he was an announcer for the P.C.L. team there.

JETER, John
    Change handler for Amusement Consultants
    Yonkers, NY

"The Jet" was a natural nickname for this lightning-quick
runner out of Grambling University. Jeter, who was
clocked at 9.5 seconds for the 100-yard dash, played in
parts of six seasons with the Pirates, White Sox, and Indians from 1969–74.   .244

JIMINEZ, Elvio
    Los Angeles Dodgers' scout/instructor in Winter
    League baseball in the Dominican Republic

Elvio qualifies as a one-game player for the Yankees in 1964.
He made good use of his limited time, going 2-for-6 that day.
    The Dominican outfielder spent virtually all of his pro-
fessional baseball career hitting well over the .300 mark.

In 1967 he hit .340 at Columbus to win the International League batting title.

JIMINEZ, Manny
      San Pedro de Macoris, Dominican Republic

While Elvio was given limited opportunity to swing at major league pitching, his older brother Manny was in and out of the big arena from 1962–1969 with the Kansas City A's, Pirates, and Cubs, hitting for a .272 average in 429 games.

As a rookie in '62, he was named to the Topps Rookie All-Star team when he hit .301 in 139 games as a regular in the A's outfield. On July 4, 1964, Jiminez hit 3 consecutive homers in a tie game halted after 9 innings for a fireworks display.

JOHN, Tommy
      Active with California Angels

Tommy's pitching arm was pronounced dead when he ruptured a ligament in his left elbow on July 1, 1974, while on the mound for the Dodgers. Two months later Dr. Frank Jobe performed revolutionary surgery when he took a tendon from Tommy's right forearm and used it to reconstruct his left elbow. Jobe told John that the odds of him ever pitching again were 100-1. He defied the odds and returned in '76. Over a hundred victories later, Tommy is still making a living as a big league pitcher. He calls himself the only right-handed southpaw because of his tendon transplant.

The left-handed sinkerball specialist, who attended Indiana State, first came up with the Indians in '61. Since that time he has pitched for the White Sox (1965–71), Dodgers (1972–78), Yankees (1979–82) and Angels from late '82 to the present. He is one of a select group in baseball history to win 20 or more games in both leagues. Tommy was 20-7 for the 1977 Dodgers and with the Yankees went 21-9 in '79 and 22-9 in '80. Some others to accomplish the feat are Jerry Koosman, Andy Messersmith, Gaylord Perry, Ferguson Jenkins, Joe McGinnity, Jesse Tannenhill and

Al Orth. His record in post-season play stands at 6-3 (2-1 in World Series). Through 1984 he has a 255-197 mark.

Despite being known for his excellent control, he tied an A.L. record on June 15, 1968, when he hit four batters in a nine-inning game. Later that season Tommy suffered a shoulder injury in a battle with the Tigers' Dick McAuliffe after plunking the Detroit infielder with a pitch.

John has authored two books: *The Tommy John Story* and with wife Sally, *The Sally and Tommy John Story,* a book that recounts the qualities of love and caring and how their Christian faith helped sustain them through near tragedy when their 3-year-old son Travis fell 27 feet from an apartment window on August 13, 1981, and survived 14 days in a coma.   255-197

JOHNSON, Alex
    Employed in family auto repair business
    Detroit MI

Just about the time the movie *It's a Mad, Mad, Mad World* was popular, this moody outfielder made his entrance into the big league world. Alex terrorized opposing pitchers and just about everyone he encountered, including managers, teammates, fans, and reporters.

The brother of former New York Giants' running back Ron Johnson, Alex was also an outstanding high school football player, but elected a career in baseball. Wherever he played he could always hit the rock with consistency. It was once said that "a bat to Alex Johnson was like a golf club to Arnold Palmer."

Baseball's angry man was around for 13 seasons (1964–76), but never remained with the same team for more than two years. Alex carried his suitcase with the Phillies, Cardinals, Reds, Angels, Indians, Rangers, Yankees, and Tigers. In 1971 psychiatrists agreed that the troubled outfielder "was unable to play because of a mental condition" and recommended that he be placed on the disabled list instead of suspended with loss of salary. He thus became the first player ever placed on the disabled list for mental illness.

In 1970 Alex edged Carl Yastrzemski for the American

League batting title while playing for the Angels. Both finished at .328, but with averages carried out to another decimal point (.3289 to .3286), Johnson was declared the batting king. This made him just the third player in major league history to win the batting title in his first year after transferring from the National League. Ed Delahanty (1902) and Frank Robinson (1966) were the others.

Johnson was named the N.L. Comeback Player of the Year in 1968 when he batted .312 following a .223 season the year before. When he departed he showed a lifetime .288 average.

JOHNSON, Bart
Chicago White Sox special assignment scout
Palos Hills, IL

Bart was once involved in a rare protest involving his uniform when he pitched with the White Sox early in the 1976 season in a game at Yankee Stadium. The Chisox invaded the Bronx wearing their new threads—Navy blue pants and blouses, clamdiggers, white hats, white lettering, and white undershirts. Yankee manager Billy Martin thought it was a no-no to wear white undershirts, expecially by the pitcher since it could be a distraction. Umpire Marty Springstead agreed, but wasn't sure. Since it was too late to check with the league office, the umpire ordered Bart to remove the white-sleeved shirt. The jersey was snipped with a scissors, and Johnson conducted his pitching chores.

Chicago manager Paul Richards protested the game which the Yankees won, 5-4. American League President Lee MacPhail ruled the white shirts were acceptable, but disallowed the protest lodged by the White Sox.

Although Bart wore White Sox and a white undershirt, his overall mark was not so bright at 39-46 between 1969–76.

JOHNSON, Bob D.
    Co-owner of B&R general contractors
    Santa Ana, CA

Bob's pitching career almost ended before it began when
he suffered a serious leg injury in a motorcycle accident in
1967 while playing in the Eastern League. For a time it
was feared his leg would have to be amputated. But fortunately he recovered and after going 13-4 in the Texas
League in 1969 Bob was invited to join the Mets, where he
made a couple of relief appearances late in the season.
    Following the miracle year of '69 he was traded with
Amos Otis to the Kansas City Royals for Joe Foy. Bob was
only 8-13 in '70, but with his 206 strikeouts, he became the
first American League rookie pitcher since Herb Score in
1955 to strike out 200. After one year in Kansas City
Johnson was shipped to the Pirates where he went 9-10 for
the N.L. East Division Champs. He pitched the most important victory of his career in the third game of the
NLCS, outdueling Juan Marichal, 2-1, giving the Bucs a
2-1 lead in a series they won in five games.
    The right-hander settled with Pittsburgh for the next
two years, then completed his seven-year voyage in 1974
after stops with the Braves and Indians.   28-33

JOHNSON, Bob W.
    Sales representative for a liquor wholesaler
    St. Paul, MN

On April 9, 1962, Bob hit the first home run in D.C. Stadium in Washington off Don Mossi (Tigers) with President
John F. Kennedy in attendance. But that is mere trivia
compared to some of the accomplishments of this utility infielder and pinch-hitter deluxe. He appeared in over 100
games at every infield position in a career that ran from
1960–1970 with the Kansas City A's, Senators, Orioles,
Mets, Reds, Braves, and again with the A's in Oakland.
    As a member of the Orioles in '63, Bob had a streak
of eight consecutive base hits. Johnson set an American
League record for most consecutive hits as a pinch-hitter

with six between June 26 and July 14 (1964). His 15 pinch-hits led the junior circuit that year.

Bob's mark of .272 in 874 games includes some interesting double-digit totals that might intrigue numerology buffs. His 11-year career includes 88 doubles, 11 triples, 44 home runs, and 66 pinch-hits.

JOHNSON, Dave
New York Mets' manager

The only man able to call both Hank Aaron and Sadaharu Oh teammates, Dave signed with the Orioles out of Texas A&M. He later earned a master's degree in mathematics from Johns Hopkins.

Johnson's 13-year career (1965–1978) was spent with the Orioles, Braves, Phillies, and Cubs. He won three Gold Gloves at second base with the Orioles between 1969–71. A four-time All-Star selection, Dave ripped 43 home runs in '73 for the Braves. Since one of his four-baggers came as a pinch-hitter, Johnson was credited with 42 homers as a second baseman which tied Rogers Hornsby's mark for most home runs by a second baseman. However, some sources credit Dave with 43 since he played the remainder of that game as a second baseman.

In 1973 he was also voted "Comeback Player of the Year" when he hit .270 to go with his 43 roundtrippers and 99 RBIs.

A licensed pilot, Dave was flying high in '78 with the Phils when he became the first pinch-hitter in major league history to hit two grand-slams in one season.   .261

JOHNSON, Deron
Seattle Mariners hitting coach

Only seven players in N.L. history can lay claim to the fact they hit four home runs in four consecutive at-bats. Deron Johnson is one of them. Playing for the Phils on July 11, 1971, he walloped three homers in an 11-5 Philadelphia victory over the Expos. The day before he cracked one in his last at bat.

Deron swung for power during his lengthy 16-year ca-

reer (1960–1976) spent mostly with the Reds and Phils. He
broke in with the Yankees after leading the Nebraska
State League and Eastern League in home runs. However,
his time in the Yankees' organization was spent mostly in
Richmond since the Bronx Bombers were rich in talent.

Johnson, who reached his zenith in '65 with the Reds
when he hit 32 four-baggers and had a league leading 130
RBIs, was named by *The Sporting News* as the All-Star
player at third base that year. In '71 Deron flexed his
muscles and hit a career high 34 roundtrippers for the
Phillies. Johnson became the first player (1973) to have a
20-homer season while playing in both leagues, hitting
one roundtripper for the Phils and 19 for Oakland. Cliff
Johnson and Dave Kingman duplicated the feat in '77.

Deron's well-traveled career has also included stops
with the A's, Braves, Brewers, White Sox, and Red Sox. He
retired with a .244 average and 245 home runs.

JOHNSON, Frank
      Security guard in San Jose, CA

This infielder-outfielder, who used to work at a rocket
manufacturing plant during the off-seasons, had a rather
slow takeoff. In 1965 he hit just .192 at Tacoma in the
P.C.L. Then he began wearing glasses and his average
soared to .308 at Phoenix the next year. Frank joined the
Giants in September (1966) and on September 7th, the first
time he was ever inside a big league stadium, poked a
12th-inning single in his first at-bat to knock in the winning run in a 3-2 victory over the Dodgers.   .211

JOHNSON, Jerry
      San Diego Padres' minor league pitching coach

Jerry's tour started in '68 with the Phillies. Before it was
over in '77, he also earned a living with the Cardinals,
Giants, Indians, Astros, Padres, and Blue Jays. He was
very effective in '71, helping the Giants to the National
League West title by going 12-9 with 18 saves.

Following his pitching days, Jerry worked as a movie
and TV stunt man, appearing in such movies as *Hooper* and

in television spots like *Little House on the Prairie* and *Hawaii Five-0* before returning to baseball as a pitching coach in the Padres' organization.   48–51

JOHNSON, Lou
    Los Angeles Dodgers Director of Community Relations and hitting instructor

"Sweet Lou," "The Cinderella Man", generated hysteria with the Dodgers in '65 and '66. In the Dodgers' late-season pennant drive, Lou propelled one big hit after another. In one game a home run beat the Giants in the 15th inning. In another, a single topped the Braves, 7-6, in the 11th after Milwaukee had taken a 6-0 lead. During the last four games of a 13-game winning streak, Lou batted .556 and in the pennant-winning game, he carried the winning run over the plate. Johnson batted .296 in the '65 World Series, including a pair of home runs. Fans throughout the country were able to watch Lou go through his hand clapping routine after each homer. His two-run shot off the Twins' Jim Kaat provided the winning margin as Sandy Koufax blanked Minnesota, 2-0, in the deciding seventh game.
    In honor of Louis Brown Johnson, in 1966 Dodger fans adopted the slogan "All the way with LBJ" as the "Cinderella Man" batted .272 with 17 home runs while the Dodgers took the N.L. pennant. Once again he waved his magic wand late in the season by belting six home runs in the September stretch run.
    Overall Lou's career record looks like a railroad timetable including all of the teams he played with in the minors and majors beginning in '53. His big league debut came in 1960 with the Cubs. He then went from the Angels to the Braves, to the Dodgers. He caught his break when Tommy Davis fractured his ankle in '65 yet almost two years to the day, "Sweet Lou" broke his ankle sliding into home plate at Dodger Stadium. Following one more stop with the Cubs, Louis Brown Johnson made his exit in '69 after tries with the Indians and Angels.
    Just as he battled his way to the big time and conquered, he has been successful in his personal war against the perils of alcoholism.   .258

JOHNSON, Stan
   Boston Red Sox scout
   Daly City, CA

In 1960 Rafer Johnson won the decathlon at the Olympic
Games in Rome. That same year outfielder Stan Johnson
played in five games for the White Sox. The next year he
was in three games with the Kansas City A's.
   Stan went 1-for-9 (.111) overall, but his one hit was a
memorable one—a pinch-hit home run for the popular
Minnie Minoso.

JOHNSTON, Rex
   Co-owner of AA-1 Painting Service, Inc.
   Paramount, CA

Rex not only played in 14 games as a flychaser with the Pirates in 1964, he also wore the uniform of the Pittsburgh
Steelers in 1959 as a running back and special teams
player.
   A member of the Trojans' 1958 NCAA baseball champs,
he graduated from USC in business administration. Rex
made a decision to leave baseball in 1966 when he refused
a $200 a month raise while at Phoenix (P.C.L.). He decided
to join the family painting business, a wise decision. Rex
revealed, "We have built the annual sales business of the
company in Industrial and Commercial Painting to $3 mil-
lion."

JOHNSTONE, Jay
   Active with the Chicago Cubs in 1984

A noted clubhouse prankster, John William Johnstone, Jr.
first arrived in 1966 with the Angels after hitting .340
that season with Seattle in the P.C.L. After hopping for a
few years between the Angels and the P.C.L., Jay earned
his tag as a regular, beginning in '69.
   The fun-loving, lefty swatter drew his unconditional release in spring training in 1973 from the White Sox. He
then spent a good part of the next couple of years in the minors mixed with a brief stay in Oakland. It looked like

Jay's obituary from baseball at age 30 when he suddenly developed into one of the tougher outs in the majors playing for the Phillies. In '75 Jay rapped 15 homers and batted .329. He set a NLCS record that year when he went 7-for-9 in a losing effort against the Reds, the seven base-hits a record for a three-game series.

Johnstone then journeyed to the Yankees, Padres, and Dodgers. In '81 he led the Dodgers with 11 pinch-hits, including three homers, two coming in back-to-back games against the Reds. His pinch four-bagger in the Fall Classic that year in Game Four brought the Dodgers back from a 6-3 deficit against the Yanks, one of the turning points in the Series.   .267

During the 1960s we became familiar with several people named Jones. Parnelli Jones won the Indianapolis 500; entertainer Tom Jones gained notoriety; James Earl Jones starred in The Great White Hope *on Broadway; and* Tom Jones *won the academy award as the movie of the year in 1963. Eight players named Jones debuted in big league box scores in the Sixties.*

JONES, Clarence
Agent for Redd Fox Productions
Santa Ana, CA

Ask somebody in Chicago to identify Clarence Jones and chances are your question will go unanswered. This would not hold true in Japan where Clarence established himself as the most prolific American home run hitter ever in the Japanese Leagues. In 1974 he became the first American player to capture a home run title when he belted 38 and repeated two years later with 36.

A first baseman-outfielder, Clarence appeared in 58 games with the Cubs in 1967–68.   .248

JONES, Cleon
New York Mets' hitting instructor

Since 1876 there have been approximately 35 non-pitchers who threw left and batted right. Cleon Jones is one of them. A natural lefthander, he became a right-handed hitter because the place where he played as a youngster in Mobile, Alabama, had a short right field barrier. To keep from losing the ball, he swung from the right side.

He played college ball at Alabama A&M for a couple of years before signing with the Mets where he rejoined Tommie Agee, who was a teammate on his high school team in Mobile.

But Cleon chose to make his living playing baseball, following other notables from Mobile to the majors such as Hank Aaron, Willie McCovey, and Billy Williams (whose cousin he married).

In 1969 Jones hit .340, leading the Mets to their surprising World Championship. Cleon was just 3-for-19 in the World Series against the Orioles, but grabbed headlines for the famous shoe polish incident in the fifth and final game of the Series when he was awarded first because the polish revealed he was struck by the pitch. Jones sparkled in the NLCS that year, going 6-for-14 as the Mets swept the Braves. Although he never had another great season like '69 he did hit .319 in 1971.

On July 18, 1975, the temperamental outfielder had a shouting match with manager Yogi Berra in the dugout, then refused to take the field in a game against the Braves. Earlier that season (May 4th) he was arrested in St. Petersburg, Florida on charges of indecent exposure. Ten days later, Board Chairman M. Donald Grant announced that he would fine Cleon $2,000 for "betraying the image of the club." At the same time, the indecent exposure charges were dropped on the grounds of insubstantial evidence.

He finished with a .281 average after playing with the White Sox in 1976.

JONES, Dalton
    Vice-president of A. L. Williams, an investment firm
    Baton Rouge, LA

The closest race in the history of baseball took place in the American League in 1967. On September 7th there was a four-way tie for first place with the Red Sox, Twins, Tigers, and White Sox clawing at each other down to the bitter

end. On September 18th the Red Sox were trailing the Tigers, 4-3, when Carl Yastrzemski homered to tie the game
in the ninth inning. In the tenth, Dalton Jones, a part-time
infielder and pinch-hitter, was inserted into the Sox lineup
because he hit so well in Tiger Stadium. The utility ace answered with a home run to give the Bosox a 6-5 win.

In nine years in the big arena with Boston (1964–69),
Detroit and Texas (1970–72), Dalton had a mediocre .235
lifetime batting avg., but was a feared pinch-swatter, an
integral part of the dream in '67. Dalton hit .289 that summer with a league-leading 13 pinch-hits. In the World
Series against St. Louis, he played four games at third
base and hit .389. One of the better pinch-hitters in Red
Sox history, Dalton batted .282 and drove in 39 runs during his hitch in Boston that ran 233 games.

One pinch-homer he'll never forget took place as a member of the Tigers on July 9, 1970. Dalton hit a grand-slam
for Detroit, but was credited only with a single because he
passed Don Wert between first and second base.

JONES, "Deacon"
    San Diego Padres' hitting coach

This "Deacon" wasn't quite as celebrated as the one who
was part of the Los Angeles Rams' Fearsome Foursome,
but he did inject his share of fear into the hearts of
opposing pitchers while playing in the minors. In 1956 he
hit a healthy .409 at Dubuque in the Midwest League, the
highest batting average in all of professional baseball that
year.

"Deacon," who studied physiotherapy at Ithaca, is the
son of a deacon in the Baptist Church. A first baseman, he
spent most of his career in the minors, but did hit .286 in
40 games with the White Sox in 1962–63 and '66.

JONES, Hal
    Los Angeles, CA

A minor league hero when he hit 34 home runs in the Eastern League in 1960 to break the team record at Reading
formerly held by Rocky Colavito, Hal wasn't so exciting as

a big leaguer. In 1961–62, this first baseman hit .216 in 17 games for the Indians.

JONES, Mack
Salesman for the R.N. Corning Co.
Atlanta, GA

Known as "The Knife" after Bobby Darin's musical hit *Mack The Knife*, Mr. Jones was around from 1961–71. In his first big league game with the Milwaukee Braves, he tied an N.L. record with four base hits. Previously Casey Stengel of Brooklyn in 1912 and Willie McCovey of the '59 Giants had picked up four hits in their major league debuts. A current fiberglass salesman, Mack was virtually shatterproof himself in '65 when he hit a career-high 31 homers in the Braves' final season in Milwaukee.

A native of Atlanta, Mack was back in town with the Braves in '66. Two years later he was sent to Cincinnati, then became the No. 2 choice of the Montreal Expos in the N.L. expansion draft. He says, "Being able to play in Montreal was the highlight of my career." Understandably so. On April 14, 1969 he hit the first major league home run in Canada, a first-inning, three-run shot off the Cardinals' Nelson Briles.   .252

JONES, Sherman
Police Sergeant/investigator
Kansas City, KS

"Roadblock" was 10-0 at Tacoma (P.C.L.) in 1960 which is where he acquired his nickname from a local sportswriter who wrote "everytime he comes in to pitch, the road to home is blocked." However, he didn't pose such a barrier in the majors, going 2-6 in 48 games from 1960–62 with the Giants, Reds, and Mets.

Sherman was the starting pitcher in the Mets' first home game ever on April 13, 1962, a 4-3 loss to the Pirates at the Polo Grounds before 12,447 fans. "Roadblock" was the loser while Tom Sturdivant picked up the win. Twenty years later (1982) he was invited to throw out the first pitch at the Mets' '82 inaugural at Shea Stadium, a nostalgic reminder of Sherman's assignment in 1962.

JONES, Steve
Vice-president of Home Federal Savings Bank
Knoxville, TN

"Baseball gave me a college education," says Steve. The educated Whittier College graduate, who also attended the University of Tennessee and the UCLA Graduate School of Business, spent portions of three seasons with three different teams (White Sox, Senators, and Royals) from 1967–69. The southpaw chucker went 5-7.

JORGENSEN, Mike
Active with St. Louis Cardinals

Mike's career almost came to a tragic end on May 28, 1979, playing for the Rangers when he was beaned by Red Sox pitcher Andy Hassler. He returned to action three days later as a pinch-hitter and suffered a relapse with a spell of convulsions. Doctors discovered a clot on the brain, and as a result, he missed the entire month of June before returning to uniform on July 1st.

Since 1968 Mike has hopscotched around with the Mets, Expos, A's, Rangers, Braves, and Cardinals. The infielder-outfielder was an Expos' hero on Oct. 1, 1974, when he belted a two-run homer off Bob Gibson at Montreal's Jarry Park to knock the Cardinals out of the National League East pennant race.

Jorgensen, who attended St. John's University in New York, was named the first baseman on *The Sporting News* National League All-Star Fielding team in 1973.

JOSEPH, Ricardo
Died in 1979 at age 39 in Santo Domingo in the Dominican Republic

Ricardo spent most of the early Sixties in the minors except for a 17-game look with the Kansas City A's in 1964.

After winning P.C.L. MVP honors at San Diego in 1967, he joined the Phillies in September.

His first major league home run came in dramatic style on Sept. 16, 1967, when he walloped an eleventh-inning pinch-hit grand-slam off Ron Perranoski to give the Phils an 8-4 win over the Dodgers. Ricardo was with the Phillies for three years and departed with a .243 average. His death resulted from a kidney ailment.

JOSEPHSON, Duane
   Real estate business, Gibson Partners of New Hampton
   New Hampton, IA

In 1964 Duane led the nation's small colleges in home runs (24) while playing at State College of Iowa in Cedar Falls. A fine hoopster who averaged over 20 points per game, Duane made his mark in baseball.

Josephson's eight-year career was spent mostly with the White Sox. In '68 he was the club's regular backstop and participated in the All-Star Game. Duane's finest season in Chisox threads came in 1970 when he swung for a .316 average. His last two years (1971–72) were spent with Boston.

The former catcher talked about his career. "Just being there was something, especially coming from a small farm town in Iowa."

Duane was forced to retire from baseball because of pericarditis, an inflammation of the heart.   .258

JOSHUA, Von
   Los Angeles Dodgers' minor league instructor/coach

The Dodgers signed Von in 1967. It looked like a good move as he proceeded to lead the Northwest League in hitting that year with a glossy .363 average. He spent the next several seasons between Los Angeles and the P.C.L. as he attempted to crack the Dodgers' outfield. Following the '74 campaign Joshua was released on waivers to the Giants where he put it all together, batting .318 in 1975.

Von's life the next few years resembled that of a gypsy. During the '76 campaign he was purchased by the Brew-

ers. Back to L.A. in '79, his topsy-turvy career ended with
the Padres in 1980.   .273

JOYCE, Dick
    Group manager of business planning for IBM
    Upper Saddle River, NJ

Dick's career literally came to a stormy end. It happened
in 1966 while pitching at Indianapolis. Suddenly a whirling tornado blew through the city. Dick pitched following
the long delay and hurt his arm. He was never the same
and admits, "I pitched on the high edge of mediocrity"
thereafter.

The tall southpaw made an impressive debut in 1965,
striking out 17 in a Northwest League encounter. Later
that year he jumped all the way to the Kansas City A's
where he lost his only decision in five games. The leap
from Lewiston to K.C. gave Dick an extra $5,000. He ex-
plained, "Charlie Finley told me that I would start in
Class A. He said, 'If you go up a classification it will be
worth an extra $5,000 to you.' When I made it to Kansas
City I wrote Finley a note to remind him of the deal. A few
days later I got a check for $5,000. Finley was very gra-
cious to me."

Dick is part of an interesting bit of trivia since he was the
starting Kansas City pitcher the night Bert Campaneris
played all nine positions. "The ballplayers knew it was a
gimmick, but Campy could play everywhere."

JOYCE, Mike
    Financial manager for Comdisco, a computer leasing
    company
    Chicago, IL

Mike Joyce, a right-hander from the University of Michigan, had a short big league stay as a member of the White
Sox in 1962–63, going 2-1 in 31 games, and batting .429
(3-for-7). In 1963 he was kept on the 28-man roster for the
White Sox rather than Early Wynn, who at the time was
one win short of 300.

JUREWICZ, Mike
    Owns and operates an agency called "Pride, Inc."
    dealing in housewares and electronics
    Lakeville, MN

Mike says, "I've never been able to get away from the
'Pride of the Yankees' syndrome." Touted as the next
Whitey Ford, this Yankee Doodle had his career cut short
by an arm injury. The southpaw appeared in just two
games with no decisions for the Yankees in 1965. Mike did
hurl a no-hitter for Columbus (Southern League) against
Charlotte that summer with Yankee Manager Ralph Houk
in the stands.

K

KANEHL, Rod
    Owns a bar
    Wichita, KS

A favorite of Casey Stengel's, "Hot Rod" was one of the
early Mets' "heroes" in 1962. The one-time Yankee farm-
hand, who spent eight years in the minors, caught the
fancy of Mets' fans in an early-season game when he
scored from second base on a passed ball.
    On July 6, 1962, Rod hit the first grand-slam homer in
Mets' history against Bobby Shantz and the Cardinals.
    Kanehl filled in all over the infield and outfield for the
fledgling Mets in their first three seasons, hitting .241 in
340 games. Following his years with the lowly Mets, he
played semipro ball for the Wichita Rapid Transit Dream-
liners, a team whose 55-6 record was at the other end of the
spectrum en route to becoming the champions of the National Baseball Congress.

KEALEY, Steve
> Student signalman for the Santa Fe Railroad
> Newton, KS

In 1968 Jean-Claude Killy won three gold medals in skiing at the Winter Olympic games in Grenoble, France, a year Steve Kealey made his jump to the majors with the Angels. Between 1968–73 Steve pitched with the Angels and White Sox, going 8-5 in 139 games, mostly as a relief specialist.

The right-hander did make four starts, including one on Aug. 21, 1969, which resulted in a 2-0 shutout over the Orioles. The details behind the game are interesting. Steve had been pitching at Hawaii (P.C.L.) that year, but was in California fulfilling military obligations. The Angels' brass asked him to stop by to throw batting practice before returning to the P.C.L. He threw well, which prompted the Angels to give him a start. Steve then blanked the Birds.

KEKICH, Mike
> Attending medical school in Juarez, Mexico, specializing in emergency and trauma care

This free-spirited southpaw who at times was into astrology, philosophy, motorcycle riding, and skiing, and later wife swapping, was around from 1965–77. The possessor of a live fastball, Mike once struck out eleven consecutive batters for St. Petersburg in a 1964 Florida State League game. The Dodgers had high hopes of making Kekich the heir to Sandy Koufax, but the unpredictable lefty was as busy perfecting his off-the-field adventures as he was his pitching skills.

In '65 Mike made the climb from the lowest minor league classification to the majors in his first year of professional baseball. That same year he was married, and while visiting Santa Barbara on his honeymoon, both he and his bride were injured riding a motorcycle.

The unsettled chucker then spent more time down on the farm. He appeared ready after going 14-4 in the Texas League in 1967, then was promoted once again to Los Angeles, where he struggled in '68 at 2-10. One of his victories was a one-hit shutout over the Mets.

His next stop was in the Bronx where he won ten games

in both 1971 and '72 for the Yankees. Wearing pinstripes, he one-hit the White Sox in '71. However, Mike's pitching exploits seemed overshadowed by his wife-swapping episode with teammate Fritz Peterson, which included trading the children and the family dogs. Mike has since been divorced from his second wife.

Kekich was traded to Cleveland in '73, then was back in the minors a couple of years later. During this period he pitched for a time in Japan and Mexico and also got into a few games with the Rangers as a reliever. After a shot with the expansion Mariners in '77 he found himself in Mexico again.   39-51

KELLER, Ron
> Certified financial planner for Unified Management Corporation
> Indianapolis, IN

The Miracle Worker won awards for Ann Bancroft and Patty Duke. Ron Keller, a nine-game chucker with the Twins in 1966 and 1968, could have used a miracle since he lost his only decision.

KELLEY, Dick
> Partner in Mercedes Benz specialty maintenance company
> Encino, CA

Dick appeared in box scores from 1964–1971 with the Braves and Padres. The left-hander was used as a spot starter and reliever and posted an overall 18-30 record. On Sept. 8, 1967, he tied an N.L. record by striking out six consecutive Phils in relief. Dick was able to complete only five of his 61 starts, but oddly enough all five were shutouts.

KELLEY, TOM
> Supervisor for United Parcel Service
> Roanoke, VA

Along with being a one-time ski instructor who competed in slalom and downhill events, Tom (no relation to Dick) zigged and zagged with the Indians (1964–67) and Braves (1971–73), going 20-22. The right-hander, who spent most of the '65 season at Portland in the P.C.L. where he enjoyed a 16-3 mark and led the circuit in strikeouts and winning percentage, no-hit Spokane, 5-0, on May 29th.

A gimpy arm kept him virtually inactive in the late 1960s, but he bounced back in '71 for his most productive season in the biggies (9-5) pitching for the Braves.

KELLY, Pat
> Partner with brother Leroy in Burger King franchise; entered divinity school to study to become a minister
> Philadelphia, PA

The brother of former Cleveland Browns' star running back, Leroy Kelly, Pat did his flychasing from 1967–82 with the Twins, Royals, White Sox, Orioles, and Indians. As part of Earl Weaver's platoon system in Baltimore, he was especially effective as a pinch-hitter. Kelly hit .288 with Baltimore in '79 and was dynamite in the ALCS, hitting .364 including a home run and four RBIs as the O's won the pennant.

Pat is the brother-in-law of Cleveland first baseman Andre Thornton because they both married daughters of an Ohio minister.

KELLY, Van
> Sales manager for the National Starch and Chemical Corp.
> Atlanta, GA

"I enjoyed every minute of my baseball career, and feel the time I spent in baseball prepared me well for my business career. I have nothing but fond memories, especially of my major league debut."

The third baseman joined the Padres in June of 1969 in a trade from the Braves' organization for Tony Gonzalez. Although his 11-game, .221 career gained him no fame, Van doubled home the game-winning run in his first game, as the Padres defeated the Dodgers for the first time ever.

KELSO, Bill
>   Coach at Rockhurst College
>   Kansas City, MO

Kelso was the name of the famous gelding who won "Horse of the Year" honors for five straight years in the early 1960s. Bill Kelso, who was signed for a substantial bonus by the Los Angeles Dodgers while attending Kansas University on a basketball-football scholarship, caught for four years in the minors before being converted to a pitcher.

He first arrived with the Angels in 1964. In 1967 he reacted like a thoroughbred out of the Angels' bullpen when he went 5-3 with 11 saves in 69 appearances, an A.L. record for most appearances by a rookie.   12-5

KENDALL, Fred
>   Last employed with a medical supplies company
>   San Diego, CA

Fred was the last of the original Padres to depart the team when he was traded to Cleveland following the '76 season. He broke in slowly with San Diego, but eventually took over as the team's regular catcher. He had his finest year in 1973 when he hit .282.

Kendall next saw action with the Red Sox after leaving Cleveland, then rejoined the Padres in 1979, where he packed it in one year later at .254.

KENDERS, Al
>   Employed in the movie set department of Warner
>   Brothers
>   Van Nuys, CA

In the early Sixties Allen Funt and his Candid Camera swept many unsuspecting guests off their feet with an array of hilarious stunts. Unfortunately, Al didn't smile too much since the Phillies' catcher hit only .174 in ten games.

TOMMIE AARON hit the first homer ever in Atlanta–Fulton County Stadium.

Controversial DICK ALLEN chats with JIM "The Toy Cannon" WYNN at first base.

LOU BROCK is the base-stealing czar with 938 career stolen bases.

In 1961, JACK BALDSCHUN led the N.L. with 65 appearances as a rookie.

Since 1900 BERT CAMPANERIS and CESAR TOVAR are the only two major leaguers to play all nine positions in a single regular season game.

Four-time Cy Young Award winner STEVE CARLTON talks with DAVEY JOHNSON, who played with home run champs Hank Aaron and Sadahara Oh.

RICO CARTY hit .366 in 1970.

CLAY CARROLL was named the Fireman of the Year by *The Sporting News* in 1972.

In the 1973 A.L.C.S. ANDY ETCHE-BARREN hit a 3-run homer in game 4 against Vida Blue.

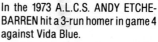

On Aug. 1, 1972, NATE COLBERT hit 5 home runs in a doubleheader.

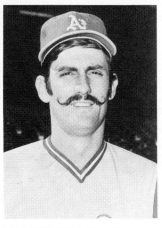

ROLLIE FINGERS is the all-time save leader with 324.

STEVE GARVEY is the National League consecutive game champ with 1207.

BOB HENDLEY (right) now coaches son, BRETT, (left) at Stratford Academy in Macon, GA.

RON HUNT was hit by pitches a record 243 times.

REGGIE JACKSON reached the 500 home run level in 1984.

ED "Krane" KRANEPOOL is the only man to play in each of the Mets' first 18 seasons.

AL LUPLOW made one of the greatest catches ever at Fenway Park in 1963.

SAM MCDOWELL led the A.L. in strikeouts and walks five times each.

ART MAHAFFEY picked off the first three men who reached base against him in the majors.

BILL MELTON was the first White Sox player in the club's history to lead the A.L. in home runs.

GENE MICHAEL was the master of the hidden-ball trick.

From 1961-67 RON PERRANOSKI was the ace of the Dodgers' bullpen.

JOHN "Boog" POWELL enjoys a 'Lite' moment on the eve of the second annual Cracker Jack Classic in Washington, D.C.

PETE ROSE was the first switch-hitter to win a batting crown in the N.L. since Pete Reiser.

NOLAN RYAN has pitched a record five no-hitters during his career.

REGGIE SMITH is the only switch-hitter to hit 180 or more homers in each league.

RUSTY STAUB joins Ty Cobb as the only two players to homer before their 20th birthday and after their 40th birthday in the majors.

DICK TRACEWSKI earned three World Series rings during his career.

On Sept. 12, 1962, BUD ZIPFEL's 16th inning home run led the Senators to victory. (Courtesy of Bud Zipfel)

KENNEDY, John, E.
New York Yankees' scout
West Peabody, MA

Ironically, John F. Kennedy and John E. Kennedy share the same birthdate of May 29th. John E. joined JFK in Washington in 1962 to begin a 12-year term as a valuable utility player.

On Sept. 5, 1962, John became just the second player in A.L. history to hit a pinch-hit home run in his first at-bat in the majors. The first to do it was Ace Parker of the Philadelphia A's in 1937.

Kennedy, who typified the perfect role player, participated as a backup infielder for the Dodgers in 1965–66. The spirited infielder then played for the Yankees, Pilots, and Brewers, before closing in 1974 after a four-year run with the Bosox.   .225

KENNEY, Jerry
Co-owns a record company with his brother
New Brunswick, NJ

When the 1969 baseball season opened in Washington on April 7th, among those on hand were new President Richard Nixon, new baseball commissioner Bowie Kuhn, the Senators' new owner, Bob Short, and the team's new manager, Ted Williams. The Yankees were the opponent that day with a new centerfielder—Jerry Kenney, a converted infielder. For one day he reminded the baseball world of the departed Mickey Mantle as he doubled and homered in the Yankees' 8-4 victory.

Jerry first came up in '67 and hit .310 in 20 games as a Yankee shortstop. He played as the Yankee third baseman until traded to Cleveland following the '72 season in a deal which saw Graig Nettles come to the Yankees. Jerry lasted just five games with the Indians.   .237

KENWORTHY, Dick
  Salesman for Renners Express
  Indianapolis, IN

If one wanted to name an All-Star team born on April Fool's Day it might look like this: Willie Montanez (1B), Rod Kanehl (2B), Dick Kenworthy (3B), Murray Franklin (SS), Rusty Staub (OF), Claude Cooper (OF), Jeff Heath (OF), Bill Friel (C), Phil Niekro (RHP), Ron Perranoski (LHP), and Hugo Bezdek (MGR).

Kenworthy was in and out of the big arena with the White Sox between 1962–68. But to Dick's dismay he fell short of qualifying for his pension. "Not getting my pension was my biggest disappointment. I had one year to go to qualify."

Dick did have some good memories. In '64 he led the Southern League in home runs with 29. He also played in Yankee Stadium against names like Mantle and Ford. This experience Dick calls "the highlight of my career."   .215

KEOUGH, Joe
  Director of Restaurant Development for Burger King
  Pleasanton, CA

Big league baseball was first introduced to the Keough clan when Marty showed up in 1956. In 1968 brother Joe arrived, followed by Marty's son Matt in the 1970s.

Joe's debut was an auspicious one with the Oakland A's. Playing against the Yankees (Aug. 7, 1968) he pinch-hit a home run off Lindy McDaniel at Yankee Stadium in his first time at bat in the majors. Following the season, he was taken by the Royals in the expansion draft. When the A.L. returned to Kansas City in 1969, Joe's bases-loaded pinch-hit single brought home the winning run in a 4-3 victory over the Twins in the Royals inaugural home opener. The next year he was blazing at .322 when he suffered a broken leg, an injury that sidelined him for the remainder of the season. Keough spent two more years with the Royals, then waltzed away in '73 with the White Sox.   .246

KERN, Bill
> Social studies teacher in Whitehall Coplay school
> district
> Allentown, PA

Bill is still somewhat perplexed about his career. After
going 4-for-16 in eight games as a Kansas City outfielder
in 1962 which included a hit in his first at-bat off Dick
Donovan and a home run off Jim Bunning, he never returned. He says, "I went to spring training in '63 and
thought I would be the starting left fielder. They didn't
seem to have anyone. To me it's a puzzle to this day."

On August 23–24 (1962), Bill hit three home runs in
back-to-back games while playing for Portland (P.C.L.).
The disappointed flychaser called it quits in '64.   .250

KERNEK, George
> Vice-president of operations for the Harrison Gypsum
> Co.
> Purcell, OK

In 1966 the St. Louis Cardinals opened spring training on
March 12th, started the regular season on April 12th,
played their first game in the new Busch Stadium on May
12th, and hosted the All-Star Game there on July 12th.
The team finished 12 games behind the pennant-winning
Dodgers that year.

What does George Kernek have to do with all that?
Probably nothing, but he did pick up 12 base hits playing
some first base for the Cards that year. George actually
started the '66 campaign as the Redbirds' regular first
baseman, a situation that changed with the acquisition of
Orlando Cepeda in mid-May.

George, who attended the University of Oklahoma on a
basketball scholarship, also played briefly with St. Louis
in '65.   .259

KESSINGER, Don
    Investment business; affiliated with a racquetball
    club; operates a baseball school
    Memphis, TN

Signed off the Ole Miss campus in 1964, Don was All-
Southeastern Conference in baseball and basketball for
three consecutive years and was named to the All-American baseball team his senior year.
    His impressive career ran from 1964–1979, most of
which was spent with the Cubs. The smooth-fielding shortstop took part in all three Cubs' triple plays in 1965 in
which the Cubbies tied an all-time major league record for
most triple plays in a season. In 1969 he set a major league
record, going 54 straight games at shortstop without an error. On June 17, 1971, he enjoyed a 6-for-6 night at the
plate, the first Cubs' player to do it since Frank Demaree
in 1937.
    The six-time N.L. All-Star also brought his sure glove to
the Cards ('76–'77) and White Sox (1977–'79). In '79 he
gained the distinction as the American League's last
playing manager as a member of the Pale Hose. Late in
the '78 season "Don Kessinger Night" was held. However,
he wasn't honored at Wrigley Field, where he had his
greatest years, but at Comiskey Park where he now was in
the twilight of his career.   .253

KESTER, Rick
    Business manager for the Douglas County school dis-
    trict
    Gardnerville, NV

Rick tried to stick but became unglued after 21 games
without a decision for the Atlanta Braves from 1968–1970.
A right-hander, Kester has a B.S. degree in finance from
UCLA.

KILKENNY, Mike
        Repairs golf equipment
        Bradford, Ontario

In 1972 Mike had to feel very unwanted or conversely very wanted as he tied a record by moving from the Tigers to the A's, Indians, and Padres. But life was more settling when he surfaced with Detroit in '69. He definitely knew he was wanted when he went 8-6 with half of his victories shutouts coming at Tiger Stadium.

Somewhat of the resident wit, Mike once was struggling with Detroit, carrying an unsightly ERA of 27.00. He was deprived of a start because of rain which led him to comment that he was in "no rush to get out there."

When used as a spot starter, he often was not told the day he was starting because of his extreme nervousness on the day of the game.   23-18

KING, Hal
        Painting contractor; baseball coach at Lake Howell
        High School in Oviedo, FL

In 1963 Martin Luther King led the civil rights march on Washington and delivered his stirring "I have a dream" speech. That year catcher Hal King was barnstorming with the Indianapolis Clowns and dreaming of making it into the big leagues someday. His dream was fulfilled as he was around from 1967–74 with the Astros, Braves, Rangers, and Reds. On June 21, 1971, the hard-working catcher was part of a home run parade for the Braves as he connected along with Mike Lum, Hank Aaron, and Darrell Evans in the eighth inning for Atlanta.   .214

KIRBY, Clay
        Vice President of E.S.I. Securities, a subsidiary of
        Epic, Inc.
        Fairfax Station, VA

There haven't been many times in baseball that a pitcher has been lifted from a game while in the process of pitching a no-hitter. Clay Kirby was, while pitching for the

Padres against the Mets on July 21, 1970. After eight innings, Clay trailed, 1-0, and was removed from the contest
in the ninth inning for a pinch-hitter by manager Preston
Gomez. Gomez's decision resulted in much second
guessing by Padre fans, and the situation was magnified
because Clarence Gaston, the pinch-hitter, struck out and
Jack Baldschun, Kirby's replacement, surrendered two
runs in the 3-0 loss to New York.

Clay started out in the Cardinals' chain, but went to the
expansion Padres. From 1969–1973 he was a rock on the
San Diego pitching staff, rarely missing a start. But the
lack of offensive support affected Clay's won-lost record.
He then spent a few years with the Reds before closing
with the Expos.   75-104

KIRK, Bill
    Sales manager for the Susquehanna Broadcasting Co.
    York, PA

Bill appeared on the mound in only one game with the
Kansas City A's in 1961, failing to gain a decision. But he
did have one game during his career he'll never forget.

"In 1960 I was pitching for Lancaster and was scheduled
to pitch the second game of a doubleheader against Binghamton. I arrived at the park ten minutes before the first
game and was told that I would pitch the opener instead. I
then proceeded to no-hit Binghamton."

KIRKPATRICK, Ed
    Recuperating from extensive injuries suffered in car
    accident
    Laguna Niguel, CA

In the winter of '81 Ed was injured in an auto accident that
left him in a coma for several months. Although he has since
come out of his coma, Kirkpatrick remains confined to a
wheelchair. The extensive brain damage suffered in the accident has affected his ability to speak. However, he can com-
municate with those around him, and is a visitor at Anaheim
Stadium from time to time. Ed has undergone several operations in his struggle to make the comeback of his life.

One of the most sought-after schoolboy sluggers in Southern California, "Spanky" was just 17 years old when he appeared in three games with the Angels in 1962. His first hit in the majors was a memorable one which gave the Angels a 1-0 victory over Chicago in 15 innings on April 15, 1963.

A versatile player who was used as a catcher, first baseman, and outfielder, he was up and down between Anaheim and the P.C.L. before going to the Royals in 1969.

Kirkpatrick was a fixture in the Royals lineup their first few years before traveling to Pittsburgh where he helped the Bucs to back-to-back National League East titles in 1974–75 as a utility player.

Prior to his accident he was employed as a representative for the Rawlings Sporting Goods Company.   .238

KLAGES, Fred
Co-owner of Titan Plastic, Inc. in Houston, TX

In 1962 Fred was voted the state of Pennsylvania's most outstanding high school football player. The heavy recruiting battle for a college football scholarship was won by the University of Maryland. But Fred decided that playing between the foul lines instead of the hash marks was the way to go.

The right-hander signed with the White Sox and went 5-4 in 14 games in 1966–67.

KLAUS, Bobby
Circulation distribution agent for the San Diego Union-Tribune
San Diego, CA

If you should ask anyone who played with Bobby Klaus to evaluate his skills you'll hear comments like "a real gamer," and "he turned the double play well." The University of Illinois All-American shortstop was a member of the Reds and Mets in 1964–65, hitting .208. At one point during the '64 season, Bobby replaced a slumping Pete Rose at second base for the Reds.

An all-around utility infielder, Bobby was playing for San Diego (P.C.L.) in '68 when Bob Skinner, the team's

manager, was named to manage the Phillies, replacing the
fired Gene Mauch. Klaus became the club's player-manager for the balance of the '68 season and was the team's
19th and final skipper in the club's P.C.L. history. His
older brother Billy was an infielder in the majors from
1952–63.

KLIMKOWSKI, Ron
Stockbroker on Wall Street with McLaughlin, Piven,
and Vogel
Westbury, NY

In Ron's first big league start with the Yankees, he pitched
eight innings of three-hit baseball at Fenway Park, but the
Yanks lost it in the 14th frame, depriving him of his moment of glory. The Morehead State product was around
from 1969–72 (Yankees and A's), going 8-12 in 90 games.
Ron spent most of the '69 season at Syracuse and was
named the I.L. Most Valuable Pitcher after a 15-7 season
and a fine 2.18 ERA.

KNOOP, Bobby
California Angels' coach

"With his fielding ability he could hit .086 and still be my
second baseman."
—Bill Rigney

That was just one of many tributes paid to this brilliant-
fielding second baseman who was with the Angels, White
Sox, and Royals from 1964–72. Billy Herman referred to
Bobby as "the greatest I've ever seen." Mickey Mantle was
once quoted, "He will make the .300 hitter extinct."
He established two major league records in 1966 by taking part in six double plays in a nine-inning game on May
1st, and snaring 12 putouts on August 30th.
The starting A.L. second baseman in the '66 All-Star
Game, Bobby teamed with Jim Fregosi in California to
form one of the better double play combos in the 1960s. A
three-time Gold Glove winner, he is the only four-time
winner of the Owner's Trophy, symbolic of the club's out-

standing player. His best season at the plate came in '66
when he led the league in triples (11) and connected for 17
homers and 72 RBIs.   .236

KNOWLES, Darold
     St. Louis Cardinals' minor league pitching instructor

Darold played with the Orioles, Phils, Senators, A's, Cubs,
Rangers, Expos, and Cardinals from 1965–1980. Although
this southpaw reliever shows a mediocre career record of
66-74, in the early '70s he was a key figure in the Oakland
bullpen as Rollie Fingers' counterpart from the port side.
In 1972 in the first of three straight championship seasons
for the A's, he was 5-1 with 11 saves and an ERA of 1.36.
Unfortunately Darold was forced out of post-season play
with a fractured thumb. The following year he more than
made up for it when he established a World Series record
by coming out of the A's bullpen in all seven games
against the Mets. He did not allow an earned run and was
credited with saves in the first and seventh games. Lifetime Darold racked up 143 saves.
     In a 1967 game for Washington in which the Senators
defeated the Twins 9-7 in 20-innings, he pitched 10 innings
of three-hit scoreless relief.

KOCH, Alan
     Attorney
     Montgomery, AL

A graduate of Auburn University, Alan was 4-11 in 42
games with the Tigers and Senators (1963–64). At the
plate he was a bit more successful, going 10-for-35 for a
.286 average.
     Life after baseball has been very successful. The right-
hander earned a master's degree in history and a degree in
law from the University of Alabama and also received a
law degree from New York University.

KOLB, Gary
    Co-owns a rustproofing business
    Charleston, WV

Gary was in and out of the biggies from 1960–1969 with
the Cardinals, Braves, Mets, and Pirates. Kolb, who lettered in football at the University of Illinois, played all
nine positions during his organized baseball career. A
catcher by trade, "Mr. Fill-in" was used by the Pirates in
'68 at second, third, right and left fields, catcher, and as a
pinch-hitter and pinch-runner.
    Gary's most memorable role as a pinch-runner came on
Sept. 29, 1963, when he pinch-ran for Stan Musial in
Musial's last game.   .209

KOLSTAD, Hal
    Teacher and coach at Leigh High School
    San Jose, CA

Elvis Presley was singing and starring in the movie *Follow That Dream* when this stocky right-hander achieved
the dream of most American boys of making it to the
majors.
    The San Jose State product had somewhat of a restless
dream, going 0-4 in 34 games with the Red Sox in 1962–63.

KOONCE, Cal
    Restaurant business
    Hope Mills, NC

Unlike Gaylord Perry, his one-time classmate at Campbell
College in North Carolina, Cal is candid about accusations
that he threw a spitter as he admits that he occasionally
"wet one up." From 1962–71, he was employed with the
Cubs, Mets, and Red Sox.
    After going 10-10 as a Cubs' rookie in '62, he never
again won in double figures. But during the Mets miracle
campaign in '69 he went 6-3 with seven saves.   47-49

KOOSMAN, Jerry
Active with Philadelphia Phillies

Jerry was pitching for his Army team in 1964 when his catcher, named John Luchese, wrote his father, a Polo Grounds usher, and recommended that the Mets scout him. By 1967 the crafty southpaw found himself in Mets flannels, losing his only two decisions. Then bang—in 1968 he was named the N.L. "Rookie Pitcher of the Year" with a 19-12 record. "Koos" shut out the Dodgers and Giants for his first two victories to open the season, making him the first Met hurler ever to pitch back-to-back shutouts. His rookie campaign was one of bliss as he chalked up seven shutouts en route to a 19-12 record. His seven blankings tied the National League rookie record held by Irv Young of the 1905 Boston Braves and Grover Cleveland Alexander of the 1911 Philadelphia Phillies. Jerry was beaten by Johnny Bench for N.L. Rookie of the Year honors by one vote. That year Koosman etched his name in the record books in a dubious way when he struck out 62 times, an all-time mark for a National League chucker.

"Koos" followed up his brilliant rookie campaign with a 17-9 log in '69 when the Mets shocked the baseball world by taking all the marbles. In the Fall Classic against the Orioles, Jerry won the second and fifth (final) games as the Mets completed their miracle. In '73 he went a mediocre 14-15, but mastered a consecutive scoreless inning streak of 31⅔ innings. In Game Five of the World Series, he combined with Tug McGraw to shut out the A's, improving his overall Series record to 3-0.

He won 20 for the first time in '76 (21-10), then plummeted to 8-20 the following season. Following a 3-15 campaign he was traded to the Twins and bounced back with a 20-13 year.

In 1983 "Koos" admitted that he was really 40 years old (born Dec. 23, 1942—not 1943) thereby correcting his "baseball age." 216-205

KOPACZ, George
    Transport driver for Gulf Mobile
    Orlond Park, IL

George, a left-handed hitting first baseman, spent most of
the 1960s in the minors aside from a brief trial with Atlanta in '66. He returned four years later with the Pirates.
George earned his advancement following a big year for
Columbus (I.L.) in which he hit .314 with 29 homers and
116 RBIs to capture league MVP honors.

KOPLITZ, Howie
    Dairy farmer
    Oshkosh, WI

Named by Topps as the "Minor League Player of the
Year" in 1961, this right-hander was 23-3 for Birmingham
(Southern Association) including a no-hitter. His plush
year was completed in fashion when he was brought up to
the Tigers where he won his only two decisions.

The next year he was back in Motown after fulfilling his
military obligations, and proceeded to go 3-0 to maintain
his flawless mark.

After winning his first seven major league decisions, he
wound up 9-7 in 54 contests including time with Washington from 1964–66.

KORINCE, George
    Employed with General Motors
    St. Catherine's, Ontario

Like Howie Koplitz, "Moose" Korince was undefeated in
his mound career with Detroit, winning his only decision
in 11 games in 1966–67.

Since "Moose" finished 1-0, it gives him the distinction
of being the only Canadian-born pitcher to finish his major
league career undefeated.

KOSCO, Andy
  Insurance business
  Poland, OH

Andy turned down scholarship offers to play both football and basketball at several Big Ten schools to sign a reported $80,000 bonus by the Tigers out of high school.

Kosco's ten-year big league journey started in Minnesota ('65) before playing with the Yankees, Dodgers, Angels, Red Sox, and Reds. Andy's best year came with the Dodgers in 1969 when he belted 19 four-baggers.

Primarily an outfielder who also played first and third base, Andy was frequently victimized by Death Valley, the 457-foot left-center alley in Yankee Stadium which cost him numerous home runs. In 1973 he was a valuable spare flychaser for the N.L. West Champion Reds banging out nine homers and hitting .280. In the Mets NLCS victory over Cincinnati, Jon Matlack shut out the Reds, 5-0, on a two-hitter with a pair of singles by Andy the only hits off Matlack that day.   .236

KOSTRO, Frank
  Owns Western Region Life Insurance Company; also
  deals in extended warranties with car dealers
  Denver, CO

During the 1960s baseball fans had to battle the confusion of distinguishing Frank Kostro from Andy Kosco. Both were right-handed hitters who began in the Detroit organization; both were about the same size and played first, third, and the outfield; both were in and out of the Twins' lineup.

Frank played for the Tigers, Angels, and Twins from 1962–1969, hitting .244. A pinch-hitter par excellence, Kostro led the A.L. in that category in '67, going 9-for-23. In his role as a pinch-swatter the similarities to Kosco once again became apparent as Frank was 34-for-142 and Andy was 39-for-144.

KRANEPOOL, Ed
> Display manufacturer
> New York, NY

Ed was signed by the Mets out of James Monroe H.S. in the Bronx for a reported $85,000 contract. After spending the summer of 1962 in the minors, Ed joined the Mets as a green 17-year-old and picked up one hit in six at-bats. The base hit, a double, was the first of 1,418 he would collect in a Mets' uniform; he is the team's all-time leader in that department. The first baseman-outfielder played in 208 games between 1962–64. Only Robin Yount (243), Mel Ott (241) and Phil Cavaretta (221) saw more action as teen-agers. In the summer of '62 Ed received special permission from N.L. President Warren Giles to sit on the Mets' bench as a non-roster player while under special tutelage in first base play from Gil Hodges.

Ed spent portions of the next two years in Buffalo, but became part of one of baseball's all-time marathon stories. On May 31, 1964, the Mets and Giants tangled in a Sunday doubleheader at Shea Stadium. The Giants won both ends, with the nightcap going 23 innings and lasting seven hours and 23 minutes, the longest game by time in baseball history until the White Sox–Brewers contest on May 9, 1984, that went 25 innings and lasted eight hours and six minutes. Aside from appearing in major league's longest doubleheader, he also played in the longest shutout game and longest game played to a decision. Kranepool was at first base for the Mets on April 15, 1968, when New York edged the Astros, 1-0, in 24 innings. He pinch-hit for the Mets on September 11, 1974, when the Mets lost to the Cardinals, 4-3, in 25 innings.

"Krane" was probably the tiredest player in the park in the '64 marathon with the Giants. The day before he played a twinbill for Buffalo. Following the double-dip he was notified that he was to join the Mets in New York. Ed drove all night and arrived in time to play in all 32 innings against the Giants. He tied a record when he batted 14 times in the 32 frames.

A part of the Mets from their early years of futility through the "miracle" of '69, Ed found himself back in the I.L. in 1970, but returned to stay for the next decade.

Following the '73 pennant-winning season, the Mets regressed to the ineptness of their early years. But "Krane" proved to be a breath of life on a team that was experiencing a sudden relapse. In '74 he was the pinch-hitter deluxe in the National League, going a torrid 17-for-35 off the bench. The next year he batted a career high .323. Ed aged graciously on the diamond. From 1974–78 he was 57-for-144 as a pinch-hitter for nearly a .400 average.   .261

KRAUSSE, Lew
Public relations and sales for American Metals Corp.
Kansas City, MO

In 1931, 19-year-old Lew Krausse threw a shutout for the Philadelphia A's in his first big league start. Thirty years later Lew was a scout for the Kansas City A's when his son, Lew Krausse, Jr., was signed to a reported $125,000 bonus by the A's out of high school. The 18-year-old righty made a big league debut against the Angels which proved to be as spectacular as his father's with a three-hit, 4-0 shutout.

Lew spent a good part of the next few years in the minors before moving into the A's starting rotation in 1966, a year which would prove his best at 14-9. He also pitched for the Brewers, Red Sox, Cards, and Braves before making his exit with a 68-91 mark.

Krausse was involved in one of baseball's most controversial incidents during the 1960s. It happened on Aug. 3, 1967, when the A's were flying from Boston to Kansas City. Lew was fined $500 15 days later by Charlie Finley for conduct unbecoming a major leaguer. Krausse was charged with rowdyism on the TWA flight.

The Major League Baseball Players' Association asked for a hearing before Commissioner William Eckert as a result of Finley's dispute with his players. Later an unfair labor practice charge was filed with the National Labor Relations Board in which Finley was accused of harassing his players in an attempt to persuade them not to go through with the hearing.

A preliminary hearing was held by Eckert on September 11–12 at which time a compromise was reached on all as-

pects of the case except the Krausse dispute. A full hearing
was requested by Krausse on September 28th, but surprisingly was cancelled when Lew withdrew his request. The
Krausse case marked the first time that the Major League
Baseball Players' Association filed a complaint of unfair
practices before the National Labor Relations Board.

KREUTZER, Frank
Salesman for Cantwell-Cleary Co.
Annapolis, MD

Frank never filed a complaint to the National Labor Relations Board. There was no need to as his career was relatively tranquil—8-18 in 78 games from 1962–69 with the
White Sox and Senators.

The southpaw out of Villanova University had his most
memorable game on July 2, 1965, when he fanned ten and
blanked the Tigers on a three-hitter. Frank also homered
to conclude his dream game.

KROLL, Gary
Insurance business
Tulsa, OK

Kroll had a lifetime 6-7 mark with the Phillies, Mets,
Astros, and Indians from 1964–69. The 6'6" right-hander
once fanned 19 batters in a California League game, only
to lose, 4-3, when he balked home the winning run. His 309
strikeouts that year were the most in all of professional
baseball. In 1964 although he worked in just 24 innings divided between the Phils and Mets, his four balks were the
most in the National League.

The Brigham Young product spoke about his career and
his successful life after baseball: "I should have been a consistent 15- to 20-game winner in the bigs, but I didn't pitch
much after I hurt my arm in 1966. I am now semi-retired.
After baseball I went into insurance and did very well. I
now oversee my own agency and invest."

KRSNICH, Mike
Employed with the Burlington Northern Railroad
Butte, MT

The younger brother of Rocky Krsnich, an infielder with
the White Sox in the late '40s and early '50s, Mike was a
flychaser with the Milwaukee Braves in 1960 and 1962,
hitting .190 in 15 games. A graduate of Central High
School in West Allis, he was the first native of the immedi-
ate Milwaukee area to play for the Braves in Milwaukee.

KRUG, "Chris"
Assistant baseball coach at UCLA

Everett "Chris" (he was born on Christmas Day) Krug
spent several years in the Cardinals' organization until
being drafted by the Cubs. The burly 6'4", 200-lb. catcher
came dancin' and prancin' with the Cubbies in 1965. Not
long after arriving he had a big day against the Cards,
picking up four hits and five RBIs in a twinbill.
    This Christmas baby made his final stop in San Diego in
1969 before riding away with a 79-game package at .179.

KUBIAK, Ted
Owner of the J.K. Cleaning Company
Concord, CA

Championships aren't won with mascots, rhetoric or
songs. They're won with players, expecially those who understand their role. Such was true of Ted Kubiak who was
a valuable infield replacement for Dick Green, Campy
Companeris, and Sal Bando for the Oakland A's World
Championship teams from 1972–74.
    Ted started out with the A's in 1967, then hopped
around with the Brewers, Cardinals, and Rangers before
returning to the A's during the '72 campaign. He closed in
San Diego in 1976.   .231

KUBISZYN, Jack
    Owns insurance agency, sells real estate
    Tuscaloosa, AL

Ray Charles was singing *Hit the Road Jack* and that's exactly what Jack did after hitting .188 in 50 games as an infielder with the Indians in 1961–62.

KUNKEL, Bill
    American League umpire

During the 1984 spring training season, Jeff Kunkel of the Texas Rangers brought the lineup card to home plate (with his name on it) where his father Bill was proudly waiting with his team of umpires. Bill says, "Baseball historians believe that this was the only time in the history of baseball that a father and son appeared in the same major league game as an umpire and player." It was surely an emotion-filled day for Bill Kunkel, the former player turned umpire. Then again, Bill's story is a tidal wave of emotion.

After toiling for several years in the minors, Bill made it to the majors, where he camped from 1961–63 as a relief pitcher with the Kansas City A's and New York Yankees. He logged a 6-6 mark in 89 relief appearances.

Kunkel, who also officiated in the NBA briefly, returned to the American League as an umpire. As one of the men in blue, he has made it to the All-Star Game and World Series.

Then the shattering news came a few years ago that he was suffering from cancer. Undaunted, he has fought back after two cancer operations. Bill has given several speeches with the message, "Cancer doesn't mean termination. Advances in technology have given us hope."

KURTZ, Hal
    Owner of several Reliable Home Appliances stores
    Queenstown, MD

"Bud" used his degree in business to its fullest advantage as a successful owner of several stores. The right-hander was in the Indians' organization for several years beginning in 1961. He made it to the big team in '68, winning his only decision in 28 games.

L

LABOY, "Coco"
Seattle Mariners' Latin American scout in Puerto Rico

The 1969 expansion helped make this 29-year-old Ponce, PR, native a big leaguer. Jose "Coco" Laboy had been playing in the Cardinal chain in Tulsa and led the P.C.L. in RBIs (100) in '68 when he was taken by the Expos in the expansion draft.

"Coco" made the most of his long-awaited chance by hitting 18 home runs and driving in 83 runs for Montreal's first-year fledglings. A very popular player in Montreal, his playing time steadily diminished as he hit just ten more roundtrippers during four more years with the Expos.   .233

LACHEMANN, Marcel
California Angels' pitching coach

In the frequently aired Lite Beer commercial, Marcel portrayed the veteran pitcher being eyed by scouts for a return trip to the biggies. Possibly it did "bring out the best" as he did return to the American League as the Angels' pitching coach in 1984. Four years older than brother Rene, Marcel's mound stay with Oakland was from 1969–1971 after Rene had already completed his tour with the A's. Marcel, who helped pitch USC to an NCAA title, was 7-4 in 70 games out of the A's bullpen.

LACHEMANN, Rene
Boston Red Sox coach

A product of the same Dorsey High School in Los Angeles as Detroit manager Sparky Anderson, "Lach" was a bat boy (1959–62) for the Dodgers as a youngster.

The enthusiastic catcher topped the Midwest League in homers (24) in his first pro season with Burlington in 1964. Ironically his only full year in the majors was his rookie campaign in 1965 as he hit .227 with nine home runs and 29 RBIs in 92 games as a 19-year-old. Rene then spent part of the '66 season with Kansas City and part of '68 with Oakland.

From 1969–72 "Lach" spent his time with Iowa (American Association) before dashing his playing hopes in favor of a managerial career which eventually brought him the job as the field boss of the Mariners. "Lach" was lionized in '82 when he led Seattle to a fourth place finish, the high water mark for the seven year old franchise.

Rene then sunk in June '83, but was named the skipper of the Brewers less than four months later. He was subsequently released following the '84 season.

LAHOUD, Joe
Executive vice-president of Pierce–Kennedy and Associates, a management consulting firm in Danbury, CT

Joe figured in one of the longest games in baseball history on July 27, 1969, when the Red Sox beat the Pilots 5-3. In the 20th inning at Seattle, Lahoud hit a two-run homer for the Red Sox. Tommy Harper belted a roundtripper in the bottom of the inning, but the Pilots came up short. However, every game wasn't so dramatic for Joe who hit .223 in his well-traveled, 11-year excursion with the Red Sox, Brewers, Angels, Rangers, and Royals from 1968–78.

The left-handed hitting outfielder jumped all the way from the Carolina League into the defending A.L. champions' lineup in 1968 when Tony Conigliaro was unable to return because of blurred vision, a result of his 1967 beaning.

In 1969 Lahoud had a three–home run game for the Bosox against the Twins.

Joe had his best season in 1974 when he hit .271 and banged out 13 homers as a member of the Angels.

LAMABE, Jack
Pitching coach for Beaumont (Texas League)

A graduate of Springfield College (MA), Jack earned a master's degree after writing a thesis titled "A study of the relationship of physical fitness to selected motor fitness items."

He wore the uniforms of seven different teams in as many years from 1962–1968. His 33-41 record was manufactured with the Pirates, Red Sox, Astros, White Sox, Mets, Cardinals, and Cubs. Jack borrowed from his thesis in '67 going down the stretch for the champion Cardinals. After coming from the Mets in mid-July he made eight appearances in August and did not allow a run. At one point he allowed no runs in 25 consecutive innings.

LAMB, Ray
Artist/sculptor for Superior Models
Balboa, CA

During the 1960s baseball fans had to digest such delectable names as Moose, Lamb, and Veale. Ray's 20-23 overall mark from 1969–1973 as a member of the Dodgers and Indians cannot be classified as a gourmet dish, but in the College World Series for U.S.C. in '64, Ray fanned ten and walked only one in six innings of relief pitching.

LAMPARD, Keith
Teacher and coach at Spring Hill High School
Houston, TX

Born in Warrington, England, Keith was one of the Astros' top draft choices in 1965. Signed out of the University of Oregon, he arrived in Houston in September '69.

In his first at-bat in the Astrodome, he hit a two-run

pinch-hit homer in the ninth inning to give the Astros a
3-2 victory over Cincinnati. It was the only roundtripper of
Keith's two-year stint with Houston in which he hit .238 in
62 games.

LANDIS, Bill
     Kings County Deputy Sheriff
     Hanford, CA

In 1967 Bill was 1-0 in 18 games during the "Impossible
Dream" year at Fenway, but missed the celebration as he
spent the late part of the season on National Guard duty in
Georgia. On the final weekend when the Red Sox clinched
the pennant in dramatic fashion, Bill was on a bivouac with
his company and had no idea of the excitement unfolding
in the Old Towne.
     After going 3-3 in '68, Landis and the Red Sox started
'69 in a most unusual way. On Opening Day he was the
winner in relief in a 5-4, 12-inning victory over Baltimore.
Following a 13-inning loss to the Orioles on the second day
of the season in which Bill was not involved, he gained
credit for the win in a 2-1, 16-inning marathon against
Cleveland. The fourth contest of the season was more routine, a 5-3 triumph in nine innings, but Landis was again
the winner in relief. After four games of the '69 campaign,
the Red Sox were 3-1 and Bill Landis was 3-0. He announced, "My goal for the season is now 161 victories."
Bill had to settle for just five in what turned out to be his
last hurrah, winding up 9-8 in 102 games overall.

LANIER, Hal
     St. Louis Cardinals coach

Hal is an example of an individual who stared adversity in
the eye and conquered it. Following a beaning in 1965, he
suffered fits of epilepsy which has been kept in check with
medication.
     The son of former pitcher Max Lanier, Hal signed with
the Giants in 1961 for a reported $50,000 bonus, turning
down numerous scholarship offers for college basketball.

As part of the deal, his father was named a scout for San Francisco.

Lanier arrived with the Giants and hit .274 in 1964, which turned out to be the best mark of his ten-year stay. He was also named the Topps All-Star Rookie second baseman that year although he played shortstop most of his career. Hal remained a fixture in the San Francisco infield through the 1971 season before completing the last two years of his big league swing with the Yankees.   .228

LAROSE, Vic
 Home construction business
 Phoenix, AZ

Do you remember the sounds of David Rose's *The Stripper?* How about Vic LaRose, who was stripped of his major league status after appearing in four games in the Cubs infield in 1968.

LARUSSA, Tony
 Chicago White Sox Manager

"He spends more time on the field now than he did as a player."

           —Don Baylor

Who would have ever dreamed when Tony roomed with Rene Lachemann in the minors that they would one day engage in battle on opposite sides in baseball history's longest game by time (8 hours and 6 minutes). On May 8, 1984, the White Sox and Brewers played 17 innings to a 3-3 draw. It was suspended to the following night, when the Chisox won the game after 25 innings, 7-6.

Tony took over as the White Sox manager late in 1979, replacing Don Kessinger. He appeared to be on the verge of being fired several times until his team took charge of the A.L. West in 1983 and ran away with the Division championship. He joins Jimmy Dykes and Al Lopez as the only White Sox managers to exceed the 5-year tenure mark. LaRussa, who is a licensed attorney in Florida, is the third lawyer-manager in the history of baseball. The other two,

Monte Ward, who managed the New York Giants and
Brooklyn in the late 1800s, and Hughie Jennings, who piloted Detroit from 1907–1920, are both in the Baseball
Hall of Fame. Former Yankee manager Miller Huggins
earned a law degree but never practiced law.

Tony, who signed an estimated $100,000 bonus contract
with the Kansas City A's in 1962, played 16 years of professional baseball, six of them in the majors. He had his
132-game stint with the A's, Braves, and Cubs between
1963–1973 and batted .199.

LASHER, Fred
> Operates a dry-wall company; recreation therapist for
> youth with drug and alcohol problems
> Merrillan, WI

This sidearm, almost submarine thrower, first inked his
name with the Twins in 1960. His big league life consisted
of time with the Twins, Tigers, Indians, and Angels primarily as a reliever. Fred did his best work with Detroit
from 1967–69, contributing five wins and another five
saves to the Bengals' '68 A.L. pennant and a couple of
scoreless innings to the World Series.   11-13

LAUZERIQUE, George
> Baltimore Orioles' regional scouting director in Latin
> America

In May of 1967 pitching at Birmingham in the Southern
League, this Cuban-born right-hander tossed a no-hitter
for seven innings, but was removed from the game because
of the policy of A's management of not allowing their
young prospects to throw more than 100 pitches in a game.
A month later in an exhibition contest against the parent
A's, George was once again taken out after delivering 100
pitches and allowing only one hit, a Bert Campaneris
single. On July 6th he did get a no-hitter, a seven inning,
1-0 gem over Evansville.

George joined the A's later that year, but could do no better
than 4-8 as a member of the A's and Brewers between
1967–70.

LAW, Ron
      Location unknown

Next to running, throwing is probably the most natural
athletic impulse we have. Ron was able to exercise his impulse in 35 games with the '69 Indians. After going 3-4,
this Canadian right-hander failed to reappear ever again.

LAWRENCE, Jim
      Ontario, Canada

In 1962 movie viewers were treated to the epic award-
winning *Lawrence of Arabia*. The following year baseball fans in Cleveland got a brief glimpse of Lawrence of
Canada, who made it into two games as a catcher with
the Indians.

LAZAR, Danny
      President of Slugger Corporation of America, a com-
      pany which produces hydraulic bar and billet shears
      Munster, IN

Danny got the most out of his athletic talents, rising to the
majors in 1969 as a member of the White Sox. But rising is
one thing, staying is another as Danny was gone after
going 0-1 in 17 games.
      His current job description indicates that Danny has prop-
erly cultivated his individual talents in life after baseball.

LEE, Bill
      Pitches for the Moncton Mets in the New Brunswick
      Senior League in Canada; construction work in Cape
      Cod area

"The people who have a thirst for winning are the people
who die young."
                                              —Bill Lee

      Bill ranks as one of the all-time zanies. He was 18-karat
crazy. During the mid-Seventies the Red Sox had a group

of players known as the Loyal Order of The Buffalo Heads.
They were Ferguson Jenkins, Rick Wise, Jim Willoughby,
Bernie Carbo and Bill "Spaceman" Lee. The eccentric
pitcher explained the reason for the term Buffalo Head in
his autobiographical book, *The Wrong Stuff*. "Jenkins
had nicknamed Zimmer (Red Sox manager) Buffalo Head,
pointing out that the buffalo was generally considered to
be the dumbest animal in creation. It was also Fergie who
had summed up Zimmer's problems with us by saying,
'The man knows nothing about pitching or pitchers. He's a
lifetime .230 hitter who's been beaned three times. He
hates pitchers. We will never see eye to eye."

The Bosox brass obviously didn't see eye-to-eye with the
Buffalo Heads as the cliquish herd each was given his
walking papers one by one. After Carbo was sold to the Indians, Lee went on strike for a day. Summoned to General
Manager Haywood Sullivan's office, Bill was docked a
day's pay. When told it would be about five hundred dollars, he snapped, "Make it fifteen hundred and let me take
the weekend off."

William Francis Lee III has always been considered
strange, the ultimate flake. The southpaw who wore number 37 wanted it changed to No. 337 since 337 upside down
spells Lee. A 12th-round selection in the 1968 free agent
draft after pitching USC to the NCAA championship, Bill
was in Boston from 1969–1978, and was a 17-game winner
for three straight seasons (1973–75). Following the '78
campaign, Bill was traded to Montreal where he was released in 1982.   119-90

LEE, Bob
    Iron worker
    Tehachapi, CA

During the same period that the Red Sox had their "Monster" in Dick Radatz, the Angels had their "Moose" in Bob
Lee, a strapping 6'3", 235-lb. right-hander who once broke
his hand punching a heckling sailor.

Bob struggled for several years in the levees and shant-
ies of the minors before making it to the bright lights of
Anaheim. He jumped from Batavia in the New York-Penn

League in 1963 where he overpowered everyone with a
20-2 record including 240 K's to the Angels. In '64 he set
an A.L. record for appearances by a rookie pitcher with 64
games. He would most likely have had more if he did not
suffer a fractured right hand in a game against Boston.
That year he posted the best ERA (1.51) in the A.L. while
saving 19 games to go with his 6-5 mark. In '65 and '66 he
was California's resident "Fireman," collecting 23 and 16
saves.

Then arm trouble struck the big guy. In a couple of years
he was gone after attempts with the Dodgers and Reds. He
finished 25-23 and was credited with 63 saves.

LEE, Leron
Active player in the Japanese League

Leron accepted a reported $50,000 bonus to sign with
the Cardinals after being selected by St. Louis in the
first round of the 1966 free agent draft. The outfielder
came up with the Cards in 1969 and also played for San
Diego, Cleveland, and the Dodgers through 1976, hitting .250.

He had his best year in 1972, hitting an even .300 for the
Padres.

Leron has been joined in Japan by his brothers Leon and
Terry who played in the minors, but never made it to the
big top.

LEE, Mike
Sales Manager for Pella Products, a window and door
company
Fallbrook, CA

Many questions have been raised regarding Lee Harvey
Oswald and the assassination of President Kennedy in
1963. There was nothing mysterious or controversial
about Mike Lee. The 6'5" lefty went 1-1 pitching for the Indians (1960) and Angels (1963).

LEFEBVRE, Jim
    San Francisco Giants' Director of Player Develop-
    ment; manager at Phoenix (P.C.L.)

As a teenager, Jim was the visiting team's batboy in
games played at the Los Angeles Coliseum. Reared in a
baseball family, his father, a California high school coach,
was a highly respected batting instructor, who had a book
published on hitting.

Jim joined the Dodgers in '65 without a portfolio of
glossy statistics. But his .250, 12–home run, freshman season earned him Rookie of the Year honors. Jim capped his
rookie season by hitting .400 in the World Series as the
Dodgers clipped the Twins. His 12 homers that year was
the lowest home-run total to lead a pennant winner since
Pee Wee Reese and Jackie Robinson had 12 each for the
Brooklyn Dodgers in 1947.

Instead of being cursed by the sophomore jinx he enjoyed
his finest of eight seasons in Los Angeles with career highs
in homers (24), RBIs (74), and average (.274).

A second baseman, Lefebvre was part of the all-switch
hitting infield the Dodgers used during the 1965–66 seasons, joining Wes Parker (first base), Maury Wills (shortstop), and Jim Gilliam (third base).

Jim rotated between second and third the next few years
prior to his release after the 1972 season. He then played
in Japan for four years before returning as a coach with
the Dodgers and Giants.　　　　　　　　　　　.251

LEHEW, Jim
    Employed with the Preston Trucking Co.
    Baltimore, MD

Password was a TV hit in 1961 when Jim got the word to
report to the Orioles. The Baltimore native, who threw
submarine style, pitched effectively in his eight appearances in '61 and '62 after winning 20 games at Pensacola
in the Florida State League. Unfortunately, his career was
cut short by an ailing back.

LEJOHN, Don
Manager at Bakersfield in the California League

"Ducky's" career was filled with starts and stops, then incredible joy at making it with the Dodgers at age 31 after sweating 11 years in the minors. In the final weeks of the '65 season, he was brought up to fill in at third base. He responded well, hitting .256 in 34 games.

LeJohn was on the World Series roster that fall and made it into one game as a pinch-hitter in his only year in the majors. "Ducky" has managed in the Dodger chain for the last several years.

LEMASTER, Denny
Co-owner of a construction company
Lilburn, GA

Denver Lemaster always appeared to be on the brink of greatness, but for some reason he never acquired celebrated status. Pitching for Jacksonville in a 1959 Sally League game, the southpaw chucker racked up 19 strikeouts, 11 coming in succession. In 1962 he graduated to the Milwaukee Braves for the first of 11 seasons in the senior circuit.

His highlight year came in '64 when he went 17-11. Denver stared greatness in the eye but blinked. After spending time with the Astros and Expos, he vanished with a 90-105 mark following the '72 season.

LEMAY, Dick
Montreal Expos' scout
Tulsa, OK

Like Sandy Koufax, Dick LeMay was a left-handed pitcher out of the University of Cincinnati. The comparison ends there as Dick was 3-8 in 45 games with the Giants and Reds from 1961–63.

LEMONDS, Dave
District manager for Marion Scientific, a medical company
Charlotte, NC

In 1965 Dave pitched and hit the Charlotte, NC, team to the National American Legion baseball championship with his father as the team's coach. The southpaw was named the "College Player of the Year" in 1968 after pitching for the University of North Carolina.

Dave's big league career was divided between the Cubs (1969) and White Sox (1972). He did not become the hero in Chicago that he had been in Charlotte, finishing at 4-8.

LEON, Eddie
Civil engineer
Tucson, AZ

Eddie was a two-time All-American shortstop in 1965–66 at the University of Arizona, where he graduated with a degree in engineering. He played the middle infield for the Indians, White Sox, and Yankees from 1968–75, dividing his time equally between second base and shortstop.

In 1970 Eddie led the A.L. in sacrifices with 23. His final average was .236 in 601 games, the last one his only one in a Yankee uniform.

LEONHARD, Dave
Owns a flower shop and garden center
Boston, MA

The first graduate of prestigious Johns Hopkins University in Baltimore to reach the majors, Dave was a long shot to make it to the big time after posting a 2-2 mark in high school and a 3-3 record in college. He was teaching high school and pitching amateur ball in the Baltimore area when he was signed by the Orioles.

He blossomed late, but was in full bloom at Elmira in 1965 when he went 20-5 and led the Eastern League in strikeouts with .209. At Rochester in '67, Leonhard was

15-3 leading the I.L. in both victories and winning percentage.

Dave was promoted to Baltimore that year and was used as a starter and reliever with the O's through 1972. He finished at 16-14 overall—not bad for a guy who was 2-2 in high school.

LEPPERT, Don
Houston Astros' coach

Don Leppert is not all that common of a name, but a pair of them, unrelated, made it to the majors. The first Don Leppert showed up with the Orioles in 1955, while this Don Leppert was a catcher with the Pirates and Senators from 1961–64, hitting .229 in 190 games.

After several minor league campaigns, this 30-year-old receiver broke into the majors by cracking a home run in his first big league at bat on June 18, 1961. Don connected for three consecutive roundtrippers on April 11, 1963, as the Senators defeated the Red Sox, 8-0.

LERSCH, Barry
Employed with an oil company
Houston, TX

The 7 Minutes was a popular novel in 1969 when right-hander Barry Lersch began a seven-year march, mostly with the Phillies. A graduate of the University of Colorado with a degree in education, Barry went 18-32. With the exception of one game in 1974 with the Cardinals, Barry spent his entire career as a member of the Phillies.

LEWIS, Allan
Coaching in winter league program in Panama

In 1974 Oakland owner Charlie Finley gained the attention of the baseball world when he used track star Herb Washington exclusively as a running "specialist." However, it was not the first time the innovative A's owner carried a designated runner. The first was Allan Lewis, the "Panamanian Express" who was around from 1967–73.

Unlike Washington, Lewis was a baseball player who hit over .300 in the minors several years. After pilfering 116 bases in 1966, Finley ordered Lewis to report to the big team. In his first appearance as a pinch-runner, Allan was embarrassingly picked off first base by Steve Hargan.

Allan participated in nine World Series games, all as a pinch-runner. In his six seasons, he came to bat 29 times and collected six hits.

LEWIS, Johnny
St. Louis Cardinals minor league hitting instructor

Ask any Mets' trivia buff, "Who broke up Jim Maloney's ten-inning no-hitter on June 14, 1966?" and they'll quickly reply, "Johnny Lewis." That certainly was his most memorable homer, but if Johnny had to pick a whole day it would probably be July 29, 1965, when he went 7-for-10 including two homers as the Mets split a twinbill with Chicago.

Lewis, who played the outfield from 1964–67 for the Cards and Mets, carried a .227 lifetime average.

LIBRAN, Francisco
Physical education teacher
Mayaguez, Puerto Rico

By 1969 the "San Francisco Sound" peaked with groups like The Grateful Dead, Country Joe and the Fish, and The Jefferson Airplane. That year Puerto Rican shortstop Francisco Libran played ten games for the expansion Padres and batted an even .100.

LINDBECK, Em
Dean of Kewanee High School
Kewanee, IL

Talk about a busy guy—meet Em Lindbeck. A former football and basketball coach at Kewanee High, Em is also the commissioner of the city, working directly under the may-

or. Lindbeck, who quarterbacked the University of Illinois
in the mid-Fifties, is equally busy at home as the father of
nine children.

Em had a lot more time on his hands as a major leaguer
since he appeared in just two games as an outfielder with
the Tigers in 1960.

LINDBLAD, Paul
    Building contractor
    Arlington, TX

Around baseball circles, Paul's name is frequently mentioned as part of a four-man gang that hurled a no-hitter
for the A's on Sept. 28, 1975, against California at the
Oakland Coliseum. He combined with Vida Blue, Glenn
Abbott, and Rollie Fingers in the 5-0, no-hit win.

He surfaced in '65 and circled around the A.L. through
the late '70s pitching for the Senators, Rangers, and Yankees. The left-hander appeared in a major league record
385 games without committing an error from Aug. 17,
1966, to April 30, 1974.

Some of Paul's brightest moments came with the A's in
'73 and '74. In three World Series games he was unscored
on and was the winning chucker in Game Three of the
1973 autumnal classic. Paul sailed away at 68-63 while
collecting 64 saves.

LINES, Dick
    Sales rep for a sporting goods company
    Fort Lauderdale, FL

In 1966 and '67 moviegoers stood in long lines to see the
James Bond flicks *Thunderball* and *You Only Live Twice*.
During both those years this Canadian-born southpaw was
busy in the bullpen for the Washington Senators, appearing in over 50 games and going 7-7 with a 2.83 ERA.

LINZ, Phil
   Owns nightclub, Avenue One
   New York, NY

"The harmonica was my only shot at the Hall of Fame."
                                          —P. Linz

Phil was noted for his witty lines like "Play me or keep me." He once was stopped by a police officer for a traffic violation and when the cop asked Linz why he wasn't wearing glasses, Phil answered, "I got contacts." The cop said, "I don't care who you know, you still have to wear your glasses when you drive."

After winning the Texas League batting title in '61 (.349) with Amarillo, Linz joined the Yankees the following year. Phil stayed in the Bronx until '65 before transferring to the Phils. His last hurrah came with the Mets in '68. In Linz's first at-bat as a Met, he hit into a triple play.

A valuable utilityman who was known as "Supersub," Phil had the reputation of making the big play with his glove and with his harmonica. It was the famous harmonica incident on Aug. 20, 1964, that gained Linz national attention.

The Yankees had just lost a doubleheader to the White Sox and were swept in four straight by the Pale Hose. The dejected Yankees, now in third place, were stalled in traffic on the team bus en route to the airport to catch a flight to Boston. Linz, who was sitting in the rear of the bus, whipped out his harmonica and wheezed the tune of "Mary Had A Little Lamb." Yankee manager, Yogi Berra, was in no mood to be serenaded after the four-game sweep. He barked at Linz, "Shove that harmonica up your ass." Phil then tossed it to Yogi who fired it back and hit Joe Pepitone on the knee.

Whether or not the incident revived the lethargic Yankees is questionable. But the pinstripers did proceed to win the pennant.

With regular shortstop Tony Kubek out with injuries, Linz played in all seven games in the Series against St. Louis. Although he hit just 11 career homers, he poked two in the Series that fall.   .235

LINZY, Frank
>   Coal miner for the Cherokee Coal Co.
>   Cowetta, OK

Many athletes have gone from the coal mines to the majors, but the opposite is true for Frank who was part of baseball's vintage rookie crop in 1965 that produced names like Jim Palmer, Joe Morgan, Tony Perez, and Rico Petrocelli. The right-handed relief specialist was named the N.L. Rookie Pitcher of the Year in '65 by *The Sporting News* after going 9-3 with 21 saves and an excellent 1.43 ERA as a member of the Giants after a quick look in '63.

On Sept. 1, 1967, Frank pitched the last five innings of a record-setting, 21-inning 1-0 victory over Cincinnati in relief of Gaylord Perry who had shut out the Reds through the first 16 innings. The contest tied a major league record with 20 scoreless innings, and also set a N.L. mark for the longest night game in time, 5 hours and 40 minutes. Linzy was the winning chucker in the game.

The hard-working hurler, who still gives everyone an honest day's work as a drag line operator, pitched until 1974. He also wore the uniforms of the Cardinals, Brewers, and Phillies, logging a 62-57 record plus 111 saves.

LIPSKI, Bob
>   Pennsylvania State Trooper
>   Scranton, PA

1963 was a big year for such singers as Bobby Vee *(The Night Has a Thousand Eyes),* Bobby Vinton *(Blue Velvet),* and Bobby Bare *(500 Miles Away From Home).*

Bobby Lipski was a few miles away from home himself that year as he made it into two games as a catcher with the Indians.

LLENAS, Winston
>   Manager at Edmonton in the Pacific Coast League

Winston came by his first name as a result of his father's admiration for Winston Churchill. An infielder-outfielder from the Dominican Republic, he was up and down be-

tween the Angels and the P.C.L. several times. Llenas
found P.C.L. pitching to his liking. In 1969 he hit .361 for
Hawaii and followed that up the next year with a .339 average and league-leading 108 RBIs.

For the Angels, Llenas was only able to swing for an
overall .230 mark in parts of six seasons from 1968–75.
But Winston's pinch-hitting success in 1973 was rather
stately when he led the A.L. in that department, going
16-for-56.

LOCK, Don
    Cattle and wheat farmer
    Kingman, KS

This big farm boy walloped a total of 122 home runs during
his eight-year stay with the Senators, Phillies, and Red
Sox which began in 1962.

A former captain of the Wichita University basketball
team, Don started out in the Yankee chain. He led the Carolina and Eastern Leagues in home runs before the Yankees swapped him to the Senators for Dale Long in 1962.

Lock, who made his big league debut on July 17, 1962,
whiffed his first two times at bat, then poked a home run
for the game's only run as Washington defeated Chicago,
1-0.   .238

LOCKE, Ron
    Assistant shift foreman for Pfizer, a chemical plant in
    Groton, CT

Ron had his single shot at glory in 1964 when he jumped
from the New York-Penn League to the Mets. The southpaw appeared in 25 games and took home a 1-2 log.

LOCKER, Bob
    Real estate business
    Lafayette, CA

It takes a special breed of man to appear in 576 games—all
in relief. That's what Bobby Locker did from 1965–75 with

the White Sox, Pilots, Brewers, A's and Cubs. The Iowa State University graduate led the A.L. in appearances (77) in '67. Wherever he went he established himself as a consistent performer.

Bobby closed with an impressive 57-39 record along with 95 saves and a 2.76 ERA.

LOCKWOOD, "Skip"
Sports psychologist consultant
Wayland, MA

Claude "Skip" Lockwood began as an infielder and even played in a few games at third base for the Kansas City A's. After hitting just .245 in the Midwest League in 1967 he switched to pitching.

Lockwood was selected by the expansion Pilots in '69. In the early '70s "Skip" had trouble winning with the Brewers, going 28-54. He apparently found a home in the Mets bullpen where he collected 39 saves combined in '76 and '77. He closed with the Red Sox in 1980 at 57-97 with 68 saves.

LOLICH, Mickey
Owns and operates a doughnut shop
Rochester, MI

"Nobody knows I'm around. Half the time, when my name is mentioned, people look around and say 'Who's he?'" cried Mickey Lolich during his distinguished, if not respected career that ran from 1963–79.

A natural right-hander, Mickey turned southpaw during his childhood years after a motorcycle fell on him when he was just a toddler and resulted in a broken left shoulder. A doctor recommended his tossing a ball left-handed to develop it. He listened and threw a ball from the left side for close to 40 years when he finally retired in 1979 with 217 victories and 2,832 strikeouts.

Like Avis, Mickey has always been number two. In 1968 when the Tigers won the pennant, Lolich won 17 games, but Denny McLain won 31. Vida Blue captured the Cy Young Award in 1971 though Lolich went 25-14 and led the league in strikeouts with 308. The next year Mickey won 20 games for the second consecutive year, but the prestigious Cy Young Award went to Gaylord Perry.

Mickey was numero uno in the hearts of fans following the '68 Fall Classic when he won three games himself. It was only the twelfth time that a pitcher collected three victories in the World Series as Lolich won the second, fifth, and seventh games. In Game Two he homered, the only four-bagger he hit in his career. Entering Game Seven, he was matched up with Bob Gibson at St. Louis who had been the victor in the seventh game in the '64 and '67 Series. Not this time, however—Mickey gave up only five hits and won, 4-1, marking the only time a southpaw had pitched three complete game victories in the World Series.

Lolich, who spent most of his career with the Tigers (1963–75), also saw action with the Mets and Padres before hanging it up. Does Mickey deserve Hall of Fame consideration? For comparison, let's match up Lolich with Don Drysdale who was inducted in 1984:

	Won	Lost	ERA	Strikeouts	Shutouts	Complete Games
Drysdale	209	166	2.95	2486	49	167
Lolich	217	191	3.44	2832	41	195

LONBORG, Jim
Dentist; graduated from Tufts Dental School in 1983
Boston, MA

In 1967 the Red Sox capitalized on their "Impossible Dream" theme that was taken from the musical *Man of La Mancha*. Jim Lonborg was an integral part of that dream when he went 22-9, leading the league in victories and strikeouts (246). This certainly came as a surprise since Jim struggled his previous two years with a combined 19-27 record.

"Gentlemen Jim" wasn't so kind to the Cardinals in Game Two of the World Series as he fired a brilliant one-hitter, retiring the first 20 batters until Julian Javier doubled. In the fifth game he allowed just three hits winning, 3-1, but lost to Bob Gibson in the final contest. Lonborg's

big year earned him the Cy Young Award and American
League Pitcher of the Year honors by *The Sporting News*.

The Boston chucker then made news during the off-
season when he suffered a broken leg in a skiing accident.
The mishap triggered the so called "Lonborg Law," a standard practice in contract phrasing adopted by team owners
stating that players would not be allowed to participate in
other sports.

Lonborg, who served up Mickey Mantle's last (536th)
home run, struggled to regain his '67 form the next few years
and for a time returned to the minors. After the '71 season,
Jim was involved in a multiplayer trade with the Brewers. In
1972 he went 14-12 for the Brewmen and appeared to have
his act together, since his 2.83 ERA was the best of his
career. He then journeyed to the Phillies where he won 17 in
'74 and 18 in '76. Pitching for the Phils on June 29, 1974 he
hit a grand-slam off Ron Taylor and the Expos.

Jim closed with the Phils in 1979 and took with him a
157-137 log.

LONG, Jeoff
> Owns business that recycles 55-gallon drums for steel
> Lakeside Park, KY

Jeoff came into organized baseball as a pitcher in the Cardinals' organization but eventually switched to first base.
His big league time was limited to 56 games with the
Cards and White Sox in 1963–64. The only home run of his
career came on May 15, 1964, as the Cards beat the
Braves, 10-6, in St. Louis. He underwent surgery for his
knee problems and was out of the game for three years before attempting a comeback in 1969.

"I was advised that I needed the knee surgery and the
decision was a bad one. I was out for the '66, '67, and '68
seasons, then had corrective surgery. It was futile coming
back with Tulsa in '69, but I appreciated the Cardinal organization for the opportunity," said Long.

Jeoff is proud of his golf ball hitting feats. In recent
years he has both won and been the runnerup in the National Long Drive championship which is sponsored by
Golf Digest magazine and the PGA Tour.   .193

LOOK, Bruce
    Management position with the Dyonics Medical Co.
    Okemus, MI

Bruce played in both the Braves' and Dodgers' chains as a
catcher after leaving Michigan State. He was then drafted
by the Twins. He made it to Minnesota in 1968 and hit .246
in 59 games as a backup receiver.

LOOK, Dean
    National Football League official; director of Instru-
    ment Makar, a medical instrument company

Bruce's older brother, Dean, was an All-American running
back at Michigan State. He signed with the White Sox, appearing in three games in 1961 as an outfielder, going
hitless in six at-bats.
    While in the minors he decided to scrap his baseball ca-
reer in favor of pro football. Dean has experienced a great
deal of success as an N.F.L. official and reached the zenith
of football officiating by working a Super Bowl.

LOPEZ, Arturo
    Mail carrier
    Park Ridge, NJ

Arturo was working as a 24-year-old bank clerk in the
Bronx in 1961, a year Hector Lopez (unrelated) helped lead
the Yankees to victory over the Reds in the World Series.
He fulfilled George Plimpton's dream by signing with the
Yankees on June 23, 1961, as a product of the annual Yankee Stadium tryout camp. The Puerto Rican–born flychaser made it into 38 games in '65, but hit just .143 as his
career went "La Bamba."

LOPEZ, Marcelino
   Maintenance worker and handyman
   Miami, FL

Talk about being a handyman, Marcelino was just that in
1965 when he went 14-13 for the Angels and was named
the American League Rookie Pitcher of the Year by *The
Sporting News.*
   Marcelino first arrived for a brief taste with the Phillies
in '63. But his main stretch ran from 1965–72 when he did
his mound work for the Angels, Orioles, Brewers, and Indians.
   The Cuban-born southpaw showed his temper while
pitching for Little Rock in 1963. He became so upset when
taken out of a game by Manager Frank Lucchesi, he threw
the baseball into the stands. Lopez was fined $27.50 by
Luchessi, who said it was "$25.00 for the throw and $2.50
for the ball." Marcelino recalled, "There were a lot of people playing out of position. I got mad and threw the ball
into the stands."   31-40

LOPEZ, Ramon
   Died Sept. 4, 1982, at age 45 in Miami, FL

Do you remember Trini Lopez? What about Ramon
Lopez? Ramon was purchased by the Angels from the
Mexican League in 1966. But in the majors he lost his
only decision in four games. Ramon returned to Mexico
and in 1970 pitched the league's first no-hitter in four
years.

LOUGHLIN, Larry
   Mechanic for I.H. Co.
   Tacoma, WA

In 1967 a new Pontiac Grand Prix cost barely $4,000. It's
doubtful that lefty hurler Larry Loughlin was able to af-
ford one with what he made as a three game reliever with
the Phillies that year.

His bat was certainly revved up as he hit safely in his only at-bat in the majors.

LOUN, Don
Sales rep. with the Glen Gary Brick Corp., the world's largest brick makers
Vienna, VA

Don earned his ticket to the big time after four winning seasons in the minors. His Sept. 23, 1964, debut with the Senators was a memorable one as he blanked the Red Sox, 1-0, on a five-hitter. Loun lost his other start that year, but in spring training of '65 he was quoted, "I'm a positive thinker and look to a long big league career." It was not to be as he never again returned to the majors.

LOVRICH, Pete
Senior clerk with Commonwealth Edison
Mokena, IL

In 1963 the Four Seasons were singing *Walk Like A Man* when Pete walked quite a few men and allowed several base hits in his one season of walking in from the Kansas City bullpen. The right-hander did pitch three innings of solid relief for the A's the day Early Wynn picked up his 300th win.   1-1

LUEBKE, Dick
Died at the age of 39 on Oct. 4, 1974, in Clinton, MO

If happiness is having a scratch for every itch, Dick was able to smile for a short time in 1962 since he was able to scratch his big league itch with the Orioles. That season the lefty hurler lost his only decision in ten relief appearances.

LUM, Mike
Hitting instructor in White Sox organization

This Hawaiian-born outfielder was around a bit longer than the popular TV series *Hawaii Five-O*. Lum, who began in the Braves organization, came in with Atlanta in 1967. His first major league hit produced the game-winning run as the Braves beat the Mets, 4-3.

An accomplished pinch-hitter, Mike has the distinction of pinch-hitting for Hank Aaron. On May 22, 1969, the Braves built up a 9-0 lead. Mike was called upon to pinch-hit for Aaron and doubled as Atlanta went on to win the game, 15-3. The Aaron-Lum connection was invoked once again on July 3, 1970. The home run champ was given a day off and Mike replaced him in right field and—would you believe—connected for home runs in three consecutive at-bats as the Braves pasted the Padres 8-1.

The Chinese-Hawaiian enjoyed his best year in 1973 when he whacked 16 home runs and knocked in 82 with a .294 average.

Traded to the Reds after the '75 season, Mike spent three years in Cincinnati before returning to Atlanta for a second try. His last shot was with the Cubs in '81.

LUND, Gordy
Manager at Edmonton in the P.C.L. in 1982

By the late 1960s, Gatorade was widely used on training tables for athletic teams throughout the country as it became a staple of the American sports diet. Shortstop Gordy Lund struggled to become a part of America's summer staple, but fizzled after 23 games with the Indians ('67) and Pilots ('69).   .261

LUPLOW, Al
Owns Smokey's Bar in Carrollton, MI

When baseball fans talk about great catches, the one that usually evokes discussion is the one Willie Mays made off the bat of Vic Wertz in the 1954 World Series. Al Luplow made one that need not take a back seat to any.

It came on June 27, 1963, at Fenway Park while Al was a member of the Indians. Dick Williams was batting for the Red Sox with two men on base and smashed a liner that was headed into the bullpen at Fenway. Luplow chased the ball in relentless pursuit and made a leaping backward catch while running at full speed. After catching the ball he flew over the wall and momentarily disappeared from sight, then got up holding the ball to complete the great catch.

Johnny Pesky, the Red Sox manager at the time, commented: "I've seen both Joe and Dom DiMaggio make some great catches, but nothing like that one."

Luplow recalled the play: "When I walked back out there the next inning I took a look at the spot I went over. I said I was nuts for doing it. I could have killed myself."

Luplow, who also played for the Mets and Pirates before leaving after the '67 season, was signed by Cleveland out of Michigan State where he also played football. In his first full season in '62 Al hit .277 and was named to the Topps Rookie All-Star team.   .235

LYLE, "Sparky"
      Employed at the Claridge Casino Hotel in Atlantic
      City, NJ

Relief pitching is a pressure position that attracts baseball's blithe spirits. Albert "Sparky" Lyle fits the bill perfectly.

A notorious clubhouse prankster, Sparky sat on birthday cakes and sawed up chairs. One day he staged a verbal argument in the Yankee clubhouse with coach Elston Howard as teammates watched nervously. Both retreated to a back room and returned with boxing gloves. The gag was on the spectators.

The arrival of spring training was always a show. He once flew into Fort Lauderdale on an air balloon. Another time he made his grand entry with his leg in a fake cast but his ultimate prank was the year a hearse pulled up to the field and out jumped Sparky from a casket.

However, on the mound he was no joke. From 1967–1982 the tobacco-chewing southpaw stamped himself as one of the great relief specialists in the history of the game. His numbers read: 222 saves, most games; relief pitcher no games started (899); and a 99-76 won-lost record.

The Orioles scouted Sparky on the sandlots and signed him after he struck out 31 men in a 17-inning game in 1963. The following year he was drafted by the Red Sox and made his debut in '67 with Boston serving the Sox well until 1972 when he was traded to the Yankees for Danny Cater and Mario Guerrero.

All he did in '72 was rack up an A.L. and Yankee record 35 saves and a 1.92 ERA, good for *The Sporting News* American League Fireman of the Year honors. It was a common scene in New York that summer when Sparky would jump out of the Toyota bullpen car, toss his warmup jacket to a batboy, and stride gracefully to the mound to the strains of *Pomp and Circumstance* and the roar of the crowd.

His bestselling book *Bronx Zoo* revealed intimate moments around the Yankee team and the turmoil that surrounded George Steinbrenner's castle in the Bronx.

With the arrival of Goose Gossage in New York, Sparky was disenchanted with his playing time. Following the '79 season he was sent to Texas in a multiplayer deal that involved Dave Righetti going to New York. His final stops were with the Phillies and White Sox where he was released after the '82 season.

Lyle joins Mike Marshall, Rollie Fingers, Bruce Sutter, and Willie Hernandez as the only five relief pitchers to win the Cy Young Award. He captured the coveted honor in 1977.

LYTTLE, Jim
Active in Japan

On June 8, 1969, 60,000 fans jammed historic Yankee Stadium for Mickey Mantle Day as the Yanks retired No. 7. Lyttle, who was the centerfielder in the Yankee lineup that day, collected a couple of base hits in the Yankees 11-2 romp over the White Sox. For a brief moment in '69, the Yankees mystique once again appeared.

The Florida State All-American was around until 1976

and also played for the White Sox, Expos, and Dodgers before going to Japan.   .248

M

MACKENZIE, Gordy
> Manager at Birmingham in the Southern Association, a Detroit Tigers affiliate

Adrenalin shot through Gordy's veins in 1961. The reason for this excitement was his promotion to the majors, even though his party lasted only 11 games as a catcher and ended with a .125 average. MacKenzie spent the early Sixties playing in the P.C.L., then while only in his twenties, became a manager at Geneva (NY-Penn League) in 1966.

MACKENZIE, Ken
> Associate Director for Programs and Yale Clubs with Yale Alumni Association
> Sidney, OH

While several of his buddies from the 1956 graduating class at Yale were climbing the corporate ladder, Ken was climbing the steep rungs of the minors. The Canadian-born southpaw appeared in a few games with the Braves in 1960 and '61, then was sold to the Mets. In one of his early outings with the newborn Mets, he struggled with his control and walked three straight batters. Manager Casey Stengel paid MacKenzie a visit on the mound and said, "Pretend it's the Harvards."

The former Yale captain does have the distinction of being the only winning Mets' pitcher in 1962 when he went 5-4. When the season ended, Ken appealed to the Mets front office for a raise, stating, "I'm the lowest paid member of the Yale class of '56."

MacKenzie also pitched for the Cardinals, Giants, and Astros before closing overall at 8-10 in 1965. He coached

the Yale baseball team for several years following his
playing days.

MACLEOD, Bill
Salesman for Bradford Associates
Salem, MA

Billy signed with the Red Sox directly out of high school in
Boston and appeared destined for success after leading the
Carolina League in victories, strikeouts, and ERA in his
first season of pro ball. But greatness never happened as
he was limited to just a couple of games with the Red Sox
in 1962 in which he lost his only decision.

The southpaw ran up quite a record in the Eastern
League, winning his last four decisions in 1964 before
going 18-0 with Pittsfield the following year.

MAESTRI, Hector
Salesman for the Miami Tobacco and Candy Co.
Miami, FL

Hector is one of only three players to play for the original
Washington Senators (1960) and the expansion Senators
(1961), joining Hal Woodeshick and Rudy Hernandez. Hector kept it sweet and simple, pitching in one game for each.
He allowed just one run in his eight big league innings,
good for a 1.13 ERA.

MAGRINI, Pete
Owns Zumwalt-Magrini Chrysler-Plymouth automo-
bile dealership
Santa Rosa, CA

There was a time when it looked like Pete Magrini would
combine with Billy MacLeod to help lead the Red Sox to
the Promised Land. While MacLeod went 18-0 at Pittsfield
in 1965, Magrini did all right for himself on the same
pitching staff, going 18-8. But like MacLeod, this right-
hander's hopes were dashed after appearing in three
games and losing his only decision.

MAHAFFEY, Art
Insurance business
Newton Square, PA

What are the chances of a pitcher picking off the first three
men who reach base against him in the majors? Art came
up in the middle of the 1960 season and worked a couple of
scoreless innings of relief against St. Louis in his debut.
He allowed base hits to Curt Flood and Bill White, then
proceeded to pick them both off first base. Mahaffey was
then given a start against the Giants and allowed a leadoff
single in the first inning, then picked off the runner at first
base.

Mahaffey, who was with the Phils from 1960–65 and
briefly with the Cards in '66, had a 59-64 career mark. On
April 23, 1961, the hard-throwing right-hander whiffed 17
Cubs, tying an N.L. record, en route to a 6-0 shutout. He
only went 11-19 with the '61 Phils, a team that lost 107
games, 23 in succession.

MALONEY, Jim
Runs automobile dealership; manager of Fresno team
in the California League
Fresno, CA

"The best game I ever pitched I got beat," says Jim
Maloney, who had his share of heartbreaks in a prestigious career that ran from 1960–1971. Maloney was referring to his 10-inning no-hitter on June 14, 1965, while
pitching for the Reds against the Mets. However, his
dreams went up in smoke when Johnny Lewis clouted an
eleventh-inning home run to give the Mets a 1-0 victory at
Crosley Field.

Maloney's trademark was his 99-mph fastball. In the
mid-Sixties his name ranked with those of Koufax, Gibson,
and Marichal.

His greatest year was 1963 when he went 23-7 with six
shutouts. On May 21st he tied a modern N.L. record when
he struck out eight straight Milwaukee Braves' batters
with Eddie Mathews and Hank Aaron among his victims.
Victory No. 20 came on September 2nd when he blanked

the Mets, 1-0, at the Polo Grounds with Pete Rose hitting the game's first pitch for a homer, the game's only run.

Two months after Johnny Lewis spoiled Maloney's no-hit bid in 1965, he no-hit the Cubs over 10 innings, this time winning on a home run by Leo Cardenas.

In '66 Jim went 16-8, including a league-leading five shutouts. He flirted with yet another masterpiece only to be once again disenchanted when he was forced to leave the game against the Pirates in the seventh frame due to an ankle injury he had suffered while legging out a triple the previous inning.

On April 30, 1969, Maloney no-hit the Astros. The following night Don Wilson of Houston returned the favor against Cincinnati. Jim also pitched an N.L. record-tying fifth one-hitter that year.

Lifetime, Maloney racked up 1,605 K's, 30 shutouts, and an ERA of 3.19. His won-lost mark stands at 134-84.

MANGUAL, Angel
    Employed with the municipal government in Ponce, Puerto Rico

When Angel was playing in Puerto Rico, he became acquainted with Roberto Clemente who was playing winter league baseball and recommended the Bucs sign the young outfielder. After hitting .320 and leading the Eastern League in home runs (26) and RBIs (102) to earn the league MVP, he made it into six games with Pittsburgh in 1969. But with Clemente blocking his way in right field, Angel was traded to the Oakland A's where he stayed from 1971–76.

Mangual was a valuable spare outfielder and pinch-hitter for the club during a dynastic period in which Oakland won five straight A.L. West titles and three World Series. His younger brother, Pepe, was an outfielder with the Expos and Mets from 1972–77.   .245

MANNING, Jim
    Computer operator for Johnson Motors, a tool and die
    company
    Weaukeegan, IL

Jimmy Clanton was singing about *Venus in Blue Jeans*
when Minnesota writers were writing about Jimmy Manning in Minnesota flannels. At age 18, Manning was the
youngest player to appear in the majors during the 1962
season. The right-hander failed to gain a decision in five
games.

MANUEL, Charlie
    Manager at Orlando in the Southern League

Charlie claims to have taken the biggest cut in baseball
history when he went from $250,000 a year as a player in
Japan to $20,000 as a scout for the Twins. He was quoted,
"And you know what, there's a lot less problems at
$20,000."

In 1980 Manuel was a hero in Japan, swatting 48 home
runs and driving in 132, but his statistics in the majors
weren't quite so hefty. An outfielder with the Twins
(1969-72) and Dodgers (1974-75), Charlie hit a slim .198
in 242 games.

The batting champ of the Midwest League in 1967 (.313),
Chuck made the Twins' roster in '69 after his surprise
showing in spring training when he tore up the Grapefruit
League. In one March game he actually called his shot,
pointing towards the outfield fence, and then producing
with a home run.

On July 20, 1969, man walked on the moon for the first
time and for the last time that season, Charlie collected a
base hit. He went hitless in his final 36 at-bats the rest of
the year and was heard muttering, "I hope I don't have to
wait for them to walk on the moon again before I get another hit."

MARANDA, Georges
Employed with a night club
Levis, Quebec

Pitching for the Giants on Aug. 21, 1960, Georges defeated the Cubs, 5-3, the day before his first child, a son, was born. A French Canadian, Georges Henri Maranda won one game each for the Giants in 1960 and the Twins in 1962. The right-hander was 2-7 overall after originally signing with the Braves organization in 1951.

MARENTETTE, Leo
Employed with Roadway, a trucking company
Toledo, OH

Astronaut Ed White walked in space from Gemini 4 in 1965 when Leo felt like he was on a space walk with his hometown Detroit Tigers. His walk was short and he did not emerge again until 1969 with the Expos. His five-game mission produced no decisions.

MARICHAL, Juan
Director of Latin American scouting for Oakland A's

After battling Juan's assortment of innumerable pitches and his frightening high kick delivery, more than one hitter soon discovered that he'd left his batting average as well as his heart in San Francisco. The first of what should eventually be a long list of major leaguers to debut in the 1960s to reach the Hall of Fame (1983), the "Dominican Dandy" became the third Latin American ballplayer to be so honored, following Roberto Clemente and Martin Dihigo.

From 1963–69 he posted 154 wins, including six 20-win seasons. In '63 he went 25-8 and in '68 was 26-9. Normally those figures pass the acid test for Cy Young laurels, but Juan had to get in line behind Sandy Koufax and Bob Gibson.

Unfortunately in the image-conscious world of baseball, Marichal is frequently associated with his bat-swinging assault against Dodger catcher John Roseboro on Aug. 22,

1965. His subsequent suspension may have cost the Giants the pennant that summer. However, he still won 22 games including 10 shutouts as the Giants finished second, two games behind Los Angeles.

The Dominican right-hander showed signs of greatness from the very beginning. In his big league debut with the Giants on July 19, 1960, he retired the first 19 Phillies he faced. He lost his no-hit bid when Clay Dalrymple singled with two out in the eighth inning. The 2-0 victory would be the first of 243, the shutout the first of a career total 52.

Juan hurled the only no-hitter of his career on June 15, 1963, against the Astros. It was the first no-hitter by a Giants' pitcher since Carl Hubbell no-hit the Pirates at the Polo Grounds in 1929. Less than a month later (July 2), he was involved in one of the classic pitching duels of all time when he hooked up with the Braves' Warren Spahn in a 16-inning marathon won by the Giants when Willie Mays homered in the 16th frame. Ironically enough, exactly 30 years before to the day (July 2, 1933), Hubbell went 18 innings in shutting out St. Louis, 1-0.

On May 26, 1966, Juan beat the Phillies, 1-0, in 14 innings, the longest 1-0 defeat in Phils' history. That season the high-kicking right-hander went 25-6 for the top winning percentage in the National League. Marichal beat the Mets 19 straight times before they caught up with him in 1967.

After a couple of losing seasons, Juan took his tiring right arm to Boston in 1974 and finished with the Dodgers (of all teams), pitching in two games in 1975.

MARONE, Lou
        International Sales Manager for Rampart America
        Toronto, Canada

While the Pirates had a shortstop named Barone for a brief period in 1960, they had a southpaw chucker named Marone in 1969 and '70 who was 1-1 in 30 relief appearances with a commendable 2.68 ERA.

MARSHALL, Dave
    Businessman
    Long Beach, CA

An outfielder with the Giants, Mets, and Padres from
1967–1973, Dave was named, along with Bobby Bonds and
Del Unser, to the Topps 1968 All-Star Rookie team after
hitting .264 in 76 games. From 1970–72, Dave joined the
Mets, but was unfortunately snuggled in between the two
Met pennant-winning seasons.

    In April 1970 Marshall beat Gaylord Perry and his
former Giant teammates with a grand-slam, providing the
Mets with a 5-2 victory.   .246

MARSHALL, Mike
    Baseball coach at St. Leo College in Florida; teaches
    exercise physiology

This controversial, sometimes cranky right-hander, originally broke in as an infielder in the Phillies' organization.
After being sold for a nominal sum to the Tigers in '66, he
was converted to a pitcher. Marshall, who holds a doctor-
ate in physiological psychology from Michigan State, has
quietly voiced his theories on pitching. The good doctor has
also been accused of doing his share of doctoring of baseballs.

    Mike cracked the Tigers' roster in 1967, going 1-3 in 37
games with 10 saves. Following another year of learning
in the minors at Toledo, he was shifted to the Pilots, where
he went 3-10 and recorded the only shutout of his career.

    From that point he went to Houston and Montreal where
he developed into one of the best relief pitchers in the
game. His ability to pitch frequently without much rest in
between became one of Mike's trademarks. With the Expos in 1972 he was 14-8 with an excellent 1.78 ERA and
a league-leading 65 games. The next year he made a record
92 appearances and saved a league-leading 31. The iron
man reliever appeared in a new record 106 games in 1974
for the Dodgers, including a major league record 13
straight from June 18–July 3. His performance earned
him the Cy Young Award, the first relief pitcher to do so.

Mike also established the A.L. record for appearances with 90 for the Twins in 1979, making him the only pitcher to lead both leagues in appearances. During his career he also saw action for the Braves, Rangers, and Mets. He finished with 187 saves.   97-112

MARTIN, Gene
>   Owns a commodity dealership; buys and sells grain
>   (foreign wheat and soybeans)
>   Leesburg, GA

Gene mailed in his signed contract to the Senators for the 1968 season from Vietnam where he was serving in the U.S. Army. Martin made it into nine games with Washington during the '68 season and showed his fiber by going 4-for-11 for a .364 average. In his fourth big league at bat, the hopeful outfielder hit a pinch-hit home run off Stan Bahnsen at Yankee Stadium.

Gene returned to the Far East where he played in Japan from 1974–79.

MARTINEZ, "Buck"
>   Active with the Toronto Blue Jays; also does post-
>   game show

The only one of the five Martinezes to come up in the Sixties who wasn't born in Cuba, John "Buck" Martinez has been in the A.L. since 1969 with the Royals, Brewers, and Blue Jays. The Sacramento State College product, who started out in the Phillies organization in 1967, was drafted by the Astros, then traded to the Royals with whom he came up in 1969.

Martinez's ears were ringing on Dec. 8, 1977 as he was traded twice the same day, first to St. Louis, then to Milwaukee. In the '76 ALCS, he went 5-for-15 against the Yankees.

MARTINEZ, Hector
Havana, Cuba

In the fall of 1962, American-Cuban relations grew perilous with the discovery of Soviet missile installations in Cuba. With the fear of nuclear war, the "Cuban Missile Crisis" was resolved when Soviet premier Nikita Khruschev agreed to have the missiles dismantled and removed.

After Hector played in seven games with the Kansas City A's in parts of the '62 and '63 seasons, he was dismantled and removed. .267

MARTINEZ, JOSE
Kansas City Royals' coach

Jose spent a decade in the minors. He was like a jockey doing his time before getting a good mount. Now it was time for him to prove he could ride when the Pirates brought him up in 1969. But his ride was relatively short (96 games) and ended the following year. Jose hit his only home run in the biggies on Sept. 8, 1969, and it came in dramatic fashion as he whacked a grand-slam in the ninth inning giving Pittsburgh a 6-2 victory. .245

MARTINEZ, Marty
Seattle Mariners coach

Versatile Marty Martinez was with the Twins in 1962, then returned in 1967 to play with Atlanta, Houston, St. Louis, Oakland, and Texas. A lifetime .243 hitter, Marty played every defensive position including one appearance as a relief pitcher with the Astros in 1969, a year he hit .308 in 78 games.

MARTINEZ, Tony
Miami, FL

Tony was heralded as a "can't miss" prospect. Several scouts labeled him as the best player to ever come out of

Cuba. The Tigers even offered to return power-hitting outfielder Rocky Colavito to Cleveland for Tony, but were denied.

Martinez never quite lived up to his billing as he played in
portions of four seasons with the Indians from 1963–1966
and hit just .171 in 73 games. In 1966 he was reported to have
married by a telephone proxy in New Jersey to Cuba even
though he hadn't seen his new bride in over seven years
since coming to the United States to play baseball.

MASHORE, Clyde
Heavy equipment operator; owns a ranch
Clayton, CA

At Mexico City in 1967, the New York Mets made Mashore
their No. 1 selection in the baseball draft. But after a brief
spring trial, the Mets returned Clyde to the Reds, the organization he came up with in 1969.

He spent most of his career lugging with the Expos
(1970–73). His first big league base hit was a homer off
Ray Sadecki of the Mets in 1970.   .208

MASON, Don
Chatham, MA

Perry Mason wound up a long run on TV in 1966, just as
second baseman Don Mason arrived on the scene with the
Giants. The fast and stylish infielder, who also played with
San Diego, took a roundabout way to the big arena. A
hockey goalie in his teenage years in New England, he attended Parsons College in Iowa, and was then signed by
the Senators before being drafted by San Francisco.   .205

MATCHICK, Tommy
Employed in a sporting goods store
Toledo, OH

Tommy won't forget July 19, 1968, when he sent a Moe
Drabowsky (Orioles) pitch into space with two outs in the
ninth, a man on base, and a full count to give Detroit a

dramatic 5-4 win and a critical victory in the Tigers' 1968 pennant drive.

Matchick enjoyed a six-year swing as a member of the Tigers, Royals, Red Sox, Brewers, and Orioles. A .215 life-time hitter, Tom was the talk of the Grapefruit League in 1967 when he hit .484 for the Bengals. The infielder appeared in three games for Detroit in the '68 Series.

MATHEWS, Nelson
    Drives a Wonder Bread truck
    Columbia, IL

Remember the advertisement "Wonder Bread Builds Bodies 12 Ways?" When "Nels" was around, he was wondering what remedy could be used to build his batting average, which stood at .223 lifetime after 306 games.

The big outfielder has fond memories of Sept. 16, 1962, when he belted his first major league home run, a grand-slammer, against Stan Williams and the Dodgers in the first inning of a 5-0 victory which snapped Chicago's ten-game losing streak.

"Nels" was traded to Kansas City and was a regular in the A's garden in '64. He had 14 homers, but also led the American League in striking out (143). He packed his lunch box the following year and drove away.

MATHIAS, Carl
    Pipefitter
    Oley, PA

You probably remember "Chubby" Checker from the early 1960s more than Carl "Stubby" Mathias, a left-hander who twisted his way in 11 games with the Indians and Senators in 1960–61, losing his only decision.

Like so many, he calls pitching in Yankee Stadium "the highlight of my career. But I don't miss the minor league bus trips and living out of a suitcase."

MAXIE, Larry
>   Toronto Blue Jays' scouting supervisor
>   Upland, CA

Peter Max designs were in vogue in the Sixties as the artist and designer was responsible for the color explosion. Right-hander Larry Maxie wore the big league colors of the Atlanta Braves in a not too explosive two-game career in 1969.

Larry fashioned a couple of no-hitters in the minors, the first coming in 1961 for Austin (Texas League). In 1965 he suffered eight straight defeats before throwing a no-hitter for the Atlanta Crackers (I.L.).

MAXVILL, Dal
>   Operates a travel agency called "Cardinal Travel, Inc"; Atlanta Braves' coach

When Dal Maxvill struggled at bat (0-for-22) in the 1968 World Series for the Cardinals, he shattered the dubious record previously held by Dodger first baseman Gil Hodges, who went hitless in 21 at-bats in the '52 Fall Classic. Dal's hard times against Tiger pitching seemed to go unnoticed compared to the publicity Hodges received, likely because Charles Dallan Maxvill gained a reputation for his slick glove, not his bat. He established an N.L. record for the highest fielding average (.9726) by a shortstop, lifetime, with ten or more years' playing time.

From 1962–1975 Dal's classy glove electrified audiences in baseball backyards throughout the majors as he spent his days with the Cards, A's, and Pirates. Although primarily a shortstop, he took over at second base late in the '64 season for the injured Julian Javier. On the final day of the campaign, Dal drove home three runs with a pair of clutch base hits as St. Louis clinched the National League pennant. Although only 6-for-26 during the regular season, he started all seven games in the World Series against the Yankees and went 4-for-20.

Dal's fourth World Series came in 1974 with the Oakland A's. He finished his career a year later with a .217 lifetime mark.

MAY, Carlos
        Post Office employee
        Chicago, IL

Lee May's younger brother was on reserve duty with the Marines at Camp Pendleton, California, when a mortar misfire nearly ended his big league career just as it was getting started. After winning the Carolina League batting title with a .330 average in 1968, he was called to the White Sox and appeared in 17 games. The following year Carlos enjoyed a banner rookie campaign, hitting .281 with 18 home runs.

Life momentarily went on the fritz for Carlos when he lost much of his right thumb in early August, the result of his military accident. Although his season was prematurely terminated, he was named the American League Rookie of the Year by *The Sporting News*. Following skin graft surgery, the determined first baseman-outfielder put together some productive seasons for the Pale Hose in the early Seventies, hitting a career-high .308 in 1972.

Carlos wore Yankee linens in '76, then returned to close his ten-year A.L. stay with the White Sox.   .274

MAY, Dave
        Sales representative for a cable television company
        New Castle, DE

This quiet, baseball-serious outfielder was around from 1967–1978. "Chopper" did his flychasing for the Orioles, Brewers, Braves, Rangers, and Pirates with his penthouse season coming in 1973: 25 homers, 93 RBIs and a .303 avg. for the Brewers.   .251

MAY, Jerry
        Owns a redi-mix company called the "Transit Mix Concrete Co. Corp."
        Staunton, VA

The 1964 movie *Seven Days in May* was a highly acclaimed suspensful political drama. That same year catcher Jerry May arrived in the majors with the Pirates and was involved in a highly emotional baseball drama.

Jerry spoke about the game he rates as the greatest thrill of his career. "It was the night Danny Murtaugh retired. We were playing the Reds and the game went into the 16th inning. Before the inning started Danny asked me if I could squeeze a runner home. I thought he was crazy since the inning hadn't even started.

"Donn Clendendon led off the inning with a double. Bill Mazeroski moved him over and made it to first base. I then came up and squeezed in the winning run."

Drama always seemed to follow Jerry. In 1969 he was injured when he crashed into the dugout at Montreal. While en route to the hospital in an ambulance, May suffered further injury when the vehicle was involved in an accident. He recalled, "A guy ran a red light. I hurt my arm which affected my career. I was injured worse in the accident than I was on the field."

Jerry was in big league box scores for ten seasons with the Pirates, Royals, and Mets.   .234

MAY, Lee
   Kansas City Royals' hitting coach

Some players need a sense of style and a bit of swagger. Lee went about his job in a rather quiet, colorless way. He played 16 full years between 1965–82 with tours of both the American and National Leagues.

From 1967–79 May was one of baseball's top run producers, averaging 28 home runs and 94 RBIs per season. The soft-spoken first baseman, who also played in the outfield, was voted the N.L. Rookie of the Year in 1967. Between May 24–28 (1969) he tied a major league record with six home runs in three games, hitting two in each game. Lee's career high in four-baggers came in '71 when he parked 39 with the Reds. He is one of six players to hit 100 homers in both leagues.

After the '71 campaign May went to Houston in a multiplayer deal. He then brought his dangerous stick to Baltimore where he was employed from 1975–80. Granted free agency after the '80 season, he drove away with the Royals in '82. His stats read: .267 average, 354 homers, 1,244 RBIs.

MAY, Rudy
> Active player (disabled list) New York Yankees in 1984

Rudy arrived in 1965 with the Angels and in his debut on April 18th he one-hit Denny McLain and the Tigers. Rudy pitched 7⅓ innings of hitless ball before Jake Wood cracked a pinch-hit single in the eighth inning. May left in the ninth, down 1-0. The Angels tied it, but lost the game in the 13th frame.

After a few mediocre seasons in California, he was sold to the Yankees, where his career took an uptown swing. He bounced around with Baltimore and Montreal, then returned to New York. His winningest campaign was in '77 with the Orioles (18-14). With the Yankees in 1980 he went 15-5 and captured the ERA title (2.47).   152-156

MAYBERRY, John
> Minor league hitting instructor for Toronto Blue Jays

It was in 1968 that Elvin Hayes scored 39 points to lead the University of Houston to a 71-69 victory over UCLA before over 52,000 fans in the Astrodome. That summer 18-year-old John Mayberry joined the denizens of the Astrodome.

John signed with the Astros after turning down numerous college basketball scholarship offers. For four years he shuttled between Houston and Oklahoma City, then was traded to Kansas City after the '71 season. In 1972 big John took over as the Royals' regular first baseman and responded by hitting .298 with 25 round-trippers and 100 RBIs.

A product of Detroit's Northwestern High School which produced Willie Horton and Alex Johnson, John spent six years at Kansas City. Twice he knocked in over 100 runs and in '75 hit a career-high 34 homers. But things went downhill after that. After trips to Toronto and New York (Yankees), it was over for John in 1982. He ended with 255 homers and a .253 average.

Mayberry has the distinction of hitting the first home

run in Kansas City's new Royals Stadium on April 10,
1973. Twice in his career he hit three homers in a game.

MCANDREW, JIM
Stripmine executive
Napierville, IL

A psychology graduate from the University of Iowa, one
would have to wonder about the psychological effect of
Jim's first season in the National League (1968). "The
Pride of Lost Nation, Iowa," Jim found life in the big city
with the Mets quite frustrating in his first few outings
since he lost his first three starts by scores of 2-0, 2-0, and
1-0. He then won for the first time by blanking the Cardinals, 1-0, but the luckless rookie then lost again by scores
of 2-0 and 2-1. Jim's 4-7 mark in '68 was quite deceiving in
light of his snappy 2.28 ERA.

The tall right-hander remained with the Mets during
the glory years, but never appeared in a post-season game.
He wound up in San Diego in 1974.   37-53

MCAULIFFE, Dick
Owns coin-operated laundry machines in apartment
complexes
West Simsbury, CT

Dick had a distinct batting stance. He stood at the plate in
the fashion of a banty rooster ready to spring. He held his
bat parallel with the ground at waist level, a lefthanded-
hitting Gil McDougald. He cocked his right foot in the air à
la Mel Ott.

McAuliffe's debut with Detroit in 1960 was spectacular.
In his first game he singled home the tying run against
Washington. The following night he homered and knocked
in two runs off Cleveland's Dick Stigman. And then, with
defeat imminent, he bailed out the Tigers with two out in
the ninth inning by hitting Frank Funk's first pitch over
the right field fence for a two-run homer that won the
game.

In 1964 the spunky shortstop set a home run record for
Tiger shortstops with 24. He became the first Detroit

shortstop to ever start the All-Star Game in 1965 and homered in the mid-summer classic that year. In '66 he also played shortstop in the July classic and made it in '67 as a second baseman when switched to the keystone sack by manager Mayo Smith.

One of the toughest players to double up during his day, Dick led the American League four different years in hitting into the fewest double plays. In 1968 he didn't hit into a DP the entire season.

Dick rounded out his 16-year career with the Red Sox in 1974–75. He showed a .247 average including 197 home runs.

MCBEAN, Al
Director of Parks and Recreation
Charlotte Amalie, Virgin Islands

Hollywood probably wouldn't buy the story of how Al McBean became a major league pitcher. In the late 1950s he was working as a newspaper photographer in his native Virgin Islands and was assigned to cover a tryout camp being held by the Pirates. He put his camera down, and decided to tryout himself. Al impressed the bird dogs and was signed to a contract.

By 1961 he was in Pittsburgh threads. The fashionable dresser became part of the Bucs' starting rotation the following year, winning 15 games. Converted to a reliever in '63, Al carried victory with him like a talisman. He was named *The Sporting News* "Fireman of the Year" in '64 with an 8-3 record plus 22 saves and an outstanding 1.91 ERA. McBean's final year with the Buccos was 1968, a year he was switched back to a starter. On July 28th he walloped a grand-slam homer off Larry Jaster of the Cardinals.

Al took his splendid wardrobe to San Diego in the expansion draft for the customary $200,000 price tag. Thus the Pirates realized a profit of $199,900 on Al since he was signed to his original contract with the organization for $100.

McBean had a brief stay with the Dodgers, then finished

his ten-year story back with the Pirates. Overall he stands
at 67-50 with 63 saves.

MCCABE, Joe
        Pan Am airline pilot
        Lebanon, IN

A 1960 graduate of Purdue, Joe was considered the top
catching prospect in college baseball that year after hitting .432 and winning Big Ten MVP honors. The Twins
outbid a dozen other teams for Joe, but he was up with
Minnesota only briefly in '64, then was traded to Washington in '65.

    Joe says, "I feel many times that I am as fortunate as
anyone living in knowing that I have already in my life
had two careers; most young boys would give nearly anything to obtain only one of them."   .174

MCCALL, Brian
        Free lance artist
        Alexandria, VA

"I think I'm a better artist than I was a ballplayer."
                              —Brian Allen McCall

    Brian's career illustrates the game's capriciousness.
Known as "Bam," this outfielder was in seven games with
the White Sox in 1962–63 and went 3-for-15. However, two
of his three hits were home runs at Yankee Stadium, both
coming in the only game he was ever penciled in a starting
lineup in the majors.

    Bam's big day came on Sept. 30, 1962, against the Yan-
kees when he took Bill Stafford deep twice.

MCCLAIN, Joe
        Production supervisor with Pharaseal Laboratories
        Johnson City, TN

Joe had a total of 30 decisions in his two-year trek. Unfortunately, 22 of them were losses. But then again Joe was

with the 1961–62 Washington Senators, a team that resembled a garage sale with worn-out items.

One of McClain's eight victories came on April 2, 1961, when he beat the Twins, 5-3, in the first game ever played at Metropolitan Stadium in Minnesota.

MCCOOL, Billy
   Salesman for the Peninsula Steel Co.
   Centerville, OH

The more you know about pitchers, the less you can trust them. Billy was the Reds' top reliever in the mid-Sixties. Plagued by arm trouble, his arm yelped for the last time at age 26.

Named to the Topps Rookie All-Star team in '64, Billy saved 21 and 18 the next two years for Cincinnati, averaging a strikeout per inning. The hard-throwing southpaw, who developed a gimpy arm, finished his seven-year run with San Diego and St. Louis at 32-42 plus 58 saves.

MCCRAW, Tom
   San Francisco Giants' batting coach

Tom had a big year in 1962 when he won the American Association batting crown (.362). Playing for the White Sox on May 24, 1967, he feasted on Twins pitching when he banged out three home runs and collected eight ribbies.

The first baseman-outfielder moved around the American League from 1963–1975 with the White Sox, Senators, Indians, and Angels. On May 3, 1968, he tied a major league mark by committing three errors in one inning.   .246

MCDONALD, Dave
   Supervisor for the Carolina Freight Company; assistant baseball coach at Gardner-Webb College in Boiling Springs, NC

Dave's father, Lester McDonald, was a star football player at the University of Nebraska in the mid-1930s, then played for the Bears and Eagles in the NFL. Dave was an All-State pigskin selection himself in Nebraska and was set to accept a football scholarship to Nebraska when he decided to sign with the Yankees.

The left-handed hitting first baseman was in pinstripes briefly in '69 after hitting 24 homers for Syracuse (I.L.), then made one more appearance for the Expos in 1971. .145

MCDOWELL, Sam
Counsels youngsters with drinking and drug problems
Pittsburgh, PA

The saga of "Sudden Sam" started and ended in Pittsburgh. The hard-throwing, hard-drinking southpaw found that mixing "fastballs" with "highballs" was fatal in the game of baseball.

McDowell signed an $85,000 bonus contract out of high school. In his first big league appearance with the Indians in 1961 he informed the American League that he was all business as he hurled six scoreless innings while walking and striking out five. The game set the pattern for his roller coaster career in which he was a league leader in strikeouts and walks, five times each. His ratio of 8.85 strikeouts per nine innings ranks him third behind Nolan Ryan and Sandy Koufax.

"Sudden Sam" fanned a career-high 325 batters during the '65 season when he went 17-11 with a league-leading 2.18 ERA. In 1966 McDowell tossed back-to-back one-hitters on April 25th and May 1st. From 1968–70 the big left-hander led the American League in strikeouts. He had a smart 1.81 ERA in '68 and was a 20-game winner the only time in his career in '70 (20-12 with the Indians).

Following the '71 season, McDowell was traded to the Giants for Gaylord Perry. He then came down the home stretch with the Yankees and Pirates where he finished in 1975. 141-134

MCFADDEN, LEON
Operates a nightclub
Brownsville, TX

With such teammates as future major leaguers Bob Tolan
and Willie Crawford, it's not surprising that Leon's Fremont High School team was the Los Angeles city champions in the early 1960s. Leon hit .215 in 62 games with the
Astros from 1968–1970.

MCFARLANE, Orlando
Location unknown

Orlando was with the Pirates, Tigers, and Angels for
portions of five seasons from 1962–68. A Golden Gloves
boxer in his native Cuba, Orlando had the eye of the tiger,
but the bat of a pussycat (.240).

MCGINN, Dan
Public relations work for the Northwestern Bell Tele-
phone Co.
Omaha, NE

Dan was a Canadian hero based on his heroics during the
first week of Expos' history. On April 8, 1969, he relieved
in the first Expos game ever against Tom Seaver and the
Mets. When he took his turn at bat he homered off Seaver,
the first four-bagger in Montreal history and the only
homer of his career. In the first big league contest ever
played in Canada, Dan entered the game and shut out St.
Louis over five innings. He also drove in the game's winning run which led to an Expos' celebration that saw Dan
carried off the field.
   McGinn, who earned a B.A. degree in communications
from Notre Dame, and was also a punter for the Fighting
Irish in the early '60s, plugged into big league parks from
1968–1972. The southpaw was 15-30 for the Reds, Expos,
and Cubs during his stay.

MCGLOTHLIN, Jim
     Died Dec. 23, 1975, at age 32 in Union, KY

Baseball fans, particularly those of the Angels and Reds, were stunned to learn of the death of Jim McGlothlin, a former pitcher who passed away at age 32, a victim of cancer.

The red-haired right-hander was blazing in his first full season in 1967 when he went 12-8 with the Angels. From May 22 to June 11 he pitched 36 consecutive scoreless innings, tossing three straight shutouts. His six shutouts set the pace in the Junior Circuit that year. Five of his whitewashings came in the first half of the season, which earned him a spot on the All-Star team.

Jim hurled two scoreless innings in the July classic played at Anaheim that summer. After floundering the next couple of years, he went to the Reds in a trade for Alex Johnson. In '70 and '72, Jim played an integral part in helping Cincy to pennant-winning seasons. He was the Reds' pitcher on June 30, 1970 when Riverfront Stadium was dedicated.

The right-hander completed his nine-year journey with the White Sox in 1973 at 67-77.

MCGRAW, Tug
     Active with Philadelphia Phillies in 1984

"The 1969 season was like being in love—you always remember the first time."
                              —Frank "Tug" McGraw

Winning has always been a love affair with this effervescent left-hander. His triumphant march from the mound to the dugout following a save was always a colorful spectacle as he repeatedly tapped his glove against his body while his face beamed with satisfaction with his fist clenched in victory.

Prior to McGraw's success (9-3) with the incredible '69 Mets, the highlight of his career would have been in 1968 when he was pitching for Jacksonville (I.L.) and beat

Buffalo, 14-1, while going 5-for-5 at the plate including a home run.

In '65 when he was 2-7, one of his wins came against Sandy Koufax, which snapped a 13-0 lifetime mark by Koufax vs. the Mets.

McGraw was also the winning pitcher of the game in which Steve Carlton struck out 19 batters and lost on Sept. 15, 1969.

During the 1970s the ex-Marine established himself as one of the all-time relief greats. In 1972 he set a Mets' club record with 27 saves, broken by Jesse Orosco in '84. The following year he spearheaded the "You Gotta Believe" slogan. His words were not phony as he led the charge to the pennant. At the end of the season Tug went on a sizzling 19-game streak in which he garnered 12 saves, 5 victories, and posted a 0.88 ERA.

Following the '74 campaign, the Mets dealt Tug to the Phillies and for the next ten years he showcased his talented wing in Philly. In 1979 he set an N.L. mark and tied an M.L. record by yielding four grand-slams in one season.

One of baseball's most engaging personalities, McGraw was a major factor in Philadelphia's 1980 championship season. After coming off the disabled list in July, he allowed only three earned runs the rest of the year in 52⅓ innings of work.   96-92

MCGUIRE, Mickey
Agent for the Metropolitan Life Insurance Co.
Dayton, OH

Mickey spent most of his career cloistered in the minors. Twice his phone rang to report to Baltimore. After appearing in a total of 16 games, the second baseman became a memory, batting .190.

MCKNIGHT, Jim
Pipe fitter for a construction company
Bee Branch, AR

Remember the hit songs *Are You Lonesome Tonight* by Elvis in 1960 and the Tokens' rendition of *The Lion Sleeps*

Tonight in 1962? An infielder-outfielder, Jim McKnight was in 63 games for the Cubs in 1960 and 1962 before saying good night at .231.

MCLAIN, Denny
Associated with a 24-hour emergency walk-in medical clinic
Sarasota, FL

"I'm not a bum, not a crook, not a dope peddler."

If Denny McLain had as much command of his personal life as he had of his pitches, he would probably be in the Hall of Fame today. But the former Detroit pitching ace, the last man to win 30 games, will never make it to Cooperstown. If convicted of 1984 federal charges of racketeering, conspiracy, extortion, possession and distribution of cocaine, and conspiracy to import cocaine, the free-wheeling ex-chucker may never make it out of jail.

Following a 38-7 record at Chicago's Mt. Carmel High School, he was signed by the White Sox in 1962. In his first pro start the talented right hander hurled a no-hitter pitching for Harlan (Kentucky) in the Appalachian League.

The next spring he was claimed on waivers by the Tigers and debuted fashionably in September 1963, when he beat the White Sox 4-3 while hitting a home run. Although primarily a starter, on June 15, 1965, at Detroit in a game against the Red Sox, he struck out the first seven Bosox batters he faced in relief and left with an impressive total of 14K's in 6⅔ innings of work.

In 1967 Denny went 17-16, but failed to win a game in September. The bespectacled, Pepsi-Cola drinking hurler discarded his goggles for contact lenses prior to the '68 season. Something helped as he became the most celebrated player in the majors that summer going 31-6, the first 30-game winner since Dizzy Dean went 30-7 in 1934.

His climb to 31 was interesting. In victory No. 29 he had one of his better days at the plate in a 7-2 win over the Angels when he banged out two singles and a triple. When he won No. 30, Reggie Jackson homered twice for the A's. Dizzy Dean, who was in attendance, met McLain after the game, wrapped his arms around the Tiger hero and said,

"They won't have this much excitement here if they win the World Series." On September 19th he recorded his 31st victory, a 6-2 win over the Yankees. Mickey Mantle hit No. 535 that day, the next to last of his career. Supposedly McLain "laid one in there" for Mickey who moved into third on the all-time list ahead of Jimmie Foxx at the time. When Denny went for No. 32 he was a 2-1 loser to the Orioles. Denny's big year earned him MVP and Cy Young honors.

The following season the self-confessed "character" was 24-9 and tied Baltimore's Mike Cuellar for the American League Cy Young Award.

But he ran into problems in 1970 when he overextended himself in some business dealings and became involved with organized gamblers. He was the victim of the first suspension imposed by Bowie Kuhn during his term as Baseball Commissioner when, on Feb. 18, 1970, Kuhn suspended McLain indefinitely for his gambling. After Denny was reinstated (July 1), he was suspended again Sept. 9, 1970, for carrying a gun during a road trip and in between received a suspension for dousing a sportswriter with ice water. The Detroit bad boy was reinstated by Kuhn at the end of the season, but was dealt away to the Senators.

After going 10-22, he completed his tumultuous career in '72 with the A's and Braves at 131-91.

MCMANUS, Jim
      Roslindale, MA

Jim hit 32 homers for Shreveport to lead the Southern Association in 1960. The left-handed-swinging first baseman was invited to Kansas City where he went 4-for-13 (.308) including a home run, but he never returned to the big leagues.

MCMATH, Jimmy
      Pressman for the *Tuscaloosa News*
      Tuscaloosa, AL

Teenager Jimmy Lee McMath came out of Tuscaloosa, AL, to hit .388 in the Midwest League in 1968, a year the

19-year-old flychaser was brought up to the Cubs and went 2-for-14 (.143).

McMath was described in a column by Chicago writer Jerome Holtzman as "a veritable fashion plate, a picture of sartorial splendor." The following season Jimmy fashioned army fatigues and never returned to the majors.

MCMULLEN, Ken
        Member of Dodgers Speakers Bureau; operates baseball camps
        Camarillo, CA

Third base demands that a player be particularly adept at fielding bunts, charging slow rollers, and scooping up the ball barehanded to make the quick throw to first. Ken McMullen graded A in all these categories in his lengthy (1962–77) tenure with the Dodgers, Senators, Angels, A's, and Brewers.

McMullen helped the Dodgers to the N.L. flag in '63 with his brilliant fielding during the second half of the season, but a pulled muscle kept him out of action for the World Series. After the '64 campaign he was traded with Frank Howard to Washington for pitcher Claude Osteen. For the next five years he was a rock at third for the Senators.

Ken's fielding exploits have always been respected. In '66 he once collected a record 11 assists in a game against the Red Sox. Offensively his best year was in '69 when he had 19 homers, 87 RBIs, and a .272 average.

After three years with the Angels, he returned to the Dodgers in '73. He was used as a backup to Ron Cey who took over the hot corner that year. Ken also developed into a dangerous pinch-hitter with a lifetime total of 10 pinch-hit home runs. He finished with the A's and Brewers at .248.

MCNALLY, Dave
   Automobile dealership
   Billings, MT

"McNally was the only player who could consistently bring General Manager Harry Dalton to his knees."
                                                            —Earl Weaver

   Following the 1975 season Dave and Andy Messersmith challenged baseball's sacred reserve clause. Their victory ultimately brought the Lords of Baseball to their knees. Although McNally had no intention of ever playing again, he fought the ancient clause on principle. Peter Seitz, the arbitrator, ruled that the option clause in their contract bound them to their teams for only one year. The decision opened the stuffy traditional baseball world to free agency, the most revolutionary concept since Alexander Cartwright laid out the 90-foot baselines.
   Dave did not play baseball in high school since the school did not field a team. But after his impeccable showing with the Billings American Legion team, he signed a reported $80,000 bonus with the Orioles.
   Late in '62, Dave was called up to Baltimore. On Sept. 26th he made an astonishing debut at age 19 by beating the Kansas City A's, 3-0, on a two-hitter. From 1968–1971 his talented left wing was the cause célèbre of the A.L., winning 22, 20, 24, and 21 games for an overall 87-31 mark.
   From Sept. 22, 1968, through July 30, 1969, Dave won 17 consecutive games including 15 straight at the start of the '69 season.
   The Orioles' greatest southpaw ever, who racked up 181 wins and 33 shutouts for them, also swung a pretty fair stick, connecting for nine home runs during his career including a grand-slam off Chuck Dobson of Oakland on Aug. 26, 1968. In the '69 World Series, he homered off the Mets' Jerry Koosman and in the 1970 Fall Classic poked a grand-slam off Wayne Granger and the Reds, the only grand-slam shot ever hit by a pitcher in a World Series game.
   McNally was also tough on the mound in post-season play. He beat L.A., 1-0, in the fourth and final game of the

'66 World Series and won two of three decisions against
the Pirates in 1971. In ALCS competition he owns a 3-2
mark, including an 11-inning, three-hit shutout against
the Twins in 1969.

Following the '74 season he was shipped to Montreal in a
trade that brought Ken Singleton to Baltimore. But Expos'
fans never saw the real McNally. Plagued by a shoulder injury, Dave called it quits after 12 starts.   184-119

MCNERTNEY, Jerry
        New York Yankees' minor league coach

An avid fisherman, Jerry cast his presence on big league
diamonds from 1964–1973.

A graduate of Iowa State University, he was with the
White Sox for four years before joining the Pilots in '69.
McNertney is the answer to the trivia question: "Who was
the Seattle Pilots' regular catcher in their one year of exis-
tence in 1969?" Jerry transferred with the franchise to
Milwaukee the next year, then in '71 he shifted to the Cardinals, where he filled in nicely for Ted Simmons who was
on military reserve duty. In 56 games that summer, Jerry
hit a respectable .289. His grand finale was with the Pirates where he finished at .237 lifetime.

MCNULTY, Bill
        Owns a men's clothing store
        Sacramento, CA

Bill wore the garish pastels of the Oakland A's in 1969 and
1972, even though his .037 average (1-for-27) was a bit rag-
tag. But his minor league performance in 1974 was a stylish Pierre Cardin.

Bill was to the P.C.L. what Steve Bilko had been two de-
cades earlier. Taking aim at the 233-foot left field screen in
Sacramento, Bill one year walloped 55 home runs with 135
RBIs and a .329 average.

MCQUEEN, Mike
    Owns bowling lanes in Pasadena and Baytown, TX

The late Steve McQueen became a full-fledged star during the Sixties for his roles in such movies as *The Great Escape* and *Bullit.* Mike made his quiet entry at age 19 in 1969, making him the youngest player in the majors that year. He made one start for Atlanta, then hung around with the club until 1972 before seeing brief action with Cincinnati in '74 where he made his great escape at 5-11 after 73 games.

MCRAE, Hal
    Active with the Kansas City Royals

Hal is without question the designated hitter deluxe in baseball history. Entering the 1984 season he had appeared in 1,156 games, has collected 121 homers, 673 RBIs, and batted .298 in his role as a DH the past 11 years.

The Royals' hitting star arrived in 1968 when he played in 17 games as a second baseman for the Reds, a move prompted by Pete Rose going on the disabled list with a fractured thumb. Hal's debut was a good one (July 11, 1968) as he collected a pair of singles off Gaylord Perry of the Giants. That winter he broke his leg playing winter ball which caused him to miss most of the '69 campaign, but came up to stay in '70 as a spare outfielder with the Reds.

McRae appeared in two World Series with Cincy and each time delivered. In the 1970 Fall Classic he went 5-for-11 and in '72 was 4-for-9.

The Royals acquired the prolific DH in a trade after the '72 season. With Kansas City he appeared in four ALCS and one World Series, with his overall Series average standing at .409. Obviously it is no fault of Hal's that he's been on the losing end each time.

A fearless baserunner, McRae had an effect on the automatic double play rule, the result of his overzealous base running in the 1977 ALCS against the Yankees when he almost cut Willie Randolph in shreds for the purpose of breaking up a double play.   .293

MCRAE, Norm
    Active player in Mexico

Norm had a relatively short, evanescent career. In 22 relief outings with the Tigers in '69 and '70, the right-hander failed to gain a decision.

Following the '70 campaign he was put in a package with Denny McLain and Don Wert as they were dealt to Washington for Aurelio Rodriguez, Joe Coleman, and Ed Brinkman.

MELTON, Bill
    Investment counselor
    Mission Viejo, CA

Bill was the first White Sox player in the club's history to lead the A.L. in home runs when he punched out 33 in 1971. It was his second straight 33-homer season.

When the Chisox acquired Dick Allen, the purpose was to provide a formidable one-two punch that would rock the 44,492 wooden seats at the South Side Stadium. But Melton came up lame, missing most of the '72 campaign with a ruptured disc.

Like many long ball hitters, Bill had a tendency to strike out frequently. He was swinging at air in late July (1970) when he tied and broke several records for whiffs, including an ignoble string of striking out 11 straight times (July 23, 24). Conversely when his stroke was right, Bill was nobody to fool with. Twice in his career he homered in four straight games. On June 24, 1969, he unloaded three four-baggers against the Pilots at Seattle.

Bill's ten-year run ended with the Angels (1976) and Indians (1977). He showed a .253 average with 160 homers.

MENKE, Denis
    Houston Astros' coach

Considered to be the hottest prospect to come out of the cornfields of Iowa since Bob Feller, Denis brought with him a well-woven basket of skills. He was 34-0 as a pitcher in high school and was plucked by the Braves for a reported $100,000 bonus.

Milwaukee brought up the heralded prospect in 1962, a year Denis played five different positions for the Braves, a club record. He tied an N.L. mark on May 23, 1964, when he received three intentional walks.

The infielder went to Houston, where he earned a living from 1968–71. In Shea Stadium on July 30, 1969, Denis and Jim Wynn hit grand slam home runs in the ninth inning against the Mets to tie an M.L. record set by Bob Allison and Harmon Killebrew of the Minnesota Twins when they unloaded against Cleveland in 1962.

A two-time All-Star (1969–70), his best season was 1970 when he hit .304 and drove in 92 runs. After two years in Cincinnati and one back in Houston, the Iowa farm boy left with a .250 average.

MERRITT, Jim
    Business printing broker for CalTar Data Forms
    Cerritos, CA

If any team holds the record for most bat boys to make the majors, it's most likely the Dodgers. As were Rene Lachemann and Jim Lefebvre, Jim Merritt was a Dodger bat boy as a youngster.

Jim arrived in '65 and partied with the Twins as they copped the pennant. He made two relief appearances against the Dodgers without a decision in the World Series. On July 27, 1966, the southpaw chucker tied an A.L. record for most consecutive strikeouts in a game with 7 and the following year racked up 181 K's, pitching four complete game victories over the Yankees.

Following the '68 campaign, Jim was shipped to the Reds for Leo Cardenas. He was too good to be true for the Crosley Field faithful, winning 17 and 20 games his first two years in the Queen City.

Merritt's arm didn't have much punch after his glittering year in '70 as he plummeted to 1-11 and was sent down to the minors before one last gasp with Texas. Prior to his final two seasons he was 75-62 but finished 81-86.

MESSERSMITH, Andy
>   Assistant coach at Cabrillo College; also coaches in
>   Palomino League
>   Soquel, CA

Like Dave McNally, Andy tested baseball's ancient reserve clause and beat it. The Dodgers renewed Andy's contract following the 1974 season under the option clause provided, but Messersmith said no thanks. After the '75 campaign he was declared a free agent by judge Peter M. Seitz whose ruling ended indefinite ownership of players by the owners and ushered in the megabuck era.

The University of California ace broke into organized baseball in sizzling fashion by throwing a one-hitter for Seattle (P.C.L.) against Tulsa. His rookie campaign in 1968 showed a 4-2 mark with the Angels.

A 20-game winner in 1971, the right hander was sent to the Dodgers after the '72 season in a multiplayer deal that saw Frank Robinson go to the Angels. On May 28, 1973, he tied a record for most strikeouts at the start of a game with six. In '74 Andy went 20-6, with 221 strikeouts and a 2.59 ERA, leading the Dodgers to the N.L. pennant. His option year in '75 was a good one (19-14), leading the N.L. in complete games (19), innings pitched (322) and shutouts (7). That year (April 25) he became the first N.L. pitcher since 1895 to hit three doubles in a game.

The man entered free agency with a solid arsenal of achievements. He was picked up by the Braves where he lodged for two years before riding out with the Yankees ('78) and Dodgers ('79).   130-99

METCALF, Tom
>   President of a lumber company; bank director
>   Wisconsin Rapids, WI

This former Northwestern University basketball player dribbled in for eight games with the 1963 Yankees. He gave the A.L. champs some help out of the bullpen, winning his only decision in eight games and also posted a 2.77 ERA that year.

MEYER, Bob
Magazine publisher
Toledo, OH

Many players find the adjustments in the real world following baseball a difficult period in their lives. Some not only adjust, they conquer. Bob qualifies in this group. He publishes a magazine titled *A Guide to Greater Real Estate Income*, a quarterly mailed to over 160,000 realtors throughout the United States and has authored several books on investment.

Bob stood on big league real estate in parts of the years 1964–70 with the Yankees, Angels, K.C. A's, Pilots, and Brewers. He fired a 12-strikeout, 6-0 no-hitter, the first ever pitched in the Honolulu Stadium while pitching for Vancouver (P.C.L.) in 1968.   2-12

MICHAEL, Gene
New York Yankees' coach

The pièce de résistance of all infield tricks is the hidden ball. Gene was the master. He says, "I pulled the hidden ball trick about five times with the Yankees. I could have done it more but I was afraid that some players would get mad at me."

A graduate of Kent State University, "Stick" was as smooth on the basketball court as he was fielding his shortstop position. He was pursued by several teams in the NBA and offered a two-year, no-cut contract by the Detroit Pistons, but chose baseball instead. After the first couple of years in the minors, Michael had to be scratching his head when he hit .215 in the Carolina League his first year before deciding to give pitching a fling. The next year he pitched in 16 games and went 1-3, but he finally got his bat in motion, hitting .304.

"Stick" shuffled in with the Pirates in '66. The next season he was involved in a trade to the Dodgers for Maury Wills. His next stop was in the Bronx where he wore Yankee pinstripes from 1968–1974. A fixture at shortstop during the period, Gene hit a career high .272 in 1969.

Michael, who managed Columbus to the I.L. pennant in

'79, has served the Yankees as a coach, general manager, and manager (1981).   .229

MIKKELSEN, Pete
     Asparagus and grape farmer
     Prosser, WA

Pete is a part of baseball trivia on two fronts, but you won't find it in a record book. Pitching for the Yankees he was the loser in the first game ever played in the Astrodome.

On July 4, 1965, he tossed a no-hitter for Toledo (I.L.), against the Atlanta Crackers, the first no-hitter ever thrown at Atlanta's Fulton County Stadium.

The Yankees' most effective relief pitcher in '64 when he went 7-4 with 12 saves, the sidearmer made four appearances in the World Series against the Cardinals, losing one decision. From 1966–72 he was with the Pirates, Cubs, Cardinals, and Dodgers.

Pete closed at 45-40 with 49 saves.

MILES, Jim
     Baseball coach at Northwest Junior College
     Senatobia, MS

Jim was up for three games with the Senators in 1968. A graduate of Delta State in Mississippi, he pitched in ten more games for Washington in 1969. Overall, the right-hander finished 0-1.

MILLAN, Felix
     Received degree in marketing management from the
     University of Puerto Rico in 1983; operates a sports-
     wear business in Rio Piedras, Puerto Rico

The warning flags were out on Felix in 1967 when he was named the International League Player of the Year and *The Sporting News* "Minor League Player of the Year" after hitting .310 at Richmond.

Felix Millan (pronounced me-yann) first came up with

the Braves in '66 for a test run. By 1969 he was the N.L. All-Star second baseman.

Nicknamed "Nacho" and "The Cat," his bat was purring on July 6, 1970, when he went 6-for-6 in a game against the Giants, the first time anyone had six hits in one contest for the Atlanta Braves.

Following the '72 season Felix was sent to the Mets where he spent the last five years of his career. "The Cat" found Shea Stadium turf to his liking in '73, batting .290 as the Mets took the N.L. pennant.

When the Mets played Houston in a 25-inning marathon in 1974, Felix tied an M.L. record when he came to the plate 12 times.

He was sold by the Mets to the Taiyo Whales in Japan on February 22, 1978.   .279

MILLER, John, A.
      Salesman   of   commercial   printing   paper   for
      Carpenter/Offutt Paper Company
      Los Angeles, CA

John did something that no other Yankee did during the club's illustrious history when he homered in his first major league at bat. But his four-bagger on Sept. 11, 1967, at Boston did not prove a quick fix to the path of pinstripe immortality.

A 32-game big leaguer, the first baseman-outfielder also showed up with the Dodgers in '69 where he homered in his last big league at bat making him the only man in major league history to homer in his first and last major league at-bats. Ironically, they were his only major league home runs.   .164

MILLER, John, E.
      Baltimore County Fire Dept.

A Baltimore native, John was signed by the Orioles out of high school in 1960. The right-hander arrived in '62, crackling with energy and enthusiasm. In parts of seasons between 1962–67, John logged a 6-4 mark.

MILLER, Larry
 Marketing consultant
 Scottsdale, AZ

Larry was around from 1964–66, going 5-14 with the Dodgers and Mets. The University of Kansas graduate tossed a no-hitter for Atlanta in 1961.

 In 1977 his daughter, Kathy, an athlete and honor student, was critically injured when she was hit by a car. Her courageous struggle to recovery was depicted in the 1981 television movie, *The Miracle of Kathy Miller*, with actor Frank Converse portraying Larry in the movie.

MILLER, Norm
 Executive position with Monterey House Restaurants
 Houston, TX

Norm wore the double knits of the Astros and Braves from 1965–1973. At times the flychaser showed some real fabric, like in the waning days of the '68 season when the home run of this Los Angeles native beat the Dodgers before the smallest crowd in the history of Dodger Stadium, 8,928. Unfortunately, his euphoria was short-lived as he suffered a broken ankle a couple of weeks later. Scheduled to be married shortly after the season, he had to go through the ceremony on crutches.   .238

MINCHER, Don
 Owns Don Mincher's All-Star Trophies and Sporting Goods
 General Manager at Huntsville (Southern League)
 Huntsville, AL

This well-muscled lefty slugger made his presence felt in the A.L. from 1960–1972 by belting 200 lifetime homers. A standout lineman in high school, big Don turned down a football scholarship from the University of Alabama to sign with the White Sox. Traded to Washington for Roy Sievers at the start of the 1960 season, he made his debut that year with the Senators.

 Mincher accompanied the Senators to Minnesota in '61

and was an integral part of the power-hitting Twins of the mid-Sixties. His lethal bat (22 home runs) helped Minnesota to their only A.L. pennant in 1965. In his first World Series at-bat, he homered off Don Drysdale to become the fourth player in WS history to homer in his first at bat.

After the '66 season, the Twins sent Mincher to the Angels for Dean Chance.

Placed in the expansion pool after the 1968 season, he became the first player selected by the Seattle Pilots. The brawny slugger poked the first home run in a major league game at Sick's Stadium in the Pilots' home opener on April 11, 1969, off Joel Horlen of the White Sox. He led Seattle with 25 roundtrippers and earned his place as the first and only member of the Pilots to appear in the All-Star Game.

Don's banner home run year came in 1970 when he walloped 27 roundtrippers with Oakland. After visits with Washington and Texas he closed with Oakland in '72.   .249

MITTERWALD, George
    Manager at Modesto in the California League

"Mitty" helped to provide the grist for good talk around Minnesota as the regular backstop for the A.L. West Division champ Twins in 1969–70. He spent most of his 11-year swing with the Twins before being traded to the Cubs for Randy Hundley following the '73 campaign.   .236

MOELLER, Joe
    Associated with apartment complex
    Manhattan Beach, CA

Joe had a caseload of injuries through his rocky stay (1962–71). The right-hander signed with the Dodgers along with his twin brother.

The effusive young chucker who was so overpowering in his first year in the Dodgers' organization, moved all the way from Class C to Triple-A. Along the way, he went 20-9, fanning 295 batters in 237 innings. But wildness got in his way, plus a bottomless starting Dodger staff that was en route to the Hall of Fame. Joe seemed headed for a starting role with Los Angeles in 1966 when he had a superb spring

training while Sandy Koufax and Don Drysdale were holding out. When Sandy and "Big D" returned, Don Sutton
was given the No. 4 starting role behind Koufax, Drysdale, and Claude Osteen. Moeller took over the miscel-
laneous assignment chores and never seemed to get un-
tracked.   26-36

MONDAY, Rick
     Released by Dodgers during the 1984 season

Rick earned instant fame. In baseball's first free agent
draft of college and high school talent, Rick was selected
by the Kansas City A's, making him the first-ever No. 1 selection. The Arizona State "College Player of the Year"
went on to a distinguished career from 1966–84.

From April 20–30, 1969, Monday tied an A.L. record
held by Lou Gehrig when he collected at least one RBI in
ten consecutive games.

The following April Rick went on a dubious streak when
he fanned nine times in two games, with seven K's coming
in embarrassing succession. During the April 29th game
when he whiffed five times against the Red Sox at Fenway
Park, a brawl broke out when Sonny Siebert hit Reggie
Jackson with a pitch. Rick later commented, "During the
fight, I swung at five guys and missed everyone of them."

Following the '71 season he went to the Cubs for Ken
Holtzman and spent the next five years at Wrigley. He
connected for a season-high 32 home runs in 1976, finishing with 241 homers and a .264 mark.

Monday had the spirit of '76 on April 25th when he
earned the title of "Mr. Red, White, and Blue" and gained
national acclaim as he saved the American flag from a possible burning in left field by a pair of protestors at Dodger
Stadium.

Rick then went to the Dodgers for Bill Buckner and
helped the club to N.L. pennants in 1977, '78, and '81. The
highlight of the '81 season and perhaps Monday's career
came in the ninth inning of the fifth game of the NLCS
when his home run off Steve Rogers of the Expos gave
the Dodgers a 2-1 victory and a berth in the World Series.   .264

MONEY, Don
   Active in Japan in 1984
   Vineland, NJ

Playing for the Brewers on April 10, 1976, Money was batting with the bases loaded in the bottom of the ninth inning, trailing the Yankees, 9-6. Dave Pagan, the Yankee pitcher, delivered the pitch, not realizing that Yankee first baseman Chris Chambliss had requested time from first base ump Jim McKean. "Time" was called, but Pagan pitched anyway and Money blasted a bases-loaded home run. When the smoke cleared the homer was nullified because "time" had been called. Batting over again, Money hit a sacrifice fly to make the score 9-7. The Brewers' celebration just moments before turned into a funeral.

Don also adds a touch to Opening Day history. On April 8, 1969, he hit two home runs as a member of the Phils in a game against the Cubs, the homers representing the first two of his career. In the same contest, Ernie Banks belted two roundtrippers, marking the first time in N.L. history that two players each hit a pair of home runs in a season opener.

Money, who hit a total of 176 lifetime roundtrippers, hit the first home run ever at Philadelphia's Veterans Stadium on April 10, 1971 against the Expos' Bill Stoneman.

Primarily a third baseman, Don broke in with the Phils in '68, but was traded to Milwaukee after the '72 campaign where he stayed through 1983. In '77 he enjoyed career highs in homers (25) and RBIs (83).

· A player with rounded skills, Don also carried a sure glove. From July 23 through Sept. 11, 1972, he established a N.L. record for the most consecutive errorless chances by a third baseman with 163. Money also set the A.L. mark for most consecutive errorless games at third base (88) from Sept. 28, 1973–July 16, 1974. During the '74 season he established an M.L. mark for the highest fielding percentage by a third baseman in a season (.9894), and for fewest errors (5) by a third sacker in a season for a player in at least 150 games.

Believe it or not, Money was originally signed by a scout named Sid Thryft.   .261

MONTANEZ, Willie
       Owns a trucking company
       Caguas, Puerto Rico

Willie looked like a reincarnated Vic Power with his
French pastry glove and fancy cha-cha footwork around
the first base bag.
    The youngest player in the majors at age 18 in 1966 as a
member of the Angels, Montanez was sent to the Cardinals' organization where he originally started.
    The Phillies acquired Willie from the Cards on April 8,
1970, to replace Curt Flood, who refused to report after
being traded on Oct. 7, 1969. In 1971 Montanez belted 30
homers and collected 99 RBIs in his first full season with
the Phillies.
    Traded to the Giants early in '75 for Garry Maddox, the
diabolic winds of Candlestick Park suited this first baseman-outfielder just fine as he hit .302 with a career high
101 ribbies in '75. But before he learned his way around
the city he was jettisoned to Atlanta for Darrell Evans
midway through the '76 season. Dividing his season from
coast to coast he hit .317 and played in a league-leading
163 games.
    The well-traveled Puerto Rican also played with the
Mets, Rangers, Padres, Expos, and Pirates before it ended
in 1982.   .275

MONTEAGUDO, Aurelio
     · Pitching coach at Peoria (Midwest League)

Aurelio never gave up. The Cuban-born right-hander was a
scarred Don Quixote, always ready to do battle with a few
more windmills, as he was in and out of the big top between
1963–1973 with the Kansas City A's, Astros, White Sox, and
Angels. The final score for his 72 battles stands at 3-7.

MONTEJO, Manny
       Las Villas, Cuba

The Berlin Wall was constructed in 1961, the year Manny,
(aka) "Pete" Montejo, crashed the wall to the majors when

he pitched in a dozen games for the Tigers without a decision from the bullpen.

MOOCK, Joe
High school teacher and baseball coach at Baker High School
Greenwell, LA

Long before the Mets had a Mookie Wilson, they had a Joe Moock. Joe, who played 13 games at third base for the New York Mets in 1967, was one of a cast of thousands tried at the hot corner by the New York team.

A selection by the Mets in the 1965 free agent draft from LSU, Moock was on top of the world in September of '67. He recalled, "I drove in the winning runs against the Dodgers at Dodger Stadium the last two games of the year." .225

MOORE, Archie
Professor of Physical Education at Indiana University
Indiana, PA

The Yankees have always had a way of making players with pedestrian ability into walking legends. But such was not to be the case with this first baseman-outfielder who appeared in 40 games in '64 and '65.

An All-American selection at Springfield College (MA), he graduated with a degree in education. The boyhood idol of this Upper Darby, PA, native was Robin Roberts, the great Phils' pitcher. On June 24, 1964, Archie's first major league hit was a pinch-hit double against Roberts, who was a member of the Orioles' staff that season.

MOORE, Barry
Cleveland, NC

Barry Goldwater failed in his bid for the White House but Barry Moore made it to Washington in 1965 to begin a six-year term spent mostly with the Senators. The southpaw chucker made his first big league start in 1966 and beat

the Kansas City A's on a three-hitter. The following year
he one-hit the Twins, the only hit a sixth-inning single by
Cesar Tovar.

Moore departed after stints with the Indians and White
Sox in 1970.   26-37

MOORE, Jackie
Oakland A's Manager

Jackie has the distinction of being the last man to manage
the Toronto Maple Leafs (I.L.) when he took over the team
the final days of the '67 season. Chances are quite probable
that he won't be the last man to manage the Oakland A's,
a job he acquired when Steve Boros was fired early in the
1984 season.

Moore's big league playing career lasted only 21 games
as a catcher with the Tigers in 1965, hitting .094.

MOORHEAD, Bob
Retired dockworker with Roadway Express
Lemoyne, PA

Bob's claim to fame is that he was the first relief hurler
ever to come out of the Mets' bullpen in a regular season
game. It happened on April 11, 1962, against the Cardinals. Roger Craig was knocked out of the game in the
fourth inning and Bob added insult to injury by allowing
five runs in three innings of work. The right-hander was
0-3 in 47 games for the Mets in '62 and '65.

MOOSE, Bob
Died Oct. 9, 1976, on his 29th birthday in an automobile accident in Martin's Ferry, OH

Bob was killed in a two-car crash while en route to a birthday party in his honor at a country club operated by his
former Pirates' teammate, Bill Mazeroski. The tragedy
marked the end of 76-71 career that filled the hearts of
Bucs' fans with excitement on many occasions.

In 1969 Moose enjoyed his finest year, going 14-3 for the

top winning percentage in the National League. Following a Pirates' game against the Mets that year at Shea Stadium on September 19th, his wife told him how excited she was about sitting directly behind actor Dustin Hoffman at the game. The very next night Bob gave Mrs. Moose more thrills when he temporarily stalled the "Miracle Mets" with a 4-0 no-hit victory. At just 21 years of age, the ex-Marine became the youngest pitcher since Bob Feller in 1940 to throw a no-hitter in the majors.

Over the next four years he played an important part in helping the Pirates to three N.L. East titles and to the 1971 World Championship. Unfortunately, many remember Bob for the wild pitch in the fifth and final game of the NLCS which allowed George Foster (Reds) to score the Series' winning run.

MORALES, Jerry
    Chicago Cubs minor league hitting instructor

This battered but unbroken warrior was hustled around big league parks between 1969–1983 with the Padres, Cubs (twice), Cards, Tigers, and Mets. Originally signed as a free agent by the New York Mets in 1966, Jerry was named the Player of the Year in the Appalachian League at the age of 17 when he hit .345.

Selected by San Diego in the expansion draft, he became a regular in the Padres' outfield by 1972. Jerry had his premier year in 1977 when he hit .290 and was a member of the National League All-Star team. He has the distinction of being the last active player in the majors who was drafted by Montreal or San Diego in the N.L. Expansion Draft in 1969. .259

MORALES, Richie
    Chicago White Sox scout
    Pacifica, CA

Whoever bats .195 better learn the art of fielding. Richie did just that. In 480 games (1967–73) he filled in around the infield with the White Sox and Padres.

MORAN, Al
Employed with Rockwell Company Contractors in Livonia, MI

Al copied Richie Morales' .195 mark over a 135-game career with the Mets in 1963–64. Al's fielding skills were good enough to make him Casey Stengel's regular shortstop in '63.

MOREHEAD, Dave
Works for the Jafco Department Store (sporting goods) Tustin, CA

Around the New England area, the trivia question "Who was the last Red Sox pitcher to hurl a no-hitter?" is frequently asked. The answer is Dave Morehead.

Despite an overall 40-64 record, Dave's career was not without its highlights. On April 13, 1963, he shutout the Senators and struck out 10 in his big league debut. One month later the right-hander beat the Senators, 4-1, on a one-hitter, allowing only a first-inning home run to Chuck Hinton. On Sept. 16, 1965, Dave no-hit the Indians, 2-0. Only 1,247 were in attendance at Fenway Park for the game which ended in a bang-bang play at first base. After giving up a walk to Rocky Colavito, Morehead juggled Vic Davalillo's tapper to the mound and bounced a throw to Lee Thomas at first for the final out. For his efforts, he was given a $1,000 raise.

Although Morehead is usually associated with his no-hitter, he did win five games for Boston in their 1967 pennant drive. In the World Series he pitched 3⅓ hitless and scoreless innings in two relief appearances.

MORGAN, Joe
Cincinnati Reds announcer

This future Hall of Famer brought with him a woven quiltwork of skills—speed, power, fielding (with his tiny glove), you name it. A total player, Joe beat the opposition in a variety of ways.

"Little Joe" began his path of glory in '65 when he won

The Sporting News Rookie of the Year honors, batting .271 with 14 homers. On July 8th he went 6-for-6, collecting two homers, a double, and three singles in a 9-8, 12-inning loss to the Milwaukee Braves. He completed his first tour at Houston in 1971 when he was traded to Cincinnati.

In Cincinnati, Morgan established himself as one of the game's superstars, winning back-to-back MVP awards in 1975–1976. The N.L. career leader in walks, the second baseman led the league in that department four different times, receiving over 100 free passes eight different years. On June 2, 1966, Joe tied an N.L. record by walking five times in a game.

The all-time home run leader among second basemen, Joe surpassed Rogers Hornsby during the '84 campaign when he walloped No. 265 as a second sacker.

An important cog in Cincinnati's Big Red Machine of the mid-Seventies, Morgan appeared in three Fall Classics with the Reds. His .333 average in the '76 World Series aided Sparky Anderson's crew to a four-game sweep of the Yankees.

In 1980 Joe returned to Houston via the re-entry draft. He continued his winning tradition by leading the Astros to their first N.L. West division title. The following year Morgan signed with the Giants. His magical presence didn't win a title for San Francisco, but in his last at-bat of the '82 campaign, he hit a three-run homer which buried the Dodgers' pennant hopes on the final day of the season. At age 39, his .289 average earned him the "Comeback Player of the Year" award. Joe then moved to the Phillies in '83, where he waved his magic wand (and his bat) in September, putting on one of the greatest clutch hitting shows in baseball history, leading the Phillies to 22 wins. In that stretch Joe hit .337. He celebrated his 40th birthday on September 19th by going 4-for-5 with two homers.

At some time in the future, this eight-time All-Star will be in big company side-by-side with baseball's greatest players as a member of the Hall of Fame.   .271

MORHARDT, "Moe"
> Athletic director, baseball and soccer coach at Gilbert H.S.
> Winsted, CT

James Meredith became the first black man to enroll at the University of Mississippi in the early Sixties. Meredith "Moe" Morhardt was enrolled in the Northwest League in 1961 and graduated with honors by winning the batting title (.339) at Wenatchee. His diploma stated "Report to the Cubs immediately."

In September Moe found himself at first base with the Cubbies. The following year Morhardt was used mainly as a pinch hitter. Overall he appeared in 25 games during his brief stay and batted .206.

A part of Moe's problem was that he was in the wrong place at the wrong time. He says, "When I came up with the Cubs it was about the time they were converting Ernie Banks to a first baseman." Ernie's grades were too high to move.

MORRIS, Danny
> Employed by Standard Oil Company
> Oakland City, IN

Danny's sensational year in 1965 was a ringing endorsement for the big time. Pitching for Wisconsin Rapids in the Midwest League he led the league in wins (16) and strikeouts (274) including a 21-strikeout game.

Unfortunately Danny's 16 wins turned into only 16 innings of total work in the majors with the Twins in 1968–69.   0-2

MORRIS, John
> Air conditioner and solar units salesman
> Phoenix, AZ

The Invaders came on the tube in 1966 when this southpaw pitcher commenced his 132-game invasion in parts of seasons from 1966–1974. When John put away his artillery he was 11-7 after stops with the Phillies, Orioles, Pilots, Brewers, and Giants.

MORTON, "Bubba"
Electrical engineer
Seattle, WA

Wycliffe Nathaniel "Bubba" Morton was a ripe 30-year-old rookie with the Tigers in 1961. The graduate of Howard University was with the Tigers, Braves, and Angels from 1961–69.

The stocky outfielder enjoyed his vintage year in 1967 when he hit .313 in 80 games for the Angels. Bubba's big day came that year when he led California to a 7-2, 11-4 doubleheader sweep over the Orioles, collecting four RBIs in both ends of the twinbill.

MORTON, Carl
Died April 12, 1983, at age 39 in Tulsa, OK

Carl's life came to a premature end when he suffered a fatal heart attack. Originally signed by the Braves as an outfielder, he switched to pitching after hitting just .227 in the Carolina League. After a 13-5 record at Shreveport in the Texas League in 1968, Carl was first up with the Expos in '69. In his first full season in 1970, the hard-throwing right-hander went 18-11 and was named Rookie of the Year, but the following season did a turnabout, losing 18 games for the third year franchise.

Traded to Atlanta after the '72 campaign, Carl was a dependable starter, winning 15, 16, and 17 games.   87-92

MOSCHITTO, Ross
Security consultant
Garnersville, NY

Summer in the City was a popular song in 1965 when this 20-year-old outfielder spent a summer in the city with the Yankees. He also wore pinstripes in '67 for a short time. For Ross, it wasn't such a hot time in the city hitting .167 in 110 games.

MOSES, Gerry
    Executive position with Ogden Foods; operates a base-
    ball camp
    Yazoo City, MS

Grandma Moses turned 100 years old in 1965. Catcher
Gerry Moses turned 19 and arrived with the Red Sox for a
quick peek after signing a reported $75,000 bonus with
them the year before. He was up long enough to pick up
one hit, a home run, in four at-bats.
    He returned in 1968 to play in six more games when he
collected six base hits, two of the home run variety, giving
him three four-baggers in his first seven hits in the bigs.
    Moses was the Boston receiver in '69 and '70, hitting
.304 in 1969, when he was selected as "The Man of the
Year" by the Bosox Club of Boston for contributions to the
success of the Red Sox and for cooperation in community
endeavors.
    From 1971–75 Gerry motored around with the Angels,
Indians, Yankees, Tigers, White Sox, and Padres.   .251

MOTA, Manny
    Los Angeles Dodgers' coach

"He could wake up on Christmas morning and rip a single
into right field."
                                        —Jim Murray

    Manny signed with the Giants in 1957. His bonus was a
plane ticket away from the ghettos of Santo Domingo and
$400, a cheap investment for a guy who has a career record
total of 150 pinch-hits.
    The pinch-hitting expert first came up with the Giants
in 1962. However, most of his career was spent with the Pirates (1963–68) and Dodgers (1969–82) plus a short visit
with Montreal in '69 when the Expos selected him first in
the expansion draft as a 30-year-old. However, in June he
was dealt to the Dodgers along with Maury Wills in exchange for Ron Fairly.
    Official records are not kept on bunting for base hits, but
Manny likely would hold the mark for a game when he col-

lected three straight bunt singles against the Mets in 1967. In his next game, he bunted safely for a fourth straight single.

The Dominican Republic native was supposed to be retired as a player in '80, but was activated by the Dodgers August 29th when Reggie Smith was disabled. At age 42 he responded with three pinch-hits in seven at-bats, leaving him with 150 lifetime pinch-swats, the major league record, eclipsing the old pinch-hit mark of 144 set by Smoky Burgess.

Overall Manny sports a .304 average.

The pinch-hitting king enjoys hero status in the Dominican Republic where there is a "Manny Mota Baseball League" named in his honor. He also owns a restaurant in Santo Domingo called "Manny Mota's Dugout."

MOTTON, Curt
    San Francisco Giants outfield and baserunning instructor; insurance agent for the Prudential Insurance Co.
    Oakland, CA

This 5'7" compact outfielder had some pinch-hitting heroics of his own during his eight-year (1967–74) A.L. safari. Originally signed by the Cubs in 1962, Curt was drafted by Baltimore and joined the Orioles in 1967 after spending most of the summer leading Rochester to the International League pennant by hitting .337.

On May 15 and 17, 1968, Curt tied a then-major league mark for hitting home runs in two consecutive pinch-hitting appearances.

In the second game of the 1969 ALCS his 11th-inning pinch-hit single knocked in the game's only run in a 1-0 victory over the Twins.

Curt glided around with the Brewers and Angels in '72 before returning to his nest in Baltimore to close out the last two years of his career with the Orioles.   .213

MUDROCK, Phil
    Employed with the Utah Structural Bonding Co.
    Salt Lake City, UT

In the early 1960s the Flintstones came to TV for a long
stay as the prehistoric family in the town of Bedrock.
Right-hander Phil Mudrock emerged in '63 for a much
shorter stay. After pitching in one inning for the Cubs, he
became an extinct species.

MUNSON, Thurman
    Died on Aug. 2, 1979, at age 32 in crash of his private
    plane at the Canton, OH Airport

An All-American catcher at Kent State, Munson was the
Yankees' No. 1 selection in the June 1968 free agent draft.
After 99 minor league games, the gruff catcher was in the
majors to stay. He was Rookie of the Year in 1970. Until
his tragic death, he was a sweat hog in pinstripes. He once
said, "I seem to attract dirt. The game was only ten pitches
old tonight and I was filthier than anybody else was all
night."
    Thurman was the first Yankee captain since Lou Geh-
rig's retirement in 1939. He was the latest in the great
catching tradition of Dickey-Berra-Howard-Munson.
    Thurman did not catch with good form and grace, but his
hard work behind the dish earned him three Gold Gloves.
During the 1971 season he tied a Yankee record with a
.998 fielding percentage when he made only one error the
entire season.
    From 1975–77 he was a rock of consistency when he hit
.300 and drove in 100 runs for three straight years, winning the A.L. MVP award in 1976.
    During post-season play (1976–78) he hit safely in 27
of 30 games, batting a healthy .341. His titanic two-run
homer in Game Three of the 1978 ALCS against the
Royals gave the Yanks a 6-5 win and turned the Series
around. In the World Series against the Dodgers, he
drove in seven runs, had eight hits, and batted a hefty
.320. In 1976 he hit .529, the best-ever Series average by
a player on a losing team. He had six straight hits in his

final six at-bats, including a 4-for-4 performance in the fourth and final game to tie the 1924 record by Goose Goslin of the Washington Senators. He missed out on the chance at both a record five-hit World Series game and record seventh straight hit when the game and Series ended with Munson on deck.

Munson, who used to refer to himself in conversation as "The Fat Kid," hit a fat .300 five times. He was a member of the All-Star squad six times.

The night following the fatal crash, the Yankees took the field against the Orioles minus a catcher in tribute to Munson. Number 15 would never be worn again by a Yankee. The attendance that night at Yankee Stadium was 51,151. .292

MURAKAMI, Masanori
Hyugo, Japan

Tokyo hosted American athletes at the 1964 Summer Olympics at a time America hosted one Japanese athlete in big league stadiums. His name: Masanori Murakami, a southpaw who pitched with the Giants in 1964 and 1965. The lefty went 5-1 in 54 games, all but one as a reliever. His return to Japan following the '65 season was prompted after a dispute over his contract between the Giants and the Nankai Hawks of the Japanese League. San Francisco signed two other players from the Land of the Rising Sun in 1964, but only Murakami made it.

When Murakami first joined the Giants he couldn't speak a word of English. Masanori was told by teammates Gaylord Perry and Juan Marichal that when manager Herman Franks comes to the mound to take the ball from him he should know what to say. What did Marichal and Perry teach Murakami to tell Franks? "Take a hike, fatso."

Almost 20 years later, Murakami attempted a comeback at age 38, but was released during the 1983 spring training.

MURCER, Bobby
New York Yankees' announcer

When this Oklahoma City wonder arrived with the Yankees for a quick taste in 1965 he was considered the heir apparent to Mickey Mantle. It was a natural thought since both were signed by scout Tom Greenwade, both were from Oklahoma, and both came up as shortstops. Following Mantle's retirement, Murcer was given Mickey's locker and ironically Bobby would eventually move to the outfield as Mickey did.

If he ever resembled No. 7 it was in 1972 when he hit 33 home runs, had 96 RBIs, and led the Ameican League in runs scored (102). Twice in his professional career Bobby homered in four straight at-bats. Playing at Toledo in 1966 he parked four consecutive four-baggers, then repeated the feat in the big arena during a doubleheader at Yankee Stadium on June 24, 1970.

On Aug. 29, 1972, Bobby hit for the cycle, making him the last Yankee to accomplish the feat.

He departed to the Giants in '75 for Bobby Bonds, spent two years in Frisco, then transferred to the Cubs until 1979 when he returned to the Bronx, where his 252-homer career ended in 1983.

On July 15, 1969, Bobby struck out four times in a game against Boston. The 4K's came on 11 strikes. How did that happen? During his fourth at-bat he had a count of 1-2 when he fouled a pitch off the plate which bounced up and hit him in the eye. The injury forced him to leave the game. Bill Robinson replaced him at the plate and took the third strike, but the strikeout was charged to Bobby.   .277

MURPHY, Billy
District manager for the Tacoma News Tribune
Tacoma, WA

A batter who hits .230 has about as much job security as a head of state in a banana republic. Billy swatted .230 for the Mets in 1966 and was ousted after 84 games.

However, the first of his 31 base hits was a memorable one, a three-run homer off Ray Sadecki.

MURPHY, Danny
Publishing business
Beverly, MA

Dan has the distinction of being the last player in big league history to make the switch from the field to the mound.

Thought to be another Babe Ruth, Dan signed a reported $125,000 bonus with the Cubs in 1960 after hitting over .600 and hurling several no-hitters at St. John's Prep in Danvers, MA.

He made his debut one day before his 18th birthday. After 34 games and a .177 average Dan returned to the minors. While at Evansville in '66 he decided to test his wing. The results were positive, which triggered his return to the big top in 1969. He worked out of the White Sox bullpen for two summers and closed at 4-4 plus nine saves in 68 appearances.

MURPHY, Tom
Commercial real estate salesman for Frost Trinen and Partners
Costa Mesa, CA

"Murf" reported to the Angels in 1968. The right-hander enjoyed his best season in 1970 when he won 16 games. In 1971 he struggled (6-17) and led the league in hitting batters with 21 nicks, the highest total in that department since 1922 when Howard Ehmke of the Tigers plunked 23.

Tom made a quick return to the minors in '72 and fired a no-hitter on August 25th for Omaha, beating Indianapolis 7-0. He then made stops with the Royals, Cardinals, Brewers, Red Sox and Blue Jays. With the Brewers he was converted to a reliever and had 20 saves in both 1974 and 1975.

MURRELL, Ivan
Active in Mexican League

Ivan was a member of Panama's soccer team in the Pan-American Games and also an amateur boxer before signing to play baseball with Houston in 1963. For the next several years, he shuttled between the majors and minors.

Ivan caught his break in '69 when he was selected by the expansion Padres.

"The Big Bull" wore a cowface to ward off the hex of several years of injuries. A cowface? Yes. Ivan wore a triple cross around his neck to avoid injuries. The cross was known as a "caravara" which means cowface.

Injury-free his last couple of years, he walked away with San Diego and Atlanta carrying his cowface and a .236 mark.

MUSER, Tony
    Milwaukee Brewers' coach

A first baseman, Tony broke in with the Red Sox in 1969 but spent most of the decade of the '70s with the White Sox, Orioles, and Brewers. His nine-year run ended at .259.

MUSGRAVES, Dennis
    Property note analyst for Shelter Insurance Company
    Columbia, MO

In 1964 Ford introduced the Mustang and sold over 100,000 of them in a few months. Dennis could have ordered a fleet of them with the $100,000 bonus he received for signing with the Mets.

Musgraves inked his name after hurling the University of Missouri to a second-place finish in the College World Series. The right-hander, who pitched in five games for the Mets in 1965, failed to gain a decision, but pitched 16 impressive innings in which he allowed just one run and put together a 0.56 ERA.

Unfortunately, Dennis underwent surgery for a bone growth on his pitching elbow after the season, which ended his career.

N

NAGELSON, Rusty
Account executive with Merrill Lynch
Little Rock, AR

Rusty entered Ohio State on a football scholarship as a
quarterback, but after being switched to the line by Woody
Hayes, he decided to concentrate on baseball. The long-
ball hitting outfielder helped lead the Buckeyes to a
second-place finish in the 1965 College World Series. His
big league stay consisted of 62 games with the Indians and
Tigers between 1968–70.   .211

NAGY, Mike
Real estate business Better Homes Realty
Bronx, NY

As a youngster raised near Yankee Stadium in the Bronx,
Mike grew up a natural-born Yankee fan. However, he
signed his name on the dotted line with the Red Sox.
  Mike was the surprise of the Bosox staff in '69 after
jumping to the bigs from the Carolina League. Of all
places, Nagy made his debut in Yankee Stadium and beat
Mel Stottlemyre, 2-1. The 21-year-old right-hander finished the year 12-2 and was named the A.L. Rookie Pitcher
of the Year by *The Sporting News*.
  The celebrated Bronx native began the '70 campaign in
the military. Mike finished the year 6-5 in Beantown. But the
rest of his ride was bumpy since he won just one more game
with Boston over the next couple of years. Nagy closed with
the Cards and Astros at age 26 with a 20-13 overall mark.

NAPOLEON, Danny
Employed with Hill Refrigeration
Trenton, NJ

On April 24, 1965, Danny belted a pinch-hit three-run
triple to lead the Mets to a 7-6 win over the Giants, giving

Casey Stengel his 3,000th victory as a manager in pro baseball. Unfortunately after 80 games covering parts of '65 and '66, he fell on his face, hitting a weak .162.

NARUM, "Buster"
Insurance, real estate, and furniture business
Clearwater, FL

"Buster" homered in his first at-bat in the majors. The right-hander out of Florida State University connected off Detroit pitcher Don Mossi in Tiger Stadium on May 3, 1963. By doing so he became the sixth of nine pitchers to homer in his first at-bat in the biggies.

Leslie Ferdinand Narum first arrived with Baltimore in 1963 and failed to gain a decision in seven games. He then took up residence with the Senators the next four years and logged a 14-27 mark. Buster didn't do much better at the plate either (7-for-118), but three of his hits were homers.

NASH, "Cotton"
Real estate business; involved in youth sports programs
Lexington, KY

In 1966 *A Man for All Seasons* was honored as the best movie of the year. It wasn't about Charles "Cotton" Nash, but the 6'6" All-American hoopster from the University of Kentucky was a man for two seasons, combining a career in both pro basketball and baseball.

After leading the Adolph Rupp-coached Wildcats to the S.E.C. title in 1964, he played with both the Lakers and Warriors in the NBA and also spent a season with the Kentucky Colonels of the ABA.

The man had another season—baseball. As a first baseman with the White Sox and Twins ('67, '69–'70) he appeared in 13 games and hit .188.

Reflecting on his career, Nash said, "If I had to do it over again, I would choose one sport and stick with it. Trying a pro career in two sports took away from my quality of play in both. I'm not sure which one I would choose as I enjoyed both equally."

NASH, Jim
    Regional manager for an insurance company; baseball
    coach at Kenesaw College
    Marietta, GA

After Jim took his current college coaching job in 1983 he was quoted as saying, "You never get baseball out of your system." In 1966 "Jumbo Jim" had a great deal of baseball in his system while operating on a full eight cylinders with the Kansas City A's when he won his first seven decisions after his promotion from the Southern League in July. Jim's efforts (12-1) gained him American League Rookie Pitcher of the Year honors by *The Sporting News*.

During a 1969 game Nash hit one between the outfielders and ignored third base coach John McNamara's signs to stop at second base in an attempt to stretch his hit into a triple. He later explained, "I'd never hit a triple before."

"Jumbo" pitched with mediocrity the next few years before he was sent to Atlanta. With the Braves he put together 13-9 and 9-7 seasons in '70 and '71. After losing all eight of his decisions with the Phils in 1972, he was released during spring training of '73, winding up his seven-year trip at 68-64.

NAVARRO, Julio
    Atlanta Braves' Latin America scout

Julio joined the Angels on Labor Day in 1962. The following day he pitched and beat the Yankees at Yankee Stadium in the first major league game he ever saw.

Julio stuck around for six seasons. The right-handed reliever also was used in the bullpen with the Tigers and Braves before closing at 7-9.

NEIBAUER, Gary

Insurance agent with City and County Insurance, Inc.
Scottsbluff, NE

Gary became a pitching casualty in 1975 after a 75-game
4-8 career that stretched from 1969–1973. The 6'3" right-
hander, who was signed by the Braves out of the University of Nebraska where he was an All Big-Eight
Conference pitcher, spent his time in the majors with the
Braves and Phillies.

When it all ended, the game left Neibauer cold, but he
has since mellowed. He says, "I have been in the insurance
business since I left baseball in 1975, at which time I
didn't care if I ever saw another baseball."

NEIGER, Al

Production superintendent for a manufacturing company
Wilmington, DE

Rated by many scouts as the best pitching prospect in college baseball in 1959 while at the University of Delaware,
the southpaw made an abrupt departure after six games
with the Phillies. "I quit baseball rather prematurely at
age 25 due to family responsibilities. However, I have
nothing but pleasant memories of my five-year career,
which was spent mostly in the minors."

NELSON, Dave

Chicago White Sox minor league instructor

Some baseball people like to talk about hitting, others enjoy the art of pitching; Dave's specialty is the running
game. If anyone understands the nuances of base running,
it's Dave Nelson, who pulled off a baserunning hat trick on
August 30, 1974, when he became one of a handful of
players in major league history to swipe second, third, and
home in one inning.

Primarily a second baseman, Davey also put in quite a
bit of time at third base. His ten-year (1968–77) sprint was
spent with the Indians, Senators, Rangers, and Royals.

Named as the second baseman on the Topps Rookie All-Star team in '68, he had his finest year in '73 when he hit .286 for the Rangers. .244

NELSON, Mel
    Oakland A's scout
    Highland, CA

Throughout the Sixties Mel was in and out of the majors with the Cards ('60), Angels ('63), Twins ('65 and '67), and Cardinals again in '68 and '69.

Nelson began his career as an outfielder and looked promising in 1955 when he banged out 27 homers and 112 RBIs for Fresno in the California League. But after hitting just .156 with Columbus in the Sally League, he disappeared from the outfield and decided that pitching might be an easier way to make a living. 4-10

NELSON, Roger
    Arcadia, CA

Roger hurled one of the more notable games in the history of minor league baseball. Pitching for Sarasota in 1964 he once retired 28 consecutive batters from the second to the 11th inning against Daytona Beach. In all he went 14 innings and struck out 22 before he was lifted. Unfortunately, his efforts were in vain as Daytona won in the 17th frame, 2-1.

Nelson broke in with the White Sox in 1967, then went 4-3 as a member of the Orioles the following year before becoming the Kansas City Royals' first selection in the expansion draft.

In '72 he conquered his shoulder miseries to go 11-6 with an excellent 2.08 ERA and six shutouts. Kansas City sent Roger to Cincinnati in a deal involving Hal McRae. Nelson found himself back in Royal blue in '76 where he finally made his exit at 29-32.

NEN, Dick
Seal Beach, CA

This first baseman spent most of his days with the Senators and Cubs from 1965–1970, but will always be remembered by Dodger fans for the home run he hit when he first came up late in the '63 season.

Going into St. Louis, the Dodgers were leading by a game. In the third game of the series the Cards held a 5-to-1 lead going into the eighth inning when Nen batted for Bob Miller and ripped a liner to centerfield for an out. But the Dodgers scored three runs in the inning and Nen was left in the game. Cards' pitcher Ron Taylor faced the pumped-up rookie in the ninth. Nen connected for his classic four-bagger, tying the score. The Dodgers went on to win in the 13th frame, sweeping the three-game set and burying the Cards for good. Dick didn't get another hit the rest of September, but nobody cared. The Dodger players voted Dick a $1,000 share of the World Series spoils.   .224

NETTLES, Graig
Active with San Diego Padres

"Some boys dream of growing up to join the circus. Some want to be a baseball player. I'm lucky to have done both." —Graig Nettles, discussing the tumultuous situation with the Yankees

The quick-witted native of San Diego was always as smooth with his choice of words as he was with his glove. His bat was also a choice piece of equipment filled with 319 home runs as an A.L. third baseman, the all-time record for most homers by an A.L. third sacker.

Nettles, who attended San Diego State on a basketball scholarship, started out in the Twins organization as a second baseman but was moved over to third to make room for a guy named Rod Carew. He first came up in 1967 with Minnesota and doubled in three at-bats. During his first few years he played the outfield as well as third base. Graig belted five home runs in four consecutive games

(September 6–9) for the Twins just four days after his arrival in the big arena from Denver in 1968.

His next stop was in Cleveland (1970–72) where he stayed until he was dealt to the Yankees.

One of the greatest third sackers in the history of the game, Graig led Ameican League third baseman in many categories throughout the 1970s. In '77 and '78 he earned Gold Gloves. His work around the hot corner in the World Series (1976–78) established numerous records.

He walloped 11 home runs in the month of April in 1974, an A.L. mark for baseball's opening month. He led the A.L. with 32 in 1976.

Graig's book, *Balls*, was published in 1984. His brother Jim was an outfielder with the Twins and Tigers in the early Seventies.   .250

NEWMAN, Fred
Retired from the Brookline, MA, Fire Department due to a back injury

Light My Fire was a big hit in 1967 when the fire went out in the big league career of Fred Newman who first arrived with the Angels in '62.

The right hander was 33-39 overall, with his best work coming in 1964 and '65 as a member of the Angels' starting rotation when he won 13 and 14 games.

NICHOLSON, Dave
Owns Nicholson's Sporting Goods
Chicago, IL

Remember Bill "Swish" Nicholson, the Cubs' long-ball hitting outfielder in the 1940s? Meet the real "Swish" Nicholson.

No relation to Bill, Dave signed the largest bonus ever given by the Orioles at the time, a reported $135,000 in 1958. He looked like a sound investment when he hit 35 round-trippers in 1959 to lead the Northern League, then jumped to the Orioles the following year.

His most productive year was in '63 when he pounded 22 homers and knocked in 70 runs for the White Sox. But it was also that season that he entered his name into the record books in several categories for his propensity to strike out. He established several dubious records including most times striking out in a season with 175, tying a major league mark by fanning four times in a game three times that year. Dave closed his seven-year jaunt with Houston and Atlanta.   .212

NIEKRO, Joe
     Active with Houston Astros

It's trivia time. What brother combination holds the record for most pitching victories in the majors? Answer: The Perrys—Gaylord and Jim (529). But the Niekros are a not-too-distant second and still closing in.

Five years younger than Phil, Joe broke in with the Cubs in 1967. Papa Niekro was on hand that year on July 5th when his two sons opposed each other in Atlanta as Phil (Braves) defeated Joe (Cubs), 8-3. It was the first time brothers had opposed each other as starters since Jesse Barnes (Dodgers) beat brother Virgil (Giants) on July 3, 1927.

Traded to Detroit prior to the 1970 season on July 2, 1970, Joe one-hit the Yankees as Horace Clarke broke up his no-hit bid with a single after 8⅓ innings. After three years in Motown, the right-hander spent time with the Braves in between stops to the minors.

Around this time he developed a knuckleball. His new pitch gave his career the shot of adrenalin it sorely needed. In '75 he found a home in Houston and has been an aging wonder ever since. Joe is the only chucker in Astros' history to put together back-to-back 20-win seasons, going 21-11 in 1979 and 20-12 in 1980. In '79 he was chosen the N.L. Pitcher of the Year by *The Sporting News*. Joe is one of three N.L. pitchers to have a 20-win season in the 1980s, joining Steve Carlton (1980 and 1982) and Joaquin Andujar (1984).

On May 26, 1976, he defeated Phil, 4-3. Joe homered that day, the only four-bagger of his career.   193-167

NIEKRO, Phil
    Active with New York Yankees

"Trying to hit Phil Niekro's knuckleball is like trying to
hit jello with chopsticks."

—Bobby Murcer

A graduate of Bridgeport H.S. (OH) in 1957 where he
was a teammate of John Havlicek, the former Boston
Celtic great, "Knucksie" has been in organized baseball
since 1958. Before signing with the Yankees at the end of
'83, he ranked first in baseball among active players in
longevity with one organization (Braves). Niekro, who
goes on like an endless highway, first arrived in 1964 with
the Milwaukee Braves and since that time has mustered
284 victories. His career-high (23-13) came in 1969 with
victory No. 23 coming on Sept. 30th, the Braves' 10th
straight win down the stretch which clinched the N.L.
West title. In that game, Hoyt Wilhelm, the guru of the
knuckler, relieved Phil.
    Niekro also won 20 games in '74 and '79 when he went
21-20, tying for the league lead in wins and leading the
National League in losses. With brother Joe also winning
21 in '79, they became the first brothers in baseball history
to win at least 20 games in the same season. Phil's performance that year made him one of six men to win 20 games
after reaching age 40, joining Cy Young, Eddie Plank,
Grover Cleveland Alexander, Gaylord Perry and Warren
Spahn. His only no-hitter came on Aug. 5, 1973, when he
sent the Padres home frustrated.
    Phil holds the career mark for wild pitches, the result of
the unpredictable flight of his fluttering knuckleball. On
August 4, 1979, he had a record four in one inning, and six
for the game, tying a major league mark set by J.R. Richard. His four wild pitches in the same frame tied Walter
Johnson's record set in 1914.
    Where did he learn the knuckleball? He says, "One day
when I was about 13 years old, my Dad and I were having a
catch in the backyard and he threw me a knuckler. The
ball hit me on the knee because I had trouble catching it.
My Dad laughed and I asked him to show me how to throw
that pitch." The rest is history.   284-238

NIESON, Chuck
   Area manager for the Hartford Insurance Co.
   Burnsville, MN

If you dig deep into the archives of Twins' history, you'll find the name of Chuck Nieson, who worked in a total of two innings in 1964. Of the six outs he recorded, five were by strikeouts.

   It's interesting to note that his recall in September that season came after he spent the season at Atlanta (I.L.) where he was 4-17 and led the league in losses.

NIPPERT, Merlin
   President of the Guarantee State Bank
   Mangum, OK

Nicknamed "Merlin the Magician" for his outstanding work out of the bullpen for Seattle (P.C.L.) in the early Sixties, there was nothing magical about this right-hander's stay in the majors as he had no record with the Red Sox in four games.

NISCHWITZ, Ron
   Baseball coach at Wright State University
   Dayton, OH

Ron was a star at Birmingham in 1960 when he had the best ERA in the Southern League at 2.41. But in the majors he looked more like a supporting player clinging to his job as he went 5-8 with the Tigers and Indians from 1961–65.

   The southpaw reliever was busy in '62 when he went 4-5 in 48 games with the Bengals.

NOLAN, Gary
    Employed with the MGM Hotel and Casino in Las
    Vegas, NV

"I don't think he ever threw a pitch that didn't hurt."
—Johnny Bench, commenting on Gary Nolan's chronically
  sore arm

Nolan signed for a reported $65,000 bonus with the Reds
out of high school in 1966. The following year he pitched as
an 18-year-old for the Reds, making him the youngest
player in the majors that year. The hard-throwing right-
hander went 14-8 with the aid of a 95-mph fastball. In one
game he fanned 15 Giants, including Willie Mays four
straight times.

The next year he started slowly because of arm problems
and began the season in the minors. After developing a
fine off-speed pitch, Nolan was 18-7 in 1970 as the Reds
copped the N.L. pennant. He shut out the Pirates in the
opening game of the NLCS as the Reds swept the three-
game set. In '72 Gary was a key member of the Reds' pitching clan, going 15-5 with an ERA of 1.99.

But his personal war with his ailing arm raged on. In '73
he only appeared in two games, but rebounded to win 15
games in both '75 and '76 for the Cincinnati World Championship teams. When the Big Red Machine cut down the
Yankees in four straight in the '76 World Series, Gary won
the final game, 7-2.

His swan song came in '77 at age 29 when he pitched for
the Reds and Angels. The battle was over at 110-70.

NOLD, Dick
    Daly City, CA

Richard Nixon was 0-2 in political races in the 1960s when
he returned to win the Republican nomination and the
1968 election. Dick Nold also began 0-2 in Washington
(1967) after pitching in seven games for the Senators. However, unlike Mr. Nixon, he never had another chance to
come back.

NORIEGA, John
    Therapist at the Davis County Mental Health Center
    Kaysville, UT

John sounds like a rugged individualist who would have
fitted well in a Zane Grey novel. When contacted he was on
a survival mission with juvenile court offenders.
    The right-hander out of the University of Utah was on a
survival mission in 1969–70 and failed to gain a decision
in 13 games for the Reds.

NORMAN, Fred
    Minor league pitching coach for Montreal Expos

Fred's story typifies the modern big money era in baseball.
Following the 1979 season in which Norman was 11-13 for
the Reds he was granted free agency. At the time the
39-year-old left-hander with a career mark of one game
over .500 received a call from his agent informing him that
the Expos had offered him a $125,000 bonus with a con-
tract calling for $450,000 for two years and another
$350,000 for a third.
    "It's ridiculous, but that's the way things are in baseball
now, and I'm more than happy to accept my hunk," stated
Norman.
    During most of the 1960s, Fred teetered around in the
minors with stops in between with the A's and Cubs.
    His next stops were with the Dodgers, Cardinals, and
Padres where he continued to struggle. Then he was
traded to the Reds where the floodgates opened a stream of
success for the late starter. From 1973–79 he won between
11 and 14 games a year, putting winning records together
for six consecutive years.

NORTHEY, Scott
    Location unknown

The son of Ron Northey, one of the top pinch-hitters of the
1950s, Scott began in the White Sox organization, then
was plucked by the Royals in the expansion draft.
    "Scooter" began the '69 season in the depths of the Caro-

lina League then jumped all the way up to the Royals where he batted .262 in 20 games, the extent of his big league stay.

NORTHRUP, Jim
Manufacturer's representative
Tracy, MI

An all-around athlete at Alma College (Michigan), he was a good enough football quarterback to be offered a tryout by the Chicago Bears of the N.F.L. To the delight of the Tigers he chose baseball and represented the Bengals in the outfield from 1964–74 with his last stops in Montreal and Baltimore in '75.

On June 24, 1968, Jim connected for two grand-slams in the same game, a feat accomplished by only six other players. Five days later he unloaded another bell ringer. Jim was in grand-slam heaven that year. In the World Series against St. Louis he hit just .250, but collected eight RBIs, including four when he blasted a grand-slam in Game Six to highlight the Tigers' 10-run inning against the Cardinals.

The following year ('69) he became the first Detroit player since Ty Cobb in 1925 to go 6-for-6 in a game. His sixth hit that day came in the 13th inning, a long, game-winning homer which went over the right field roof at Tiger Stadium. The lefty slugger hit a career high 25 four-baggers that year.

In his final full season in Tiger flannels (1973) he hit .307, the only time he topped the .300 mark in his career. On July 11th he enjoyed a second eight-RBI day in a game against Texas with two home runs, a sacrifice fly and a fielder's choice. Jim accomplished all those things hitting in the leadoff position that game.

Northrup closed at .267 lifetime with 153 home runs.

NOSSEK, Joe
Chicago White Sox Coach

One of the arts of baseball is sign stealing. Joe has gained the reputation as the best in business. But he didn't qualify for this text by stealing signs.

After winning All-American honors at Ohio University, Nossek was in and out of the A.L. with the Twins and A's from 1964–69, plus one game for the Cards in 1970. The flychaser finished at .228. He appeared in six World Series games for the Twins in '65.

NOTTEBART, Don
    Retired from carpet business
    Houston, TX

It was obvious to baseball savants that Don was headed in the right direction when he won 18 games four different years in the minors. His big league career spanned the Sixties, going 36-51 with the Braves, Colt .45s–Astros, Reds, Yanks, and Cubs.

"Notty" was in a generous mood in 1961 when he tied an all-time N.L. record by serving up three grand-slams that year. He was traded to Houston after the '62 season, and on May 17, 1963, hurled the first no-hitter in the franchise's history when he beat the Phillies, 4-1. The lone run came as a result of an error.

His next win didn't come until July 15th when he beat the Mets, 8-0. With two out in the ninth inning and two strikes on the batter, Jim Hickman, Don sprained his ankle on the mound and was forced to leave the contest. A reliever came on to throw the third strike to Hickman, but Don was credited with the strikeout. Despite the fact he struck out the final batter of the game to complete the 8-0 victory, he was not credited with a shutout because he did not finish the game.

NYE, Rich
    Veterinarian
    Chicago, IL

Although Nottebart's shutout which wasn't a shutout is strange, how about Rich Nye, who in 1969 (Cubs) picked up victories number two and three before his first win of the year. How did it happen you ask? Very simple—Rich gained credit for a win on September 2nd of a game which was the completion of a suspended game from June 15th.

The lanky left-hander from the University of California was named to the Topps Rookie All-Star team after going 13-10. His 13 victories were the most wins by a Cub rookie since Dick Drott won 15 in 1957.

Unfortunately Nye was able to win just 13 more games the next three seasons as an arm injury put the hex on his career. He finished 26-31 after stops in Montreal and St. Louis. It seems fitting that he spent some time with the Cardinals since he later graduated from the University of Illinois in veterinary medicine and today has a practice which specializes in the care of exotic birds.

NYMAN, Jerry
    Professional outdoorsman
    Kalispelle, MT

A professional outdoorsman? That's right. When contacted, Jerry replied, "I run a baseball school in the summer, hunt in the fall, and helicopter ski in the winter."

The southpaw hurler out of Brigham Young University was with the White Sox and Padres from 1968–70, going 6-7 with two of his six victories shutouts.

O

O'BRIEN, Syd
    West coast manager for the Petroleum Publishing Co.
    Long Beach, CA

For every several thousand O'Briens named Pat and Mike, there is probably one named Sydney. Syd was named after a Jewish man who once saved his father's life.

This utility infielder played with the Red Sox, White Sox, Angels, and Brewers from 1969–72, hitting .230.

ODOM, "Blue Moon"
    Employed with IBM
    Fountain Valley, CA

Players are frequently in search of intimations of good luck. John "Blue Moon" Odom was part of that lot. He wore number 13 until he went through a long dry spell in pursuit of his 10th victory in 1968. He switched to number 10 and one-hit the Senators, 4-1, on August 10th. By the time he hung it up in 1976, it was irrelevant what number he wore since he finished a consistent 84-85.

Possibly the best performance of his career came during the pressure-packed '72 ALCS when he blanked the Tigers on three hits in the second game. In the fifth and deciding contest he was the starter and winner, 2-1. In Game Three of the 1972 World Series, he continued to sizzle, but was a hard-luck 1-0 loser to the Reds despite his 11 strikeouts. Two years later he won the fifth and final game of the '74 Freeway Series between the A's and Dodgers.

John also saw action for the Indians, Braves, and White Sox. On July 28, 1976, he pitched a combined no-hitter with Francisco Barrios (White Sox) to beat his original A's, 2-1.

O'DONOGHUE, John
    Chemical plant employee
    Independence, MO

John enjoys the distinction of being the first Kansas City native to play for the A's in that city when the A's brought him up in 1963. Despite a 4-12 record at the All-Star break in '65, he was named to the A.L. All-Star team that summer, but did not participate.

The University of Missouri product spent the summer of '67 in Cleveland and helped himself to a 8-2 victory of the Tigers on June 1st with a grand-slam off Denny McLain.

O'Donoghue moved around to the Orioles, Pilots, Brewers and Expos before finishing with a 39-55 mark.

OLIVA, Tony
     Minnesota Twins' coach

Baseball Digest's scouting report on rookie prospects in 1964 said of Tony Oliva: "Fair hitter, can make somebody a good utility outfielder." Fifteen years, 220 homers, and a .304 lifetime average later, Tony would hardly be classified as a fair hitter.

He was the first-ever rookie batting champion in the A.L. when he batted .323 in '64. He also established a rookie record by collecting 217 hits. In addition, Tony belted 32 home runs and had 94 RBIs. The following year he won his second straight batting title (.321) and led the Twins to the World Series. Tony's second batting crown marked the only time in baseball history that anyone had won consecutive batting titles at the start of their career.

But Tony's special talents were hampered by a shoulder separation in 1968 and a cartilage tear in his knee four years later. Aside from battling opposing pitchers, he had to deal with the surgeon's knife seven times for knee problems.

The determined Cuban won his third title (.337) in 1971 and won Player of the Year honors for a second time. Although the Twins were swept three straight by the Orioles in both the '69 and '70 ALCS, Tony wasn't at fault as he swatted a torrid .440 in six games.

Tony's actual name was Pedro, but once he used his brother's passport to enter the United States to play pro ball in 1961 he's been known as Tony Oliva ever since. His name quickly gained fame in organized baseball circles when he won the Appalachian League batting title hitting .410, a prediction of things to come.

OLIVARES, Ed
     Professor at Inter American University in San German, Puerto Rico

The celebrated musical *West Side Story* about rival Puerto Rican gangs walked off with all the honors in 1961 at the Academy Awards, a year that saw Puerto Rican–born outfielder Ed Olivares walk out of the big leagues after a

24-game story spread over two seasons with the Cardinals. .143

OLIVER, Al
   Active with the Philadelphia Phillies

Al Oliver's license plate reads: "Al Hits." He sure does. Al is the only player in modern major league history to have combined 200 hits and 100 RBIs in a season in both the American and National Leagues.

A product of Kent State University, Al hails from Portsmouth, Ohio. The first baseman-outfielder came up with the Pirates in '68, his first full season coming in '69 when he was named to the Topps Rookie All-Star team. He later switched to the outfield and established himself as one of the game's top hitters in the '70s.

Oliver's early career was spent with the Pirates (1968–77). When he was traded to Texas in 1977 he blitzed through the A. L. with averages like .324, .323, .319 and .309. In the spring of '82, he returned to the N. L. when the Rangers traded him to Montreal. All he did was lead the N. L. in batting (.331). Oliver, who was sent to the San Francisco Giants prior to the '84 season, was dealt to the Phillies later in the campaign.

The eight-time All-Star was an integral part of the Pittsburgh "Lumber Company" which won five N. L. East titles in six seasons from 1970–1975. While a member of the Rangers he had a day (Aug. 17, 1980) that sounds almost fictitious when he established a big league record with 21 total bases in the Rangers' doubleheader sweep over the Tigers. He doubled, tripled, and homered in the first game, then homered three times in the nightcap.
   "Al Hits!" .305

OLIVER, Bob
   Quality control inspector for Smith Tool; assistant
   baseball coach at Loyola High School
   Anaheim, CA

In 1965 Emmett Ashford broke the color line as the first black umpire in major league baseball. That same year

Bob broke in with the Pirates, but he spent most of the decade in the minors.

Oliver's big chance came in 1969 when he was taken aboard the expansion Royals. A noted mosaic painter, he created havoc for the Angels on May 4, 1969, when he went 6-for-6 (four singles, a double, and a home run), leading the Royals to a 15-1 win.

Bob's penthouse season came in 1970 when he whacked 27 homers and had 99 RBIs. His eight-year march wound down with the Angels, Orioles, and Yankees in 1975.   .256

OLIVER, Nate
    Station agent for Bay Area Rapid Transit (B.A.R.T.)
    Oakland, CA

The musical *Oliver* was named the best picture of the year in 1968. This musically inclined infielder, who was at one time in great demand as a singer, sang the national anthem before games on occasion and even recorded an album.

"Pee Wee" was with the Dodgers (1963–67), Giants ('68), Yankees and Cubs ('69).

Nate writes: "At present I am doing very well. I am no longer singing. However, I am back in baseball as a member of the Oakland A's Speakers Bureau and as a clinic director. I'm in a position to help young people, and am very pleased the way things have gone for me."

The early 1960s saw the arrival of the brothers Olivo. Both were relief pitchers who arrived at advanced ages. In February of 1977 the Olivo brothers both died in their native Dominican Republic just 12 days apart.

OLIVO, Diomedes
    Died Feb. 15, 1977, at age 58 in Santo Domingo, DR

Next to Satchel Paige, Diomedes would have to be the second oldest rookie in major league history as he was reported to be "about 42" when he joined the Pirates' bullpen for four games in 1960.

The I.L. MVP in '61 with Columbus, Diomedes appeared

in 62 games for the Pirates in '62 and was 5-1 plus seven saves. He was with the Cardinals the next season and finished 5-6 overall. That same year (July 22nd) he tossed a no-hitter pitching for Atlanta (I.L.) and beat Toronto, 1-0. Since he was "about 45," his performance most likely makes him the oldest pitcher ever to throw a no-hitter in professional baseball.

OLIVO, Frederico
    Died Feb. 3, 1977, at age 49 in Santo Domingo, DR

"Chi Chi" was well past his 30th birthday when he came up with the Braves in 1961. After a two-year hiatus in the minors, "Chi Chi" returned to the Braves, where he finished in '66 at 7-6, plus 12 saves in 96 games. On July 26, 1964, he won his only two games of the season on the same day when he got credit for both wins in a double-header sweep of the Mets in New York (11-7 and 15-10).

OLLOM, Jim
    Salesman for Westco Bakery Products
    Everett, WA

The big southpaw was drafted from the Yankees by Minnesota after sputtering in the minors. In 1966 he put it all together and went 20-8 at Denver (P.C.L.), racking up 137 K's. Ollom was the first pitcher to win 20 games in the P.C.L. since Leo Kiely won that many for the San Francisco Seals in 1957. He lost his only decision in 24 games with the Twins in 1966–67.

O'RILEY, Don
    Budweiser beer truck driver
    Kansas City, MO

Don started as a catcher in the Kansas City semipro league until 1964 when his team found itself in an emergency situation and his manager asked him to give pitching a try. He did and was quite successful in his new role. Don enjoyed the life of O'Riley in 1969 at Omaha, going

12-4 for the A.A. champions. But his big league stay (1969–70) lasted only 27 games as a member of the Royals.   1-1

ORSINO, John
    Baseball coach and director of intramural program at Fairleigh Dickinson University; Deputy Director of Bergen County Community Action program in Hackensack, NJ

"Horse" worked his way up through the Giants organization, starting in 1957. The big catcher divided the '61 and '62 seasons between San Francisco and Tacoma (P.C.L.). In 1962 he hit .327 at Tacoma and earned his permanent passport to the big top, where he made it into 18 games for the N.L. champion Giants.

Traded to Baltimore that winter, John made his bat his ally in spring training in 1963 when he blasted five home runs in five at-bats over a two-game period. John went on to have his finest year in '63 when he poked 19 of his career total 40 roundtrippers.

After two more seasons in Baltimore, he finished with the Senators in 1967.   .249

ORTEGA, Phil
    Taxicab driver
    Mesa, AZ

A right-handed pitcher of Mexican and Yaqui Indian descent, Filomeno Coronado Ortega signed a $70,000 bonus contract with the Dodgers out of Mesa H.S. in 1959. He was a hot item back then, thanks to his blazing fastball and was sought by all 16 clubs.

The "Chief" had his first full season in the majors in 1964 and went 7-9 with three shutouts for Los Angeles. His first big league victory was an impressive 1-0, four-hit shutout over the Braves.

Following the season he joined Frank Howard in a swap to Washington for Claude Osteen. Ortega, who was a 12-game winner for the Senators in '65 and '66, last pitched with the Angels in '69.   46-62

ORTIZ, Jose
     Insurance salesman; postgame host for the Ponce
     winter league baseball team
     Puerto Rico

It's been said that the team is more important than the individual. Such is true in the sometimes cold world of baseball. A good example is Jose Ortiz, a speedy outfielder who
batted .301 while playing for the White Sox (1969–70) and
Cubs ('71), then was among the missing.

OSINSKI, Dan
     Steel fabrication salesman
     Oak Forest, IL

Dan had to have nerves of steel to continue playing after a
freak accident he experienced on the mound. On April 13,
1963, he was nearly skulled by J. C. Martin's line drive in
the 13th inning. The ball hit the little finger of his right
hand and bounced into the air to Joe Koppe, who turned
the liner into a double play.
     The hard-throwing relief specialist wore the jerseys of
the A's, Angels, Red Sox, White Sox, and Astros from
1962–70, going 29-28 in 324 games.

OSTEEN, Darrell
     Beverly Hills, CA

Sammy Ellis says, "Darrell found the world too interesting." This right-hander, no relation to Claude, enjoyed
success in the minors but was off in the ozone, losing all
four of his decisions with the Reds from 1965–67. Osteen
closed with the A's in 1970, winning his only decision.   1-4

OTIS, Amos
     Released by Pirates in 1984

In 1969 the Mets could have started an all-Mobile (AL) outfield with the likes of Tommie Agee, Cleon Jones, and
Amos Otis. However, after the '69 season, the World

Champions were in need of a third baseman and swapped Amos and Bob Johnson to Kansas City in exchange for Joe Foy. It did not turn out to be one of the better deals in Mets' history.

Otis went on to become an All-Star five times, a Royals Player of the Year three times and a three-time Gold Glove winner in centerfield. He collected over 2,000 career hits and has pilfered over 350 bases. He owns almost every Royals' lifetime offensive record.

In 1971 he hit .301 and led the league with 52 steals, establishing an A.L. record for being caught stealing just eight times, the fewest ever for a player with at least 50 steals. Amos batted .303 in '73, with a career high 26 homers.

During the 1980 World Series against the Phillies, Amos batted .478 (11-for-23), with three home runs and seven RBIs. He became the 16th player in Series history to homer in his first at-bat when he connected off Bob Walk in the second inning of Game One.   .277

O'TOOLE, Dennis
Assistant Director of Motor Carriers for the Kentucky State Government Department of Transportation
Erlanger, KY

"I was trying to fight that off, not live it down but live up to it," said Dennis in response to the pressures of following his older brother Jim to the majors.

Denny, 12 years younger than Jim, had been a batboy for the Reds in the early Sixties. The young right-hander who came up to the White Sox at age 20 in 1969, was never able to get his foot solidly planted. He appeared in 15 games with the Pale Hose from '69–'73 and never gained a decision.

OTT, Billy
Policeman
New York, NY

Like the great Mel Ott, Billy Ott was an outfielder. Playing for San Antonio in 1962 he looked like the second coming of Mel when he banged out 33 doubles, 12 triples, 23 home runs, and 88 RBIs. However, the switch-hitting

St. John's University alumnus hit just .164 in 32 games with the Cubs in '62 and '64.

OYLER, Ray
Died on Jan. 26, 1981, at age 42 in Seattle, WA

The epitome of the good-field, no-hit player, Ray played shortstop with the Tigers (1965–68), Pilots ('69), and Angels ('70), hitting an anemic .175. Ray proved that a team could win without a good-hitting shortstop when he batted a ghastly .135 for Detroit in 1968 in 111 games, the lowest average for a major league shortstop playing in at least 100 games. He made way for Mickey Stanley in the World Series that fall, but did appear in four games as a late-inning replacement.

When Oyler was drafted by the Pilots in the 1969 expansion pool, a Seattle disc jockey, noting Ray's .135 bat, decided the weak-hitting infielder needed help in the form of a fan club. The Ray Oyler Fan Club was formed and had a large membership. It may have helped, since Ray improved his batting to .165 and hit seven of his 15 career homers with the Pilots.

At the time of his death, he was employed with a Seattle grocery company.

P

PACIOREK, John
Physical education teacher
San Marino, CA

On the final day of the '63 season, this 18-year-old strong-boy outfielder found himself in the lineup of the Houston Colt .45s. All he did was go 3-for-3, draw two walks, knock in three runs, and score four as Houston devoured the Mets, 13-4. Because of a back ailment that required surgery, he never returned to the majors, finishing with a 1.000 avg.

John had three brothers involved in organized baseball. His brother Tom has had a long and distinguished career, brother Mike was a first baseman in the Dodgers' and Braves' organizations, while Jim, an outfielder, is currently in the Brewers' system.

PAEPKE, Dennis
Automobile salesman
Crestline, CA

As a catcher and outfielder with the Kansas City Royals in parts of four seasons from 1969–74, "Pap" hit .183 in 80 games. His father, Jack Paepke, was a coach with the Angels from 1961–66.

PAGE, Mike
Dock foreman for Mezzo, Inc.
Greenville, SC

The Beatles were singing *Paperback Writer* when this 28-year-old outfielder had kind of a paper lion career (20 games) with the Atlanta Braves in 1968.   .179

PALMER, Jim
ABC baseball announcer; Jockey underwear representative

Known as "cakes" in the Baltimore clubhouse because of his Jockey underwear commercials, Jim could have easily been called "pancakes." He got into the habit of eating them for breakfast on days he was pitching in 1966 while running up an eight-game winning streak.

Jim signed a reported $60,000 bonus with the Orioles in 1963. His first win came on May 16, 1965, in relief against the Yankees. He also hit his first big league home run that day against Jim Bouton. The 6'3" right-hander went 15-10 in '66 and also had his pancakes for breakfast on the day he shut out Sandy Koufax and the Dodgers, 6-0, in the second game of the '66 W.S. Palmer's shutout made him the youngest pitcher to win a complete World Series shutout game. He was 20 years, 11 months old at the time.

The next two years were like a bad dream for Jim. Plagued by an assortment of back and shoulder injuries, his career almost terminated. Suddenly, two years later, there was life in a moribund career.

From 1969–79 Palmer was the right-hander supreme in the American League and was a major part of the successful Orioles' franchise. Eight out of nine years Jim was a 20-game winner, his personal high coming in '75 when he went 23-11. A three-time Cy Young Award winner (1973, '75, '76), he also posted the best ERA in the A.L. twice.

In eight ALCS games covering six different years he stands 4-1 with a 1.96 ERA. Covering six World Series he is 4-2 with a 3.20 ERA.

Palmer's only no-hitter came on August 13, 1969, when he no-hit Oakland, 8-0, only four days after coming off a six-week stretch on the disabled list. An oddity about his career is that he never gave up a grand-slam in almost 4,000 innings pitched.

Palmer's frequently publicized disputes with manager Earl Weaver established the pair as baseball's odd couple. Ironically, they would renew their marriage in the broadcast booth.

This future Hall of Famer's record stands at 268-152.

PALMER, Lowell
    Liquor distributor
    Sacramento, CA

During his playing days, Lowell had a private investigation agency in Sacramento. He actually was in constant search of success. From 1969–74 Lowell went 5-18 with the Phils, Cards, Indians, and Padres. His first big league win came on June 29, 1969, when, pitching for the Phillies, he shut out the Expos on three hits.

In 1967 the right-hander was pitching for Tidewater (Carolina League) when he was scheduled for induction into the Army but it was delayed. Lowell had time to make one more start, and made the most of it by throwing a no-hitter.

PALMQUIST, Ed
     Construction business
     Los Angeles, CA

In 1960–61, the right-handed reliever was 1-3 in 36 games spent mostly with the Dodgers and briefly in Minnesota.
     Palmquist celebrated his 27th birthday on June 10, 1960, by making his major league debut and allowing just one hit in four innings of relief work against Cincinnati.

PAPA, John
     Chemical sales representative for Guard-All in Norwalk, CT.

When John made his debut on Opening Day in 1961 for the Orioles, the first batter he faced was Ted Kluszewski, the original hulk. Playing in the first game ever for the Angels, "Klu" greeted Johnny with a home run. Baltimore catcher Gus Triandos ran out to the mound and told the shaken Oriole chucker, "Welcome to the big leagues, rookie." Papa's teammates added insult to injury by blowing up Kluszewski's picture and putting it in Papa's locker stall.
     John made a total of three trips from the bullpen in '61 and '62 for the Birds without being involved in a decision. He says, "I can always say that I played in the first game in the history of the California Angels' franchise."

PARKER, Wes
     Los Angeles Dodgers' instructor; baseball announcer; actor
     Santa Monica, CA

When Bruce Bochte retired from baseball while still in his prime after the 1982 season, it brought to mind the name of Wes Parker, who 10 years earlier retired while still in his early 30s to "enjoy the whole spectrum of life." Unlike Bochte however, Wes never returned.
     Parker had a solid career (1964–72), spent entirely with the Dodgers. The smooth-fielding Dodger first baseman

made just 45 errors in his career, which adds up to a .996 fielding percentage, the best of any first baseman playing in at least 1,000 games. In 1968 he was charged with just one miscue in 1,009 chances for a .999 fielding percentage and came close to being the first regular playing first sacker to make it through a season without an error. The one error was debatable as it came on a bad-hop grounder hit by Norm Miller off the carpet in the Astrodome. Dodger broadcaster Vince Scully almost jumped out of the radio booth when the error was called.

A career .267 hitter, Wes put together a big season at the plate in 1970 when he hit .319. He collected 111 RBIs to become the first switch-hitter in 35 years in the N.L. to drive in at least 100 runs. With 10 homers that season, he became the first major leaguer to drive in at least 100 runs with 10 or less home runs.

On May 7, 1970, Wes hit for the cycle with a single and triple batting left-handed, and a double and homer hitting from the right side.

Parker joined the Reds' telecast crew following his retirement, then began a career as an actor. He says, "My baseball career was the ideal training ground for my acting career as both professions are hotbeds of insecurity."

PARSONS, Tom
>Foreman for Green Hills Sausage Company
>Salem, OR

This 6'7" right-hander was known as "Long Tom." It was a long time between victories for Tom as he was 2-13 pitching in 40 games for the Pirates and Mets between 1963–65. Most of that was accumulated with the Mets in '65 when he had a 1-10 record.

PATEK, Fred
>Employed with Star Com Communications, a long distance telephone service
>Kansas City, MO

Baseball is a game in which size doesn't matter. Freddie Patek, the diminutive 5'4" shortstop, is living proof. When asked how it felt being the smallest player in the majors, he responded, "It beats being the smallest player in the minors."

Nicknamed "Flea," Patek was not chosen until the 35th round of the first free agent draft in June of 1965. He worked his way up the Pirates' ladder and was with the Bucs from 1968–70 until traded to the Royals. Throughout most of the Seventies, Freddie was the Kansas City short-stop. In the '76 and '77 ALCS against the Yankees he was 7-for-18 (.389) both years, only to lose the rubber fifth game to the Yankees each time. When the Royals finally beat the Yanks in 1980, he was with the Angels, where he closed in 1981.

The little man had some big days. On July 9, 1971, he hit for the cycle and on May 6, 1972, he tied a major league mark by taking part in five double plays in a nine inning game. The miniature shortstop enjoyed a gigantic day on June 20, 1980, when he hit three home runs and a double to lead the Angels to a 20-2 blowout over the Red Sox at Fenway.　　　　　　　　　　　　　　　　　.242

PATTERSON, Daryl
　　　Inspector for Pacific Gas and Electric
　　　Clovis, CA

Born in the little town of Coalinga, California, which suffered through the devastating earthquake in 1983, Daryl spent parts of five seasons (1968–74) in the big top as a reliever with the Tigers, A's, Cardinals, and Pirates. As a rookie member of the World Champion Tigers in '68, the right-hander had a pair of wins with seven saves and a fine 2.12 ERA in 38 games and hurled three scoreless innings in two appearances out of the bullpen against the Cardinals in the World Series.　　　　　　　　　　　　　　11-9

PATTIN, Marty
　　　Baseball coach at the University of Kansas

Marty made history on April 8, 1969, when he was the starting and winning pitcher in the first game ever played by the Seattle Pilots. The All-American from Eastern Illi-

nois University worked five innings that night in Seattle's
4-3 win over the Angels, a fitting accomplishment since
Marty came up the year before with the Angels.

The right-hander shifted gears with the Pilots to Milwaukee and was a 14-game winner for the Brewers in 1970
and 1971. The next two years he was with the Red Sox
where Marty won a career-high 17 in '72.

Pattin was traded to the Royals after the '73 campaign
and spent the rest of his career in Kansas City as a starter
and long reliever.   114-109

PAUL, Mike
    San Diego Padres minor league pitching instructor;
    real estate salesman
    Tucson, AZ

Early in the 1968 season Mike was pitching for Reno (California League) while commuting back and forth to classes
at the University of Arizona. Following a two-hit shutout
in which he struck out 14, he put his books on hold and
jetted to Cleveland where in his first appearance, he
pitched three scoreless innings in relief to gain a save in a
3-1 triumph over Minnesota. Following stops with the
Rangers and Cubs he was gone at 27-48.

While pitching in Tampico, Mexico, the umpires would
frequently call time as a train chugged through the outfield just behind second base and exit through a gate in the
left field fence. Intrigued by this, Mike once gave the train
engineer an autographed baseball card of his and in exchange was allowed to drive the train to the fence.

PENA, Jose
    Last active in Mexican League

Jose worked in 61 games, all from the bullpen, while with
the Reds and Dodgers from 1969–72. After pitching with
the Reds in '69, he returned to the Mexican League.   7-4

PENA, Roberto
Automobile mechanic
Santiago, Dominican Republic

Roberto isn't the greatest of baseball heroes, but he was a true "hero" back in his native country during the winter following the '68 season when he saved a woman from a shark attack in the waters off the coast of the Dominican Republic.

The peppy shortstop was a baseball hero on Opening Day of the 1965 campaign at Wrigley Field as he singled, doubled, and homered in his major league debut with the Cubs. He went 3-for-6 in the game against the Cards which ended after 11 innings in a 10-10 tie due to darkness. Unfortunately, his glove had the snap of a toothless shark as he committed three errors in seven chances.

Roberto also played with the Phillies, Padres, A's, and Brewers (1965–71), hitting .245.

PEPITONE, Joe
Public relations for "Adam and Eve" hair replacement center
Scarsdale, NY

In his book *Joe, You Coulda Made Us Proud*, the life story of this Brooklyn-born Italian is vividly told. His extracurricular activities might make Bo Belinsky blush.

Joe could also frolic with the guys. His trip to West Point with Mickey Mantle in a rented limousine to play in an exhibition game against the cadets has become a classic story. The pair missed the team bus and had to rent a limousine in which they dined on vodka and orange juice as they traveled north. When they arrived on the right field line at the Point, they were not in the best condition to play baseball.

Pepitone broke in with the Yanks in 1962. The swinging single gave pinstripe fans a ray of hope that the Bronx Bomber legacy would survive, but Joe's bat was about as predictable as his moves after midnight. From 1962–73 he batted a mediocre .258 with 219 roundtrippers. Many who played the game would relish those figures, but for "Pepi," it was like an A student who got by with C's.

Joe hit 27 homers in 1963, followed up with 28 the next season and in the World Series against the Cards, he hit a grand-slam in Game Six to lead the Yanks to an 8-3 win. "Pepi," who had a career-high 31 roundtrippers in '66, led the league in fielding at first base in '65 and '66, then was switched to the outfield in '67 when Mickey Mantle went to first base. His Yankee days ended after the '69 season.

Joe split the '70 campaign with the Astros and Cubs. He stayed in Chicago until 1973 before playing in three games for the Braves that year, the last stop for Joseph Anthony Pepitone.

PEPPER, Don
Sales representative for CCC Associates, Saratoga Springs, NY

Sgt. Pepper's Lonely Heart's Club Band was heard by millions of Beatles fans in the late Sixties, but Don Pepper was heard from in just four games as a member of the Tigers in 1966, going hitless in three at-bats.

In *Sports Illustrated*'s annual rookie prospects issue, the husky first baseman joined Johnny Bench on the cover in the spring of 1968. The magazine batted .500 in its predictions.

PERAZA, Lou
Philadelphia Phillies' scout in Puerto Rico

Throughout the Sixties, Lou played in minor league towns rubbing elbows with a host of career failures. The right-hander appeared for the Phillies in eight games in 1968 without a decision.

PEREZ, Marty
Insurance agent for Rogers and Associates
Decatur, GA

The cousin of former Cleveland pitcher Mike Garcia, Marty had short trials with California in both 1969 and '70 before being purchased by the Braves. For the next five years he played shortstop and second base for Atlanta before being traded to the Giants in '76.

Before it ended in '78, Marty was also with the Yankees for one game before crashing with the Oakland A's.   .246

PEREZ, Tony
Active with Cincinnati Reds

To borrow from Tom Wolfe, Tony had the right stuff. Aside from talent, that would include consistency, endurance, and determination.

Atanasio Rigal Perez joined the Reds in '64. He came up as a first baseman, but switched to third in '67 where he remained for the next five years. In the All-Star Game that summer his 15th-inning home run off Catfish Hunter gave the N.L. a 2-1 victory in the longest game in All-Star history. Ironically it would be the only base hit he would ever collect in the seven All-Star Games he played in.

Tony had his best year in 1970 when he belted 40 home runs, 129 RBIs, and swung for a .317 avg., all career highs.

Between 1970–76, Tony was one of the leaders of the "Big Red Machine" that won five N.L. West titles, four N.L. pennants and two World Series.

A streak hitter throughout his career, he was 0-for-15 in the '75 World Series against the Red Sox before breaking loose with a pair of four-baggers in Game Five, then hitting a key two-run homer in the seventh and deciding game.

Traded to the Expos following the '76 season, Perez stayed in Montreal until granted free agency at the end of the '79 campaign before going to Boston where he spent his next three summers. After his release he was picked up by the Phillies for the '83 season, then was sold to the Reds. Tony has 371 homers and a .279 batting average.

PERKINS, Cecil
Owns Ceba Distributors, Inc. (decorating products)
Martinsburg, WV

In The Heat of the Night was named best picture in 1967, a summer the Yankees threw right-hander Cecil Perkins into the heat of a couple nights, losing his only decision in two appearances.

PERRANOSKI, Ron
    Los Angeles Dodgers' pitching coach

During a good part of the Sixties, the Dodgers spelled relief "Perranoski." From 1961–67, the Paterson, NJ, native was the workhorse of the Los Angeles bullpen, leading the N.L. in games pitched in 1962 (70), 1963 (69), and tying for the N.L. lead in 1967 (70).

Ron's golden year was 1963 when he used his screwball to go 16-3 (.842) the top percentage by a Dodger pitcher since Preacher Roe's 22-3 in 1951.

From 1961–65 he had a collective ERA of 2.48. A so-so start with the Dodgers in '65 led to trade rumors, but Perranoski put a stop to that. From August 7 to September 28 he hurled 47⅔ innings in relief with a microscopic ERA of 0.38.

On Sept. 12, 1966, he tied an N.L. record for most consecutive strikeouts by a relief pitcher when he sent six Cardinal batters back to the dugout in succession.

Traded to Minnesota after the '67 campaign, the reliever deluxe went on to lead the A.L. in saves for the Twins in both 1969 and '70 when he had 31 and 34 respectively. Both seasons he was named by *The Sporting News* as the A.L. Fireman of the Year.

His last couple of years were spent with the Tigers, Dodgers again, and the Angels in '73. He finished 79-74 with 179 saves.

PERRY, Bob
    Civil Service employee at an Army base
    New Bern, NC

In 1963, Melvin Gray "Bob" Perry homered off Whitey Ford at Yankee Stadium in the first game he ever played in the big leagues. Overall, the outfielder hit .266 in 131 games for the Angels in 1963–64.

PERRY, Gaylord
  Owns and operates a peanut farm
  Williamston, NC

"The league will be a little drier now folks,"
—Gaylord Perry at his press conference announcing his
retirement

In his book *Me and The Spitter,* Gaylord made a public
confession how he used to load it up. He explained, "My favorite method was wetting up the back of my thumbnail
area at the same time I was wetting my first two fingers
with a natural and legal lick. Then I'd wipe the two fingers
dry, just in case anyone was watching. But while I was getting my sign from the catcher, I'd flick those fingers over
the back of my thumb and get the ball ready for my super
pitch."

The only pitcher to win the Cy Young Award in both
leagues, Gaylord signed with the San Francisco Giants for
a reported bonus of $90,000. His 21-year career took him to
San Francisco (1962–71), Cleveland (1972–75), Texas (1975–
77), San Diego (1978–79), Texas again and finally to the
Yanks (1980), Atlanta ('81) and Seattle ('82–'83). During
that time he racked up 314 wins against 265 losses.

In 1964 at age 28, when he stood at 24-30, Gaylord
hardly seemed a candidate for 100 career wins, let alone
300 and a probable Hall of Fame berth. After turning age
30, he won 239 games. Only Cy Young (318) and Warren
Spahn (277) won more after reaching 30.

On Sept. 17, 1968, Perry tossed a no-hitter at Candlestick Park against the Cardinals to beat Bob Gibson 1-0 before Ray Washburn of the Cards no-hit the Giants 2-0 the
next day.

On July 3, 1973, the Perry brothers faced each other in
Detroit, marking the first time in A.L. history that brothers opposed each other. Jim was not the pitcher of record,
but Gaylord took the loss.

One aspect of his career that was quietly overlooked was
his strikeout total. On July 22, 1966, he set a Giants' record when he whiffed 15 Phillies. When Gaylord retired on
September 24, 1983, at age 45, he had a career total of

3,534 strikeouts, ranking him third on the all-time list behind Steve Carlton and Nolan Ryan.

PETERSON, "Cap"
    Died May 16, 1980, at age 37 in Tacoma, WA

In the early 1960s, Marty Robbins was singing about the west Texas town of *El Paso* when baseball fans in that city were singing the praises of Charles "Cap" Peterson, who hit .335 with 29 homers and a league-leading 130 RBIs as he was named the MVP of the Texas League.

A versatile player who saw action in both the infield and outfield, Cap was around from 1962–69, with the Giants, Senators, and Indians.

"Cap" died of kidney disease in his native Tacoma in 1980.   .230

PETERSON, "Fritz"
    Pro Financial Services in Chicago; deals with disability insurance for athletes

Although he will probably best be remembered for the wife-swapping episode with Yankee teammate Mike Kekich, Fritz had a respectable 11-year run from 1966–76, mostly with the Yanks.

His given name of Fred was also his father's and grandfather's so he became Fritz to avoid confusion. A one-time semipro hockey player with a master's degree from Northern Illinois University, Peterson had the misfortune of wearing pinstripes for nine seasons in which the Yankees never made it into a World Series.

In 1970 he won his 20th game on the final day of the season, 4-3, over the Red Sox at Fenway Park. While Lindy McDaniel was saving the game, Fritz was so nervous he hid under Ralph Houk's desk in the clubhouse. When the game ended, everybody found Peterson under the "Major's" desk. He was later quoted: "I sure wanted that 20th. Did you ever see a list of 19-game winners."

This southpaw with excellent control was traded to Cleveland in 1974, closing in '76 with the Rangers.   133-131

PETROCELLI, Rico
    Salesman for Ziff Company; co-owner of the Lynn
    team of the Eastern League

There is something uncomfortably strange about the parallels drawn between Rico and Harry Agganis, the Red
Sox first baseman who died unexpectedly in 1955. To begin
with, each wore No. 6 while spending their entire careers
with the Red Sox.

Each played the infield for the Sox, both being elevated
from the Boston farm system. Both lived in Lynn at one
time or another. Rico was born on June 27. Harry died on
June 27.

The Petrocelli-Agganis connection seemed ended until a
few years ago when Rico and Mike Agganis, the nephew of
Harry, got together to purchase the Lynn Sailors of the
Eastern League.

Americo Petrocelli was around Fenway briefly in '63,
then from 1965–76. Originally a shortstop, he moved over
to third base in 1971. In 1969 he joined Ernie Banks as the
only shortstops in baseball history to belt 40 home runs in
a season and he still had less than 100 RBIs when he drove
in 97. That season his .980 fielding avg. was tops in the
A.L. for shortstops as he committed just 14 errors.

Although just 4-for-20 in the '67 World Series, the
Brooklyn-born infielder hit a pair of roundtrippers against
the Cardinals. Both came in Game Six including the third
of a record three in the fourth inning, following homers by
Carl Yastrzemski and Reggie Smith. In the '75 WS against
the Reds, Petrocelli swung for a .308 average. He joins Yaz
as the only Red Sox players to appear in both the '67 and
'75 World Series.

Rico adjusted well after being shifted to third base. His
.976 fielding avg. was the best in the A.L. in '71 and at one
stretch established a major league record at third base by
going 77 consecutive games without an error. He had 210
homers and a .251 mark.

PFEIL, Bobby
      Partner in a chain of shoe stores called Sports Shoe
      Reseda, CA

During his career, Bobby worked in the animation department at Walt Disney's studio in the off-season. Bobby was
in fantasyland when his father saw him play profession-
ally for the first time on April 17, 1966, leading Tulsa to a
doubleheader sweep at Phoenix with a single, double, and
triple in each game.
      While with Eugene (P.C.L.) in 1970, Bobby was sched-
uled to play all nine positions in a game against Tacoma.
After playing eight different positions through the first
eight innings, he took the mound for the ninth. However,
he was unable to pull off the stunt when Tacoma Manager
Whitey Lockman protested that Bobby wasn't certified to
pitch and the umpire agreed.
      In the majors Bobby saw action at every infield position,
in the outfield, and as a catcher while hitting .242 in 106
games with the '69 Mets and '71 Phillies. Pfeil hit only two
homers in 281 at-bats but they came in the same game in
1971.

PFISTER, Dan
      Staff member of the Yankee Baseball School
      West Hollywood, FL

In Dan's first big league start on April 24, 1962, he hurled
a three-hitter for the Kansas City A's, but was a hard-luck,
1-0 loser to the Tigers. The right-hander was with the A's
from 1961–64 and finished 6-19.

PHILLIPS, Adolpho
      Panama

"He has the ability of Willie Mays and he could make a for-
tune playing baseball, if he wanted to play baseball."
                          —Leo Durocher on Adolpho Phillips

Adolpho's career ran from 1964–72 with the Phillies,
Cubs, Expos, and Indians. The Panamanian outfielder

who was traded to the Cubs after playing in two games
with the Phils in '66, hit .260 with 16 home runs that summer, and his 32 stolen bases were the most by a Cub since
1903. At one point that year he struck out nine times in
succession, an N.L. record.

On June 11, 1967, he looked like Willie Mays in a doubleheader against the Mets when he belted four homers
(three in the second game) in the twinbill victory. In the
nightcap, which was won by the Cubs, 18-9, both clubs
combined for 11 four-baggers to establish a N.L. record.
That day Phillips received numerous standing ovations
from Cub fans at Wrigley Field with cheers of "Olé—
Adolpho—Olé".

But when he began to fade after that, Cubs' fans might
have shouted "no mas—Adolpho—no mas." He was traded
to Montreal early in '69 where he stayed until the end of
the '70 campaign before finishing with Cleveland in
1972.   .247

PHILLIPS, Dick
    Assistant General Manager at Vancouver (P.C.L.) in
    1983

"Puppy Dog" was past his 30th birthday when he scooted
in with the Giants in 1962 before joining the Senators in
'63, '64, and '66 hitting .229 in 263 games.

During the '63 season when the Senators visited Comiskey Park to play the White Sox, Dick was honored by his
hometown fans of nearby Racine, Wisconsin. He was given
many gifts including a new automobile. A spokesman for
the group honoring Dick said "He's a nice guy, and we're
proud he's in the big leagues."

A veteran of the Korean War, Dick won MVP honors in
three different minor leagues, the Northern, Southern Association, and Pacific Coast League.

PHOEBUS, Tom
    Liquor distributor
    Bradenton, FL

Trivia: Since 1945 four pitchers broke in hurling two consecutive shutouts. How many can you name?

    Answer: Dave "Boo" Ferris (1945), Al "Red" Worthing-
ton (1953), Karl Spooner (1954), and Tom Phoebus (1966).

    Tom's first whitewash came on September 15th (2-0)
against the Angels in front of his native Baltimore fans,
the second against the Kansas City A's five days later by a
4-0 score.

    It was an unforgettable year for Phoebus since earlier in
the season he tossed a no-hitter for Rochester in the I.L.

    Tom started the '67 campaign where he left off in '66,
with three consecutive early-season shutouts. He finished
14-9 and was named the A.L. "Rookie Pitcher of the Year"
by *The Sporting News*.

    On April 27, 1968, Tom no-hit the Red Sox, 6-0. The next
year the right hander went 14-7 for the pennant-winning
Orioles.

    Phoebus was a winner in relief in Game Two of the 1970
World Series against the Reds, in his final appearance
ever in an Orioles' uniform. He finished in '72 after pitching for the Padres and Cubs.   56-52

PICHE, Ron
    Montreal Expos' scout
    Quebec, Canada

Claude Raymond, who first arrived in the majors in 1959,
was joined in the Milwaukee Braves bullpen by a second
French Canadian, Ron Piche (pronounced Pee-Shay), in
the early Sixties. Primarily a reliever, Monsieur Piche
was with the Braves for portions of four seasons (1960–63)
and also with the Angels and Cardinals, going 10-16 in 134
games.

PIERCE, Tony
 Employed with Coca-Cola
 Columbus, GA

The long and successful 18-year pitching career of Billy
Pierce ended in the mid-Sixties after 211 victories. It was
at this time that another southpaw named Pierce began a
brief two-year stay with the A's in their final season in
Kansas City and their maiden one in Oakland. However,
an ailing left wing kept Tony from a longer stay.   4-6

PINA, Horacio
 Active in Mexico

Horacio was a busy man between 1968–74 with the Indiana, Senators, Rangers, A's, Cubs, and Angels. The reliever made 314 appearances.
 In '73 with the World Champion Oakland A's he pitched
two scoreless innings in the ALCS against Baltimore, and
in the World Series against the Mets, was unscored on in
three frames.   23-23

PINIELLA, Lou
 New York Yankees' coach; owns two restaurants, The
 Tree House and Sweet Lou's,
 Woodbride Center, NJ

The marquees outside Yankee Stadium on Saturday, June
16, 1984, read: "Sweet Lou—Final Game 4:00 P.M." A
crowd of 37,583 paid tribute to the popular outfielder who
retired after 17 years of big league service.
 Many years before in the Orioles' minor league system,
he was told by Earl Weaver that he would never make it to
the big time because of his temper. Clearly, Lou proved
Earl wrong.
 Piniella was signed to an Indians' contract in 1962 out of
the University of Tampa where he had enrolled on a basketball scholarship. He was drafted by the Senators soon
after, then was traded to the Orioles where he had one at
bat in 1964. In '66 Lou was sent to the Indians, where he
finally made it into a few games in '68 before being se-

lected by the expansion Pilots who subsequently sent him
to the Royals on April 1st. But the joke was on the Pilots as
Lou went on to capture "Rookie of the Year" honors,
hitting .282. His five years in Kansas City were well spent
as he twice batted over .300.

After the '73 season Lou was traded to the Yankees. For
the next 11 years, the Tampa native was a steady performer for Steinbrenner's cranky family. His competitive
countenance was always quite evident as he flung bats,
threw helmets, kicked dirt, and jawed with umpires.

Lou was not the most graceful flychaser who ever
roamed the hallowed garden in Yankee Stadium and certainly didn't make fans forget DiMaggio or Mantle but he
was a distillation of the Yankee work ethic. His incredible
play in the 1978 playoff game at Fenway Park against the
Red Sox will long be remembered. Playing right field in a
blinding sun, he speared a line-drive single by Jerry Remy
before it got past him in the ninth inning to save the tying
run. In five ALCS covering 18 games he had a .305 avg.
and after four World Series (22 games) he showed a glittering .319 mark.

Teammate Don Baylor said it best: "If you want a guy to
drive in a run with a runner on second base, he'd be in my
top three."   .291

PLASKETT, Elmo
    Works in the Department of Recreation; Pittsburgh
    Pirates scout
    Frederikstead, Virgin Islands

Elmo became yesterday's news quite fast. A .200 hitter, it
was all over after 17 games as a Pirates' catcher in '62 and
'63. But Elmo did not leave us totally cold. On April 26,
1963, he teamed with Al McBean to form the first all-
Virgin Islands battery in major league history.

PLEIS, Bill
> Los Angeles Dodgers' scout
> Kirkwood, MO

Bill Pleis was the winner in relief in the Twins' first-ever victory in Minnesota, 5-4, over Washington on April 22, 1961. Known as "Shorty" and "Bulldog," William Pleis III spent six seasons as a left-handed reliever with Minnesota going 21-16 from 1961–66.

PLUMMER, Bill
> Manager at Chattanooga in the Southern League

They say it's amazing how much could be accomplished if nobody cares who gets the credit. As a backup catcher to Johnny Bench for the powerful "Big Red Machine" from 1970–77, Bill didn't grab many headlines, but when he was needed, he could always be found.

Originally in the Cardinals' organization, Plummer was drafted by the Cubs, for whom he played two games in 1968. He joined the Mariners in 1978 where his 10-year career came to an end with a .188 average.

POINTER, Aaron
> PAC 10 football official; employed with the Pierce
> County Recreation Center
> Tacoma, WA

You've heard of the famed singing Pointer Sisters? Well meet and greet the Pointer brother.

Aaron never became as well known as his sisters, but had the opportunity to sign autographs as a big leaguer with Houston in '63, '66, and '67. Pointer spent his first season playing for Salisbury in the Western Carolinas League and hit .402. If such an average could have been accomplished on the major league level, the name Pointer would have been a household item long before the girls began singing.   .208

POPOVICH, Paul
Los Angeles Dodgers minor league instructor

The Dodgers have produced their share of heroes, many of whom are enshrined in the Hall of Fame. You won't find Paul's name there, but in 1968 he was one of the more popular Dodgers. At one game 50 fans named Popovich, none related, turned out to honor their hero.

The sure-handed fielder was around from 1967–75 with the Cubs (twice), Dodgers, and Pirates. Before signing a reported $40,000 bonus contract with the Cubs in 1960, "Pop" attended West Virginia University on a basketball scholarship where he was a teammate of Jerry West.

On June 11, 1969, Paul was traded twice in the same day. He was swapped along with Ron Fairly by the Dodgers to Montreal for Maury Wills and Manny Mota, but before he had a chance to wear an Expos uniform, Paul was dealt back to the Cubs for outfielder Adolpho Phillips.

A .233 lifetime swatter, he swung a potent stick in the '74 NLCS playoffs for the Pirates against his former Dodgers. Paul went 3-for-5 for the Series, including a perfect 3-for-3 in pinch-hitting roles.

POSADA, Leo
Los Angeles Dodgers minor league instructor

In the 1950 Pan American Games, 14-year-old Leopoldo Posada was the youngest competitor as a member of the Cuban cyclist team, finishing fifth in the 1,000-meter cycle race.

Leo later concentrated on baseball, spending most of his career in the minors. An outfielder, he did play in 155 games with the Kansas City A's from 1960–62, hitting .256.

On Labor Day of '61 the Tigers wished that Leo had been off riding his bicycle as he paced the A's to a doubleheader sweep with an 8-for-9 day.

POULSON, Ken
General superintendent in residential construction
Simi Valley, CA

During the Sixties the Barbie Doll became the bestselling doll of all time. The Mattel Toy Company decided to give her a friend named Ken, which also became a bestseller.

It would be nice to say that Ken became one of the best choices for the Red Sox, but the truth is he had a five-game jog and collected one base hit in five at-bats.

POWELL, "Boog"
U.S. Anglers Marine charter fishing business
Key West, FL

"Hey—you're Boog Powell."

John Wesley Powell has enjoyed a renaissance of sorts in the public eye, as a steady Lite Beer commercial performer.

As a high school football player, Boog blocked for George Mira who would eventually quarterback Miami University and the San Francisco 49ers. The 6'4", 250-pound bruiser signed with the Orioles out of high school and first came up late in '61 after leading the I.L. in home runs (32) for Rochester. From 1962–74 he was a monument at first base for the Orioles.

Boog's first four-bagger came on May 2, 1962. A few innings later he parked another one. Three days later he walloped two more in a game, making him just the second player in major league history and the first in A.L. annals to twice hit two homers in a game to account for the first four home runs of a career. The only other player to accomplish this was Gus Bell of the 1950 Pirates.

On August 10, 1963, Boog became the first Oriole to hit three home runs in a game. The year before he pulled a first by walloping a ball over the hedge in centerfield at Memorial Stadium in Baltimore, a 469-foot drive against Boston's Don Schwall.

Powell hit 339 homers, his high coming in 1964 with 39. In a doubleheader in 1966 against Kansas City, he drove in 11 runs. Overall he rapped 34 homers, and collected 109 RBIs for the World Champion Orioles, who swept the Dodgers in the Series. In the World Series Boog continued his assault, batting .357.

His only .300 season was '69 when he hit .304 and legged out an inside-the-park home run against the Pilots at Sick's Stadium. It must have been a sight observing Boog, who played between 270–280 pounds, thunder around the bases.

In 1970 he was named the A.L. MVP after leading the Orioles to another flag with 35 roundtrippers, 114 RBIs, and a .297 average. In the ALCS against the Twins he hit a sizzling .429 as the Birds swept Minnesota and homered twice in the World Series as Baltimore took the Reds in five games.

Mr. Powell spent '75–'76 in Cleveland, then closed with the Dodgers in '77 with a lifetime .266 average.

PREGENZER, John
> Teacher at Franklin Pierce High School; umpires
> baseball games and referees basketball games
> Tacoma, WA

Sargent Shriver and Pete Rozelle were among the members of the John Pregenzer Fan Club, one of the most unusual and enthusiastic fan clubs in baseball history.

John was an unheralded 6'5" right-handed pitcher who was purchased by the Giants for $100 from Pocatello, Idaho. When a lady named Novella O'Hara heard of this, she offered to purchase John for $110. But Novella was told that the Giants didn't sell their players to their fans, so she started a fan club which grew to over 3,000 members.

One of the plans called for a John Pregenzer Day at Candlestick Park, but since he was farmed out to Tacoma before the big day, it was changed to "Bring Back John Pregenzer Day." A Bay Area restaurant owner made plans for John to be a dinner guest at his establishment. But after John was sent out, he hung a sign in the window which read: "John Pregenzer was going to eat here."

While slightly overwhelmed with all the attention, John managed to win his only two decisions in 19 appearances out of the Giants' bullpen in 1963–64. There has been no word if the fan club has made plans for a "Whatever Happened to John Pregenzer Day?"

PRESCOTT, "Bobby"
     Pittsburgh Pirates' scout in Panama

Bobby Lewis had a hit single, *Tossin' and Turnin'*, in 1961, the same year George Bertrand "Bobby" Prescott had one hit, a single, in 12 at-bats (.083) for the Kansas City A's. The 30-year-old rookie never returned, but the Panamanian outfielder had P.C.L. pitchers tossin' and turnin' in '62 when he banged out 32 homers for Hawaii.

PRICE, Jim
     Freelance sports announcer
     Detroit, MI

Jim Price was to Bill Freehan what Bill Plummer was to Johnny Bench. Freehan's backup catcher from 1967–71, Jim hit .214 in 261 games for the Tigers. Needless to say, his Nehru jacket wardrobe style was a bit more colorful than his statistics.

Price never had a stolen base in his five years, but he would have had one if the only game in which he stole one had not been washed out by rain.

In the last couple of years, Jim has worked the Cracker Jack classic and college WS for ESPN.

PRIDDY, Bob
     Retired from the jewelry business
     Pittsburgh, PA

A star high school quarterback from McKeesport, PA, Bob spurned over 50 football scholarship offers to sign with the Pirates as an infielder but inept hitting in the minors led to his switch to the mound.

Bob arrived for a nine-year jaunt that ended in 1971 after pitching for the Pirates, Giants, Senators, White Sox, Angels, and Braves.   24-38

PRINCE, Don
> Owns independent insurance agency, Paramount
> Insurance Services
> Wilmington, NC

We heard a lot about Majestic Prince, the 1969 Kentucky
Derby winner. However, we didn't hear so much about
Don Prince, a right-hander who hurled a scoreless inning
in relief for the Cubs in '62.

PURDIN, John
> Co-owns a construction company
> Sarasota, FL

When Walter O'Malley received two letters in the same
week suggesting that Dodger scouts look over a young
pitcher soon to be discharged from the Air Force in Ger-
many, he dispatched Cliff Alexander, Walt Alston's brother-in-law. Alexander inspected Purdin in a backyard
warmup and signed him for $8,000 without even seeing
him in a ball game.

The tall, slender right-hander was promoted to the
Dodgers late in September of 1964 and made his debut
with a two-hit shutout over the Cubs. At this point,
Purdin's story looked like a Hollywood script, but life became a bit more realistic for O'Malley's boy. By '69 it was
all over at 6-4 in 58 games.

Q

QUALLS, Jim
> Owns a livestock feed service
> Quincy, IL

The "Chicago Seven" went on trial for inciting riots at the
1968 Democratic Convention at the time the "Chicago
Eight" were given a shot at the center field position for the

'69 Cubs. Among the eight Cubbies was 22-year-old Jim Qualls, who hit .250 in 43 games. He also showed up with the Expos and White Sox before quietly making his exit at .223 with 63 games under his belt.

Jim had a total of 31 hits, but one stood out like a rose in a daisy patch: he busted up Tom Seaver's potential perfect game on July 9, 1969, with a single to left center in the ninth inning before 50,709 disappointed fans at Shea Stadium.

QUEEN, Mel
Los Angeles Dodgers minor league pitching coach

The son of former pitcher Mel Queen, Mel Jr. began as a third baseman in the minors, then shifted to the outfield before going to the mound. In '63 he hit 25 home runs for San Diego in the P.C.L., but in the big arena Mel only batted .179 in 269 games. As a pitcher in 140 contests he was 20-17 with a 3.14 ERA while on tour with the Reds ('64-'69), and Angels ('70-'72). In his first big league start in '67 he shut out the Giants and went on to win 14 games that year.

QUILICI, Frank
Minnesota Twins' announcer

Frank emerged as the youngest manager in the majors in July of '72 at age 33 when he replaced Bill Rigney as skipper of the Twins. He remained the Twins' pilot through the 1975 season.

A graduate of Western Michigan University, Frank came up in '65. Although he hit only .208 in 56 games, Quilici assumed a place in the starting lineup the final couple months of the season as the team won its only A.L. pennant. In Game One of the W.S. he collected two basehits in one inning as he singled and doubled in the Minnesota six-run third inning en route to an 8-2 victory against the Dodgers.

Fame was fleeting for Frank as he was demoted to Denver the following year. However, he returned to fill in

around the infield from 1968–70 before being named a
coach, then eventually manager.

QUIRK, Art
    Director of Marketing for Financial Industry Systems
    Hartford, CT

What do Pete Burnside, Jim Beattie, and Art Quirk have
in common? All three were Dartmouth graduates who
made it to the big leagues. Art went 3-2 in 14 games mixed
with the Orioles ('62) and Senators ('63).
    On July 4, 1961, the southpaw hurled a no-hitter pitch-
ing for Rochester (I.L.) against Syracuse.
    A member of the Board of Directors of The American
School for the Deaf, Art was previously employed with
such corporate giants as AT&T, IBM, and Xerox.

R

RADATZ, Dick
    Employed with Triple P Packaging Company in Bos-
    ton
    Brockton, MA

At 6' 6", 240 pounds, Dick "The Monster" Radatz could in-
spire fear. He used his size (and his fastball) like a wrench.
    The tale of this Monster begins in Fenway Park in 1963
against the Yankees. The Red Sox were ahead by a score of
2-1 when Boston starter Earl Wilson loaded the bases.
    Enter Radatz. His assignment was simply to retire
Mickey Mantle, Roger Maris, and Elston Howard. Ten
pitches and three strikeouts later his mission was accomplished, the attack completed.
    "That was the first time I threw my arms out in tri-
umph," says Radatz. "It got to be my trademark."
    Between 1962–65 he either won or saved 149 of Bos-
ton's 286 wins.

In '62 he finished 9-6 with 24 saves and was named the A.L. Fireman of the Year by *The Sporting News*. Radatz won the honor again in '64 when he established an A.L. record 16 victories in relief and saved a league-leading 29.

Then came '66 and a trade to Cleveland. Dick also played briefly for the Cubs, Tigers, and Expos before retiring in 1969 at 52-43 with 122 saves. In 694 innings pitched, he struck out 745, better than a strikeout per inning.

A graduate of Michigan State with a degree in education, Dick was a schoolteacher in the off-season and most likely didn't experience too many discipline problems in the classroom.

RADER, Doug
Texas Rangers' manager

As the subject of a 1983 article in *Sports Illustrated* by Ron Fimrite titled "He's Not Just a Wild and Crazy Guy," Rader was quoted, "People still want to hear things that happened 10–15 years ago. I know I'll never shake my reputation, but I'd be very happy if it just vanished."

But then again how does a guy who once suggested that kids should eat baseball cards of good players shake such a zany, eccentric image?

The "Red Rooster" had a reputation as a cut-up and prankster off the field. But between the foul lines he was all business. Doug was a solid-fielding third baseman throughout his career (1967–77), mostly with the Astros. Between 1970–74 he won two N.L. fielding titles and Gold Glove awards from *The Sporting News*. In '73 he swung a heavy stick, clouting 22 homers and 90 RBIs.

The last lap of his career was spent with the Padres and Blue Jays before taking over as manager at Hawaii (P.C.L.) in 1980. Doug was named to manage the Rangers in 1983.

Rader attended Illinois Wesleyan on a baseball and basketball scholarship. While in college he played semipro hockey in Peoria. To protect his amateur standing he played under the names Dominic Bulganzio and Lou D'Bardini.   .251

RAFFO, Al
    Teaches Spanish, ecology, economics, and sociology;
    also coaches the baseball team at Marion County H.S.
    Jasper, TN

Al seems to be much busier preparing lesson plans for the
plethora of subjects he teaches than he was in the majors
when he was 1-3 in 45 games as a Phillies' reliever in 1969.
But while at Reading (Eastern League) in '67, the 6'5"
right-hander once had a stretch of 39 scoreless innings.

RAKOW, Ed
    Restaurant business
    West Palm Beach, FL

A native of Pittsburgh, Ed was playing football for a semipro team called the Bloomfield Rams in the Pittsburgh
area during the 1950s. He was the team's quarterback, but
lost his job to another young signalcaller, an NFL reject
named Johnny Unitas. Rakow (pronounced Rock-oh) decided to give baseball a shot and in 1958 went to Green
Bay as a pitcher, not a QB, and led the Three-I League in
victories with 15. He made it to the majors with the Dodgers in 1960, losing his only decision in nine games.
    Prior to the '61 campaign Ed was traded to Kansas City.
After three years as a member of the A's staff, he was with
the Tigers and Atlanta Braves, finishing up a seven-year
36-47 career.

RANEW, Merritt
    Owns and operates a horse breeding ranch
    Leesburg, GA

Merritt was involved in one of the worst on-the-field
brawls in the history of the P.C.L. while playing for
Seattle on May 11, 1966.
    Ranew was hit over the head with a bat by Vancouver's
Santiago Rosario and suffered serious injuries, resulting
in surgery for removal of a blood clot on his brain.
    Ranew successfully sued the Vancouver club when the

case came to court in 1969. Ironically he was drawing his
salary from the Vancouver team in '69.

The left-handed hitting catcher was in and out of the
majors from 1962–69 with the Colt .45's, Cubs, Braves,
Angels, and Pilots. Merritt's best year came in '63 as a
member of the Cubs when he hit .338 in 78 games and led
the league with 17 pinch-hits.   .247

RATH, Fred
> Vice-president of Lincoln Property Co.
> Little Rock, AR

In the late Sixties a song was written by a group called
Steam titled *Na, Na, Hey, Hey—Kiss Him Goodbye*. A decade later the song would gain more attention when it became the theme song of fans at Comiskey Park in Chicago.

By this time Fred Rath, a right-handed pitcher out of
Baylor University, had long ago said his goodbyes to the
fans at Comiskey Park after having lost his only two decisions in eight games with the South Siders in '68 and '69.

RATLIFF, Gene
> Salesman with Frito-Lay
> Macon, GA

In the summer of '65 Gene was singing along with the
Rolling Stones' *I Can't Get No Satisfaction* after he made
four pinch-hitting appearances for the Astros and struck
out each time. Gene recalled, "It was a little different than
batting practice."

RATLIFF, Paul
> Television actor
> Glendale, CA

This offbeat character, who frequently spoke in old-style
English using words like "forsooth," is probably best remembered for the punch he threw with his fist, more than
for his punchless lifetime .205 bat.

A catcher, Paul first arrived with the Twins for 10

games in 1963 at the age of 19. He returned to the minors for the rest of the decade before coming back in 1970 and hitting .268 in 69 games for the A.L. West Division champion Twins.

He was celebrating the Twins' division title at a party and decided he didn't want pitcher Dave Boswell at the gathering. Ratliff then lambasted Boswell who was holding a glass at the time which shattered in Boswell's hand, cutting it to the extent that he was unable to pitch in the ALCS.

Paul finished in '71–'72 with the Brewers.

RAUDMAN, Bob
         Cross-country motorcycle racer
         Granada Hills, CA

This motorcycle racer, who finished as high as third in the national championships in the 500 C.C. class in 1967, was in high gear the year before with Tacoma of the P.C.L. with 20 home runs and 84 RBIs.

Outfielder Robert Joyce "Shorty" Raudman, who stood 5'8½", joined the Cubs late in '66 for eight games. He had a chance in eight more games in '67, finishing at .200 overall.

RAY, Jim
         Automobile salesman
         Houston, Texas

April 15, 1968 has been proclaimed as "baseball's longest night" as Houston outlasted the Mets 1-0 in 24 innings. Jim allowed just two hits and struck out 11 in working seven scoreless innings in the game.

He worked effectively out of the Astros' bullpen from 1968–73.

"Sting Ray" completed his swim in '74 with the Tigers compiling a 43-30 record plus 25 saves.

REAMS, Leroy
General agent for Midland National Life Insurance Co.
Oakland, CA

Even the most fanatic of Phillies' fans would have a difficult time remembering Leroy who struck out as a pinch-hitter in his only big league appearance in '69.

REBERGER, Frank
California Angels' minor league pitching coach

Frank went unsigned after pitching at the University of Idaho in '66. The 6'5" right-hander known as "Crane" asked for a tryout with the Cubs and was signed to a contract.
He was 14-15 with the Cubs, Padres, and Giants from 1968–72. Frank, who was out of baseball for a decade, worked as a rancher in his native Idaho and for a time operated a charter fishing boat in Puerto Rico before taking his current position.

REDMOND, Wayne
Elder in an apostolic church (Solomon's Temple Annex Church)
Detroit, MI

"In a hierarchy every employee tends to rise to his level of incompetence."
—Laurence Peter

Detroit manager Charlie Dressen called Wayne the next Willie Mays. The slender outfielder did have mannerisms similar to "The Say Hey Kid" and he did hit 31 home runs in 120 minor league games. However, Wayne eventually reached his level of incompetence. The quiet and religious-minded young man went hitless in seven at-bats with the Tigers in '65 and '69.
Minister Redmond sometimes conducts the chapel service for the Detroit Tigers before Sunday home games.

REED, Bob
　　School teacher
　　Flint, MI

During the Sixties Donna Reed had her popular long-running television show. Signed in 1966 out of the University of Michigan, Bob's act in the big show ran briefly in Detroit in '69 and '70 after going 2-4 in 24 games.

REED, Jack
　　Cotton, soybean, and catfish farmer
　　Silver City, MS

On June 24, 1962, the Yankees defeated the Tigers, 9-7, in 22 innings in a game which lasted seven hours. Jack Reed, a Yankee reserve outfielder tagged as "Mickey Mantle's caddy" from 1961–63, broke up the game with a homer off Phil Regan. The only one of Reed's 222-game career, it was the latest ever hit in a game until Harold Baines of the White Sox poked his 25th-inning shot in the 1984 marathon against the Brewers. "I enjoyed every minute I was there in the big leagues. The home run was the highlight of my career since I was more or less a filler."

　　Reed was signed by the Yankees out of the University of Mississippi where he also was a defensive back on the gridiron.   .233

REED, Ron
　　Active with Chicago White Sox

Believe It or Not Department: Ron Reed was the starting and winning pitcher for the Atlanta Braves in games when Hank Aaron hit career home runs No. 500, 600, and the record-breaking 715!

　　A basketball star at Notre Dame where at one time he held the single-season scoring record, Ron combined a career in pro baseball and basketball for a couple of years in the mid-Sixties. The right hander, who was signed by the Braves in '65 and was also a member of the Detroit Pistons in the NBA from 1965–67, decided to give up his NBA career to concentrate on baseball. His Pistons' coach, Dave

DeBusschere, understood the situation since he had made the same decision in reverse just a few years before. In Ron's final NBA game he scored 22 points as he replaced DeBusschere, his player-coach, who was ill that night.

He had his best year in 1969 when he went 18-10 for the N.L. West champion Braves.

Traded to St. Louis in '75, his next stop was Philadelphia where he became a key member of the Phils' four N.L. East Division champions in five seasons from 1976–80 and the 1980 World Championship. During his eight years in Philly he recorded 90 saves, the second best all-time total in Phils' history. Ron's biggest save might have been the one he recorded in Game Two of the '80 World Series.   146-140

REESE, Rich
Senior Vice President of Sales for the Jim Beam Distilling Company
Northbrook, IL

On Aug. 3, 1969, Rich hit a pinch-hit grand-slam to beat Baltimore, 5-2, and snap the 17-game winning streak of the Orioles' Dave McNally. The Twins' big first baseman also connected for pinch-hit slammers on June 7, 1970, and July 9, 1972, to set an all-time A.L. record.

Reese enjoyed his best year in 1969 when he batted .322 for the A.L. West champion Twins. Most of his career (1964–73) was spent with Minnesota, but finished with the Tigers at .253.

REGAN, Phil
Seattle Mariners pitching coach

Phil was nicknamed "The Vulture" by Sandy Koufax one night when the Dodgers' great southpaw left a 1-1 game after 11 innings, and Phil relieved to pick up the victory.

"The Vulture" feasted with the Tigers (1960–65), Dodgers (1966–'68), Cubs (1968–'72) and White Sox ('72). In '66 he was deadly when he went 14-1 and had an ERA of 1.62 with Los Angeles. He was voted "Fireman of the Year" and "Comeback Player of the Year" for his performance.

Regan received countless bird-like good-luck charms from Dodger fans. It was a gag around the Dodger clubhouse to put one of Phil's vultures atop the locker of the starting pitcher, but for them, it wasn't too funny.

Phil was once again voted "Fireman of the Year" in '68 when he racked up 21 saves for the Cubs. Twice that season he won both games of doubleheaders, a rare feat. Oddly enough, he did this split between two different teams. On April 21st he beat the Mets twice in relief while still with the Dodgers, then on July 7th, he won a pair against the Pirates as a member of the Cubs.

Phil, who was frequently accused of throwing the "grease ball," finished 96-81 plus 92 saves.

REICHARDT, Rick

Chartered life underwriter for Provident Life and Casualty; owner of a chain of Joe's Deli restaurants
Gainesville, FL

Rick was one of the most sought-after youngsters in baseball history when he signed a reported $200,000 bonus with the Angels in 1964. The 6'3", 215-pound rock out of the University of Wisconsin starred on both the gridiron and the baseball field. He was the Big Ten's leading pass receiver in 1963 with 26 receptions and played with the Badgers in the classic 1963 "VanderKelen" Rose Bowl, which Wisconsin lost to USC, 42-37.

Unfortunately, Rick's promising career almost ended before it started when he was sidelined by a kidney disorder in 1966, which resulted in the removal of his right kidney. He was forced to miss the final two months of the season after hitting .288 with 16 home runs in 89 games.

The shortened year was a memorable one for this Frank Merriwell. On April 19th he hit the first home run at Anaheim Stadium off Tommy John of the White Sox. On April 30th, the Angels trailed the Red Sox at Fenway when they erupted for 12 runs in the eighth inning with Rick hitting two four-baggers himself in the inning.

Reichardt returned for three more years with the Angels, then was traded to Washington in 1970. His 11-year ride came to an end in 1974 with the Royals.   .261

REID, Scott
Chicago Cubs' scout
Phoenix, AZ

Like Reichardt, Scott also enjoyed a prolific college career
as he helped lead Arizona State University to a College
World Series championship. The outfielder hit .147 in 38
games in '69 and '70 as a member of the Phillies.

RENICK, Rick
Manager at Memphis (Southern League)

Rick homered against Mickey Lolich in his first big league
at bat on July 11, 1968, as a member of the Twins.
The versatile Ohio State University product played the
infield and outfield for five seasons (1968–72) with Minnesota.   .221

RENIFF, Hal
Clerk at a Stop and Go convenience store
Ontario, CA

This stocky right-hander was with the Yankees from
1961–67, splitting his final season with the Mets.
The nephew of Joe "Moon" Harris, who played in the
majors from 1914–28, Hal was 21-23 with 45 saves during
his career.

RENKO, Steve
Attending real estate school
Overland Park, KS

Selected by the Mets in the 1965 free agent draft, Steve
was also drafted as a quarterback by the Oakland Raiders
of the NFL after starring at the University of Kansas,
where he played with future NFL great Gale Sayers in the
same backfield. A three-sport performer for the Jayhawks,
Steve decided to pitch curve balls instead of footballs.
The 6'5″ right-hander started out as a first baseman for
Williamsport. Realizing that .169 hitters usually end up in

the unemployment office, he decided to be a pitcher. From 1969–83 he compiled a 134-146 mark with the Expos (1969–76), Cubs ('76–'77), White Sox ('77), A's ('78), Red Sox ('79–80), Angels ('81–'82), and Royals ('83).

Steve tossed a trio of one-hitters during his career, two coming a month apart in '71 for Montreal and twice won 15 games in a season.

REPOZ, Roger
Quality control supervisor for Fabrica International, a carpet company
Anaheim, CA

Signed by the Yankee organization in 1960, the left-handed hitting outfielder earned his living with the Yankees, A's, and Angels from 1964–72. In '69 Roger's bat was most definitely in repose when he hit just .164 in 103 games for the Angels, the lowest batting avg. in major league history for an outfielder playing in at least 100 games.

Roger attended Western Washington State College and was named MVP in the N.A.I.A. tournament in 1959.

RETTENMUND, Merv
Texas Rangers' hitting coach

Mervin Weldon Rettenmund had the opportunity to write his own ticket while at Ball State University where he broke the school's rushing records held by NFL star running back Tim Brown. Merv was drafted by the Dallas Cowboys, but decided to go the baseball route.

By 1968 Rettenmund was a top prospect in the Baltimore organization after winning I.L. MVP honors and being named Minor League Player of the Year by *The Sporting News*.

His first full season came in '69. The following year he hit .322 with 18 homers.

Merv proved that a steady diet of playing time was quite agreeable when he hit .318 in 141 games in '71. Rettenmund also played for the Reds ('74–'75), Padres ('76–'77) and Angels ('78–'80). With the Padres in 1977, he was the

busiest and most effective pinch-hitter in the N.L. going
21-for-67.   .271

RETZER, Ken
    Assistant manager and racquetball instructor for
    Alton Nautilus and Fitness Center in Alton, IL

Baseball historian Lee Allen calculated that the game between the Indians and Senators on September 6, 1963, was
game No. 100,000 in major league annals. Ken was a part
of that game, collecting a couple of basehits and knocking
in two runs to help Washington to a 7-2 victory. The four-
year (1961–64) catcher later presented the game's first
pitch to Allen for the Hall of Fame.   .264

REUSS, Jerry
    Active with the Los Angeles Dodgers

Are you surprised to see this 35-year-old lefty in this book?
Jerry was picked by the Cardinals in the second round of
the free agent draft in 1967.
    The guitar-playing southpaw, who joined the Cards in
1969, has traveled to Houston ('72–'73), Pittsburgh ('74–
'78), and Los Angeles ('79–'84). In his big league debut, he
hurled seven shutout innings and allowed just two hits to
gain the victory. Jerry helped the Pirates to N.L. East
titles in '74 and '75 by winning 16 and 18 games respectively. He missed much of '84 with injuries, but has a lifetime mark of 178-147.
    In 1980 the St. Louis native went 18-6 for the Dodgers
and also was the winning pitcher in the All-Star Game
that summer. On June 27, 1980 he no-hit the Giants at
Candlestick Park. Reuss was denied a perfect game when
Jack Clark reached base on an error by shortstop Bill
Russell with two out in the first inning.

REYNOLDS, Archie
>   Production well testing in Saudi Arabia for Otis Engi-
>   neering Company; owns two country and western
>   nightclubs
>   Fort Worth, TX

Do you remember Archie Bell and the Drells and their hit
song *Tighten Up?* How about Archie Reynolds and the
Cubs, Angels, and Brewers (1968–'72)? Maybe not, since
Archie was 0-8 during that period. He must have tightened
up!

REYNOLDS, Bob
>   Employed with Mail Dispatch, Inc.
>   Seattle, WA

On the field baseball chatter traditionally has been filled
with the words "Hum, babe!" From 1969–'75 it was "Hum,
Bob!"
   The hard-throwing right-hander known as "Bullet"
heard those infield sounds with the Expos, Brewers, Cardinals, Orioles, Tigers, and Indians. "Bullet Bob" was sizzling with his blistering fastball in '73 and '74 with the
A.L. East champion Orioles when he went 7-5 both seasons. In '73 he also added nine saves and posted the best
ERA for the Birds at 1.86. Overall he was 14-16 plus 21
saves and a 3.11 ERA.

REYNOLDS, Tommie
>   Coach at Denver (American Association)

A minor league terror with the bat, Tommie could never
solve the puzzle of big league pitching. The Midwest
League batting champ (.332) in 1963, Reynolds hit a lifetime .226 in the big leagues on and off from 1963–72 with
the Kansas City A's, Mets, Oakland A's, Angels, and
Brewers.

RIBANT, Dennis
Insurance salesman for Lincoln National Life
Santa Ana, CA

Did you know that Dennis was the first starter in Mets' club history who had a winning percentage when he went 11-9 in 1966?

A one-time hockey player with the Detroit Red Wings' organization, Dennis was playing at Hamilton, Ontario, but chose baseball after dislocating his arm on the ice.

Ribant's odyssey took him to the Mets, Pirates, Tigers, White Sox, Cardinals, and Reds before he skated out at 24-29.

When Dennis first joined the Mets, Casey Stengel came to the mound to remove him from the game. Dennis protested, "I can get him out. I got him out last time." But Casey took the ball and commented, "He led off the inning and you've faced eight men since then."

RICHARDS, Duane
Supervisor for the Manufacture Engineering Department of Natco
Richmond, IN

In 1960 we listened to the sounds of Duane Eddy's guitar with the popular *Because They're Young*. That summer a young right-hander named Duane Richards made a pair of relief appearances with the Reds without a decision. Duane never returned to the majors.

RICHARDSON, Gordie
Owner of a meat processing plant
Colquitt, GA

Patience is a virtue for anyone in organized baseball. Gordie is proof in living color.

After starting in the Braves' organization in 1957, it appeared that this lefty was destined to a life in the Texas League where he was voted Pitcher of the Year in 1962. But a 9-3 mark at Jacksonville through the first half of the '64 season brought him his promotion papers as a spot starter and reliever for the Cardinals, a team that took it all that year.

Gordy also worked out of the Mets' bullpen in '65 and '66, finishing 6-6 in 69 games.

RICHERT, Pete
Accounts executive for KCMG radio, Palm Springs, CA

Talk about an auspicious debut: Pitching in relief for the Dodgers on April 12, 1962, Pete took over for Stan Williams who was roughed up for four runs by the Reds in the second inning. The southpaw came in with two out and Eddie Kasko on second, then fanned Vada Pinson on three pitches to retire the side. In the third inning he struck out four batters. He whiffed Frank Robinson, Gordy Coleman, Wally Post, and Johnny Edwards. Coleman made it to first when the third strike slipped past catcher John Roseboro. In the next inning Pete whiffed Tommy Harper, giving him six strikeouts for the first six batters he faced in the majors.

He also wore the linens of the Senators ('65–'67), Orioles ('67–'71), Dodgers again ('72–'73), Cards, and Phils ('74).

On April 24, 1966, Pete tied an A.L. record by striking out seven straight Detroit batters while on the mound for Washington. During his stay in Baltimore, Richert was converted to a reliever and was a pivotal performer with the Birds between 1969–71. His finest year came in 1970 when he was 7-2 plus 13 saves in 50 appearances with an excellent 1.96 ERA. He totaled out at 80-73 plus 51 saves.

RICKETTS, Dave
St. Louis Cardinals' coach; teaches and coaches basketball at John Fisher College in the off-season Rochester, NY

In 1955 Dave and his brother Dick led Duquesne University to the NIT championship. Dick, who pitched for the Cards in 1959, was an All-American choice and also spent three years in the NBA.

Dave was also a crack hoopster and at one time held the NCAA record with 42 consecutive free throws. Like his brother, Dave was signed by the Cardinals. He first came up in '63, but for the next few years was back and forth between St. Louis and Triple-A.

Dave was a backup catcher for the '67 and '68 N.L. champion Cardinals before finishing his trek with Pittsburgh in 1970.   .249

RICO, Fred
    Hair stylist
    North Hollywood, CA

Known as "Fred the Barber" as he often cut the hair of his teammates, Fred was cut himself after playing in 12 games as an outfielder and hitting .231 in 1969 for the Kansas City Royals.

RIOS, Juan
    Factory worker
    Mayaguez, Puerto Rico

They Shoot Horses Don't They was in cinemas in 1969 when Juan had his one shot in the biggies with the '69 Royals. Rios hit .224 in 87 games while filling in at second and third base and shortstop.

RIPPLEMEYER, Ray
    Pig farmer
    Valmeyer, IL

It would be nice to say that Ray went about his business with nary a ripple. But the truth is that he spent most of his organized baseball career in the minors. On the big league level he was 1-2 in 18 games for the Senators in 1962 and at the plate he was 3-for-6 with a home run.

A former basketball player at Southern Illinois University, Ray has done some college basketball officiating.

RITCHIE, Jay
>   Car salesman for Don Andeson's Oldsmobile–Datsun
>   dealership
>   Salisbury, NC

"Picking Willie Mays off first base in 1967 was my biggest thrill," says Jay. That certainly is original.

The tall North Carolinian who broke in with the Red Sox in '64 was soon off to Atlanta for a couple of seasons before closing with the Reds in 1968 at 8-13, all in relief.

From May 5–20 in '67, Jay retired 28 consecutive hitters in four trips to the mound from the bullpen. The string was broken on an error.

ROARKE, Mike
>   St. Louis Cardinals' pitching coach

Like E. F. Hutton, when Mike speaks people listen.

Known as Bruce Sutter's personal tutor, Mike has developed a reputation as an outstanding pitching coach among big league pitchers.

A catcher with the Tigers from 1961–64, Roarke walked away with a .230 avg. in 194 games.

While at Boston College in the early 1950s, he captained both the football and baseball teams. On one Opening Day in Washington, President Kennedy took cover in the clubhouse area during a rain delay and expressed great interest in Mike, remembering him from his gridiron days at Boston College.

ROBERTS, Dale
>   Industrial electrician with GTE
>   Versailles, KY

In 1967 this southpaw hurler worked in a couple of games for the Yankees without a decision.

While Jay Ritchie's highlight was picking Willie Mays off base, Dale's biggest thrill was getting Whitey Ford's locker when he was up with the Yankees.

ROBERTS, Dave A.
Owns Rain-Chek, a lawn sprinkler systems business
Houston, TX

Do you like real esoteric trivia? Dave Roberts was the last
pitcher to ever face Hank Aaron when the home run
champ retired from the game on Oct. 3, 1976. At the time,
Dave was on the Tigers' pitching staff.

His long swing (1969–81) was spent with the Padres,
Astros, Tigers, Cubs, Pirates, Mariners, and Mets. Dave's
plush year came in '73 when he was 17-11 for the Astros.   103-125

ROBERTS, Dave. L.
Supervisor for the National Foundation of Emotion-
ally Handicapped Children
Northridge, CA

Who's on first? What's on second?
Not to be confused with Dave A., Dave L. Roberts was a
first baseman-outfielder with the Astros and Pirates for
portions of three seasons from 1962–66, hitting .196 in 91
games.

The Panamanian-born Roberts hit 38 home runs for
Oklahoma City in 1965 to lead the P.C.L.

ROBERTSON, Bob
Public relations work for a grocery chain
Lavale, MD

This husky, broad-shouldered redhead was around between 1967–79, mainly with the Pirates. Labeled as another Ralph Kiner, Bob led the Western Carolinas League
and the Southern League in both homers and RBIs in '65
and '66.

Originally a third baseman, Bob had a quick look with
the Bucs in '67. He missed the entire '68 campaign with a
kidney obstruction. In '69 powerful Bob led the I.L. in
homers (34) for Columbus, then joined the Pirates' "Lumber Company" crew as a long ball-hitting first baseman.

In 1970 he had career highs in home runs (27), RBIs (87),

and a .287 average as the Pirates took the N.L. East. But the '71 World Championship season would have to be considered his scrapbook year, as he banged out 26 four-baggers. A month earlier he garnered a major league record eight assists in a game from his first base position. In the NLCS he single-handedly destroyed the Giants in the second game with a three-homer show and also added a double to drive home five runs in the Pirates' 9-4 victory. The following day Bob homered again as the Pirates beat Juan Marichal, 2-1. In the World Series against Baltimore his bat continued to smoke as he added a couple of round-trippers.

He finished up in 1979 after playing with Seattle and Toronto, totaling 115 homers.   .242

ROBERTSON, Daryl
    Lieutenant in the Salt Lake County Sheriff's office
    Midvale, UT

"I was just there—that's it."

Those were the words of infielder Daryl Robertson who was Cripple Creek, Colorado's contribution to the majors. He made it into nine games with the Cubs in 1962 and batted .105. That's it!

ROBERTSON, Jerry
    Athletic Director at Washburn University
    Topeka, KS

This 6'2" right-hander was on the pitching staff of the expansion Montreal Expos in '69. Jerry struggled to a 5-16 season, but in seven of those defeats, the hapless Expos were shut out.

Robertson's first win came on June 8th when he defeated the Dodgers, 4-3. The victory snapped the Expos' 20-game losing streak, three short of the league record of 23 by the Phillies in 1961, a team managed by Gene Mauch—who also happened to be the manager at Montreal in '69.

Jerry's last lap came with the Tigers in 1970 without a decision.

ROBERTSON, Rich
     Accountant for Hewlett-Packard
     Palo Alto, CA

The Miranda decision requiring that police officers read criminal suspects their rights was passed in 1966, a year Rich had a chance to read his rights in his first big league contract with the San Francisco Giants.

A graduate of Santa Clara, the right-hander was the Giants' first-ever free agent selection in 1965. Rich spent parts of six seasons in the swirls of Candlestick with the Giants.   13-14

ROBINSON, Bill
     New York Mets' hitting coach

After a fine minor league record in the Braves' organization and a brief trial with the parent team in 1966, Bill was traded to the Yankees for Clete Boyer.

After three seasons in which Robinson batted under .200 he was back in the minors. He resurfaced again with the Phillies in 1972. By this time his bat had matured and in 1973 he belted 25 homers and hit .288.

At the start of the '75 season Robinson was traded to Pittsburgh. In both the '76 and '77 campaigns, he hit over .300, his best year coming in 1977 when he hit .304 with 26 home runs and 104 RBIs, all career highs. In '77 Bill hit grand-slams twice in a three-day period, tying a N.L. record. Robinson last played with the Phils in '83, finishing at .258 with 166 home runs.

ROBINSON, Floyd
     Liquor store owner
     San Diego, CA

The White Sox were the first team to have names of players on the back of their uniforms when innovative Bill Veeck started the practice in 1960. One of the players in uniform that year for the Pale Hose was a little outfielder with a skillful bat named Floyd Robinson.

Floyd hit over .500 in high school in San Diego but was

considered to be too small (5'9″) by major league scouts. He
signed a contract worth $500 with the local P.C.L. team
and spent several seasons there, with time out to serve in
the Marines.

In three of his first four years in Chisox threads, Floyd
hit over .300. On July 22, 1962, he went 6-for-6, all singles,
in a nine-inning game. That year he led the league in doubles (45), the best total by an American Leaguer since
Hall-of-Famer George Kell had 56 in 1950.

Robinson carried his bat to Cincinnati, Oakland, and
Boston where he closed with a .283 avg.

ROBLES, Rafael
San Pedro de Marcoris, Dominican Republic

Rafael has the distinction of being the first-ever Padres'
batter on April 8, 1969, when he led off the bottom of the
first for the infant San Diego club and reached base safely
as second baseman Joe Morgan booted his ground ball.

In parts of three seasons Rafael hit .188 in 47 games.

RODGERS, Bob
Montreal Expos' manager

"Buck" worked his way through the Tigers' organization,
then was chosen by the Angels in the expansion draft. His
first glimpse of the big leagues was in 1961. The following
year, Rodgers caught 150 games to break the rookie record
set by Hall of Famer Mickey Cochrane and was behind the
dish the remainder of the decade for the Angels.

At the age of 31, he joined the Twins as a coach in 1970.
He also coached and managed in the minors before replacing George Bamberger as skipper of the Brewers on Sept.
7, 1980. "Buck" was subsequently replaced by Harvey
Kuenn in 1982.   .232

RODRIGUEZ, Aurelio
>   Last active in Mexico in 1983
>   Sonora, Mexico

In 1969 the Topps Gum Co. printed their baseball card set with a picture of Aurelio. The only problem was that the picture on the card was actually the team's batboy. However, Aurelio was a real live, bona fide player who appeared in box scores from 1967–83 with the Angels, Senators, Tigers, Yankees, White Sox, and Orioles.

1968 was the year of the pitcher in major league baseball, but Rodriguez, who hit .242 in 76 games, had the longest consecutive-game hitting streak in the A.L. that season (16 games). The streak did not cause Joe DiMaggio to lose sleep.

Blessed with a rifle arm and cat-like quickness, the Mexican third baseman snapped Brooks Robinson's string of 16 consecutive Gold Gloves at the hot corner when he captured the award in 1976.

He was involved in the blockbuster trade which saw Denny McLain go to the Senators after the '70 season.

Rodriguez remained a fixture at third for Detroit throughout the 1970s, leading A.L. third basemen in fielding percentage in both '76 and '78.

Before being granted free agency on November 7, 1983, he also played with the Padres, Yankees, White Sox, and Orioles. In the 1981 World Series, he batted .417 (5-for-12) for the Yankees against the Dodgers.　　　　　.237

RODRIGUEZ, Ellie
>   Coach for Arecibo in the Puerto Rican winter league;
>   coaches amateur baseball
>   Bayamon, PR

Ellie Howard went to the Red Sox in 1967, but the Yankees had another Ellie behind the plate in 1968 when Ellie Rodriguez was in the lineup for nine games.

Born in Puerto Rico, Rodriguez moved to the Bronx as a youngster and became a Golden Gloves boxer. He failed to make the grade at a couple of Yankee tryout camps, but was signed by the Kansas City A's. Ellie was then drafted

by the Yankees from K. C. in 1964 and climbed through
the Yankee farm system.

After the '68 season he went to the Royals in the expansion draft and also saw action with the Brewers, Angels,
and Dodgers through 1976. He was selected to the All-Star
squad twice, but never played.   .245

RODRIGUEZ, Bobby
Caracas, Venezuela

Two For The Road was in cinemas in 1967 when Bobby
was on the road to a 57-game trip that began in Kansas
City. The right-hander, who was 4-3 overall, moved from
Oakland to San Diego to the Cubs in 1970.

ROGGENBURK, Garry
Boston Red Sox minor league pitching coach

"Roggy" was one of the leading scorers for the Dayton University Flyers basketball squad in the early 1960s. He co-
captained the Flyers' 1962 NIT champs before signing
with the Twins.

The first of his big league victories was the easiest. It
came on April 26, 1963, pitching for Minnesota against
Detroit. Garry entered the game in the bottom of the
eighth and retired the only batter he faced. He was pinch-
hit for in the top of the ninth and was the beneficiary of a
five-run Twin rally to beat the Tigers, 7-5. The 6'6" southpaw hurler was around from 1963–69 (Twins, Red Sox, Pilots) and went 6-9 in 79 games.

ROHR, Billy
Attorney specializing in aviation insurance claims
Redondo Beach, CA

Billy came within one out of pitching a no-hitter in his big
league debut on April 14, 1967, against the Yankees at
Yankee Stadium with Jacqueline Kennedy in attendance.
Rohr held the Yankees hitless for 8⅔ innings before Elston Howard singled on a 3-2 pitch with two out in the

ninth. Rohr beat Whitey Ford and the Yanks that day, 3-0, but just missed being the first chucker in major league history to toss a no-hitter in his debut.

Billy never completed another start or won any more games that year. He pitched in only nine more games for the Red Sox and 17 for the Indians before returning to the minors in 1968.   3-3

ROHR, Les
     Employed with Modern Refrigeration Company
     Billings, MT

Les was the Mets' first round choice in the 1965 free agent draft and the second player selected overall after Rick Monday. The left-hander was born in England where his father was stationed in the Air Force during World War II. He came to the United States when he was just a few months old.

Les was the talk of Montana when he put together a staggering 38-0 record in American Legion baseball. Bing Divine of the Mets' front office was quoted, "If I ever saw a young pitcher who looked like a 20-game winner, this is it."

When Rohr made his big league debut on Sept. 19, 1967, he became the 54th player to crack the Mets lineup that season, breaking the previous mark of 53 players used by the 1944 Brooklyn Dodgers. He was also the 27th pitcher used by the Mets in '67, which tied the major league record previously set by the 1915 Philadelphia Athletics and the 1955 Kansas City A's.   2-3

ROJAS, "Cookie"
     California Angels' advance scout

When asked recently about the 1964 Phillies' late-season collapse, Cookie responded, "I don't think we should talk about 1964."

Although primarily a second baseman, Cuban-born Octavio Rojas played in 70 games that year in the outfield and batted .291. The remainder of the 39 games he played that season were split around the infield. It would appear that he could talk as an authority figure about '64.

Cookie, who was around from 1962–77 after arriving

with the Reds, spent most of his career with the Phils (1963–69) and Royals (1970–77) with a stop at St. Lou- is.   .263

ROJAS, "Minnie"
Huntington Park, CA

March 31, 1970, was a dark day in Minnie's life. That's when a truck hit the car which he was driving. His two young daughters were killed in the accident and he was left paralyzed.

Named *The Sporting News'* A.L. "Fireman of the Year" in 1967 when he won 12 games and saved a league-leading 27 in his 72 appearances, "Minnie" was 23-16 lifetime with 43 saves. His 1966–68 career was spent entirely with the Angels before being plagued by arm trouble.

ROLAND, Jim
Owner of Jim Roland's Sporting Goods
Murphy, NC

Jim had his 10-year stay in the A.L. with the Twins (1962–68), A's (1969–72), Yankees, and Rangers ('72).

The left-hander, who made the long jump from the Class B Carolina League to Minnesota, was used mainly in re- lief. In his first big league start on April 21, 1963, he re- corded his only shutout, blanking the White Sox, 7-0, on three hits while allowing nine walks.

Pitching for the Oakland A's on Oct. 2, 1969, he defeated the Seattle Pilots in the last game the Pilots played before moving to Milwaukee.   19-17

ROLLINS, Rich
Director of Group Sales for the Cleveland Cavaliers of the NBA
Broadview Heights, OH

In his first full season with the Twins in '62, Rich hit .298, walloped 16 homers, collected 96 RBIs, and appeared in both All-Star Games. The following year the third baseman hit a handsome .307, the only time in his career that he batted over .300.

A .269 lifetime hitter, Rich remained with the Twins through '68 before finishing up with the Pilots, Brewers, and Indians in '69–'70.

ROMAN, Bill
Employed with IBM
Chicago, IL

Bill had the satisfaction of hitting a home run in his first big league at-bat when he connected as a pinch-hitter on Sept. 30, 1964. It proved to be the only four-bagger of his career.

Following the '65 season, Bill, a graduate of the University of Michigan with a degree in aeronautical engineering, retired to take a position as a design analyst for the Continental Aviation and Engineering Corporation.   .143

ROMO, Vicente
Pitching in the Mexican League

The older brother of Enrique Romo, who worked out of the Mariners' and Pirates' bullpens just a few short years ago, Vicente made one appearance with the Dodgers in '68.

Romo started the '69 campaign with Cleveland. He was the winning pitcher in their first victory after five losses. Fortunately for Vicente, he was traded to the Red Sox during a losing streak that took them to 1-15.

Vicente went into some disappearing acts while with Boston and eventually was gone altogether to the White Sox. His next excursion was with the Padres where it seemed all over in 1974, but after pitching several years in the Mexican League, Vicente reappeared in 1982 with the Dodgers.

ROOF, Phil
Seattle Mariners' coach

Three men played with the Milwaukee Braves and Milwaukee Brewers. They are Hank Aaron, Felipe Alou, and Phil Roof.

Phil worked behind the plate for 15 seasons from 1961–77 with the Braves, Angels, Indians, A's, Brewers, Twins, White Sox and Blue Jays. A .215 lifetime hitter, Roof had a reputation as a catcher with a strong, accurate arm who handled pitchers well.

He was one of five brothers to play pro ball and his brother Gene came up with the Cards in '81.

ROOKER, Jim
   Pittsburgh Pirates' announcer

Jim's profile might support the case that left-handed pitchers often take a long time to develop into good ones, since he was past his 30th birthday when he established himself as a solid hurler with the Pirates, winning between 13 and 15 games from 1974–1977.

Rooker, who began his career as an outfielder, floundered in the low minors for several years before switching to the mound. After winning 14 games and leading the I.L. in strikeouts (206) in 1968, he got the call to Detroit where he made a couple of relief appearances.

In '69 he struggled to a 4-16 record with the Royals and most likely wondered if he shouldn't have remained an outfielder as he hit .281 with four home runs, including two in one game on July 7th.

On July 4, 1970, Rooker had the Yankees no-hit until Horace Clarke singled in the ninth inning

Following the '72 season Jim was sent to Pittsburgh, where he was a 15-game winner in both '74 and '76.

His last big day in the sun came in Game Five of the 1979 World Series when Jim battled Mike Flanagan of the Orioles and won the crucial contest.   103-109

ROSARIO, Santiago
   Ponce, Puerto Rico

A first baseman, who hit .235 in 81 games for Kansas City A's in 1965 in his only big league season, Santiago was involved in the unfortunate incident at Vancouver (P.C.L) in 1966 when he hit Seattle's Merritt Ranew over the head with his bat. The Puerto Rican native was suspended from professional baseball for a year after the wild melee.

ROSE, Pete
Cincinnati Reds' player-manager

Pete's first season in pro ball was not an indication of what was to come as he hit only .277 in 85 games playing at Geneva in the New York-Penn League. Never the most graceful-looking performer, Pete climbed the ladder of success on pride, desire, and hustle. He has doubled as a reincarnated Ty Cobb since 1963 with the Reds ('63–'78), Phils ('79–'83) and Expos ('84).

The N.L. Rookie of the Year in 1963, Pete collected his first major league hit on April 13th that year off Bob Friend of the Pirates. Bill Virdon, who was in center field for the Bucs that day, was Pete's manager in 1984 when he picked up hit No. 4,000.

Although Rose made his debut as a second baseman, he has made a tour of the diamond. He is the only player in major league history to have played more than 500 games at five different positions—second base from '63–'66, left field from '67–'71, right field from '72–'74, third base from '75–'78, and first base '79 to the present. He owns a record for the highest fielding percentage by an outfielder, lifetime, 1,000 or more games (.992). He is also the only player to win fielding percentage titles at three different positions (1B, 3B, outfield).

Rose won the batting crown in 1968 (.335), edging Matty Alou on the last day of the season. Pete was also the first switch-hitter to win a batting crown in the N.L. since Pete Reiser compiled a .341 avg. in 1941. In '69 Rose nipped Roberto Clemente for the batting crown (.348), also on the final day of the season.

Named the N.L. MVP in 1973 with his .338 avg. and league-leading 230 hits, the season ended in frustration for this competitive genius when the Mets clipped the Reds in the NLCS.

Two years later he got post-season revenge, taking it out on the Red Sox when he batted .370 (10-for-27) in the '75 Fall Classic and he was voted the MVP.

In 1978 the Cincinnati gem broke out of a 5-for-44 slump and went on a 44-game hitting streak, a N.L. record for a single season. The streak ran from June 14–Aug. 1, eclipsing Tommy Holmes' 37-game run.

Granted free agency on Nov. 2, 1978, the brash superstar signed with the Phillies a month later for 3.2 million dollars.

The essence of durability, Pete missed only 91 games in his entire career entering the '84 season. Only Rose and Charley Gehringer have had two playing streaks of 500 or more games. He has collected 100 hits or more for 22 consecutive seasons (1963–84), a major league record.

Not known as a power hitter (158 homers) he unloaded against the Mets on April 29, 1978, when he belted three homers at Shea Stadium en route to a 14-7 romp.

Pete could also be daring on the bases. Playing for the Phils in 1980, he once stole second, third and home in the same inning.

In 1984 Rose established the record for most games played in M.L. history (3,309). He will undoubtedly break Ty Cobb's 4,191 hit mark down the road.   .305

ROSS, Gary
      Owns Ross Liquor
      Encinitas, CA

At one time the Pirates' brass told Gary that he wasn't good enough to play in the majors. On June 24, 1968, the right-hander beat the Pirates while pitching for the Cubs in his first big league game.

Ross was in and out of the majors for portions of 10 seasons with the Cubs, Padres, and Angels. He finished 25-47.

ROWE, Don
      San Francisco Giants' minor league pitching coach

The New York Titans became the New York Jets in 1963 when Don Rowe became a New York Met. In 26 games that season, Don failed to gain a decision.

Prior to taking his current position with the Giants, he

was a teacher and coached baseball at Golden West College in California for several years.

ROWE, Ken
Baltimore Orioles minor league pitching instructor

This Rowe also had a 26-game career. His came between 1963–65. After hopping around with sundry minor league clubs from 1953–62, he earned his shot with the Dodgers. The Orioles purchased Ken late in the '64 season, a year the right-hander established a P.C.L. record by appearing in 88 games for Spokane. Ken then appeared in six more contests with the Orioles to bring his season total to a record 94 games.   2-1

ROZNOVSKY, Vic
Vice president and foreman of a construction company
Fresno, CA

In Vic's career (1964–69) he hit just .218 overall. However, there were some bright spots for this reserve catcher with the Cubs, Orioles and Phils.

He participated in a record-tying feat with Boog Powell when they hit back-to-back pinch-hit home runs for Baltimore. In '67 Vic was ol' reliable, going 6-for-20 as a pinch-hitter for the Orioles.

RUBERTO, "Sonny"
School photographer and territory manager for National School Studios
Indianapolis, IN

John "Sonny" Ruberto swung a light stick with the Padres in '69 and '72 with a .125 avg. in 17 games. He became a minor league manager at Lodi (California League) in 1970 at the age of 24.

From 1971–76 Sonny was a popular figure in Indianapolis (AA) as a catcher.

Along with his baseball career, he worked as a radio commentator and also operated a photography studio.

RUBIO, Jorge
    Mexicali, Baja California, Mexico

Herb Albert and the Tijuana Brass rose to fame in the mid-Sixties, selling more instrumental records than any other artist in history. During this period the California Angels had great hopes for this guitar playing Mexican born pitcher.

A natural right-hander, the ambidexterous hurler actually won two games in the Mexican League throwing from the port side. Called up to the Angels, he won two games, including a 15-strike-out, 2-0 shutout over the Indians on the final day of the '66 season. However, he was "South of the Border" after losing his only two decisions in 1967.   2-3

RUDI, Joe
    Rancher
    Baker, OR

Who can ever forget Joe's brilliant catch in the second game of the 1972 World Series as a member of the A's against the Reds? Then again when you think of those Oakland dynasty years (1972–74), Joe was always a menace to N.L. opponents at World Series time with an overall .300 avg. and a decisive home run in the final game of the '74 Series off Mike Marshall of the Dodgers.

Joe, who received his baptism with the Kansas City A's in 1967, fluttered between the majors and minors for three seasons before becoming a permanent fixture in the Oakland outfield for several years.

Joe's first start ever came on May 8, 1968, the night Catfish Hunter hurled a perfect game. In 1972 the clutch-hitting left fielder led the A.L. in base hits (181) and in triples (9), then had career highs in homers (22) and RBIs (99) in 1974. His 287 total bases and 39 doubles topped the junior circuit in '74. From '74–'76 he was named to the All-Star fielding team.

From 1977–80 Rudi was with the Angels, before spending one year each in Boston and Oakland. Joe retired after the entire 1983 season on the A's disabled list with an

Achilles tendon injury. He closed with a .264 avg. along with 179 home runs, 12 of them grand-slams.

RUDOLPH, Ken
> Minor league manager in Cubs' and Cards' organizations in recent years

Ken was first up with the Cubs in 1968 after catcher Gene Oliver was lost for the season with a leg injury. But the rookie backstop spent 14 days without seeing any action. He was a little busier the next few years (1969–77) with the Cubs, Giants, Cardinals, and Orioles.   .213

RUIZ, "Chico"
> Died in an auto accident on Feb. 9, 1972, in San Diego, CA at age 33

"Bench me or trade me." That was the ultimatum "Chico" once gave Reds' manager Dave Bristol. Sound a little off the wall? Maybe—but that was Hiraldo "Chico" Ruiz, the utility infielder who was around from 1964–71 with the Reds and Angels.

Ruiz was known for his alligator shoes, his custom bench cushion, and a small battery-operated fan to provide comfort during the hot months. He once pasted large stars on the dugout roof for every game he failed to start. In 1968 his daily ritual with the Reds consisted of forming a large ball out of a stack of gum wrappers.

"Chico" had a serious side to him as shown in 1971, when he was accused by Angels' teammate Alex Johnson of pulling a gun on him in the California clubhouse. Chico reportedly told Alex, "I hate you so much I could kill you."

His premature death was caused when his car skidded off a San Diego highway and hit a utility pole.

RUSSELL, Bill
> Active with the Los Angeles Dodgers

When Jim Palmer drew his release from the Orioles early in the 1984 season, Russell became the major leagues' ac-

tive longevity king with the same team, since he has worn
Dodger blue since 1969.

Bill was drafted in the 37th round by the Dodgers from
the little town of Pittsburg, KS, where his high school
didn't even field a baseball team. He was signed at a
hometown tryout camp by Los Angeles.

When the dean of the Dodgers made his big league debut, he went 4-for-4. Since then Bill has risen to ninth on
the all-time Dodger hit list. From 1974–83, "Mr. Durable"
has averaged 138 games a year. He is the sole survivor of
the longest running infield act ever: Steve Garvey (1B),
Davey Lopes (2B), and Ron Cey (3B).

His finest year was 1978 when he hit .286 and had 179
hits. Russell was the hero of the fourth and deciding game
of the LCS, driving in the winning run with two outs in the
10th inning to give the Dodgers a 4-3 victory over the Phils
and their second consecutive N.L. pennant. In the W.S., he
hit .423 against the Yankees.

In the 1974 NLCS Bill established a record with seven
base hits in a four-game series as the Dodgers defeated the
Pirates.

During the 1984 season Bill became the all-time leader
in games played by a Los Angeles Dodger with 1,953.
Through '84 his career mark is .264. He played his 2000th
game for the Dodgers on the final day of the '84 season.

RUSTECK, Dick
    High school teacher
    Portland, OR

The Beatles were singing *Eight Days a Week* at the time
this left-hander pitched in eight games for the New York
Mets in 1966. Dick was only in the big arena for one day
when he pitched the Mets to a 5-0 shutout over the Reds,
thus becoming the first Met to hurl a shutout in his first
major league start.

The Notre Dame graduate finished 1-2.

RYAN, Mike
    Philadelphia Phillies' coach

You most likely know about a few four-decade players. What about a three-century family in baseball?

Mike Ryan of the Ryan clan of Haverhill, MA, first arrived in the majors 75 years after his grandfather's cousin, John Ryan, first came up to Louisville in 1889 in what was then known as the American Association. Should Mike remain in uniform in some capacity until the year 2000, the Ryans would be the first and only baseball family to be a part of the major league scene for parts of three centuries.

Mike was with the Red Sox through the pennant-winning '67 season, then was traded to the Phillies for pitcher Dick Ellsworth. He was in Philly through '73, finishing out his 11-year career with the Pirates in '74.

On May 2, 1970, Tim McCarver had to leave a game against the Giants when he suffered a broken bone in his hand when he was hit by a foul tip. Mike replaced him behind the plate, and before the inning was over he also suffered a broken bone in his hand from a foul tip.   .193

RYAN, Nolan
    Active pitcher with the Houston Astros; also engages
    in cattle breeding and banking
    Alvin, TX

For the past 17 years, the "Ryan Express" has roared through the major leagues. At this writing Nolan and Steve Carlton continue to wage a competitive struggle as baseball's all-time strikeout king.

Someone once said that Ryan could throw his fastball through a car wash without getting the ball wet. Lee (Bee Bee) Richard will attest to that. Playing for the White Sox against the Angels on Sept. 7, 1974, he struck out on a called third strike that was officially clocked at 100.8 mph from "The Express."

Lynn Nolan Ryan, Jr., has used his tools to record five no-hitters during his career. An oddity here is that five different catchers caught Nolan's no-hitters; Jeff Torborg, Art Kusyner, Tom Egan, Ellie Rodriguez, and Alan Ashby. Four of his no-hitters were as a member of the Angels, the other was in Houston threads. When Nolan no-hit the Tigers on July 15, 1973, he was so overpowering that Detroit first baseman Norm Cash came to the plate with a paddle, but umpire Ron Luciano threw the paddle out of the game. In the ninth inning Norm returned carrying a piano leg wrapped in tape—a "beggar's bat." That was also thrown out. Four days later he almost duplicated Johnny Vander Meer's feat of two successive no-hitters when he no-hit the Orioles for the first seven innings. A bloop single leading off the eighth by Mark Belanger spoiled Ryan's historic bid. Ryan is one of four chuckers to hurl no-hitters in both leagues, joining Cy Young, Jim Bunning, and Tom Hughes. In addition to his five no-hitters, he has authored nine one-hitters and 18 two-hitters.

In that '73 campaign, "The Express' racked up 383 K's, a modern M.L. record for most strikeouts in a season.

Four times during his illustrious career, Nolan collected 19 strikeouts in a game and twice has struck out the side in a minimum nine pitches.

He has recorded two 20-win seasons. One came in 1974 when he posted a 22-16 log for the Angels, making him the first A.L. pitcher since Ned Garver of the 1951 Browns to win 20 games for a last-place team.

Pitching for the Mets in the 1969 NLCS against Atlanta, he was the winner of the pennant-clinching third game with seven innings of relief work in which he struck out seven batters, the most ever in an LCS game by a relief pitcher. In Game Three of the '69 Fall Classic against the Orioles, he was credited with a save in a 5-0 shutout.

Overall Nolan has been with the Mets ('66, '68–'71), Angels ('72–'79), and Astros ('81–'84), compiling a 231-206 record.

S

SADECKI, Ray
Sells light fixtures and ceiling fans
Kansas City, KS

Did a pitcher ever have tougher luck than Ray did in 1968?
That year the left-hander went 12-18 for the Giants, losing
eight times while the Giants were being shut out. On five
other occasions the club got him only one run to work with.

A lifetime 135-131 performer, Sadecki broke in with the
Cards in 1960 as a 19-year-old rookie. In '64 he was a
20-game winner for the World Champion Cardinals and
won the opener of the WS against the Yankees.

Early in the '66 season he was traded to San Francisco
for Orlando Cepeda, but after pitching four years in the
swirling winds of Candlestick Park, Ray went to the Mets
(1970–74) where he was used as a spot starter and reliever
seeing action in four games in the '73 W.S.

Before his career toppled in '77, Ray made one more stop
with the Cards and also worked for the Braves, Royals,
Brewers, and Mets again.

SADOWSKI, Bob
Inspector for Chrysler Corp.
Ballwin, MO

Unrelated to the three Sadowski brothers who arrived in
the Sixties, Robert F. Sadowski, aka Sid, was an infielder-
outfielder with the Cards, Phils, White Sox, and Angels
from 1960–63.

Bob's biggest day in the majors will never be recorded,
since it came during an exhibition game on April 8, 1962,
when playing for the White Sox he hit three homers
against the Reds.

In 1961 Bob's I.L. Buffalo team swept Louisville in four
games of the Junior World Series. "Sid" got his team off to
a fast start in the Series when he belted two home runs in
the first inning of the first game.

Throughout the Sixties My Three Sons *was one of the most popular television shows. During this period the three sons of Mr. and Mrs. Sadowski of Pittsburgh, PA, performed in baseball's big show.*

SADOWSKI, Bob
Sales representative for C.F.S. Continental Foods
Chamblee, GA

In 1965 Braves' fans in Milwaukee knew the team was entering a lame duck season, with the franchise slated for transfer to Atlanta the following year, but 33,000 still showed up at County Stadium for the team's final home opener on April 15th when Bob defeated the Pirates, 5-1, on a four-hitter.

Overall the right-hander went 20-17 with Milwaukee (1963–65) and the Red Sox ('66). In '64 he had his best season, winning nine games and saving five others.

SADOWSKI, Eddie
Management position with a container manufacturing company
Anaheim, CA

Okay, Red Sox fans, meet catcher Eddie Sadowski, the guy who wore No. 8 before Carl Yastrzemski wore it and retired it.

Originally up with the Red Sox in 1960, "Sado" saw most of his big league action with the Angels from 1961–63. When he was called up to the Angels in June of '61, it came on the same day as the birth of his first son. He celebrated with a pair of doubles and a home run in his first game.

Eddie's last shot came with Atlanta in '66.   .202

SADOWSKI, Ted
Home repair business
Pittsburgh, PA

Ted made headlines right from birth as he was pictured in a Pittsburgh paper as an "April Fool's Baby" and was also

the hospital's biggest baby at over 11 pounds. Twenty-four
years later this right-handed chucker was grabbing a few
headlines upon his entry to the majors. He was around
from 1960–62 with the Senators and Twins, going 2-3.

Jim Sadowski, a nephew of the three Sadowski brothers,
pitched briefly for the Pirates in 1974.

SALMON, "Chico"
Coaches amateur baseball in Panama; coached the
Panamanian team in the 1984 World Amateur Base-
ball Series

"Play me or keep me" was the ultimatum issued by this
Panamanian-born utilityman to Orioles' manager Earl
Weaver. Rutherford Eduardo Salmon was really in no
hurry to go anywhere since he was able to collect three
World Series checks between 1969–72 as a member of the
O's.

From 1964–68 Chico was employed by the Indians, but
went to the Pilots in the expansion draft. Fortunately, he
was traded to Baltimore for pitcher Gene Brabender.   .249

SAMUEL, Amado
Electronic repairman with General Electric
Louisville, KY

Amado "Sammy" Samuel came out of the Dominican Republic to play in the infields of the Braves and Mets, but
didn't sweep anybody off their feet, hitting .215 in 144
games.

SANDERS, John
Head baseball coach at the University of Nebraska

Colonel Sanders and his Kentucky Fried Chicken outlets
were showing up everywhere when John strutted in for
one game as a pinch-runner for the Kansas City A's in
1965. John today labors a somewhat anonymous role as
head baseball coach for the football-conscious Cornhusk-
ers.

SANDERS, Ken
      Real estate business
      Milwaukee, WI

In 1971 Ken was the relief pitcher extraordinaire in the
A.L. as a member of the Brewers when he appeared in 83
games and set an A.L. record by finishing 77 of those contests. The right-hander was just 7-12, but his league-
leading 31 saves and excellent 1.92 ERA made him the
choice of *The Sporting News* as the A.L. Fireman of the
Year.
   Ken's long march began in '64 and ended 12 years later.
When it was over Sanders had established an A.L. record
of playing for eight different clubs in the A.L. (A's, Red
Sox, Brewers, Twins, Indians, Angels, Royals, and Yankees) plus a stop with the Mets.   29-45

SANDS, Charlie
      Owns Charlie's, a restaurant
      Charlottesville, VA

This ex-Marine landed on A.L. shores in 1967 by making
one pinch-hitting appearance for the Yankees, but most of
his combat came with the Pirates, Angels, and A's from
1971-75. The left-handed hitting catcher hit .214 during
his 93-game battle. He rates his biggest thrill as "being a
member of the '71 Pirates Championship team."

SANGUILLEN, Manny
      Representative of Davimos Sports, a company which
      handles the business affairs of professional athletes

Although Johnny Bench was the premier catcher in the
N.L. during the 1970s, this always-smiling Panamanian
receiver would have to rate as the No. 2 backstop of the
era. A free swinger who rarely struck out, Manny was
tough in the clutch.
   A lifetime .296 hitter, Sanguillen played a key role as
the Pirates won five N.L. East titles in six seasons from
1970-75. Three times during that period he was selected to
the N.L. All-Star squad, appearing once in the mid-sum-

mer classic in '72. In the '71 World Series he hit .379 as the Buccos beat the Orioles in seven games.

Manny first broke out in his friendly smile in '67, then became a regular two years later. He held the Bucs' backstop job until 1976, then was involved in a unique trade in which he went to the Oakland A's along with an estimated $100,000 for Manager Chuck Tanner. After just one season in the A.L., Manny finished back in Pittsburgh in 1980.

SANTIAGO, Jose
Announcer for Santurce in the Puerto Rican winter league; runs amateur baseball program for the government of Puerto Rico

Jose has the distinction as being the only pitcher in World Series history to lose a game in which he homered. Playing for the Red Sox in the '67 Fall Classic, he belted one off the Cards' Bob Gibson in the opening game of the Series, but couldn't get any help from his teammates, losing 2-1.

Not to be confused with Jose Guillermo Santiago who pitched for the Indians and K.C. A's from 1954–56, Jose Rafael pitched for the K.C. A's (1963–65) before winding up with the Red Sox from 1966–70.

In '67 Jose was 12-4 with five saves for the Bosox, helping Boston achieve their "Impossible Dream."

After a 9-4 mark in '68, "Sandy" developed elbow problems and never won another game in the majors.   34-29

SANTO, Ron
Owns a chain of Union 76 truck stops and Kentucky Fried Chicken franchises
Glenview, IL

In 1973 Ron was the first player to take advantage of the rule which stated that a player with 10 years of big league service and five years with the same team could refuse to accept a trade to a team he didn't want to be traded to. This veteran Cubs' third baseman vetoed a trade to the Angels since he wanted to remain in Chicago where he had business interests. He eventually accepted a deal that sent him

crosstown to the White Sox. The rule has since been referred to as the "Santo Clause."

Ron's 15-year career was an impressive one—a .277
mark with 342 home runs. The five-time All-Star choice
led N.L. third basemen in assists for seven consecutive
years (1962–68). He broke several of his own assist records,
creating the standard of 393 in 1967.

Santo, who hit over 30 home runs with 100 RBIs four different times, made his debut on June 26, 1960, when the
Cubs were in the middle of another June swoon, muddled
in a nine-game losing streak. Starting at the hot corner
that day, Santo led the Cubs to a doubleheader sweep
against the league-leading Pirates, going 3-for-7 with 5
RBIs.

A durable performer, he never was in less than 154
games from 1961–1971, playing in 1,595 of his team's
1,618 games. During the '66 season he had a hitting streak
of 26 games, but he was sidelined with a fractured left
cheekbone when hit by a pitch from Jack Fisher of the
Mets. Ron missed a few games, then returned to extend his
streak to 28 games. The disciplined swatter also led the
N.L. four times in bases on balls.

Santo would most likely trade several of his records for a
chance to play in the World Series. Like his illustrious
teammates Ernie Banks and Billy Williams, he was denied the opportunity to show his skills in October.

SANTORINI, Al
Union carpenter; owns business called "Al Santorini's
Pavement Marking"
Union, NJ

Al tossed a no-hitter pitching for Austin in his first year in
pro ball, but didn't know it until sometime following the
game as the official scorer changed a hit to an error on the
second baseman at the request of the second sacker, current Toronto manager Bobby Cox, who stated, "I should
have had the ball easy."

Santorini arrived in '68 with Atlanta, then went to San
Diego in the expansion draft. His six-year big league stay
ended with the Cardinals at 17-38.

SATRIANO, Tom
Certified public accountant
Los Angeles, CA

A member of the 1961 USC NCAA baseball champions, Thomas V. Satriano became the first player signed to an Angels' contract directly from a college campus. Although the V. stands for Victor, it could represent versatile in describing his life in the big top. Primarily a catcher, Tom roamed the infield for the Angels until 1969 when he went to Boston and closed in 1970 with a .225 avg.

On Aug. 11, 1968, Tom enjoyed one of the finest offensive days in Angels' history, going 5-for-5 with two singles, two doubles, and a home run. He was due up next in the ninth inning with a chance to go 6-for-6, but missed the opportunity when Rick Reichardt was thrown out at second base attempting to stretch a single into a double.

SAVAGE, Ted
Schoolteacher
St. Louis, MO

Ted Savage lived up to his name early in '67 when he was told by the Cardinals he was being returned to the minors. Upset at hearing the news, he smashed the ukelele he was playing into several pieces against his locker. The Cards then traded him to the Cubs instead of sending him down.

After winning the I.L. batting title in 1961 with a .325 avg. and being named the MVP of the league, he arrived with the Phillies in 1962. From there, Ted was also with the Pirates, Cardinals, Cubs, Dodgers, Reds, and Brewers before finishing with the Royals in '71.   .233

SCHAAL, Paul
Owns a pizza restaurant; also a licensed chiropractor
Kansas City, KS

Paul has certainly sampled life. How many chiropractors in this world also own a pizza parlor? As a player his off-season occupations included jobs as an electronics technician and a car salesman.

The Angels' infielder suffered a skull fracture on June 13, 1968, when he was beaned by Boston's Jose Santiago. Schaal suffered a one-inch fracture and a punctured eardrum. It was feared the injury would end his career, but Paul's confidence was not fractured. He returned and was picked up by the Royals in the expansion pool.

In the early years of the Royals, Paul manned the hot corner with his best season coming in '73 when he hit .288 in 121 games. Paul swung back to the Angels in '74 where he wound up his 11-year stay with a .244 average.

SCHAFFER, Jimmie
Kansas City Royals' coach

Jim's first big league home run was a grand-slam shot as a member of the Cards against the Cubs at Wrigley Field in 1961. But Jim's career was not lined that often with such fancy trimmings.

From 1961–68, Schaffer bounced around with the Cards, Cubs, White Sox, Mets, Phillies, and Reds, hitting .223 in 314 games. Although Jim's position was solely a catcher, he once played all nine positions in a game for Decatur in 1955.

SCHEINBLUM, Richie
Owns a jewelry store
Villa Park, CA

New York City-born Richie Scheinblum was once quoted as saying, "The only good thing about playing for the Indians is not having to make road trips to Cleveland."

The C.W. Post College graduate skated around with the Indians, Senators, Royals, Reds, Angels, and Cards between 1965–74. A .263 lifetime hitter in the majors, Richie tore the American Association apart in 1971, hitting a torrid .388 for Denver.

Scheinblum looked like a budding star for the Royals in '72 when he batted .300 playing in the outfield on a full time basis. That summer he also played in the All-Star Game and was named the right fielder on *The Sporting News* All-Star Team.

SCHERMAN, Fred
    Employed with Psychrometics Co., which designs and
    manufactures gauge labs
    Dayton, OH

The Saturday Evening Post, 148 years old, folded in 1969
when Fred unfolded a neat (1969–76) career that saw him
go 33-26 plus 39 saves. The southpaw hurler from Ohio
State served the Tigers his first four seasons. In '71 Fred
went 11-6 and saved 20 for the Bengals in 69 appearances.
That year he finished second in appearances and third in
saves in the A.L.
    Scherman closed with the Astros and Expos.

SCHILLING, Chuck
    Math teacher at Seldon Junior High School in Center-
    each, Long Island

Time and again the sophomore jinx has crept up and
plagued the best of first-year players. This Brooklyn-born
second baseman is a classic example.
    During his rookie season for the Red Sox in 1961, Chuck
hit .259 and committed a skimpy eight errors in 854
chances, establishing an A.L. fielding record for second
basemen. But the next year he went hitless in his first 31
at-bats.
    Schilling remained in Boston until 1965 then announced
his retirement following the season when he was traded to
Minnesota.
    Chuck says, "My first big thrill was my first M.L.
home run, a grand-slam against the Twins." He adds, "I
was not very big to begin with. But I was able to hang in
there."   .239

SCHLESINGER, Rudy
    Cincinnati, OH

Playing for Eugene (P.C.L.) Rudy was hit on the head by a
Larry Sherry fastball, which caused him to suffer blind-
ness for a few days. Although he regained his sight, a blind

spot remained which forced him to abandon a promising
career.

Schlesinger's only exposure to the limelight was in 1965
when he made one pinch-hitting appearance for the Red
Sox.

SCHMELZ, Al
          Commercial real estate broker
          Paradise Valley, AZ

When Al took the mound for the Mets in his big league debut on Sept. 7, 1967, he became a part of baseball history.
He was the 25th different pitcher for the Mets that year,
tying the N.L. record set by the 1912 Reds and 1946
Phillies.

A member of the 1965 NCAA champion Arizona State
team, Al had no decisions in his only two games for the
Mets in 1967.

SCHNEIDER, Dan
          Schneider and Talerico Insurance Agency
          Tucson, AZ

One of the most sought-after pitchers in the country after
compiling a 13-1 record at the University of Arizona, Dan
was signed to a reported $100,000 bonus by the Braves in
1962. The left-hander who displayed his good sinkerball
with the Braves and Astros for parts of five different years
from 1963–69 finished 2-5 in 117 games.

SCHOEN, Gary
          Sales supervisor for Coors Beer distributor
          Scottsdale, AZ

During the 1960s singer-entertainer Wayne Newton gained
popularity for his hit song *Danke Schoen*. Also arriving on
the scene, although not so popular, was Gerry Schoen. The
right-hander was the starter and loser in his only game for
the Washington Senators in 1968.

SCHREIBER, Ted
    Staten Island, NY

Ted has the distinction of making the final out ever in the
Polo Grounds on Sept. 18, 1963, when he grounded into a
double play as a member of the Mets. The St. John's product saw action at second, shortstop, and third base in 39
games, hitting .160.

SCHURR, Wayne
    Inspection engineer with Magnavox
    Hudson, IN

Flipper came on TV in 1964 when this right-handed flipper
arrived on the scene with the Cubs for 26 appearances that
summer, failing to gain a decision.

SCHRODER, Bob
    Hospital pharmacist; runs baseball clinics
    Hattiesburg, MS

In the late Sixties Otis Redding was singing about sittin'
on the *Dock of the Bay*. From 1965–68 infielder Bob
Schroder did a lot of sitting on the bench in the Bay Area
with the San Francisco Giants as he made it into a total of
138 games, hitting .217.

SCHWALL, Don
    Stockbroker
    Pittsburgh, PA

As an All-Big Eight Conference basketball star at the University of Oklahoma, 6'6" Don Schwall once outscored and
outrebounded Wilt Chamberlain of Kansas in a game. As a
big league chucker from 1961–67, he outpitched several
opponents during that period.
    Schwall was a 23-game winner at Alpine in the Sopho-
more League in 1959. By 1961 he was named the A.L.
Rookie of the Year by the baseball writers for his 15-7 season with the Red Sox. The following year he fell off to 9-15

and was traded to Pittsburgh for first baseman Dick Stu-
art.

Converted to a reliever, Schwall won nine games and
saved four more in '65 before finishing with the Braves in
'67.   49-48

SCHWARTZ, Randy
Mortgage banker for Pacific Northwest Mortgage in
San Diego
Northridge, CA

After being named to the All-American team in '64 when
he led the nation in home runs and RBIs for UCLA, the big
left-handed hitting first baseman was signed by the Kansas City A's and was named "Player of the Year" in the
Midwest League in 1965.

His playing time in the big arena was limited to 16
games for the A's in the '65 and '66 seasons and he had to
settle for three singles in 18 at-bats for a .167 avg.

SCOTT, Dick
Repair parts manager with Davis Water and Waste
Industries
Thomasville, GA

Movie viewers were treated to a blend of adventure and excitement in the *Dirty Dozen*. Dick Scott didn't have much
of either in a dozen trips to the mound as a member of the
Dodgers and Cubs in the '63 and '64 seasons, failing to
gain a decision.

SCOTT, George
Manager in the Mexican League

"You've got to understand, man, baseball ain't an easy
game to play."
                                        —George "Boomer" Scott

Defensively, baseball appeared an easy game to play for
George since his eight Gold Gloves are the most of any first

baseman in baseball history. But offensively, his bat was about as predictable as March weather in Boston.

The MVP of the Eastern League in 1965, Scott jumped to the majors in '66 and played all 162 games for the Red Sox. He surprised the Fenway faithful as he hit 27 homers and drove in 90 runs. "Boomer" continued his fine play without missing a beat in '67, batting .303 and walloping 19 four-baggers with the pennant-winning Bosox.

Then his average plummeted to .171 with three homers and 25 RBIs in '68. His anemic average established the dubious record of being the lowest in M.L. history for any first sacker playing in at least 100 games.

"Boomer" spent three more seasons in Boston before going to the Brewers where he hit a career high .306 with 107 RBIs in 1973. Two years later the husky first baseman enjoyed his greatest campaign, leading the A.L. with 36 home runs and 109 RBIs. After the next season he was shipped back to Boston where he stayed for another couple of years.

The 6'2", 215-pound slugger, who finished in '79 with the Royals and Yankees, poked 271 home runs and swung for a .269 avg.

SEALE, Johnnie
    Co-owner of a construction company, Ben Seale and
    Sons Construction
    Durango, CO

When Johnnie Seale of Durango, CO, arrived at the Tigers training camp, he was immediately dubbed the "Durango Kid" because he showed up wearing cowboy boots and a cowboy hat. In '64–'65 Seale made eight appearances out of the Detroit bullpen, winning his only decision.

He writes, "I'm hoping you'll hear about one of my boys in the major leagues someday."

SEAVER, Tom
    Active with Chicago White Sox

If any pitcher has been in virtually total command of himself on the mound, it's been this son of a former member of the U.S. Walker Cup golf team. Tom is a master of his trade who has the ability to dissect the fundamentals of pitching and analyze each and every section of his craft.

George Thomas Seaver was originally selected by the Dodgers out of USC in the 22nd round of the 1965 free agent draft, but eventually signed a reported $40,000 bonus contract with the Atlanta Braves on Feb. 24, 1966. However, the Braves were unaware that they were violating a rule prohibiting a major league team from signing a player while his school's (USC) baseball season was in progress. On March 2, 1966, Commissioner William Eckert nullified Seaver's contract with the Braves but Tom lost his collegiate eligibility at USC.

There was nothing terrific about Tom when he made his debut on April 13, 1967, as he allowed four runs and six hits in five innings, twice hitting Matty Alou with pitches. But he ironed out his problems and even pitched in the All-Star Game that summer. His 16-13 record his freshman season earned him Rookie of the Year honors.

Seaver won his first of three Cy Young awards in 1969, going 25-7 with a 2.21 ERA. Shea Stadium became the Mecca of the baseball world as a horde of fans made a steady pilgrimage to Flushing, NY, to watch the Mets capture their first pennant and World Series.

Between 1968–1976 Tom struck out 200 or more each season making him the first in big league history to whiff 200 or more batters for nine consecutive years. On April 22, 1970, he tied an M.L. record by fanning 19 San Diego Padres, including the last 10 in a row, also a record.

In 1977 Mets' Board Chairman M. Donald Grant made a "win or else" statement regarding the annual Mayor's Trophy Game against the Yankees. Seaver commented, "We're in a losing streak and at our bottom level and the Chairman worries about an exhibition game. I never thought I wanted to be traded away from the Mets. I do now." The following day Seaver publicly apologized, but on June 15, 1977, he was traded to the Reds for Doug Flynn, Pat Zachry, Dan Norman and Steve Henderson. His stay in the Queen City lasted from 1978–82, during which time he went 61-43 while posting a 14-2 mark during the strike-shortened season in 1981. The only no-hitter of his career came on June 16, 1978, pitching for the Reds against the Cardinals.

In 1983 he returned to the Mets and went 9-14.

The Mets' brass failed to protect Tom in the Compensation Draft in 1984 and he was chosen by the White Sox. He won 15 games for them, pushing his career totals to 288-181.

SECRIST, Don
Coal miner for Arch Minerals Company
Dubuque, IL

While pitching for Knoxville (Southern League) on June 19, 1966, Don came within one out of hurling complete games of a twinbill against Asheville. In the first contest he tossed a 3-0 shutout and in the nightcap held a 4-2 lead with two out in the final frame but was unable to retire the last out and was removed from the game.

Don's big league swing wasn't quite so newsy. As a member of the White Sox (1969–70), the southpaw relieved on 28 occasions and was a loser once.

SEGUI, Diego
Active in the Mexican League

Okay, you baseball univacs. Did you know that Diego is the only player to wear the uniforms of both the Seattle Pilots and Seattle Mariners? What probably is more important is that this Latin antique continues to function in high level fashion in the Mexican League as he nears his 50th birthday.

The durable Cuban first arrived with the Kansas City A's in 1962 where he remained for four years before a one-year stint with the Senators. It was then back to the A's. In '68 Diego was 6-5 with a fine 2.39 ERA, but was the losing pitcher when Denny McLain chalked up victory No. 30. Segui was the rock of the Pilots' staff in '69, pitching in 66 games, all but eight as a reliever, winning 12 and saving another dozen.

Traded back to the A's in 1970, he was a combination of fire and ice as he won 10 games and posted the best ERA (2.56) in the American League. The next few summers were spent with the Cardinals and Red Sox, and in 1977 was the starting pitcher in the first game ever in Mariners' history.

SELMA, Dick
Salesman for United Distributing Company; pitching coach at Fresno City College
Fresno, CA

Dick can brag that he was the starting and winning pitcher in the San Diego Padres' first game in '69 when he beat the Astros, 2-1, on a five-hitter with 12 strikeouts. The right-hander can also boast about a few other things. When Dick made his debut with the Mets in 1965 he beat St. Louis, 6-3, then followed with a 10-inning, 1-0 decision over the Braves, setting a then-Mets club record of 13 K's.

Selma was around from 1965–74 with some time spent in the minors. Following a 9-10 season in '68 (Mets), Dick joined the Padres. However, a few weeks after the victory mentioned above, he found himself with the Cubs. It was during that '69 season in Chicago that he gained national attention when he led daily cheers for the bleacher bums at Wrigley Field.

Dick had the Cubs' fans cheering on May 13th that year when he blanked the Padres, 19-0, in a game which tied the record as the most lopsided shutout in N.L. history.

The next year he traveled to Philadelphia where he won 8 games and saved 20 in 73 busy appearances for the Phils before closing with the Angels and Brewers at 42-54 lifetime.

SEMBERA, Carroll
Owns a tavern
Shiner, TX

This right-handed reliever was nicknamed "The Pencil" because of his slight build. Carroll scribbled a 3-11 mark in 99 games with the Astros and Expos between 1965–70.

SEVCIK, John
  Construction equipment sales business
  Minneapolis, MN

It could have been twins with the Twins when John and his identical twin brother Jim were signed by Minnesota after helping lead the University of Missouri to a second-place finish in the 1964 College World Series.

John was around for just 12 games in 1965. The catcher hit .063 with one hit, a double, in 16 at-bats.

SEVERINSEN, Al
  Construction company supervisor
  Medford, NY

Al most likely holds the distinction of being the only player in pro baseball history to be the losing pitcher in a game he also worked as an umpire. On May 13, 1967, Al was with Stockton (California League) when one of the regular umpires failed to show up for the game. The Brooklyn-born right-hander proceeded to work the bases as an umpire to assist the home plate ump. Midway through the game a local amateur ump replaced Al on the bases. He then returned to the bullpen and was subsequently charged with the loss after being summoned in the late innings.

In the big top Al was 3-7 plus 9 saves in 88 games with the Orioles and Padres between 1969–72.

SEYFRIED, Gordy
  Shipping and receiving clerk for Procter & Gamble
  Long Beach, CA

Pitching for Denver (American Association) in 1961, Gordy once beat Omaha, 30-8, in a complete-game effort in which he allowed 19 hits and collected a single, double, and home run. On the big league level he allowed just one earned run in nine plus innings of work for the Indians in 1963–64 for an excellent 0.93 ERA. But all he has to show for his efforts in five games is an 0-1 record.

SHAMSKY, Art
Sports announcer for WNEW-TV in New York City

Only three players in baseball history have hit two extra-inning homers in the same game. Vern Stephens did it in 1943 with the Browns. Willie Kirkland of the Indians accomplished the feat in 1963, and Art Shamsky pulled it off for the Reds against the Pirates on Aug. 12, 1966. Inserted as a substitute in mid-game, he homered in the 8th inning and also connected in the 10th and 11th frames to give him three for the day. Despite Art's heroics, the Reds lost the contest, 14-11, as both teams combined for 11 four-baggers at Crosley Field in Cincinnati.

Shamsky was back on the bench the next day, but the day after he tied an M.L. record with a fourth roundtripper in four at-bats with a pinch-homer. He finished the season with 21 home runs but played in only 96 games.

Art was traded to the Mets after the '67 campaign where he played a key role in the '69 miracle, batting an even .300 in 100 games. His bat was smokin' in the NLCS against Atlanta as he hit .538 (7-for-13).

Following the '71 season Shamsky was shipped to the Cardinals. His eight-year jog was completed in '72 after stops with the Cubs and A's.   .253

SHANNON, Mike
St. Louis Cardinals' announcer

Mike, who was born and raised in St. Louis, played some quarterback at the University of Missouri. During his nine-year run with the Cardinals from 1962–70, he was a member of three N.L. championship teams and two World Series winners.

Originally an outfielder, Shannon replaced veteran Ken Boyer at third base in 1967. A career .255 hitter, he had his best season in '66 when he hit .288 with 16 home runs. It's poetic justice that this St. Louis man picked up the first base hit in the new Busch Stadium in 1966. His four-bagger in Game One of the '64 Fall Classic against Whitey Ford and the Yankees led to a 9-5 victory.

Shannon possessed one of the strongest throwing arms

during his playing days, but his career was cut short with a kidney ailment and he took a job in the Cards' front office before joining the broadcasting team.

SHAW, Don
Insurance business
St. Louis, MO

On April 8, 1969, Montreal beat the Mets, 11-10, in the first game ever in Expos' history. Don Shaw was the winner that day in relief but won just one more game for Montreal that year.

The southpaw, who had a respectable rookie year with the Mets in '67, beat Pirates' relief ace Elroy Face twice in one day, winning a pair of 10-inning games.

Don also pitched for the Cards and A's in 1971–72.   13-14

SHEA, Steve
High school teacher; baseball coach
Amherst, NH

Generally speaking, it is not in the best interest of a rookie pitcher to make his debut with the bases loaded in the ninth inning and nobody out. But Steve walked right into that situation on July 14, 1968, while pitching in relief for Houston. However, he worked his way out of the jam and then set the Reds down in the 10th to gain credit for the victory.

Steve's 40 big league games were spent with the Astros and Expos. His 4-4 record plus six saves were all earned with Houston.

SHELDON, Rollie
Senior claims representative for the All State Insurance Co.
Lees Summit, MO

Rollie jumped from Class D in 1960 where he went 15-1 to Yankee Stadium in 1961. Signed by the Yanks out of the University of Connecticut, he went 11-5 in '61. He slipped

to 7-8 the following year which prompted his return to the
minors for more prepping.

Back with the Bronx Bombers in '64, the right-hander
worked a couple of scoreless innings in relief in the World
Series against the Cardinals. He then made stops with the
A's and Red Sox before closing at 38-36.

SHELLENBACK, Jim
> Minnesota Twins' minor league pitching coach

An auto accident almost ended Jim's career, which began
with the Pirates in 1966. It was Oct. 1, 1967, when he was
severely injured in a car mishap.

Only a few days before the accident, Jim went 11 innings to beat the Dodgers on a six-hitter in his first big
league start.

Shellenback eventually recovered from his injuries. Early in the '69 season he was sent to the Senators where his
manager was Ted Williams. Ironically Jim's uncle Frank
(Shellenback), who pitched for the White Sox in 1918–19
and is the all-time leader in P.C.L. history with 295 victories, was William's first manager at San Diego in 1936.
When it ended in 1977, Jim had also seen action with the
Rangers and Twins.   16-30

SHIRLEY, Bart
> Real estate business
> Miami, FL

Bart earned his medals on the gridiron more so than the
baseball diamond. As a sophomore in 1960 he led Texas to
the Cotton Bowl when he tossed the winning touchdown
pass against Arkansas, giving the Longhorns a 13-12 victory.

Shirley was also a baseball star in college and elected to
stay with the game. From 1964–68 he bounced back and
forth like a yo-yo between the Dodgers, Mets, and the minors. In 75 games in the big top, the infielder hit only .204.

SHOCKLEY, Coston
Construction superintendent for I.A. Construction
Corporation
Georgetown, DE

John Coston Shockley has one of the more memorable
names of the era, if not one of the more memorable careers.
As a first baseman he hit .197 in 51 games for the Phils
and Angels in '64 and '65.

In his first season in pro ball at Magic Valley in the Pioneer League (1961), he hit .360 and was waving a magical
bat at one stretch when he had 23 hits in 27 at-bats. In '64
with Arkansas (P.C.L.), he led the league in homers (36)
and RBIs (112).

SHOEMAKER, Charlie
National Sales Manager for Billard Barbell Co.
Reading, PA

Charlie says, "I often think back on my career in baseball
and feel very lucky that I was one of the few to have had the
opportunity to be a small part of the great sport of baseball."

A second baseman, Shoemaker's part was worth 28
games in three trials with the Kansas City A's between
1961–64.   .258

SHOPAY, Tom
Runs the Country Kiddie School, a nursery school
Miami, FL

Shopay was brought to the Bronx late in the '67 season
when Tom Tresh underwent knee surgery. The outfielder
played in eight games that year for the Pinstripers and
belted two home runs. One of his four-baggers knocked in
the winning runs in a game against the Twins.

It would be another decade before Tom's next big league
roundtripper. Drafted by Baltimore from the Yanks in '69,
Tom spent most of the 1970s shuttling between Rochester
and Baltimore.

Always around when needed by the Orioles, he was
much in demand as an after dinner speaker.   .201

SHORT, Bill
    Owns Easy Living Pools, a pool construction company
    in Sarasota, FL

Pitching for the Yankees in his major league debut on
April 23, 1960, Bill defeated the Orioles, 3-2, at Yankee
Stadium.
    He bounced up and down and all around the majors with
Baltimore, Boston, Pittsburgh, the Mets and Reds through
1969, finishing 5-11 in 73 games.
    Normally used as a reliever, Bill started a game for the
Orioles in 1966 and shut out the Twins, 2-0, giving the O's
a key victory in their drive for the A.L. pennant.

SIEBERT, Sonny
    San Diego Padres' minor league pitching coach

Were you awake when the Cards beat the Mets, 4-3, on
Sept. 11, 1974, in a 25-inning night game that lasted 7
hours and 4 minutes? At 3:13 A.M. Sonny Siebert became
the winning pitcher of the long affair.
    Sonny's career was long running as he was around from
1964-75, mainly with the Indians and Red Sox. He also
wore the knits of the Rangers, Cards, Padres, and A's in
his twilight years.
    After averaging over 18 points per game at the Univer-
sity of Missouri, Wilfred "Sonny" Siebert was drafted by
the St. Louis Hawks of the NBA. But he also led the school
to a second-place finish in the College World Series and
chose to sign a reported $35,000 bonus contract with the
Indians as an outfielder.
    His 16-8 mark in '66 led the A.L. in winning percentage.
On June 10th he hurled a 2-0 no-hitter over the Senators,
the only no-hitter pitched in the majors in '66.
    Although "Sonny" struggled at the plate in the low mi-
nors at the outset of his career, he often found major
league pitching to his liking. He hit .266 in 1971 including
six of his career 12 home runs. Two of those four-baggers
came in one game that year on September 2nd.   140-114

SIEBLER, Dwight
   Owner of Hotentot-Supreme Aire
   Omaha, NE

At the time Sonny Siebert was grabbing headlines at Missouri, Dwight Siebler was doing likewise at Big Eight conference rival Nebraska. But Dwight's act in the big show was limited compared to Siebert's. The ex-Cornhusker was 4-3 in 48 games with the Twins from 1963–67.

Dwight's first start ever, on Aug. 29, 1963, turned into a feast as he defeated the Senators, 10-1, on a three-hitter. He also enjoyed the support of the Twins' record-setting eight home runs that day.

SIMMONS, Ted
   Active with Milwaukee Brewers

Ted has the distinction of being the only active player to switch-hit home runs in the same game in both leagues. It is a reflection of his sharp hitting skills that he carried with him since his first taste of honey in '68.

He was the Redbirds' regular backstop for the entire decade of the '70s. In 1979 he set a St. Louis record for catchers with a personal-high 26 home runs.

Simmons holds the N.L. record for most home runs by a switch-hitter (172).

Prior to the '81 season, Ted went to the Brewers with Rollie Fingers and Pete Vuckovich for Sixto Lezcano, David Green, Larry Sorensen and Dave LaPoint.

Ted's .308 average in '83 was the best in baseball among switch-hitters. As a designated hitter that year, he led the way at .329.

Simmons appeared in five All-Star Games. His only World Series ironically came against the Cardinals in 1982, the team with which he spent most of his big league life.   .288

SIMPSON, Dick
    Food products salesman in Los Angeles
    Venice, CA

"I'm the Simpson they should have called Suitcase."
    Along with several trips to the minors, this fleet-footed
outfielder wore the uniforms of the Angels, Reds, Cardinals, Astros, Mets,and Pilots, hitting .207 from 1962–69.
    He once put pitcher Pedro Ramos in his place. For years
Ramos laid claim to be the fastest runner in baseball. On
the final day of the '62 season at Cleveland, Simpson won a
75-yard dash race, running away from other contestants
headed by Ramos.

SIMS, "Duke"
    Employed with Robinson, Inc., a plastic pipe business
    Binghamton, NY

"Duke" became part of the hallowed history of Yankee Stadium when he hit the last home run by a Yankee in the original stadium before renovations began after the '73 season.
    Catcher Duane "Duke" Sims first arrived in '64 with the
Indians. He was with the Indians until the end of the 1970
season, then bounced around with the Dodgers, Tigers, Yankees, and Rangers before leaving in 1974 with a .239 average.
    He swatted 100 home runs, one of which made history in
the House that Ruth built.

SIMS, Greg
    Employed with Consolidated Freight
    Sacramento, CA

Greg was a switch-hitting outfielder and appeared in
seven games for the Astros in 1966, going 1-for-6 (.167).

SINGER, Bill
    Vice President of Coast Development
    Newport Beach, CA

An assorted list of calamities obstructed the career of this
6'4" right-hander.

From 1964–66 the Dodgers gave Bill three late season recalls. He responded well each time.

In his first full season in '67, he was 12-8. For a two-month stretch he was the hottest pitcher in baseball, going 10-2 from mid-July to mid-September.

The "Singer Throwing Machine" sewed up one victory after another in '69 en route to a 20-win season. His 20th victory came on the final day of the season when the Dodgers scored a run in the bottom of the ninth inning to give Bill a 5-4 win over Houston.

At the start of the '70 campaign Singer contacted infectious hepatitis and didn't see any action until June. In one of his first starts he was working on a no-hitter until the Braves' Clete Boyer singled with two out in the eighth inning. A few weeks later, on July 20th, he got his no-hitter in a 10-strikeout performance over the Phillies. But bad luck struck again as he finished the season where he had started it (on the disabled list) after suffering a broken finger.

Singer struggled the next couple of years, then was involved in the blockbuster deal in which he went to the Angels. Bill found life better across town winning 20 games in '73. He appeared to be on track but was again disabled in '74.

After pitching for the Rangers and Twins, he finished with the Blue Jays in 1977.   118-127

SIPIN, John
 Owner/operator of an indoor baseball/softball batting
 range—Grand Slam USA
 Watsonville, CA

A second baseman of Filipino and Irish descent, John had a noteworthy major league debut when he was called up to San Diego in 1969 as he hit triples in his first two big league at-bats off Ken Holtzman of the Cubs. Oddly enough, they were the only triples of his career.   .223

SISK, Tommie
   Owns a land title business
   Provo, UT

Tommie had scouts salivating at the Anaheim American Legion Tournament in 1959 when he pitched a nine-inning no-hitter for the Legion All-Stars against the Los Angeles Dodgers' rookie team. Three years later he was a big leaguer with the Pirates, where he stayed until 1968.

The right-hander led the Bucs' staff in '67 with 11 complete games and two shutouts. The number "3" was wild for Tommie that year as he went 13-13 and had a 3.33 ERA.

Tommie returned home as a member of the expansion Padres, but the summer of '69 was a long one for Sisk as he was winless until September and finished up at 2-13. He last pitched for the White Sox in 1970, winding up 40-49. Tommie is not related to the current Mets' reliever.

SIZEMORE, Ted
   Vice President of Rawlings Sporting Goods
   Creve Coeur, MO

"You have to have an unselfish player batting behind you to steal a lot of bases, and I did in Ted Sizemore," said Lou Brock after his record-breaking 118 steals in 1974.

A graduate of the University of Michigan where he played basketball with Cazzie Russell, Ted counted future NBA players such as Spencer Haywood, Mel Daniels, and Ralph Simpson among his roundball teammates at Pershing High School in Detroit.

Not selected until the 40th round of the 1966 free agent draft, Ted took over at second base for the Dodgers in 1969 and was selected by the Baseball Writers as the Rookie of the Year after hitting .271 in 159 games. During the course of the season he tied an M.L. mark by hitting three bases-loaded triples. Although he spent much of the 1970 season on the disabled list he hit a career high .306 in 96 games.

He was then traded to the Cardinals in a deal that involved the controversial Richie Allen. Sizemore spent five summers in St. Louis before returning to the Dodgers in '76. On July 12, 1976, he poked two pinch-hits in one inning. When Ted first came up with the Dodgers in '69 he wanted number 5 but was unable to wear it because it was already taken by Jim Lefebvre. Sizemore settled for number 41 since 4 and 1 added up to 5. He was given number 5 when he returned in 1976.

In 1977 he was off to Philadelphia where he was instrumental in helping Philly to two consecutive N.L. East titles with his steady play at second base. In the '78 NLCS he batted .385.

Ted's last stops were with the Cubs ('79) and Red Sox ('80).   .262

SLAUGHTER, Sterling
Staff manager for Mountain Bell
Tempe, AZ

The guy with the stately name did have a stately debut as a starter with the Cubs on Memorial Day in '64. After four relief appearances Sterling hurled a one-hit, 2-0 shutout over the Milwaukee Braves with late-inning relief help from Lindy McDaniel. Four days later he beat the Braves, 5-2, on a five-hitter.

But unfortunately because of a bad arm, Slaughter was around only in '64 when he went 2-4 in 20 games. The right-hander was the first All-American ever out of Arizona State, where in 1963, he capped off a 26-4 college career with a 22-strikeout performance against Colorado State.

SLOCUM, Ron
Location unknown

In a pro career in which he played every position except pitcher, Ron played throughout the infield and caught for the Padres from 1969–71. When he was called up in September of '69, he singled and homered in his first two big league at-bats. His 80-game run ended with a .150 avg.

SMITH, Charley
Sporting goods business
Sparks, NV

When a man is traded for a legend it can have a haunting effect throughout his life. Such is true for Charley Smith who went from the Cardinals to the Yankees following the '66 season in exchange for Roger Maris, the single-season home run champ. It really wasn't fair to Charley, even though he collected 10 hits in 30 pinch-hit appearances for the Yankees in 1968.

A third baseman, Smith's career spanned the entire decade of the Sixties with the Dodgers, Phils, White Sox, Mets, Cards, Yankees, and Cubs. He started out as a shortstop and first arrived with Los Angeles in 1960 after a big season that summer at Spokane in which he hit .322 with 20 homers and 106 RBIs. Charley is one of only two players to play for both New York teams and both Chicago teams. The other man was Dick Tidrow.   .239

SMITH, Dick, A.
Restaurant manager
Medford, OR

Fate tried to conceal him by naming him Smith, but any man who makes it to the big leagues can only be concealed for so long.

From 1963–65 Dick became a mini celebrity as a player with the Mets and Dodgers, hitting .218 in 76 games.

SMITH, Dick K.
Biology teacher; head baseball coach and assistant football coach at Lincolnton (NC) H.S.

In 1969 retired Green Bay Packers' football coach Vince Lombardi was being mentioned as a potential candidate to replace William Eckert as Baseball Commissioner. But Lombardi ended up in Washington as head coach of the Redskins.

Dick K. Smith also came to Washington in '69. A one-time star receiver on the gridiron for North Carolina State, he hit .107 in 21 games as a Senators' outfielder.

SMITH, George
St. Petersburg, FL

We all should have the exhilarating experience in life that
George had on July 10, 1966. With one out in the 10th in-
ning, he hit a grand-slam for the Red Sox, beating Juan
Pizarro and the White Sox by a score of 10-6.

The second baseman began in pro ball in the mid-Fifties.
George also spent time barnstorming with the Indianapo-
lis Clowns before making the long, slow climb through the
Tigers' farm system.

He was a Tiger from 1963–65 before becoming the regular second baseman for the Red Sox in 1966, his fourth
and final season in the majors. His career came to an
end in spring training in 1967 when he tore cartilage in
a knee.   .205

SMITH, Jack
Hair stylist at the Marriott Hotel
Atlanta, GA

Houdini once said, "Nothing is a lock." That could be applied in baseball to those who have performed nobly in the
minors but came up short in the bigs.

In 1962 Jack was named the MVP of the American Association after going 17-7 with a 2.06 ERA in 71 relief appearances for Omaha.

But in the big show with the Dodgers and Braves
(1962–64) he was somewhat less effective, going 2-2 plus
one save in 34 relief trips.

SMITH, Nate
Location unknown

Detective Eddie Egan uncovered the French connection in
1962, a year the Orioles uncovered this Chicago native
late in the season.

Drafted by Baltimore from the Dodgers' organization,
this catcher singled in his first at-bat in the majors. Nate
hit .222 in his five-game stay.

SMITH, Pete
　　Guidance and placement counselor at the Putnam
　　Northern Westchester B.O.C.E.S.
　　Brewster, NY

One of the basic axioms in the game of baseball is to run
everything out. Because of Pete Smith's clever thinking,
he turned a routine play into a triple play when the principle was violated.

Pitching for the Red Sox at Fenway Park in 1963 he allowed Felix Torres's pop bunt to drop and turned it into a
triple play when the Angels' batter forgot to run. However,
Pete's shrewdness didn't extend his career. The Colgate
University grad lost his only decision in seven games
while with the Red Sox in '62 and '63.

SMITH, Reggie
　　Retired in 1984 as an active player in Japan

There is enough trivia about Reggie Smith to carry a baseball buff from happy hour until closing at the local speakeasy.

1. He is one of five players to hit World Series home
runs for both an American and National League team.
Smith homered twice for the Red Sox in 1967 and hit three
for the Dodgers in the '77 Fall Classic and another the following year.

2. Reggie and Frank Robinson are the only two men to
play for both the A.L. and N.L. in the All-Star Game and
for the A.L. and N.L. in the World Series.

3. Reggie Smith and Ted Simmons are the only players
in big league history to switch-hit homers in one game in
both leagues.

4. Mr. Smith is the only switch-hitter to hit 100 or more
homers in each league.

The most notable of the nine Smiths to debut during the
1960s, Reggie originally was signed by the Twins in 1963
but after hitting .257 in the Appalachian League, he was
left unprotected and was drafted by the Red Sox.

Reggie led the I.L. in batting (.320) in 1966 at Toronto.
For the next several years he was a fixture in the Fenway
garden after first coming up as an infielder. Three times

he hit over .300 in Boston. On four occasions he homered from both sides of the plate in the same game.

From 1974–76 Reggie was with the Cardinals. His first two years in the N.L. were good ones, as he batted over .300 each season. On May 22, 1976, the switch-hitting slugger poked three homers. A few weeks later he was traded to the Dodgers where he stayed until 1981. Reggie closed in '82 with the Giants with a .287 avg. and 314 homers.

By the way, what is Reggie's real first name? Answer: Carl.

SMITH, Willie
Foundry worker
Anniston, AL

Willie provides a little trivia himself. He is the only black in big league history to accomplish the pitcher-player feat of appearing in at least 20 games as a pitcher and 20 as a fielder. From 1964–71, Willie batted .248 in 691 games and was 2-4 as a pitcher with a 3.10 ERA in 29 games. His major league tour was spent as a member of the Tigers, Angels, Indians, Cubs, and Reds.

Smith became known as "Wonderful Willie" while with Syracuse (I.L.) in 1963 when he hit .380 and was 14-2 on the mound.

On June 8, 1964, playing for the Angels at Cleveland, Willie had a game that was symbolic of his profile. In that contest he pinch-hit, then played the outfield and finished his busy day by relieving on the mound in the eighth inning. During that season the always-smiling, always-joking, all-around player was 9-for-15 as a pinch-hitter and eventually won a job as a regular in the Angels' outfield. He led the way during the club's 11-game winning streak and finished the year batting .301.

SNYDER, Jim
Chicago Cubs field director of player development

Attorney General Bobby Kennedy began his fight against organized crime in 1961. That same year infielder Jim

Snyder began his futile battle against some pretty good pitching in the majors when he arrived with the Twins. He swung at a few offerings he should have refused and disappeared in '64 after hitting .140 in 41 games.

SOLAITA, Tony
Active in Japan

Football has its "Throwin' Samoan" in Jack Thompson. Baseball had its 'hittin' Samoan (at times) in Tony Solaita.

The first major leaguer from American Samoa, Tony was cloistered in the Yankee farm system from 1965–73 with the exception of one game in 1968 in which he struck out in his only at-bat. Before the Yanks brought him up he was a living terror in the Carolina League that summer when he hit a league-leading 49 home runs and 122 RBIs for High Point–Thomasville.

Drafted by the Royals in 1973, the muscular Samoan played with Kansas City, the Angels, the Expos and Blue Jays through 1979.

On Sept. 7, 1975, while with the Royals, he became the first player ever to hit three home runs in a game at Anaheim Stadium.

Solaita, who reportedly is the owner of the only car wash in American Samoa, signed a three-year contract to play in Japan in 1980.   .255

SORRELL, Bill
Real estate broker for Ann Winton and Associates
San Diego, CA

A third baseman/outfielder named Bill Sorrell became a major leaguer with the Phillies in 1965. He also wore the knits of the Giants and Royals before ending in 1970 after 85 games and a .267 average.

SOUTHWORTH, Bill
   Cardiologist
   Webster Groves, MO

The name Billy Southworth is a notable one in baseball as
that of the long-time player and then successful manager
of the powerful St. Louis Cardinal teams of the early
1940s. This Billy Southworth is a distant cousin. His big
league career is only distantly comparable as he made it
into three games with the Milwaukee Braves as an 18-
year-old in 1964, hitting .286 (2-for-7). One of his two hits
was a home run.

SPANSWICK, Bill
   Transportation broker for Spanswick Associates
   Enfield, CT

Known as "Crow," Bill Spanswick, who attended Holy
Cross, grew up in New England rooting for the Red Sox. In
1964 he got the opportunity to pitch for his favorite team
when he went 2-3 in 29 games. The previous year Bill led
the P.C.L. in strikeouts (209) pitching for Seattle.

SPARMA, Joe
   Vice-president of National Accounts for Worthington
   Steel Co.
   Columbus, OH

Only a select few have had the opportunity to participate
in both a World Series and a Rose Bowl football game.
   Joe was used briefly in the '68 World Series in Game
Four as a reliever against the Cardinals. He was denied
the opportunity to participate in the Rose Bowl despite
teaming with Paul Warfield in leading Ohio State to the
Big Ten title in 1961 as he passed for over 200 yards in a
50-20 victory over arch rival Michigan, the most points
ever scored by Ohio State against Michigan. However, in a
controversial decision that year, the Ohio State faculty
voted that the Buckeyes could not go to the Rose Bowl.
   Sparma was on a roll in 1967, going 16-9 with five shutouts, all of which were thrown at Tiger Stadium. He went

10-10 during Detroit's championship season in 1968. He
beat the Yankees, 2-1, on September 17th to clinch the
team's first pennant since 1945.

The right-hander was in Detroit one more year before
closing with the Expos in 1970 after losing his battle with
arm trouble. At age 28 he was done at 52-52.

SPENCE, Bob
    Commercial real estate salesman
    Fountain Valley, CA

Bob's .202 average in 72 games suggested youthful un-
readiness. Unfortunately, he never had the chance to mature, as the White Sox first baseman out of Santa Clara
University was among the missing following his brief run
from 1969–71.

SPENCER, Jim
    Owns a restaurant
    Baltimore, MD

Often, first round selections have turned out to be lemons.
But there was nothing sour about Jim, who was plucked by
the Angels in the first free agent draft in 1965.

Spencer earned his promotion to California in 1968 after
leading the Texas League in home runs (28) and RBIs (96)
for El Paso. A smooth-fielding first baseman with a Golden
Glove, Jim established an A.L. record for the highest
fielding percentage (.995) by a first baseman in a career.

Early in '73 Jim was sent to the Rangers. Before it was
all over he would also see action with the White Sox, Yankees, and A's. During the 1977 season, Jim had two 8-RBI
games for the White Sox. One came in early May when the
Chisox demolished the Indians 18-2.

With the Yankees in '79 he batted .288 and belted 23
homers in only 106 games. Jim closed with the A's in '82 at
.250.

His grandfather, Ben Spencer, played with the Washington Senators in 1913.

SPIEZIO, Ed
Furniture and appliance business
Joliet, IL

On April 8, 1969, the San Diego Padres played their first game ever in the history of their franchise. In the fifth inning of the game, Ed Spiezio hit a home run off the Astros' Don Wilson for the first base hit in Padres' history.

Spiezio was with the Cards (1964–68), Padres (1969–72) and White Sox ('72). The third baseman played a backup role for the N.L. pennant-winning Cardinals in '67 and '68, participating off the bench in World Series competition those years. .238

SPINKS, Scipio
Houston Astros' scout
Oklahoma City, OK

When Scipio was around there was a certain kind of electricity in the air. He was colorful and had the ability to hum that seed. But everything came unplugged after a brief (1969–73) career with the Astros and Cardinals.

The cousin of former pitcher Wayne Simpson, Scipio was blazing on May 8, 1969, when he hurled a no-hitter for Oklahoma City (American Association), but lost the game, 2-1, to Omaha on eight walks and his own throwing error. 7-11

SPRAGUE, Ed
Owner of the Stockton team in the California League

Unlike the majority of big leaguers who have mediocre careers, Ed did not fade into obscurity. He was the subject of a lengthy feature story in *Sports Illustrated* as the owner of the Stockton team in the California League, while his wife had become the owner of the Lodi Club in the same league.

Ed was around the majors as a pitcher from 1968–76 with the A's, Reds, Cards, and Brewers.

He was discovered by a scout while playing catch one day in the Army. The scout was impressed with Sprague's

live arm and enrolled him in Dick Howser's baseball
school in Florida. His grades were good and he was subsequently signed by the Cardinals. The 6'4" right-hander
was later drafted by the A's, the team he first came up
with. On July 28, 1968, the rookie hurler was given a
"day" in his honor by his friends from nearby Hayward
where he lived.   17-23

SPRIGGS, George
    Operates a school bus service
    Tracy's Landing, MD

We're sure you remember the popular movie and hit song
of the mid-Sixties, *Georgie Girl.* Well, meet Georgie
Spriggs who was around between stops in the minors with
the Pirates and Royals (1965–70).
   The speedy flychaser was voted MVP of the American
Association in 1970, but was not really able to cut the pie
in the big arena as he departed with a .191 mark overall.

SPROUT, Bob
    Plant manager at A.M.P., an electrical supply manu-
    facturing company
    Lancaster, PA

Baseball has sometimes been referred to as the art of the
instant. It was real instant for Bob—one game. The 6'1"
southpaw was just 19 years old when he had his chance
with the Los Angeles Angels in 1961. He lasted four innings, allowed two runs, and was not involved in the decision.

STAEHLE, Marv
    State Farm insurance agent
    Buffalo Grove, IL

If you followed baseball in the 1960s you could be pretty
sure the leaves would soon change when Marv appeared in
box scores since he was one of those guys who experienced
several September callups. Some years he could have been

called "Mr. September" with such lofty batting averages
as .429, .412, and .400. Then there were years he looked
like "Miss September" struggling with averages like .111
and .133. From 1964–71 Marv occupied a spot on the
White Sox, Expos, and Braves' rosters.   .207

STAFFORD, Bill
   Vice-president for Wendy's Hamburgers
   Plymouth, MI

In 1961–62 Bill was an important cog in the Yankees' two
World Championship seasons, going 14-9 each year. On
the final day of the '61 season he shut out the Red Sox, 1-0,
on October 1st with the game's only run coming on Roger
Maris's historic 61st homer. In Game Three of the '61
Series against the Reds, Stafford pitched well into the seventh inning of a 3-2 Yankee victory, but was not involved
in the decision. The game was won on Maris's ninth-inning
blast. The next year Stafford went the distance to beat San
Francisco in the third game of the Fall Classic with
Maris's single driving in two runs.
   Bill was never able to capture those numbers again although he did go 5-0 in '64 with the Pinstripers. His last
two years ('66–'67) were spent with Kansas City.   43-40

STAHL, Larry
   Employed with the Peabody Coal Company
   Smithton, IL

Playing for the Kansas City A's in 1966, Larry once hit a
503-foot moon shot off Jose Santiago of the Red Sox. It was
the longest homer ever hit at the Kansas City Park by a
left handed hitter. But tape measure jobs and fancy batting averages were really not part of Larry's portfolio. A
minor league beast who hit .366 at Jacksonville and .336
at Salt Lake City, Larry was quite tame in the majors,
swatting .232 from 1964–73 with the A's, Mets, Padres,
and Reds.

STALLARD, Tracy
    Coal business sales representative
    Herald, VA

Tracy carved his niche in baseball history on Oct. 1, 1961, when he gave up home run No. 61 to Roger Maris. It would be nice to write that Tracy deserves to be remembered for more, but with a 30-57 career mark, including a league-leading 20 losses for the Mets in '64, he generally isn't. But it should be noted that Stallard pitched well the day he surrendered Maris's immortal clout as the four-bagger was the only run of the game.

    If anybody had a knack of being in the wrong place at the wrong time it was Tracy. He was the losing pitcher for the Mets in the marathon 7-hour, 23-minute game against the Giants on May 31, 1964. The luckless right-hander happened to be on the mound the day Jim Bunning hurled a perfect game against the Mets.

    Stallard did win once in a while. In a 1963 game for the Mets, he beat the Reds, 4-1, in Cincinnati. The Mets went on to lose the next 22 consecutive games. But on July 30, 1963, he was the winning pitcher against the Dodgers halting the horrendous streak. The 5-1 victory came on Mets' manager Casey Stengel's 73rd birthday. Ironically, the Pirates lost 22 in a row in 1890 the year of Stengel's birth.

    When the sun set, Tracy had pitched with the Red Sox (1960–62), Mets ('63–'64), and Cardinals ('65–'66).

STANEK, Al
    Senior buyer for Hamilton Standard
    Holyoke, MA

How many of us get the chance to play with our boyhood idols? Al Stanek did when he pitched 11 games for the San Francisco Giants in 1963 and was a teammate of Billy Pierce, his childhood hero.

    The next year Al led the P.C.L. in strikeouts (220) pitching for Tacoma.

STANGE, Lee
Boston Red Sox minor league pitching coach

Only 17 pitchers in baseball history have registered four strikeouts in an inning. Lee Stange is one of them. Pitching for the Indians on Sept. 2, 1964, he whiffed four Senators in the seventh inning.

"The Stinger" was an all-around athlete at Drake University where he played the three major sports. A knee injury ended his career as a quarterback on the gridiron and forced him to choose baseball as his vocation.

Stange first arrived with the Twins in '61 after winning 20 games in the Carolina League the year before. His best year in Minnesota came in '63 when he was 12-5 with a 2.62 ERA.

In the mid-Sixties he was employed in Cleveland before being traded in June of '66 to the Red Sox for Dick Radatz. Lee did some unheralded, but steady work for the Red Sox in their surprising 1967 A.L. championship season. Used both as a starter and a reliever, he won eight games while compiling a 2.77 ERA, the best of the staff.

The following year he was the Bosox' top reliever. It all ended in 1970 with the White Sox at 62-61

STANLEY, Fred
Oakland A's director of instruction

Fred had the reputation as one of the best little utilityman in the A.L. during a good part of his career. He first arrived with the Pilots in 1969 and went with the franchise to Milwaukee in 1970. After stops with Cleveland and San Diego, he settled in with the Yankees as a utility infielder in 1973.

As a member of the Yankees, "Chicken" participated in three ALCS and three World Series. In the '76 LCS against the Royals, he was 5-for-15 in five games.

Primarily a shortstop, Fred tied a big league mark on April 29, 1975, when he started five double plays from his shortstop position.

He finished with Oakland in 1982.   .216

STANLEY, Mickey
Manufacturer's representative
West Bloomfield, MI

Although Fred Stanley played 14 years as a shortstop, outfielder Mickey Stanley got more publicity concerning the
seven games he played for the Tigers in the 1968 World
Series when he moved into the shortstop position to replace light-hitting Ray Oyler to allow veteran Al Kaline,
who had been injured, to join Jim Northrup and Willie
Horton in the Detroit outfield. The move by Manager
Mayo Smith was a good one. Mickey committed two errors,
but at times his fielding was termed "brilliant."

A crackerjack centerfielder, Stanley was named four
times to the A.L. All-Star fielding team by *The Sporting
News*. On July 13, 1973, he tied an A.L. record with 11
putouts from his centerfield position. In both the '68 and
'70 seasons, he went the entire year without committing
an error. In 1976 his .992 career fielding average was the
highest in M.L. history by an outfielder.

The Grand Rapids, MI, native hit .248 from 1964–78
with the Tigers. His best season at the plate came in '71
when he hit .292.

STARGELL, Willie
Pittsburgh Pirates' minor league hitting instructor

If the Lord ever created the perfect leader for a baseball
team it was Willie Stargell, who performed from 1962–
1982. Whether it was a stern word, a pat on the back, or
just plain fatherly advice, "Pops" was there when needed.

On the field his bat did the talking. On May 22, 1968,
Willie had three homers, a double and single to lead the Pirates over the Cubs, 13-6, at Wrigley Field. On Aug. 1,
1970, he walloped two homers and three doubles in Atlanta to tie the major league record for most extra base
hits in a game. Final Score: Pirates 20, Braves 10.

The Dodgers' weren't very happy when Stargell came to
town. On June 24, 1965, Willie powered three four-baggers
and a double in a 13-3 blowout, making him the first
player ever to hit three homers in a game at Dodger Sta-

dium. He is the only player to ever hit a ball completely out of Dodger Stadium into the parking lot, and he did it twice (Aug. 6, 1969 and May 8, 1973). Stargell showed off his power at home also. Only 18 homers were ever hit over the right field roof at Forbes Field and Willie accounted for seven of them.

The all-time Pirates leader in home runs (475), RBIs (1,540) and extra base hits (953), he combined with Roberto Clemente to smash a collective 462 home runs from 1962–72. "Pops" led the N.L. in roundtrippers in 1971 (48) and 1973 (44). In '71 he started the year at a torrid pace, smashing 11 home runs in the month of April to join Graig Nettles and Mike Schmidt as the only players to smack 11 homers in April. On Sept. 17, 1973 Willie had four long hits (2 doubles, triple, homer) for the fourth time, a N.L. record.

On March 7, 1979, Willie hit the first spring training home run of the year against a Japanese League team. He also hit the final homer of the year seven months later in the seventh and final game of the World Series as the Bucs beat the Orioles. Although plagued by an arthritic knee late in his career, Stargell was a terror in the '79 Series, hitting .400 with 3 homers and 7 RBIs. The '79 season was not Willie's greatest statistically, but it was one in which the recognition of his great career finally came as he was honored as the Major League Player of the Year and the Man of the Year by *The Sporting News* and was also named co-MVP of the National League by the Baseball Writers Association.

His number 8 was the sixth retired by the Pirates. He joins Billy Meyer (1), Danny Murtaugh (40) and three other Bucs who he will some day join in the Hall of Fame: Pie Traynor (20), Roberto Clemente (21), and Honus Wagner (33).

Willie has done volunteer work for Job Corps and Neighborhood Youth Corps in conjunction with Pittsburgh's war on poverty.   .282

STARRETTE, Herm
    San Francisco Giants' pitching coach in 1984

Pitching for Aberdeen in 1958, Herm recorded a 30-inning
victory over a young St. Cloud hurler named Gaylord
Perry. Nothing so unusual would happen to him on the
major league level.

    From 1958–66 Starrette attempted to crack the Ori-
oles' staff as a reliever, but except for three chances
(1963–65) he spent his time attempting to perfect his
craft in the minors. His 27-game trip, all in relief,
terminated at 1-1.

STAUB, Rusty
    Active with New York Mets; owns Rusty's Restaurant
    New York, NY

This gourmet chef cooked up some pretty impressive numbers during his stay, which began in 1963. For instance,
Rusty is the only player to play 500 or more games for four
different teams (Colt .45s/Astros, Expos, Tigers, and Mets).
He is also the only player to accumulate at least 500 basehits for four different teams.

    Daniel Staub was nicknamed "Rusty" by the nurses at
the hospital of his birth for his auburn hair. Staub signed a
reported $100,000 bonus with Houston in 1961 along with
his older brother, who never made it to the majors. The
pair had led their New Orleans team to the American Legion National Championship in 1960 beating Dave Mc-
Nally and his Billings, MT, team.

    Rusty's first home run in the majors came on June 3,
1963, a two-run shot off Don Drysdale, giving Houston a
2-1 victory over the Dodgers at Colt Stadium. His time
with the Astros was well spent as he was named the team's
MVP in '66 and '67.

    A favorite with Montreal fans, Staub was labeled "Le
Grand Orange" during his Canadian stay from 1969–71.
The guy with the fiery red hair and freckles belted 59
homers and batted a combined .296 with the Expos.

    On April 6, 1972, Rusty was traded to the Mets for in-
fielders Mike Jorgensen, Tim Foli and outfielder Ken

Singleton. In 1975 he was traded to the Tigers for Mickey Lolich and for the next four years was used basically as a designated hitter. He then made brief stops in Montreal and Texas before returning to the Mets in 1980.

During the '83 season Rusty collected 24 pinch-hits for the Mets, a club record. At one point during the season he had eight consecutive pinch-hits, tying Dave Philly's record.

His lone World Series was in '73 with the Mets and he responded by hitting .423 (11-for-26).

His one home run in 1984 allowed him to join Ty Cobb as the only players to homer before their 20th birthday and after their 40th.   .279

STEEVENS, Morrie
Property tax consultant for Klein and Barenblat
San Antonio, TX

Morrie lost both of his big league decisions in 22 games while with the Cubs in '62 and Phils in '64–'65. Steevens had some glossy moments in the minors, hurling no-hitters in the Northern League and P.C.L. At San Antonio he won 15 games in the Texas League in '62.

"Pitching to Stan Musial, who was my idol as a kid, was my highlight," says Morrie.

STENHOUSE, Dave
Baseball coach at Brown University

Dave Stenhouse has the credentials to lecture on the subject of patience since he waited until age 28 to debut in the big top.

A graduate of the University of Rhode Island with a degree in industrial engineering, Dave spent seven patient years working his way up through the Reds' minor league organization. He then was involved in an off season trade to the Senators.

His rookie year in '62 was a pleasant one as he became the ace of the Senators' staff. With a 10-4 record in mid-season, he was named to start the second All-Star Game

that summer. He was still in storyland on August 5th
when he was honored with a "day" at Fenway Park in Boston by 1,000 fans of his native Westerly, RI.

But Dave crashed after the All-Star break, going just 1-8
to finish his rookie campaign at 11-12. Overall he closed at
16-28 when it ended in '64.

His son Mike is currently an outfielder with the
Minnesota Twins while another son, Dave, is in the minors.

STEPHEN, "Buzz"
    Manages Porterville Monument Works and Swim-
    ming Pool Supplies
    Porterville, CA

In 1969 Edwin "Buzz" Aldrin became the second man to
set foot on the moon in the July 22nd Apollo XI lunar mission. The year before Louis "Buzz" Stephen set foot on
major league soil when he made two starts for the Twins,
going 1-1.

That was it for "Buzz" as the Fresno State product went
to the Pilots in the expansion draft but never again played
on major league ground.

STEPHENSON, Jerry
    Los Angeles Dodgers' scout
    Fullerton, CA

In 1964 Notre Dame quarterback John Huarte was the
winner of the Heisman Trophy. As a high school quarterback in Anaheim, CA, his favorite receiver was Jerry
Stephenson, whose father Joe was a catcher with the
Giants, Cubs, and White Sox in the mid-1940s.

Jerry, a hard-throwing right-hander, struggled in the
minors in 1963 at 4-20. But he was given a brief shot
with the Bosox in September. The bulk of his time came
in parts of four seasons (1965–68) with the Red Sox. His
next stops were with the Pilots ('69) and Dodgers
('70).   8-19

STEPHENSON, Johnny
Baseball coach at Southwestern Louisiana University

Johnny Stephenson came up with the Mets in 1964. That year he was the final out in Jim Bunning's perfect game against the Mets. The third baseman-outfielder switched to catching and was behind the plate in and out of the majors with the Mets, Cubs, Giants, and Angels for 10 seasons through 1973.   .216

STEWART, Jimmy
Cincinnati Reds' advance scout

You might recall that Jimmy Stewart, the actor, starred in such 1960s movies as *Mr. Hobbs Takes a Vacation* and *Man Who Shot Liberty Valance.*

Jimmy Stewart, the baseball player, appeared primarily in a utility and pinch-hitting role with the Cubs (1963–67), White Sox ('67), Reds (1969–71), and Astros ('72–'73).

Stewart, who became the Cubs' regular second baseman in 1964 following the untimely death of Kenny Hubbs, played in a utility role in 1970 for the N.L. pennant-winning Reds as he hit .267 in 101 games playing all over the field. As a pinch-hitter Jimmy went 13-for-39 (.333). His one homer that year was a 3-run pinch-swat to defeat Tom Seaver, 7-5, at Shea Stadium.

Jimmy is a graduate of Austin Peay State College in Tennessee where he also played basketball.

STIGMAN, Dick
Vice-president and manager of the Continental Loose
Leaf Company
Minneapolis, MN

When contacted, Dick supplied us with a pamphlet titled *How to Be Born Again.* He also stated, "It's the most important thing that has ever happened to me."

Dick Stigman, the father of nine children (ages 8 to 21), has certainly touched base in the various corners of life. His baseball existance consisted of a seven-year retreat with the Indians, Twins, and Red Sox from 1960–66. It ob-

viously was not the most important thing in his life, but he
did work up an overall 46-54 record. He also was selected
to the A.L. All-Star team as a rookie. Despite finishing his
freshman season at 5-11, the southpaw chucker was
named to the Topps Rookie All-Star team.

At the start of the '62 campaign, Dick went to the Twins
along with Vic Power for Pedro Ramos. He went through a
born-again baseball revival in Minnesota, going 12-5 in
'62 following up with a 15-15 season.

STILLWELL, Ron
High school teacher/baseball coach at California Lu-
theran College
Thousands Oaks, CA

Eye damage which affected his vision, along with other assorted injuries, led to the aborted 14-game career and premature retirement of this infielder, who hit .211 with the
Senators in 1961–62.

He was signed by Washington to a reported $40,000
bonus out of USC after he helped lead the Trojans to the
1961 NCAA title. His son Kurt may fulfill his father's
dream of a more extended career. A shortstop, Kurt was selected by the Reds in the first round of the 1983 free agent
draft, the second player chosen overall.

STINSON, Bob
Landscaping business and shipyard employee
Seattle, WA

"Scrap Iron" was the nickname given to Clint Courtney,
the hard-nosed bespectacled catcher who performed with
several teams during the 1950s. Gorrell Robert Stinson
was tagged with the same moniker early in his career by
Fresco Thompson of the Dodgers' front office because of
Stinson's ability to bounce back within a few days after
suffering a broken jaw in 1967 at Albuquerque.

Originally a centerfielder in the Dodgers' organization,
Bob first arrived from Spokane in 1969 in a late-season recall. After stops with the Cards, Astros, and Expos, the
switch-hitting backstop shared the receiving in Kansas

City in '75 and '76, helping the Royals to their first A.L. West title. His final four years were spent with the expansion Mariners.

STONE, Gene
Duarte, CA

Everyday People by Sly and the Family Stone went to the top of the charts in 1969, the same year this first baseman was attempting to become an everyday person with the Phillies. Unfortunately Gene "danced to the music" of only 18 games, hitting .214.

STONE, George
Baseball and football coach at Farmerville H.S.
Ruston, LA

This 6'3" left-hander, who played college basketball at Louisiana Tech, scrapped his jump shot in favor of a career in baseball. Pitching for the Braves (1967–72) and Mets (1973–75), he went 60-57 while playing a key role in helping both clubs to division titles.

In '69, he won a career-high 13 contests including a crucial 4-3 victory in the final week of the season in which his only home run in his nine-year career was the game winner.

George was traded to the Mets after the '72 campaign. He proceeded to have his most effective year (12-3; 2.80). In post-season play in '73 he allowed just one run in seven innings against the Reds. He was a starter in the fourth game of the NLCS and won, 2-1, in 12 innings at Cincinnati. In the World Series against Oakland, the sizzling Mets' hurler pitched three scoreless innings of relief in two appearances.

STONE, Ron
Insurance company general manager
Eugene, OR

Says Stone, "After leaving baseball, I moved to Eugene for the great outdoors. I'm an avid hunter and fisherman. I'm also a licensed pilot, and am currently single. I enjoyed my years in baseball, but it's over and I'm enjoying life today, and making more money than when I played."

Signed by the Kansas City A's in 1963, Ron had a clause in his contract which stipulated he would receive a $5,000 bonus when he made it to the majors for 60 days. After hitting .273 in 26 games in 1966, he was sent down to the minors on his 59th day.

Three years later the outfielder returned to play from 1969–72 with the Phillies winding up with a .241 average.

STONEMAN, Bill
Assistant to Montreal Expos' club president John McHale

What do Grover Cleveland Alexander, Lefty Grove, Dizzy Dean, Bob Gibson, Whitey Ford, and Don Drysdale have in common? Answer: All are Hall of Famers, but none ever threw a no-hitter.

On the other hand, William Hambly Stoneman III, with a career mark of 54-85 as a member of the Cubs, Expos, and Angels (1967–74), will never get any votes for the Hall of Fame but did hurl a no-hitter. Wait a minute—make that two!

Bill went to the expansion Expos in 1969 and earned a spot in the starting rotation. He lost his first two starts so ineptly, no one could have guessed what was to come next. But Bill then took the mound at Philadelphia and not only picked up his first complete game, but no-hit the Phils, 7-0, fanning eight and allowing five walks. He followed that performance with a six-hit, 2-0 shutout over Bob Gibson and the Cardinals.

Stoneman's best year was '71 when he went 17-16 and led the N.L. in games started with 39. In '72 he fell to 12-14, but had his best ERA at 2.98. On Oct. 2, 1972, Bill pitched his second no-hitter, a game which was very similar to his first no-hitter. He beat the Mets by a 7-0 score with 9 strikeouts and 7 walks.

STOTTLEMYRE, Mel
>   New York Mets' pitching coach; owns a sporting goods
>   store
>   Yakima, WA

Brought up in 1964 during mid-season, Mel helped the
Yankees to their 14th A.L. flag in 16 years as he went 9-3.
On September 26th the young right-hander hurled a 7-0,
2-hit shutout at Washington and went 5-for-5 at the plate
in the same game. In the World Series he defeated Bob
Gibson, 8-3, in Game Two. "Stott" made two other starts.
After a no-decision effort in the fifth game, his third
matchup against "Gibby" came in the seventh game
which the Cards won, 7-5.

The next two seasons were Jekyll and Hyde years for
Mel. A three-time 20-game winner, his first came in '65
(20-9), leading the league in complete games (18) and innings pitched (291). A good-hitting pitcher, Mel had the
most memorable of his seven career homers on July 25,
1965, an inside-the-park grand slam off Bill Monbouquette
of the Red Sox in a 6-3 victory at Yankee Stadium.

Durable, consistent, and a good fielding pitcher, Mel
rarely missed an assignment between 1965 and '73, averaging between 35 and 39 starts every year. At age 33 a
torn rotator cuff abruptly ended his career. It was over for
the man who helped to maintain the prestigious tradition
of the Yankees during a dark era. He was 164-139, with a
2.97 ERA. In his lifetime 360 appearances, he relieved
only four times. Mel owns the A.L. record of 272 starts
without a relief job.

A few years ago, Mel's 10-year-old son Jason died of leukemia. This kind of personal battle is much tougher to
handle for a man than facing the Killebrews, Yastrzem-
skis, and Kalines. He says, "This has given me a new per-
spective on what's important, and maybe the maturity to
laugh at the small things that go wrong in life."

STOWE, Hal
    Owns a seafood restaurant, Stowe's Fish Camp
    Gastonia, NC

Hal once won a game without throwing a pitch. It was on
July 14, 1964, when, pitching for Charlotte (Southern
League), he entered the game in the ninth inning and
picked the runner off first base for the third out. His team
scored the winning run in the bottom of the ninth and he
was credited with the win.
    Considered one of the finest pitching prospects to join
the Yankees since Whitey Ford, Hal was signed out of
Clemson University. However, the southpaw was limited
to just one inning in relief for the Yanks in 1960.

STROUD, Ed
    Housing Inspector in Community Development for
    the city of Warren, OH

In 1962 the story of prisoner Robert Stroud was told in the
movie *Birdman of Alcatraz*. That year Speedy Ed Stroud
began his term in professional baseball after spending four
years in the Army.
    Known as both "The Creeper" and "The Streak," Ed
was a terror on the bases in the minors, leading three different leagues in stolen bases.
    Stroud surfaced with the White Sox briefly in '66, then
was traded to the Senators early in '67. For the next few
years he was a mainstay in the Washington outfield before
finishing his six-year term back with the Pale Hose in
1971. A .237 career hitter, Ed's best year was in 1970
when he hit .266 with 29 stolen bases.
    In May of 1968 Frank Howard went on one of the great-
est home run streaks in baseball history walloping ten
four-baggers in 20 official at-bats over a six game stretch.
During that period Ed banged out four homers in eight
games which went virtually unnoticed. While "Hondo"
went on to belt 44 that year, Ed settled for the four he hit
during his eight-game run.

STUBING, Larry
    California Angels' hitting instructor

There are those who made a career out of minor league life. Larry is one of those guys, a veteran of long bus rides and all-night diners since 1956.

Known as "Moose," the 6'3", 220-pound strongboy looked to be on his way to the bright lights in '64 when he whacked 35 homers and 120 RBIs for El Paso in the Texas League. But his only shot in the majors came in '67 with the Angels. Larry sputtered, going hitless in all five at-bats, striking out four times.

SUAREZ, Ken
    Sales manager for Turbine Cassings
    Arlington, TX

This rifle-armed catcher was out of Florida State University where he won All-American honors. Ken brought his gun to the big leagues with the Kansas City A's, Indians, and Rangers from 1966–73. A lifetime .227 hitter, Ken played the role of the spoiler on June 16, 1973. Playing for the Rangers against the Orioles, he broke up a Jim Palmer no-hitter with one out in the ninth after Palmer had retired 25 straight batters.

SUDAKIS, Bill
    Owns the Majestic Trophy store
    Fountain Valley, CA

When "Suds" first came up to the Dodgers in '68 he arrived in St. Louis after a tiring all-day journey from Albuquerque. Dodger manager Walt Alston said to Bill, "Get into that uniform in a hurry—you're batting fifth." The Texas League Player of the Year went out and calmly singled in a run and homered, leading L.A. to a 3-0 victory over the Cardinals and the Dodgers' nemesis, Larry Jaster.

The next game he got two hits including a triple. During his first week he hit a torrid .444. He finished the year hitting .276 in 24 games down the stretch and looked to be the answer to the Dodgers' revolving door at third base.

Following the '68 season, Bill visited his eye doctor because he was experiencing difficulty with his contact lenses. "No wonder," his doctor told him, "you've been wearing your left lens in your right eye and vice-versa."

With his contact lenses hooked up properly, he hit .234 in his jaunt that lasted until 1975 with the Dodgers, Mets, Rangers, Yankees, Angels, and Indians.

SUKLA, Ed
Scout with the Major League Scouting Bureau
Santa Ana, CA

The Los Angeles Angels officially became the California Angels on September 2, 1965. The next season they played their home games at Anaheim Stadium. On Arpil 20, 1966, the Angels won their first game at the "Big A," a 4-3 decision over the White Sox. Ed was the winner in relief of Dean Chance that day.

"Slats" was with the Angels between 1964–66, at which time appearing in 39 games out of the bullpen, going 3-5.

SULLIVAN, John
Toronto Blue Jays' coach

Hitless in eight at-bats in brief trials with the Tigers in '63 and '64, John was in the Bengals' opening day lineup to start the '65 campaign, replacing catcher Bill Freehan who was out with an ailing back. It turned out to be John's party as he homered off Wes Stock of the Kansas City A's.

In 1973 he began his minor league managing career by leading Kingsport to the Appalachian League title. In 1975 he piloted Waterloo to the Midwest League pennant with a 93-35 overall mark, a modern-day record for professional baseball.

John led Omaha to a division title in '77 and copped the pennant the following season. His high grades brought him to the Royals and Braves as a coach before his current position with the Blue Jays.   .228

SUTHERLAND, Darrell
    Employed with the First National Bank of Oregon
    Portland, OR

The basketball player of the year in Southern California in
1959, Darrell went on to Stanford University where he
graduated in 1963. The 6'4" right-hander was 10-1 at Buffalo (I.L.) in '64, then surfaced with the Mets where he
picked up his checks until 1966.
    Darrell budgeted the remainder of his time with the In-
dians in '68, finishing 5-4 in 62 games. His brother, Gene,
was a member of the UCLA NCAA championship basketball teams in the Lew Alcindor era. Another brother,
Gary, listed below, had a longer stay in the majors.

SUTHERLAND, Gary
    Cleveland Indians' scout
    Monrovia, CA

Actor Donald Sutherland has been an ardent fan of the
Montreal Expos and is often seen watching the team's
games. From 1969–71 he had a namesake in the Expos'
lineup as Gary was generally the team's regular second
baseman in their first three seasons.
    An excellent utilityman, "Suds's" career extended from
1966–78 when he wore the threads of the Phillies, Expos,
Astros, Tigers, Brewers, Padres, and Cardinals.   .243

SUTTON, Don
    Active with Milwaukee Brewers in 1984; 1985 season
    status not settled

The all-time Dodger leader in strikeouts (2,652) and victories (230), Don arrived with the Dodgers in '66 after
prepping only one year in the minors where he combined a
23-7 mark with Santa Barbara and Albuquerque.
    Named *The Sporting News* Rookie Pitcher of the Year in
1966, Don went 12-12 and racked up 209 strikeouts, the
most by an N.L. rookie chucker since Grover Cleveland
Alexander in 1911. The young right-hander then experienced three successive losing seasons.

In 1970 Don went 15-13 and was over .500 every season
until 1979, peaking at 21-10 in '76 and twice winning 19
games. Sutton has five one-hitters to his credit, third best
on the all-time N.L. list. He still ranks as the Dodgers' all-
time leader in eight pitching departments and only he and
Don Drysdale have won 200 or more games in Dodger blue.

On June 24, 1983, Sutton notched his 3,000th career
strikeout, placing him in a select group of hurlers. During
the '84 season, he became the only pitcher in M.L. history
to strike out 100 or more batters in 19 consecutive seasons.

In NLCS competition he is 3-1 and is 2-2 in World Series
play. Through '84 he was 280-218.

SWOBODA, Ron
    Sports announcer for KTVK–TV in Phoenix, AZ

"Rocky" symbolized the Mets' unpredictable image. Hard-
working, ungraceful, and competitive, he kidnapped the
hearts of Mets' fans during his stay at Shea Stadium.

Swoboda's story began in 1963 when he signed for a reported $35,000 bonus with the Mets out of the University
of Maryland. He impressed manager Casey Stengel in
spring training when he hit a ball over the training camp
fence and through an office window. Casey was quoted, "If
a man can hit a ball over buildings he can make my team."
However, Ron was sent down when as Casey noted, "He
commenced to stop hitting balls over buildings."

"Rocky" became a semi-regular in the Mets' outfield in
1965 and showed promise with 19 homers as a rookie.

A lifetime .242 hitter, his career-high .281 was in '67.
But it was in 1969, when he hit just .235 with nine homers,
that he would become the darling of Flushing with his
timely heroics.

On Sept. 13, 1969, "Rocky" hit the first grand-slammer
of his career in the eighth inning of a 5-2 win over the Pirates. Two nights later Steve Carlton fanned a record 19
Mets, but the Mets "amazingly" won 4-3 on a pair of
homers by Swoboda.

He was 6-for-15 in the World Series against the Orioles,
with a double in the eighth inning of the fifth and final
game as the Mets rallied for a 5-3 win.

It would be difficult to underestimate the still reverberating excitement from his circus sliding catch of Brooks Robinson's liner to right field in the ninth inning of Game Four as the unforgettable catch kept the Orioles from going ahead and enabled the Mets to score a 2-1, 10-inning victory.

A couple of years later he found himself with the Expos, then rode out in Yankee pinstripes where it was over in 1973.

T

TALBOT, Fred
        Construction worker
        Falls Church, VA

In Jim Bouton's book *Ball Four Plus Five*, Bouton wrote about Talbot: "When I telephoned Fred at his home in Virginia to ask what he was doing he said, 'Well, I'm still living,' and hung up." Talbot's shortness with Bouton might have had something to do with an incident that occurred in 1969 when Fred was a member of the Pilots.

On July 9th that year Talbot connected for a grand-slam off Eddie Fisher and the Angels. Because of a local "Home Run for the Money" contest, it made an Oregon resident $25,000. Fred soon received a telegram telling him a check for $5,000 would be on his way from the lucky winner. However, it turned out to be one of several jokes played on Fred by Bouton that summer.

Talbot arrived in 1963 for one game with the White Sox before going on tour in the A.L. until 1970 with the Kansas City A's, Yankees, Pilots, and Oakland A's. 38-56

TALTON, "Tim"
        Member of North Carolina Conservation and Development Commission
        Pikeville, NC

Herbert Khaury, better known as Tiny Tim, became a successful novelty artist in the late Sixties and was a frequent guest on *Laugh-In* and the *Tonight Show*.

Nobody ever referred to Marion Lee Talton, a 6'3", 200-pound first baseman-catcher as tiny, but he was known by the name "Tim." It would be convenient to say that "Tim" tiptoed through the A.L., while Tiny Tim "tiptoed through the tulips," but in reality Talton's steps, though not long, were loud and clear.

In 1966 Tim hit .340 in 37 games with the Kansas City A's, but after one more season he was gone with an overall .295 avg. in 83 games including a solid .333 as a pinch-hitter with 19 hits in 57 at-bats.

TARTABULL, Jose
    Manager at Sarasota (Gulf Coast League) in Astros'
    organization

One of the refined parts that made the Red Sox machine mesh in '67 was this Cuban-born outfielder who spent nine years in the A.L. with the Kansas City A's, Red Sox and the A's once again, in Oakland.

Jose hit .277 as a K.C. rookie in 1962. A .261 career hitter, Jose hit .312 as a part-time player in Kansas City in 1965. With the Red Sox in '67, Jose participated in all seven games of the World Series against the Cardinals, going 2-for-13.

Tartabull's son, Danny, is a highly regarded shortstop in the Seattle Mariners' organization.

TATUM, Jarvis
    Self-employed (garden work)
    Fresno, CA

California baseball crowds are known to exit early, and so are some players, like Jarvis Tatum.

This speedy outfielder, who was once clocked in the 100-yard dash in under 10 seconds, hit .232 in 102 games for the Angels from 1968–70.

TATUM, Ken
   Vice-principal at Pelham H.S.
   Pelham, AL

After pitching Mississippi State to a couple of SEC championships, Ken climbed through the Angels' chain as a starting pitcher and joined the Angels in late May of 1969. He must have thought he was in fantasyland, going 7-2 plus 22 saves in 45 appearances. His ERA was a dreamlike 1.36 and even had two separate streaks of 24 consecutive scoreless innings. Ken also hit .286 and a pair of home runs.
   The following campaign he was again effective, winning seven games while saving 17, but at the end of the season he was traded to Boston in a deal which saw Tony Conigliaro come to Anaheim.
   Plagued by a sore arm, he never managed to regain his old form and was gone in 1974 after a stint with the White Sox.   16-12

TAYLOR, Carl
   Hair stylist
   Venice, FL

"Hey—You're Carl Taylor!"
   The half-brother of slugger Boog Powell, Carl Means Taylor was a catcher and outfielder and also dabbled in the infield with the Pirates, Cardinals, and Royals from 1968–73. After signing a reported $50,000 bonus in '62, he worked his way up in the Pirates' chain.
   Carl made his first start on May 10, 1968, as Roberto Clemente's sub in right field and got two hits that helped beat the Phillies. In '69 he looked like Clemente as he hit .348 in 104 games and proved to be a reliable pinch-hitter, going 17-for-41 off the bench.
   Taylor picked up the nickname "Senator" after accusing the Pirates of not playing him regularly because of politics.   .266

TAYLOR, Chuck
        Owner of the Western Auto and Ace Hardware Store
        in Smyrna, TN

As a rookie with the Cardinals in 1969, Chuck went 7-5 in
his role as a spot starter and reliever. The remainder of his
eight-year jog was spent primarily in the bullpen.

Following brief stops with the Brewers and Mets, this
right-hander spent his last four years (1973–76) with the
Expos.   28-20

TAYLOR, Gary
        Dearborn, MI

Born in Detroit in October of '45, a few days after the Tigers won the World Series by defeating the Cubs, Gary became a member of his hometown Tigers' mound staff in
1969. The right-hander out of Central Michigan University lost his only decision in seven games.

TAYLOR, Ron
        Toronto Blue Jays' team physician

This "Diamond Doc" helped the Mets perform major surgery on the N.L. in 1969, winning nine and saving 13 in 59
trips out of the bullpen. In the NLCS he was credited with
a save for Tom Seaver in the opening game and was the
winner in the second contest. In the World Series he saved
Game Two for Jerry Koosman, a 2-1 decision over the Orioles.

        Dr. Taylor began his baseball career in 1956 in the Indi-
ans' organization while earning a degree in electrical engineering from the University of Toronto in 1961. The next
season he arrived in Cleveland. His debut on April 11,
1962, was quite unusual in that he hooked up in a 12-in-
ning scoreless duel against the Red Sox before giving up a
grand-slam to Carroll Hardy and losing, 4-0.

        The Canadian-born right-hander was traded to the Car-
dinals at the end of the season and became a workhorse in
the Cards' bullpen. In 1964 Ron went 8-4 for the World
Champions and in Game Four of the World Series, pitched

four scoreless innings against the Yankees to gain the
save in a 4-3 victory as St. Louis tied the Series up at 2-2.

Dr. Taylor made a house call with the Astros before joining the Mets in '67 where he hung his shingle for five years.

He last pitched for the Padres, winding up 45-43 in 491
games with 72 saves and a pair of World Series rings.

TENACE, Gene
Milwaukee Brewers minor league hitting instructor

Reds' pitcher Gary Nolan was given a rude welcome in the
opening game of the 1972 World Series when Gene Tenace
of the A's whacked a two-run homer in the second inning
and a bases-empty shot in the fifth off the Cincinnati ace.
It marked the first time in World Series history that a
player hit home runs in his first two World Series at-bats.
The two homers accounted for all the RBIs in a 3-2 victory
over the Reds. In Game Four Tenace homered again in another 3-2 win. In the fifth game Gene poked a three-run shot
in a 5-4 loss. He turned Riverfront Stadium into a temple of
gloom when he knocked in a pair of runs with a single and
double in the A's third 3-2 victory of the Series in Game
Seven. Tenace's rampage produced a .913 slugging percentage, a World Series record for a seven-game Series.

Gene broke in with Oakland in 1969. The next season
was spent at Iowa in the A.A. where his development as a
catcher was aided by his manager, Sherman Lollar.

Originally signed as a shortstop by the Kansas City A's,
Gene's 1972 heroics actually began in the ALCS against
Detroit, when he went only 1-for-17 but his lone hit
knocked in the winning run in a 2-1 victory that won the
A.L. pennant for Oakland.

The hero of '72 didn't make much noise in the '73 and '74
Fall Classics, but in '73 he tied a record held by Babe Ruth
when he was walked 11 times. On Sept. 1, 1974, he played
a whole game at first base for the A's without a chance in
the field.

Granted free agency in '76, Fury Gene Tenace was
signed by the Padres where he played from 1977–80 before
making stops at St. Louis and Pittsburgh.

A lifetime .241 hitter, Gene hit 201 four-baggers during
his career. The proper pronunciation is "Ten-Ah-Chee."

But Gene's grandfather many years before gave up trying to get people to use the proper Italian way of pronouncing the family name.

TEPEDINO, Frank
Sporting goods business
Hauppauge, NY

Like Jason of Jason and the Argonauts fame, Frank embarked on a quest in 1967 as a member of the Yankees. His travels also took him to Milwaukee (Brewers) and Atlanta (Braves) between 1967–75.

Originally with the Orioles' organization, this Brooklyn-born first baseman was drafted by the Yankees. In '67 he came through with pinch-hit singles in both ends of a July 4th doubleheader. The 19-year-old prospect was rewarded the next day with a ticket to Greensboro in the Carolina League.   .241

THIES, Dave
Co-owns Thies and Talle Enterprises, Inc., a real estate investments company
Edina, MN

Dave found himself on some big league real estate in 1963, losing his only decision in nine appearances for the Kansas City A's. If he has one distinction it was on April 20, 1961, when he beat Vancouver in the first professional game played in Hawaii.

Subsequent to leaving baseball in 1964 after two shoulder operations, Dave received his master's degree in industrial relations from the University of Minnesota.

THOENEN, Dick
Owns The New Past Time Tavern
Medford, OR

Dick made like Michael Jackson and beat it after working in one inning of one game for the Phillies in 1967. The 6'6" right-hander walked away without a decision.

THOMAS, Carl
> Owns a sand and gravel business
> Phoenix, AZ

There have been many sweet performers in spring training who turned sour during the regular season. Carl Thomas qualifies in such a group.

The big right-hander out of the University of Arizona was the surprise sensation of the Indians' 1960 spring training camp when he hurled 17 consecutive scoreless innings. But after four relief appearances in which he had a fat ERA of over 7.00, Carl was on the outside looking in, never to return. He did win his only decision, if that's any consolation.

THOMAS, Lee
> St. Louis Cardinals' Director of Player Development

Lee won't forget a ground-rule double he hit for the Red Sox on Easter Sunday (1965) at Fenway. When Thomas's ground-rule double hopped into and out of the right field seats, onto the field bounded a black Labrador Retriever named Chief. The friendly canine reached the ball ahead of Baltimore right fielder Curt Blefary and jumped back into the stands where he gave the ball to a youngster.

The *Boston Globe* had a verse the next day:

> A black retriever named Chief
> He really isn't a thief
> Jumped from the stands
> Showed a fast pair of fangs
> And left Blefary saying, 'Good grief!'

Lee left a few teams saying good grief during the course of his career, especially from September 1–10 (1961) as a member of the Angels when he went on a torrid stretch, 23-for-39, for a .590 pace. On September 5th he had a record-breaking day that no Angels' player has ever matched when he collected nine hits and 19 total bases in a doubleheader at Kansas City. Overall he went 9-for-11, including three homers and eight RBIs.

James Leroy "Lee" Thomas, who joined the Yankees' organization in 1954, hit .390 at Amarillo (Texas League) in 1960 then opened the '61 campaign with the Yankees. However, he was soon dealt to the expansion Angels and became a regular, hitting .284 with 24 home runs. He was even better in '62 at .290 with 26 roundtrippers and 104 RBIs.

During his trek which lasted through '68, he wore the garb of the Yanks, Angels, Red Sox, Braves, Cubs, and Astros.

TIANT, Luis
    Owns chicken farm in La Piedad, Mexico; New York Yankees' scout in Mexico

Luis was a fun guy who had the ability to loosen up a team during sensitive moments. Once while he was a member of the Red Sox, Tommy Harper pulled a bonehead play in the outfield that led to a Boston defeat. Needless to say, the locker room was a morbid chamber following the game. Then came Luis to the rescue. He got up off his chair and went to the john. He flushed the toilet and yelled, "Goodbye, Tommy!" The clubhouse erupted in laughter.

His book *El Tiante* tells the life story of this colorful Cuban. When he first broke into organized baseball in 1959 with the Mexico City Tigers, he looked like "El Horrible" going 5-19, but he improved steadily and found himself in Cleveland knickers in 1964 after a 15-1 mark at Portland (P.C.L.). In his first major league start he shut out the Yankees on three hits and finished at 10-4 in his maiden season.

The 1968 season was one in which Denny McLain, Bob Gibson, and Don Drysdale delivered some remarkable performances. Don't forget "El Tiante," who went 21-9 with a 1.60 ERA, the best in the American League. He also racked up a league-leading nine shutouts and had a string of 41 consecutive scoreless innings. His last whitewashing came on September 25th as he fired a one-hitter against the Yankees, the only base hit a two-out single in the first inning by Mickey Mantle in Mantle's final game ever at Yankee Stadium. Another of his shutouts was a 1-0,

10-inning win over the Twins, in which he established an A.L. record for most strikeouts (19) in a 10-inning contest.

After falling to 9-20 in '69, he was traded to the Twins. It looked like Luis was about to wash out, but he battled back after a short visit to the minors.

In Beantown he was voted the A.L. Comeback Player of the Year in '72 by *The Sporting News* going 15-6 with a league-leading 1.91 ERA, a year the cigar-chomping right-hander hurled four consecutive shutouts. Three times he was a 20-game winner in the Hub.

In 1975 Luis went 18-14 for the A.L. champs and beat the A's, 7-1, on a three-hitter in the opening game of the ALCS. In the classic World Series against the Reds, he shut out Cincinnati in Game One and was also a winner in the fourth game.

Granted free agency, Luis was grabbed by the Yankees. In his two years in pinstripes he combined for a 21-17 record. His last hurrah came with the Pirates ('81) and Angels ('82). He was all done at age 41—at least that was his listed age—a subject that always raised controversy.   229-172

TIEFENTHALER, Verle
   Maintenance worker for Ralston Purina Co.
   Carroll, IA

The "Go-Go" White Sox were the A.L. pennant winners in 1959. Three years later they were a fifth-place team, finishing below the Angels, a team that didn't even exist in '59.

Right-hander Verle Tiefenthaler didn't have too much to do with the White Sox downward skid in '62, since he had no decisions in three relief appearances that season, his only exposure to the big leagues. The year before he won 13 games and saved 14 in helping Tacoma to the P.C.L. pennant.

TILLMAN, Bob
   Executive with a food brokerage company
   Gallatin, TN

On July 30, 1969, Hank Aaron hit career home run No. 537 for the Atlanta Braves to move past Mickey Mantle into third place on the all-time list of home run hitters. In the same game, a 19-0 romp over the Expos, Aaron's team-mate, catcher Bob Tillman, blasted Nos. 63, 64, and 65 of his career while Jim Wynn and Denis Menke each stroked grand-slams.

Bob came up with the Red Sox in 1962 and remained in Boston until '67. His 17 four-baggers in '64 established a single-season record for Red Sox catchers until Carlton Fisk hit 22 in '72. His next stop was with the Yankees. The final three years of his nine-year career were spent in Atlanta.   .232

TILLOTSON, Thad
Business agent for Teamsters Union, Local #748
Modesto, CA

Johnny Tillotson was singing *Poetry in Motion* in 1960 when Thaddeus Asa Tillotson put his right arm in motion in the Dodgers' organization, winning 19 games in the California League. He spent several more years in the minors before making it to the big time with the Yankees in 1967. On May 16th the Yankees held a pre-game ceremony honoring Mickey Mantle for recently having hit career homer No. 500. That day against the Indians, Thad came out of the bullpen in the top of the ninth inning in a 3-3 tie game and retired a batter to end the inning.

He led off the bottom of the 11th frame with his first and only big league hit and eventually scored on a base hit by Mantle as the Yankees won, 4-3, with Thad gaining credit for his first big league win. After winning his first three decisions for the Yankees in '67, he lost his last nine to tie the Yankee record for the longest 1-year pitcher's losing streak with Bill Hogg who dropped nine in a row in 1908.

He finished in '68 at 4-9 after pitching in 50 games.

TIMBERLAKE, Gary
Employed with the Olin Chemical Co.
Brandenburg, KY

Gary says, "The biggest thrill of my baseball career was being called up by the Seattle Pilots in June of 1969. I replaced Steve Barber, who was injured. My biggest disappointment was going on six months active duty with the Army Reserves two weeks later."

The left-hander made two starts in his short stay and wasn't involved in a decision. He never returned after fulfilling his military commitment.

TIMMERMAN, Tom
    Employed in metal fabricating sales
    Breese, IL

If you like numerical oddities you'll love Tom's figures. He finished 35-35 with 35 saves. At the plate he was 8-for-88. In his role as a starter he had 8 complete games.

All of the above was accomplished from 1969–74 with the Tigers and Indians. In 1970 Tom relieved 61 times for Detroit, winning six games while saving 27 more and was voted "Tiger of the Year" by the Detroit sportswriters.

His last two years were spent in Cleveland.

TISCHINSKI, Tom
    Construction worker
    Kansas City, MO

"Tish" was used primarily as a bullpen catcher during his stay with the Twins from 1969–71. He had a lifetime avg. of .181 in 82 games.

On Aug. 21, 1970, the University of Missouri product hit the only homer of his career, a game-winning blow in a 4-3 Twins' victory over Washington.

TOLAN, Bobby
    Manager at Beaumont in the Texas League

There have been back-to-back no-hitters twice in major league history and Bobby Tolan is the only man to play in all four games. As a member of the Cardinals in '68, Bobby played in the Perry-Washburn no-hit tilts and also appeared in both consecutive no-hitters in 1969 tossed by Jim Maloney (Reds) and Don Wilson (Astros) when Bobby was on the Reds' roster.

Tolan, whose first audition came in 1965 with the Cardinals as a 19-year-old, spent the next four years as a spare outfielder in St. Louis. The day after the Tigers' seventh game victory over the Cards in the 1968 World Series, Bobby was swapped to the Reds for Vada Pinson.

His Cincy debut on April 7, 1969, was noteworthy. Pete Rose led off the bottom of the first inning with a home run and Bobby followed with another four-bagger off Don Drysdale. The pair would pull off the feat three different times, an M.L. record for back-to-back homers to lead off a game by the same two players. Unfortunately, the homers off Drysdale that day were the only runs the Reds could put across the plate in a 3-2 loss to the Dodgers in the final season opener at Crosley Field. Bobby finished '69 batting .305 with 21 homers and 93 RBIs.

In 1970 Tolan was named to *The Sporting News* N.L. All-Star team after hitting .316 with a league-leading 57 stolen bases. In the NLCS against the Pirates he continued to sizzle, going 5-for-12 in the Reds' three-game sweep. Three of his hits came in the second game, including a home run, as he scored all three runs in Cincinnati's 3-1 victory.

Bobby's groove was interrupted in '71 when he missed the entire season because of a torn Achilles tendon. But he bounced back in '72 to capture Comeback Player of the Year honors, hitting .283 in aiding the Reds to another pennant. After slumping to .206 in '73, Bobby drifted around with the Padres, Phillies, and Pirates. He finished in San Diego in 1979 with a lifetime .265 average.

Tolan's excellent speed was a family trait as his uncle, Eddie Tolan, was a double Gold Medal winner in the 1932 Olympic Games.

TOMPKINS, Ron
Division manager for Interstate Brands Corporation
Chula Vista, CA

In 1965, when Billy Joe Royal had a hit song, *Down in the Boondocks,* Ron Tompkins had no decisions in five games for the Kansas City A's. The 6'4" right-hander, known as "Stretch," then did a long stretch down in the boondocks before spending the 1971 season in the Cubs' bullpen and losing his only two decisions in 35 games.

TOPPIN, Rupe
Location Unknown

Ruperto Toppin was born on Pearl Harbor Day in Panama City.

In 1962 Rupe came to the majors. The right-hander bottomed out after two appearances in relief for the Kansas City A's.

TORBORG, Jeff
New York Yankees' coach

Only two catchers in baseball history have caught no-hitters in both major leagues—Gus Triandos and Jeff Torborg. The current Yankee coach was on the receiving end of Sandy Koufax's perfect game for the Dodgers against the Cubs in 1965 and was behind the dish for Bill Singer's no-hitter for the Angels in 1970. Three years later he called the pitches for Nolan Ryan's no-hitter for the Angels against the Royals.

An expert handler of pitchers, Jeff also caught Don Drysdale's fifth straight shutout in "Big D's" string of six in 1968.

Torborg received a reported $100,000 bonus from the Dodgers in 1963 after earning All-American honors at Rutgers University. The next year he found himself in Dodger Stadium as a backup catcher, a role he played in Los Angeles until 1970. He then spent three years with the Angels.

A lifetime .214 hitter in his 10-year journey, Jeff remained in the majors following his playing days as an Indians' coach from 1975 until replacing Frank Robinson as the Cleveland manager in June of '77. The hapless Indians went on a seven-game winning streak when Jeff took over. But in July of '79 he was replaced at the helm by Dave Garcia. Ironically, Cleveland went on a 10-game winning streak after Jeff was axed.

TORRE, Joe
    California Angels television announcer

Wherever Joe went he seemed to accept the mantle of leadership. Labeled "The Godfather" during his tenure as a Mets' manager, Joe received the respect of the baseball world almost immediately when he made his major league debut with the Milwaukee Braves on Sept. 25, 1960, as a pinch-hitter for Warren Spahn and promptly singled off Harvey Haddix. He had been promoted from Eau Claire where he won the Northern League batting title (.344).

Torre started the next year at Louisville, but was summoned to the big arena early in the '61 season. In his first start on May 21st, he went 3-for-8 in a doubleheader against the Reds with a single, double and home run.

The nickname "Chicken-Catcher Torre" never caught on and rightly so, since there was nothing chicken about this rugged Italian who terrorized N.L. hurlers until 1977 with the Braves (1960–68), Cards (1969–74), and Mets (1975–77), to the tune of a .297 avg. and 252 home runs.

Named as catcher on *The Sporting News* All-Star team three straight years (1964, '65, '66), Joe caught Warren Spahn's 300th victory. When he hit .321 in '64 for the Braves, he became the first big league catcher in nine years to bat over .300, hit 20 or more home runs and collect at least 100 RBIs. His 36 four-baggers in '66 were the most ever hit by a Braves' backstop.

When the Braves made their move to Atlanta, he introduced himself to the South on Opening Night (April 12, 1966) by hitting a home run off the Pirates' Bob Veale, the first regular-season homer in Atlanta's Fulton County Stadium.

The Braves traded Torre to the Cardinals for Orlando Cepeda on March 17, 1969. It was in St. Louis that Joe went on his celebrated diet and went on to win a batting championship in addition to playing solid first and third base for a club which had Tim McCarver and later Ted Simmons behind the plate. While Joe's waistline diminished, his offensive statistics ballooned. His dream year came in 1971 when he was named MVP after winning the batting crown (.363) and also leading the N.L. in hits (230) and RBIs (137), all three figures being personal highs for him.

Following the '74 season, Joe returned home when he was traded to the Mets. He was named the Mets' player-manager on May 31, 1977, replacing Joe Frazier. He retired as a player 18 days later. In 1982 he took over as the Atlanta skipper and stayed through the '84 season, compiling an overall record of 257-229. He led the Braves to the N.L. West Division title in '82.

The only thing that seems to have escaped Joe's career is a World Series, unlike his brother Frank who played in the '57 and '58 Fall Classics with the Braves.

TORRES, Felix
Employed with the General Electric Company
Santa Isabel, Puerto Rico

For a baseball player, making it to the big top at any age is the culmination of a dream, usually after many years of hard work. Felix joined the Angels in '62 as a 30-year-old third baseman. He stayed with the club for three years, hitting .254 in 365 games.

During the '63 season his name entered the defensive record books twice. He went through a stretch of 12 consecutive games without making a putout at his position, but he also tied an M.L. mark that year when he started four double plays in a game from his position.

TORRES, Hector
Coach at Florence (South Atlantic League)

How Tall is a Giant was the title of a television documentary in 1958 centering on the Monterrey, Mexico, team that won the Little League World Series that year. The hero of the squad was a 12-year-old named Hector Torres who pitched the Monterrey team to the title. His father, Epitacio Torres, was one of Mexico's all-time great power-hitting outfielders from 1944–1958.

Just four years after Hector's heroics at Williamsport, he found himself in the Midwest League as a shortstop with Decatur, an affiliate of the Giants.

Hector's big league debut came with Houston in 1968, a year in which he won honors as the Topps Rookie All-Star shortstop. He hit just .223 in 128 games, but his fielding drew such praises by his peers as "the quickest shortstop I've ever seen", and "the best arm I've ever seen at shortstop".

He was with the Cubs, Expos, and Padres, before closing with the Blue Jays in 1977. On June 27, 1977, he hit the first A.L. grand-slam in Canada in a game against the Yankees.

As a member of the Expos he was once used on the mound, but was unable to recapture his 1958 Little League heroics as he allowed five hits and two runs in the one inning he worked.   .216

TORREZ, Mike
Active with New York Mets and Oakland A's in 1984

There is something about the game of baseball that manufactures heroes and goats simultaneously. For instance, for every Bobby Thomson there's a Ralph Branca. For every Bucky Dent, there's a Mike Torrez. Unfortunately, Mike may always be remembered for serving up Bucky Dent's three-run homer in the 1978 playoff game at Fenway Park between the Yankees and Red Sox rather than his overall endurance record of over 3,000 innings pitched and a 184-155 mark.

Mike was first up with the Cards in '67 but he split the next five years between the minors and St. Louis. In the middle of the '71 season he was swapped to Montreal where he fashioned a 40-32 record from '71–'74 before being moved to Baltimore.

Mike was in Baltimore for just one season, but had his best year, going 20-9 in '75 while leading the league with a .690 winning percentage. Before the righthander could get comfortable, he was put in a package with Don Baylor and was sent to Oakland for Reggie Jackson and Ken Holtzman on April 2, 1976. That year Mike went 16-12 and at one point hurled three straight shutouts over 38⅓ scoreless innings, establishing A's team records in both categories.

He joined the Yankees the following April and played a

key part in the Yankees' drive to the pennant and World
Series victory over the Dodgers that year. In the World
Series the well-traveled chucker posted two complete game
victories over the Dodgers. Granted free agency, he signed
with the Red Sox where he lodged from 1978–82, going
60-54.

Traded to the Mets in '83, he suffered through a 10-17
season, then was released early in '84 before being picked
up by Oakland. With the exception of the Mets, Mike was a
winner wherever he went, with a 185-160 record.

In 1983 his ex-wife had a book published titled *High Inside* chronicling her marriage to Mike and her life as a
wife of a major league player. Mike was quoted about the
book: "I hope she makes a lot of money out of it so I can cut
off her alimony."

TOTH, Paul
Sales manager for Z and Z Beer Distributing Company
Toledo, OH

In the early Sixties, Peter, Paul, and Mary became the
most popular folk singing group of the decade with such
hits as *Blowin' in the Wind* and *Puff, the Magic Dragon*.

Right-hander Paul Toth came up with the Cards at
about the same time in '62, before blowing into the Windy
City and working as both a starter and reliever for the
Cubs in '63 and '64. His career went puff after he went 9-12
in 43 games.

TOVAR, Cesar
Major league baseball scout
Caracas, Venezuela

On Sept. 22, 1968, Cesar duplicated Bert Campaneris's
feat by playing all nine positions for the Twins in a game
against the A's. Ironically the first batter he faced was
Campaneris. Of more significant note concerning the one
scoreless inning he worked was that he struck out Reggie
Jackson.

Primarily an outfielder, this jack of all trades also

played at second and third base. He indirectly caused an uproar in 1967 when he hit .267. That same year Carl Yastrzemski was a runaway MVP winner when he copped the Triple Crown, but wasn't a unanimous choice since Cesar received one first-place vote.

Tovar was a key member of the Twins' back-to-back A.L. West championship clubs in '69 and '70. On May 18, 1969, he and Minnesota teammate Rod Carew ran wild in the second inning against the Tigers as they both stole home against the embarrassed battery of Mickey Lolich and Bill Freehan. In 1970 Cesar hit an even .300 while leading the A.L. in both doubles (36) and triples (13). The next season, the versatile Venezuelan continued to roll as he hit .311 and led the league in base hits (204).

Tovar should be nicknamed "Mr. Spoiler" as he is the all-time leader in collecting the only hit in five one-hitters. He broke up no-hit bids by Dave McNally, Mike Cuellar, Catfish Hunter, Barry Moore, and Dick Bosman.

From 1973–76 he wore the uniform of the Phils, Rangers, A's, and Yankees.   .278

TRACEWSKI, Dick
Detroit Tigers' coach

It was a merry year for Dick in 1963, his first full year in the majors as a member of the Dodgers. It was a year in which he was married, hit his first major league home run, started all four games in the Dodgers' World Series sweep over the Yankees, and welcomed the birth of his first child. He and his wife named the baby girl Joy—what else after a year like that?

In the '63 World Series "Trixie" started all four games at second base for the Dodgers as they swept the Yankees. His diving grab of a force-play throw, erasing Elston Howard in the fifth inning of the final game with the score tied 0-0, was one of the great plays of the Series.

A utility infielder, Dick also appeared with Los Angeles in the '65 autumnal classic against the Twins before going to Detroit for Phil Regan. His role in the Motor City was similar to what he did with the Dodgers. He earned his third World Series ring playing with the Tigers in 1968, although he hit just .156 in 90 games.

Dick's eight-year swing terminated in '69 with a .213 average and three World Series rings.

TRESH, Tom
Assistant Placement Director at Central Michigan University; owner of a Kentucky Fried Chicken franchise
Alma, MI

Tom epitomizes the 1960s, having played in the big arena from 1961–69. He arrived on the scene 12 years after his father, Mike, departed after a 12-year career spent mostly with the White Sox. There are some similarities in the father-son duo. Both wore number 15; Mike played 1,027 games against Tom's 1,192. Although Mike swung for a .249 avg. vs. Tom's .245, Tom carried a more powerful stick as he outhomered his dad, 153 to 2.

In 1962 Tom was voted the A.L. Rookie of the Year playing for the Yankees, primarily at shortstop. The switch-hitter had 20 homers, 93 RBIs, and hit a career-high .286. In the World Series against the San Francisco Giants, he garnered nine hits, including a big three-run homer in Game Five to give the Yankees a 5-3 win and a 3-2 lead in the Series.

Tresh appeared marked for pinstripe immortality when he followed up his rookie campaign with 25 home runs in '63, when he moved to left field. On September 1st he became only the eighth player in big league history to homer from both sides of the plate in a game. The eager Yankee parked a two-run homer in Game One of the '63 World Series against the Dodgers, depriving Sandy Koufax of a shutout.

Historically the Yankees have not been known to play the running game. However, in 1964 Tom pilfered 13 bases in 13 attempts, by no means a threat to Lou Brock, but nevertheless a record total of stolen bases in a season without once being caught.

On June 6, 1965, Tresh put on one of the great homer shows in Yankee Stadium history when he walloped four

roundtrippers in a doubleheader against the White Sox.
Three of his four-baggers came in the second game. That
season he led the sixth-place Yanks in runs (94), hits (168),
doubles (29), home runs (26), RBIs (74), and hitting (.279).
He followed up with 27 home runs in '67.

A damaged knee which required surgery in 1967 pre-
vented the popular Yankee from performing to his potential. The injury, which he received in an exhibition game
in '67, seemed to handicap Tom thereafter. His next two
seasons were depressing as he batted .219 and .195 respectively.

His final year was in his native Detroit. He was gone at
age 31. But he says, "Hey—I had a good career."

TREVINO, Bobby
    Monterrey, Mexico

The Summer Olympics were held in Mexico City in 1968,
and the name Trevino came into prominence that year
when the "Super Mex," Lee Trevino, won the U.S. Open
Golf tournament. Bobby Trevino played in 17 games in the
Angels' outfield that summer, hitting .225.

The brother of current Braves' catcher Alex Trevino,
Bobby gained as many headlines in the spring of '69 at El
Paso (Texas League) as did Lee Trevino, the popular El
Paso native. The reason was a 37-game hitting streak
which tied the all-time league record set by Ike Boone in
1923.

TURNER, Ken
    Hawthorne, CA

On May 7, 1967, Ken was within one out of hurling the
first nine-inning perfect game in P.C.L. history, pitching
for Seattle against Tacoma, when pinch-hitter Al Spangler
doubled with two out in the ninth inning. However, nothing so dramatic happened to Ken in the majors as he went
1-2 in 13 games for the Angels in 1967.

TYRIVER, Dave
 Manager of a men's clothing store
 Oshkosh, WI

You probably remember Andy Williams' rendition of *Moon River* in 1962. You probably don't remember Dave Tyriver, a right-hander who appeared in four games without a decision that year for the Cleveland Indians.

U

UECKER, Bob
 Milwaukee Brewers' announcer; does Miller Lite Beer commercials

Bob was asked by the sports staff of the *USA Today* newspaper to list his five greatest thrills as a player. He answered: 1. Getting out of a rundown; 2. Driving home the winning run by walking with the bases loaded; 3. Watching a fan in the upper deck; 4. Showing up for most games; 5. Catching the games on the radio that I didn't show up for.

When a man has that kind of sense of humor it doesn't really matter if he hit .200 lifetime with the Braves ('62), Cards ('64–'65), Phillies ('66–'67), and Atlanta Braves ('67). However, there was nothing funny about this baseball comedian as far as the Braves were concerned on September 1, 1964, when he hit a ninth-inning homer for the Cards to beat the Braves 5-4. It was Uecker's only four-bagger of the year and it kept the Cards in the pennant race. A frequent guest on Johnny Carson's *Tonight Show,* Ueck was a celebrity on June 21, 1967, when he racked up 5 RBIs, 4 of them on a grand-slam, as the Braves beat the Giants 9-2.

His book, *Catcher in the Wry,* was published in 1983. An interesting man this Mr. Uecker, especially for a guy who hit .200

UHLAENDER, Ted
     Vice-president of T&M Distribution Company; also
     owns business called "Travel Music" (equips cars with
     tapes, cassettes, etc.)
     McAllen, TX

The story goes that Ted was once on a fishing trip with
Twins' teammate Frank Kostro, who landed a big one.
Tiring after a struggle to reel in the fish, Kostro handed
the line to his teammate saying, "Here, Ted, You-land-
'er."
   After winning the P.C.L. batting title (.340) for Denver
in 1965, Ted was brought up to the Twins. He was a regular in the Minnesota outfield for the rest of the decade,
then following two seasons in Cleveland, he checked out
with the N.L. champion Reds in 1972.
   A business administration graduate from Baylor University, Ted majored in statistics. His statistics were a .263
avg. in 898 games.

UMBACH, Arnie
     Attorney
     Opelika, AL

Arnie first caught the eye of big league scouts as a 17-year-
old in 1960 at the All-American Amateur Baseball Association Tournament when he pitched his Alabama team to a
5-0 victory over the host Johnston, PA, team, striking out
a tournament record 24 batters.
   The Auburn University right-hander was up for one
game in '64 in which he gained a victory for the Milwaukee Braves. Arnie returned two years later, losing his only
two decisions.   1-2

UNSER, Del
     Vice-president of a wholesale baseball and softball
     firm in Pleasant Hill, CA; Philadelphia Phillies' hit-
     ting coach

When a man embarks on a new career, he normally experi-
ences obstacles and trials similar to those of a rookie base-

ball player. Del, who was released from baseball in 1982, compares his new position with Westar to being a "rookie" as the company challenges such established sporting goods giants as Rawlings and Wilson in the production of hard-balls and softballs. One of Westar's innovations is the "IncrediBall," a ball made out of nylon fabric wrapped around a soft polyurethane core which promises to take the "sting" out of learning new skills.

As a rookie outfielder in 1968, Del hit .230 for the Senators to win Rookie of the Year honors from *The Sporting News*. On August 20th that year he led off the game with a homer, his first big league four-bagger and only one of the season. He then followed up with four straight singles for a 5-for-5 day.

The son of Al Unser who was a catcher from 1942–45 (Tigers and Reds), Del was an All-American outfielder in 1966 at Mississippi State. Unaffected by the sophomore jinx, the speedster shot up to .286 in '69, a year he also led the A.L. in triples (8), the lowest total in history for a league leader. Before it ended, Del jumped around with the Indians, Phils, Mets, Expos, and Phils a second time (1979–82).

If he develops the same reputation with Westar that he did as a pinch-hitter late in his career, Wilson and Rawlings should take heed. Unser tied a major league record for hitting three consecutive pinch-hit home runs on June 30, July 5, and July 10, 1979.   .258

UPHAM, John
        Teacher at the University of Windsor
        Windsor, Ontario

On May 19, 1967, 81-year-old Pat Pieper, the Cubs' field announcer for 51 years, put down his megaphone and left the field to move up to the press box for the first time. For Canadian-born John Upham, it might not have been as historic a game, but he did come off the bench to pick up a pinch-hit single.

Both a pitcher and an outfielder, the southpaw lost his only decision in seven games for the Cubs, but did hit .308 in his 21 games for the Cubbies in 1967–68.

UPSHAW, Cecil
     Employed with Coca-Cola Bottling Company
     Atlanta, GA

Sometimes a man is having so much fun he tends to over-
look things that could pose a danger to his well-being.
Cecil Upshaw, the 6'6" Centenary College basketball star
pulled a prank at the beginning of the 1970 season that
cancelled his season and almost his career.
     The Braves opened the 1970 campaign in San Diego. On
April 9th, Upshaw and his cousin, pitcher George Stone,
who were Atlanta teammates, were walking down the
street when Cecil decided to make like "Dr. J." and im-
press Stone, also a college basketball standout. Demon-
strating his ability to dunk a basketball, Cecil caught a
finger in a metal awning and wound up spending a couple
of months in the hospital. He suffered severed arteries in
his ring finger, and for a time it was feared the finger
would be amputated. Fortunately, the finger was saved
through skin and nerve graft surgery.
     Upshaw broke in with the Braves in '66 and in a couple
of years he became the ace of the club's bullpen. In 1969 he
won six games and saved another 27 in 62 appearances as
Atlanta won the N.L. West. No doubt Cecil's untimely accident the following year hurt the Braves' chances to re-
peat as they fell to fifth place.
     A sidearmer in the Ewell Blackwell style, he made a
strong comeback in '71, winning 11 games and saving 17.
He then hopscotched around with the Astros, Indians,
Yankees and White Sox, finishing 34-36 with 86 saves.

VALDESPINO, Sandy
     New York Yankees' minor league coach and instructor

When a guy like Rod Carew praises a man for helping his
career, it is quite a compliment. When Rod was a rookie

second baseman in 1967, Sandy taught him the art of bunting. He has never forgotten that. Only two years before, Sandy was a rookie himself, hitting .261 as a part-time player and pinch-hitter for the A.L. champion Twins.

The flychaser transferred leagues in '68 when he joined the Braves. After stops with the Astros, Pilots, Brewers, and Royals, the former I.L. batting champ completed his seven-year swing in 1971 with a .230 avg.

VALENTINE, Bobby
New York Mets coach; owns two restaurants in Connecticut

Bobby is the only player in Connecticut high school football history who was selected as an All-Stater three different years. Approximately 250 colleges were interested in his services, but he chose baseball when he was the No. 1 choice of the Dodgers in the 1968 free agent draft.

The bubbly, always smiling Stamford native arrived for five games with the Dodgers in '69. For the next three years he swung back and forth between the majors and minors. He was the whirling dervish of the P.C.L. in 1970 when he won the batting title (.340) at Spokane and was named the league's "Player of the Year" after leading the league in seven offensive departments.

In 1973 Valentine was sent to the Angels in a deal that involved Frank Robinson and Andy Messersmith. It was on May 17th that year that Bobby collided with tragedy when he crashed into the centerfield wall at Anaheim, breaking both the tibia and fibula bones in his right leg. He was hitting .302 at the time.

What might have been, never was. At age 29 Valentine was gone in 1979 after also seeing action with the Padres, Mets, and Mariners. The current Mets' coach does see a positive side to his story. He says, "When I came back, I was forced to learn a lot of new positions in order to stay in the lineup. I played every position except pitcher." .260

VALLE, Hector
Bookstore Auxiliary I
Mayaguez, Puerto Rico

Valley of the Dolls became the bestselling novel of all time during the Sixties when Puerto Rico-born catcher Hector Valle was trying to sell himself to the Dodgers.

In 1965 he had his only big league exposure and responded well, hitting .308 in a brief trial. Defensively, Hector was a Silver Glove winner in 1966 when he led all minor league catchers in fielding as he committed just one error in 543 chances for Spokane in the P.C.L.

VAUGHAN, Charlie
Employed with Burton Auto Supply
Weslaco, TX

In 1966, this 18-year-old southpaw from Texas made his first major league start as a member of the Atlanta Braves. In that contest, the Braves beat the Astros, 12-2, as Charlie allowed just two runs in seven innings to gain the victory.

It wasn't until '69 that the Braves gave Charlie another start. In that one he lasted just one inning and wasn't involved in the decision.

VAUGHAN, Glen
Has an insurance agency, Vaughan and Company Insurance Co.
Houston, TX

Arky Vaughan had a celebrated career as a Pirates' shortstop during the 1930s. Glenn "Sparky" Vaughan, the nephew of the great shortstop, who was signed for a reported $100,000 bonus by the Colt .45s, hit .167 in 1963. He started the '64 season at Oklahoma City, but early in the campaign he entered the Army. He then gave up his baseball career and returned to the University of Houston to earn his degree.

VEALE, Bob
   New York Yankees' minor league pitching coach

Bob is credited as the first one to make the profound statement that "Good pitching will beat good hitting, and vice
versa." But there was nothing silly about this intimidating moundsman.
   It all started when the Pirates, who were playing at
Wrigley Field in May of 1958, asked Bob to work out. He
was signed on the spot. It proved to be a pleasant marriage
as the 6'6" southpaw had a productive career (1962–72) in
Pittsburgh linens.
   Bob is the only pitcher in Pirates' history to get 200 or
more strikeouts in a season and he did it three times (1964,
'65, '66). In '64 he led the majors with 250 strikeouts and
won a career-high 18 games. On June 1, 1965, the bespectacled hurler set a Pirates' record by fanning 16 Phillies at
Forbes Field.
   If he had a weakness, it was his generosity in giving up
too many free passes, as he led the league four times in
that category. However, in 1,926 career innings pitched,
Veale gave up a total of 91 home runs, an average of one
every 21.2 innings, the best ratio over the past 30 years.
   Bob, who was 120-95 lifetime, worked out of the bullpen
in his twilight years. From Sept. 7, 1970, to May 28, 1973,
he never lost a game, while going 10-0 in relief. His last
couple of years were spent with the Red Sox where he shut
down in 1974.

VELAZQUEZ, Federico
   Texas Rangers' scout in the Dominican Republic

Expansion in 1969 opened the door for many players who
otherwise might never have had the chance to make it to
the big leagues. One of them was Federico, who made it
into six games with the Pilots that season. He was out of
the Majors until 1973 when he played 15 games for Atlanta and hit .348 as a 35-year-old catcher.   .256

VERBANIC, Joe
Owns All-Pro Fire Protection, a company which designs and installs sprinkler systems
Eugene, OR

Bob Uecker did an impersonation of Whitey Ford in a beer commercial. Joe Verbanic, after a trade from the Phils, was the man called up from the minors when Whitey retired early in the '67 season. Nobody really expected Joe to replace the future Hall of Famer and he didn't as he won only 11 games for the Pinstripers between 1967–70, missing the '69 season with an ailing arm.   12-11

VIDAL, Jose
Santo Domingo, Dominican Republic

Jose has the distinction of being the first player in the history of the California League to win the Triple Crown, hitting .340 with 40 homers and 162 RBIs. But on the major league level, from 1966–69, the Dominican outfielder appeared in a total of 88 games with the Indians and Pilots hitting only .164. Jose batted above .300 several years on the Triple-A level.

VINEYARD, Dave
Carpenter
Left Hand, VA

Dave's 19-game party wasn't all wine and roses since he went 2-5 in 1964 with the Orioles.

Two years earlier he was considered one of the top prospects in the Baltimore organization before he suffered a serious industrial leg injury in the off-season and was in a leg brace for several months. Dave hurled two I.L. no-hitters, at Rochester ('66) and Toronto ('67).

VINSON, Charlie
Warehouse employee for the Giant Food Company
Jessup, MD

Only a few baseball fans got the chance to view Charlie, since he was around with the Angels for only 13 games in '66.

His quick stay in September provided some newsworthy items. Although he hit just .182, he beat the eventual World Champion Orioles twice in his first three games. Charlie doubled home the game winner with his first major league hit, then beat them again a couple of days later with his first and only big league home run.

VON HOFF, Bruce
Salesman for "Transportation Equipment"
Tampa, FL

Pitching for the Astros' minor league affiliate in the Florida State League in 1965, Bruce was working on a no-hitter in the ninth inning when he was removed from the mound by manager Billy Goodman under orders of parent Astros' General Manager Paul Richards, who didn't want any of the young Houston prospects throwing more than 110 pitches in a game. He did get a no-hitter in '66 for Durham (Carolina League).

Although winless (0-3) in his brief trials with Houston in '65 and '67, Bruce made an impressive first big league start in '67, allowing just four hits in eight innings in a 2-1 victory over the Dodgers. He was not credited with the win.

VOSS, Bill
Insurance business
Irvine, CA

This Southern California native had four trials with the White Sox between 1965–68. He hit a grand-slam on June 30, 1968, to lead Chicago to a 12-0 rout over Detroit, but then was hit in the jaw by a Pete Richert pitch four days later and was out the rest of the season.

Bill returned home in '69 and enjoyed his finest season, hitting .261 in 133 games as a regular in the Angels' outfield. On April 18th that year he became the first Angels' player ever to hit a grand-slam in Anaheim Stadium. His eight-year stay concluded in '72 after also seeing action for the Brewers, A's, and Cardinals.   .227

W

WAGNER, Gary
Environmentalist; regional manager for S.C.A. Chemical in Boston
Jackson, NJ

Gary was around the majors with the Phillies and Red Sox from 1965–70 and went 15-19. But it was a miracle that the right-hander was around at all. At the age of 12, Gary was kicked in the face by a horse on the family farm in Illinois. He was unconscious for a month and was given little chance to survive. However, he recovered from his injuries, which included a jaw that was shattered in five places and the loss of several teeth. He still carries a scar on the right side of his chin.

Wagner went on to Eastern Illinois University where he played basketball and soccer, and was a shortstop on the baseball team. In his collegiate pitching debut, he filled in on the mound and hurled a no-hitter.

Gary's rookie season in the big top turned out to be his most successful (7-7 plus 7 saves) as he made 59 trips in from the Phillies bullpen.

WAKEFIELD, Bill
Director of purchasing for Kranslo Water Recreational Products
San Francisco, CA

Bill was the starting pitcher for the Mets in the first night game ever played at Shea Stadium in 1964, his only season in the big arena when he went 3-5 in 62 games for the Mets with a club-leading 3.60 ERA.

Wakefield rates his top thrills as pitching in the Hall of Fame Game at Cooperstown and appearing in Jim Bunning's perfect game.

WALKER, Luke
Sheriff's deputy
Texarkana, TX

Though Bill Wakefield hurled the first pitch in a Shea Stadium night contest, Luke Walker goes one better as he was the pitcher who delivered the first pitch in a World Series night game (against the Orioles on October 13, 1971).

Luke was a member of the Pirates (1965–73) and Tigers ('74) during his big league stay, with his best year coming in 1970 when he logged a 15-6 mark.

Had the "Star Wars" sagas come out a few years earlier, Luke Walker most certainly would have acquired the nickname "Sky." As it was, he was just plain old Luke Walker.   45-47

WALLACE, Don
Principal of Cheyenne Mountain Junior High School
Colorado Springs, CO

In 1967 George Wallace announced his candidacy for President on the American Independent Party ticket. That year Don Wallace, an off-season schoolteacher with a degree in education from Oklahoma State was a big league candidate as he made it into 23 games as an infielder for the Angels and was hitless in six at-bats.

In the 1961 College World Series, Don was named as the All-Tournament shortstop.

WALTERS, Charley
Sports reporter for the *St. Paul Dispatch*

Charley's profile is one of those "Hollywood wouldn't buy it stories." A native of Minneapolis, Walters made a strong impression on the Twins' minor league officials when he attended the club's tryout camp in August of 1965, and was signed to a contract.

In '68 Charley found himself in the Class A Midwest League. The following year he was a member of the Twins on Opening Day. But that's where the script ends, as he had no decisions in six games.

Charley has covered the Twins as a writer. It is unusual that a beat reporter for a big league club can boast of having pitched for the team.

WALTERS, Ken
Employed with a trucking company
San Ramon, CA

On May 16, 1960, Ken became just the 14th outfielder in big league history to record two assists in one inning while playing for the Tigers. Before it was over Ken appeared with the Phils ('61) and Reds ('63), finishing up at .231.

WALTON, Danny
Pipefitter/welder
Los Alamos, NM

Danny was an aggressive, colorful Enos Slaughter–type of player. He arrived for a couple of games with the Astros in '68, then returned to the farm for more prepping. In 1969 he was selected as the "Minor League Player of the Year" when he hit .332 and led the American Association with 25 homers and 119 RBIs at Oklahoma City. Late that year he was traded to the Seattle Pilots.

Walton moved with the franchise to Milwaukee in 1970 and became a popular figure with the fans for his long ball hitting, but still had trouble solving big league pitching.

He closed in 1980 after also appearing with the Yankees, Twins, Dodgers, Astros again, and Rangers. During the '70s he twice led the P.C.L. in homers between visits to the majors.   .223

WANTZ, Dick
      Died on May 13, 1965, at age 25 in Inglewood, CA

The California Angels have had an uncanny link to tragedy. Minnie Rojas and Ed Kirkpatrick were disabled in
auto accidents; Chico Ruiz and Mike Miley were killed in
car crashes; Lyman Bostock died from gunshot wounds;
Jim McGlothlin lost his battle with cancer; and Dick
Wantz passed away as a result of a brain tumor.
      Wantz, who was the surprise of the Angels' 1965 spring
training camp, made the opening day roster after coming
to spring training as a non-roster player. The tall right-
hander made it into just one game in a relief role before he
began suffering from migraine headaches which led to the
discovery of the tumor. A trophy in his honor was established and given to the most dedicated and improved
players in the Angels' organization.

WARD, Jay
      Manager at Spartanburg in the South Atlantic League

Jay and the Americans sang *She Cried* in '63, a year Jay
Ward was jumping with joy as a Twins' rookie. The rookie
went 1-for-15, but his first major league hit was a two-run
double which gave Minnesota a 2-0 victory over the A's.
      Following another shot in '64, Jay was crying for more
playing time since he didn't return until six years later
with the Reds.   .163

WARD, Pete
      Owns a travel agency
      Lake Oswego, OR

Pete is one of 164 major league players born in Canada
where his father, Jim Ward, had been a NHL standout
many years ago for Montreal. He moved to Portland as a
youngster and was a boyhood friend of future Heisman
Trophy winner Terry Baker.
      Ward broke in with the Orioles in 1962 and collected a
two-run, pinch-hit single in his first at-bat to beat the
Twins and prevent Camilo Pascual's 20th victory. Ward

was then swapped to the White Sox in a trade that brought
Luis Aparicio to Baltimore.

Pete's first full season was a celebrated one as he was
named the A.L. Rookie of the Year by *The Sporting News*
for his 22 homers, 84 RBIs, and .295 average.

His career took a sudden downward turn after a whip-
lash injury in an auto accident early in 1965. An ailing
back plagued Ward the remainder of his career. Used primarily at first and third base and sometimes in the outfield, Pete was the top pinch-hitter in the A.L. in 1969,
going 17-for-46.

Pete made his exit with the Yankees in 1970.   .254

WARDEN, Jon
Involved in school sales for fund raising through mag-
azine subscriptions
Loveland, OH

Jon has been on the receiving end of some pretty fat checks
that came by surprise. As a relief pitcher with the Tigers
in '68, he went 4-1 and had three saves. At age 22 he was
the youngest player on either roster during the World
Series and was also the only one who failed to get into a
game in the seven-game Series. However, like Mickey
Lolich, Al Kaline, and the rest of the Tigers, he received
his full winner's share of $10,936.66. Warden also had a
big day in 1977 when he won $63,000 in the Ohio Lottery.

Jon had a memorable debut in '68 when he came out of the
bullpen to strike out Carl Yastrzemski. He was credited with
the victory when Gates Brown belted a pinch-hit home run.

Jon went to the Royals in the expansion draft, but a rotator cuff injury destroyed his career as he never appeared in
the majors again. He returned to college and received a
teaching degree from Ohio State.

WARNER, Jack
General foreman for Arizona Public Services Utility
Phoenix, AZ

The Cubs groomed Jack Dyer Warner as a reliever from
the time he was in the low minors. Early in 1963 Jack

struck out 41 batters in 35 innings pitching in relief for Salt Lake City of the P.C.L.

But in the big arena the stocky right-hander lost his only two decisions in 33 appearances out of the Cubs' bullpen between 1962–65.

WARNER, "Jackie"
Glendora, CA

The Seattle World's Fair, with its 600-foot high space needle, opened a six-month run in 1962, a year the Angels had high hopes for outfielder John Joseph "Jackie" Warner. He broke into pro ball with San Jose that summer and hit home runs his first two times up for the Bees.

Warner, who began the 1966 season as the Angels' right fielder, hit his first big league homer in the ninth inning on April 14th to give California a 2-1 victory over the White Sox. The win snapped the Angels' 12-game losing streak at Comiskey Park, dating back to June of 1964. But "Jackie" had just that one season in the limelight, hitting .211 in 45 games.

WARWICK, Carl
Owns real estate company, Carl Warwick and Associates
Houston, TX

Less than 40 non-pitchers in big league history have batted right-handed and thrown left-handed. One player on this list is Carl Warwick, who is best remembered for his pinch-hitting accomplishments with the Cardinals in the 1964 World Series when he was 3-for-4 and drew a walk in five at-bats off the bench. His pinch-single drove home the go-ahead run in a 9-5 Cards' win in the opener.

A graduate of Texas Christian University, Carl moved around and also played for the Dodgers, Colt .45s, Orioles, and Cubs, hitting .248 in his six-year stay.

WASHBURN, Greg
> Maintenance planner for Mobil Oil Company
> Coal City, IL

Greg had a fleeting taste of the big leagues as a pitcher with the Angels, going 0-2 in eight games.

WASHBURN, Ray
> Chairman of health, physical education, athletics, and recreation at Bellevue Community College in Bellevue, WA

Pitching for the Cardinals, Ray no-hit the Giants on Sept. 18, 1968, at San Francisco less than 24 hours after Gaylord Perry no-hit the Cards.

St. Louis trainer Bob Bauman recalled, "I was working on Washburn on the rubbing table just before the game. I told him, 'You are going to pitch a no-hitter today because you're going to get even with those guys.'"

The right-hander, who was with the Cards (1961–69) and Reds ('70) going 72-64, signed with St. Louis after pitching Whitworth College to the NAIA championship in 1960.

Ray's highlight year was 1968, when he won a career-high 14 games, pitched a no-hitter and was the winner in Game Three of the World Series against the Tigers.

WASLEWSKI, Gary
> Assistant Manager of the Hartford Insurance Co., Southington, CT

Gary had been cloistered in the minors since 1960 when he got the call to the Red Sox during the 1967 season while Boston was in the middle of a blistering pennant race. His contribution to the pennant was a 2-2 mark in 12 games. In the World Series against the Cardinals, he pitched three innings of perfect relief in Game Three and was given the starting nod in the sixth game. Although he pitched well, he did not get credit for the 8-4 Boston victory which forced a seventh game.

After just a 4-7 log in '68, Gary was employed with

the Cards, Expos, Yankees, and A's before closing in
'72. 11-26

WATKINS, Bob
Compton, CA

You probably saw the movie *Butch Cassidy and the Sun-
dance Kid.* Do you remember the line, "Who in the hell are
those guys?" That's what Bob might have been saying that
same year (1969), when he made five relief appearances
with the Astros and was shelled for 13 hits while walking
13. 0-2

WATKINS, Dave
Physician in private practice; staff member at the
Amelia Brown Frazier Rehabilitation Center in Lou-
isville, KY

Dave only hit .176 in 69 games for the Phillies in 1969. But
look what the former catcher is doing today.

In 1972 he received a B.S. degree in biology. Four years
later Dave graduated from the University of Louisville
School of Medicine before completing a four-year residency
program in physiatry. Dave specializes in physical medicine and rehabilitation, working primarily with stroke victims and patients with spinal cord and head injuries.

Dr. Watkins' greatest achievements will not be found in
a baseball encyclopedia.

WATSON, Bob
Oakland A's minor league hitting instructor

Bob has two noted distinctions: 1, he is the only man to hit
for the cycle in both leagues —Astros (1977) and Red Sox
(1979); and 2, he scored baseball's one millionth run on
May 4, 1975, as a member of the Astros in a game against
the Giants. After the game, Watson's shoes and the home
plate that he scored on were sent to the Baseball Hall of
Fame in Cooperstown, NY.

Originally a catcher, Bob moved to the outfield and first

base. Most of his career was spent with Houston (1966–79) before stops with the Red Sox ('79), Yankees (1980–82) and Atlanta ('82–'84). He finished at .295 with 184 homers.

The "Bull" was a dangerous performer in post-season play. In two ALCS with the Yankees he batted .375, including a .318 performance against the Dodgers in the 1981 W.S. Seven times in his career he hit over .300.

WATT, Eddie
Minor league pitching coach at Reading (Eastern League)

Eddie Watt almost had his lights put out when he got hit by a thrown ball in rundown practice during spring training in 1967. As a result of the play, he suffered a broken nose and an eye injury.

The right-hander was shining early in the 1965 season. Pitching for Elmira, he tossed a no-hitter on Opening Day, then in his third start he hurled another no-hit game.

Watt was the key man in the Orioles' bullpen from 1966–73, with his best year coming in '69: 5-2 with 16 saves and a sparkling 1.65 ERA in 56 games. Eddie closed in 1975 after stops with the Phillies and Cubs.

Overall he went 38-36 with 80 saves. His World Series mark isn't so bright (0-3).

WEAVER, Floyd
Employed with Babcock and Wilcox boiler manufacturer in Paris, TX

The Chiffons were singing *He's So Fine* and *One Fine Day* in the Sixties. Floyd had one fine day when he made his debut in '62 with the Indians and went five innings striking out eight without allowing a run, and he was credited with the victory. Overall the right-hander went 4-5 with the Indians, White Sox and Brewers and ended in 1971.

WEAVER, Jim
Sales executive for Consolidated Business Forms
Lancaster, PA

The Clint Eastwood movie *The Good, the Bad, and the Ugly* appropriately describes this Angel southpaw, who gave up Reggie Jackson's first major league home run.
"The Good"—3-0 in '67.
"The Bad"—0-1 in '68.
"The Ugly"—out of the majors.

WEBSTER, Ramon
Panama

Ray began his cruise in 1967. The left-handed hitting first baseman sailed around with the A's (twice), Padres, and Cubs before he shipwrecked in 1971 at .244.

WEEKLY, Johnny
Died at age 37 in an automobile accident on November 14, 1974 in Walnut Creek, CA

An outfielder, Johnny hit the first pinch-hit home run in the history of the Houston club. He was around from 1962–64 when the team was called the Colt .45s before they became the Astros in '65.   .207

WEGENER, Mike
Employed with Southern California Edison; family dog grooming business
Laguna Niguel, CA

Early in the '69 season Expos' manager Gene Mauch said about Wegener, "Nobody can hit his pitches when he's right."
Unfortunately, Mike wasn't "right" too often as he struggled during his two years in Montreal with an 8-20 mark. In fairness to Wegener, however, he did undergo elbow surgery after the '69 campaign. He was "right" one day against the Mets when he fanned 15 in 11 innings.

On July 18, 1970, the 6'4" right-hander gave up Willie Mays' 3,000th career base hit. Mauch, his Expos' manager, had been on hand in 1951 as a member of the Boston Braves when Willie picked up the first base hit of his career, a home run off Warren Spahn.

WEIS, Al
Manager of a furniture warehouse
Chicago, IL

"There goes my chance of ever playing in a World Series" is what Al said to himself when he was traded to the Mets prior to the start of the 1968 season after having spent six years as a utility infielder with the White Sox. A year later he would not only play in a World Series, but become an unlikely hero for the Mets.

A prototype fine-fielding, light-hitting infielder, Al did hit .296 in 103 games for the White Sox in '65. That same year he indirectly contributed to the Orioles' failure to capture the A.L. pennant when he was involved in a collision at second base with Frank Robinson. "Robby" slid hard into Weis in an attempt to break up a double play and cracked his head on Weis' knee. Frank suffered double vision for a period of time. After the mishap, Al had to have knee surgery. The following year he slumped to .155 in 129 games, the lowest batting avg. ever for a second baseman who played in at least 100 games.

Al's W.S. heroics in '69 last in the memory of Mets' fans. He emerged a national hero when he hit .455 (5-for-11), including a game-winning single in Game Two. In the fifth game, his seventh-inning home run tied the contest as New York went on to a 5-3 victory and captured the Series.

Weis closed his 10-year career in '71 at .219 with just seven home runs.

WENZ, Fred
Wholesale liquor distributor
Somerville, NJ

Freddie Cannon was singing about *Palisades Park* when Fred began his roller coaster ride in pro baseball. By the late Sixties he made it to Fenway Park as the heir apparent to Dick Radatz. The 6'3" hard-throwing right-hander, known as "Fireball," struck out nearly one hitter per inning in his short but pleasant ride, which also saw him work out of the Phillies' bullpen in 1970 and finish undefeated at 3-0 in 31 games.

WERHAS, John
Ministry work for professional athletes
Los Angeles, CA

When the Dodgers moved to the West Coast before the start of the '58 season, they worked hard to establish a new identity. They also worked hard to find a regular third baseman. Johnny was the seventh different third sacker the Dodgers employed between 1958–1964 when he took the field on Opening Day in 1964.

The former USC baseball and basketball star gained All-American honors when he helped the Trojans to the NCAA baseball crown in 1958. He was also a fifth-round selection of the NBA Lakers, but chose to sign with the Dodgers.

But John was never really able to establish a foothold in the majors, even though he usually had a highly vocal and enthusiastic Trojan rooting section at Dodger Stadium.

Following a brief fling in '64, John was back in '65 and '67 with the Dodgers before finishing his 89-game stay with the Angels in '67 at .173.

WERT, Don
Advertising business; baseball coach at Franklin and Marshall College
New Providence, PA

There are many theories in baseball that say what it takes to produce a winning team. One is that a team can't win it all with little offensive productivity at third base. Don Wert contradicts that theory as he hit an even .200 in 150 games at the hot corner for the World Champion '68 Tigers.

Don was around Detroit from 1963–70 and with the Senators in 1971. You'll probably stump your friends if you ask them who the Detroit third baseman was in the 1968 World Series. Answer: Don Wert.   .242

WHITAKER, Steve
On staff of Yankee Baseball School in Florida; real estate business
Ft. Lauderdale, FL

Steve was the last player to homer for the Seattle Pilots when he connected on Oct. 2, 1969, in a 3-1 loss to Oakland on the final day of the season.

The outfielder was a ray of light during a dark Yankee era from 1966–68. When he first came up in late August (1966) he walloped a titanic shot off Detroit's Earl Wilson that landed in the third deck at Yankee Stadium. The next day he had an inside-the-park homer off Johnny Podres, then the following day capped off his 72-hour binge with a grand-slam off Mickey Lolich. Unfortunately, there would be just 15 more four-baggers in pinstripes.

After one year with the Pilots, Steve slid out with the Giants in 1970.   .230

WHITBY, Bill
Warehouseman for Ryder-Tie Trucking Company in Charlotte, NC

Bill Whitby would have to look back at 1964 as a highlight season when he made it to the majors and worked in four games out of the Twins' bullpen. But maybe he looks back at 1965 as a better year as he hurled a no-hitter for Charlotte (Southern League) and met and married the winner of the Miss Charlotte Hornets Beauty Contest.

WHITE, Elder
>   Technician for Beasley Oil Co.
>   Ahoskie, NC

In 1962 former football star Byron "Whizzer" White was appointed to the United States Supreme Court, where he has remained for the past 23 years. That same year the Cubs moved Ernie Banks from shortstop to first base and appointed Elder Lafayette White to be the Opening Day shortstop. Elder's tenure lasted only 23 games.   .151

WHITE, Mike
>   Area supervisor for the Pierce County Parks Dept.
>   Tacoma, WA

The son of Joyner "Jo-Jo" White, an outfielder for the Tigers during the 1930s, Joyner Michael White played in the Houston outfield from 1963–65, hitting .264 in 100 games. Mike's career almost went up in smoke when he tore up his knee in spring training in 1958 as a 19-year-old. As a result his pro debut was put on hold for a year.

In a game early in the 1964 season, Mike's father, Jo-Jo, had to have mixed emotions as Mike connected for four hits, including a game winning double, to lead the Colt .45s to a victory over the Braves, the team where Jo-Jo was employed as a coach.

WHITE, Roy
>   Assistant to the General Manager, New York Yankees

If there was ever a man who viewed Yankee history from a variety of angles, it was this classy pro.

Roy Hilton White got things going by hitting safely in his first big league at-bat on Sept. 7, 1965, with a pinch-hit single off Dave McNally. The switch-hitting Yankee came on board during a dismal period of pinstripe history following the collapse of the Yankee dynasty. In 1968 the once-powerful Yankees had a team batting average of .214, the lowest in the majors. Roy's .267 avg. and 62 RBIs, certainly not Ruthian figures, were enough to lead the Yanks in both categories.

Individually the heady Yankee enjoyed his best season in 1970 with 22 homers, 94 RBIs, and a .296 avg., all career highs. A second baseman throughout his minor league career, he switched to the outfield and in 1971 set a record by being the only outfielder in Yankee history to field 1.000 for a single season. Roy also established an A.L. record that year with 17 sacrifice flies.

Roy survived the gloomy years and became a part of the Yankee pennant-winning teams from 1976–78. In '76 he led the A.L. in runs scored with 104.

In the 1978 ALCS against the Royals, the popular Yankee hit a sixth-inning home run to break a 1-1 tie in the fourth game as the Yanks beat the Royals to capture the A.L. pennant. In the '78 Fall Classic against the Dodgers he batted .333 (8-for-24) scoring a Series-leading nine runs.   .271

WHITFIELD, Fred

> Employed in the shipping department of Anderson
> Electric Co. in Lees, AL

Twice released from the lowest level in the minors by the Pirates and Orioles, Fred caught on with the Cardinals in 1962. His .266 avg. earned him a spot as the first baseman on the Topps Rookie All-Star team.

Traded to Cleveland after the season, he spent the next five years as the Tribe's first sacker. In 1965 he hit 26 four-baggers and drove in 90 runs while hitting .293. Ten of his homers and 26 of his RBIs came against the Yankees.

Fred picked up where he left off when he hit game-winning homers off the Yankees in the first two games against them in '66. He concluded his journey in 1970 after playing for the Reds and Expos, hitting a lifetime .253 with 108 home runs.

Not a bad career for a guy who was twice released from Class D.

WICKER, Floyd
    Poultry farmer
    Snow Camp, NC

Pink Floyd was one of the bands which led a second wave English invasion in music in the late Sixties when outfielder Floyd Wicker appeared in a ripple of games for the Cardinals. He was also with the Expos, Brewers, and Giants before washing out in 1971.   .159

WICKERSHAM, Dave
    Insurance business
    Overland Park, KS

If there was ever a definitive name of the 1960s, it was Dave Wickersham, who was around from 1960–69 as a member of the A's, Tigers, Pirates, and Royals. His best year was in 1964 when he went 19-12, but would have been a 20-game winner, had it not been for an incident with umpire Bill Valentine.

In his final start of the year (Oct. 1, 1964) Wickersham was pitching for Detroit against the Yankees. With the score tied 1-1 in the seventh inning, Phil Linz of the Yankees was called safe at first base. In an attempt to call Valentine's attention to the play, Dave put his hand on the ump which called for his automatic ejection. The Tigers went on to a 4-2 victory with Mickey Lolich getting credit for the win. Wickersham never won more than 12 games in any other season.

Dave can boast that he won the first game in the history of the Royals' franchise when he hurled five innings of scoreless relief in a 4-3 victory over Minnesota.   68-57

WILLHITE, Nick
    Oil and gas broker
    Englewood, CA

Nick was one of those guys who was in the wrong place at the wrong time. He had a tough time cracking the Dodgers' pitching staff with names like Sandy Koufax and Claude Osteen in front of him.

The left-hander out of Colorado State University made

an impressive pro debut in 1960 when he threw a three-hit shutout with 14 strikeouts for Reno in the California League.

Nick arrived in the majors in strong fashion on June 16, 1963, when he pitched a five-hit shutout for the Dodgers over the Cubs. But between 1963–67 he could put together only a 6-12 log in 58 games for the Dodgers, Senators, Angels, and Mets.

Ted Williams was just completing his illustrious career while Billy Williams was virtually beginning it in the Sixties after coming up in '59. One of the top songs on the record charts in 1960 was titled Stay *by Maurice Williams. Six players named Williams debuted in the '60s, but most had only a brief stay.*

WILLIAMS, Billy
Owner of Billy Williams's Men's Boutique
Oakland, CA

The Cubs' Billy Williams built his consecutive-game playing streak to 1,117 games during the Sixties. This Billy Williams was a graybeard 35-year-old veteran with over 15 seasons in the minors when he got his first chance to play in the big time in 1969 as he appeared in four games for the Seattle Pilots. The aging outfielder had been struggling in the minors since 1952. After going hitless in 10 at-bats with the Pilots, Billy was gone.

WILLIAMS, Don. R.
Pet supplies salesman
San Diego, CA

Do you remember Don F. Williams, a right-hander who had no decisions for the Pirates and A's in the late Fifties and early Sixties? How about Don R. Williams who had no decisions in three relief appearances for the Twins in 1963?

Interestingly enough, when Don R. was called up by the Twins, the Dallas–Fort Worth team needed a pitcher to replace him and they signed Don F.

WILLIAMS, George
> Assistant foreman at Cadillac Motors
> Detroit, MI

The Marvellettes were singing *Please Mr. Postman* while
George kept changing his address as a member of the
Phillies, Astros, and A's in between trips to the minors.
The second baseman hit .230 in 59 games from 1961–64.

WILLIAMS, Jim A.
> Santa Ana, CA

Jimmy led the Midwest League in 1967 in homers (17) and
RBIs (70). However, he didn't lead the majors in much
since he was around for only 24 games in '69 and '70 as a
Padres' outfielder.   .282

WILLIAMS, Jim F.
> Toronto Blue Jays' coach

Jim's cup of coffee came in '66–'67 with the Cardinals. A
14-game major leaguer, Williams hit .231 in his brief stay.
  He began a successful minor league managing career in
1974, capturing the P.C.L. "Manager of the Year" honors
in both 1976 and 1979 as his '79 Salt Lake City team won
the league championship.

WILLIAMS, Walt
> Recreation supervisor for Cordell Community Center;
> umpires youth baseball leagues
> Brownwood, TX

Walt was known as "No-Neck" for his fireplug-like stat-
ure. The stocky little outfielder is well remembered for his
boundless enthusiasm and hustling style.
  Originally in the Houston organization, Walt was up
with the Colt .45s briefly in 1964. The next two years he
hit .330 each season for Tulsa, winning the P.C.L. batting
title in '66.
  He then became White Sox property and became a regu-

lar in 1967. After being named to the Topps Rookie All-
Star team in the outfield with Reggie Smith and Rick Monday, "No-Neck" spent more time in the minors. Playing for
Hawaii he went on a streak of 11 consecutive base hits in
late May of '68, one short of tying the league record, but
was able to console himself by winning $1,000 in a payoff
from an Indianapolis restaurant owner when he hit a ball
through a hole in the right field fence.

Walt returned to Chicago for four more seasons and enjoyed his finest year in '69, hitting .304. He then went to
the Indians and Yankees before sprinting out in 1975.

"No Neck" hustled over to Japan where he became
known as "Mr. Energyman" by the fans for his hustling
brand of play.   .270

WILLIS, Dale
        President of Southeast Lift Equipment
        Tampa, FL

Not many pitchers can leave the game and boast that they
struck out more batters than they pitched innings. Dale
Willis can, as his numbers read 47 strikeouts in 44 innings
with the Kansas City A's in 1963. The reliever out of the
University of Florida, lost his only two decisions in 25 appearances that summer.

WILLIS, Ron
        Died Nov. 21, 1977, at age 34 in Memphis, TN

Ron's magnetic personality and great sense of humor
made him a popular after dinner speaker. From 1966–70
he was a popular relief pitcher with the Cardinals, Astros,
and Padres. His best season was in '67 when he helped the
Cards to the World's Championship as he won six games
and saved 10 others while recording a fine 2.67 ERA in 65
games.

Prior to his death he was the general manager for the
Memphis team in the Southern League.   11-12

WILSON, Bill
    Construction supervisor
    Broken Arrow, OK

You might think that a 9-15 record plus 17 saves in 179 games, all in relief, is not much to talk about, but Bill's record is quite an accomplishment: He underwent three arm operations in 1966 to correct a circulatory block in his arm, enduring the ordeal of having a vein transplanted from his leg to his arm.

The Marshall University right-hander was around from 1969-73 with the Phillies.

WILSON, Don
    Died Jan. 5, 1975, at age 29 in Houston, TX

There are some obvious parallels that one can draw between Don Wilson and J.R. Richard. Both were big, hard-throwing black right-handers; both pitched all of their careers in Houston; both were natives of Louisiana; and both had their careers suddenly end at a relatively young age.

Don was found dead in his car in the garage adjacent to his home in Houston while his young son died in the house. The Medical Examiner ruled the deaths to be accidental, the result of carbon monoxide poisoning.

On June 18, 1967, big Don no-hit the Braves, 2-0, striking out Hank Aaron three times along the way. The following year he had games against the Reds where he fanned 18 and 16 batters.

Wilson tossed his second no-hitter on May 1, 1969, against the Reds, coming on the heels of Jim Maloney's no-hitter the night before. Don carried a vendetta into the game at Crosley Field since nine days earlier Cincinnati humiliated the Astros in Houston, 14-0.

Late in the '74 season he just missed out on a third no-hitter. He had the Reds no-hit through eight innings, but trailed in the contest. Houston manager Preston Gomez lifted Wilson for a pinch-hitter but Don was subsequently charged with the defeat.

His uniform number (40) was retired by the Astros following his death.   104-92

WILSON, "Neil"
     Inspector with T.L.&M. Associates
     Lexington, TN

Neil Sedaka had a hit in *Breaking Up Is Hard To Do* when
Sammy O'Neil "Neil" Wilson was crying, "Breaking in is
hard to do" as he went hitless in 10 at-bats in six games as
a Giants catcher in 1960.

WINE, Bobby
     Atlanta Braves' coach

Labeled as a "good-field (.972), no-hit (.215)"-type player,
Bobby was a fixture at shortstop for the Phils throughout
most of the Sixties (1960–68). In '63 he earned a Gold
Glove at shortstop and was named to the N.L. All-Star
fielding team by *The Sporting News*.
     At the start of the '69 season Bobby was sent by the Phils
to the expansion Expos as a replacement for pitcher Larry
Jackson, who announced his retirement after being chosen
by Montreal from the Phils. In 1970 he established an M.L.
record for shortstops by participating in 137 double plays.
     Wine's playing career ended in 1972 when he was re-
leased by the Expos. Two weeks later he rejoined the Phils
as a coach.
     Bobby's son, Rob, a catcher from Oklahoma State Univer-
sity, was a first-round draft choice by the Astros in 1983.

WISE, Rick
     Retired
     Hillsboro, OR

Rick's career contains a potpourri of trivial information.
His portfolio goes from 1966–82 as a member of the Phils
('66–'71), Cards ('72–'73), Red Sox ('74–'77), Indians ('78–
'79), and Padres ('80–'82). During his impressive 188-181
career, Wise gained many distinctions. Here are a few:

1. He joins Gaylord Perry, Doyle Alexander, and Mike
    Torrez as the only pitchers to beat all 26 teams in the
    post-expansion era.

2. On June 23, 1971, he no-hit the Reds 4-0 and became the first pitcher in major league history to hit two home runs and pitch a no-hitter.

3. On Aug. 28, 1971, Rick hit a solo home run in the fifth inning and a grand-slam in the seventh as the Phils beat the Giants, 7-3. It was Wise's second two-homer game of the season, tying a major league record for pitchers.

Prior to the '72 season, the 6'2" right-hander went from the Phillies to the Cardinals for Steve Carlton. After winning 16 games for the Cards each of the next two seasons, he was swapped to Boston for Reggie Smith. He won a career-high 19 games for the pennant winning Red Sox in 1975 and in the ALCS was the starter and winner in the third and final game as the Red Sox ended the A's dynasty. Rick was the winner in relief of Game Six of the classic Red Sox–Reds Series when Carlton Fisk homered in the twelfth inning.

WISSMAN, Dave
Foreman for Dole Brothers, a general contractor
Shelburne Falls, MA

In 1964 Mary Wells had a popular tune in *My Guy*. That year Pirates' manager Danny Murtaugh decided that Dave Wissman wasn't going to be one of his guys in the Bucs' outfield after Dave hit .148 in 16 games.

WITHROW, "Corky"
Employed with State of Kentucky Dept. of Mine and Minerals as an oil and gas inspector
Owensboro, KY

Movie audiences in 1963 were treated to Alfred Hitchcock's masterpiece, *The Birds*. Outfielder Raymond "Corky" Withrow didn't frighten anyone as a member of the Birds in St. Louis, going hitless in nine at-bats in six games. However, he did cause pitchers in the Texas League some concern in 1962 as he hit 34 homers for Austin.

WOJCIK, Johnny
  Ministry and counseling work
  Louisville, KY

In 1962 it was "Here's Johnny" as Johnny Carson began his long run as host of the *Tonight Show*. It was also the year the Kansas City A's introduced John Wojcik, who looked like a celebrity as he hit .302 in 16 games.

  After short stays with the A's in '63 and '64 and a .218 avg. in 41 games, it was "Where's Johnny?"

WOLF, Wally
  Broker for a lumber company
  Corona Del Mar, CA

Wally's odyssey to the big leagues was quite unusual. A copyboy at the *Los Angeles Times* in the early Sixties, with designs on being a sportswriter, he was also a little-used utility infielder for the baseball team at USC. The Trojans reached the College World Series and Wally was brought in to pitch in relief. He performed well and impressed scouts as he helped his team capture the championship.

  Wolf was then signed to a $100,000 bonus by the Astros. He looked like a good investment after a 16-3 mark in the Carolina League, but he developed a sore arm and was out of pro ball for a few years.

  In 1969 the Angels gambled on Wally and assigned him to El Paso (Texas League) where he went 9-4. He was home in his native L.A. for military duty in late August when he went to Anaheim Stadium to pitch batting practice. He impressed Angels' manager "Lefty" Phillips and was activated. Overall, Wally relieved in a total of six games without a decision in 1969–70.

WOMACK, "Dooley"
  Carpet business
  Columbia, SC

This control artist who threw curveballs at various speeds was around from 1966–70 with the Yankees, Astros, Pilots, and A's. Horace Guy "Dooley" Womack became a member of the Yankees' bullpen in 1966. He performed admirably, going 7-3 with a 2.64 ERA in 42 games for the last-place Yankees.

In '67 Womack slipped to 5-6, but had 18 saves and at one point hurled 26 consecutive scoreless innings.   19-18

WOOD, Jake
    Supervisor for Abraham & Straus
    Red Bank, NJ

As a rookie in 1961, Jake played in all 162 games for the Tigers at second base and was named to the Topps Rookie All-Star team after hitting .258. His 14 triples were the most in the A.L., as were the 141 times he struck out.

Wood's first big league hit was a home run off Jim Perry on Opening Day in '61, the most active year of his six seasons in Detroit. He closed in '67 with the Reds at .250.

WOOD, Wilbur
    Owns a fish store in Boston, MA

It is interesting that of all the knuckleball pitchers of note—the Niekro brothers, Hoyt Wilhelm, Dutch Leonard, and Charlie Hough—only Wilbur Forrester Wood threw left-handed. The Cambridge, MA, native signed with the Red Sox in 1960, then spent most of the next few years in the minors. By the time he was sold to Pittsburgh in 1964 he was 0-7.

Wilbur's next stop was Chicago where he made his mark with the White Sox from 1967–78 with his iron-man, rubber-armed achievements. A 20-game winner for four consecutive years (1971–74), in 1971 he made 14 of his starts with only two days' rest. From 1968–70 he led A.L. pitchers in games pitched.

Wood baffled A.L. batters in 1971 when he went 22-13, including seven shutouts and a handsome 1.91 ERA. He won 24 games each of the next two seasons. In '72 he started 49 games, just two short of the all-time record of 51 held by Jack Chesbro in 1904.

Named the A.L. Pitcher of the Year by *The Sporting*

News in '72, he also set the dubious record of striking out 65 times, most ever by a pitcher in big league history.

Wilbur went 24-20 in '73, again leading the A.L. in victories, games started, and innings pitched. He became the first pitcher to win and lose 20 since Walter Johnson was 25-20 in 1916. On July 20th that year, the knuckleball ace started both games of a doubleheader against the Yankees, but was knocked out in each game, losing both.

On May 9, 1976, Wilbur suffered a broken left kneecap which sidelined him for the season when he was hit by a line drive off the bat of Ron LeFlore in Detroit. He retired after the '78 campaign at 164-156.

WOODS, Ron
   Inglewood, CA

Perseverance paid off for Ron, who spent several years in the low minors at such outposts as Hobbs, Kinston, and Batavia before making the Tigers' roster in 1969. Traded to the Yankees early in '69 for Tom Tresh, Woods only hit .183 in the Bronx, but was a pest to Baltimore pitcher Mike Cuellar on July 8th, when Cuellar three-hit the Yankees with Woods collecting all three hits.

In '71 the speedy outfielder was jettisoned to Montreal for Ron Swoboda. With the Expos he was used as a part-time player through 1974 and finished at .233.

WOODSON, Dick
   District manager for GF Furniture Systems, Inc.
   Georgetown, TX

This right-hander did his tossing for the Twins (1969–74) and Yankees ('74), compiling a 34-32 log. As a rookie in '69 he helped Minnesota to the A.L. West title, going 7-5 in his role as a spot starter and reliever. In one game that summer Woodson threw a couple of pitches close to Reggie Jackson's head. Enraged, Jackson charged the mound and tackled him. Believe it or not, rookie Twins' skipper Billy Martin played the role of peacemaker in the altercation.

WOODWARD, Woody
New York Yankees' vice-president

A first cousin to actress Joanne Woodward, William "Woody" Woodward was another of those good-field, no-hit type of players during his excursion which lasted from 1963–71 with the Braves and Reds.

Woody's screen test came a week after signing for a $50,000 bonus in June of '63. Denver, the Triple-A affiliate of the Braves, hosted the parent club in an exhibition contest and proceeded to blow out the big guys by a 16-1 score. Woody impressed by collecting four hits and five RBIs including a home run to lead the rout.

A product of Florida State University where he gained All-American honors, Woodward was promoted to the Braves not long after his exhibition game performance.   .236

WRIGHT, Clyde
Operates pitching school; distributor for Olympic Gold sporting goods
Anaheim, CA

In 1904 Jack Chesbro won 41 games, an increase of 20 victories from the 21 he had won in 1903. In 1970 Clyde Wright was a 22-game winner for the California Angels. The year before he struggled to a 1-8 mark in a campaign interrupted by military duty. Records may not be kept in that category, but his increase in victory total of 21 wins would likely be a record from one season to the next.

After going 9-0 at El Paso in '66, he was brought up to the Angels and, in his first start ever, defeated the Twins, 8-1, on a four-hitter. "Skeeter," as he was sometimes called, had his vintage year in 1970 (22-12) which won him "Comeback Player of the Year" honors.

On July 2, 1970, he was elected to the NAIA Hall of Fame for his heroics at Carson-Newman College in Jefferson City, Tennessee, where he helped lead the school to the NAIA championship in '65.

The day after his NAIA Hall of Fame election, Clyde hurled a no-hitter to beat the A's, 4-0, the first no-hitter by an Angels' pitcher since Bo Belinsky's masterpiece in

1962. About the only thing that went wrong for Wright in
1970 was his being charged with the loss in the All-Star
Game that summer.

He rode out with the Brewers ('74) and Rangers ('75) at
100-111.

WYATT, John
Owns and operates apartment buildings
Kansas City, MO

John managed to stick around big league real estate from
1961–69, with the A's ('61–'66), Red Sox ('66–'68), Yankees and Tigers ('68), and A's again ('69) after investing a
great deal of time barnstorming with the Indianapolis
Clowns, and pitching in the low minors and Mexican
League. But by 1963 John was one of the bullpen aces in
the A.L. collecting a career-high 21 saves. The following
season he won his first two decisions with a pair of scoreless innings in both ends of a doubleheader against
Minnesota and went on to post a 9-8 mark with 20 saves
while establishing an A.L. record with 81 appearances.

He was an integral factor for the A.L. champion Red
Sox in '67, carrying a 10-7 record with 20 saves. He was
credited with the victory in Game Six of the World Series.　　　　　　　　　　　　　　　　　　　　　　42-44

WYNNE, Billy
Insurance business
Jacksonville, FL

The sign at the Williamston, NC, city limit reads: "Home
of Gaylord Perry, Jim Perry, and Billy Wynne." Billy
didn't quite make as big a name as did the Perry brothers,
but the right-hander was with us from 1967–71 as a member of the Mets, White Sox, and Angels, going 8-11.

WYNN, Jim
Marketing division of Houston Astros

"The Toy Cannon" did his firing from 1963–77 and at
times was quite explosive. However, in one of his first

games in the majors he must have felt like a cap gun when Frank Thomas of the Mets pulled the hidden ball trick on him. Thomas asked Jim, "Please step off the bag a second so I can kick the dust out of it." Wynn did—welcome to the big leagues!

You can count Houston home run hitters on one hand. "The Toy Cannon" is one of them as he provided power for the Astros during his Texas stay (1963–73). In 1967 he had a career-high 37 homers, but also led the N.L. in striking out 137 times. On June 15th that year he belted three four-baggers in a game against the Giants in the Astrodome.

Two years later Jim poked 33 roundtrippers for the N.L. West fifth-place Astros even though opposing teams would often pitch around him in the Houston lineup. He drew 148 bases on balls, tying the all-time N.L. mark set by Eddie Stanky in 1945.

Jim went to the Dodgers in 1974 and quickly became a favorite of the L.A. fans when he homered in the first three games of the '74 season. On May 11th he became the first Dodger since Don Demeter to hit three homers in a game. Jim went on to hit 32 homers and collect 108 RBIs, helping L.A. to the N.L. pennant and earning the "Comeback Player of the Year" award in the N.L. by *The Sporting News*.

Before his final explosion in 1977, Wynn also played with the Braves, Yankees, and Brewers. When "The Toy Cannon" was emptied, it had fired a .250 avg. and 291 home runs.

Y

YASTRZEMSKI, Carl
Representative of a Boston area meat company; special events broadcaster for Channel 7 in Boston

Gods are not easy to replace. That's how Red Sox fans must have felt when Ted Williams retired in 1960. But somebody was watching over that tiny playpen in Boston called Fenway Park when there suddenly appeared a man named

Carl Yastrzemski who at times seemed to have supernatural powers. For example:

1. Only "Yaz," Hank Aaron, Willie Mays, and Stan Musial have collected 3,000 hits and 400 home runs. (Yaz had 3,419 hits and 452 homers.)
2. In 1980 Carl became the first A.L. player to have 20 straight years of 100 or more games.
3. He is the only player in modern M.L. history who recorded more than 3,000 hits, but never had a 200-hit season.
4. Holds record for the lowest league-leading batting average in big league history when he hit .301 for Boston in 1968, the "year of the pitcher."
5. After turning 40 in 1979, "Yaz" hit 49 homers before his retirement at age 44 following the '83 season. That established a record for most home runs after age 40, previously held by Stan Musial (46).
6. Won the Triple Crown in 1967 (.326; 44; 121).

The pressure of trying to replace Williams in left field did not affect Yastrzemski!

Signed as a shortstop after his freshman year at Notre Dame, Yaz led the Carolina League with a .377 avg. at Raleigh in 1959. But playing second base and shortstop, he also led the league in errors with 45. Who would ever think at that point that he would be named to the A.L. All-Star fielding team six times?

His collective accomplishments are well taken but he is probably best remembered for his clutch hitting, and individual game and pennant drive heroics.

Nobody was ever more clutch than this Southampton, NY, native at the end of the "Impossible Dream" '67 season when he collected 10 hits in his last 13 at-bats. In the last 19 games Yaz batted .444 with 26 RBIs. On the last weekend of the season, his timely home run against the Twins on Saturday led to a 6-4 Boston win. Carl's 44 homers that year were the most ever for a lefty swatter in Boston.

In the '67 Fall Classic Yaz went 10-for-25 (.400) with three homers and in the '75 World Series against the Reds hit .310. The magnificent slugger batted .455 (5-for-11) against the A's in the ALCS that year.

On May 19, 1976, captain Carl hit three home runs in a game for the only time in his career. He hit two more the next day to tie a big league record of five in two games.

He will join Johnny Bench in Cooperstown in 1989.
.285

YELLEN, Larry
  Taxicab driver in New York City

Right-hander Larry Yellen, out of the same Lafayette High School in Brooklyn as Sandy Koufax, finally realized his goal of making it to the majors when he pitched in 14 games with the Astros in '63 and '64 without a decision.

YOUNG, Don
  Machinist for Flimline Manufacturing
  Scottsdale, AZ

Larry Yellen came out of the same high school as Sandy Koufax while Don Young made his major league debut facing Sandy Koufax on Sept. 9, 1965, hitting in the leadoff spot and playing centerfield for the Cubs. Like all the other Cubs that night, he went hitless as the Dodger great hurled a perfect game.

In '69 the Cubs tried several players to solve their centerfield dilemma. Young was used in 101 games. Overall he hit .218 after his trials in '65 and '69.

Z

ZACHARY, Chris
  Manufacturer's sales representative for Contract Office Furniture
  Knoxville, TN

This right-hander did his pitching for the Astros, Royals,

Cards, Tigers, and Pirates from 1963–73. The Texas League "pitcher of the year" in '65, Chris did some effective work out of the A.L. East champion Tigers' bullpen in 1972 with a 1.42 ERA in 25 games.   10-29

ZEPP, Bill
Marketing representative for Chrysler Corp.
Westland, MI

The thunderous volume of Led Zeppelin made the group the most successful of the heavy metal bands starting in 1969. *Stairway to Heaven* became their best known hit. At the same time right-hander Bill Zepp, a graduate of the University of Michigan, climbed the stairway to the majors, making four appearances out of the Twins' bullpen that year.

In 1970, he played an important role as the Twins repeated as A.L. West champions with a 9-4 record. In one game that year Bill started for the Twins and beat the Tigers, 4-3, in his native Detroit on Al Kaline Day. It was an emotional day for Bill, since Kaline was his boyhood hero.

Zepp did get a chance to pitch for the Tigers in 1971 and went 1-1.   10-5

ZIMMERMAN, Jerry
Baltimore Orioles' regional scouting supervisor for Pacific Northwest and Western Canada
Milwaukee, OR

You couldn't leave the name of Bob Dylan out of this book. The most influential pop musician of the Sixties, Dylan legally changed his name from Robert Zimmerman to Bob Dylan in August of '62. He left his Minnesota home for New York City at the time Jerry Zimmerman arrived in Minnesota for a seven-year run (1962–68) after breaking in with the Reds in 1961.

Jerry had the reputation of a good-fielding catcher. His .997 fielding avg. for the 1965 A.L. champion Twins topped all A.L. catchers.   .204

ZIPFEL, "Bud"
> Insurance business—Midwest Capitol Associates, Inc.; also owns a real estate business, Bud Zipfel Enterprises
> Belleville, IL

The Zone Improvement Plan was introduced by the Post Office Department in 1962. It remains debatable if ZIP has helped speed our mail delivery. What may not be debatable is that "Bud" Zipfel was delivered to the majors so quickly, that he believes it affected his career.

Bud explained, "I grew up in the Yankee chain. I was being groomed to replace Moose Skowron at first base. But the Yankees lost me in the expansion draft to the Washington Senators. Each team had to put 15 guys on the block from their 40-man roster. Gil McDougald said, 'I'll always be a Yankee,' and refused to go on the block. I then replaced McDougald and was picked by the Senators."

Washington selected Zipfel and Bud lamented, "It was a bad stroke of events for me. Washington sent me to Houston (AA), then brought me up the same year (1961). As a result I didn't mature like I should have plus I had lost my organization," referring to the Yankees.

On Sept. 12, 1962, Tom Cheney of the Senators set an M.L. record by striking out 21 Orioles in a 2-1 victory. "Bud" singled home the first Washington run in the first inning, then provided the game winner with a 16th-inning home run.

Overall, Marion Sylvester Zipfel batted .220 in 118 games for the Senators.

Things happened too fast for "Bud." His profile is symbolic of the 1960s, an exciting baseball era that kept us entertained while American society was in transition.

Bibliography

Allen, Maury. *Bo-Pitching and Wooing*. New York: The Dial Press, 1973.

Baseball Encyclopedia. New York: MacMillan, 1974, 1979.

Baseball Research Journals. Virginia: Society for American Baseball Research, 1976–1983.

Benaugh, Jim. *Incredible Baseball Feats*. New York: Grosset and Dunlap, 1975.

Berke, Art and Paul Schmitt. *This Date in Chicago White Sox History*. New York: Stein and Day, 1982.

Boswell, Tom. *How Life Imitates the World Series*. New York: Doubleday and Co., Inc., 1982.

Brown, Bob and Phil Itzoe. *Baltimore Orioles 1974 Yearbook* (20th Anniversary Edition). 1973.

Carroll, Bob. "Nate Colbert's Unknown RBI Record." *The National Pastime* (SABR).

Clifton, Merritt. "The Freshman Class of 1964." *The National Pastime* (SABR), 1983.

D'Agostino, Dennis. *This Date in New York Mets History*. New York: Stein and Day, 1981.

Davids, L. Robert. *Great Hitting Pitchers*. Virginia: Society for American Baseball Research, 1979.

Eckhouse, Morris and Carl Mastrocola. *This Date in Pittsburgh Pirates' History*. New York: Stein and Day, 1980.

Hawkins, John. *This Date in Detroit Tigers History*. New York: Stein and Day, 1981.

————. *This Date in Baltimore Orioles and St. Louis Browns' History*. New York: Stein and Day, 1983.

Irving, Elliot. *Remembering the Vees-Richmond Virginians 1954–64*. Virginia: Cumberland Printing, 1979.

Javna, John and Gordon. *60s*. New York: St. Martin's Press, 1983.

Karst, Gene and Martin J. Jones, Jr. *Who's Who in Professional Baseball*. New Rochelle: Arlington House, 1973.

Kiersh, Edward. *Where Have You Gone Vince DiMaggio?*. New York: Bantam, 1983.

Leptich John and Dave Baranowski. *This Date in St. Louis Cardinals History*. New York: Stein and Day, 1983.

Lewis, Allen and Larry Shenk. *This Date in Philadelphia Phillies History.* New York: Stein and Day, 1979.

Marazzi, Rich. *The Rules and Lore of Baseball.* New York: Stein and Day, 1980.

Michelson, Herbert. *Charlie O.* Indianapolis, New York: Bobbs-Merrill Co., Inc., 1975.

Neff, David, Roland Johnson, Richard Cohen and Jordan Deutsch. *The Sports Encyclopedia: Baseball.* New York: Grosset and Dunlap, 1977.

Nelson, Kevin. *Baseball's Greatest Quotes.* New York: Simon and Schuster, 1982.

O'Connor, Anthony. *Baseball For the Love Of It.* New York: Macmillan, 1982.

Onigman, Marc. *This Date in Braves History.* New York: Stein and Day, 1982.

Salant, Nathan. *This Date in New York Yankees History.* New York: Stein and Day, 1979.

Terrance, Vincent. *Complete Encyclopedia of TV Programs 1947–79, Vol. 2.* New York: Barnes, 1980.

The Encyclopedia Americana Annuals. New York: Americana Corp., 1960–69.

Turkin, Y. and S.C. Thompson. *The Official Encyclopedia of Baseball.* New York: Dolphin Books, 1977.

Walton, Ed. *This Date in Boston Red Sox History.* New York: Stein and Day, 1978.

_____. *Red Sox Triumphs and Tragedies.* New York: Stein and Day, 1980.

Weaver, Earl, with Barry Stainback. *It's What You Learn After You Know It All That Counts.* New York: Doubleday and Co., 1982.

FIORITO, Len
> Employed in the transportation department at *The Seattle Times*; freelance writer
> Seattle, WA

One of just two profiled in this book who failed to make it into a major league game, Len was not signed out of high school by anyone. He entered college where he studied to become a schoolteacher. His education was interrupted by military duty in the mid-1960s during the Vietnam War. Following Navy duty he entered the newspaper business, working in both the editorial and circulation departments at the *Seattle Post-Intelligencer* where he remained until he joined the *Times* following the 1983 merger of the two newspapers.

In the early 1970s, inspired by Roger Kahn's book *The Boys of Summer*, he began tracking down hundreds of other major leaguers of the 1950s. He became one of the early members of the Society of American Baseball Research through which he met Rich Marazzi of Ansonia, CT. The two then collaborated on the book *Aaron to Zuverink—A Nostalgic Look at the Players of the 1950s* which was published in 1982. Len and his wife Patti have two children, a daughter, Gina (8), and a son, Steve (3).

MARAZZI, Rich
> Baseball writer; schoolteacher; umpire
> Ansonia, CT

The second non-player to be profiled in this book, Rich is a baseball junkie who, like Steve Hamilton, dreamed of playing in Yankee Stadium. Unlike Hamilton his fantasy was never achieved. A fairly solid catching prospect in high school and college, Marazzi's goals drifted away with each passing curveball. The New Paltz (NY) graduate (1965) decided that teaching and umpiring would be safer professions since they didn't carry batting averages.

Labeled in college as a headsy defensive catcher whose bat had about as much sting as a wet newspaper, Marazzi has pursued his baseball interests as a columnist and author. He has authored *The Rules and Lore of Baseball; The*

Stein and Day Baseball Date Book 1981; and co-authored *Aaron to Zuverink.*

Rich is married to the former Loisann Kelly. They have two children, Richie (10) and Brian (7).